Jesus Monotheism

Volume 1

Electronic copies of this volume and other accompanying resources are available at:

www.JesusMonotheism.com

Jesus Monotheism

VOLUME 1—Christological Origins:
The Emerging Consensus and Beyond

Crispin Fletcher-Louis

CASCADE *Books* · Eugene, Oregon

JESUS MONOTHEISM
Volume 1. Christological Origins: The Emerging Consensus and Beyond

Copyright © 2015 Crispin Fletcher-Louis. All rights reserved. Except for brief quotations in critical publications or reviews, no part of this book may be reproduced in any manner without prior written permission from the publishers. For hard copy, write: Permissions. Wipf and Stock Publishers. For electronic copy, write: Crispin Fletcher-Louis, crispin@whymanity.com.

Cascade Books
An Imprint of Wipf and Stock Publishers
199 W. 8th Ave., Suite 3
Eugene, OR 97401

www.wipfandstock.com

ISBN 13: 978-1-62032-889-7

Cataloguing-in-Publication Data

Fletcher-Louis, Crispin H. T.

    Jesus monotheism : volume 1. Christological origins : the emerging consensus and beyond / Crispin Fletcher-Louis

    xx + 368 p. ; 23 cm. Includes bibliographical references.

    ISBN 13: 978-1-62032-889-7

    1. Jesus Christ—History of doctrines—Early church, ca. 30–600. 2. Jesus Christ—Cult—History. 3. Jesus Christ—Persons and offices. I. Title.

BT198 F56 2015

Manufactured in the U.S.A.   07/28/2015

For Ian Dighé

Contents

Preface | xiii
List of Abbreviations | xvii

Part 1 | 1

CHAPTER 1 Christological Origins: An Introduction to a New Emerging Consensus | 3

  1. An Early Divine Christology | 3

     i. Paul and an Early High Christology in Twentieth-Century Scholarship | 6

     ii. "Christological Monotheism" | 8

     iii. Cultic Devotion | 15

     iv. Conclusion: Consensus on the Shape and Date of an Early High Christology | 21

  2. The Origins of Christ Devotion and "Christological Monotheism" | 24

     i. A Lack of Precedent in Jewish Monotheism | 25

     ii. Hurtado's Explanation of Christological Origins | 26

     iii. Bauckham's Explanation of Christological Origins | 29

CHAPTER 2 Unconvincing Objections and Fresh Support for the Emerging Consensus | 31

  1. Unconvincing Objections to the Emerging Consensus | 31

     i. No "Christological Monotheism" in Paul? | 32

II. The Numerical Theology of 1 Cor 8:6 and the Emerging Consensus | 39

III. No Genuine Worship of Christ? | 56

Introduction to Part 2 | 61

CHAPTER 3 The *Shape* of NT Christology: Questions and Problematic Arguments | 65

1. Incarnation | 66
2. The Distinct Identities of God the Father and the Lord Jesus Christ, the Son | 88
3. The Son of Man Title in the Gospels | 101
    I. The Emerging Consensus's Rejection of the Apocalyptic Son of Man Theory | 105
    II. Hurtado on the "Son of Man" | 106
    III. A Pre-Christian Son of Man Expectation | 109
    IV. Daniel 7:13 and the Son of Man Expression. | 112
    V. A Nontitular Expression? | 123
    VI. Conclusion: the Emerging Consensus on the Son of Man | 126

CHAPTER 4 The *Origins* of NT Christology. Questions and Problematic Arguments | 128

1. No Precedent in Pre-Christian Judaism for "Christological Monotheism"? | 128
2. Lack of Opposition to Early Christology | 132
3. Psalm 110 and the Identification of Christ with *Yhwh-Kyrios* | 138
4. The Origin of a Belief in Christ's Role as Agent of Creation | 141
5. Problems with Hurtado's Explanation of the Christ Cult | 148
    I. Lack of Textual Support for the Theory | 148
    II. Opposition to the Role of Visions in Some Parts of Early Christian Life | 149

CONTENTS

    III. Social Scientific Studies and Innovations in
Early Christianity | 152

6. Conclusion: In Search of an Explanation of the Origins
of Christ Devotion | 156

7. Conclusion to Chapters 3 and 4 | 156

EXCURSUS A Theological Problems Posed by the Emerging
Consensus | 158

    I. Religious Experience and Revelation | 159

    II. The Worship of Jesus and Idolatry | 160

Introduction to Part 3 | 167

CHAPTER 5 The *Similitudes of Enoch* and a Jewish
"Divine" Messiah | 171

1. The Enochic Son of Man, Christology, and
the Enoch Seminar | 172

2. Hurtado: No Precedent for Christ Devotion in the *Similitudes* | 179

    I. Jesus the Son of Man and the Origins of Christ Devotion | 180

3. Bauckham: The *Similitudes* as a Partial Precedent for
"Christological Monotheism" | 182

    I. Jesus the Son of Man and the Origins of "Christological
Monotheism" | 186

4. The Enoch Seminar: Continuity between the "Parables"
and NT Christology | 189

5. Provenance: A Marginal, Sectarian Text? | 191

    I. Related Texts Describing a "Transcendent" Messiah
or Figure | 193

    II. The Old Greek Translation of Daniel 7:13 | 195

    III. The *Similitudes* and Enoch's Transformation in *2 Enoch*
and *3 Enoch* | 199

6. The *Similitudes* a Mainstream Second Temple Text | 201

7. Conclusion | 203

CHAPTER 6   The King, the Messiah, and the Ruler Cult | 206

1. William Horbury: Jewish Messianism, Ruler Cult, and Christ Devotion | 207
2. Some Weaknesses of Horbury's Model | 214
3. High Priestly and Royal Messianism | 220
    I. The Divine "Glory" of the (High Priestly) Messiah | 230
    II. A Dubious Royal Interpretation of Dan 7:13 and Ps 110 | 233
    III. Dan 2:46, 7:13–14 and the True Humanity Receiving Worship | 237
    IV. Conclusion | 247
4. Conclusion to Chapters 5 and 6: Messianism and the Origins of "Christological Monotheism" | 248

CHAPTER 7   A "Divine" and Glorious Adam Worshipped in Pre-Christian Judaism? | 250

1. Introduction to a Critical Study of the Worship of Adam Story | 256
2. Arguments against the Story's Relevance for Early Christology | 257
3. A Pre-Christian Date for the Worship of Adam Story | 258
    I. A Jewish, Hebrew-Speaking Provenance? | 263
4. Is the Worship of Adam Story "Untypical" of Pre-Christian Judaism? | 266
5. Is Adam Actually "Worshipped" in this Story? | 269
6. The Story's Place in First-Century Jewish Practice and Belief | 276
7. A Scriptural, Theologically Coherent Explanation of the Story | 281
    I. The Worship of Adam Story and Daniel 2–7 | 285
8. Conclusion | 291

EXCURSUS B   On the Absolute Distinction between Creator and Creation | 293

1. An Absolute Qualitative Distinction between God and All Reality | 294

2. No Absolute Qualitative Distinction between the Creator and Creation? | 296

  I. "Divine" Creatures as Creative Agents | 297

  II. "Divine" Angels? | 298

  III. "Divine" Human Beings? | 299

  IV. The Worship of "Divine" Agents? | 303

  V. Problems with Bauckham's Proposals | 305

3. Towards a New Model of "Exclusive Inclusive Monotheism" | 309

Bibliography | 317

Scripture and Ancient Document Index | 339

Preface

IN 1988 I ENTERED the fraught world of modern theology and biblical studies a naïve Bible-believing Evangelical. I was confronted by a disturbing curriculum: Jesus' followers had been wrong about their Lord's return, Christ did not believe that he had to die for anyone's sins, the Gospels were largely created by the early church (and historically inaccurate), and belief in Jesus' deity only emerged late in the first century. None of the cardinal tenets of orthodox Christianity could be believed without question or serious modification.

But I had arrived at Oxford at a time when many of the assured results of modern critical scholarship were fair game. With N. T. (Tom) Wright, Ed Sanders, Christopher Rowland, John Ashton, Rowan Williams, Alister McGrath, and their ilk for teachers, my theology was molded in a melting pot of rigorous scholarship and wide-open creative possibilities. We were taught to think for ourselves and to question everything. And I was captivated by the light of a bright new future for biblical studies, for theology, and for the church.

This is a book about the issue at the heart of it all: Christology—the earliest beliefs about Christ and the ways his followers devoted their lives to him. I offer, over the course of four volumes, a "new paradigm" that describes and accounts for the origins of the belief in his deity. The foundations for the conceptual structure of the new paradigm were laid in the intellectual crucible that was Oxford in my undergraduate years. For the most part, the new paradigm is a synthesis of my teachers' seminal insights. Mix together Sanders on the centrality of the priesthood and the Temple in ancient Jewish life, with Wright's observations on Adam, Israel, the Messiah, and the overarching shape of the biblical story, and Rowland's groundbreaking discussion of Jewish apocalyptic; stir whilst listening to Kallistos Ware and Geoffrey Rowell lay out the basics of patristic Christian orthodoxy. Then add in a sprinkling of Margaret Barker (a muse to many of us, albeit from beyond the immediate confines of Oxford) on the cosmology and religious experiences nurtured by Israel's Temple, and you have all the ingredients of the new paradigm (bar a few fresh observations of my own).

There are two ideas that constitute its heart. Firstly, I contend that in Israel's Scriptures (and for first-century Judaism) the one God has already revealed himself to be an incarnational and scandalously humanity-focused God. Secondly, I propose that, within the context of a fresh understanding of the shape of Jewish monotheism, a straightforward explanation of Christological origins is now available: the historical Jesus believed himself to be uniquely included—as one who served as Israel's royal and priestly Messiah and as a fully divine person—within the identity of the one God (as the "Son" of the "Father"). Jesus' own monotheism was this new, radically refashioned "Jesus monotheism." These two theses offer a satisfactory account for the primary sources and historical data that no other currently available models can.

I arrive at these conclusions not through a reactionary return to pre-critical arguments and dogmas, but by revisiting some assumptions about biblical theology that predate the critical period; questionable assumptions that are deeply rooted in those strands of the Christian tradition where post-Enlightenment scholarship has flourished. Early on in my own studies I concluded that a third way between the critical dismantling of orthodoxy and a defensive conservative reaction was needed. In the heat of debate unspoken assumptions shared by both sides are often the real cause of the conflict. On the matter of Christological origins, it seems to me that both those of us for whom Christian "orthodoxy" has become a toxic brand and those of us at the forefront of the fight to defend it have, in various ways, missed the theological shape and force of the texts. So the route I lay out to the new paradigm will seem to many a surprising one. I offer what I hope is ultimately an attractive alternative to the models currently on offer. The new paradigm builds on recent insights and advances by many specialists in the field (whose contributions will, in particular, be the focus of this first volume). There are places where it at least has the virtue of greater historical simplicity than other models, and no doubt some will find it theologically appealing. However, *it is not a cheap account*; it has its intellectual and existential (personal, political, economic, and ecclesial) costs. I hope not to push and cajole readers to an old place long since abandoned, but to introduce readers to a new terrain. The journey there is neither quick—this is the first of four volumes—nor easy.

Initially I had hoped, on leaving a position as the principal of a small college in 2012, to write a short book that would set out in an accessible form the main parts of the view of Christological origins that I have long taught my students (and that I had begun to sketch in some shorter, discretely focused publications since the publication of my doctoral thesis in 1997). That was to be a series of propositions, without meticulous argument, with but a brief introduction setting the scene. The project grew rapidly. The laying out of the propositions that comprise the new paradigm now takes up Volume 3, which covers the biblical and Jewish material, and Volume 4, which covers the New Testament material. A summary of the new paradigm is available on my www.academia.edu page and at www.JesusMonotheism.com. Volumes 1 and 2 prepare the ground for a full presentation of the new paradigm (in Volumes 3 and 4).

Volume 1 maps out the current state of scholarship as the context for the new paradigm. It has two main aims. On the one hand, it sets out the convincing arguments of Larry Hurtado and Richard Bauckham for an early high Christology. On the other hand, it explores the ways in which Hurtado and Bauckham (and the others in what I call the "emerging consensus") are unable to account satisfactorily for some of the hard data of the primary sources. That data, especially some non-Christian Jewish material which the emerging consensus scholars have not treated adequately, points towards a new approach.

Volume 2 takes up the evidence of those Jewish texts (studied in Part 3 of Volume 1) and returns to the New Testament to consider the possibility that its divine Christology is built on pre-Christian precedents. A long chapter is dedicated to a focused case study—the hymn in Phil 2:6–11—and another to a survey of texts in the Synoptic Gospels where Jesus is presented with, or claims for himself, a divine identity. Volume 2 also offers some new insights into these early Christian texts, but it will attempt to show that, without a wholly new paradigm, some key components of New Testament Christology are really hard to explain.

For the new paradigm I am indebted not just to Oxford, but also to the many who have made the United Kingdom the powerhouse of Christology research that it has been for the last twenty-five years; above all to Larry Hurtado and Richard Bauckham. Between them, they have changed the field forever. In fundamental ways their work paints a picture from which we must all start. And, over the course of the last twenty years, their publications have both confirmed and challenged my thinking in equal measure. Along with N. T. Wright, they are dialogue partners throughout this book. Other colleagues, friends, and conversation partners have made vital contributions to the sharpening of my thinking: Eddie Adams, Colin Gunton, Karen Kilby, Loren Stuckenbruck, Robert Hayward, Mike Thate. Larry graciously read and commented on an earlier version of several chapters. Others have given me invaluable feedback throughout the writing process:

especially, Jim West, Joseph Longarino, Ed Gerber, Simon Gathercole, Gabrielle Thomas, and Chris Kugler.

Robin Parry, my editor at Wipf and Stock, invited me to write a book on Christology about fifteen years ago. He has been patient, and when, in the autumn of 2012, I said I had something for him, I had no idea it would take this long, nor the number of times I would ask him if he minded increasing the size and the number of volumes.

Finally, thanks goes to my colleagues and the students of Westminster Theological Centre; for taking up the baton so successfully as I stepped down at a critical juncture in the new college's life. In countless ways the new paradigm is indebted to my experience in spearheading the WTC experiment, but if I had not stepped down this book would never have happened.

Ash Wednesday, 2015
Camelot

List of Abbreviations

Series

AB	Anchor Bible
AGAJU	Arbeiten zur Geschichte des antiken Judentums und des Urchristentums
AJEC	Ancient Judaism and Early Christianity
BETL	Bibliotheca Ephemeridum Theologicarum Lovaniensium
BZAW	Beihefte zur Zeitschrift für die alttestamentliche Wissenschaft
CHANE	Culture and History of the Ancient Near East
CSCO	Corpus Scriptorum Christianorum Orientalium
EJL	Society of Biblical Literature: Early Judaism and its Literature
FRLANT	Forschurgen zur Religion und Literatur des und Neuen Testament
GAP	Guides to Apocrypha and Pseudepigrapha
HSS	Harvard Semitic Studies
ICC	International Critical Commentary
JSJSup	Journal for the Study of Judaism Supplement
JSNTSup	Journal for the Study of the New Testament Supplement
JSOTSup	Journal for the Study of the Old Testament Supplement
LNTS	Library of New Testament Studies
LSTS	Library of Second Temple Studies
NETS	Albert Pietersma and Benjamin G. Wright. *A New English Translation of the Septuagint and the other Greek Translations Traditionally Included under that Title.* Oxford: Oxford University Press, 2007.
NIBC	New International Biblical Commentary

NovTSup	Novum Testamentum Supplement
NTOA	Novum Testamentum et Orbis Antiquus
OGIS	Wilhelm Dittenberger, *Orientis graeci inscriptiones selectae: supplementum sylloges inscriptionum graecarum*. 2 vols. Leipzig: Hirzel, 1903
SBLDS	Society of Biblical Literature Dissertation Series
SCS	Septuagint and Cognate Studies
SJLA	Studies in Judaism in Late Antiquity
SJS	Studia Judaeoslavica
SNTSMS	Society of New Testament Studies Monograph Series
SSEJC	Studies in Scripture in Early Judaism and Christianity
STDJ	Studies on the Texts of the Desert of Judah
SUNT	Studien zur Umwelt des Neuen Testaments
SVTP	Studia in Veteris Testamenti Pseudepigrapha
TSAJ	Texts and Studies in Ancient Judaism
UCSD	University of California San Diego
WBC	Word Biblical Commentary
WUNT	Wissenschaftliche Untersuchungen zum Neuen Testament

Ancient Sources

Old Testament Pseudepigrapha

1 En.	*1 Enoch*
2 Bar.	*2 Baruch (Syriac Apoclaypse)*
3 Bar.	*3 Baruch (Greek Apocalypse)*
2 En.	*2 Enoch*
3 En.	*3 Enoch*
Add Esth	Additions to Esther in the Septuagint
A.L.D.	Aramaic Levi Document
Artap.	Artapanus
Apoc. Zeph.	*Apocalypse of Zephaniah*
Apoc. Abr.	*Apocalypse of Abraham*
Apoc. Sedr.	*Apocalypse of Sedrach*
Asc. Isa.	*Ascension of Isaiah*
Ezek. Trag.	Ezekiel the Tragedian's *Exagoge*

Jos. Asen.	*Joseph and Aseneth*
Jub.	*Jubilees*
L.A.B.	*Liber antiquitatum biblicarum* (Pseudo-Philo)
L.A.E.	*Life of Adam and Eve*
Let. Arist.	*Letter of Aristeas*
Pr. Man.	*Prayer of Manasseh*
Ps. Sol.	*Psalms of Solomon*
Ps. Phoc.	*Pseudo-Phocylides*
Sib. Or.	*Sibylline Oracles*
T. Dan	*Testament of Dan*
T. Gad	*Testament of Gad*
T. Jos.	*Testament of Joseph*
T. Jud.	*Testament of Judah*
T. Levi	*Testament of Levi*
T. Mos.	*Testament of Moses*
T. Naph.	*Testament of Naphtali*
T. Reub.	*Testament of Reuben*
T. Sim.	*Testament of Simeon*

Josephus

C. Ap	*Against Apion (Contra Apionem).*
Ant.	*Jewish Antiquities*
J.W.	*Jewish War*

Philo

Abraham	*On the Life of Abraham*
Alleg. Interp.	*Allegorical Interpretation*
Creation	*On the Creation of the World*
Decalogue	*On the Decalogue*
Embassy	*On the Embassy to Gaius*
Dreams	*On Dreams*
Flight	*On Flight and Finding*
Heir	*Who is the Heir?*

Migration	*On the Migration of Abraham*
Moses	*Life of Moses*
QE	*Questions and Answers on Exodus*
Spec. Laws	*Special Laws*
Cherubim	*On the Cherubim*
Sacrifices	*On the Sacrifices of Cain and Abel*
Unchangeable	*That God is Unchangeable*

Rabbinic Sources

m. Hor	*Mishnah Horayot*
m. Kil.	*Mishnah kil'ayim*
Gen. Rab	*Genesis Rabbah*
Eccl. Rab.	*Ecclesiastes Rabbah*
Pirqe R. El.	*Pirqe Rabbi Eliezer*

Classical Sources

Div. Jul.	Suetonius, *Julius Caesar (Divus Julius)*
Rep.	Plato, *The Republic*
Rhet.	Aristotle, *Rhetoric*
Var. Hist.	Aelian, *Historical Miscellany (Varia Historia)*

Early Christian Writings and the Church Fathers

1 Clem.	*1 Clement*
Apoc. Pet.	*Apocalypse of Peter*
Barn.	*Epistle of Barnabas*
Ep. Apost.	*Epistle of the Apostles*
Gos. Bart.	*Gospel of Bartholomew*
Leg.	Athenagoras, *Plea for Christians (Legatio pro Christianis)*
Pol. Phil.	Polycarp, *To the Philippians*
Praep. Evang.	Eusebius, *Preparation for the Gospel (Praeparatio Evangelica)*

PART 1

CHAPTER 1

Christological Origins

An Introduction to a New Emerging Consensus

It is an exciting time to be studying NT Christology. There are few subjects in biblical studies where it is possible to say that there is a clear and steady movement towards a consensus. But it is hard to disagree with Cambridge scholar Andrew Chester who, in a recent critical review of the field, describes a newly emerging consensus about the early date and character of a belief in Jesus' divinity.[1] In this chapter I describe that "emerging consensus."

1: An Early Divine Christology

In the modern period, specialists have disagreed widely on the conceptual shape and historical origins of Christology (and many have insisted on a plurality of NT Christolog*ies*). In particular, there has been a long-running debate about the phenomenon that scholars traditionally call a "high Christology" (the belief that Jesus was somehow divine and was treated as such by his followers). Most have thought that a high Christology was reached only after significant theological development of thought and, therefore, in a different time, place, and circumstances to those of Jesus himself and his earliest Jerusalem-based followers. On this view, during his ministry in Galilee and Judea the disciples must have had either no Christology—no very strong beliefs specifically about Jesus—or a "low" one in which Jesus is simply a created being (a prophet, or even the long-awaited Jewish messiah). In other words, if the historical Jesus had *any* sense of his own special vocation he only believed he was a specially chosen *human being*, and as

---

1. See Chester, "High Christology," 38, 50.

such was, like all human beings, subordinate to God his Creator and Lord. There is now, however, a newly emerging consensus that a "high Christology" goes back to the earliest period of the church and that it was adopted by the Jerusalem-based disciples in the early years, or even the first months, of the movement after Jesus' death.

This new consensus has been achieved in particular by the endeavors of the late Martin Hengel (of Tübingen), Larry W. Hurtado, Richard Bauckham, and others who have developed the arguments they have put forward. Hengel argued that a fully high Christology must have been formed within eighteen years of Christ's death and, in all probability, within four or five years.[2] With three monographs and other supporting articles Hurtado has pushed back the origins of the Christian transformation of Jewish monotheism much further; to perhaps even the first months of the new movement.[3] At the very earliest phase of the post-Easter church Jesus' followers worshipped their master in ways that, as good orthodox Jews, they had previously reserved exclusively for the one God of Israel. That early high Christology is present throughout the NT, finding particularly clear expression (in different but mutually illuminating ways) in Paul's letters, the Johannine corpus, Hebrews, and Revelation.

In its early stages, Hurtado's project was spurred on by an article by Richard Bauckham, who showed that in some texts the worship of Jesus sets him apart as a uniquely divine being over against the angels who are not to be worshipped.[4] In recent years Bauckham has played tag-team with Hurtado, complementing Hurtado's arguments for a "binitarian" or dyadic shape to the church's earliest Christology, but also stressing the considerable evidence that for the NT authors Jesus is firmly included within the *identity* of the one Jewish God.[5] Bauckham has promised a two-volume study of early Christology so we await a full statement of his views, which differ from Hurtado's on some points. Aside from their differences, between them

---

2. See Hengel, *Son of God* (1976); *Between Jesus and Paul* (1983); *Studies in Early Christology* (1995); *Studien zur Christologie* (2006), and the treatment of Hengel's contribution in Chester, "High Christology," 24–26; Deines, "Christology," and Frey, "Eine neue religionsgeschichtliche Perspektive."

3. Hurtado's principal publications are: *One God, One Lord* (1988, 2nd ed. 1998); *Lord Jesus Christ* (2003); *How on Earth Did Jesus Become a God?* (2005). See also his *God in New Testament Theology* (2010).

4. Bauckham, "Worship of Jesus" (1983).

5. Bauckham's principal publications are: *God Crucified: Monotheism and Christology in the New Testament* (1998) and *Jesus and the God of Israel: "God Crucified" and Other Studies on the New Testament's Christology of Divine Identity* (2008) (that includes a reprint of *God Crucified*). For the agreements and some points of disagreement between Bauckham and Hurtado now see Bauckham, "Devotion to Jesus Christ" (2014).

1. INTRODUCTION TO A NEW EMERGING CONSENSUS 5

Hurtado and Bauckham are bringing about a sea change in the study of Christology. An increasing number of New Testament scholars now accept their principal findings.[6] Even those who take issue with important aspects of their work now accept their main contention: a high Christology was a very early phenomenon and not one brought about by a Hellenization of Christian theology.[7]

Some scholars still seem committed to views that Hurtado, Bauckham, and others have shown to be inadequate.[8] And amongst those who are now indebted to the Hurtado-Bauckham early dating and divine identity "emerging consensus" there remain points where agreement is lacking. Disagreements arise, in particular, around the issue of the *origins* of an early high Christology: what caused the post-Easter church to Worship Hurtado argues the new Christian form of monotheism was a response to powerful revelatory experiences, such as visions in the context of worship. Bauckham stresses, on the other hand, the importance of early Christian interpretation of (Israel's) Scriptures and has insisted that beliefs about Jesus came first, and then the worship of Jesus was a necessary outworking of those beliefs. And whilst there is not yet agreement on the *origins* of an early Christology, others have also raised important questions about the conceptual *shape* of the Christology that Hurtado and Bauckham describe.

In large part, this four-volume book is intended to be an argument *in support of* much of the Hurtado and Bauckham paradigm; addressing the

---

6. The following are notable publications that reflect the approach taken by Hengel, Hurtado, and Bauckham: Chester, *Messiah and Exaltation* (2007), esp. 80–120; "High Christology," (2011), esp. 33–40; Fee, *Pauline Christology* (2007); Gathercole, *Preexistent Son* (2006); "Paul's Christology" (2011); Vollenweider, "Jesus als Träger des Gottesnamens im Neuen Testament" (2008); "Christozentrisch oder theozentrisch?" (2011); McDonough, *Christ as Creator* (2009); Schröter, "Trinitarian Belief," (2013); Tilling, *Paul's Divine Christology* (2012). Frey, "Eine neue religionsgeschichtliche Perspektive" (2013) summarizes and strongly endorses Hurtado's thesis, adding a commentary with an emphasis on the history of modern German scholarship. N. T. Wright—e.g., *Paul* (2005) 73, 86–96, *Paul and the Faithfulness of God* (2013) 619–773, esp. 647–56—can be included here, although in important ways his perspective challenges some aspects of the approach taken by Hurtado and Bauckham.

7. In this category there belongs, for example, Daniel Boyarin—esp. his *Jewish Gospels* (2012) and see also his earlier *Border Lines* (2004) and "Enoch, Ezra" (2013). Even Bart Ehrman, in his recent popular-level book, shifts from his earlier view to accepting that a divine Christology appears early on in the Christian movement (Ehrman, *How Jesus Became God*), though in many other respects his discussion is rather out of touch with the work of the emerging consensus.

8. For recent examples of the old paradigm see, e.g., Reumann, *Philippians*, 359, on the "name" in Phil 2:9–10 and the continued voice given to the work of P. M. Casey in Crossley, *Reading the New Testament* (2010). For all its considerable strengths, Litwa's *Iesus Deus* (2014) sometimes passes by the main findings of the emerging consensus.

objections and the doubts of its detractors. Equally, my own work has led me to a new paradigm that explains the central findings of Hurtado's work—the *early* dating of a "high Christology"—with some significant modifications to the Hurtado-Bauckham perspective, especially on the question of the *shape* of the earliest Christology. To set the scene for my own proposals, this first chapter offers an introduction to the study of Christology by laying out essential, defining components of the emerging consensus view. In chapter 2 I consider some arguments against the emerging consensus that are easily answered and provide fresh evidence to support the case from 1 Cor 8:6. In Part 2—chapters 3 and 4—I consider some outstanding, unanswered problems and objections to the new view. Part 3—comprising chapters 5 to 7—offers a fresh examination of Jewish traditions that some have turned to for help in explaining the historical origins of Christ devotion, and Part 4 (Volume 2) will return to a fresh examination of some NT texts in the light of Part 2. The new paradigm will be fully laid out in Parts 5 and 6 in Volumes 3 and 4.

There are, of course, other subjects that properly belong in a comprehensive study of NT Christology. Ideally, we should consider the evidence for a trinitarian shape of some NT texts.[9] But space constrains us. As my argument progresses, I will however, say quite a bit about two other topics that are tightly connected to Christology: anthropology and soteriology. Neither of these will be treated thoroughly or systematically, but I hope that by the end of the presentation of the new paradigm readers will have a better sense of the ways that the earliest Christians' beliefs about Jesus were inextricable from a revolution in their understanding of themselves. For Jews who believed in Jesus and for whom there had already been an expectation that God would act decisively in history, there was also a revolution in the understanding of what salvation really meant. In other words, to understand Jesus' *person* (as both a divine and a human being) we have to say some things about the peculiar nature of his *work* and, also, about the fresh light he shed on God's original purposes for humanity.

I: Paul and an Early High Christology in Twentieth-Century Scholarship

There is a fascinating, if complex, modern history of the study of early, New Testament-era Christology. To simplify matters, we can orient ourselves to

---

9. On which see the important discussions in Gorman, *Cruciformity*, 63–74, and Watson, "Triune Divine Identity."

the history of debate by focusing on Paul and Pauline Christology, which provides the earliest easily datable evidence.

Throughout the Pauline letters there are passages that connect the risen Lord closely to the one God of biblical faith, ascribing to Jesus language and prerogatives that put him way above ordinary human beings. There is also evidence of prayer, acclamation, and praise directed to Christ that suggests Paul and other Christians treated him as a divine being. In the past, two different strategies have been adopted to explain remarkably exalted, transcendent language for the risen Jesus and a pattern of early Christian "Christ devotion." Older scholarship, exemplified by the classic study of W. Bousset (*Kyrios Christos*, 1913), reckoned that for Paul Jesus had become a "divine" being under the influence of Greco-Roman religion, where a variety of beings were accorded a divine (or semidivine) identity. In other words, for Paul (and other "Hellenistic" Christians) "the placing of Jesus in the center of the cultus of a believing community . . . is conceivable only in an environment in which Old Testament monotheism no longer ruled unconditionally and with absolute security."[10] Any passages in the Gospels that seemed also to portray Jesus as a "divine" being were also explained with recourse to the influence of Hellenistic religion.[11]

The Hellenization explanation of the origins of high Christology does not fit well with the fact that Paul's thought is biblical and Jewish through and through. Paul has an avowed continued commitment to the biblical belief in one God (Rom 3:30; 1 Cor 8:4; Eph 4:6) and the rejection of idolatry (Rom 1:21-23; 1 Cor 10:7, 14; 12:2; 1 Thess 1:9-10). This has led some to the conclusion that for Paul Jesus Christ is not really "divine" in the Jewish sense; that the risen Jesus is close to the one God, that he can take over divine *functions* without being divine *in nature*; he functions as a mediator between God and his people, but was not included within the identity of the one God. In recent decades, this approach to Paul (and other portions of the NT, too) has been associated in particular with the work of James D. G. Dunn.

In his 1980 classic study of Christology, *Christology in the Making*, Dunn made a subtle, hard-to-describe argument for an unconventional understanding of the shape of Pauline Christology. He claimed that Pauline language that has traditionally been taken to ascribe preexistence and incarnation to Jesus is really traditional Jewish language for Wisdom, that had already functioned as no more than a (literary, poetic) personification of one of God's own attributes in some Jewish texts. He then judged that

10. Bousset, *Kyrios Christos*, 147. Bousset's major study of Pauline Christology (*Kyrios Christos*) was originally published in German (in 1913) and then appeared in an English translation in 1971. I refer in this study to the English translation.

11. See, e.g., Bousset, *Kyrios Christos*, 69-118.

what might seem to us to be statements about Christ as a distinct "divine" person are really statements about Christ *as Wisdom*. This means that such statements do not, for Paul, threaten Jewish monotheism, since talk of divine Wisdom is really simply talk of the wisdom of God in the same way that the OT talks of the spirit of God. Pauline statements that seem to ascribe preexistence and divinity to Jesus are really talking about Wisdom, with Christ identified secondarily with Wisdom. With John's Gospel incarnational Christology appears at the climax of a long process of developing ideas about Jesus within the new movement and Dunn insists that in John "Christ was the incarnate Logos, a self-manifestation of God, the one God insofar as he could make himself known in human flesh—not the incarnation of a divine power other than God...."[12] For John's Gospel, that is, Jesus is not a distinct divine person (as if the Son existed in an eternal relationship with the Father). There is, therefore, no belief in Paul in a personal preexistence for Christ and no belief in the Incarnation in the classic sense that that doctrine came to be described in later Christian orthodox theology.

The new emerging consensus agrees with Dunn that Paul (and the Synoptics) belong firmly within a Jewish religious context and that NT Christology cannot be explained, as Bousset argued, with recourse to the influence of a Greco-Roman model. *But, against Dunn, the emerging consensus argues both that Jesus was fully and firmly included, as a divine being, within a monotheistic theological framework, and that a high Christology is very early.* It is already present throughout the Pauline material and goes back to the early years or months of the post-Easter Jerusalem-based church.

To explain how the emerging consensus has moved so decisively beyond the paradigm offered by Dunn we need to consider the two focal points of its argument. First, it is argued that Paul and the earliest Christians adopted a scriptural hermeneutic to express their belief that Jesus belonged firmly within the parameters of the identity of the one God—what Bauckham and others have called "Christological monotheism." Secondly, following in particular the work of Hurtado, the earliest Christians gave to Jesus cultic devotion in a way that must mean that *as biblically faithful first-century Jews* they believed he was a fully divine being.

II: "Christological Monotheism"

There is a passage in Paul's letters that seems to offer an interpretative key to all his other Christological statements. It places Jesus squarely within the identity of the one God of Israel. And it does so in a way that assumes Paul's

---

12. Dunn, *Christology* (2nd ed., 1989), xxx.

readers will need no further explanation because he is appealing to an established, widely accepted credal statement.

In 1 Corinthians 8 Paul takes up the issue of believers in the Corinthian church eating food that has been offered to an idol in a pagan temple. For Jews with a pious scruple against participation in idolatry, participation in a meal that appears to endorse the worship of other deities—at a dinner party or at a restaurant attached to a temple, for example—would be unthinkable. On the other hand, there seem to be Christians in Corinth who take the view that because other gods do not in fact exist, they are now free to eat meat that has previously been offered to an idol, without being harmed. Over the course of three chapters Paul steers a careful, middle course between competing, polarized views on this pressing practical question.

The details of the full argument need not concern us here. It is Paul's opening, ground-rule setting, theological statement that has become a key text for the emerging consensus. In 1 Cor 8:3–6 he says,

> 3 *ei de tis agapą ton theon, houtos egnōstai hyp' autou.* 4 *Peri tēs brōseōs oun tōn eidōlothytōn, oidamen hoti ouden eidōlon en kosmǭ kai hoti oudeis theos ei mē heis.* 5 *kai gar eiper eisin legomenoi theoi eite en ouranǭ eite epi gēs, hōsper eisin theoi polloi kai kyrioi polloi,* 6 *all'*
>
>> (a) *hēmin <u>heis theos</u> ho patēr*
>>
>>> (b) *ex hou ta panta* (c) *kai <u>hēmeis</u> eis auton,*
>>
>> (d) *kai <u>heis Kyrios</u> Iēsous Christos*
>>
>>> (e) *di' hou ta panta* (f) *kai <u>hēmeis</u> di' autou.*

... 3 and if anyone loves God, he is known by him. 4 Concerning, therefore, the food of idols, we know that no idol in the world really exists and that there is no god except one. 5 For, even if there are many so-called gods, whether in heaven or on earth—as there are in fact many gods and many lords—6 but,

> (a) <u>for us</u>, there is <u>one God</u>, the Father,
>
>> (b) from whom are all things (c) and to/for whom <u>we</u> live,
>
> (d) and <u>one Lord</u>, Jesus Christ,
>
>> (e) through whom are all things (f) and through whom <u>we</u> live.

The whole of this passage, beginning with the love of God in verse 3, evokes the Jewish monotheistic confession laid out in the opening line of the daily prayer known as the Shema:

> Hear, O Israel, the LORD/*Yhwh* our God, the LORD/*Yhwh* is One.

The first verse of the Shema is written in Hebrew and Greek:

> Deut 6:4 (Heb.): *Shema Yisrael Yhwh elohenu Yhwh ehad.*

> Deut 6:4 (LXX): *Akoue, Israēl; Kyrios ho theos hēmōn Kyrios heis estin.*

Paul does far more than evoke the Shema. As my underlining of shared vocabulary shows, 1 Cor 8:6 is a reworking of the Shema in which the identity of the one God is split in two, through the glossing of the word *theos* ("God") with "the Father" and *Kyrios* ("Lord") with "Jesus Christ." Paul still believes there is one God (v. 4)—he has not become a ditheist—but given the way the Shema has been opened up and reinterpreted, the one God is now mysteriously two.[13]

This is such a remarkable passage because the Greek word *kyrios*, whose basic meaning is "Lord" (or sometimes "master"), is used in this instance as the Greek translation of the Hebrew word *adonay*, which, in turn, substitutes for the name of God written as the untranslatable Hebrew Tetragrammaton (four-letter word) *Yhwh*. Any Greek-speaking Jew who hears a Christian say what 1 Cor 8:6 says is bound to hear those words as a claim that *Yhwh* is now somehow identified with Jesus Christ.

Surprising though this may seem, it is in keeping with the many instances in which Paul cites, or alludes to, a scriptural text in which *kyrios* is the word used for the name of God so that Jesus Christ is effectively identified with *Yhwh-Kyrios*. To take, as an example, one well-known case, in Rom 10:9–13 Paul interprets the words of Joel 2:32—"all who call on the name of the Lord (Gk. *Kyrios*, Heb. *Yhwh*) will be saved"—to mean that believers who call on Jesus' name are in fact, by so doing, calling on the name *Yhwh-Kyrios* (cf. 1 Cor 1:2; 2 Tim 2:22).[14] There is ongoing discussion

---

13. See Wright, *Climax*, 120–36; *Paul*, 662–66; Hurtado, *One God*, 97–98; *Lord Jesus Christ*, 114; *How on Earth?*, 48–49; Bauckham, *God Crucified*, 36–40; *God of Israel*, 100–104, 141, 210–18; Fee, *Pauline Christology*, 89–94.

14. The other "Yahweh" texts now marshalled as evidence for Paul's identification of Christ with Israel's one God are: Rom 14:11 (Isa 45:23); 1 Cor 1:31 (Jer 9:23–24); 1 Cor 2:16 (Isa 40:13); 1 Cor 10:21–22 (Mal 1:7, 12; Deut 32:21); 1 Cor 10:26 (Ps 24:1 [LXX 23:1]); 2 Cor 3:16 (Exod 34:34); 10:17 (Jer 9:23–24); Phil 2:10–11 (Isa 45:23); 1 Thess 3:13 (Zech 14:5); 1 Thess 4:6 (Ps 94:1–2). Discussion of these texts can be found

about which of all the possible texts that might witness to this scriptural hermeneutic actually contain an identification of Jesus with *Yhwh,* since in quite a few cases an OT text that refers to *Yhwh-Kyrios* is cited without any Christological interpretation (e.g., Rom 4:7-8; 9:27-29; 10:16; 11:3, 34; 15:11; 1 Cor 3:20; 2 Cor 6:18).[15] Discussion of the extent and precise meaning of texts that have a Christological interpretation will no doubt continue. But given the presence of so many examples, we can conclude with Chester that: "cumulatively they certainly represent a clear emerging pattern."[16] And the existence of the other non-Christological *Yhwh-Kyrios* texts shows that for Paul Jesus is not simply equated with *Yhwh* without remainder; rather, Jesus is somehow a unique manifestation of *Yhwh* (Israel's one god).[17]

That Paul (and his Jewish-Christian predecessors) adopted a self-conscious identification of Jesus with the four-lettered, ineffable name of God is also the natural conclusion of the climax to the hymn about Christ in Phil 2 (discussed below and in chapter 8). There, honoring Christ Jesus' humble, obedient service unto death, God "highly exalted him and gave him the name above all names" so that, in language echoing the words describing the nations' submission to *Yhwh* in Isa 45:21-25, "at the name of Jesus, every knee should bend, in heaven and on earth and under the earth" (vv. 9-11). *For a biblically literate and faithful Jew, the name given here to Christ must somehow refer to God's own name, Yhwh.* The name above all names must have in mind the name of Israel's god (*Yhwh*) that is in view throughout the passage from Isaiah to which Phil 2:9-11 alludes (see "*Yhwh-Kyrios*" in Isa 45:18-19, 21, 24-25).[18] The passage is famous as an uncompromising

---

in Capes, *Yahweh Texts*; Hurtado, *Lord Jesus Christ*, 111-18; Bauckham, *God of Israel*, 186-91; Fee, *Pauline Christology*, 20-25, 43-50, 56-69, 89-94, 123-24, 127-34, 177-80, 189, 257-58, 264-66, 352-59, 396-98, 408-10, 563-71, 631-38. See also the use of Ps 34:8 [33:9 LXX] in 1 Pet 2:3, Isa 8:13 in 1 Pet 3:15, and Ps 102:25-27 in Heb 1:10-12.

15. For Paul citing an OT passage where *Kyrios is* used as a translation substitution for the divine name (as in the Septuagint) see: Rom 4:7-8 (Ps 32:1-2 [LXX 31:1-2]); 9:28-29 (Isa 1:9); 10:16 (Isa 53:1); 11:34 (Isa 40:13); 15:11 (Ps 117:1 [LXX 116:1]); 1 Cor 3:20 (Ps 94:11 [93:11]); 2 Cor 6:17-18 (Isa 52:11; 2 Sam 7:14). For a fuller list of *Yhwh* texts that have God as referent see Bauckham, *God of Israel*, 189-90.

16. Chester, *Messiah*, 106.

17. See Bauckham, *God of Israel*, 186-94, cf. N. T. Wright, *Fresh Perspectives*, 73, 92. It is not clear to me why Fee rejects the identification of Jesus Christ with *Yhwh* that is the unavoidable implication of 1 Cor 8:6 and other *Yhwh-Kyrios* texts (Fee, *Pauline Christology*, 564-71).

18. Most now think that Jesus is "given" the name *Yhwh* in Phil 2:9 (see, e.g., Bauckham, *God of Israel*, 24-25, and Hurtado, *Lord Jesus Christ*, 112; *How on Earth?*, 50, 94-95). This is problematic and in chapter 8 I will suggest an alternative reading that nevertheless incorporates the key insight that in vv. 9-11 Jesus is identified, as *Kyrios*, with *Yhwh*.

statement of the exclusivist claims for *Yhwh*'s identity as Creator and Lord of history. And yet now, in a quite extraordinary way, language that in Isaiah describes the categorically unique identity of *Yhwh-Kyrios* is used for the position and identity of the Lord Jesus Christ.

Returning to 1 Cor 8:6, the inclusion of "Jesus Christ" within the identity of the one God—as defined by the Shema—is not simply a matter of Christ's *exaltation* to a position at God's right hand. The "high Christology" of 1 Cor 8:6 is not just a claim for Jesus' *postresurrection* identity. In addition to the "binitarian" glosses on the words "God" and "Lord," Paul ascribes to the Lord Jesus Christ a role in creation. God the Father is the one who initiates creation—"*from* whom are all things and for whom we live" (v. 6b-c). But to the Lord Jesus Christ is also ascribed creative agency when Paul says that he is the one "*through* whom *are all things* and *through whom* we live" (v. 6e-f).[19] Similar language to describe the Son (who is the image of the invisible God, the firstborn of all creation) as creative agent is used in the Christ hymn in Col 1:15-17.

In an influential study of 1 Cor 8:6, Phil 2:6-11, and Col 1:15-20, N. T. Wright coined the expression "Christological monotheism" to describe the way these passages contain "an explicitly monotheistic statement, of the Jewish variety (i.e. creational/covenantal monotheism, as opposed to pantheism or Deism), in which we find Christ set within the monotheistic statement itself."[20] In his work, Hurtado has talked of a "binitarian mutation" of Jewish monotheism, though his analysis of 1 Cor 8:6 and related material is on the same lines as that offered by Wright.[21] Perhaps because of the negative connotations of the English word "mutation" and the questions begged by the theological neologism "binitarian," others have taken up Wright's "Christological monotheism" as a more appealing rallying cry for this new understanding of Pauline Christology.[22] For reasons that I will come to in Parts 5 and 6, I find "Christological monotheism" a less-than-perfect label for the phenomenon that Wright and others have identified. So, until I explain my preferred expression ("Jesus monotheism") I will place the expression "Christological monotheism" in scare quotes.

19. See esp. Bauckham, *God of Israel*, 102, 104, 213-18 on the wider Jewish and Hellenistic parallels and the use of similar language for God himself in Rom 11:36.

20. Wright, *Climax*, 114, cf. 99, 114, 116, 129, 132, 136.

21. Hurtado *One God*, 97-98; *Lord Jesus Christ*, 114; *How on Earth?*, 48-49.

22. See, for example, Bauckham's use of the expression in *Jesus* (18-19, 28, 30, 38-40, 101). In his most recent work Hurtado prefers the word "dyadic" to "binitarian" (see Hurtado, "Revelatory Religious Experience"; "Ancient Jewish Monotheism," 384) and sometimes prefers to talk of a "variant form" rather than a "mutation" of monotheism (*Lord Jesus Christ*, 50, n. 70).

This understanding of the "Christological monotheism" of 1 Cor 8:6 (and closely related passages) now provides an economical explanation of other prominent features of Paul's letters and other parts of the NT. Bauckham has argued that it is not just identification with the divine name that gives to Jesus a divine identity. Israel's one God has a personal identity (like a human identity) defined by various relationships that should then govern our understanding of NT statements about Jesus. In particular, the one God of Israel rules over all creation and is Lord of all human history, and as such appears on a high and lofty throne above the rest of reality. No other being (like an angel, for example) ever has such a sovereign position, so statements that put Jesus Christ at God's right hand, on God's throne, or that refer to him being over "all things (*ta panta*)" also intend his inclusion *within the unique divine identity*.[23]

The *enthronement* of Christ, with a particular debt to a Christological interpretation of Psalm 110:1—"The Lord said to my Lord, sit at my right hand," the most cited OT text in the NT—brings Hebrews and Revelation into the discussion of early "Christological monotheism" (e.g., Heb 1:3, 13; Rev 4–5; 7:15–17; 22:3). The Christology of Hebrews and Revelation, though later than the Pauline material, is very much in keeping with what is already present in Paul. Here we also find Jesus' inclusion in the divine identity expressed through his inclusion in the creative work of God (Heb 1:2–3, 10–12, cf. Rev 3:14). Christ is also eternal—the *alpha* and *omega*, first and last—in the way that Israel's one God, alone, is eternal (Rev 1:17; 22:13, cf. 1:8; 21:6; Isa 44:6; 48:12; and Heb 1:8). Bauckham has also endorsed the minority view of the likes of Christopher Rowland that the name given to the eternal Son in Heb 1:4 is not, as most have supposed, the expression "Son," but the divine name, *Yhwh*.[24] In the same vein, David Lincicum has now added further support to a divine identity understanding of Revelation's Christology by arguing that the title "alpha and omega" for Jesus (in Rev 22:13) is partly indebted to a creative interpretation of the Greek letters Iota Alpha Omega, which were sometimes used in Greek biblical manuscripts as a translation of the Hebrew *Yhwh*.[25] In any case, in Rev 22:3–4 God and the Lamb share the same divine name. So, in their own ways Hebrews (1:3–4,

---

23. For Israel's God as ruler over all things, see the texts in Bauckham, *God of Israel*, 23 n. 44. For Christ over all things, see: 1 Cor 15:27–28; Eph 1:22; Phil 3:21; Heb 1:2; 2:8. For Christ's creative work in sustaining "all things," see John 1:3; 1 Cor 8:6; Eph 1:10; Col 1:16–17, 20; Heb 1:3.

24. Bauckham, *God Crucified*, 34; *God of Israel*, 25, 200, 239. See already Rowland, *Open Heaven*, 113.

25. Lincicum, "Alpha and Omega."

13; 2:5-9) and Revelation (esp. 5:9-14) echo the *exaltation* of Christ over all creation that is the climactic moment of the Christ hymn of Phil 2:6-11.

Time and again we find divine *action* or *functions* ascribed to Christ in a way that now makes sense if Christ belongs within the divine identity and if he fully participates in the divine nature. For example, sometimes God is said to transform believers (1 Cor 15:38; 2 Cor 5:1; Rom 8:11), but in Phil 3:20-21 this is Christ's responsibility. In biblical and Jewish literature God sits in (heavenly) *judgment* (e.g., Dan 7:9-11, cf. Rom 14:10), but in 2 Cor 5:10-11 all must appear before the judgment seat *of Christ*.[26]

In 1 Cor 8:6 God is the Father, and although the Lord Jesus Christ is not called "the Son," his identity as God's (preexistent, eternal) Son seems to be assumed (cf. 1 Cor 1:9; 15:28). At any rate, the one-God-the-Father and one-Lord-Jesus-Christ of the "Christological monotheism" in 1 Cor 8 now explains the way Paul regularly describes the divine subject in similar language, without explanation or apology, and often quite casually in greetings and final blessings. In 1 Thess 3:11 he can pray, for example, "May our God and Father himself and our Lord Jesus Christ direct our way to you" (cf., e.g., Rom 1:7; 15:6; 1 Cor 1:3; 2 Cor 1:2-3; Gal 1:3; Eph 1:2-3; 6:23). Paul's divine identity Christology needs no explanation: his readers, including and especially those from a Jewish background, apparently understood and did not question it.

Furthermore, the way Paul spoke (and wrote) so freely of Christ's inclusion in the divine identity led to language that at first seems clumsy, but on fuller reflection is probably designed to express a profound theological mystery. So, for example, the prayer in 1 Thess 3:11—in what is probably Paul's first letter—nicely illustrates the conscious ambiguity of a God who is *one*, yet now, for Paul and his fellow Christians, mysteriously *two*. Ordinarily, grammar would dictate that *two* subjects (God, who is the Father, and the Lord Jesus Christ) require a verb in the plural. But in the Greek of 1 Thess 3:11 the verb "direct" (*kateuthynai*) is a singular: *two* persons grammatically expressed as *one* acting subject. Two in one. English translations cannot convey the arresting use of such odd grammar, but it would not be missed by first-century Greek speakers. Again, a similar phenomenon occurs in the book of Revelation where, as Bauckham has noted, "mention of God and Christ is followed by a singular verb (11:15) or singular pronouns (22:3-4; and 6:17)."[27] To these texts we might add that a similar strategy may

---

26. For this sharing of divine attributes and prerogatives in Paul see Fee, *Pauline Christology*, 576-85.

27. Bauckham, *God of Israel*, 142. Bauckham's inclusion of 6:17 here assumes the variant reading *autou* is the original. Those manuscripts at 6:17 that have a plural pronoun (*autōn*) instead of the singular (*autou*) are best explained as a correction to the

be at play in Col 1:20, where there is perhaps deliberate ambiguity between God and the beloved Son in the phrase "reconciling all things to *him*."[28]

III: Cultic Devotion

Twentieth-century study of the New Testament has long recognized that the Christology of the early church was not just a matter of propositional truth claims. Christ is also the focus of worship and prayer. There was a cult of Christ.[29] In the early second century, the Roman magistrate Pliny the Younger described in a letter to the Emperor Trajan the practice of Christians chanting hymns "to Christ as to a god" (*Epistles* 10.96.7) and the New Testament itself provides first-century evidence of this practice. For Wilhelm Bousset and the generations of scholars in the twentieth century influenced by his approach to the history of religions, the Christ cult could only be understood as a development arising from a shift from a Jewish to a Greco-Roman context where the worship of Jesus as a divine Lord (*kyrios*) came about under the influence of the cult of divine heroes and deities. And this must have happened some time after the early years of the Aramaic-speaking, Palestinian-based, "primitive community" phase of the new movement.[30]

Building on the work of Martin Hengel, Hurtado and Bauckham have successfully argued that Christ devotion in fact goes back to the earliest period of the (post-Easter) Christian community, perhaps even to its earliest months, and that it is a phenomenon attested across the whole of the NT, with no evidence of any early Christians objecting to the practice.[31]

---

more difficult, original text that deliberately used odd Greek to make the point that the one God is now one God in two persons.

28. Commentators usually argue for one or the other, but the passages in 1 Thessalonians and Revelation suggest deliberate ambiguity. Jesus' words in Matt 28:19 may also intend a similar ambiguity. Are believers are to be baptized into the one "name" (as the singular Greek *to onoma* implies: "Father, Son, and Holy Spirit") or, into three names (as the Greek of what follows is naturally read: "*The* Father, *the* Son, and *the* Holy Spirit")?

29. See, e.g., Bousset, *Kyrios Christos,* 129–38, for cultic devotion to Jesus attested in, but also antedating, Paul.

30. See discussion of Bousset's paradigm and its influence in Hurtado, *Lord Jesus Christ,* 13–25. Bousset's paradigm now finds expression, with more cautious claims about historical *origins,* in Litwa, *Iesus Deus* (2014).

31. See Hengel, *Between,* 79–96; *Studies,* 227–92; *Studien,* 185–258. For Hurtado's view that it probably goes back to the earliest months of the post-Easter church, see *Lord Jesus Christ,* 118, 136. For Bauckham on worship directed to Christ, see his *God of Israel,* 127–81.

Hurtado categorizes six kinds of evidence for this Christ devotion. And in view of other contributions to the emerging consensus we can add here a seventh. The relevant evidence both illustrates early Christian *practice* and also the pattern of *belief* that Bauckham has emphasized.[32]

First, then, there is a "well established pattern of prayer in which Jesus features prominently, either as a recipient or as a unique agent through whom prayer is offered."[33] Paul in his letters pens "prayer-wish passages" in which God and Jesus are together invoked, as in the passage from 1 Thessalonians that we discussed in the previous section (1 Thess 3:11-13, cf. 2 Thess 2:16-17; 2 Thess 3:5).[34] In a similar vein, many of his letters conclude with a prayerful benediction invoking God and Christ together (Rom 16:20; 2 Cor 13:14; Gal 6:16-18; Eph 6:23-24; Phil 4:20-23; 1 Thess 5:23-28). These formulaic, matter-of-course prayers probably reflect well-known patterns of corporate prayer (or "liturgical" practice), though on other occasions we encounter spontaneous, individual, and very personal prayers (2 Cor 12:8-9; Acts 7:59-60, cf. Acts 1:24; 13:2).

Secondly, there is invocation and confession of the kind found in Paul's exclamation in Aramaic in 1 Cor 16:22-23: "If anyone has no love for the Lord, let him be accursed. *Marana tha!* ("Our Lord, come!"). The grace of the Lord Jesus be with you." This is an example of Paul himself "calling on the (name of) the Lord (Jesus)," which other texts, along with the context in 1 Cor 16:22-23, show was a basic, constitutive practice of the Spirit-filled Christian life, defining Jesus' followers over against others (non-Christian Jews and pagans) (see Rom 10:9-13; 1 Cor 1:2, 13, 15; 12:3; 2 Cor 12:8; Acts 9:14, 21; 22:16; 2 Tim 2:22; Rev 22:20). As an invocation for the Lord Jesus to come—whether now or in the eschatological future is a matter of interpretation—this confession and calling on Jesus as Lord anticipates a universal confession, by "every tongue," in the eschatological future (Phil 2:11). In the present, it is reflected in texts that speak of a proclamation "in his name" of a "repentance for the forgiveness of sins" (Luke 24:47, cf. Acts 2:38; 10:43). Several of the texts show that an invocation of the name of the Lord Jesus was an established feature of early Christian ritual and spirituality (1 Cor 1:2, 13, 15; 12:3; 16:22-23; Acts 22:16) that reflected the older, biblical practice of "calling on the name of *Yhwh-Kyrios*" (e.g., Gen 4:26; 12:8; 1 Sam 12:17-18):

---

32. For fuller discussion see, Hurtado, *One God*, 83-124; "Binitarian Shape"; *Lord Jesus Christ*, 134-53; Bauckham, *God of Israel*, 127-51; Fee, *Pauline Christology*, esp. 488-95, cf. 122-23, 170, 196-98, 362, 409, 412-13, 574-76.

33. Hurtado, *Lord Jesus Christ*, 140.

34. See especially now Fee, *Pauline Christology*, 51-55; 65-68; 73-77; 465-66; 493-95, 574-76.

it reveals both the character of early Christian devotional practice and of the Christological interpretation of scriptural *Yhwh* texts.

The 1 Cor 8:4-6 redefinition of the Shema should be included here as evidence for a distinctive (Jewish) Christian confession of Jesus as Lord. The way the redefinition of the Shema is used by Paul—at the beginning of his argument over food offered to idols—suggests early Christians used the words of 1 Cor 8:6 in their own version of the daily meditation on God's oneness (that priests proclaimed in the daily Temple service and ordinary Jews prayed in the morning and evening).[35] Omitting the word "But" (Gk. "*all*'") with which the verse now starts in the traditional division of the text, verse 6 contains a tightly constructed formula in two balanced thirteen-word halves. Some of the terminology in the confession is uncharacteristic of Paul's own writing and this is consistent with other evidence, to which we shall come in the next chapter, that the confession goes back to the earliest Aramaic- and Hebrew-speaking group of believers.

Hurtado's third and fourth categories are baptism and the Lord's Supper. Both, in their own way, are rituals focused on Jesus as Lord and can be compared with pagan rites dedicated to a deity. Baptism involved invocation of Jesus' name (Acts 2:38; 8:16; 10:48, cf. 1 Cor 6:11; Jas 2:7) and a Christ-focused dying with Christ and being clothed with him (Rom 6:4; Gal 3:27). The regular meal in memory of Jesus is the "Lord's Supper" (*kyriakon deipnon*) (1 Cor 11:20), focused on the "cup" and "table of the Lord" Jesus (1 Cor 11:27; 10:21), which Paul himself compares with pagan cult meals and the eating of sacrifices in the Jerusalem Temple (1 Cor 10:14-22). "This is not merely a memorial feast for a dead hero. Jesus is perceived as the living and powerful *Kyrios* who owns the meal and presides at it, and with whom believers have fellowship as with a god."[36]

Hurtado's fifth category is the "hymns" that celebrate Christ's identity and work. Singing "psalms (*psalmois*), hymns (*hymnois*), and spiritual songs (*ōdais*)" (Col 3:16-17; Eph 5:18-20, cf. 1 Cor 14:26) was a feature of early Christian gatherings. Newly created hymnic material in Phil 2:6-11, Col 1:15-20, John 1:1-18, Eph 5:14, and 1 Tim 3:16 is generally reckoned to reflect the Christ-focused content of that verbal praise. In these passages the hymn is *about* Christ, just as biblical psalms are also often *about* Yhwh/God.

There is also evidence that the earliest Christians directed hymns and praise *to* Christ. The prose hymn in Phil 2:6-11 is *about* Christ, but it is "difficult to make sense" of the hymn's climax "except on the basis that it

---

35. For the recitation of the Shema in first-century Temple liturgy, synagogue services, and daily prayer see Waaler, *The Shema*, 123-205.

36. Hurtado, *Lord Jesus Christ*, 146, cf. Fee, *Pauline Christology*, 491-92; Dunn, *Worship*, 50-51.

is assumed and expected that Christ will be acclaimed and worshipped in the same way as God (and that this will itself be to the glory of God)."[37] When Acts 13:2 says "*While they were worshipping the Lord (Kyrios) and fasting, the Holy Spirit said . . . ,*" the Lukan pattern of freely using *Kyrios* for the risen Christ (e.g., Luke 24:34; Acts 1:6; 7:59-60) means Luke thinks the Christians in Antioch were "worshipping *Jesus*" in a way that must have included corporate singing (cf. 2:47; 10:46; 16:25). The same goes for the injunction to address "one another in psalms and hymns and spiritual songs, singing and making melody *to the Lord* with your heart . . ." (Eph 5:19, cf. Col 3:16). Indeed, Christ-*directed* praise is explicit in the doxologies in 2 Tim 4:18; 2 Pet 3:18; Rev 1:5-6 (cf. Heb 13:21; 1 Pet 4:11), in the words of thanks to "Christ Jesus our Lord" in 1 Tim 1:12, and in the climactic scene of future universal prostration and confession *to* Christ—in the hymn *about* him—in Phil 2:10-11. In Revelation 5:9-14, the future worshipful recognition of Christ's divine sovereignty is already a reality in heaven in the praise offered by every creature in heaven, on the earth, and in the world below to both the "one who sits on the throne *and to the lamb*" (that in turn parallels the worship given to God in 4:8-11 and that anticipates the worship of both God and the Lamb in 7:9-17 and 14:4).

It is true that we do not have the actual words of hymns directed *to* Christ that all these passages surely envisage. Paul only records hymns *about* Christ. But then this is not surprising. The literary context of Paul's letters suits hymnic material in the *third* person ("*he* humbled himself . . ."; "*who* is/*who* being . . ."), not the *second* person or vocative ("You are . . ."; "O Lord Jesus"), since Paul is already writing in the *second* person to a particular community of believers. A change of address to include hymnic material directly to Christ ("You, O Lord, are . . .") would be odd. Paul and his fellow Christians prayed both *for* Christ or *about* Christ (in "wish-prayers" and benedictions) and to Christ (e.g., Acts 7:59-60; 2 Cor 12:8-9), so we are not surprised to find the kind of circumstantial evidence just noted that they sang songs both *to* Christ and *about* him.

Psalms in the Greek Bible are regularly labeled with the same terms used to describe Christian corporate worship in Col 3:16-17 and Eph 5:18-20.[38] And because, as we have seen, early Christians were in the habit of applying biblical *Yhwh-Kyrios* texts to Jesus, it is likely that biblical psalms were sung and applied to Christ in the same way. This practice is reflected in the catena of biblical texts applied to Christ in Heb 1:5-13, where Christ is the "Son" (of

---

37. Chester, "High Christology," 39.

38. For the *psalmos* and *ōdē* see, e.g., LXX Pss 4:1; 17:1; 29:1; 41:9; for the *hymnos* see, e.g., LXX Pss 6:1; 53:1; 60:1.

Ps 2:7 and 2 Sam 7:14), the "firstborn" (who fulfills the word of LXX Deut 32:43), "God" (as in Ps 45:6-7), and the "*Kyrios*" (of Ps 102:25-27).[39]

Hurtado's last category is prophecy, which serves and is directed by God, the Spirit, and *the Lord (Jesus)* in the Pauline churches (1 Cor 12:4-6). So, as Hurtado points out, "[g]iven the negative stance of biblical tradition against prophecy in the name of any other deity (e.g., Deut. 13:1-5), and the lack of any parallels of prophetic oracles delivered in first-century Jewish group worship in the name of any figure other than God, this attribution of prophecy to the exalted Jesus is simply extraordinary."[40]

To these six categories we should make explicit a seventh; the offering of the physical gesture of *proskynesis* (prostration) to Christ.[41] In the Bible and in the wider ancient world, *verbal* acclamation and praise of a deity or of divine ruler (in the Greek and Roman worlds where kings and emperors were worshipped) could be accompanied by the physical gesture of prostration. The precise interpretation of this gesture varies according to context. In some circumstances *proskynesis* merely honors a superior or one from whom a kindness is sought (as is the case in Gen 23:12; 33:3-7; 2 Sam 18:21; Matt 18:26). But in most cases in the Old and New Testaments *proskynesis* is reserved for the one God and there are clearly statements, from the Decalogue onwards, prohibiting it being given to another deity (Exod 20:5 = Deut 5:9, cf., e.g., Exod 23:24; 34:14; Lev 26:1; Matt 4:9-10). After the deification of the Macedonian king Alexander the Great (356-323 BC), *proskynesis* was often a key feature of the cult of the ruler/Ruler Cult in the Greek and Roman worlds. So, in the first century, when Roman emperors were regularly accorded the same honors as the gods, the action was charged with political and religious sensitivities, especially for Jews who refused to offer *proskynesis* to the emperor Gaius Caligula (Philo *Embassy* 116-18, cf. Esth 3:1-6; LXX Add Esth 13:12-14). In Jewish and Christian apocalyptic literature there is also a topos in which prostration before an angel is prohibited to make clear that the angel is not God, since such a gesture should only be done before God himself (e.g., *Apoc. Zeph.* 6:14-15, cf. Tob 12:15-22).[42]

Against this background, prostration to Jesus seems to be another key element of the Christ-devotion pattern. In Phil 2:10, the future recognition and acclamation of Jesus will be accompanied by a bending of the knee. The author of Luke-Acts is at pains to stress that even though they are agents of divine power, the early Christians rejected an obsequious or reverential

---

39. On which see Bauckham, *God of Israel*, 233-53.
40. Cf. Hurtado, *Lord Jesus Christ*, 151.
41. Discussed in Hurtado, *How on Earth?*, 139-51.
42. See Bauckham, "Worship of Jesus"; Stuckenbruck, *Angel Veneration*, 75-103.

proskynesis that would have implied they were worthy of receiving the kind of honors given to a god (Acts 10:25–26, cf. 14:8–18). But Jesus himself happily receives *proskynesis* as he ascends to heaven at the end of Luke's Gospel (Luke 24:50–53). In Revelation prostration before an angel is specifically prohibited (Rev 19:10; 22:8–9). But the wicked are depicted giving *proskynesis* to demons, to the beast, to the dragon, and to the image of the beast (Rev 9:20; 13:4, 8, 12; 14:9, 11; 16:2), whilst in heaven there is a right and proper angelic *proskynesis* that accompanies the songs of praise offered to the enthroned Lamb (Rev 5:14, cf. Phil 2:10). Similarly, Hebrews proclaims the divine identity of Jesus the Son with the claim that he is worthy of *proskynesis* from the angels (Heb 1:6).

In none of the Gospels is there a fully conscious, corporate, worshipful prostration before Jesus until after his resurrection (see Matt 28:9, 17, and Luke 24:53). However, in John and Matthew there are cases where Jesus receives *proskynesis* during his earthly life (Matt 2:2, 8, 11; 8:2; 9:18; 14:33; 15:25; 20:20; John 9:38) and in Mark the pagan soldiers mockingly treat Jesus as a divine ruler by rendering to him *proskynesis* (and royal acclamation) (Mark 15:19).[43] In these cases, especially the passages in Matthew where the Old Testament suggests a divine epiphany, the Gospel writers have likely included the language of prostration to suggest that, although Jesus was not yet fully recognized for who he was, at various times and places the veil was lifted and people (and demons in Mark 5:6) gave to Jesus an honor that, with hindsight, they would have realized was entirely fitting for the one who was "God with us."[44]

Together these seven phenomena constitute a constellation or *pattern* of devotional actions that amounts to a "worship" appropriate to one who is included within the identity of the one God of the Hebrew Scriptures. (In Part 6 I will return to this pattern of cultic devotion and propose that we add an eighth item to the inventory. But this list of seven will do for now.) Indeed, frequently Jesus is accorded reverence that in Jewish tradition is reserved for God. Such reverence is specifically *denied* to other figures (mediatorial beings such as angels or exalted patriarchs), but is now given to Jesus. Along the way, the devotional pattern means the treatment of Jesus in the first century was in various ways *analogous* to the treatment of gods and divine beings in the Greco-Roman world. But the fact that, as we have seen, the Lord Jesus Christ is firmly included within the identity of the one

---

43. Compare the *proskynesis* to Jesus by the demonized man in Gentile territory in Mark 5:6 that for Mark probably signals a worshipful recognition of Jesus at least in the terms that would be normal outside of Jewish territory.

44. Compare the discussion in Bauckham, *God of Israel*, 130–31, 179–80, 204.

God of Israelite faith means that the devotion to him cannot be denied the full significance it would have in the Jewish context.

IV: Conclusion: Consensus on the Shape and Date of an Early High Christology

Together, the arguments for a "Christological monotheism" and the worship of Jesus create a weighty and solid case for a high Christology of divine identity in the early years—and in the thoroughly Jewish context—of the Christian movement. In all this, practice is inseparable from belief. Christ devotion necessarily entails a binitarian (or "dyadic") shape to Jewish monotheism and "Christological monotheism" inevitably required a Christ devotion (that was, at the same time a one-God-of-Israel devotion). I agree with Bauckham that in terms of the *origins* of the early church's Christology, belief preceded practice: his earliest followers worshipped Jesus in recognition of Jesus' inclusion in the identity of the one God. So, in this study I will often refer to "Christological monotheism" assuming that readers know that that theology necessarily entailed a particular and novel transformation of existing biblical patterns of worship.[45]

The peculiar beliefs about Jesus and his inclusion within the identity of the one God are reflected in the *form* that Christ devotion took. For a (non-Christian) Jew the early Christians treat Jesus the way Israelites were expected to treat the one God himself.[46] Before long the earliest believers were rubbing shoulders with, and evangelizing, non-Jews. In many and various ways (that I will not review at this juncture, but will grapple with in later chapters) what the early Christians did to Jesus meant that non-Jews in the wider pagan environment would justifiably conclude that Jesus was being treated as a god or a divine ruler (like the Roman emperor). For example, calling Jesus the Son of God and announcing his arrival (including his birth) as "good news" would evoke the language of the cult of the

---

45. For Bauckham's subordination of the *practice* to the *belief* see *God Crucified*, 13–16 (= *God of Israel*, 11–13). I agree with Bauckham in so far as practice followed belief *at the origins* of "Christological monotheism." However, it was probably also the case that sometimes some new converts first had a powerful encounter with God in the context of an early Christian community at worship and prayer that then led to a new confession of faith. Sometimes people (then and now) have an encounter that produces new behavior before it brings about clearly articulated new beliefs.

46. This, of course, has to be qualified in some important respects. For example, Jesus is not worshipped as one who now resides in the Jerusalem Temple and he does not receive animal sacrifices on a physical altar (though he does receive metaphorical sacrifices in Rev 14:4).

(divine) emperor.[47] *But the early Christians were not ditheists.* The worship of Jesus was not expressed through the setting up of a new temple shrine to him. Jesus is not *added* to an existing pantheon. The birth of Christianity was not marked by the worship of a new Mediterranean god, but by the belief that the one unique God—*Yhwh-Kyrios*—had climatically, at the end of Israel's history, appeared in fully human and a highly personal form. The NT texts adopt various strategies to ensure that the grammar of their devotion remained firmly within the boundaries of a belief in one God.

By the same token, this distinctive "binitarian" worship of one God without two cults is mirrored in the distinctive *language* of NT Christology. The twoness of the one God's identity is expressed through the intimate, relational language of the Father and the Son, not through wholly separate names of discrete, potentially competing, divine entities (e.g., Zeus and Apollo). Glory given in worship to Jesus Christ the Lord goes through Jesus to God the Father (Phil 2:11; 1 Pet 4:11). The Son is the visible image and form of a Father who is invisible (explicitly in Col 1:13–15 and implicitly in Phil 2:6; Heb 1:3; Rev 1:13–16; 4–5) and as such the Son shares and manifests God the Father's glory (Heb 1:3, cf. Phil 3:21; 2 Cor 3:12–4:4; Col 1:19). Both are responsible for creation, but everything comes *from* the Father, *through* the Son (1 Cor 8:6; Col 1:16; Heb 1:2; John 1:3). Scriptural texts that employ more than one word to refer to Israel's God in a way that seems, on the face of it, to entail an unnecessary redundancy are taken to refer to the two divine entities Jesus Christ the Son and his Father. For example, in the reworking of the first line of the Shema in 1 Cor 8:6 the two words that denote Israel's deity—"God" and "Lord" ("Hear, O Israel the *Lord* your *God*, the *Lord* is one")—are each taken to refer to different entities, or persons, within the divine identity ("*God* the Father" and the "*Lord* Jesus Christ"). Hurtado has pointed out that a similar creative interpretation of two referents for God in Isa 45:23 ("God" and "to me") may have precipitated a "Christological midrash" on that *Yhwh-Kyrios* text in Phil 2:9–11.[48] Later Christian and rabbinic texts, and material in Philo of Alexandria, suggest that this method of scriptural interpretation was already being used in some Jewish circles to explore the ways in which the one God could be manifest in two discrete entities or forms.[49] A similar creative scriptural hermeneutic

---

47. For recent explorations of the way some passages would be read or heard in a Greco-Roman context see esp. Peppard, *Son of God* (2012), and Litwa, *Iesus Deus* (2014).

48. Hurtado, *How on Earth?*, 92.

49. Justin Martyr, in his *Dialogue with Trypho* says that Gen 19:24 ("And *the LORD* rained on Sodom and Gomorrah brimstone and fire *from the LORD* out of heaven") refers to two separate divine beings (*Dial.* 56). This interpretation of Gen 19:24 is

1. INTRODUCTION TO A NEW EMERGING CONSENSUS

is used in the way that, as we have seen, God and Christ appear together as the subject of a singular verb (Rev 11:15), as the antecedent to a singular pronoun (Rev 22:3-4; 6:17), with each described as joint occupants of a singular throne (e.g., Rev 22:1, 3).

Whilst Hurtado's work has shown that what Christians did to Jesus is in many ways equivalent to both the pagan treatment of their gods and also Israel's own worship of the one God *in the cultic context*, recent voices in the ongoing debate have helpfully stressed that Christ devotion extends beyond the kind of cultic categories identified by Hurtado that we have just reviewed. For example, in his discussion of *Pauline Christology* (2007) Gordon Fee points out that there is not just a "cultic" devotion to Christ in Paul; there is also a total life commitment that is thoroughly *personal*.[50] For Paul "to live is Christ; to die is gain" (Phil 1:20) and the ideal life is lived in undivided devotion to the Lord (1 Cor 7:35, cf. vv. 32-34), straining forward towards the time of permanent communion with him (1 Thess 5:9-10; 2 Cor 5:8; Phil 1:23). Everything else is rubbish compared with a personal, individual, "gaining Christ, and being found in him" (Phil 3:8-9).

Some of this has precedent in the piety of OT psalmody where the psalmist longs for God (e.g., Pss 42:2; 63:1; 84:2). But the Christ devotion attested in the NT is essentially more quotidian, personal, and all-life encompassing than the *event*-focus of the Jewish cult and its daily, weekly, and annual festivals and liturgies. For "Paul's radically changed world view, everything is done in relation to Christ. The church exists 'in Christ,' and everything that believers are and do is 'for Christ,' 'by Christ,' 'through Christ,' and 'for Christ's sake.'"[51] Christ devotion was *process*, not just *event*.

Chris Tilling has now strengthened this wider perspective on Pauline Christology through a careful monograph-length comparison of the relationship in biblical and contemporary Jewish literature between Christ and the believer (along with the rest of reality), on the one hand, and the relationship between God and his people (along with the rest of reality), on the other hand.[52] Tilling helpfully shows that there is need to move beyond the focus on *cultic* devotion in Hurtado's work and to pay attention to all

---

reflected in talmudic debates about the Two Powers in heaven heresy (on which see Segal, *Two Powers*, 118-19, 130-31, 159-62, 221-22). In turn, writing in the first century, Philo of Alexandria says that Gen 31:13 (LXX) ("I am the God who appeared to you in the place of God") refers to two Gods (*On Dreams* 1:227-29). (The Hebrew Massoretic text lacks "in the place of God"). See Segal, *Two Powers*, 159-62.

50. The point was made also by Bousset, *Kyrios Christos*, 153, 157, 159-60.

51. Fee, *Pauline Christology*, 489, cf. 412-13, 488-90.

52. Tilling, *Christology*, (2012). See also Tilling, "Misreading" and Bauckham's observations in his most recent article ("Devotion to Jesus Christ," 191-92, 199-200).

the ways in which the early Christian understanding of the "Christ relation" (as he calls it) mirrors the biblical and Jewish "God relation." Together with Fee's comments, Tilling's contribution anticipates a defining element of the new paradigm that I will present in Parts 5 and 6.

2: The Origins of Christ Devotion and "Christological Monotheism"

At the heart of the new emerging consensus there is a confident claim that a high Christology appeared at the very start of the life of the new movement (after Jesus' death). Though there are voices of discontent and various objections raised in some quarters (which I will review in chapter 2), it is hard to gainsay the coherent pattern of Christ devotion that Hurtado and Bauckham have demonstrated. In turn, the nature of the pattern has implications for its origins. Because key passages in Paul, to one degree or another, reflect traditional pre-Pauline liturgical language (1 Cor 8:6, cf. Phil 2:6–11), which in one case apparently goes back to the Aramaic-speaking church (in the case of the "*marana tha*" in 1 Cor 16:22), overwhelmingly the evidence points to a very early origin.[53] We do not have to wait until John's Gospel or texts that may have been written late in the first century (such as Revelation and Hebrews) to find a high Christology.

It is true that there is no evidence of an organized pattern of devotion during Jesus' lifetime. Yet, there is no extant evidence for any form of (post-Easter) Christianity that rejected or opposed the behavior that evidently became the norm. Neither is there clear, indisputable evidence of stages of development towards "Christological monotheism." So it is likely that a high Christology was precipitated by "a veritable explosion in devotional innovation as well as in christological beliefs in the very few earliest years (perhaps even the earliest months)" impacting the whole church in its early Aramaic (and Greek-speaking) Palestinian environment.[54] And, we might

---

53. For some, e.g., M. Hengel, the Christ hymn in Phil 2:6–11 has been the primary evidence for an early, pre-Pauline high Christology of preexistence and incarnation (see his *Studies*, 278, 288–89, 379–83). However, placing so much weight on Phil 2 assumes the hymn is pre-Pauline and that it does not fit well in its current context in Philippians (so too Hurtado, *How on Earth?*, 104–7). It is questionable whether it is pre-Pauline and in recent years commentators have increasingly recognized the many ways that Phil 2:6–11 is carefully integrated into the rest of the letter. (I will argue in later chapters that its Christology is a particularly appropriate one for the Philippian context). So it is better to allow the breadth of evidence, including now especially the confession in 1 Cor 8:6, to bear the burden of the case for early origins.

54. Hurtado, *Lord Jesus Christ*, 136. Later Hurtado suggests the "first few weeks" of the church's new life for the origins of binitarian monotheism (*How on Earth?*, 203).

add, there is no obvious external stimulus or change of circumstances that would plausibly explain a shift from seeing Christ as a messiah and prophet to the worship of him in a way that implied his divine identity. For example, an influx of Greek-speaking Jews into the nascent Palestinian movement (see Acts 6) does not readily account for a significant change in the way Jesus is treated. There is no evidence that, by comparison to their Aramaic and Hebrew speaking compatriots, Greek-speaking Jews had significantly different views about the identity of God and the way that he alone should be worshipped that would explain the birth of Christ devotion.

So, in his recent review of the current debate Chester concludes that there is now a growing "scholarly consensus . . . that . . . a Christology that portrays Christ as divine emerges very early, in distinctively Jewish terminology and within a Jewish context."[55] However, beyond basic agreement that there was a "binitarian" high Christology at the beginnings of the life of the church, consensus starts to disappear. Serious problems and questions arise, particularly when we consider the issue of origins: where did it all come from, when exactly, and why? We will consider some of these problems in chapters 3 and 4. On such questions there are some key judgments where Hurtado and Bauckham are in agreement, and Hurtado has made some specific proposals to explain *why* an early high Christology came about.

I: A Lack of Precedent in Jewish Monotheism

In recent decades, a number of other scholars have stressed the continuities between early Christian beliefs about Jesus and pre-Christian Jewish ideas surrounding various divine mediator figures (angels, Wisdom, the Logos, and exalted patriarchs, for example). Some have argued that much of what we find in "Christological monotheism" is anticipated in Jewish traditions surrounding these divine mediators. Worship of Jesus and his inclusion in the divine identity could then be understood, in part, as a case of Jesus being judged the fulfillment of existing hopes for a unique divine mediator.[56]

However, both Hurtado and Bauckham—each in their own way— stress the lack of precedent or real analogy for a high Christology in first-century Judaism. Hurtado insists that there is no evidence of Jewish worship of a figure other than the one God that could provide a precedent for the worship of Jesus alongside and in addition to the worship of the one God

---

55. Chester, "High Christology," 38.

56. Scholars who have stressed continuity (without necessarily signing up to all the conclusions of the emerging consensus) include C. Rowland, J. Fossum, W. Horbury, A. Chester, A. Y. Collins, S. Vollenweider and D. Boyarin.

of Israelite faith. There are passages in various texts that describe angelic and/or human reverence towards various human beings (the Enochic Son of Man-Messiah in *1 En.* 37-71, the high priest in Ben Sira/Sirach 50 and Adam in the *Life of Adam and Eve* 12-16, for example), which some of us (myself included) have adduced as evidence for a partial precedent for a worship of Jesus. However, Hurtado dismisses the possibility that these texts provide such a precedent. There may be some *literary* scenes that "are interesting as illustrating the speculative directions and forms that ancient Jewish thought could take toward exalted symbolic figures."[57] However, none of these provide evidence of Jews worshipping "a second figure alongside . . . in addition to their God" that can be shown to reflect concrete behavior in a way that explains the "full *pattern of religious behavior* practiced in early Christian groups."[58]

Similarly, for Bauckham, Jewish monotheism entails a clear line of absolute distinction between the one God and all other reality. Jewish monotheism is "strict" and "exclusive," with God wholly separate as Creator from his creatures over whom he is sovereign. Because his identity as Creator and Ruler of all things defines his identity—*who* he is—he does not *share* his role as Creator and Ruler with another. And because worship is what you do to recognize the identity of this God, it is unthinkable, from theological first principles, that biblically faithful Jews could ever have worshipped anyone, or anything, other than God. So, along with Hurtado, Bauckham thinks there is no real evidence for a worship other than the worship of God himself that anticipates the worship given to Jesus.

II: Hurtado's Explanation of Christological Origins

So what caused the apparently unprecedented variant form of Jewish monotheism that we call "Christological monotheism"? Hurtado argues that there are *four* explanatory factors and forces.[59] First, there is *Jewish monotheism* itself. Although its exclusive worship of God did not *cause* or stimulate the worship of Jesus, it did impose a *constraint* on Christ devotion that led to a distinctive pattern of including Jesus in the worship of the one God. Christians did not create an additional, separate Jesus cult and add it to

---

57. Hurtado, "Binitarian Shape," 194 (see 193-94 generally for comments on *L.A.E.* 13-14, *1 En.* 37-71, and obeisance to Moses in *Ezekiel the Tragedian* 68-82, and *How on Earth?*, 126).

58. Hurtado, *Lord Jesus Christ*, 39-40 (see generally 38-42, 137).

59. Ibid., 27-78.

the existing worship of the one God. That would have entailed, in effect, a ditheism (rather than a "binitarianism").

Secondly, there was (the historical person) Jesus of Nazareth. Hurtado shares the view of the overwhelming majority of modern scholars that Jesus did not think of, or present, himself in divine terms. And he certainly did not endorse or demand the kind of worship of him that went with the early church's "binitarian" modification of Jewish monotheism. But the historical Jesus caused a polarization between supporters and opponents that can best be explained by both his teaching and messianic self-claims. So Jesus' ministry is an important presupposition of the later worship of him.

A satisfactory account of the *shape* and *origins* of early (high) Christology can remain quite agnostic as to both Jesus' precise "aims or purposes" and the contents of his message, "in particular what specific claims he may have made for himself."[60] Jesus' ministry is obviously a presupposition of Christ devotion, but the "particularizing focus on Jesus" in evidence across the NT does not "account for the binitarian devotional pattern we see so quickly in evidence."[61] So whilst a factor, Jesus' historical life was not sufficient, of itself, to explain Christ devotion.

Thirdly, Hurtado theorizes that the decisive factor that caused the binitarian mutation in monotheism and worship of Jesus was powerful revelatory experiences that led his followers to conclude that the risen and exalted Jesus should now be worshipped:[62]

> Within the early Christian circles of the first few years (perhaps even the first few weeks), individuals had powerful revelatory experiences that they understood to be encounters with the glorified Jesus. Some also had experiences that they took to be visions of the exalted Jesus in heavenly glory, being reverenced in cultic actions by the transcendent beings traditionally identified as charged with fulfilling the heavenly liturgy (e.g., angels, the "living creatures," and so on). Some received prophetic inspirations to announce the exaltation of Jesus to God's right hand and to summon the elect in God's name to register in cultic actions their acceptance of God's will that Jesus be reverenced. Through such revelatory experiences, Christological convictions and corresponding cultic practices were born that

---

60. Ibid., 55 (see further 53–63 and *How on Earth?*, 134–51).

61. Hurtado, *Lord Jesus Christ*, 64.

62. Hurtado, *One God*, 114–23; *Lord Jesus Christ*, 64–74; *How on Earth?*, 179–204; "Origins," 10–16; "Resurrection-Faith," 128–130 and "Revelatory." At this point Hurtado's work is anticipated by older German scholarship: see, e.g., Bousset, *Kyrios Christos*, 50–51.

amounted to a unique "mutation" in what was acceptable Jewish monotheistic devotional practice of the Greco-Roman period.[63]

Powerful visionary experiences of the exalted Jesus included God's direction to worship Jesus. These combined with Spirit-inspired songs, prophetic oracles, and "charismatic exegesis" of the Old Testament to create the kind of Christological material that is now reflected in the New Testament and in subsequent Christian literature. This whole process is reflected in accounts of visionary experiences that describe or assume the place of Jesus in the heavenly realm (e.g., Acts 7:54–60; 2 Cor 12:1–4; Gal 1:13–17; Rev 4–5).

Here Hurtado joins the chorus of a growing number of scholars who have recently insisted that in explaining various features of earliest Christianity we should pay more attention to the role of visions, dreams, and other forms of religious experience than NT scholarship has traditionally allowed. Although most have not taken up this part of Hurtado's work on Christology, it has at least won the support of A. Chester, who also claims it offers the best explanation of the origins of an early divine Christology.[64]

Fourthly, Hurtado reminds us that an early high Christology has its origins in a wider Roman-era religious environment.[65] Early Christian binitarian monotheism, like Jewish monotheism itself, stands *over against* Roman religious practices and so it is likely, for example, that in the Christian literature of the late first century onwards, "son of God" language for Jesus reflected a reaction to the use of the same language for the Roman emperor.

There are also important points of more open cultural and religious engagement with the Greco-Roman world. For example, the Gospels are a striking innovation in the Jewish environment. They are quite unlike any texts in the rabbinic corpus, which sometimes included short stories from the lives of rabbis, without ever connecting those short stories into a coherent account of a life that might then be held up as authoritative or paradigmatic. Rabbinic tales of famous rabbis are used to point to true fulfillment and interpretation of Torah, not to attract the readers' attention to those rabbis themselves. The central focus throughout the Gospels on Jesus himself means they are generically most like the biographies of the Greco-Roman world and this in turn reflects the way the Gospels function as an expression of early Christian devotion to Jesus.[66]

---

63. Hurtado, *How on Earth?*, 203.

64. See Chester, *Messiah*, 99–105; "Christ of Paul," 120–21; "High Christology," 47–50, cf. also Eskola, *Messiah*, 182–202 and Ehrman, *How Jesus Became God*, 171–246.

65. Hurtado, *Lord Jesus Christ*, 74–77.

66. Ibid., 75, 274–77, 313, with reference to wider scholarly discussion of the genre of the Gospels, especially the important contribution made by R. A. Burridge,

III: Bauckham's Explanation of Christological Origins

Bauckham has promised a two-volume work on Christology and so far has only laid down a few key judgments that would contribute to a full explanation of the origins of Christological monotheism. Some of these, especially the judgments that are distinctively his own, will be highlighted in the following chapters.

At the outset, however, it is worth highlighting a major difference between Hurtado and Bauckham. Bauckham is apparently unconvinced by the proposal that powerful religious experiences were a factor leading to "Christological monotheism." Instead, he seems to think that the actual life of Jesus was more important than Hurtado allows. He has boldly argued in several separate studies that all four canonical gospels should be treated as reliable historical eyewitness testimony to the life of Jesus.[67] In these, he has mounted a full-frontal assault on the form-critical paradigm that has dominated Gospel studies in the last hundred years, with its view that the Gospels are in large measure the creation of the early church and a reflection of the various stages of the church's life and development. Bauckham thinks that pretty much everything in the Gospels (especially in the Synoptics, but also, with qualification, in John's Gospel) is historically reliable testimony.[68]

For many modern Gospel interpreters the Synoptics have a low Christology. Indeed, for Hurtado the Synoptic Gospels are clear that Jesus did not claim a divine identity during his earthly life (even though the Gospels are, in their own way, a testimony to the wider pattern of Christ devotion). However, Bauckham argues from a range of passages in the Synoptics that the older, traditional (precritical) view that the Synoptics have a Christology no different to the one in John is a more faithful interpretation of the evidence. Furthermore, whilst some modern scholars have seen a high Christology in some Synoptic passages and have usually judged the "divine" elements of Jesus' biography to be the product of a Hellenization of the early Christian movement, for Bauckham the Gospels represent the historical realities of Jesus' very *Jewish* life.

He has not yet explained how the Gospels' accounts of Jesus' life account for the precise shape of "Christological monotheism." That is, he has not yet explained in detail how the life of Jesus as told by Matthew, Mark, Luke, and John produces the kind of statements we find in 1 Cor 8:6 and

---

"Gospel Genre."

67. See esp. Bauckham (ed.), *Gospels for All Christians,* (1998) and his essay therein ("For Whom?"), and *Jesus and the Eyewitnesses,* (2006), *Testimony of the Beloved Disciple,* (2007).

68. See also his short sketch of Jesus' life in *Jesus: A Very Short Introduction* (2011).

Phil 2 and the distinctive pattern of worship of Jesus that we see throughout the NT. The route from the Gospel accounts of the life of Jesus (taken as historically reliable throughout) to "Christological monotheism" and Christ devotion may seem to some readers utterly straightforward. However, in chapters 3 and 4 I will pose some historical and theological questions of Bauckham's model of Christological origins. In the end, the new paradigm that I will outline in volumes 3 and 4 will find some common cause with Bauckham's approach to the Gospels as historically accurate accounts of Jesus' life, though along the way I will make interpretative and historical judgments that part company with him.

CHAPTER 2

Unconvincing Objections and Fresh Support for the Emerging Consensus

NOT EVERYBODY IS CONVINCED. In this chapter I review some arguments against the emerging consensus's claims for earliest Christian beliefs and practices, in particular those to which it is possible to give a confident rebuttal. In addition to a review of some of the most recent arguments in defense of the emerging consensus, I add some fresh insights into one key text (1 Cor 8:6). In chapters 3 and 4, on the other hand, I will outline some questions and objections that have not yet been satisfactorily addressed. These call into question some aspects of the work of Hurtado, Bauckham, and of other voices in the emerging consensus.

1: Unconvincing Objections to the Emerging Consensus

From the pen of a one-time-Pharisee 1 Cor 8:6 is startling and so it is not surprising that some have voiced objections to the binitarian "Christological monotheism" interpretation of that and similar passages in Paul. The arguments against the emerging consensus attack both ends of the case.

Some accept, as Bousset did, that with Paul we have (limited) evidence of an early Christian worship of Christ, but they are unconvinced by the arguments for a "Christological monotheism." From a dismissal of the case for a genuine "Christological monotheism" it is possible to move to dispense with the case for a genuine "worship" of him: if Jesus was not (as Bauckham claims) included within the divine identity, then whatever the earliest Christians did to Jesus it was not "worship" *in the biblical sense of the word.*[1]

1. See Bousset, *Kyrios Christos*, 119–210. Dunn (*Theology of Paul*, 260) suggests it

Alternatively, the argument can go the other way: if it can be argued, as some do, that there is actually not much hard evidence of an actual worship of Jesus, that suggests he was not really included within the divine identity.[2]

The arguments for a "Christological monotheism" and a worship of Christ are, inevitably, interconnected. However, Bauckham has made a good case for thinking that beliefs about Jesus preceded the worship of him. So, following his lead and because the argument for the emerging consensus really hinges on the case for and against a pattern of Christological *belief* I start this chapter with the radical paradigm shift in Jewish monotheism that we find in the NT.

I: No "Christological Monotheism" in Paul?

Objections to the case for a "Christological monotheism" in the earliest material in the NT are of two kinds. Firstly, there are those who really do not give the case a full or plausible hearing. For example, Maurice Casey reviewed some of the evidence for the case in a conference paper fifteen years ago. Whilst he made many valuable observations, his rejection of the case for worship of Christ in Pauline churches rested on critical judgements about the shape of Pauline theology that really are unpersuasive, especially in the light of subsequent publications by Bauckham and Hurtado. For example, to say that the use of Isa 45:23 in Phil 2:10–11 is "an unusual piece of midrash, and we should not read it into the daily life of all Pauline churches" sounds, in view of all the evidence reviewed in the last chapter, an implausible case of special pleading.[3]

Similarly, but more recently, Adela Yarbro Collins's dismissal of the case for "Christological monotheism" in Paul suffers a lack of real engagement with the arguments. She says that such an interpretation of Phil 2 amounts to an "overinterpretation,"[4] and prefers to explain Phil 2:6 as a description simply of the preexistent (royal) *messiah* who is "in the form of God," but not fully on God's own level. As coauthor with John Collins of a recent book on *King and Messiah as Son of God*, she makes many insightful observations on the relationship between NT Christology and the wider

---

may be best to think of Christ as only *venerated*, not worshipped, in Paul, appealing to the later distinction between veneration of the saints and worship of God in the eighth-century second Council of Nicaea (787 AD).

2. For this double-pronged approach against the emerging consensus, see McGrath, *Only True God* (2009) and Dunn, *Worship* (2012).

3. Casey, "Christological Development," 225.

4. Collins, "How on Earth?" 63.

historical context of biblical, Jewish, and contemporary Greco-Roman traditions of kings, messiahs, and divine rulers. However, for her explanation of Pauline preexistent Christology in terms of a preexistent royal messiah and preexistent Wisdom she is heavily dependent on the preexistent messiah of the *Similitudes of Enoch* (*1 En.* 37–71). We will discuss the *Similitudes* in chapters 5, 6, and 8. Suffice to say at this juncture, the Messiah-Son of Man in that text is nowhere described as the "form of God" and he does not receive or possess the kind of equality with God *as a distinct individual divine being* that is a major theme of the Philippians hymn. Although there may be a hint of Wisdom language in parts of 1 Cor 8:6, there is no real Wisdom Christology in Phil 2:6.[5]

But the most serious flaw in her argument is the failure to discuss all the evidence. She omits discussion of Col 1:15–20 and strangely fails to engage with the arguments for a redefined Shema in 1 Cor 8:6. She does not even mention the use of Deut 6:4 in 1 Cor 8:3–6.[6] And without considering the possibility that the name given to Christ in Phil 2:11 is God's own name, she seems to reduce the Christology of that passage to the functional and political, but not fully divine.[7] So it is hard to take seriously the rest of her argument for a Christology that does not include Jesus Christ the Son and Lord in the identity of the one God. She devotes just a few pages to the question of the worship of Jesus in the New Testament and raises several important points that might count against Hurtado's argument.[8] But she does not engage with either the full extent of the evidence for Christ devotion nor its conceptual relationship with the evidence for a "Christological monotheism."

A more serious, developed argument against the "Christological monotheism" and Christ devotion reading of Paul comes from Dunn's former pupil James McGrath.[9] McGrath proposes that Paul has not "split the Shema" in 1 Cor 8:6, rather he has *expanded* the Shema by adding Jesus *alongside* its confession of the one God. Paul refers to the Shema in 1 Cor 8:4, then he offers a "paraphrase" in v. 6 in which, as in v. 4, there is still just one God—the Father. Then outside of the linguistic parameters set by Deut 6:4, Paul provides an *additional* affirmation: there is also one Lord. For this

---

5. See Collins and Collins, *King*, 208–9, appealing to *1 En.* 48:2–3, 6 for the combination of Wisdom and preexistent messiah in one figure.

6. She briefly discusses 1 Cor 8:6 in Collins and Collins, *King*, 112, 147, 208.

7. Ibid., 174.

8. Ibid., 173–74, 211–13.

9. McGrath, *Only True God*, 38–44 (cf. further McGrath, "Intertextual Echoes," 78–79). Dunn has endorsed McGrath's arguments on 1 Cor 8:6 in *Worship*, 108–9, and Schnelle (*Apostle Paul*, 191) agrees that there is no splitting of the Shema, only an inclusion of the one Lord "in the linguistic and conceptual domain of the one God."

construal McGrath can point to the ways in which Jews meditated on the reality of one God and concluded that, for example, for the one God there is also one Temple (Josephus *C. Ap.* 2:193, cf. *Ant.* 4:200–201). The fact that Israel had one Temple obviously reflects and witnesses to its belief in one God, but "one Temple" is in no sense part of the one God. In the same way, McGrath argues, the "one God" of biblical faith now also has one Lord (Jesus Christ) in 1 Cor 8:6. The Lord Jesus Christ then is not to be identified with the *Kyrios* of the Shema (that substitutes for the Tetragrammaton), but is a mediator, and agent of creation, *alongside the one God*.[10] He is a messianic *kyrios*, not the fully divine *Kyrios*.

There are various problems with McGrath's argument. In the first place, it is hard to see how the verse can speak of a purely messianic, mediatorial Lord, given that he is described as an agent of creation. There is no parallel in contemporary Jewish thought for the idea that there is a messianic Lord "through whom are all things." Such language could only be used for one who fully expresses the divine identity.

McGrath complains that if Paul has done what Wright, Hurtado, and Bauckham claim he has done in 1 Cor 8:6 Paul should have explained himself.[11] But this is to miss a feature of Paul's high Christological material generally and the specific context and content of 1 Cor 8:6 in particular. Time and again, a high Christology (whatever exactly we make of it) in Paul is presented as a presupposition that Paul assumes his readers will share.[12] It does not need to be argued for and Paul is not arguing for it. He argues *from* a high Christology for this or that particular aspect of the Christian world view. This is especially the case in 1 Cor 8:6.[13] There Paul begins by affirming the perspective of those who believe they are free to eat food offered to idols because there is only one God, whilst acknowledging also the subtleties (or difficulties) of the question of the existence of other gods (1 Cor 8:4–5). He then launches into a long, multipronged argument that the strong in faith need to take thought for circumstances in which eating idol food would be a mistake. He cites a Christian version of the Shema at the outset because he wants to ensure that he and his readers are on the same page throughout the argument up to the end of chapter 11, where the focus is still on proper Christian conduct around the dining table. A redefined monotheism that puts Jesus Christ within the identity of the one God does not need to

10. McGrath finds a similar construction in 1 Tim 2:5 (*Only True God*, 41–42).

11. Ibid., 39–40.

12. See e.g., Fee, *Pauline Christology*, 92, 148, 500–501.

13. To date, the best treatment of 1 Cor 8:6 in relation to the argument that follows is Wright, *Climax*, 132–35; *Paul*, 661–70. In later chapters I will offer observations on Phil 1–3, 1 Cor 8–9 and Col 1–3 that reinforce Fee's point.

be argued for now, in the context of an issue surrounding meat offered to idols; it is the very bedrock of Paul's faith and at the heart of the message he preaches.

Indeed, a careful look at the form and content of 1 Cor 8:6 indicates that here Paul is almost certainly quoting a well-known early Christian confession (in the same way that traditional early Christian hymns in Phil 2 and Col 1 are quoted as a basis for the particular pastoral injunctions that follow them. There is a clear syntactical break between vv. 5 and 6 and although traditional versification begins at v. 6 with "but" (*all'*), in Paul's original letter that word functions more as a connecting word between what has preceded and what Paul is about to write in the rest of the verse. So the "but" (*all'*) functions in a similar way to the "who" (*hos*) with which the hymns in Phil 2 and Col 1 are introduced (Phil 2:6: "*who* being in the form of God . . ."; Col 1:15 "*who* is the image of the invisible God").

Beyond the initial "but," 1 Cor 8:6 is a confession that is an unmistakable self-standing formula. According to the conventions of Greco-Roman rhetoric, it is an isocolon composed of an equal number of words (13 in v. 6a–c and 13 in v. 6d–e) and syllables (8 + 11 in v. 6a + b–c and 8 + 11 in v. 6d + e–f) in each of its two halves.[14] It contains no verb in the Greek; an ellipsis that reflects both the lack of a verb in the main clause of Deut 6:4 and the way in which the confession functions as a well-known and much used summary of the church's early faith. Several linguistic elements within the confession are also uncharacteristic of Paul suggesting he is reliant on older church teaching.[15] So, the verse should be added to the string of other passages in 1 Corinthians where Paul cites or alludes to well-established Christian tradition, that is sometimes even anchored in the early Christian account of the life and teaching of Jesus, and that frequently has a confessional or liturgical form (see 1 Cor 7:11–12; 9:14; 11:23–25; 12:3; 15:1–7).

In any case, whatever we make of the prehistory of the confession in 1 Cor 8:6, it is unlikely in the extreme that Paul could get to this point in his relationship with the Corinthian Christians without a clear presentation of his understanding of Israel's one God in the light of Christ. McGrath's complaint only has force if Paul's pastoral letter (that we call 1 Corinthians) functioned for its readers as an outline of Paul's theology. We, as modern scholars, may want it to serve such an end. But it did not function that way for Paul. And as it is, it is a mistake to imagine that Paul would not also

---

14. Cf. Aristotle *Rhet.* 1410a. I take it that the longer text in P.46 that adds the words "and one holy spirit, in whom all things and we in him" is a later addition.

15. Paul nowhere else uses the phrase *heis theos ho patēr* ("one God the Father") (though Eph 4:6 comes close), nor the simple expression *di' autou* ("through him"), preferring longer *dia* + genitive phrases (1 Thess 5:9; Rom 5:1, 11; 15:30; 1 Cor 15:57).

need to explain a Christologically "supplemented Shema" (along the lines of McGrath's interpretation of 1 Cor 8:6) to a mixed Jewish-Gentile community of believers in the same way that we should assume he has in fact already explained a "redefined Shema."[16] As it is, and as we shall see shortly (below), 1 Cor 8:6 contains a carefully structured traditional formula, that Paul quotes in the belief that all parties in Corinth (including those evidently aligned to Peter and Apollos—see 1 Cor 1:12; 3:4–6, 22; 9:5) could sign up to; a shared theological starting point *that would have been taught as a fundamental piece of Christian catechesis at conversion.*[17]

To prepare the ground for that several-chapter-long argument Paul recalls the faith once delivered to the Corinthian saints that included a redefined Shema that is *both* an affirmation of those who deny the existence of other gods and also a call now to live a life conformed to the pattern and identity of the one God that includes (the pre-existent and yet crucified) Jesus within it. The way this redefined monotheism functions in the context of 1 Cor 8–10 was a key component of the original argument for a "Christological monotheism" put forward by N. T. Wright in his 1991 article.[18] And in the course of my presentation of a new paradigm for Christological origins in Part 4 I will sharpen up Wright's observations and show just how carefully Paul's argument in the chapters that follow is grounded in the confession in 1 Cor 8:6. In any case, McGrath has not explained how the expanded-Shema interpretation explains the relationship between 1 Cor 8:6 and Paul's unfolding argument in 1 Cor 8–10 better than a redefined Shema interpretation.

On the other hand, McGrath conducts an interesting thought experiment that he thinks counts against the split-up Shema interpretation. He proposes that if Paul had wanted a clear statement with Father and Son both existing as parts of the identity of the one God he could have omitted the confusing second "one" and written:

> There is one God:
> the Father, from whom all things,
> and the Son, through whom are all things.

---

16. The argument that in an oral culture the Corinthian readers would not hear the subtlety of Paul's alleged "splitting" of the Shema in 1 Cor 8:6 is also, therefore, beside the point (against McGrath, "Intertextual Echoes," 78–79).

17. For the "*eis auton*" ("to/for him") with reference to God compare the liturgical contexts of Rom 11:36 (for God) and Col 1:17, 20 (for Christ, the image of the invisible God). Another sense of "*eis theon*" ("against God") occurs in Rom 8:7, though see Eph 1:5 and 4:15. For the "from him," "to/for him" and "through him" combination see Rom 11:36, and compare the similar use of prepositions as a whole in Col 1:15–20.

18. See Wright, *Climax*, 132–35.

The fact that this is *not* what Paul says certainly invites careful reflection. But the fact that this is not what Paul says does not lead to the conclusion McGrath advocates. Paul could only have adopted that form of language by abandoning the biblical revelation. This hypothetical formulation makes no specific reference to the identity of the God revealed to Israel and might just as well be a confession of a completely new religion, created out of nothing. On the other hand, a similar kind of thought experiment casts considerable doubt on McGrath's interpretation of what Paul actually said. If Paul really wanted to say what McGrath thinks he is saying (in an *expanded* Shema) Paul should surely have written something like this:

> But for us there is one God, the Father and Lord,
> from whom all things and we to/for him,
> and (there is also) one Christ (or "messiah"), Jesus the son (but not Lord),
> through whom all things and we through him.

If 1 Cor 8:6 does not identify the *Yhwh-Kyrios* of the Shema with Jesus Christ then it is not at all clear what the word *kyrios* is doing as a part of Jesus' name or title. It is redundant as a reference to Jesus' role as a messiah, since Jesus' messiahship can be conveyed in the word "Christ."[19] And coming, as it does, after the language in v. 5 in which Paul acknowledges the existence of so-called "gods" and (divine) "lords (*kyrioi*)," to speak of Jesus as a *kyrios* who is *added* to an *expanded* Shema (as McGrath proposes) would mean, as Bauckham points out, that Paul is in effect repudiating biblical and Jewish faith altogether by introducing a new, additional, *kyrios*—Jesus—to the one God (who, as every Jew knows, is the only true Lord).[20]

As it is, Bauckham has also drawn attention to other details of the text that support the split-open-Shema interpretation. Firstly, a careful reading shows that every part of 1 Cor 8:6 after the introductory "but" maps onto Deut 6:4. The Shema is more a declaration than a traditional prayer. In the Greek of the LXX the first line is: "Hear O Israel, the LORD (*Kyrios*) our (*hēmōn*) God, the LORD (*Kyrios*) is one." We have already seen how the words "*Kyrios*," "God," and "one" are picked up in the different parts of 1 Cor 8:6. The "our" (*hēmōn*) of God's people is picked up both in the first word of the formula in 1 Cor 8:6 ("for us," *hēmin*), and also with the "*we* (*hēmeis*) to him" and "*we* (*hēmeis*) through him" parts at the end of the first and the end of the second half (vv. 6c & 6f), demonstrating that throughout 1 Cor 8:6 the individual parts of Deut 6:4 are in mind.[21] We might add that in calling

---

19. For the messianic sense of "Christ" in Paul, see, e.g., Wright, *Climax*, esp. 18–55, and now Novenson, *Christ*, and my discussion of "Christ" in Phil 2:11 in chapter 8.

20. Bauckham, *God of Israel*, 212–13.

21. Ibid., 103, 212.

the Corinthians back to this confession Paul himself implicitly performs the opening "*Hear*, (O Corinthians)." So all this counts strongly against the view that the "one Lord Jesus Christ" part of 1 Cor 8:6 is simply added to the Shema (in simplified form) in the first half of the verse.

Secondly, the way Paul has split up the Shema is parallel to the way he has split up the confession of Rom 11:36. In that Romans passage Paul writes of God: that "all things are *from* him and *through* him and *to/for* him." With the same three prepositions used in a similar way in 1 Cor 8:6, it rather looks as though the confession is a deliberate combination of two confessional formulae. The first—the Shema—defines God's relationship to his people (salvation history). The second—the formula that Paul uses in Rom 11:36 (which is quite likely a pre-Christian Jewish formula)—has a wider scope that also embraces God's relationship to creation. As a thoroughgoing statement that the Lord Jesus Christ is now included in the divine identity *both* the Shema *and* the prepositional phrasing of the formula in Rom 11:36 are split up to create a balanced dyadic account of the divine identity.

Thirdly, the conceptual structure of the relationships between "God the Father" and creation, on the one hand, and the "Lord Jesus Christ" and creation, on the other, also points to Jesus' *inclusion* in the identity of the one God.[22] At the beginning and the end of the work of creation there is God the Father, who is the one *from whom* and *for whom* creation takes place. *In between* that beginning and end, there is placed the Lord Jesus Christ as the one *through whom* creation takes place. This implicit thought sequence reflects Paul's *inclusion* of the Lord Jesus Christ *within* the identity of the one God himself.

The intense scrutiny to which 1 Cor 8:6 has now been subjected, and the alternative approaches of Dunn and McGrath, on the one hand, and the likes of N. T. Wright, Richard Bauckham, and Gordon Fee, on the other, should establish one thing about which none of us should disagree. In the matter of the Christian version of Deut 6:4 in 1 Cor 8:6 there can be no "overinterpretation." The theological, religious, and political stakes do not get any higher. Both sides of the debate cannot both be right. Whatever one makes of Phil 2:6–11, there can have been no Christological grey area once somebody decided to bring the Lord Jesus Christ into such close proximity to the opening line of the Shema. Either they meant, in doing so, to simply say that the one God has one messiah (who is also a "Lord"), as McGrath claims. Or, they made a more radical claim that Jesus Christ is actually to be *included* in the identity of the one God and that he is therefore also the LORD (*Yhwh-Kyrios*). What other interpretative options do we have? In view of all

---

22. Ibid., 218 and compare Fee, *Pauline Christology*, 91.

the points made above, it is really hard to see how the confession in 1 Cor 8:6 does not say, quite boldly and unashamedly, the latter not the former.

II: The Numerical Theology of 1 Cor 8:6 and the Emerging Consensus

Ever since reading N. T. Wright's first presentation of the case for a "Christological monotheism" in 1 Cor 8:6 I have been persuaded by the main thrust of the interpretation subsequently developed by Bauckham and others. This verse and the Wright interpretation of it serves as a touchstone for the argument that I will develop throughout this book. And because I will ask this verse to be historically and theologically load-bearing for key parts of the new paradigm that I offer in Parts 5 and 6, I venture in this section into some unconventional interpretative territory where further confirmation for the "Christological monotheism" reading of 1 Cor 8:6 can be found.

In the last couple of decades, mostly at the fringes of the scholarly community, a new interpretative tool for biblical scholarship has appeared: *numerical criticism*. Broadly speaking this is simply the study of numerical patterns and structures in biblical texts. At its most simple level, this produces the observation that, for example, in the case of 1 Cor 8:6 the numerical structure of the verse (minus the opening "but") shows that we are dealing with a traditional confessional formula (see above). There are other liturgical pieces in the NT that show a similar use of numerical patterns. There are seven affirmations in the doxology in Rom 11:33–36a, seven petitions of prayer in the Lord's prayer Matt 6:9–13, seven OT passages in the catena of Scriptures in Heb 1:5–13, and the hymn in Col 1:15–20 can be neatly divided up into balanced halves of fifty-five words each.

But for many practitioners of numerical criticism there is now a recognition that, like the allegorical meaning sometimes conveyed through parables (both those ascribed to Jesus and those of his Jewish contemporaries), numbers and numerical structures can have deeper symbolic significance. This is because there was a closer connection between numbers and words in antiquity than there is today. In the Jewish tradition the practice of interpreting texts through their numerical structures and the possibility that a letter can signify a number is known as "gematria". Similar practices were used in the Greco-Roman world and, indeed, were well-known across the ancient world. As it happens, both Hurtado and Bauckham have themselves observed that sometimes in NT texts and in later early Christian literature numerology was used to invest texts with a deeper Christological meaning than is at first obvious at surface reading. Hurtado has made new proposals for a possible gematria on Jesus' name in a famous passage in the letter of Barnabas (*Barn.* 9:7–8),[23] and Bauckham has taken up the work of Martin Menken to show how John's Gospel encodes Christological (and other) claims through numerical structures.

In a similar vein, I now offer some fresh observations on 1 Cor 8:6. We have already touched on the way the verse's confessional formula has a neatly balanced two-part structure. This is how the formula can be laid out in terms of a symmetry between the words and syllables of the two halves:[24]

v. 6a–c : 13 words (5 words in 6a + 8 words in 6b–c)

(19 syllables: 8 + 11 in v. 6a + b–c)

v. 6d–f: 13 words (5 words in 6d+ 8 words in 6e–f)

(19 syllables: 8 + 11 in v. 6d + e–f)

Total: 26 words

(38 syllables)

There is no great significance in the 19 + 19 = 38 syllable structure. It simply contributes to the confession's memorable and easily recitable form. However, I propose that the numerical word structure (of 13 + 13 = 26 words) makes a profound contribution to the confession's claim that the identity of the one God is now two-in-one. That is, the confession's numerical structure helps it to carry and convey the mysterious new *shape* of Jewish monotheism. At the same time, the way the formula employs a clever numerical structure suggests the confession was formulated in the earliest Hebrew- and Aramaic-speaking bilingual Christian community in Palestine. So reflection on the text's number symbolism also makes a vital contribution to the quest to understand the historical *origins* of "Christological monotheism."

Some may fear that I am about to set sail from the terra firma of sober biblical criticism into the never never land of imaginative Bible code speculation. So it is as well that, before I explain these claims for the theological

---

23. Hurtado, *Artifacts*, 114–16 (see further 147–50) and Hurtado's private contribution to M. C. Parsons's intriguing proposals for gematria on the numerical value of Jesus' name (18) in Luke 13:4, 11, 16 (Parsons, "Numerology," 34 n. 40).

24. The "for us" picks up the "Hear O Israel . . ." and the "the LORD *your* God" of the Shema and so properly acts as a part and beginning of the confession. N. T. Wright draws attention to the word and syllable count, discounting the initial "but," in *Climax*, 130 n. 26.

significance of the numerical structures in the confession in 1 Cor 8:6, I provide a basic introduction to biblical number symbolism and the latest scholarship on it.

Recent study, especially the pioneering work of Casper Labuschagne, has shown that in the Hebrew Bible care is taken to convey meaning through numerical structures.[25] Everyone knows that the OT gives certain numbers symbolic value (seven, twelve, and forty, for example), for both literary, organizational, and temporal structures (such as the seven days of creation and the twelve tribes of Israel) and in the world of Israelite daily life and worship (the seven-branched temple lampstand and twelve-month liturgical calendar, for example). The Creator creates an ordered world. He is celebrated as the one who has "arranged all things by measure and number and weight" (Wis 11:20, cf. *T. Naph.* 2:3).[26] And so it is fitting that the worship of him, and the writing of Scriptures that witness to him, should also reflect the way he creates in and through a human creativity that similarly so arranges things.

It is now clear that sometimes numerical structures are only apparent when one reads the original Hebrew and that other numbers, not spelt out at the surface of the biblical text, may be intentionally expressed through the text's layout and careful choice of words. This is especially so with liturgical material (such as psalms, prayers, and blessings), but also in narratives (especially in divine speeches). The opening chapter of the Hebrew Bible offers a wonderful example of a narrative text with a strongly liturgical flavor full of numerical patterns that witness to God as the one who creates by bringing about order.[27]

In the ancient world the skill of counting and measuring (for the sake of accounting and architectural design) overlaps with the art of writing (in the composing of literature, poetry, and liturgy) in a way that is strange to the modern world. The Hebrew *scribe* (*sopher*) can serve as both an *enumerator* (a book keeper) and *a secretary,* because the verbal root *spr* can mean both *to count* (in *qal*) and *to report* or *to recount* (in *piel*). In various ways, the fact that a scribe (or a similarly skilled reader) was trained to

---

25. See Labuschagne, *Numerical Secrets* (2000); "Numbers as an Organizing Principle" (2009) and also P. van der Lugt, *Cantos*, vol. 1 (2006), 84–87; Knohl, "Sacred Architecture" (2012), cf. Menken, *Numerical Literary Techniques* (1985). By no means are all of the numerical structures Labuschagne identifies convincing. In what follows I have selected some of the more convincing examples that he and others have identified.

26. For a keen interest in God as the one who measures, or who creates *with attention to measure,* in contemporary Judaism see Kister, "Measurements Ordained by God."

27. See esp. Cassuto, *Genesis*, vol. 1, 13–14 and Levenson, *Creation,* 67–68, and compare e.g., W. Brown, *Seven Pillars,* 37.

count provided an impulse to see aspects of a text that modern readers are programmed to ignore.

In the first place, scribes and ancient readers paid attention to the number of words in a portion of text (a colon, a strophe, or other subunit) or in a whole text. For one thing there were practical reasons to do so: copyists could ensure there were no mistakes if the required number of words were reproduced in a scroll or codex and scribes could be paid by the number of words they copied. But the number of words in a portion of text could also be chosen to convey symbolic meaning.

Ancient Hebrew had no separate system of written signs for numbers (as we do with our "1," "2," "3," and so on). So the consonantal (written) letters of the Hebrew alphabet doubled up as a set of numbers (*aleph* = 1, *bet* = 2, and so on). The letters of the Hebrew alphabet written on a scroll or tablet could either be a set of numbers or a piece of literature, or in some cases could be intended to be taken both ways.[28] In a similar way, in Greek isopsephy letters are given numerical value.[29] Alternatively, the number of words in a portion of text could be correlated to the numerical value of a word. At some point in Jewish history (perhaps already in the Tannaitic period—see *m. Aboth* 3:23) the art of reading hidden numerical meanings out of Hebrew (and Greek) words and number patterns came to be called gematria. But Labuschagne prefers to talk of "logotechnical" composition techniques and argues that *numerical criticism* needs now to be treated as an important subdiscipline of *literary criticism*. Certainly we can use the word "gematria" without assuming that the more fanciful mystical speculations that that word implies are necessarily involved.

Some instances of "logotechnical" composition are well known: in Rev 13:17-18 reference to the number of the beast as 666 is gematria for Nero Caesar (in Greek) and for first-century readers with a basic understanding of Hebrew, the fourteen-generation schema in Matthew's genealogy (Matt 1:1-17) helps communicate the claim that Jesus is the true son of David, a name which has the consonants in Hebrew (*dwd*) that add up to 14 (because *dalet* (= 4) + *waw* (= 6) + *dalet* (= 4) = 14).[30]

---

28. For the historical evidence for such a practice, which has roots in the wider ancient Near East, see Lieberman, "Mesopotamian Background," and Menken, *Numerical Literary Techniques*, 12.

29. On Greek isopsephy see Barry, *Greek Qabalah*, 23-24.

30. For this to work we have to assume that David's name is not written (as it sometimes was in the first century) in a *plene* spelling with an additional *yod: dwyd*. Labuschagne, "Numbers as an Organising Principle," 601-2, points out the organizing numerical principle in Matt 1 is already present in Ps 3, the first Psalm of David in the psalter.

Labuschagne has shown that other special Hebrew words and their numerical value were used to enrich the Scriptures' sacred value and depth of meaning. In a sense, like the beautifully decorated texts of the medieval age, such structures enable the Scriptures to have an iconic function: their structure (*form*) points to the realities of which their *content* speaks. Perhaps by using numbers to give the text an iconic structure—even to include numerical references to the names of God (see below)—ancient Jewish scribes were thereby able to avoid actual visual representations of God which would contravene the scriptural prohibition against idolatry.

In any case, the numerical value of the name of God, *Yhwh*, that was likely understood in antiquity as a form of the verb "to be" (*hayah*), was highly prized as a number providing structure in poetry, prayer, and divine speech. By a simple addition of the alphabetic positional values of its letters, the Tetragrammaton has the numerical value twenty-six:[31]

yod (= 10) + *he* (= 5) + *waw* (= 6) + *he* (= 5) = 26

Alternatively, by counting the sum of the digits and removing all the zeros—another method of letter counting in the ancient Near East known as "*mispar katan*" in Jewish tradition—the Tetragrammaton has the numerical value seventeen:[32]

yod (= 1) + *he* (= 5) + *waw* (= 6) + *he* (= 5) = 17

Labuschagne suggests that the numerical value seventeen for God's name can also be arrived at through gematria on the Hebrew for "I am." Using the same verbal root for the name of God, this would be '*hwh*, which has the numerical value seventeen:

aleph (= 1) + *he* (= 5) + *waw* (= 6) + *he* (= 5) = 17

The number seventeen is important in its own right because it is the seventh prime number. Both twenty-six and seventeen are also attained by adding the numerical values of the Hebrew word for "glory" (written in *scriptio defectiva*) because letters from the eleventh letter in the alphabet onwards can either be employed for the tens and hundreds (*kap* = 20, *lamed* = 30, . . . *qop* = 100, and so on) or treated as a continuation of the first ten letters (*kap* = 11, *lamed* = 12, . . . *qop* = 19 . . .). So the Hebrew word "glory," *kavod*, is either:

---

31. Independently of Labuschagne, Herbert Rand has drawn attention to the importance of the number 26 in Scripture (Rand, "Numerological").

32. Labuschagne, *Numerical Secrets*, 89–90; "Numbers as an Organising Principle," 586.

kap (= 11) + *bet* (= 2) + *dalet* (= 4) = 17

or

kap (= 20) + *bet* (= 2) + *dalet* (= 4) = 26[33]

Thus, the numbers seventeen and twenty-six signified both the name of God and God's own (divine) glory, indeed implying an identification between God's name and his glory (cf. Isa 43:7; 59:19; Phil 2:10-11). The appearance of patterns and blocks of seventeen or twenty-six words in the literary structure of a text then creates a divine watermark, reminding the attentive reader of God's presence through his revealed word and in other ways.

For example, Psalm 136 repeats the call to give thanks to God for his steadfast love in twenty-six parallel verses.[34] In a more subtle example, the importance of the numbers seventeen and twenty-six can be seen in their structural function in the composition of Ps 8 (a Psalm much used by the early church according to the NT: Matt 21:16; 1 Cor 15:27; Eph 1:22; Heb 2:6-8, cf. Mark 12:36).[35] In the first place, we can observe that Ps 8 in Hebrew has seventy-seven words (or seventy-two discounting the heading): a sure sign that its author has thought about the number of words used. The main body of the Hebrew of the Psalm then begins and ends with a *seven*-word proclamation focused on God's name: "O *Yhwh*, our sovereign, how majestic is your name in all the earth (*Yhwh 'adonenu ma 'addir shimka bekol ha'arets*)" (vv. 2a, 10). In between the opening and closing verses there is a numerical structure that uses both the numerical values of *Yhwh*, which in the case of the number twenty-six applies also to the word *glory* that is used in v. 6 and the word *your majesty* in v. 2b [*hwdk* = 26]. The poetic unit in vv. 4-5 has seventeen words and the one in vv. 6-9 consists of twenty-six words. So the majestic *name* that is the primary subject of the psalm is not only "in all the earth" (vv. 2, 10), it is also present in the very text of the psalm itself, whose structure serves, like an icon, as a testimony to the reality of which it speaks.

Both the Shema and its Christological reworking in the confession in 1 Cor 8:6 are focused on the identity of Israel's one God, *Yhwh-Kyrios*. As a *confession that is to be repeated* (as Paul does here in his argument over the

---

33. Or, if *kavod* is written in *plene* spelling its value was taken to be 32 (*kap* [= 20] + *bet* [= 2] + *waw* [=6] + *dalet* [= 4] = 32).

34. For a fuller discussion of texts that have twenty-six in their structure see Labuschagne, *Numerical Secrets*, 75-104, and the more detailed analysis of the Psalms and other texts on Labuschagne's website: www.labuschagne.nl.

35. For what follows and further observations on the numerical structure of Ps 8, see Labuschagne, *Numerical Secrets*, 145-46, and van der Lugt, *Cantos*, vol. 1, 144.

one God in relation to idols) *and that is, in turn, based on the biblical form of the Shema—the confession that was deeply ingrained in every Jew's liturgical and theological imagination—it cannot be a coincidence that the confession in 1 Cor 8:6 is composed of twenty-six words, the numerical value of* Yhwh.

In the first place, this means that the confession then functions as an example of a phenomenon that is already attested to in the Hebrew Bible: the numerical value of a key word in a text provides the numerical structure of that text. For example, Ps 48 is a Psalm of *Zion* that exalts Israel's capital as the place of *Yhwh's* habitation. "Zion" in Hebrew has the numerical value forty-eight—*tsade* (= 18) + *yod* (= 10) + *waw* (= 6) + *nun* (= 14) = 48—and the number forty-eight plays a key role in the Psalm's artful literary and numerical structure.[36] Indeed, its position as the forty-eighth Psalm in the Masoretic numbering of the Psalter probably reflects an editor's awareness of its numerical structure. Similarly, the book of Ecclesiastes is organized around the number thirty-seven, which is the numerical value of the word *hebel* ("vanity") that occurs thirty-seven times in the book.[37] In one section of Proverbs (10:1—22:16), the number of lines (375) is equal to the numerical value of the Hebrew name of Solomon, to whom the sayings are ascribed at the start (in Prov 10:1): *shin* (= 300) + *lamed* (= 30) + *mem* (= 40) + *he* (= 5). Similarly, in the section of Proverbs copied by Hezekiah's men (Prov 25:2–29:27, cf. 25:1) there are 140 lines, which is the numerical value of one spelling of Hezekiah's name: *yod* (= 10) + *het* (= 8) + *zayin* (= 7) + *qof* (= 100) + *yod* (= 10) + *he* (= 5).[38]

The numerical structure in the Matthean prologue is another example of this phenomenon, and recent studies have identified the presence of more sophisticated NT examples, especially in contexts that reflect the liturgical patterns of Christ devotion. For example, Martin Menken has pointed out that in John 1:1–18—which, of course, is often judged to be or to reflect a Christ hymn—there are 496 syllables. As the ancients knew, the number 496 is a special number because it is both the thirty-first triangular number (being the sum of the numbers one to thirty-one) and a perfect number (being equal to the sum of its divisors). And it is especially chosen because 496 is

---

36. Psalm 48 has three cantos, with the second containing fifty-eight words framed by the first and last each containing twenty-four words (that adds up to forty-eight). The word Zion appears three times (in vv. 3, 12, and 13). See Labuschagne, "Numbers," 602–3 and the document "General Introduction to Logotechnical Analysis" at www.labuschagne.nl/aspects.pdf (pp. 14–16) and the numerical analysis at www.labuschagne.nl/ps048.pdf. For other examples of this phenomenon in the Hebrew Bible see Corley, "Numerical Structure," 48–49, 51.

37. See Labuschagne, *Numerical Secrets*, 138–40.

38. See the commentators noted in Corley, "Numerical Structure," 51.

the numerical value of the key word for the Logos and the Son in John 1:14 and 18: *monogenēs* ("only, only begotten").[39] The famous and mysterious reference to 153 fish in John 21:11 quite likely reflects the importance of the number seventeen as the value of God's name, since 153 is both the seventeenth triangular number (attained by adding up all the numbers one to seventeen) and the product of nine times seventeen.[40] Outside the NT, the early second-century *Epistle of Barnabas* (9:8) provides an explicit Christological interpretation of the 318 servants of Abraham in Gen 14:14. This is treated as three hundred—the value of the Greek letter *tau* that symbolizes the cross—and eighteen, which is the value of the Greek letters iota (I = 10) plus eta (H = 8). Hurtado has drawn attention to the possibility that in the background of Barnabas's interpretation there is the practice of writing the name of Jesus as a *nomina sacra*, abbreviated in Greek scripts to iota eta (IH) which shares the numerical value of the Hebrew word for life: *kh* (= 8) + *yod* (= 10).[41]

Returning to 1 Cor 8:6, we can now see that the twenty-six-word structure makes clear that, even though it is a reworked Shema that includes the Lord Jesus Christ within the divine identity, the confession is still a declaration of the identity of *Yhwh-Kyrios*. Through the use of exactly twenty-six words the reworked first line of the Shema says: *together, the one God the Father and the one Lord Jesus Christ constitutes the identity of the one God, Yhwh-Kyrios*. In other words, the confession implies that what Israelites have daily proclaimed through the confession of Deut 6:4 was a provisional statement of the divine identity now more fully revealed to include the *Kyrios Iēsous Christos*.

---

39. See Menken, *Numerical Literacy*, 20–21, 29, and see further Bauckham, *Beloved Disciple*, 274–76. Besides the numerical structure of the two halves of the hymn in Col 1:15–20, it is perhaps significant that the Philippians hymn can be divided into two halves comprising ninety syllables (vv. 6–8) and ninety-one syllables (9–11). If the first line of the poem, as it was usually known, started "*Christ Jesus* being in the form of God" instead of Paul's "*who* being in the form of God," both halves would have ninety-one syllables. Ninety-one syllables may have been chosen as the product of seven times thirteen, since thirteen is the numerical value of the Hebrew *ehad* ("one"). But I am much less confident of this than I am in my analysis of 1 Cor 8:6. For possible numerical structures in John 17 see Labuschagne, *Numerical Secrets*, 120–21.

40. Patristic-era interpreters noticed that 153 is the seventeenth triangular number (see e.g., Parsons, "Numerology," 38–41, and Culpepper, "Designs for the Church," 388, on Augustine's interpretation), but seem not to have understood the relationship to God's name in Hebrew. 153 is also a hexagonal number, as other ancient interpreters noticed (see Evagrius of Pontus, *De Oratione*, Prologue), perhaps connecting it to God's work on the sixth day of creation.

41. Hurtado, *Artifacts*, 114–16, 147–50.

Lest there be any doubt that the use of twenty-six words is deliberate and that it functions in this way, there is more to the numerical structure of the confession that spells out the point beautifully and memorably. The confession has two carefully balanced halves, each comprised of thirteen words. In the conceptual flow of the sense of each half, the word "one" comes first (although it is not strictly the first word in each clause): "for us *one* God . . . and *one* Lord . . . ." The ellipsis of the verb—"for us *(there is)* one God . . ."—accentuates the stress on the word "one" in both halves. In Hebrew the numerical value of the word "one" (*'ehad*) is thirteen, since *aleph* (= 1) + *het* (= 8) + *dalet* (= 4) = 13! So the numerical structure of the reworked Shema encodes both the name of God, *Yhwh*, and the key, climactic word at the end of the Shema (". . . *Yhwh-Kyrios* your God, is *one*!").

Furthermore, in this ingenious use of *both* the numbers twenty-six and thirteen, the confession says, emphatically, that *Iēsous Christos* is placed inside a split Shema, not outside of it. The 13 + 13 = 26 word structure confirms all the other reasons for thinking that Jesus Christ is firmly placed inside the Shema; within, that is, the identity of the one God. By this structure the formula makes, subtly but clearly, some profound claims. It does this through an equation that can be laid out this way:

"*one*" $^{\text{v. 6a: 13 words}}$ + "*one*" $^{\text{v. 6b: 13 words}}$
= (the singular, *one*) *Yhwh-Kyrios* $^{\text{v. 6a + 6b: 26 words}}$

As this formula attempts to show, the numerical structure of the confession in 1 Cor 8:6 tags numerical values to concepts or divine identities. The formula can be unpacked by considering each of its two sides separately.

The left hand side of the equation looks at the divine identity in terms of its constituent *parts*; as an internally *differentiated* whole. Conceptually, the left-hand side of the confession says there are the *two* entities (or persons): the one God the Father and the one Lord. The oneness or singularity of each of these is encoded in the thirteen words of each half of the confession.

The right hand side of the equation looks at the divine identity *as a whole, as an undivided unity* (composed of differentiated parts). The addition of the two thirteen-word halves adds up to twenty-six: *the number on the right hand side of the equation*. Twenty-six is also numerical value of *Yhwh* whom every Jew knows, and whom the Shema emphatically declares to be, *one*.

So, through the arithmetic tagging of concepts and identities, the two layers of the confession say that one God the Father and one Lord Jesus Christ *together comprise the one God of Israelite faith*. In the case of this divine identity "one plus one" really does, however mysteriously, "make *one*".

This also means, therefore, that by the use of twenty-six words for the *whole* and through the two parts of the verse adding up to twenty-six, the confession prevents anyone concluding that "*Kyrios* Jesus Christ" is in fact *Yhwh* without remainder. Both God the Father and the *Kyrios* Jesus Christ, together, are *Yhwh-Kyrios*. This, of course, is consistent with the way *Kyrios* substitutes for the Tetragrammaton in the rest of Paul's letters: the *Yhwh-Kyrios* of Israel's Scriptures is *both* the one God of Israel (with no specifically Christological denotation intended in some Pauline texts) and *also*, in some now much-studied texts such as Rom 10:9–13, *Yhwh-Kyrios* is (manifest as) Jesus Christ. This is consistent with other texts that speak of God the Father and the Son sharing the divine name (Rev 22:3–4 and perhaps Matt 28:19).

I have not been able to find any comparable use of numerical structures quite like this one in 1 Cor 8:6. Numerical criticism of ancient Jewish and Christian texts is in its infancy, so perhaps there are others yet to be discovered. Nevertheless, recent analysis of passages in the Psalms by Labuschagne and P. van der Lugt suggests that 13 + 13 = 26 was an established numerical structure that would have been known to some first-century scribes.[42] The most interesting case is Ps 11 where the central colon, v. 4ab, has the two-part statement:[43]

Yhwh behekal qodsho, Yhwh bashamayim kis'o

Yhwh (is) in his holy Hekhal, *Yhwh*'s throne (is) in the heavens.

Psalm 11:4a has thirteen consonants, so does 11:4b. The choice of a 13 + 13 = 26 structure might have been deliberately chosen for the central statement of this Psalm to express the mystery that God both rules from the heavens and he is seated, enthroned in his sanctuary on earth. Although he is *in a sense* in two places at the same time, *Yhwh* is still one.

It may, of course, be that the author of the confession in 1 Cor 8:6 was unaware of such a Hebrew Bible precedent for his formulation and that he discovered the theological potential of a 13 + 13 = 26 structure for himself. In any case, there are three implications of the numerical structure of the

---

42. See van der Lugt, *Cantos*, vol. 1, 85 and his comments on the role of 13 in the numerical structure of Pss 16, 18, 29 and 37 (*ad loc*) and *Cantos*, vol. 2, 119 (on Ps 54). Labuschagne sees evidence of a 26 + 13 pattern, that he calls the *Yahweh echad* structure, in some texts (*Numerical Secrets*, 128–30). There is also a 13 + 13 = 26 in the outer branch of the menorah pattern (vv. 2–3 + vv. 7–8) in Ps 67 (see Labuschagne, www.labuschagne.nl ad loc).

43. See van der Lugt, *Cantos*, vol. 1, 166. In his analysis of Ps 11 (available at www.labuschagne.nl) Labuschagne points out that the expected, normal Hebrew world order (*kis' Yhwh bashamayim*) would have been just twelve letters in v. 4b.

Christian version of the Shema in 1 Cor 8:6. In various ways it strengthens and clarifies the claims of the emerging consensus.

(i) 1 Cor 8:6 and the Origins of "Christological Monotheism"

The confession in 1 Cor 8:6 strengthens the emerging consensus case for a very early high Christology. As we have already seen, numerous features of 1 Cor 8:6 reveal the use of a pre-Pauline formula. And we can now see that the way 1 Cor 8:6 reworks the first verse of the Shema, with a carefully crafted numerical structure and mirroring of the two halves of the formula, confirms that *Paul is reminding the Corinthians of an established early Christian confession.*

Furthermore, we can now say that the number symbolism in 1 Cor 8:6 points to an origin for this kind of liturgical, arithmetic composition in a bilingual, Greek- and Hebrew-speaking, environment. Theoretically, it could have been formulated in a community that used both Greek and Hebrew in Antioch or Damascus. But it is more likely to have been composed in the trilingual church in Jerusalem.

Any judgment about its likely origin of course depends on how one imagines the development of earliest Christianity. If we follow the picture recently painted by Richard Bauckham of the faithful transmission of the gospel story from the earliest eyewitnesses to Jesus' life, who after his death were based in Palestine and Jerusalem, through to the Mediterranean-wide Greek-speaking church, then an obvious context for the creation of the confession presents itself.[44] The confession makes good sense as the work of someone like John Mark who, there is every reason to believe, as Bauckham shows, wrote up Peter's account of Jesus' life in Greek in the gospel that now goes by his name. Even if we do not follow early Christian tradition on the authorship of Mark, someone like John Mark with a competency in both Greek and Hebrew and a position of standing amongst the leaders of the Jerusalem church most likely created the confession in 1 Cor 8:6.[45] Bauckham's reconstruction of the role of the Jerusalem church has not yet

---

44. See Bauckham, *Eyewitnesses,* and his "Devotion to Jesus Christ," 194 n. 72 where he plausibly postulates "something like a 'school' of Christian exegesis in the early Jerusalem church, where many of the christological readings of biblical texts that we find throughout the NT writings originated."

45. And so the confession also adds weight to the view that Hebrew was a living and widely used language in first-century Palestine (on which see Safrai, "Spoken and Literary Languages"). For bilingualism or trilingualism in Roman Palestine see van der Horst, "Greek," and Sterling, "Judaism," 271–74, and, above all now, the important studies in Randal Buth and R. Stephen Notley, *Language Environment.*

persuaded everyone. But in any case, consideration of ecclesial politics and the nature of Paul's relationship to the Corinthian church suggests that the confession Paul cites most likely originated in the mother church in Jerusalem. Even if it was not composed there, it must have been approved of by the leaders of the Jerusalem church, especially Peter.

Paul appeals to the confession in 1 Cor 8:6 as common theological ground with his readers as he attempts to address the issues surrounding food offered to idols. *As a radical redefinition of the Shema—the cardinal expression of Jewish monotheism—it is unlikely to have had the authoritative position that Paul assumes for it had it not been approved by all leaders and parties in the nascent Christian movement.* Paul may have taken issue, on occasion, with the position adopted by some from the Jerusalem church on matters of Torah observance, but there is no evidence of substantial disagreement on Christology. And in this letter to the Corinthians Paul is most anxious to dig out from the young church any root of partisan divisiveness. Throughout, he is deferential to Peter (1 Cor 1:12; 3:22; 9:5; 15:5), who was held in high esteem in the Corinthian church. So it is surely highly unlikely that he would resort to such a distinctive and radical Christological confession if he was not confident that Peter (and those aligned to him) would have fully endorsed it. Peter, and also Apollos—"a man well-versed in the Scriptures" (Acts 18:24, cf. 1 Cor 1:12; 3:4–6, 22; 4:6; 16:12)—would be just the kind of early believers to appreciate the number structure of the Greek confession. It is highly unlikely that Peter would have endorsed such a reworking of the Shema if he did not believe that, at the very least, it was *consistent with* the confession of the Jerusalem church.

So, Paul's appeal to the confession in 1 Cor 8:6 works best if it was a key component of the catechetical package for young converts from the earliest days of the Christian movement and that all first-century church planters and pastors understood it. As a reworked Shema we should also bear in mind the possibility that such leaders and their converts not only *understood* it intellectually, but that they also prayed it on a daily basis in a way that continued the Jewish practice of praying the Shema itself. Does that mean that the underlying Hebrew symbolism of the numerical structure of the confession was explained to new Gentile converts in Corinth? Why not? One does not need a full and proper command of the Hebrew language to understand the point of the numbers thirteen and twenty-six in the confession. And the numerical structure of its neatly balanced two halves could have been taught as an aid to learning the confession by heart. It is likely that sometimes subtle and sophisticated instances of gematria were the work of an highly educated scribal elite. However, we know that in the first-century Greek-speaking world the placing of numerical codes in words was the stuff of social media banter and tabloid satire. The phenomenon appears in lovers' graffiti discovered at Pompeii and Pergamum and could be used in anti-imperial street talk.[46] There is every reason to suppose that in the first century the confession in 1 Cor 8:6 was memorable and widely known precisely because it had a pleasing numerical structure that appealed to the rank and file in (Greek speaking) churches across the Mediterranean world. So, the confession is important evidence of the vital connection between early Christian liturgical creativity—that expressed a worshipful devotion to Christ—and the education and training of new believers.[47]

If, then, Paul was confident that some among his readership would know the full significance of the confession's numerical structure, his appeal to it means he can subtly remind the Corinthians of the need for unity and love between all members and strands of the new movement; among both Hebrew-speaking Jews and Greek-speaking Jews and Gentiles (cf. 1 Cor 12:13). "Remember," 1 Cor 8:6 says, "our core theological confession is one that works in both Greek and Hebrew: do not forget, you gentile olive tree that you have been grafted into the Hebrew-speaking people to whom God first revealed himself."

Of course, all these possibilities cannot now be proven. But they are possibilities that we cannot ignore and they lend weight to the many other reasons for thinking that the theology and devotional patterns exemplified by 1 Cor 8:6 go back to the earliest Christian community in Palestine. In Parts 5 and 6 I will present evidence that the confession in 1 Cor 8:6 is not completely without precedent in the Jewish tradition. And in a future study I will offer further evidence to support the claim that 1 Cor 8:6 attests the earliest beliefs about Jesus in the post-Easter community. For now we should note the way a creative use of Hebrew in an early Christian liturgical piece written in Greek has a likely parallel in another Pauline passage.

Colossians 1:15–20 preserves a hymn about Christ. The immediate literary context that Paul has provided in his letter to the Colossians is replete with biblical language.[48] The hymn itself draws on a number of OT passages, most obviously in the "image of God" phrase in v. 15 and in the "in him all the fullness of God was pleased to dwell" of v. 19 (cf. Ps 68:16 [LXX 67:17]).

---

46. For example, one line of graffiti at Pompeii reads "*philō ēs arithmos phme*" ("I love her whose number is 545"). See further Suetonius *Nero* 39:2, Deissmann, *Light*, 277, and the discussion in Barry, *Greek Qabalah*, 128–29, who concludes that in the Greek and Roman worlds in the first century, isopsephy was "in common use and knowledge of it was widespread among ordinary people even though Greek was not their first language" (129).

47. On that connection now see Gordley, *Teaching through Song*.

48. On which see esp. Beetham, *Echoes of Scripture*.

Besides the obvious evocation of Gen 1:26–27 in v. 15 (cf. Col 3:10), the "be fruitful and multiply" of Gen 1:28 is also echoed in the phrases "in the whole world bearing fruit and growing" and "bearing fruit in every good work and growing" of Col 1:6, 10. Following up an ingenious article by C. F. Burney almost a hundred years ago, some commentators now see beneath the hymn's Greek surface a creative speculation on the different possible meanings of the first word of the Hebrew text of Genesis.[49]

The first word of the Hebrew Bible—*bere'shit*—has two elements—the preposition *beth* and the noun *re'shit*—and it invites interpretative explanation because the grammatical relation between those two elements and the rest of the verse and chapter that follows is unclear. How *bere'shit* should be translated is a crux interpretum even today. As another witness to the creativity of the early Christian bilingual community the Colossian hymn assumes a creative inner-biblical exegesis that combined speculation on the different possible meanings of *bere'shit* in Gen 1:1 with the language for Wisdom in Prov 8:22–31. (For "wisdom" in Colossians see 1:9, 28; 2:3, 23; 3:16; 4:5, cf. "*philosophia*" in 2:8). That creative exegesis of the first word of the Hebrew Bible is reflected in the Colossian hymn because the beloved Son is identified with every possible meaning (the "fullness" of the meaning, we might say) of both the *beth* and the *re'shit* of Gen 1:1. For the different possible meanings of *re'shit* Christ is the "firstborn" (vv. 15b, 18c), "beginning" (v. 18c), "sum-total" (v. 17b), "head" (v. 18a), and the one who is "preeminent" (v. 18e). For the different possible meanings of the *beth* of *bere'shit* the hymn says that all of creation was created "in," "through," and "for/to" him in v. 16a, 16f (and echoed again in the account of salvation in 19a, 20a).[50] This, of course, emphatically places the beloved Son in the position temporarily prior to (because he is "before all," v. 17a) and metaphysically superior to the Adam who was created to be the image of God on the sixth day. As with the confession in 1 Cor 8:6 and passages in Hebrews (1:2–3)

---

49. Burney, "APXH of Creation," cf. Wright, *Climax*, 110–13; Stettler, *Kolosserhymnus*, 4–5, 155–59. The questions posed against Burney's thesis in McDonough, *Creator*, 85–86, do not amount to a strong or decisive argument against it.

50. Whilst many in the last century have been reluctant to acknowledge that such a creative interpretation of Genesis 1 underlies the text, its presence is entirely consistent with other indications that Genesis 1 is at the forefront of Paul's mind here. It also goes with the evidence of 1 Cor 8:6 and 1 Cor 16:22–23 that Paul relied on liturgical and confessional material that went back to the earliest Aramaic- and Hebrew-speaking bilingual or trilingual environment of the Palestinian church (see chapter 2 above). For an intriguing suggestion that an interest in the *bere'shit* of Gen 1:1 has influenced the characterization of the preexistent Enochic Son of Man (at *1 En.* 39:8; 48:3; 62:7) see Waddell, *Messiah*, 66–67.

and John's prologue (1:2–3), the beloved Son preexists and had a hand in the creation of the cosmos.

So the likely presence of a creative interpretation of the Hebrew of Gen 1:1 underneath Col 1:15–20 suggests that both that text and the confession in 1 Cor 8:6 came from a bilingual community. Even though both passages appear in letters written to communities of Greek speakers who would be largely oblivious to these clever linguistic patterns, Colossians and 1 Corinthians suggest that in matters of early Christian liturgy and Christ devotion there was a conservative impulse: Paul is committed to the faith once for all given to the church as it is enshrined in pieces of prayer and praise that go back to the earliest believers who read their Bibles in the original Hebrew. (Though in the case of Colossians, the use of Scripture in the rest of the letter and Paul's concern that the young church should not get blown off track by the competing claims of the local synagogue (see Col 2:8—3:4), suggests that some readers may well have had the biblical literacy to see the use of Gen 1:1).[51] Christ devotion was not simply the overflow of a Spirit-filled enthusiasm unable to contain its gratitude for God's mighty acts in and through Christ. It was also nurtured through a sober, reflective exegesis of Scripture in reliance on well-established Jewish scribal techniques and interpretative tools.

It is even possible that the numerical theology of the confession in 1 Cor 8:6 goes back behind a Greek-speaking life-setting and that what is achieved in the Greek of the confession reflects the creativity of a Christological reworking of the Shema in its original Hebrew form. With the divine name pronounced *adonay*, the first verse of the Shema has a seventeen-syllable structure (with a balanced 5 + 7 + 5 phrasing):

she|ma'|yis|ra|'el| ad|o|nay| 'el|o|he|nu| ad|o|nay| 'e|had

It is highly unlikely that this seventeen-syllable structure would have escaped the notice of the many scribes who had made countless copies of the verse for phylacteries and tefillin used by ordinary Israelites down through the pre-Christian centuries.[52] Its numerical syllabic structure goes with the fact that the first portion of text included in the Shema (Deut 6:4–9) contains *seven* distinct commands and with the (possibly deliberate)

---

51. So the presence of a Hebrew language layer of meaning to these texts cannot be dismissed on the grounds that Paul's readership would miss it (so Lincoln, "Colossians," 605; Gordley, *Colossian Hymn*, 20).

52. The seventeen syllables in a 5 + 7 + 5 phrasing means the first verse of the Shema has the structure of a Japanese haiku. This, though, must be a pure coincidence, unless such a seventeen-syllable structure reflects some innate neurological patterns common to us all.

organization of Deuteronomy such that Deut 6:4 contains the book's seventeenth occurrence of the expression "YHWH Elohenu."[53]

Once the mathematical problem of Jesus' inclusion within the identity of the one God first confronted his early followers, they were bound to ponder the possibility that there was a way of construing the Shema that enabled them to express their newfound conviction that God, though still one, was now in fact two. That they came up with the kind of numerical structure that we have now uncovered in the confession in 1 Cor 8:6 is hardly surprising. So we should reckon seriously with the possibility that for those first Jewish followers who were not confident Greek speakers there was a confession which made a similar claim in a Hebrew version of a reworked Shema. In that case, the confession in 1 Cor 8:6 would simply be Greek speakers' form of the "Christological monotheism" version of the Shema already used by the earliest Hebrew- and Aramaic-speaking Christians in Palestine. James, Jesus' brother, who sometimes held the senior position as leader of the Jerusalem community, would have endorsed the theology of the confession in 1 Cor 8:6 even if he was unable to recite it with polished Greek pronunciation and phrasing.

In any case, 1 Cor 8:6 (along with Col 1:15–20) must now be added to the Aramaic *marana tha* invocation in 1 Cor 16:22–23 *as evidence that confirms the view of the emerging consensus that the earliest, highest (or fullest) Christology was worked out in the first phase of the life of the church that was based in Palestine and Jerusalem.*

(ii) 1 Cor 8:6 and the Character of Early Christian Theology

Discovering this numerical theology in the confession in 1 Cor 8:6 is important because it shows that the earliest Christians were self-conscious about the mysterious nature of their newfound faith. One plus one cannot, according to the unchanging laws of mathematics, make one. The ancients knew that as well as any elementary school student today. And as Jews committed to belief in one God, all the evidence adduced in the last chapter shows that the early Christians adopted a view of Jesus Christ that forced them to reckon with a puzzle: how now can we remain faithful to our belief in one God whilst believing that Jesus Christ is fully divine yet also distinct from the one who is the Creator, Christ's own "Father," and the one who sent him into the world?

The numerical theology of the confession in 1 Cor 8:6 not only provides an ingenious way of expressing the conviction that God is both one

---

53. I am grateful to Casper Labuschagne for this later observation.

but also now two, it also does so in a way that unashamedly celebrates the apparently illogical nature of this theological position. It provides in a beautiful, barely hidden code the mysterious, paradoxical, and incomprehensible nature of this new "Christological monotheism" with a statement that defies mathematical logic. The confession's numerical code entails a playfulness that confounds any demand that the divine identity now be expressed in a formulation that conforms to a strict human logic.

An apparently strange mathematical logic is fitting for an account of entities that do not exist within ordinary space and time (where the mathematical laws as we know them apply). For first-century Christians, a formulation that contains an apparent mathematical impossibility would likely have been deemed appropriate for a truth claim about *this one God*, since he (as the Bible and now the formulation itself reminds us) is the Creator of all things. As the Creator of all things, he is the Creator of all earthly realities, as the numerical structures of biblical texts, especially Genesis 1, testify (cf. Wis 11:20). So it is entirely fitting that the confession of his true identity should defy or transcend earthly, human mathematical logic.

(iii) 1 Cor 8:5 and the Deity of Christ in Rom 9:5

As we have seen, the numerical theology of the confession in 1 Cor 8:6 means that whilst Jesus Christ is identified with the *Yhwh-Kyrios* of the Shema, he is by no means *Yhwh-Kyrios* without remainder: *Yhwh-Kyrios* is the one God constituted by *both* Jesus Christ *and* the Father. This, of course, is consistent with the way in which Paul can use the word *Kyrios* that substitutes for *Yhwh* in Greek translations of the Hebrew Bible *both* for Christ *and* for Israel's one God when no Christological point is in view. By the same token, the reworked Shema in 1 Cor 8:6 implies a firm inclusion of Jesus Christ within Paul's understanding of the word "God." "We know," says Paul, "there is no God but one" (1 Cor 8:4) and this God is constituted as both the (one) Father and (the one) Jesus Christ. So, 1 Cor 8:6 encourages a revisiting of the possibility that Paul would use the word "God" for Christ at other times.

Romans 9:5 includes a statement that has traditionally been taken to mean, quite straightforwardly, that Paul thinks of Jesus as the Christ who, according to the flesh, comes from Israel, but who is also "over all *God*, blessed forever" (so NIV, ESV, similarly KJV, NRSV, against RSV and NEB). The grammar of Paul's Greek strongly favors this reading and good exegetical arguments support it.[54] Although some punctuate their translation so as

---

54. See, e.g., Fitzmyer, *Romans*, 548; N. T. Wright, "Romans," 629–31; Waddell, *Messiah*, 172–77.

to avoid the use of the word "God" for Christ and Paul prefers to identify Christ Jesus with *Yhwh-Kyrios*, the traditional reading of Rom 9:5 is consistent with OT texts that use "God" language for the messiah (Ps 45:7; Isa 9:5).[55] One such text (Ps 45:7) is explicitly used to refer to Christ in Heb 1:8. Here, and in other instances of the use of the word "God" for Christ (John 1:1, 18; 20:28, Titus 2:13; 1 John 5:20; 2 Pet 1:1, cf. Col 2:2), the language goes beyond anything that was said of Israel's royal messiah or king inasmuch as *this* Christ is "*over all* blessed for ever."[56]

Certainly—and this is the key point here—the traditional reading of Rom 9:5 is consistent with the understanding of the reworked Shema in 1 Cor 8:6 that we have now gained.[57] We are bound to wonder why Paul preferred in most cases to use *Yhwh-Kyrios* for Christ. But Rom 9:5 and now 1 Cor 8:6 show that Paul had no principled objection to the use of the word "God" for Christ. This, in turn, means that even when he does not make explicit any thought for Christ in his talk of "God," Paul has, deeply ingrained within his reconfigured understanding of the one God revealed to Israel, a redefinition of the divine identity that means he speaks simply of "God" and thinks, *inter alia*, that "God" means "Christ" (who is also the *Kyrios*). This conclusion is critical for the question of worship directed to the Lord Jesus Christ, to which we now turn.

III: No Genuine Worship of Christ?

The confession in 1 Cor 8:6 is not a bare, detached piece of propositional theology. As a reworked Shema—the basic prayer-confession of Jewish daily life—it is testimony to the shape of early Christian devotion. Perhaps, to emulate the use of the Shema which at some point in its history became a central feature of the synagogue service, Christians in the churches founded by Paul (and Peter) proclaimed the confession in 1 Cor 8:6 twice a day or whenever they prayed formally and as a community. We do not know. But

---

55. See Horbury, *Jewish Messianism*, 148, and the discussion of such texts in chapter 5 below.

56. Besides the exegetical observations in Wright, "Romans," 629–31, note the way in which Rom 9:5 picks up the position of Christ in relation to "all (things)" in 8:32–39, with overt allusion, in particular, to Ps 110:1 in 8:34.

57. This implication of our numerical analysis of 1 Cor 8:6 would be further reinforced if the thirteen words of each half carry a reference also to the Hebrew word *'el* ("g/God"). The numerical value of *'el* is thirteen by the method of gematria known as "*mispar siduri*" (*aleph* = 1 + *lamed* = 12). Labuschagne argues that the number thirteen provides the numerical structure to Ps 94 which is addressed to "*Yhwh*, God (*'el*) of vengeance" (v. 1; see his analysis of that psalm at www.labuschagne.nl).

as a reworked first line of the Shema, the confession in 1 Cor 8:6 tells us what these early Christians thought they were doing whenever they talked about, prayed to, or praised their God. Combined with all the other texts gathered by Bauckham that show that Paul included Jesus Christ within the divine identity, 1 Cor 8:6 means we now have to reckon with a free-flowing grammar of cultic devotion to God (the Father) and Christ (the Son). For Paul God-talk was Christ-talk and Christ-talk was God-talk.

When we start with a clear grasp of early Christian belief—the nature of Christ's relationship to Israel's God—we are bound to conclude, against the arguments in particular of James Dunn, that texts that might otherwise be questionable do indeed have in view worship directed to Christ. So, for example, when Paul speaks of "psalms and hymns and spiritual songs, singing and making melody *to the Lord (ho kyrios)* with your heart . . ." (Eph 5:19, cf. Col 3:16) there can be no doubt that Paul has in mind worship directed *to Jesus*, whose identity is inseparable from the one *Yhwh-Kyrios* of Israelite faith, revealed also as God the Father. The same goes for the statement in Acts 13:2 that the church in Antioch was "worshipping the Lord." We do not need to choose between a worship of God and worship of the exalted Christ here, since for Luke the two are one.[58] All down through Christian history readers of the NT have assumed that such texts describe a worship of both God and Christ. It is only relatively recently that *some* modern scholars have lodged objections. Those objections are understandable given the directions taken by theology in the modern period and the conviction that Jewish monotheism could not have possibly allowed such a thing. But it is time now to dispense with the doubts and recognize that, at least on this point, age-old Christian piety has rightly discerned Scripture's theological grammar.

James Dunn has recently claimed that there is not as much *proskynesis* language for Christian behavior towards Jesus in the NT as might be expected.[59] But it really depends how much you expect, and for several reasons it is not surprising that there are not more instances of this phenomenon in NT texts. The Greek verb *proskyneō* (and its cognate noun *proskynēsis*) describe a physical gesture that usually assumes a particular place and concrete, physical direct object such as a cult statue or human ruler. For Jews at least this means *proskyneō* is what you do at the end of a pilgrimage in the (idolless) Temple in Jerusalem (John 12:20; Acts 8:27) where God meets his people.

58. Dunn inclines towards worship of God, but *not* Jesus here (*Worship*, 14). In Acts *Kyrios* clearly refers to Jesus in some texts (e.g., 1:20; 2:36; 4:33); to God, as distinct from Jesus Christ, in others (3:20, 22), and in other cases there is deliberate ambiguity (2:21, 47; 5:9).

59. Ibid., 8–12.

Almost all of the instances of *proskynēsis* for worship of Jesus occur before his exaltation to heaven (Matt 2:2, 8, 11; 28:9, 17; John 9:38, cf. Matt 28:9, 17; Luke 24:52). This is what we should expect. In this phase of the Christian story *proskynesis* to Jesus is cognate to *proskynēsis* to a divine-human ruler. It probably signifies for the Gospel writers more than the claim that Jesus is a divine ruler, but as a space-, time-, and person-specific gesture it makes sense within the context of such wider, ancient Near Eastern patterns of worship. Everything, of course, then changes once Jesus is believed to have been exalted to heaven. It makes little sense that his disciples on earth would now offer him *proskynesis*. The only beings that would naturally behave that way are angelic and heavenly beings. Indeed, the angels and elders in heaven offering *proskynēsis* to Jesus is exactly what we do find in texts that describe worship in the heavenly world (see Rev 5:14, cf. 4:10).[60]

The argument of Lionel North, taken up by James McGrath, that there is not proper worship of Christ in the NT because there is no sacrifice to him is also unconvincing.[61] As Bauckham points out, North fails to provide Jewish evidence that, as he claims, "it was sacrifice that was the acid test and criterion of deity."[62] The fact that the decalogue prohibits *proskynēsis* to idols, with no mention of sacrifice, shows that a variety of actions in different contexts were deemed definitive of "worship" in the full sense. It is true, and a matter of some importance, that in the NT sacrificial language is almost always used to describe action towards God, but not Jesus. However, there are exceptions. For example, sacrificial language is used for devotion to Christ when it says that the redeemed are "firstfruits," for both God *and the Lamb* (Rev 14:4).[63]

But, in any case, we can no longer bracket out Christ from the divine identity in texts that use sacrificial language for devotion "to God" (such as Rom 12:1; Phil 4:18). These cannot now be read apart from the clear statement in 1 Cor 8:4–6 that the identity of the one "God" includes Jesus Christ. It will not do to insist that because Christ in his death is the sacrificial victim he cannot in some way also be in view as a recipient of the subsequent

---

60. Dunn's claim that the verb *latreuein* ("to serve, worship") is not used for worship of Jesus in the NT (*Worship*, 13, 27) is misleading. As Bauckham has pointed out (*God of Israel*, 142), that is exactly what happens in Rev 22:3.

61. North, "Jesus and Worship," cf. McGrath, *Only True God*, 29–36, and Dunn, *Worship*, 56.

62. Bauckham, *God of Israel*, 204 n. 51, quoting North, "Jesus and Worship," 198.

63. D. M. Litwa also points out that in the Greco-Roman world there were gods who did not receive a sacrificial cult (*Being Transformed*, 276, with specific reference to the evidence of passages in Philo).

"sacrificial" offerings of his followers.[64] Hebrews and Revelation have no problem in presenting Jesus as both sacrificial victim and priest.[65] So there would be no conceptual difficulty in his also being the one who receives the sacrifice. This is especially the case when, given the particular kind of sacrifice that is in view, Jesus is neither the victim nor priest. When sacrificial language is used for Christian worship, quite clearly the point is not that Christians are offering Christ as a sacrificial victim to Christ-as-God: another kind of sacrifice is in view and a more sophisticated understanding of Christ's inclusion in the divine identity is at play.

The fact that the Lord Jesus Christ can play multiple roles in the divine and salvific economy needs to be explained, but individual elements within the whole should not be explained away or ignored simply because they do not fit a narrow, modern understanding of what is possible for an individual, personal identity.[66] Rather, this aspect of early Christology needs to be fully recognized for the ways that it defines the peculiar character of "Christological monotheism." And in that regard the emerging consensus probably has not yet given enough attention to the peculiar character of NT Christology. This is one of several weaknesses and outstanding problems in the emerging consensus which we discuss in the next two chapters.

---

64. As North seems to in "Jesus and Worship," 200.

65. For Christ both priest and victim in Hebrews see 9:11–14. In Rev 1:12–13 Christ is dressed as the high priest (cf. Josephus *Ant.* 3:153–59); in Rev 5:6, 12; 7:14 he is the sacrificially slain lamb. In Part 6 I will argue that Christ is both priest and victim in Rom 3:21–26.

66. As Dunn points out (*Worship*, 56), God's own role in the sacrificial drama cautions against the assumption that Jesus did not himself receive sacrifice. Whilst God is obviously the one who receives the sacrifice of Christ's death, he is also the one who puts him forward (see, e.g., Rom 3:25; 8:3).

PART 2

THE PRESENCE OF A "Christological monotheism" and a genuine worship of Christ in the Christianity that created the New Testament cannot be doubted. As we saw in the last chapter, some of the arguments against the work of Hurtado and Bauckham do not stand up to scrutiny. The rest of this study will provide more evidence to support the central claims of the "emerging consensus," especially the argument that a fully divine Christology and worship of the Lord Jesus Christ goes back to the earliest phase of the nascent movement (immediately after Jesus' death).

However, there are also questions that the emerging consensus has not yet satisfactorily addressed. Some of these present themselves for the first time in the light of all that Hurtado, Bauckham, and others working in dialogue with them have achieved. In addition, because aspects of their work are problematic, it is understandable that some specialists are not persuaded. In the next two chapters I lay out some questions and problems that I reckon still need to be addressed. My aim is to prepare the ground for the new paradigm that will be presented in Parts 5 and 6. Parts 3 and 4 will also build on the arguments of the next two chapters by sensitizing us to some specifics of the primary textual data and the questions that any comprehensive account of Christological origins needs to address.

For the sake of conceptual clarity, I divide the problems and questions into matters that pertain to the conceptual *shape* of Christology (chapter 3) and issues around a satisfactory account of the origins of a high Christology (chapter 4). Questions of shape map loosely onto what have been traditionally labeled theological concerns. They have to do with *who* the early Christians believed the Lord Jesus Christ was (belief) and the nature or character of their behavior towards him (practice). Questions surrounding the origins of Christology are matters of pure history: what caused "Christological monotheism" and the individual elements within it (such as Christ's preexistence, identification with *Yhwh-Kyrios*, and his active role in the work of creation)? Questions of origin and shape are interrelated and my own wrestling with the problems that I outline in the next two chapters has been one impetus to towards a new paradigm, in which, I believe, a clearer understanding of the shape of the earliest Christology provides a more satisfactory account of its origins.

Both my interest in the shape and the origins of NT Christology are strictly historical in the sense that this study attempts to accurately describe and explain the cause (or causes) of an historical phenomenon. For the most part my arguments will ask nothing of readers' own personal, confessional commitments. But at the end of Part 6 we will be forced to address the issue of the intersection of history (what we can say about the past) and theology (what we are invited to believe and do in the light of the past). And because the leading voices of the emerging consensus, to one degree or another, admit a personal, confessional interest in the enterprise, there is an excursus after these two chapters on some theological questions and issues arising from Hurtado's work.

At the outset, it is worth saying that, underlying all the specific issues that will be covered in Part 2, I discern a weakness in the underlying conceptual structures within which many in the emerging consensus work. Its leading voices seem to have theological assumptions that reflect the tendencies of a distinctively Western and especially a Protestant (and, in particular, a Reformed) theological vision that construes the relationships between God, the world, and humanity in terms that militate against the essentially incarnational shape of NT Christological material. There is an emphasis on divine sovereignty that is not balanced by the biblical vision of God's presence in space and time. There is also a lack of discussion of what it means to be human.[1] This means, in practice, that the fully rounded shape of NT Christology, which includes both the human and the divine poles of the identity of Christ as a distinct person, is, in some ways, obscured. In turn, a lack of recognition of the incarnational character of key NT texts has left the emerging consensus struggling to explain the origins of NT Christology. My reasons for saying this here, at the start of chapters 3 and 4, will become fully clear with the presentation of the new paradigm in Parts 5 and 6. However,

---

1. Bauckham has commented on the vision of humanity in Gen 1–2 in the context of a discussion of a biblical theology of the environment and has warned, with some passion, against any notion that human beings transcend creation in a way that might then justify our dominance of it for our own purposes (*Living with Other Creatures*, 1–12). His comments there obviously have implications for what he might say about Christology and theological anthropology, but as far as I can tell he has not addressed that relationship explicitly.

some of what I say here in Part 2—and at other points in Volumes 1 and 2—will help explain why I flag up this theological framework issue at the start.

It is an opportune time to be engaged in the quest for Christological origins, and we are all indebted to the pioneering labors of those who have gone before us. There are many who have contributed to the emerging consensus. For the sake of clarity and simplicity I concentrate in this and the next chapter on the work of Hurtado and Bauckham. A fuller, more accurate discussion would need to interact more widely. It would be more nuanced and respect the significant diversity of views on some important matters among those that I have placed in the "emerging consensus" camp.

Also, some of my criticisms of the work of Hurtado and Bauckham could equally be made of many more than just those who have aligned themselves with their work. At times my observations might be better directed at judgments and assumptions that are made by a wider and well-established scholarly tradition; that on some points the leading voices of the scholarly consensus are simply representative of scholarship in the modern period. Nevertheless, if that is the case, in their work—especially in Hurtado's several books on the subject—we have two fine, carefully laid out, and up-to-date representative examples of the modern approach to Christological origins.

To the extent that my own approach—laid out in Parts 3–6—takes issue with the emerging consensus, it will do so from two quite separate vantage points. In some respects the rest of this multivolume study will advocate a well-established alternative point of view—on this or that question of Christological origins—to the view adopted by the leading voices of the emerging consensus. I will, for example, argue for much greater *continuity* between a divine Christology and pre-Christian Jewish precedents, taking sides with a group of scholars whose voices were once more loudly and clearly heard before the chorus of the emerging consensus became so strong. I will also argue, with the appeal to the work of others, for a greater role for Greco-Roman religious patterns at the epicenter of the "big bang" that created "Christological monotheism."

On the other hand, my second vantage point, from which a whole new vista of historical and theological possibilities can now be viewed, will come from a set of proposals that have not yet had any role to play in the search for Christological origins (except, of course, for the fact that they have figured in some of my own earlier publications). Some of those proposals will draw on scholarship outside of New Testament studies done by others with no immediate thought for Christological origins—especially in Old Testament/Hebrew Bible studies. Some of the proposals are my own. And the effect of all that I say from this second vantage point will challenge the whole field of NT Christological studies in the modern period. I will challenge assumptions and judgments that (almost) everyone in the field has made, not just Hurtado and Bauckham. So, it will also become clear, looking back on the work of Hurtado and Bauckham from the other side of the new paradigm that I will offer, that in taking issue with aspects of their work, as I do in the next two chapters, my criticisms could be equally leveled at a wider selection of twentieth-century specialists. In part, they bear the brunt of two whole chapters of deconstructive analysis simply because they are currently the leading, most articulate, and persuasive voices in the field. But in part, they have this unfortunate honor because they are the scholars with whom I am most fully in agreement, and whilst the new paradigm will be just that—a *whole* paradigm that is *new*—it presumes and consolidates the arguments for many of the key findings of the emerging consensus. So I concentrate in Part 2 on weaknesses in the work of Hurtado and Bauckham in the hope that my own "new paradigm" can be clearly differentiated from the model (or model*s*) they each offer.

My primary aim in Part 2 is to show that on some key points the arguments of the emerging consensus do not work. Another way is needed. My criticisms of the emerging consensus will continue in Parts 3 and 4 (on to the end of volume 2) where I will begin to stake out the ground for a new paradigm.

CHAPTER 3

The *Shape* of NT Christology
Questions and Problematic Arguments

IN HIS PREFACE TO his magnum opus *Lord Jesus Christ: Devotion to Jesus in Earliest Christianity,* Larry Hurtado explains that his work is devoted to "an historical analysis of the beliefs and religious practices that constituted devotion to Jesus as a divine figure in earliest Christianity."[1] One aspect of that analysis is an explanation of the "Forces and Factors" that gave birth to Christ devotion (matters of *history*).[2] Another aspect is a description of the shape of Christ devotion; both what behavior it entailed and what was believed about Christ (matters of *theology*). The "belief" side of the picture has to do with issues such as preexistence, Christ's role in the work of creation, the significance of key titles ("Christ," "Son," "Lord"), and the portrayal of the one worshipped in individual New Testament texts, in extracanonical sources, and in the principle witnesses to second-century Christianity. These themes take up the bulk of Hurtado's book. The study is wide ranging and is complemented by three other book-length publications. Others working in his wake have concentrated on discrete themes and specific texts.

The genius of his work is the way that in his search for Christological origins he cuts a swathe through the thicket of complex interpretative issues (surrounding the meaning of titles, the relationship between literary layers of primary texts, and the degree to which one or other text is indebted to Jewish and Greco-Roman traditions) by focusing on a few, indisputable features of early Christian life and practice. He has convincingly shown from his discussion of a complex pattern of devotional practices focused on Jesus that already in the thoroughly Jewish context of the new movement Christians redefined the *shape* of monotheism. The *shape* of the early church's

---
1. Hurtado, *Lord Jesus Christ,* xiii.
2. A subject that is covered first and foremost in the book's first chapter.

worshipping life bespeaks a new binitarian *shape* to monotheism. (From that discussion of the shape of the earliest Christian practice and belief he proceeds to an investigation of the origins of the "mutation.")

It is not surprising that, with the breadth of its scope, there are aspects of Hurtado's description of early Christian beliefs about Jesus that are less convincing than others. There are ways he misses important features of the data that point to a richer Christology with a conceptual center around Jesus' person and his uniquely incarnational life story. To some extent similar questions and problems are raised by Bauckham's work.

1: Incarnation

The burden of Bauckham's and Hurtado's work has meant a primary focus on what early Christians, after Easter, believed about Jesus as one now exalted to God's right hand. Paul's letters reveal early Christian beliefs about the risen and exalted Jesus, and the way he was reverenced as one seated at God's right hand in heaven. We have no record of Paul's view of the historical Jesus *per se* (though there are scattered references in his letters to Gospel traditions). And Paul and other New Testament authors worship Jesus in the present tense; addressing Jesus or speaking of him where they find him— exalted in heaven. So, as it is the earliest datable evidence for Christian life and thought, it is understandable that any description of the earliest divine Christology should focus on Paul's view of Christ's divinity as one now exalted to God's right hand.

Both Hurtado and Bauckham are clear that, contrary to a few minority voices, Paul also had a Christology of incarnation and preexistence.[3] However, *in all that Hurtado has written about Christ devotion, incarnation figures minimally.* It is not a factor in the origins of Christ devotion and does not seem to be an important contributor to the binitarian mutation in monotheism for which Hurtado has carefully laid out so much evidence. Whatever we make of the issue of *origins,* for Hurtado it is not clear how *the Incarnation is really constitutive of the divine Christology that he thinks stands at the heart of Christ devotion.* My point here is not that Hurtado's understanding of New Testament Christology falls short of some kind of theological orthodoxy in which incarnation must be central. It may be that in what follows my comments will serve the interests of readers who are systematic theologians. But that would be a by-product of my real concern,

---

3. See Hurtado, *Lord Jesus Christ*, 121, 123, 395, 514; *How on Earth?*, 98, 104; Bauckham, *God of Israel*, 41–44, 254–68. The most vocal voice denying a preexistence in Paul in recent decades has been J. D. G. Dunn.

which is to highlight some ways in which Hurtado's account does not really do justice to some New Testament evidence that a belief in the Incarnation was central to the *shape* of the earliest Christology.

Philippians 2:6-11 celebrates the life of the one who, "being in the form of God," became a man (on earth) from preexistence (in heaven). In his recent and comprehensive study of Pauline Christology, Gordon Fee has demonstrated how often this understanding of Christ's identity appears in Paul's letters.[4] He has also helpfully stressed that, throughout, Paul's incarnational Christological statements reflect his *presuppositions*.[5] Paul does not *argue for* an incarnational, preexistent Christology; he assumes that his readers accept it and that he can appeal to it in the development of this or that argument. Indeed, the presence of a *preexistent* and *incarnational* Christology is usually acknowledged for several other key NT texts, the most obvious being John's Gospel and the Johannine letters.[6] *There is no evidence that anyone in the early church objected to the idea that Christ came from heaven, in other words, from preexistence.* (Many NT scholars, including Hurtado, mistakenly believe—it will be argued in chapter 9—that there is no Christology of personal preexistence in the Synoptic Gospels. But there is no obvious evidence from the Synoptics that anyone in the early church actually opposed such a Christology.) This suggests that incarnation was a key, uncontested element of Christology from the beginning and that it was rather important for the shape of Christ devotion and "Christological monotheism."

Our critical questions in this section are directed primarily at Hurtado, with a brief comment on Bauckham's work at the end. (Bauckham's account of "Christological monotheism" also seems somewhat nonincarnational in places, but some of what he says moves in the direction I will go in the rest of the study, and it would be unwise to be too dogmatic about his perspective before we have his fuller account of NT Christology). The full force of my comments will become clearer in later chapters in Volumes 1 and 2, though they are best appreciated looking back from the vantage point of the new paradigm that I will lay out in Parts 5 and 6. There, I will argue that what precipitated "Christological monotheism" was the first followers' sudden "realization"—as a result of the event that the NT calls the resurrection—that

---

4. Fee, *Pauline Christology*, 148, 246, 500. Most Pauline scholars would see it in Rom 8:3; Gal 4:4; 1 Cor 10:4, 9. Some, e.g., Fee, also argue for its presence in Rom 1:3-4 (*Pauline Christology*, 242-43) and 2 Cor 8:9 (163-64). See further Gathercole, *Preexistent Son*, 23-31.

5. See Fee, *Pauline Christology*, 92, 148, 163-67, 500-501. On this point see also Hurtado, *Lord Jesus Christ*, 125; Gathercole, *Preexistent Son*, 31.

6. See also Heb 1-2; Jude 5-7 (on which see Gathercole, *Preexistent Son*, 36-43); 1 Tim 1:15; 3:16; 2 Tim 1:9-10.

the man they had given their lives to follow over the course of the previous three or so years was in fact a preexistent and personal divine being who had come to earth as the unique bearer of the identity of the one God. In other words, Christ's resurrection precipitated an epistemological shift; no one thought it marked an ontological change in Christ's identity from nondivinity to divinity (or semidivinity to full divinity). Incarnation (along with the resurrection) not only precipitated the *origins* of Christ devotion, it also defined the distinctive shape of the "Christological monotheism" that warranted that devotion: the one who was preexistent and who became a man before rising to new life has his own *personal* identity as distinct from the identity of another whom the NT calls God *the Father*. The brief observations I offer here then, are intended to prepare the ground for the new paradigm in which the Incarnation stands front and center of the earliest beliefs about Jesus and the worship of him. My concern at this stage is primarily *the shape* of the earliest beliefs about Jesus, but to that end it is necessary to make a few comments on Hurtado's understanding of their origins.

The way Hurtado downplays the role of the Incarnation can be seen when we reflect on several aspects of his account of Christ devotion. First, there is the relationship between the *origins* of Christ devotion and the *shape* of Christological belief. Hurtado has a particular understanding of the historical origins of Christology that affects his perspective on the shape of Christ devotion (or perhaps the relationship is the other way around—it is hard to tell). In a recent article, responding to an earlier one of mine in which I drew attention to the incarnational lacuna in his model, Hurtado says "*'preexistence' and 'incarnation' are nowhere portrayed in the NT as the basis for worshipping Jesus.*"[7] If I understand him correctly, his point is both an historical and a theological one.

For Hurtado the actual historical origins of Christ devotion (and the binitarian mutation of a simpler pre-Christian monotheism) are to be found in the immediate post-Easter period in response to what was perceived to have happened at Easter. He says that it is as a result of Jesus' resurrection and exaltation to divine glory—and experiences of Jesus in that heavenly position—that Christ devotion first began.[8] God did (or was believed to have done) something to the earthly, mortal Jesus, which means after his resurrection and exaltation to heaven Christ was deemed worthy of worship. At that point in history he was "made to share in divine glory and transcendence and was therefore to be reverenced in terms and actions

---

7. Hurtado, "Response," 5 (italics added).

8. Hurtado, *One God*, 117–22; *Lord Jesus Christ*, 71–72; *How on Earth?*, 192–94.

3. THE SHAPE OF NT CHRISTOLOGY

characteristically reserved for God."[9] The resurrection of Jesus was probably seen as a vindication of the messianic self-claims Jesus made during his ministry,[10] but it was *not* in any sense a divine confirmation of a divine identity that Jesus already possessed (since Jesus' belief that he was Israel's "messiah" did not mean he thought he was "divine"). Despite popular Christian assumptions to the contrary, the resurrection was not seen in the NT "as an expression of Jesus' inherent power or divinity so much as the exercise of 'God's' power on Jesus' behalf."[11] (Obviously, in the New Testament Jesus is not said to raise himself from the dead and he is nowhere described scaling the heights of heaven in his own strength, finally to clamber atop the divine throne—as if he were the king of Babylon in Isa 14:13-14.) Christ devotion is a *theocentric* phenomenon inasmuch as it is a response to what God has done to Christ at his exaltation. So, in this sense, *historically*, a belief that Jesus had come to earth from heavenly and divine preexistence (the Incarnation) was not the "basis"—the historical impetus or a theological warrant—for the worship of him. For Hurtado, belief in Jesus' preexistence and Incarnation came along after the initial perception that Jesus had been exalted to divine glory (which was sufficient basis for the worship of him).

We will come in the next chapter to consider and critique Hurtado's account of the historical factors that precipitated Christological origins. For now his view of the resurrection and exaltation of Christ in relation to Christological *origins* is relevant because of the implications it has for the *shape* of the Christology of the New Testament. In keeping with the fact that the worship of Christ was not historically based on a belief in his Incarnation, Hurtado also seems to dismiss the possibility that when believers worshipped Christ in the decades after the first explosion of a new faith and practice they did so in virtue of—or "on the basis" that—he was God incarnate. In other words, the way it was at the origins of Christ devotion shaped the way it was thereafter.

Hurtado illustrates his point that Christ's preexistence and Incarnation were not the basis of Christ devotion with some observations on Phil 2:6-11:

> Even in Philippians 2:6-11, where most scholars concur in finding a direct reference to Jesus' divine preexistence (vv. 6-8), the *basis* for the universal acclamation of Jesus as *Kyrios* is clearly

---

9. Hurtado, *One God*, 107, cf. 93-95 (on Acts 2:33-36 and Rom 1:3-4), 120-21.
10. Hurtado, "Resurrection," 44-45.
11. Hurtado, *God in New Testament Theology*, 57, cf. "Resurrection," 47.

stated as God's exaltation of him and bestowal on him of "the name above every name." (vv. 9–11)[12]

It is true that in Phil 2:9–11 the gift of the highest name and God's exaltation of Christ is the *basis* of a universal and cosmic *proskynesis* and acclamation. But that is not all there is to that hymn and there is plenty of evidence that in fact preexistence and incarnation were precisely the "basis" for a worship of Christ in the early decades of the church.

For that evidence we can start with Phil 2:6–11. To be sure, in Phil 2:9–11 the exaltation of Christ and the bestowal of the name above all names defines the *content* of the universal acclamation of him. He is greeted with bended knee and the acknowledgement that "Jesus Christ is *Lord*." That "Lord" surely refers back to the "name above all names" that he has just received (as Hurtado and most other commentators now reckon). But there are three reasons to doubt that the hymn as a whole *bases* the worship of Christ on his resurrection in the way that Hurtado thinks.

Firstly, the *proskynesis* and acclamation in vv. 10–11 is a future, eschatological one that is not yet, from the historical horizon of Paul's letter, a reality. (They are probably envisaged taking place in the future scenario that is also in view in 3:20–21; when Christ will come from heaven as the church's savior and transform believers' bodies to conformity to his glorious body.) There can be no doubt that the name given defines the *character* of that future worship. Specifically, it defines the content of the acclamation and confession (of Jesus *as Lord*, v. 11) and the *proskynesis* to him recognizes his universal lordship. But whether it is right to say that the giving of a new name defines the *basis of*—the *reason for*—that worship is another matter; and one which needs more careful thought.

This takes us to our second point and the identity of the "name" bestowed in v. 9. If the name given is the divine name *Yhwh-Kyrios* (as Hurtado, Bauckham, and the majority now think) we would surely have to admit that *in the eschatological future* all creation will worship Christ because of what he became at his resurrection and exaltation. He would then be worshipped because, as the one uniquely identified with the divine name, he participates in or manifests the divine identity. Jesus' receipt of the divine name would be another way of saying that he entered into divine glory at his resurrection. However, I doubt very much that Phil 2:9–11 has in view a transformation of Jesus' identity at his resurrection and exaltation that suddenly warranted worship of him only in the third phase of his biography. For reasons that I

---

12. Hurtado, "Response," 5. In a longer essay dedicated to Phil 2:6–11 Hurtado argues that vv. 9–11 are the "apex of the narrative" and the "intended point of the whole drama" (*How on Earth?*, 89–91).

will lay out fully in chapter 8, it is highly unlikely that the "name" above all names that he receives in v. 9 is *Yhwh-Kyrios*. It would be quite unparalleled for Jesus to be given the name *Yhwh-Kyrios* at his resurrection and exaltation in a way that implies he was not already identified with, and in possession of, that name in heavenly preexistence. And although there is recourse to the language of Isa 45:23 in vv. 10–11—and that is a critical component of the hymn's profound Christology—the identification of Christ with the *Yhwh-Kyrios* of Isa 45 is not framed in a way that means the name given in v. 9 has to be *Yhwh-Kyrios*.

One reason for thinking that in v. 9 the name given is *not* the divine name *Yhwh-Kyrios* is the fact that *according to Phil 2:6–11*, for Paul (and by implication for all those who accorded that hymn authority) *the worship of Christ is based initially, and primarily, on his preexistent divine identity, his incarnation, and his obedience in submitting to death on the cross.* Phil 2:6–11 is a two-stanza hymn. The first stanza *praises Christ* directly in the present, at the time of Paul's writing to the Philippians. As he writes words of encouragement to the Philippians Paul slips, as so often in his letters, into the mode of worship in 2:6–11. And that worship begins with the praise of Christ (not with praise of God the Father). The hymn's *second* stanza praises Christ only indirectly, since its initial focus is on *God's action* to and for Christ, and then secondarily on the description of the universal worship that Christ will one day receive. (Insofar as the hymn describes the interaction of two distinct divine "persons" we may say that the first stanza focuses on the praise of the Son and the second on the praise of God "the Father"—esp. in vv. 9–10a, with a climactic intertwining of the praise of both in their respective actions on behalf of the other in vv. 10b–11.)

If the second stanza begins and ends with a focus on God the Father, it is the first stanza that is Christocentric throughout. It makes a number of claims for Christ that, in the very nature of those claims and by virtue of their poetic form, constitute the basis of the worship of him that the hymn expresses. The first claim is that Christ in preexistence exists "in the form of God," a statement which is generally acknowledged now to claim for Christ a divine identity.[13] The translation and meaning of the first verse is hotly debated (and will be explored in chapter 8). But almost everyone now agrees that the (divine and preexistent) Christ is commended for doing the right thing on the matter of "equality with God." (He either refused to grasp after it, to treat it as booty, or regarded it not as something to be taken advantage of.) The preexistent Christ is not "sent" by God in this text, but, quite remarkably, makes his own choices that drive forward the story of

---

13. Hurtado agrees on this point (see his *How on Earth?*, 97–102).

his incarnation, death, and resurrection. So, the preexistent decision and action that issues in the Incarnation *is the basis of* the worship of Christ in the first stanza. In his incarnate life, he chooses to live a life of service (as a slave), in humility and obedience. The stanza is focused entirely on Christ not on God the Father. What Christ does will ultimately be to the glory of God the Father in verse 11. But in Phil 2:6–7 Christ is praised *for the choices he himself makes—choices that bring about and then characterize his peculiar human life: being obedient unto death, having taken the form of a slave, having emptied himself; all from a position in eternity where he does not misjudge the matter of equality with God.* In a later chapter we will consider the earth-shattering significance of these choices and actions, and how they would be heard by the first readers of Philippians. But for now, as we consider the emerging consensus case which (rightly) puts so much store by the evidence of Phil 2:6–11, we are bound to conclude that on the matter of Christ devotion *incarnation was the thing.* In the present, *Paul himself praises Christ in Phil 2 on the basis of his preexistence and the Incarnation.* And he expected his Philippian readers to do the same.

A quick glance at the primary NT evidence for the worship of Christ also suggests that belief in Jesus' incarnation was a key component of, and somehow therefore it was regularly viewed as the *basis for*, the worship of him. In all the texts that are usually adduced as evidence of early hymns to Christ *incarnation* is definitive of the identity of the one worshipped (Col 1:15–20; 1 Tim 3:16; John 1:1–18, cf. Heb 1–2). *Incarnation is the theological constant of the primary textual evidence for the character—the shape—of the early Christian praise of Christ as a divine being.* In two texts there is also an interest in Jesus' exaltation (Phil 2:9–11; 1 Tim 3:16), but that does not figure in either Col 1:15–20 or John 1:1–18. In three texts Christ is praised for his *deeds*, especially for his (salvific) work at the cross and also for his work of creative power in preexistence (Phil 2:7–8, Col 1:16–18, 20; John 1:3–4, 12–13, 16). Praise for Christ's redemptive work during his earthly life and death may also be in view in Phil 2:6–8. (This is a matter of dispute but I will argue for a strongly soteriological interpretation of the Incarnation in Phil 2:6–11 in chapter 8). Praise for Christ on the basis of what he does should be understood primarily against the OT background of the praise of the God of Israel, who is typically worshipped because of his mighty acts, especially at creation and in protecting and saving his people Israel. And in a first-century Greco-Roman context it chimes in also with the wider pagan belief that the gods (and divine rulers) are beings of immense power who should be worshipped in gratitude for their deeds for the benefit of humanity (that is, for their benefactions).

3. THE SHAPE OF NT CHRISTOLOGY

In one New Testament passage that likely preserves an early Christ hymn, the praise of Christ is overwhelmingly taken up with Christ's incarnational movement into human history. In John 1:1-18, that is, there is no interest in his death, resurrection, and exaltation. He is also praised for his participation in God's work of creation and for the salvation he offers (in John 1:3, 12-13). But those two are subsidiary themes beneath the major theme: the Incarnation of Christ as a distinct divine being, the Son, who makes known God the Father.

Because this issue is so important it is worth touching also on the evidence of the book of Revelation. Although there is no explicit incarnational statement in the early chapters of Revelation, the worship of Jesus in chapter 5 is clearly *based on* what Christ has done *in his earthly life*. He enters the heavenly scene *as the lamb who was slain* and he is deemed "worthy" of his position in heaven, and to receive worship, because he is the one who has conquered (5:5) and because by his blood he has ransomed a people for God (5:9, cf. 1:5-6). In the first-century Greco-Roman context the worship of Christ in this chapter echoes and contrasts with traditions surrounding the divine (and *human*) emperor. Jesus is depicted as the founder of a new people and so the worship of him evokes the way divine rulers from the Hellenistic period onwards were worshipped as founders and saviors of city-states. The *basis* for the worship of Christ here then is what Christ did as a result of his humble, vulnerable (lamblike) life that culminated in a sacrificial death. He is not worshipped because he has been *glorified* by God after his death.[14] He has been restored to life—so although slain, yet now *standing*—and is still a lamb. This is a far cry from the image of a mortal *transformed* and *glorified* in heaven, radiant in heavenly garments, imbued with the presence of God, that we sometimes find in Jewish apocalypses (e.g., 2 *En.* 22:8-10, cf. Rev 1:12-16). As in the hymns reviewed above, in Rev 5 Christ is deemed worthy of universal praise *because of the things he did in life and death*. In the broader context of the Christology of Revelation and other New Testament documents this is probably best understood as a worship of Christ for deeds done in and through the Incarnation.

When we pan back from a particular focus on Christ hymns to consider the complex pattern of Christ devotion we of course find that there are aspects of the whole that do not have to do with the Incarnation: the exclamation "*Marana tha*" in 1 Cor 16:22-23 and the fact that Christians would prophesy in Jesus' name are phenomena that assume Christ's divine identity as one now exalted to heaven. Theoretically early Christians could have engaged in such practices without believing that Jesus was a preexistent being

---

14. Against Hurtado, *One God*, 103.

who came to earth in the Incarnation. However, given that Phil 2:6–8 and other texts in Paul show that the whole sweep of Christ's life was framed at its start by preexistence and incarnation this strongly implies that, as with the hymnic material just reviewed, all the different elements of the earliest devotion to Jesus were focused on his earthly (incarnate) identity. In any case, there are other aspects of the Christ devotion complex that seem to have in view his human life in a way that surely means that the earliest believers made that phase of his life the central focus of their devotional life.

Here I have in mind the Lord's Supper and the baptism of new converts into his death and resurrection that nurtured believers' identification with, faithfulness to, and love for Christ *in his earthly life, death, and resurrection*. Within both the biblical tradition (with its cultic rites that included ritual washings and meals that effected communion with God and atonement for the peoples' sins), and in the wider context of ancient Greek and Roman religious life, Christian baptism and the Lord's Supper may both reasonably be taken to imply that the human Jesus (who is also the "Lord") is regarded as a divine being. If we follow the logic of Hurtado's own understanding of Christ devotion the very act of celebrating Christ's (life,) death and resurrection in these rites ascribes to his humanity a divine identity. Within a Jewish context such rites ascribe to their central actor a divine identity. And, of course, in these rites it is very much Jesus' life and death *as a human being* that is at the forefront of believers' attention. Although baptism and the Lord's Supper are not explicitly said to be a celebration of Christ's incarnation, they certainly focus on his earthly life and deeds—on his death, his body and his blood, his going down into the realm of death to emerge victorious the other side—in a way that is consistent with the hymnic evidence that Christ was worshipped for his identity and action *in the Incarnation*.[15]

In view of all this evidence, it is surprising that Hurtado can say quite so categorically that "'pre-existence' and 'incarnation' are nowhere portrayed in the NT as the basis for worshipping Jesus."[16] And it is surprising that in a major study devoted to "the beliefs and religious practices that constituted devotion to Jesus as a divine figure in earliest Christianity" (as Hurtado describes his *Lord Jesus Christ* in its preface) Hurtado does not explore the theme of incarnation in the Christ hymns and related literature.[17]

Although Hurtado is clear that Paul and others believed in Christ's preexistence, his view of the relationship between the worship of Christ and

---

15. For devotion to Christ in the Pauline understanding of the Last Supper see Tilling, *Divine Christology*, 97–104.

16. Hurtado, "Response," 5.

17. I quote from Hurtado, *Lord Jesus Christ*, xiii.

Christ's preexistence and his becoming a man has profound implications for the shape of Christ devotion. It gives the strong impression that the Incarnation, as a defining aspect of the biography of the eternal Son, is not actually constitutive of the identity of the one worshipped. It is hard to see how, in any sense, Jesus the man is really the recipient of early Christian worship. With Hurtado's model, the problem can be framed with this question: *in what sense, if any, does the worship of Jesus include worship of him as a human being; as a uniquely divine human being, as God incarnate?* The Christ of postresurrection faith, who is seated at God's right hand, is *identified* with Jesus of Nazareth, but what really does that identification mean for Hurtado? There are several other features of New Testament Christology that illustrate this problem: his treatment of the historical Jesus, his understanding of the Synoptic Gospels, those statements outside the Gospels that ascribe to Jesus a sinless identity, and those that ground a soteriology in the Incarnation.

First, then, to the historical Jesus. Hurtado presents an account of Christological origins that rests on no particular understanding of the historical Jesus, beyond a basic set of propositions about his actual existence and his impact on his followers, which Hurtado believes will "command a fairly wide assent" among critical New Testament scholars.[18] Hurtado does not venture a comprehensive account of Jesus' aims, intentions, or self-understanding. However, he is clear that the reason the earliest Christians came to worship him was not because they came to see that the historical Jesus was worthy of worship in the light of anything he did, said, or anything that they believed was *intrinsic* to his life (and death). The earliest Christians worshipped Jesus after his death and resurrection *because they believed God directed them so to do in the context of powerful religious experiences.* Christ devotion was based *on what God was believed to have done to* Christ at his resurrection and exaltation, not on anything explicit or implicit in his words, deeds, or in his own self-claims.[19]

If we combine these two features of his work—no particular account of the historical Jesus and no basis for Christ devotion in Jesus' historical life—we find that on his model there is no logical connection between the *fact* of Christ devotion and the *character* of the life of Jesus of Nazareth. This means, in turn, that it is hard to see how the worship of *the Lord* Jesus Christ can really be the worship of *Jesus of Nazareth* in any meaningful sense. In effect, the earliest believers worshipped the "Lord

---

18. Ibid., 54 (further, ibid., 53-64, *How on Earth?*, 134-37). In this regard his approach to the origins of Christology echoes that of Bousset, who begins his *Kyrios Christos* with the beliefs of the "Palestinian primitive community," with no separate discussion of the Jesus of history or of the origins of the Gospel portrayal of him.

19. A point stressed in Hurtado, "Resurrection."

Jesus-glorified-and-transformed Christ." The risen and exalted Christ was not worshipped because he had lived a life as a peculiar kind of human being, a uniquely *divine* human being. The exalted Christ is not reverenced because first-century Christians believed that the specific, historically contingent words and actions of Jesus of Nazareth were uniquely worthy of—or that they revealed some deeper, eternal—divine status and identity. Inevitably, then, Hurtado's model creates the impression that there is only a weak connection between the human Jesus of Nazareth and the exalted and now divine Christ. Certainly, in terms of the terminology of traditional Christian discourse, the structure of the relationship between the historical Jesus and the Christ of early Christian faith seems to be adoptionist: for Hurtado, the Jesus of history is raised up from a position and status that was *not* intrinsically worthy of worship, to one that God now *declares* to be, or that he *renders* (in some way), worthy of worship. For Hurtado, after the resurrection and exaltation, "'God' in some profound way now includes a *glorified human.*"[20] That is quite a statement. But it is not quite the same thing as saying that the divine identity now includes a distinct preexistent person whose identity is defined by a biography that includes a particular historical human life (as narrated in, for example, Phil 2:6–11). What is at issue here is whether this assessment of the shape of Christ devotion (and the Christology it implies) fully does justice to the claims of the New Testament.

If we say very little about the historical life and identity of Jesus, we inevitably drain the word "Jesus" in "Lord Jesus Christ" of meaning.[21] Indeed, a lack of clarity on the historical Jesus raises pressing questions also for the use of the word "*Christ*" in that expression (and in others like it that define the shape of Christ devotion). What does it in fact mean for the earliest Christians to worship the "Lord Jesus *Christ*"? Is "Christ" in that expression no more than a personal name that only denotes the now glorified and transformed Jesus?

In the wake of a recent study by Matthew Novenson, it is likely that the word "Christ" in Pauline texts has titular force and, as such, it both denotes Jesus and *connote*s his messianic identity?[22] If the word is titular, we are bound to consider, once again, the relationship between the Christ of Christ devotion and the Jesus of history. For the Bible and for first-century Jews "the messiah" (or "the Christ" in Greek texts) always refers to a human

---

20. Hurtado, *God,* 113.

21. In later chapters (esp. chapter 8 and in Part 6) I will attempt to show that the occlusion of the historical Jesus from our understanding of Christ devotion has obscured the origins of New Testament Christology. It has left vital historical questions unanswerable just as much as it has distorted the shape of New Testament theology.

22. Novenson, *Christ among the Messiahs* (2012).

(though sometimes a *preexistent being who comes to earth as a human*). So, as with the word "Jesus" in "Lord Jesus Christ," we are bound to ask: how is the *identity* of this (divine) person—who is worshipped in ways continuous with the worship of the one God of biblical revelation—constituted by his being a messiah (*Christos*)? Did Paul of Tarsus worship the "Lord Jesus Christ" because, in part, he believed he was the messiah "of the seed of David, according to the flesh" (Rom 1:3)? That surely is now the natural conclusion from texts that make the Lord Jesus *Christ* the recipient of devotion (e.g., Phil 2:11; 1 Cor 8:6). In that case, how do we avoid concluding that a particular understanding of the historical Jesus—as the claimant to Israel's royal throne—does in fact make a vital contribution to the shape of Christ devotion: the earliest Christians worshipped a human king (albeit one now exalted to heaven)? And because "messiah" is a title for a human leader of God's people we are now bound to wonder what a *nondivine* title is doing as a part of the name of the one who receives praise and a whole-life devotion in the Pauline churches?

Other related questions now present themselves. One sure finding of twentieth-century scholarship is that there are problems with a straightforward judgment that the historical Jesus believed himself to be and proclaimed himself as the royal messiah. There is some prominent Gospel evidence that Jesus wanted to challenge or redefine royal messiahship (e.g., Mark 8:29–30; 12:35–37). Of course, there is also the added complexity that in first-century Judaism "messiah" can refer to a priestly or a prophetic figure, not just to a king. So what did it really mean for the first Christians to call Jesus "the Lord Jesus *Christ*," and to render him devotion as such? For Paul and others, was there more to Jesus' messianic identity than simply a belief that he was the one who had come to restore the booth of David?

But above all, there is now a problem with any view that the words "Jesus" and "Messiah" (in Lord Jesus *Christ*) refer only to the risen *and exalted*—that is *glorified* and *transformed*—Jesus. The effect of Novenson's work is to problematize any approach to Christ devotion that takes "Christ" (and also *Jesus*) as simply denotative, with no clear reference to a particular understanding of the historical Jesus and his messiahship. His work strongly suggests that the expression "Lord Jesus Christ" did have in view the mortal, human, Jesus of Nazareth and a view of him as Israel's true king (or prophet or priest).

Hurtado's perspective on the relationship between *Christ* devotion and the *Jesus* of history seems to be determined by three judgments. With the first judgment—an *historical* one—there can be no quarrel: the overwhelming evidence shows that there was no worship of Jesus of Nazareth during his earthly life. Secondly, Hurtado concludes from that datum that Jesus of

Nazareth neither asked to be worshiped nor did he claim a divine identity (despite texts in John to the contrary, especially 5:17–23, where Jesus says the Son should be honored the way the Father is honored). Thirdly, and crucially, he makes an historical judgment about the nature, the shape, of first-century Jewish theology: given the constraints of Jewish monotheism, it would not have been historically possible for the historical Jesus to have believed himself, and to have presented himself as, one worthy of worship.[23] This third judgment obviously supports, and perhaps precedes, the second.

Together, these three judgments, mean, in effect, that Hurtado is conceptually consistent in eschewing any thoroughgoing investigation of the historical Jesus. Since the historical Jesus did not claim a divine identity, and he was *not* worshipped as some kind of "divine man," any investigation of Christ devotion does not need to be overly concerned about the particularities of the life of Jesus of Nazareth. His aims, objectives, and achievements were not in focus when the first Christians worshipped the exalted Christ. Paul and his peers did not worship Jesus the Zealot, or Jesus the charismatic, or Jesus the teacher of subversive wisdom, or the prophet of a world-ending (apocalyptic) judgment, or Jesus the Messiah who came to restore Israel and bring her back from her long years in exile. They worshipped none of these modern reconstructions of the human Jesus of history, because they worshipped the exalted, glorified Jesus.

Of course, in all this Hurtado's model in some ways typifies the approach to Christian origins that has dominated modern scholarship. It exemplifies the way that, despite the interpretative assumptions of two thousand years of Christian theology and popular piety, when the New Testament texts are studied carefully in their Jewish historical context, the enlightened, critical historian inevitably finds a deep ditch between the Jesus of history and the Christ of faith. On careful analysis, we are bound (so the assured results of modern criticism have invariably told us) to conclude that Paul was not much interested in the historical Jesus. In this wider scholarly context it is hardly surprising that Hurtado's work has not produced the conclusion that actually for the first Christians, especially for Paul, the shape of Christ devotion was determined by a particular historical view of Jesus himself. (Neither is it surprising that, in all the critical interaction Hurtado's work has received, his views about the historical Jesus have not been the target of

---

23. In personal correspondence, Hurtado explains that John 9:35–38 anticipates the reverence given by the readers of John, but is more likely a story that has been "refracted through the post-Easter beliefs and practices of churches" than an entirely accurate account of an event in Jesus' life. Given the constraints of biblical and Jewish monotheism, it would have been "inappropriate for the mortal Jesus to demand worship and inappropriate for it to be offered."

critical scrutiny). Many others, of course, have argued that the resurrection was the decisive moment in the shift from a "low" Christology (or from *no* "Christology") to a high one. No one in the modern period has made a thoroughgoing case for thinking that actually Jesus' own view of himself and the particular manner of his life and death (his aims, motivations, and goals) determined the shape of a "Christological monotheism."

So, in reflecting on the implications of Hurtado's stance on the historical Jesus for his portrayal of the one whom the earliest Christians worshipped, we should remember that in some ways his work can be taken as illustrative of the modern guild's perspective on Christological origins. However, in other ways, Hurtado's model is distinctive and the decisive judgments about Jesus and the Gospels that he makes accentuate the problems which all modern New Testament scholars have had in explaining New Testament Christology. He stands at a point where the ditch is particularly wide and deep. For example, we will see in a later section in this chapter that Hurtado takes a particular, and unusual, stance on the expression "son of man" (that most have seen as a title—Son of Man) in the Gospels. That stance strongly supports his view that the human life and identity that we call Jesus of Nazareth does not provide much in the way of a particularizing force to the expression "the Lord *Jesus, Christ*" of Christ devotion.

The quest for the historical Jesus is fraught with difficulties and some might plead in Hurtado's defense that it is unreasonable to expect that on top of all that he has achieved he must simultaneously produce an historical Jesus reconstruction to boot. To be sure, any comprehensive presentation of an account of (a theory about) the historical Jesus is no mean feat. I simply make the point to illustrate the fact that for Hurtado the words "Jesus" and "Christ" in "Lord *Jesus Christ*" lack specific content; they do not have a *particular* historical life of Jesus of Nazareth in view, nor a particular understanding of what it would mean for that life to be messianic.[24] And the lack of any real role for the historical Jesus in Christ devotion reflects Hurtado's view that the Incarnation is not really a constitutive element of its shape.

In view of the Herculean task now required of anyone who would offer a fully persuasive account of the historical Jesus some of us might content ourselves with an unpacking of the narrative of Jesus' life given by the Gospels; if only to buy time for further work on the Jesus of history. But the problem of Hurtado's agnosticism about Jesus does not disappear when we turn to the Gospels, because in his view these cannot be straightforwardly correlated to the content of binitarian faith. Hurtado agrees with

---

24. For other reasons of his own, Bauckham also distances himself from the academic study of the historical Jesus (see *Eyewitnesses,* 1–5, and "Review Article").

the majority of NT scholars that John's story of Jesus' life is overlaid with a Christology that postdates Paul and the early high Christology that arose with the first believers. So it cannot be presumed that when Paul speaks of the Lord Jesus Christ he has in mind a specifically Johannine account of Jesus' life in explicitly incarnational terms.

On the other hand, for Hurtado, *the Synoptics*, which can more reasonably be taken to refer to a Pauline-era account of Jesus' life, *do not have an incarnational Christology*. The Jesus of Matthew, Mark, and Luke is a thoroughly human figure: a prophet, messiah, royal son of David, and so forth. *There is no incarnational pattern in the Synoptics*: Jesus is not a preexistent divine being who comes to earth in the way that Phil 2:6–11 describes and that other Pauline passages assume.

This, of course, is not an unusual scholarly position. However, it is not the only way the Synoptics have been read in the modern period. Nor, as we shall see in chapter 9, is it the most likely.[25] In any case, to arrive at his nonincarnational reading of the Synoptics, Hurtado makes a number of critical decisions, evident in both what he does and what he does not say. Hurtado offers no discussion of the possibility that some texts that speak of Jesus' having "come" refer to his coming from heaven, *from preexistence*, to earth (e.g., Mark 1:24 par. Luke 4:34; Matt 8:29; Mark 2:17 par. Matt 9:13; Luke 5:32; Matt 5:17; Luke 12:49; Matt 10:34 par. Luke 12:51; Matt 10:35; Mark 10:45 par. Matt 20:28; Luke 19:10).[26] There is no discussion of the possibility that some texts identify Jesus with preexistent Wisdom. For example, the "Johannine thunderbolt" in Luke 10:21–24 (par. Matt 11:25–27) has often been thought to express a conspicuously high Christology with a debt to Wisdom language, but for Hurtado it simply describes an intimate relationship between Jesus and God, his Father.[27] Hurtado does not comment on Jesus' remarkable claim that "all things have been handed over to me by the Father," who is "Lord of heaven and earth" (Luke 10:21–22 = Matt 11:25–27). Whilst some have heard Jesus speak in Luke 13:31–35 as divine Wisdom or God's own *Shekinah*, for Hurtado that passage simply has Jesus speaking as a prophet.[28] In a similar vein, there is also a particular problem with Hurtado's treatment of Jesus' use of "s/Son of m/Man" language, which I discuss separately below.

---

25. For recent publications that take a different view see esp. Gathercole, *Preexistent Son*, and Hays, *Reading Backwards*.

26. On which, see now Gathercole, *Preexistent Son* (2006) and the discussion in chapter 9 below.

27. Hurtado, *Lord Jesus Christ*, 339, 363.

28. Ibid., 194.

There are places where Hurtado thinks that Jesus has a transcendent power, with godlike superiority over the elements. In those passages the Synoptics comes close to ascribing divinity to him.[29] But they are a long way from the binitarian theology that defines the shape of the earliest Christology in Paul. There are also a few places where the Synoptics demonstrate a transcendent view of Jesus—passages in Matthew where Jesus receives *proskynesis,* for example—that are "paradigmatic anticipations" of the reverence for Jesus of the later church.[30] But, crucially, Hurtado thinks that this special material in Matthew, like the high, preexistent Christological material in John, is a later development in the Synoptic tradition that reflects the Christ devotion of the early church. (By the same reasoning, the blind man's worship of Jesus in John 9:35-38 is a reflection of a later church piety, not a reliable record of something that happened historically; much less evidence of some basis in the life of Jesus for the origins of Christ devotion.)

This all means, in other words, that for Hurtado *any divine Christological material in the Gospels cannot explain the origins of Christ devotion.* It does not antedate the origins of Christ devotion. Hurtado reaches for his novel explanation of the *origins* of Christ devotion—God's direction to Jesus' followers through certain visionary and other powerful religious experiences after Jesus' resurrection-exaltation—*because the earliest disciples' memories of the life (and death) of Jesus (as reflected in the Gospels, specially the Synoptics) did not itself call for such a treatment of him.*[31] And again, as with the relationship between the historical Jesus and the Christ of Christ devotion, this perspective has implications for the *shape* of NT Christology. It surely means, in effect, that whilst there is worship of the *(resurrected and) exalted Jesus,* that worship does not have the life, identity, self-consciousness, words, and actions of the man whose life is (faithfully?) told in the Synoptics as its focus.[32]

Hurtado's reading of the Synoptics, as with his stance on the historical Jesus, is conceptually consistent with the other pillars of his model. They are, far more than John, a fitting and accurate testimony to the shape of Christ devotion. The Synoptics, that is—devoid of any incarnational Christology—tell us who it is that the earliest believers worshipped. They did not worship a human Jesus who thought he was a divine man worthy of worship. The

---

29. See ibid., 285-86.

30. On Matthew's *proskynesis* material see ibid., 337-38; *How on Earth?,* 145-51. On the Matthean and Lukan postresurrection material see *Lord Jesus Christ,* 331-32, 345 respectively.

31. See esp. Hurtado, *How on Earth?,* 149; "Response," 12, and "Resurrection."

32. Here Bauckham is clearer that Jesus' divine actions are at the heart of the treatment of him (e.g., *Theology of the Book of Revelation,* 62).

earliest Christians worshipped the one that the Jesus of the Synoptics *became*, at his exaltation. The human life of Jesus is tagged to Christ devotion, but is not *constitutive* of it.

Indeed, this means Hurtado's model requires an account of Christological origins that is developmental and more complex than at other times he claims it really was. It surely means that the Christology of John's Gospel is a later development from the earliest exaltation Christology, since in John Jesus really does think that he is a divine man who is worthy of worship (John 5:23, cf. 9:35–38). And all that Hurtado says about the Synoptics in relation to the evidence for an early Christ devotion in the letters of Paul means that between those two sets of data there is also inconsistency that needs explanation. On the one hand, the Synoptic Gospels do *not* contain a preexistent, incarnational Christology. On the other hand, Phil 2:6–11 attests to a very early Christology that antedates the Synoptics, and that *does* contain such a Christology. Surely, if Hurtado is right about the Christology of the Synoptics and of Phil 2, then the Synoptics are evidence of an early *low* and nonincarnational Christology *before the development towards the kind of preexistence Christology that is now reflected in Phil 2* (and in other places). If there was a sudden explosion of high Christological devotion in the earliest months and years of the post-Easter church, why is it only with John's Gospel that the preexistent, incarnational Christology is present in the written life of Jesus? If, on the other hand, the nonincarnational Christology of the Synoptics is simply faithful to the way it was with the historical Jesus, then why do John (and to a lesser extent Matthew), but not Luke and Mark, see fit to overlay Jesus' own Christology with their own? Does that difference not strongly suggest, as most have argued in the modern period, that there were many (like Luke and Mark) who, for quite some time in the early years of the church, did not share the preexistence incarnational theology that others began to develop?

Furthermore, Hurtado *does* actually see the Synoptics as evidence of Christ devotion. That is, inasmuch as the Gospels are generically *Lifes* of Jesus, comparable to the *Greco-Roman "Bios" or "Vita"* that was sometimes used to recount the lives of those regarded as divine men, the Gospels attest to a treatment of Jesus that goes far beyond anything that Jews ever wrote for a rabbi.[33] But once again, Hurtado presents the strange situation wherein, on the one hand, the Synoptics "promoted and reflected the intense devotion to Jesus" of the early church,[34] but, on the other, they *do not*

---

33. Hurtado, *Lord Jesus Christ*, 274–77.

34. Ibid., 346. The significance of this claim is then illustrated in the use Hurtado makes of the Synoptics in his search for evidence of opposition to Christ devotion in "Opposition to Christ-Devotion" (reprinted and slightly edited in *How on Earth?*, 152–78).

contain the Christology of incarnation and preexistence that constituted the Christology of Christ devotion that we find in Paul and other parts of the NT. Of course, these oddities would disappear if the Synoptics *did* contain a Christology of incarnation and preexistence (a possibility to which we shall come in chapter 9).

These criticisms may seem to be overly analytical and unfair to a model that is bound to have tensions in the nature of the historical exercise, even apparent contradictions. But there really is a gaping incarnation-shaped-hole at the center of the Hurtado model of Christological origins that has far-reaching historical (not to mention *theological*) implications that have not yet received the scholarly attention they deserve. The problem can be seen, lastly, by reflecting a little more deeply on the relationship between *who* Christ is and *what* he does (what has traditionally been called the relationship between his person and his work).

Clear statements of Christ's preexistence and incarnation in the NT are inextricable from a particular claim for the salvific, atoning activity of Christ *in his life, death, and resurrection*. So, for Paul, God sends the pre-existent Son because, between them, the law and sinful Adamic flesh are unable to fulfill God's own righteous decree. The identity and action of *the Son* who comes from God, gives to enslaved humanity the power to become *sons*, living new lives by the Spirit of the Son and in intimacy with the Father (Rom 8:3-4, 14-16; Gal 4:4-7). This is basic also to the logic of John's incarnational theology since those who receive the Logos get to become children of God, born from above, not by the will, or flesh, of man (John 1:11-13).

It has sometimes been argued that behind such Pauline and Johannine texts there was a primitive confessional formula that connected the sending of the Son to God's salvific purposes (see also John 3:16-17; 1 John 4:9). In any case, they are important because they appear to say that it is not just the *action* of the incarnate Son that is the basis of salvation. If anything, the focus is more clearly on his *identity*; as one who is the unique *divine Son* who has come from God. As Richard Bell has recently argued, commenting on 2 Cor 5:14-21, because "Christ is the pre-existent and incarnate Son of God, he is able fully to stand in our place where 'no other person can stand in our place.'"[35] It is true that some do not see a divine identity in Paul's sonship language, but the approach exemplified by Bell fits well with our observations on the Christ hymns (above) and it will be supported by our investigation of Phil 2:6-11 in chapter 8.[36]

35. Bell, "Christology," 23, quoting from Hofius, "Gottesknechtslied," 423.

36. For Bell's approach see also, e.g., Cranfield, *Romans*, vol. 1, 381-82; N. T. Wright, "Romans," 580; *Paul*, 658, 660-61, 694 (criticizing Hurtado's denial of a divine Son of God in Paul) and 696, 701; Hays, "Story of God's Son," 186, 194-95; Fee, *Pauline*

Whilst several texts have traditionally been taken to mean that for Paul Christ's salvific work depends on his identity as the eternal, *divine* Son of God, it is possible that in two Pauline texts his divine sonship is grounds also for a particular claim to his unique humanity. In one breath Paul can say "God was in Christ—reconciling the world to himself," and in the very next breath that "for our sake he made him to be sin *who knew no sin*" (2 Cor 5:19, 21).[37] The way 2 Corinthians speaks of Christ's sinlessness implies that for Paul it was a "non-negotiable presupposition" and so a well-known component of the earliest views about Jesus.[38] It obviously only has any point if it is a statement about his *humanity*.

The Son's sinlessness is also likely to be assumed in the language of Rom 8:3, where Paul says the Son is sent "*in the likeness* of sinful flesh." In other words, for Paul, Christ was both fully human—as a man of flesh and blood, whose life was hampered in ways that all human life has been since Adam's first sin—but also uniquely, unlike the rest of humanity, not actually constituted in his essence by a sinful human nature. (How it is, for Paul, that Christ is both sinless and nevertheless present in his humanity "in the likeness of sinful flesh" is not clear and, of course, has led to fascinating debates among later theologians.) In both texts Paul probably assumes a traditional early Christian view that during his life Jesus was in some way (that he does not spell out) free from personal sin (cf. Heb 4:15; 1 Pet 2:22), even whilst he was fully identified with sinful humanity. In this case, Paul's point is likely to be that this unique, sinless-divine humanity means that *who* Jesus was (in his being, his ontology) uniquely enabled him to carry through the salvific work of God in his life and death (cf. 1 John 3:5). In the immediate context, Paul's point is that the Son is the means by which God the Father "gets the job done" (freeing believers "from the law of sin and death"—8:2, condemning sin in the flesh—8:3, so that "the righteous requirement of the law might be fulfilled" in believers who "walk according to the Spirit"—8:4). At the climax of a lengthy treatment of sin, death, and the law (chs. 5–7), Paul's primary focus is on what God has done in Christ. But his soteriological assertions are predicated on a statement of Christ's mysterious identity: he is both the eternal divine Son and the one who came "in the likeness of sinful flesh" so that, in his identification with the rest of humanity, they would have access to a life (in the Spirit) free from sin (8:2, 4–10), death (8:2, 6, 10–11), and the law's condemnation; the life, that is,

---

Christology, 220 (on Gal 4:4–6).

37. For this translation of 2 Cor 5:19 see Bell, "Christology," 11, cf. N. T. Wright, *Paul*, 675–76.

38. Fee, *Pauline Christology*, 167.

that properly belongs to the Son, even in his sinless humanity. Paul's dense train of thought assumes *both* Christ's identification with humanity after Adam (hence the phrase *"in the likeness of* sinful flesh") *and* his making available a human life that is free from sin, as Adam's was supposed to have been, hence the multiple allusions to Adam's original vocation and identity in all that follows (8:18-32).

The way such material makes a connection between incarnation (Jesus' "who" and his "whence") and salvation (his "what") requires a Christology that sees in the life of Jesus of Nazareth a divine life, identity, and action. Inasmuch as this material represents a snapshot of one aspect of the complex phenomenon that is NT Christology, it is the incarnate (and, therefore, in some sense *historical*) life of Jesus that fills most of the picture frame.

It is hard to find much interaction with this material in all that Hurtado has written on the origins of Christ devotion. As far as I can tell, he has nowhere discussed NT statements of Christ's sinlessness, which are surely a remarkable component part of the earliest "beliefs and religious practices that constituted devotion to Jesus as a divine figure."[39] To be sure, most of the sinless statements do not appear in explicitly devotional contexts. But the one in 1 Pet 2:22 appears in a passage that has sometimes been reckoned to reflect early Christian liturgical material (2:21-25).[40] Hebrews 4:14-15 relates belief in Jesus' sinlessness to "our confession," and in his recent book on Pauline Christology, Gordon Fee has highlighted the ways the material in 2 Cor 5 reflects a *devotion* to Christ in Paul.[41] It may also be that in the Christ hymns it simply goes without saying that the *incarnate* Christ lives a perfect, sinless life. How could it possibly be otherwise for a man who is described (in those hymns) as a manifestation of the one God of biblical faith?

Whilst Hurtado does not comment on the sinless theme, he thinks that sonship language for Jesus, which is a key element of the texts that speak of preexistence in relation to Christ's saving work, "did not function primarily to express Jesus' divine nature."[42] In a couple of places he has discussed Christ's preexistence and he thinks it is "clear" that the way some

---

39. The words come from Hurtado's own description of the subject matter of the historical analysis that is his magnum opus (*Lord Jesus Christ*, xiii).

40. See Martin, *Hymn of Christ,* 19; Osborne, "Un état de la question," 60-71.

41. See Fee, *Pauline Christology*, 196-98.

42. Hurtado, *Lord Jesus Christ*, 107. See further Hurtado, "Son of God," where the emphasis, for Hurtado, in Rom 8:3 is on Christ's *status* as God's Son for the benefit of believers who also become God's sons (in 8:14, 29). Hurtado's rejection of a divine sense of "s/Son of God" in Paul seems in part to be a reaction to the arguments of the old history of religions school that divine sonship in Paul stemmed from Hellenistic notions of a divine hero or demigod (see his "Resurrection," 46 n. 29, and "Son of God," 218-21).

NT texts attribute "preexistence to Jesus proceeds from the conviction that he is the eschatological agent of redemption."[43] To be sure, eschatological redemption is a theme in the key texts. But in the texts that we have it is far from obvious that the relationship between preexistence and eschatological redemption "proceeds" the way Hurtado claims. In the cases he cites (Col 1:16–17; Heb 1:2; John 1:1–3) the texts themselves quite straightforwardly say that eschatological redemption (Jesus' "what"—Col 1:18–20; Heb 1:3d, 2:5–18; John 1:11–12) proceeds from his preexistent identity, as the unique preexistent and divine Son, the "invisible image of God," and "the Logos" (from his *"who"*). Taken as a whole, the New Testament claims that belief in Jesus' preexistence proceeds from his own claim to preexistence (in John, if not also in the Synoptics), and in the texts under review here Christ's preexistence is an aspect of his identity that undergirds his salvific work at the cross, not his exalted position in heaven or his role as agent of some future, yet to be completed, eschatological salvation.

We should also consider the possibility that for Paul and others it is because Christ, the Son, is a preexistent divine being that he is capable of being a sinless human being and that, as such, he is capable of fulfilling the work of salvation: in other words, that the work of salvation already done at the cross is predicated on his *preexistent divine identity*.[44] All this is both vital to a fully rounded understanding of the *shape* of New Testament Christology. It also has implications for the origins of Christ devotion since it suggests that, in fact, the worship of Christ was a response to beliefs about his eternal and incarnate identity, and that that identity was revealed in the peculiar character of his work (of salvation).

I have suggested that Hurtado's view of the relationship between the earthly and the exalted Jesus can usefully be labeled "adoptionist." This is not an obvious feature of Bauckham's model, where there is a greater stress on the Son's eternal *inclusion* in the divine identity, and Christology is much less a matter of a *worship* of Jesus (that only started after Christ's resurrection). However, there are places where Bauckham's exegesis also seems less interested in the Incarnation than we might expect from the New Testament texts.

In his *Jesus and the God of Israel*, Bauckham stresses Christ's participation in the work of creation and unique sovereignty of God. The stress,

---

43. In Hurtado, *Lord Jesus Christ*, 124 (see more fully 118–26). See also *How on Earth?*, 102.

44. Traditionally, Christian theology has brought the virgin birth stories into the discussion at this point. For Hurtado, these affirm Jesus' role as the fulfillment of Israel's history and hopes (*Lord Jesus Christ*, 318–30), but they have nothing to tell us about a belief in Jesus' divine identity. He does not discuss the important article by C. E. B. Cranfield ("Virgin Birth") that argues for a contrary view.

3. THE SHAPE OF NT CHRISTOLOGY

throughout, is on the identity of the risen and exalted Christ. However, Bauckham does believe that the Synoptics, not just John, accord Jesus a divine identity during his earthly life. Indeed, the last chapter of *Jesus and the God of Israel* deals with a passage that could be taken as evidence against the central thesis: the Markan cry of dereliction, where Jesus appears, on the face of it, to be very much *outside* the divine identity. A careful reading of that chapter suggests that with Bauckham's work we have a quite different problem to the ones evident in Hurtado's treatment of Jesus and the Gospels.

As a counter to the argument from Mark 15:34 that Mark does not have a Christology of Christ's full divine identity, Bauckham provides a provocative reading of that text that attempts to show that here too there is a Christology of divine identity.[45] His argument is revealing of Bauckham's wider perspective and assumptions. There are places in the essay where Bauckham affirms Jesus' distinct identity as a discrete individual, in distinction to the "Father," as his fully divine "Son." But it is striking that his discussion nowhere includes an affirmation of Jesus' *humanity*. Indeed, at its heart, Bauckham's exegesis of the cry of dereliction—if I understand him rightly—is rather docetic. Jesus' question to God (". . . why have you forsaken me?") is not asked "on his own account."[46] Rather it is a willing, conscious, act of identification with the godforsaken. Jesus chooses *from his divine identity* to voice the words of a godforsaken Israel and all of humanity's godforsaken individuals. In other words, this is the *divine* Son of God speaking *on behalf of* others with whom he identifies himself. This is not a human Jesus speaking of his own (very real) experience of divine abandonment.

This way of reading Mark 15:34 certainly avoids the problem that the verse might otherwise pose for Bauckham's model. But it also seems to remove any real distinction between Jesus and God (the Father) and to undermine any possibility that (even if, for Mark, this is the story of a fully *preexistent* and divine Son) in his earthly life Jesus is genuinely and fully a human being. For Bauckham, this is not, apparently, the human Jesus crying out, but rather simply "God's unique act of self-identification with the godforsaken."[47] I doubt this reading will convince most interpreters. It contrasts starkly with another recent reading of Mark 15:34 by Joel Marcus, who argues that the cry of dereliction shows that in his death Jesus, in effect,

---

45. Bauckham, *God of Israel*, 254-68.
46. Ibid., 261.
47. Ibid., 267. I struggle to see how divine "identification" with the godforsaken equates to "incarnation" (as does ibid., 267). Israel's god is perfectly capable of identifying with his people without thereby having to take on human flesh as one of them. And it is not obvious to me how Bauckham's understanding of "incarnation" in this passage achieves, or offers, any kind of meaningful salvation.

"becomes in some ways a man possessed" by a demon, or Satan.[48] Whatever we make of Marcus' provocative approach—and I think at an exegetical level there is much to be said for it—Bauckham seems to abstract the verse from the Markan narrative, where it comes at the climax of an account of Jesus in thoroughly human terms. To be sure, there are times in Mark where Jesus has a divine identity (that I will discuss in Parts 4 and 6). But in the chapters leading up to the cross the accent is on his ordinary humanity and there is a sense of divine withdrawal and imminent suffering. I struggle to think of any obvious parallels to Jesus' speaking a verse from Scripture in the way that Bauckham argues he does on this occasion. It is true that there are passages in the NT where Christ is explicitly identified with others. But these are primarily statements of identification *with the people of God*, not, that is, with the godforsaken.

In later chapters, as I press into the evidence for an incarnational Christology at the heart of New Testament theology, I will sometimes have occasion to question Bauckham's discussion of texts where, as with his treatment of Mark 15:34, he emphasizes Christ's divine identity in a way that seems to preclude a faithful account of Christ's full humanity (within an incarnational framework). Bauckham emphatically insists on the absolute distinction between Israel's God and the rest of the reality, which is an undeniable feature of the primary texts. However, he construes that distinction in a way that is questionable. Sometimes that seems to be to the detriment of his interpretation of the New Testament and certainly, as we shall see in Part 3, it hampers his interpretation of some of the Jewish texts where already, before Jesus, Jewish monotheism appears to have an "incarnational" aspect or tendencies.

2: The Distinct Identities of God the Father and the Lord Jesus Christ, the Son

In working so hard to convince the academy of a fully *divine* Christology, Hurtado and Bauckham have emphasized all the ways in which early Christian practice and belief treats Jesus *in the way that the one God of Israelite faith was treated*. The picture that emerges draws our gaze to the similarities and commonalities *between*, and to the *identification of*, Jesus and God.[49] *But other aspects of Jesus' identity are either missed or, in some cases, played*

---

48. Marcus, *Mark*, vol. 2, 1063; "Identity and Ambiguity," 140–47. See also Brown, *Death*, vol. 2, 1047–51, against various attempts to avoid the natural reading of cry of dereliction.

49. This is also a feature of Tilling's *Christology*.

down; texts that complicate the picture in giving "the Lord Jesus Christ" an identity quite distinct from "God the Father" are undervalued.

This may seem a surprising criticism to make of Hurtado's work, since throughout he has spoken of the twoishness of the early Christian version of monotheism.[50] He has boldly pioneered the emerging consensus with the insistence that the earliest Christian monotheism was "binitarian." So it would seem to be counterintuitive that his model would suffer a lack of recognition of distinctions between God the Father and the Lord Jesus Christ. Indeed, in this section Bauckham will bear the brunt of my critical questions. However, in some ways Hurtado's model is, once again, in my sights.

We may start, for example, with a little reflection on the wider implications of our comments on Hurtado's work in the last section. If my observations have been anywhere near the mark, then some of Hurtado's judgments about Christ's identity inevitably weaken the sense that he has his own distinct divine identity. For Hurtado, the Christ of Christ devotion is divine and treated as a distinct figure in heaven after the resurrection and exaltation, but not because of his own intrinsic identity in the Incarnation and from preexistence. The *divine* Christ is divine because of what God has done to him. He is not worshipped the way Roman emperors were worshipped; because of individual human deeds and a uniquely virtuous character. Inasmuch as it is Jesus of Nazareth who defines the identity of the second figure who became the object of Christian worship, it is a *glorified* Jesus, not the human Jesus who was a distinct first-century Jewish man with his own unique biography. For Hurtado, the glorification and transformation that take place at the resurrection both exalt Christ to a position of worship but also seem to strip him of aspects of the human identity he had as Jesus of Nazareth (whether that be the Jesus of Nazareth of actual history or the Jesus of Nazareth of the Gospel stories).

The title of Bauckham's first book on Christology, *God Crucified*, seems to elide the distinction between God the Father and the Lord Jesus Christ and to ignore the fact that the NT only ever speaks of *Christ* crucified, not of "God crucified." And, as we shall see, others have questioned whether Bauckham's model stresses the identification of Christ and God *at the expense* of the distinctions between them. Indeed, in a recent book-length response to both Bauckham's and Hurtado's work, James Dunn has forcefully pressed the need for more attention to the distinctions between the Lord Jesus Christ and God the Father.[51]

50. Bauckham criticizes Hurtado for a twoishness that seems in the end not to amount to the inclusion of Jesus Christ within the identity of the one God (Bauckham, "Devotion to Jesus Christ," 197-98).

51. Dunn, *Did the First Christians Worship Jesus?* (2010), see esp. 4, 21-22, 28, 39,

Such criticisms do not lead, as Dunn thinks, to the conclusion that there is not a full inclusion of Jesus in the divine identity, nor a worship of him as such. But given the way Jesus Christ is fully included in the divine identity, the full portrayal of him, even at times in ways that seem to place him *outside* the divine identity, needs to be considered afresh. For reasons that I hope will become clear in this and subsequent chapters, I think it is not simply that their paradigm (or paradigm*s*) have been incomplete. As my argument for a new paradigm unfolds, I will argue that the distinction between the divine "persons" is a vital aspect of the theological *shape* of NT Christology that needs to be given more attention than it has received in the emerging consensus. I will propose that, instead of leaving it on one side until the divine identity of Christ is fully established, reflection on this aspect of the relation between Jesus and the God of Israel leads to a clear understanding of the *origins* of "Christological monotheism." Far from it being a problem (as Dunn assumes) for the view that the NT has a fully divine Christology, this part of the conceptual shape of early Christian belief actually points us towards a more secure understanding of the historical origins and conceptual intelligibility of such a Christology.

In all probability there is a problem here that is much wider than the work of Hurtado and Bauckham. Modern scholarship has tended to envisage a chain of being, or an ontological ladder, reaching down from God through divine mediators to ordinary creatures, including human beings.[52] Then it is assumed an entity cannot have an ontology of more than one rung on the ladder; its position is static.[53] The study of Christology has then boiled down to the question of the location of Christ's rung on that ladder of being; whether there is a "high" or a "low" Christology in any given text. Bauckham (and in his own way Hurtado) have made a persuasive case that he should be placed firmly at the top rung of the ladder. Or, rather, that (as Bauckham has stressed) that it is even a mistake to think of a ladder of being at all: Christ's identity is to be found outside, above, and beyond the world (and whatever ladders it may contain). The ladder image too easily buys into a Greco-Roman model where there is a sliding scale of divine identities, from the high God at the top down through lesser divine beings each receiv-

---

43–58, 136–42, and see Gorman, *Cruciformity,* 18 n. 26, pointing out the problem in Bauckham's book title. The title of Bauckham's longer book—*"Jesus and the God of Israel"*—avoids the dangers of the first title.

52. For my comments here compare Rowe, *Early Narrative Christology*, 19–23.

53. This problem surfaces also in the study of Jewish angelology. See, for example, Philip Alexander struggling to comprehend the possibility that Qumran community members could think of themselves as both human and angelic (in Alexander, *Mystical Texts,* 46).

ing a level of honor, praise, and cultic worship in respect of their position in an ever changing divine hierarchy.

But, against both Bauckham and the usual assumptions of modern NT scholarship, careful study of Paul for example, suggests it is a category mistake to assume Christ's identity, or ontology, must be limited to one position or another in all reality (in and outside of the cosmos). If we were to assume (against Bauckham) that the early Christians did have a ladder-of-being model then we should resist thinking that their Christology placed Jesus Christ at just one position on the ladder. Certainly, it is hard to avoid the impression that the NT endorses a basically Jewish and biblical view that there is a tiered universe with the Lord Jesus Christ sometimes located on the divine tier (as co-creator) and at other times described taking up the identity of heavenly beings—angels—and that in the Incarnation, above all, he becomes fully human. (A nice example of Christ's multi-tiered identity is Luke 9:26, where the Son of Man comes "in his own glory, the glory of the Father and of the holy angels.") Christ, in other words, appears to have an ambiguous or multifaceted identity and this, I will be arguing, is a central—theologically and historically definitive—aspect of NT Christology. Beneath the *appearance* of an ambiguous identity, we will actually see that there is a clearly defined, if complex, identity, and that there were biblical categories that meant that this complexity made very good sense to his first-century Jewish followers.

The evidence that Jesus Christ has a distinct identity and that he is not simply, or straightforwardly, to be included in the divine identity is not hard to describe.[54] He is, for example, the object of God's resurrection action; he does not raise himself from the dead. And there are texts that firmly subordinate Christ to God (1 Cor 3:21–23; 11:3; 15:24–28), and sometimes *kyrios* for Christ seems to function "not so much a way of *identifying* Jesus with God, but if anything more a way of *distinguishing* Jesus from God."[55] For example, Paul addresses praise and prayer to "the God (and) *Father of our Lord (kyrios)*" in a way that suggests the Lord Jesus Christ is not himself the recipient of devotion (Rom 15:6; 2 Cor 1:3; 11:31; Col 1:3; Eph 1:3, 17, cf. 1 Pet 1:3). And in other texts, Christ is the one who leads the praise of his people; praise that is directed *to God*, not to himself (Heb 2:11–13).

For Paul and other NT writers, the risen and exalted Christ is as much a *mediator* between God and humanity as he is a member of a dyadic Godhead. He is the one who enables prayer and worship to God: devotion to

---

54. For what follows, see Dunn, *Worship*, and compare Hays, *Reading Backwards*, 27–28, on material that suggests Jesus' "non-identity with God."

55. Dunn, *Worship*, 254.

God is offered *in his name* (Eph 5:20; Col 3:17) and *through him* (Rom 1:8; 7:25; 16:27; 2 Cor 1:20; Jude 25), and he is an intercessor between God and his people (Rom 8:34; 1 John 2:1). He models prayer and teaches his followers how to pray (Mark 1:35; 6:46; Matt 6:5-8; Luke 3:21; 5:16; 6:12; 11:2-4).

Of course, there is also material in the Gospels that portrays Jesus as one sharply *separated* from God in his earthly life. Jesus prays to God, speaks of his ignorance of matters known only to God (Mark 13:32), and directs others to God's kingdom (not to his own divine kingdom). In the cry of dereliction in Mark 15:34 and Matt 27:46—"My God, My God, why have you forsaken me"—Jesus voices a total estrangement from God. On the face of it, that cry is a real problem for the view that Mark and Matthew have a fully divine Christology in which Jesus is never other than the one God in human form. At the very least, because this verse gives Jesus a distinct identity *as one who is fully human* and set over against "God," it surely is unwise to say, without further ado, that for the Markan Jesus, "God was crucified."

In the previous section we discussed Bauckham's problematic attempt to repulse the argument that Mark 15:34 tells against his construal of a Christology of divine identity. In view of the problems with his approach to that kind of passage, it may be more promising to explore other possibilities that nevertheless share his stance that in the Synoptics Jesus is fully identified with *Yhwh-Kyrios*. Bauckham argued that the text describes the divine Christ fully identifying himself with a godforsaken humanity. It is true that there are passages in the NT where Christ is explicitly identified with others. But these are primarily statements of identification *with the people of God*, not, that is, with the godforsaken. And with such passages we get the impression that for his earliest followers after his death there was as much of a belief in Christ's inclusive identification with his followers as there was a belief in his inclusive identification with God.[56] The church is Christ's body (Rom 12:4-5, 27; Eph 5:23; Col 1:24) and his identity is now present in and through his people; especially in 2 Cor 4:10-11 and Col 1:24, and in all the Pauline passages that use incorporative language for the relationship between Christ and believers. We need to explain how such texts fit with Christ's identification with *Yhwh-Kyrios* in other places. Do they mean that it is not just that Jesus Christ is now included in the divine identity, but so too, in fact, is the church—his body—in some way? In other words, does the distinctive shape of a monotheism that includes the human life of the Lord Jesus Christ within the divine identity now entail a salvation that includes some sense of *theosis*; of believers in Jesus now taken up into the life of the one God?

---

56. See especially the recent discussion of Hays, "Story of God's Son," esp. 195-96.

If there is some sense—for Paul and for others—that the eternal Son's *particular* identity includes a unique human life, that would both make sense of his experience of suffering at the cross and the effects of his human life on those he came to save. In the cry of dereliction it really is the human Jesus who, in his total identification with humanity *as a distinct divine and now human person set apart from God the Father*, experiences the full effects of sin for the divine-human relationship.[57] And by virtue of the eternal Son becoming what we are, he enables us to become what he is; *in a way that is not true of the identity and work of the Father (apart from the work of the Son)*.

If, on the other hand, it is not the case that Christ's humanity is really constitutive of his identity and precisely in such a way that salvation has as its goal the embracing of human beings within the divine identity, then we are left with the pressing question: how do we articulate the relationship between God, Jesus, and the redeemed in such a way that we respect the inclusive, overlapping identities between God, Christ, and his people that the texts just reviewed describe? There is a real danger that we too quickly draw a sharp and fixed line that serves to include Christ within the divine identity, but that does so in a way that jeopardizes his identity in relation to the church and the rest of reality. This seems to be the way Bauckham leans. Again, the issue is not whether Bauckham (or Hurtado) have a theology that is sufficiently appealing to a currently fashionable Eastern Orthodox belief in *theosis*.[58] The issue is whether Bauckham's exegesis and aggregation of his exegetical observations does sufficient justice to the nature of the primary texts. As my argument progresses, I will indicate that there are places where it seems not to, particularly in view of the considerable evidence that an early Christian belief in (something like an Eastern Orthodox) *theosis* is both anticipated by strands of Second Temple Judaism and, ultimately, is well grounded in the shape of Old Testament theology and spirituality.

On a separate, but related, point, more thought could be given to the possibility that different parts of Christological phrases—"Jesus," "Christ," "Lord," and "Son"—might *connote* different aspects of the identity of the one person (whom they all *denote*). This point is accentuated if, with N. T. Wright and M. Novenson, we see in Paul's use of the word "Christ" not just Christ's name, but a title that gives to Jesus a *messianic* identity that also

---

57. To some that may sound like a woefully anachronistic reading of Mark that owes little to proper historical exegesis but everything to the concerns of systematic theology. In a future study, beyond the scope of this one, I hope to set out reasons for thinking that it is a rather good summary of Mark's understanding of the cross.

58. For that fashion see, above all, Finlan, *Theosis*; Gorman, *Inhabiting*, but also N. T. Wright, *Paul*, 546, 781, 955, 1021–23, 1031.

makes him the human *representative* of his people.[59] As such, Christ's representative identity may need to be seen as more than *mere* representation or mere divine self-identification with humanity. Because he is the messiah, what is true for Christ is true also for those who are "in" him and who share his faith, *because they are included in his identity*.

A similar point can be made for "s/Son of God" language. Sometimes "Son (of God)" refers to the one who is preexistent (see Rom 8:3, 29; Gal 4:4, cf. John 3:17) and even the counterpart to "the Father" within a dyadic-but-singular and fully divine identity (Heb 1:2, 5, cf. Matt 11:25–27 = Luke 10:21–22; John 1:14; 17:1, 11, 21). At other times, though, "son" language evokes Jesus' royal messianic, and therefore, *human* identity (John 1:49; Rom 1:3; Heb 1:8).[60] Given the imperial connotations of the word *kyrios* (as reflected in Acts 25:26 for Nero), we should also bear in mind the possibility that on occasion Paul and others speak of Jesus as *kyrios* simply because he is the supreme ruler in the earthly, human (not just in the cosmic) realm; not, that is, because he is, necessarily, *Yhwh-Kyrios*. There are texts where *kyrios* (not *Kyrios*) is simply a designation of the ideal ruler who is, as such, "a savior, Christ the Lord (*kyrios*) (born in the city of David)" (Luke 2:11). This is the true human king, who is Israel's god's answer to the false claims of the Roman emperor.[61] This aspect of Paul's Christological language for Jesus' *distinct* divine identity will become particularly clear in our examination of Phil 2:6–11 (in chapter 8).

Some of all this evidence for the multifaceted role of Christological titles is noted by Hurtado, though more could be made of it.[62] An older generation of scholarship, exemplified by the work of Bousset, assumed that a high, transcendent or divine Christology could not coexist with a human,

---

59. N. T. Wright, *Climax*, esp. 18–55; "Romans," 416–19; *Resurrection*, 333–38, 393–98, 553–83; Novenson, *Christ*, esp. 26–28, 66, 117–19, 124–29, 131. And compare Hays, *Conversion*, 101–18. Texts that are marshalled to support this view are Rom 1:1–4; 8:17; 9:5; 15:7–12; 1 Cor 15:23–28; 2 Cor 5:10; Gal 3:16. Wright's argument for a representative *royal* messianism behind the use of "*christos*" for Jesus founders on the lack of strong and widespread evidence that the royal messiah was expected to be a representative figure (cf. the criticism of Chester, "Christ of Paul," 114). But the conceptual point stands once the representative function of the high priest messiah is appreciated (a point I will come to in later chapters).

60. Hurtado touches on the messianic use of sonship language in *Lord Jesus Christ*, 104, 109.

61. For this use of *kyrios* see also *Ps. Sol.* 17:36. The word "savior" or "deliverer" (*sōtēr*) in Luke 2:11 has strongly political connotations, as its use in Acts 5:31; 13:23 for Israel's judges (cf. Judg 3:9, 15; Neh 9:27) and in Phil 3:20 (discussed in chapter 8) both show. The word was a standard term for the ideal ruler in the Greco-Roman world.

62. He notes the imperial context of meaning for the Greek word *kyrios*, but seems to distance the NT use of *kyrios* from it (Hurtado, *Lord Jesus Christ*, 108–9).

messianic Christology. Again, it was assumed that Christ had to belong on just one rung of the ladder of being. And that judgment perhaps also reflects dualistic modern assumptions which have not yet been fully exorcised from scholarship.[63]

None of this means that we have to dismiss the undeniable evidence that Jesus Christ belongs within the divine identity or that he is worshipped as such. At other times *kyrios* for Jesus is clearly the *Kyrios* that stands in for the Tetragrammaton in the Septuagint. But it does suggest that the *Lord Jesus Christ* has his own identity which is not exhausted by his inclusion within the divine identity. To say that Jesus is a *representative* messiah does not mean that Jesus *only seems to be* (in a docetic fashion) a human king and Israel-in-miniature. It could mean that in fact his identity is constituted, in part, by his being the (true) king and the (true) Israel, summing up in himself all that is good and holy and true in Israel the nation, in her human rulers and, indeed, in the rulers of the wider (pagan) world.

When we attend carefully to those texts that speak unavoidably of Christ's inclusion in the divine identity we also find the language emphasizes Christ's distinction from God the Father. For example, in 1 Cor 8:6, God the Father is the *source* of creation, but the Lord Jesus Christ is its (personal) agent. In other texts Christ is the one who *sustains* creation (Col 1:16-17, 20; Heb 1:3) in a way that seems uncharacteristic of biblical language for God. And, of course, he is the Son, not the Father. It is not just that Jesus is inserted into the existing understanding of the divine identity, it is that *with the inclusion of Jesus within the identity of the one God, that identity is now understood in a substantially different way.* On one reading of the evidence we are invited to conclude that the divine identity now includes an individual human life in a way that means it is right and proper to speak of a humanity within the divine identity.[64] And that unique human life that manifested the humanity within the divine identity enables other human beings to be now gathered up into the divine life and identity.

In their major publications to date, neither Bauckham nor Hurtado have given as much attention to all this evidence for Jesus Christ's distinct identity as they might. And some of what they say suggests that their

---

63. See Bousset, *Kyrios Christos*, 30-35, for the claim that the early church rejected belief in a royal, Davidic messiah in favor of a transcendental messianism. There is still a hint of this in the argument against a royal messianism in Pauline Christology in, for example, Chester, "Christ of Paul."

64. On this point, and in criticism of the work of the emerging consensus scholars, compare Rowe, "Name of the Lord?," 167-73. In the previous section I noted but questioned Hurtado's view that the divine identity includes a "*glorified* human" (Hurtado, *God*, 113).

conceptual categories constrain them from recognizing the ways the NT distinguishes the identities of God the Father and the Lord Jesus Christ, the Son. Hurtado has emphasized the notion that Christ is God's unique *agent* and that Christ devotion has come about as a modification of existing Jewish traditions in which God gives responsibility for engagement with the world to a principal agent figure.[65] The problem here is that, in the first-century Jewish context, an agent is not a person. An agent is one who subordinates, or screens off his own personal interests, in the service of the one he represents. Or, alternatively, the agent never had any distinct personal interests and capabilities that have to be screened off. An angel, for example, may be said to be a divine agent (as God's *messenger*), but is not a "person" who acts of his own volition. (One function of the story of the fall of the angelic watchers in *1 En.* 6–15 is to explore the catastrophic consequences of any attempt by angels to act in their own independent self-interests. The sinful watchers leave behind their duties in heaven to have intercourse with women on earth.) So by grounding the origins of Christology in the modification of a Jewish divine agency tradition, Hurtado inevitably risks playing down the ways the Lord Jesus Christ does have his own personal identity in the drama of salvation (and at creation).

Bauckham minimizes the presence of a divine agency tradition in the Jewish sources and rejects its significance for Christological origins. Nevertheless, his own conceptual categories for the relationship between Christ and God are sometimes not far removed from Hurtado's.[66] For Bauckham "Jesus himself is the eschatological manifestation of YHWH's unique identity to the whole world . . . ."[67] In another place he says, "it was because Jesus *functioned* as God in early Christian religion that he was worshipped. All *the divine functions* in relation to the world—as Saviour, Lord and Judge—were *exercised by Jesus*, of course on *God's behalf*."[68] At the climax of the Christ hymn in Philippians, Christ is worshipped because of what he does: "he exercises the

---

65. See esp. the whole of Hurtado, *One God,* and also his *Lord Jesus Christ,* 31, 204, 393-94.

66. For Bauckham on principal agents see *God Crucified,* 16-22 (= *God of Israel,* 14-17) and compare N. T. Wright, *Paul,* 626, 633, 651-54, 684-85.

67. Bauckham, *God of Israel,* 193.

68. Bauckham, *Theology of the Book of Revelation,* 62 (italics added) and compare his "Divinity," 17: "in the New Testament it is primarily as sharing or implementing God's eschatological Lordship that Jesus is understood to belong to the identity of God." This approach is particularly prominent in his exegesis of Phil 2:6-11 (in "Philippians 2:9-11" and *God of Israel,* 42, 197-210).

3. THE SHAPE OF NT CHRISTOLOGY

unique divine sovereignty over all things," and he brings to full eschatological expression and recognition the universal sovereignty of the one God.[69]

My criticisms of Hurtado's treatment of Phil 2:6-11 in the last section apply here also. For Bauckham, the basis for the universal acclamation in Phil 2:10-11 is Christ's identification with God in his sovereignty. It may well be that that is part of the matter, and certainly Phil 2:11 emphasizes the way the glory given to Christ goes to the Father. But the hymn opens with praise of Christ as a distinct divine being—one who is "in the form of God"—who in preexistence and in the Incarnation reckoned and acted in ways that demonstrate a unique, personal, divine identity *distinct* from God the Father. Much more thought needs to be given to the way this remarkable passage ascribes to the Lord Jesus Christ a distinct personal identity that for the most part did not include a participation in the Father's unique divine sovereignty.

The point here is not to gainsay the truth of all that Bauckham says. I do not disagree that there is a strong sense that the divine functions, unique to the one God of Israel, are now carried out by the Lord Jesus Christ. And furthermore, in highlighting Bauckham's use of functional language we should not miss the fact that Bauckham argues trenchantly *against a functional understanding of Christ's relationship to God insofar as that has been understood in the modern period as necessarily entailing Jesus' exclusion from the unique divine identity.* The problem is that such statements (in the previous paragraph) do not say all that the NT texts ask us to say. And for Bauckham, what would traditionally be called the inner-trinitarian relationship between God the Father and the Lord Jesus Christ, the Son, seems to be primarily a functional one: the divine Jesus *functions* as one who *"exercises"* God's own divine functions *"on God's behalf."* The problem with this model is that it easily obscures the ways God the Father and the Lord Jesus Christ are distinct *persons* in the drama of both creation and salvation. And so it is understandable that Dunn complains that Bauckham has produced a picture of the divine relations which recalls the "modalism" of some later trinitarian theology (in which there is only one God who operates in different modes, first as the Father, then as the Son at the Incarnation).[70]

To be fair to Bauckham, even in the relatively short volume he has written on Christology, he finds space to point out that the NT goes beyond such a functional Christology to highlight the novelty of the early Christian

---

69. Bauckham, "Philippians 2:9-11," 130, cf. 130-31, 135 and his *God of Israel*, 42, 199-201.

70. Dunn, *Worship*, 142. There is not a little irony in Dunn's complaint since, in its own way, Dunn's understanding of Christ as Wisdom could also be deemed modalist. Dunn, far more than Bauckham, denies the existence of Christ as a preexistent divine person with his own distinct identity.

"inclusion in God of the interpersonal relationship between Jesus and his Father" (and indeed with the Holy Spirit).[71] What is at issue here is not whether in fact the NT meets the standards of a later trinitarian orthodoxy. My point is simply to say that seeing the relationship between God and the Lord Jesus Christ in terms primarily of the latter *acting on behalf of the former, as his agent*, risks minimizing all the ways the NT envisages distinct divine identities within the one divine identity. Having rejected one kind of functional Christology—where Jesus acts on God's behalf and therefore is *not* divine—there is a danger that we are still left with another kind of functional Christology that does not fully respect the way the NT texts describe distinct identities within the one God. Is the divine Son only ever the agent of the Father? Is his identity only ever referred back to God, with no reciprocal relationship of the Father now defined by the Son? Why does the NT use the highly *personal* language of a Father and a Son, and give the latter a distinct name, or honorific title ("the Lord Jesus Christ"), if he is primarily or simply the one who functions, as agent, on God's behalf?

In chapter 8 I will offer a reading of Phil 2:6–11 in which the distinct divine identity of Christ is very much at the heart of the hymn's Christology: alongside the Incarnation (see my comments in the previous section in this chapter), the basis for the worship of Christ is his distinct personal identity. Philippians 2:6 is remarkable for the fact that it does not say, as other New Testament passages sometimes say, that Christ was "sent" (by God) from preexistence. In this passage, Christ sets off from his heavenly home by *his own* initiative and volition. And insofar as he has an "equality with God" in preexistence, v. 6 stresses his distinct personal identity (echoing the way divine human rulers and Rome's emperors were regarded, by virtue of their personal charisma, power, virtue, and deeds, equal to the Olympian gods and worthy of their own cultic honors—see chapter 8). In Phil 2:9–11, Christ certainly participates in, or manifests, God's own unique sovereignty, but only as one of a number of roles and privileges that give him a discrete divine identity.

As Bauckham's language that I have just cited notes, traditional Christian theology has spoken of distinct *persons* within the Godhead. Understandably, NT scholars today are shy of using such language because it carries linguistic, philosophical, and cultural associations in the patristic period and for subsequent Christian discourse that should not be imported anachronistically into NT exegesis. Nevertheless, in large part, traditional Christian theology's talk of distinct *persons* is simply an attempt to do justice to all the ways that the New Testament texts themselves distinguish

---

71. Baukham, *God Crucified*, 74 (see further, 74–77) (= *God of Israel*, 55, 55–57).

clearly between the activities, biographies, and identities of God the Father and the Lord Jesus Christ.

Hurtado helpfully stresses the way Christ devotion does not entail the addition of a new deity, with a separate cult, to the one God already revealed to Israel: "Jesus is characteristically reverenced by early Christians as part of their worship of the one God of the biblical tradition."[72] However, Jesus' death and resurrection are marked in baptism and the "Lord's Supper" as distinct, new rites. Baptism may in part replace circumcision as the rite that marks the individual's inclusion in the covenant community. But both baptism and, more clearly, the regular celebration of the "Lord's Supper" are new rites that go beyond anything that was expected of Israel in its worship of the one God of biblical tradition. Both are focused squarely on Jesus (the Lord) whose death is remembered and in whose name baptizands are initiated into the faith. With these two we obviously do not simply have Jesus Christ take up the position that was already occupied by *Yhwh-Kyrios* in one of Israel's existing cultic rituals. They happen without reference to the Jerusalem Temple and in both cases they mark the creation of a new covenant that extends, or replaces, the one at Sinai. To be sure, these rites do not mean that with Christ devotion Jesus is treated as a new deity with his own separate cult. God the Father is not excluded from these rites; he is present at them. But they go with all the evidence that the earliest believers gave Jesus Christ a quite distinct identity, both as a divine being and as a human being (who had died an atoning death on a cross). So in these cases, *the shape of Christ devotion emphasizes the fully distinct personal identities of those that make up the one divine identity.*

My point can be further illustrated with some observations on 1 Cor 8:6. It is not clear why, if we follow all the things that Bauckham has said about "Christological monotheism," Paul does not in fact say in 1 Cor 8:6:

> ... for us, there is *one Lord God*:
>
> the Father, from whom all things and we for him,
>
> and Jesus Christ the Son through whom all things and we through him.

Formulated this way, with just one "one," the confession is a simpler evocation of Deut 6:4 and a more straightforward and emphatic statement of Christ's inclusion in the divine identity. As far as I can tell, this simpler form of a freshly expounded statement of Jewish monotheism (that starts with a brief evocation of the Shema) would also say all that Bauckham

---

72. Hurtado, *Lord Jesus Christ*, 138.

thinks Paul and his fellow believers felt compelled to say. It says very well the kind of things that Bauckham claims lie at the heart of "Christological monotheism": Jesus Christ the Son shares in and implements God's divine functions in relation to the world.

But, as it is, the confession that we actually have in 1 Cor 8:6 goes out of its way to make clear that there is *one* God the Father and *one* Lord Jesus Christ. So the fact that Paul does *not* speak in 1 Cor 8:6 of one God who is both Father and Son (and *Kyrios Christos*) quite understandably leads James McGrath to conclude that Paul does not in fact include the Lord Jesus Christ in the identity of the one God.[73] We have seen that for all sorts of reasons McGrath's own view of 1 Cor 8:6 is untenable. But McGrath's reading at least shows that in so emphasizing the distinction of "persons," and as a confession that asks to be treated as a piece of essentially biblical and Jewish theologizing, the confession strains the credibility of a claim that Christ belongs within the divine identity. *So in the creation of the confession in 1 Cor 8:6 there must have been very good reasons for so stressing the distinction between "one" God the Father and "one" Lord Jesus Christ.* And so we should be careful to avoid, in reaction to the kind of arguments put forward by McGrath, an interpretation of 1 Cor 8:6 that so emphasizes the identification of God and Jesus Christ that the distinction of identities is obscured.

Bauckham acknowledges *that* there is an intradivine relationship between Father and Son, and perhaps will have more to say in future publications on why that should be or why the NT church came to that view. It is a measure of the success of the emerging consensus in arguing for the genuine worship of Christ and his inclusion in the divine identity that these distinctions between the "persons" should now be the focus of our attention. In the modern period, the distinctions between "God the Father" and "the Lord Jesus Christ, the Son" have been deemed reason to reject the Christian dogma of Christ's full deity. In asking for a renewed focus on the distinctions this is not my purpose at all. Rather, once we have established (as I hope I have done in chapters 1–2) Christ's full deity in the primary witnesses to the theology of the early church, it is incumbent on us, in a fully rounded account of the theological shape and historical origins of NT Christology, to explain why the "persons" are so carefully distinguished. And as this study proceeds, I will argue that this distinction is in fact a crucial piece of the jigsaw puzzle that explains Christological origins and, indeed, that it is entirely right and proper that we do speak of the "persons" within the divine identity and economy. That language is appropriate, even necessary, once we see the *historical* realities that shaped "Christological monotheism." It

---

73. McGrath, *Only True God*, 39.

is not just that the later church fathers had good reason, within their own cultural and philosophical contexts, to speak of distinct persons. When we set early Christian beliefs in their first-century Jewish and Greco-Roman contexts, we will find that *as historians* (whether or not we also aspire to be theologians) the distinction between two divine *persons*, the Son and the Father, is language without which it is rather hard to explain the unique brand of Jewish monotheism that is earliest Christianity.

3: The Son of Man Title in the Gospels

In considering the *shape* of the Christology of the emerging consensus we come, finally, to the expression *ho huios tou anthrōpou,* that is traditionally translated "the Son of Man." The Jesus of the Gospels avoids speaking of himself as the messiah (or *"Christos"*), but frequently speaks in a peculiar fashion of "*ho huios tou anthrōpou.*" Why he does that and what the expression means has been one of the most hotly debated subjects in modern-era New Testament scholarship.

Although the group of scholars that I have described as an "emerging consensus" are by no means a self-defined community with an agreed position on every issue of New Testament Christology, they mostly share a common approach to "the Son of Man problem." They resist the view that when Jesus talks of the *ho huios tou anthrōpou* he lays claim to the identity, or to the title, of a widely expected heavenly figure. So they depart from the once widely accepted view that Jesus refers to a figure well-known to first-century Jewish apocalyptic literature.

For most of the twentieth century it was a matter of no real contention that "the Son of Man" was a figure of eschatological hope first described in Dan 7:13, where Daniel sees "one like a son of man" coming to, or from, God (the "Ancient of Days" as he is called in v. 9) on clouds. At least two Gospel Son of Man sayings clearly refer to the cloud-borne "one like a son of man" in Dan 7:13 (Mark 13:26; 14:62 and pars.). There are portions of two non-Christian Jewish apocalypses from around the time of the Gospels (the *Similitudes of Enoch—1 En.* 37–71—and *4 Ezra* 13) that elaborate on Dan 7:13, describing a Son of Man figure who is a heavenly, preexistent messiah, endowed with divine prerogatives (such as divine glory and a heavenly throne). In the Gospels too the Son of Man can be described as coming from heaven to earth (e.g., Mark 13:26; Matt 16:28; 24:39; Luke 18:8), with the Father's own "glory" (Mark 8:38, cf. 13:26; Matt 25:31). He is seated on a heavenly throne (Matt 19:28; 25:31) with power, and appears in the company of his own angels (e.g., Mark 8:38; 13:26–27 and pars.; Matt 13:41;

25:31), with authority to exercise divine judgment (Matt 16:27; 25:31–46; John 5:27, cf. Mark 8:38; Luke 12:8–9; 18:8; 21:36). His future appearance will be universal or cosmic (Luke 17:24, 30 and par., cf. Matt 24:30). The fact that he can be said to send *his* angels to administer the end-time judgment (Matt 13:41–42, cf. Matt 16:27 & Mark 13:26–27; Matt 24:30–31) also implies he is set over the angels, like God himself. And he comes in, or with, the clouds (Mark 13:26; 14:62 and pars.), in a way that recalls God's own exclusive mode of appearance and transportation.[74]

So most scholars have thought that with this expression the Jesus of the Gospels refers to a pre-Christian figure created by the imaginative world of Jewish apocalyptic; the "apocalyptic Son of Man." And the traditional modern view has been that in using the "Son of Man" expression the Jesus of the Gospels speaks not of the earthly royal messiah who would rule like David and restore the nation's political fortunes, but of a transcendent, heavenly messiah of a world-ending apocalyptic hope. As such *ho huios tou anthrōpou* is a title that ascribes to Jesus a set of established, broadly agreed-upon ideas and hopes. It is a title that refers to the tradition that flowed out of Dan 7:13 (and that perhaps preceded the first mention of the "one like a son of man" figure in Dan 7:13), and a whole set of "Son of Man" ideas and expectations is in mind even when a Son of Man saying has no obvious reference to Dan 7:13.

Sayings that describe a future coming of the Son of Man from heaven to earth are quite clear (esp. Mark 8:38; 13:26 and pars.). They must refer to a future return of Jesus after his death and resurrection; at the "parousia." Furthermore, one implication of the apocalyptic Son of Man theory is the possibility that in some sayings Jesus has already come from heaven to earth as the Son of Man during his earthly life. The apocalyptic Son of Man theory lends itself, in other words, to a preexistent and incarnational Christology. An incarnational coming is clear in John 3:13 ("No one has ascended into heaven except he who descended from heaven, the Son of Man") and, arguably, is also a feature of several Synoptic sayings where a coming in the present is most naturally analogous to the future coming from heaven to earth. Three Synoptic sayings could be read this way:

> For the Son of Man *came* not to be served but to serve, and to give his life as a ransom in the place of many. (Mark 10:45 and par.)

---

74. Cf. Exod 13:21; 19:9; 24:16; 34:5; Lev 16:2; Num 11:25; 12:5; 14:14; Deut 1:33; 2 Sam 22:12; Pss 97:2; 104:3; Isa 19:1; Jer 4:13; Ezek 1:4; Nah 1:3.

> The Son of Man *has come* to seek and save that which is lost. (Luke 19:10)[75]

> The Son of Man *has come* eating and drinking, and you say, "Look! A glutton and a drunkard, a friend of tax collectors and sinners!" (Luke 7:34 = Matt 11:19)[76]

The possibility that a past and now present coming Son of Man carries this incarnational sense is contentious because most have thought that the Synoptics otherwise lack an incarnational Christology. That is an issue to which we shall return in a later chapter (chapter 9). Whatever we make of the Christology of the Synoptics as a whole, the incarnational reading of present "coming" Son of Man sayings fits with other features of the Son of Man sayings. Besides the "divine" features of the Son of Man expression already noted, it fits with the way that it is *as the Son of Man* that Jesus has the authority to forgive sins already in the present (Mark 2:10 and pars.) and that he has Lordship over the Sabbath that allows his disciples to somehow transcend the usual boundaries of Torah (Mark 2:28 and pars.).

In one Synoptic passage the Son of Man is probably a way of talking about Jesus' present heavenly identity that stands behind his empirical earthly identity (Luke 12:8–9):

> 8 And I say to you, whoever confesses me before men, the Son of Man will confess him before the angels of God. 9 And the one who denies me before men will be denied before the angels of God.

In this passage "the Son of Man" can be taken as a way of talking about Jesus' true, heavenly identity, which is unrecognized on earth. On analogy to Jesus' view that disciples have an angelic self or counterpart in heaven—the most likely import of Matt 18:10, Jesus really is, already in the present, the heavenly Son of Man of apocalyptic tradition.[77] On earth his Son of Man identity goes unrecognized and he is even reviled by some (Luke 12:10), but in heaven his witness is decisive in the divine courtroom (cf. Dan 7:9–14).

The story of Jesus' transfiguration before three specially chosen disciples in Matthew, Mark, and Luke (Mark 9:2–9 and pars.) can also be read as a sneak preview of Jesus' soon-to-be fully revealed identity as the divine

---

75. Compare God's action in Ezek 34, esp. vv. 11–12, 16, 22.

76. On these texts see discussion in Fletcher-Louis, *Luke-Acts*, 239–46; Gathercole, *Preexistent Son*, 167–70, and chapter 9 (in Volume 2).

77. See Fletcher-Louis, *Luke-Acts*, 235–37. A similar Christology is also present in the longer text of the Son of Man saying in John 3:13 (on which see Fossum, *Invisible God*, 149–50).

Son of Man given the way that title is used in the immediately surrounding narrative as Jesus' own preferred Christological self-designation: Mark 8:31, 38 before the transfiguration and 9:9, 12 after it (a possibility to which we return in chapter 9). So the transfiguration reveals to a select few what will be manifest to all when the Son of Man comes in the divine glory of the Father (8:38).

Whether or not it is right to see in any Son of Man sayings an incarnational Christology, there is plenty of evidence to support the traditional view that the title ascribes to Jesus a transcendence well beyond what would be expected of an ordinary human messiah. Indeed, the fact that some divine prerogatives are ascribed to the Son of Man, especially in what will be *given to* him, or *revealed about* him, in the future, suggests for the early church's memory of Jesus, the Son of Man title was continuous with a post-Easter high Christology.[78] There are unmistakable lines of literary and conceptual connection between some Gospel Son of Man sayings and passages in Paul that suggest the title lies not far beneath the surface of the texts which we now reckon as principle witnesses to a "Christological monotheism." For example, the coming of the Lord Jesus as a thief in the night in 1 Thess 5:1–11 is anticipated by the coming of the Son of Man as a thief in Luke 12:39–40 (and par.). And it has sometimes been suggested that the Christ hymn in Phil 2 relies on the heavenly Son of Man idea when it describes Christ in preexistence as a heavenly, primal man figure (in v. 6).[79] It is in keeping with the way the expression is used in all four Gospels that on one occasion in John Jesus receives *proskynesis* (from a man whom he has just healed of blindness) *precisely as the Son of Man* (John 9:35–38).

As we consider the shape of the Christology now proposed by voices in the emerging consensus, one implication of the apocalyptic Son of Man theory should be stressed. If, against the emerging consensus, we were to accept the apocalyptic Son of Man theory then we also have to reckon on the fact that it is the title that defines the *shape* of the Christology of the Gospels. If the Son of Man is indeed a title, *it is the title that appears most often. It is the title Jesus himself prefers.* When Peter and Caiaphas think in terms of Jesus as the "Messiah" or the "Son of God" (Mark 8:29; 14:61 and pars.), Jesus talks instead about the Son of Man (Mark 8:30; 14:62 and pars.). *And it is the title that, for Jesus, fully expresses the heart of his own Christological self-claim:* when everything comes to a head with the authorities, Jesus lays

---

78. Compare Nickelsburg, *1 Enoch 2*, 74–76, on the Son of Man tradition behind Pauline texts such as 1 Thess 1:10, 2:19–20; 4:13–18; 5:1–11; 2 Thess 2:1–12; 1 Cor 15:23–28.

79. See e.g., Cullmann, *Christology*, 174–81. I discuss the primal man reading of Phil 2:6 in chapter 8.

down the gauntlet with the Son of Man title. Quite possibly, it is the title that provokes the charge of blasphemy (Mark 14:64 and par.). Judging by the evidence of John 9:35-38 we might conclude that the worship of Christ began with the conviction that he is the Son of Man.

However, for the most part the emerging consensus rejects (or ignores) the main claims of the apocalyptic Son of Man theory. The expression has no real significance for the origins of Christ devotion and it does not make a significant contribution to the shape of "Christological monotheism." This is a viewpoint that sets Hurtado, Bauckham, and their colleagues apart from the rest of New Testament scholarship: both historically *in the modern period*, and still today, theirs is a distinctive, and probably still a *minority*, view of the Son of Man expression.[80] It obviously fits well with the other ways in which the incarnational shape of the earliest Christology is downplayed.

I: The Emerging Consensus's Rejection of the Apocalyptic Son of Man Theory

The Son of Man questions are complex and intimidating. A survey of recent scholarship on the Gospels, the historical Jesus, and Christological origins suggests some are coy about the subject. And with all the disagreement and uncertainty surrounding the expression, it is unsurprising that there are no grand Christological theories that base much on a Son of Man title in the Gospels (or, for that matter, in the life of the historical Jesus). And at this juncture I do not engage its many fascinating and contentious issues. My purpose is simply to draw attention to the way the emerging consensus has really failed to get to grips with the Son of Man expression. Once again, my primary concern is that we faithfully represent the shape and character of the New Testament texts. The outcome of my analysis of the emerging consensus on this topic suggests that the "apocalyptic Son of Man" theory remains the most likely. That obviously also has a significant bearing on the *origins* of "Christological monotheism."

Of all the voices in the emerging consensus, Hurtado's is the boldest in laying out a set of claims for the meaning of the expression and its role in Christological origins. Probably on some points he goes further than most in the emerging consensus would go, but overall his approach is in keeping with the minimalist approach to the s/Son of m/Man problem that is

---

80. For representative examples of a continued adherence to the apocalyptic Son of Man thesis see e.g., J. J. Collins and A. Y. Collins, *King*, 75-100, 149-203; Marcus, *Mark*, vol. 1, 528-32; Nickelsburg, "Son of Man" (1992); "Son of Man" (2010); Walck, "The Parables and the Gospels"; *Parables of Enoch*; Schnelle, *Apostle Paul*, 148-53.

also represented in the work of Bauckham, N. T. Wright, Richard Hays, and others.[81] And a careful consideration of Hurtado's proposals sheds valuable light on distinctive features, and also some serious weaknesses, of the approach to Christological origins that is now in the ascendency.

II: Hurtado on the "Son of Man"

In his *Lord Jesus Christ* Hurtado provides an excursus on the expression that demolishes every part of the older apocalyptic Son of Man theory.[82] Building on the work of those, since the pioneering challenge by Ragnar Leivestad,[83] who have rejected the apocalyptic Son of Man consensus, Hurtado says, in essence, that in the Gospels the expression *ho huios tou anthrōpou* is simply the distinctive way that Jesus referred to himself. The words have no titular force. It denotes Jesus, but it connotes nothing much at all. Hurtado would know what he knows about Christology whether or not the historical Jesus himself had used a similar distinctive Aramaic expression.

Hurtado's route to this conclusion can be laid out in the following six steps.

1. Whatever Dan 7:13 meant for its original author, there was no pre-Christian Son of Man apocalyptic title. The *Similitudes of Enoch* cannot be confidently treated as a pre-Christian text (as it used to be) and, as everyone agrees, *4 Ezra* is a post-Christian text. In any case, in those Jewish texts the son of man is not a title. There is no evidence that Jews were waiting for *the* Son of Man, as such.[84]

2. In the early church the expression was not a confessional title for Jesus. His earliest followers preferred to speak of him as "Lord," "Christ," and "Son." Neither is it ever used as an honorific title by anyone else for Jesus, as in "You are the Son of Man."

---

81. Gauging the views of these scholars can be hard since what they do *not* say is often more telling than what they do say. See Bauckham, "Son of Man" (reprinted in Bauckham, *Jewish World*, 93–102); Wright, *New Testament*, 280–99; *Jesus*, 360–67, 512–19, 624–29; Hays, *Reading Backwards*, 18–19.

82. Hurtado, *Lord Jesus Christ*, 290–306, cf. 19–20. A further sketch and defense of his approach is provided in Hurtado and Owen, "Summary" (2011). In his older work, reflected in his commentary on Mark—*Mark* (1984, reprinted 1995)—Hurtado's approach was less radical, accepting, for example, that in the Gospels the expression is a title.

83. Leivestad, *Der apokalyptische Menschensohn* (1968) and "Apocalyptic Son of Man" (1971–72).

84. A point reiterated in Hurtado, "Fashions," 307–13.

3. The alleged connection between the expression and Dan 7:13 really was not important to the early church. "Outside the canonical Gospels, the early Christian writers who refer to Jesus as 'son of man' seem completely unaware of any association with Daniel 7 or Jewish apocalyptic figures."[85]

4. There are, at most, just two Gospel texts where "the son of man" is a part of a "likely allusion" to Dan 7:13, Mark 13:26, and Mark 14:62 (with, of course, the parallels to both these in Luke and Matthew).[86] But these are "comparatively late New Testament texts."[87] And in any case, "son of man" language in Pss 8 (v. 4, Heb. v. 5) and 80 (v. 17, LXX 79:18) is as likely to be relevant for the Gospel expression as any reference to Dan 7:13.

5. In the Gospels, "'the son of man' essentially functions as a semantic equivalent for the emphatic first-person pronoun ('I/me/my')."[88] We can happily substitute the first person pronoun with no difficulty or loss of meaning.

6. The Gospel writers chose the unusual, indeed totally unprecedented, Greek expression *ho huios tou anthrōpou* to reflect the fact that Jesus was remembered as having spoken of himself in Aramaic in a distinctive way; with an expression that had a particularizing self-referential force. So *ho huios tou anthrōpou* is a way of conveying Jesus' own distinctive idiolect. And this brings us to the boldest feature of Hurtado's approach. In the last forty years a number of English scholars have argued that the historical Jesus used an Aramaic expression with no titular force but that by the time we get to the Gospels that expression has become, by one route or another, a title in the Greek of the Gospels.[89] *Hurtado goes one step further: the expression is not even a title in the Gospels.*[90]

---

85. Hurtado, *Lord Jesus Christ*, 297.
86. Ibid., 298.
87. Ibid.
88. Ibid., 293.

89. For a review of this approach (advocated by G. Vermes, B. Lindars, and M. Casey) see ibid., 299-301, and compare now M. Casey, *Solution* (2007).

90. He has changed his mind on this since writing his Mark commentary (cf., e.g., Hurtado, *Mark*, 37-38). For a similar view see Leivestad, "Apocalyptic Son of Man," 244-47, 253, 256-58, 260. Casey takes the usual line that the expression in the Gospels is a title (*Solution*, 3, 6, 11, 224).

At this point there seems to be something of an ambiguity in Hurtado's position. On the one hand, he says the "expression's primary linguistic function is to *refer, not to characterize*."[91] It only refers to Jesus. It does not convey additional information about him (as the apocalyptic Son of Man theory would have it). Because the expression has no titular force, its meaning is wholly determined by the wider narrative since it simply refers to the man whose life is laid out in the stories told about him (which define his identity).

On the other hand, he says "the semantic force of the expression is an emphatic reference to Jesus as human being, *the* human being/descendent."[92] It means in effect something like "the man" or "this man."[93] That surely means that while it denotes Jesus, it connotes his humanity; his being a member of the human race. It would naturally be taken by first-century readers as a way of talking about Jesus as he operates "in the human/historical sphere" as opposed to talking of him as God's "Son" which discloses his higher significance, even his "intrinsic divinity."[94] It *refers* to Jesus and emphasizes his *human* character.

There are numerous ways in which Hurtado's brief treatment of "the son of man" is enlightening and incisive. It is a welcome relief to have an approach that does not require complex arguments about which of the many Son of Man sayings goes back to Jesus and which come from the early church. His view that the expression is neither a title in the Gospels nor in its Aramaic equivalent on the lips of Jesus is simpler, and therefore more attractive, than complex theories about translation mistakes and the accretion of new meaning on the linguistic journey from Jesus to the Gospels. And several of his arguments against the apocalyptic Son of Man theory are weighty and must be answered by any who would go back down that road.

Hurtado is partially right on his first point: we cannot now say that there was a pre-Christian Jewish "Son of Man" *title*. He is absolutely right on his second point: there is a real lack of evidence that "the Son of Man" was an established and widely used title for Jesus in the early church. Anyone who believes that *ho huios tou anthrōpou* has titular force in the Gospels must explain why it is then that the likes of Paul preferred to use other titles for Jesus. They must also explain why the Gospel writers retained a title for Jesus that was not in use in the later church. And yet they must also explain why it is that even in the Gospels *ho huios tou anthrōpou* is never predicated

---

91. Hurtado, "Summary," 166.
92. Hurtado, *Lord Jesus Christ*, 305–6.
93. Hurtado, "Summary," 167.
94. See Hurtado, *Lord Jesus Christ*, 306, where he seems to contradict other statements to the effect that "son of God" does not claim a divine identity for Jesus.

of Jesus. We never read "I am the Son of Man," nor "I, the Son of Man," nor "Jesus is the Son of Man." Also, if the expression is a title it is quite puzzling that Jesus is the only one who uses it. On the apocalyptic Son of Man theory this is all rather strange and has not yet been explained in a way that is wholly convincing.

It is also a real problem for the apocalyptic Son of Man theory that so many of the Gospel Son of Man sayings appear to be unconnected to Dan 7:13. And because these come early on in the Gospel story it is hard to see how, for first-century readers, the sayings that do refer to Dan 7:13 could govern the meaning of the others.

However, Hurtado's points 3-6 (as I have laid them out above) really are unpersuasive. Furthermore, Hurtado is almost certainly wrong to be cautious about the dating of the *Similitudes of Enoch* and even though he is right to insist that there is no evidence for a pre-Christian "Son of Man" *title*, that point cannot bear the significance for the NT that Hurtado asks of it. And the force of Hurtado's second point is somewhat blunted, if not quite nullified, by his first point, as I will explain below. Some observations on each of his main points helps sharpen up our critical analysis of his model as a whole. And because the Son of Man expression will figure prominently in the new paradigm, some comments on individual sayings and patterns in the way they appear in the Gospels will help clear the ground for a new approach (that wraps up the strengths of the older apocalyptic Son of Man theory in a new understanding of Jewish apocalyptic and of Daniel 7).

III: A Pre-Christian Son of Man Expectation

On Hurtado's point 1. Everyone now agrees that there is no evidence for a "Son of Man" *title* in pre-Christian Judaism. Although there is a clear interpretation of Dan 7:13 in *1 En.* 37-71 and *4 Ezra* 13 we do not find the title "*the* Son of Man" in any extant Jewish texts. However, it is now generally agreed that there is a definite Son of Man figure in those two apocalyptic texts.[95] And this is the really important point for New Testament studies. Focusing solely on the issue of a Son of Man *title* misses the real point of the comparative

---

95. Pace Hurtado, *Lord Jesus Christ*, 296 n. 90, the variety of Ethiopic expressions usually translated "Son of Man" in English editions of *1 En.* 37-71 almost certainly reflects just one linguistic form in the Greek (and beneath that in the Aramaic or Hebrew original) for which the Ethiopic used three translation variants (see. e.g., Nickelsburg in Nickelsburg and VanderKam, *1 Enoch 2*, 113-15; Hannah, "Elect Son of Man," 141). At any rate, one distinctive Son of Man figure (also called the Elect One and the messiah) is certainly in view throughout the text as we now have it (see Waddell, *Messiah*, 48-103; Nickelsburg and VanderKam, *1 Enoch 2*, 113-16).

non-Christian texts. The really important historical questions are separate from the existence or nonexistence of a Son of Man title. Were there Jews before Jesus who eagerly read Dan 7 and hoped and prayed for "the coming of the one like a son of man" of Dan 7:13? (If there were, there are a variety of linguistic forms—in Aramaic, Hebrew, and Greek—that they might have used to refer to that figure.) Did those Jews go beyond the simple plain sense of Dan 7 and agree amongst themselves on some distinctive characteristics of the figure who would come? And could talk, in Jewish Christian Greek texts, of *ho huios tou anthrōpou* readily be taken as a reference to both Dan 7:13 and to a constellation of expectations circulating (some fixed, some floating in the realms of debate) around that visionary text?

The answer to each of these questions is now emphatically "yes." The first two questions are so important that I devote the whole of chapter 5 to them. There are many who have lately agreed with Hurtado's position that the *Similitudes* and *4 Ezra* should not determine our interpretation of Gospel "s/Son of m/Man" sayings. At one time there were firm historical grounds on which to base that stance. In the 60s and 70s of the last century it became clear, with the eventual release of relevant information about the Dead Sea Scroll texts, that the *Similitudes* were not, apparently, included in the version of the Aramaic book of Enoch used by the Qumran community. On that evidence it seemed likely that *1 En.* 37–71 (the *Similitudes*) were in fact a later, post-Christian, addition to the Enochic corpus.[96] However, in recent years the pendulum has swung back to the older dating of the *Similitudes*. Most specialists now think it is pre-Christian and in chapter 5 I will lay out the reasons to be confident of that dating.

For many in the modern period there have probably also been theological reasons to downplay any role for the *Similitudes*. The fact that many in the modern period have been allergic to all that an "apocalyptic" Jesus seems to imply (in terms of a dualistic, world-denying attitude to the present and God's dealings with the world) is well known.[97] There is also an issue that has been talked about less openly, much less written about, but that is sometimes the proverbial elephant in the room: the *Similitudes* and *4 Ezra* are not a part of the Old Testament. If we have to interpret the Gospel Son

---

96. This was the position from which Leviestad launched his assault on the apocalyptic Son of Man consensus (see his "Apocalyptic Son of Man," 244). J. Milik's edition and commentary on all the Enochic material in the Qumran Library (*Books of Enoch*—1976), in which it was argued that the *Similitudes* is a Christian text from "around the year AD 270 or shortly afterwards" (96, cf. 89–98), then lent authority to the argument against the apocalyptic Son of Man theory. Nobody agrees with Milik's extreme position today.

97. On that allergy see Koch, *Rediscovery*, 57–97, and the strenuous efforts of the Jesus Seminar scholars to reconstruct an nonapocalyptic Jesus.

of Man sayings in reliance on a nonbiblical Jewish text, that poses grave problems for our biblical theology. If we have a high view of Scripture as the locus of divine revelation it will not do to have a Jesus whose self-consciousness and self-claims are essentially indebted to a noncanonical (and probably sectarian) Jewish text. This problem was even more acute when some argued that the apocalyptic Son of Man idea came ultimately from a stock of themes common to all ancient oriental religions; from a wider "Anthropos" or *Urmensch* myth.[98] The *Similitudes*-is-not-Scripture issue ought perhaps to be aired more openly than it has been. I will return to it, and to the implications of an apocalyptic understanding of Jesus and the Son of Man expression, in later chapters. There I will argue that the *Similitudes* is vital for an understanding of the Son of Man expression, but not because the Gospel writers (or Jesus himself) were *reliant* upon it. I will also explain why I think generations of modern scholars have fundamentally misconstrued the nature of Jewish apocalyptic (for which the *Similitudes* is an important witness) and that it is time for a reappraisal of its theological significance for Jesus and earliest Christianity.

For now, in this dialogue with Hurtado, it is enough simply to note that his treatment of the evidence for some kind of relationship between the Gospels and the *Similitudes* is weak. Most now think that Matthew's Gospel has some kind of relationship to the Enochic Son of Man material. In Matt 19:28 and 25:31 we have the Son of Man seated on his "throne of glory" as judge of the nations and of Israel, in the company of his angels. There is none of that in Dan 7 itself. But in every respect these distinctive features of Matt 19:28 and 25:31 have a parallel in the *Similitudes* (see esp. *1 En.* 55:4; 61:8-11; 62:3-5; 69:27, 29). Many now think that Matt 19:28 and 25:31 have been created under the influence of the *Similitudes*, perhaps even that Matt 19:28 and 25:31 directly quote from it. A good case can also be made for the view that Matt 13:36-43; 16:27-28, and 24:30-31 all rely on it.[99]

Indeed, evidence for contact between the Gospels and the *Similitudes* is not confined to Matthew. The appearance of the Son of Man title at the trial of Jesus (in Mark 14:62 and pars.) can be compared with the scene of final judgment in *1 En.* 62-63. The Son of Man of John 5:27 acts as a divine judge in a way that parallels his position in Matt 13:36-43; 16:27-28; 19:28; 25:31, and in the *Similitudes*. Sayings in which the Son of Man comes, or descends, from heavenly preexistence can be paralleled to the way that in the

---

98. On the early-twentieth-century German scholarship of the history of religions school that convinced itself of this theory see Hurtado, "Fashions," 307-13.

99. The seminal work on this topic is Theisohn, *Der auserwählte Richter*, and see now Walck, "Parables and the Gospels," 323-24, 329-33; *Parables of Enoch*, cf., e.g., Dunn, *Jesus Remembered*, 756-57.

Similitudes (and in *4 Ezra*, but not in the Dan 7 itself) Daniel's man figure has become a preexistent heavenly being before his decisive revelation at the end of days. Until that revelation the Son of Man is hidden from the world:

> For from the beginning the Son of Man was hidden, and the Most High preserved him in the presence of his might, and he revealed him to the chosen. (See esp. *1 En.* 62:7)

A similar interest in the Son of Man's hiddenness before revelation may also be present in several Gospel Son of Man passages (Mark 8:31—9:12; Luke 7:34; 9:58 and par.; Luke 12:8–10).[100] In Mark as a whole, Jesus reveals himself to those whom he chooses, his disciples: especially the inner group of three (Peter, James, and John), ahead of a fuller, wider, revelation of his identity as Son of Man (see esp. Mark 9:9, 12 and 14:62). And the mysterious relationship between Jesus and the Son of Man—are they simply one and the same, if so why does the former speak of the latter as if he is somebody else?—has a striking parallel in the relationship between the Son of Man and the visionary Enoch himself—they are separate throughout *1 En.* 46-70 and then, mysteriously, Enoch becomes the Son of Man in ch. 71.

None of this evidence for some kind of influence from the *Similitudes* to the Gospels (or a common tradition surrounding the interpretation of Dan 7:13 shared by both) is discussed by Hurtado. It calls into question one key premise of his rejection of the apocalyptic Son of Man theory: if some texts that use the "s/Son of m/Man" expression definitely assume a Jewish apocalyptic Son of Man tradition, then it is likely that others, if not all, do too. The possibility that in the earliest Gospel tradition Jesus' true identity (as the divine Son of Man) was hidden from others also invites more attention than the emerging consensus has given it.

IV: Daniel 7:13 and the Son of Man Expression

On Hurtado's points 3 and 4, Hurtado overstates the lack of evidence for a reference to Dan 7:13 in the Son of Man sayings.[101] Contrary to Hurtado's statement quoted above (at point 3), outside the canonical Gospels we find two early Christian writers who refer to Jesus as the "one like a son of man" of Danielic expectation and post-Danielic traditon. In Rev 1:7–13, Dan 7:13

---

100. Cf. Walck, "Parables and the Gospels," 313, 318; A. Y. Collins, "Secret Son of Man."

101. Some connection between "the Son of Man" title and "son of man" language in Ps 8 is quite likely, but is inextricable from the connection to Dan 7:13, for reasons that I will explain in Volume 3.

is quoted in v. 7, and in v. 13 Jesus is identified as the "one like a son of man" whom Daniel saw. A later passage in Revelation (14:14–16) makes the Danielic man figure an agent of end-time judgment in a way that is entirely in keeping with the interpretation of Dan 7:13–14 that we find in the *Similitudes* and *4 Ezra*.

Similarly, there are good reasons for thinking that in Acts 7, Stephen evokes Daniel's vision and the apocalyptic tradition associated with it. Speaking to the Sanhedrin, who are at the point of stoning him, Stephen's words—"Behold, I see the heavens opened, and the Son of Man standing at the right hand of God" (7:56)—must evoke Daniel's original vision. For one thing, Acts 7:56 recalls the two passages in Luke's first volume where the Son of Man is without a doubt Daniel's Son of Man (Luke 21:27; 22:69). Secondly, Acts 7:56 goes back beyond those Gospel verses to Daniel itself. Stephen's words cannot be treated simply as a fulfillment of Jesus' own prophecy in Luke 22:69 (since the Son of Man is "standing" at the right hand of God, not *seated* as in Luke 22:69).[102] The scene in Acts 7 is obviously apocalyptic: Stephen has a vision and he sees the "heavens opened"—a stereotypical formula of the apocalyptic genre (cf. *T. Levi* 5:1; *Jos. Asen.* 14:2; Rev 4:1). So we are bound to recall Daniel's original vision in Dan 7, where Daniel, in effect, sees into an open heaven (in vv. 9–14) and "one like a son of man" appears in God's presence (not seated, so presumably he is upright and standing). Stephen sees again, with greater clarity, what Daniel saw. Daniel saw "one like a son of man." Stephen sees that now, in wake of all that has happened at the end of history and with the dawning of the kingdom, that the one whom Daniel saw only vaguely as an unnamed "one like a son of man" is in fact (the risen and exalted) Jesus of Nazareth. So Acts 7:56 is best taken as a claim, by Stephen, that Jesus is *that* Son of Man; the one whom Daniel prophesied would appear at the final judgment. And because there is now good evidence (in the *Similitudes* and related material discussed in chapter 5) that there was a lively tradition surrounding Dan 7:13 in pre-Christian Judaism, Stephen in effect proclaims to the Sanhedrin, "Jesus is the Son of Man figure that some us have been waiting for!"

Returning to the Gospels, even if we decided that there is no interaction specifically with the *Similitudes* in New Testament texts, there is far more evidence of a conscious reference to Dan 7:13 in the Gospels than Hurtado acknowledges. Reference to Dan 7:13–14 in the description of the Son of Man coming on clouds, with power and glory and angelic emissaries in Mark 13:26–27 (not just Mark 13:26) and to his coming "with the clouds of heaven" in Mark 14:62, really are certain (not just a "likely allusion").

102. *Pace* Hurtado, *Lord Jesus Christ*, 293 n. 83.

With most commentators we can also include a reference to Dan 7:13 in Mark 8:38 (and pars.). That verse also evokes the scene of eschatological judgment in Dan 7:9–14, the Son of Man's glory recalls the gift of glory to him in Dan 7:14 (as also in Mark 13:26; Matt 25:31, cf. John 12:23; 13:31; Luke 9:32; Rev 1:13–16), and, as in Mark 13:27, the appearance of "the holy angels" picks up the description of myriads of angels in Dan 7:10.

Texts where the Son of Man has his own angels (Mark 13:26–27; Matt 13:41–42; Matt 16:27; Matt 24:31) and his own throne (Matt 19:28; 25:31), his own glory, and authority over the Sabbath (Mark 2:28), to judge (Matt 13:36–43; 16:27–28; 25:31–46; John 5:27), and to forgive sins (Mark 2:10) can all be treated as typically Jewish examples of creative biblical interpretation. In all these cases, the Jesus of the Gospels is presented as one who appeals to Dan 7:13 *with an interpretation of that verse in its original context*. In Dan 7:14, the "one like a son of man" is given "authority" (*exousia* in the Greek). So although Jesus' particular interpretation of that "authority" (*exousia* in Mark 2:10) as something that enables the Son of Man to forgive sins might have been unusual, we have every reason to believe his audience could get the point. To speak of the Son of Man's "glory" spells out the logic of Dan 7:14 where the one like a son of man is given glory by God. In Dan 7:9 Daniel sees the placing of multiple thrones. The Ancient of Days takes his seat on one of them. Jesus of Nazareth can hardly have been the only first-century Jew who wondered who it was that sits on the remaining thrones. The text invites interpretation, so we are not surprised to find the Jesus of the Gospels concluded that the "one like a son of man" would also sit on a heavenly, glorious throne. Similarly, when Jesus talks of the Son of Man with judicial authority, he would naturally be heard to be referring to Dan 7:14, where the "one like a son of man" is given "dominion, glory, and kingship." What does that mean if it does not mean the authority to judge? Lastly, by giving the "one like a son of man" his own angels, Jesus concludes that if the Danielic son of man figure is enthroned as God is enthroned then he should, by rights, also have a share in power and authority that comes through an angelic entourage.

In John 5:27 there is also an unmistakable reference to Dan 7. This is a peculiar "Son of Man" saying because the logical structure of the verse makes a clear claim for Jesus *on the basis that he is the "Son of Man"*:

> "And he has given him authority (*kai exousian edōken autō*) to execute judgment, *because* he is (the) Son of Man (*huios anthrōpou*)."

The logic of the verse demands reference to a specific well-known figure. Indeed, for multiple reasons, there really is no escaping an explicit

3. THE SHAPE OF NT CHRISTOLOGY 115

reference to Dan 7:13-14. The anathrous form of the Son of Man expression in John 5:27 is unusual, but it reflects the form of the Greek text of Dan 7:13, which says:

> "... I saw one like a son of man (*huios anthrōpou*) coming with the clouds of heaven."

And Jesus' words "and he has given him authority" (*exousian edōken autō*) are an exact verbal echo of Dan 7:14: "And to him was given dominion, glory, and kingdom." The echo is unavoidable when we check the Greek translations of Daniel where it is explicitly "authority" that is given to the man figure and one Greek translation (the Old Greek) has a four-word phrase that is an almost word-for-word parallel to the first four words of John 5:27a. In the Old Greek of Dan 7:14 we read:

> *kai edothē autō exousia* (and authority was given to him).

So it is surprising that Hurtado has nothing to say about the possibility that John 5:27 should be included in an inventory of texts that refers to Dan 7:13-14.[103]

A reference to Dan 7 can also be heard, if not so loudly and clearly, in other Son of Man sayings. Mark 10:45 is likely meant as an interpretative comment on the talk of "service" to the one like a son of man in Dan 7:14 Jesus challenges the expectation, based on a straightforward reading of Dan 7:14, that, as the Son of Man, he has come "to be served." On the contrary, *his* kind of Son of Man-ship means he will be the servant (though, strictly speaking, in Mark he has already received the "service" of the angels in Mark 1:13).

Talk of the Son of Man "coming" also evokes the "coming" of the "one like a son of man" in Dan 7:13 (in Mark 10:45; Luke 7:34 and par.; Luke 18:8; 19:10; Matt 16:28; 24:39; 25:31). To be sure, it is puzzling that in Dan 7:13 the coming is apparently a "going (up)" *from earth to heaven* and in the Gospel texts it is a "coming (down)" from heaven to earth. But for a first-century Jewish mind-set steeped in the Scriptures and open to a creative interpretation of them, there is every reason to suppose that all the texts that speak of a "coming" of the "Son of Man" will have evoked Dan 7. Other texts connect to Dan 7 in less obvious, but nonetheless important ways. Luke 12:8-10, for example, seems to assume that the "Son of Man" belongs in a heavenly law court scene (as per Dan 7:9-14).

Stepping back from the minutiae of individual texts, it is worth reflecting on Hurtado's treatment of the relationship between Dan 7:13 and the

---

103. For John 5:27 and Dan 7:13-14 see Ashton, *Understanding*, 357-63; Reynolds, *Apocalyptic*, 132-40.

Gospels as a whole. His way of handling this issue does not really do justice to the relationship between the Gospels and the Scriptures. All four Gospels make a two-fold claim for Jesus' life, in the context of which it is highly unlikely that "the S/son of M/man" only *denotes* Jesus with neither a more specific connotation nor a reference back to Dan 7:13.

Firstly, the Gospels present the life of Jesus in the broader context of an eschatological fulfillment of biblical prophecies of an end-time restoration of the nation and the healing of creation. Secondly, they ascribe to Jesus himself a rich tapestry of biblical identities and purposes, that all go to give Christological focus to the claim for the inauguration, in Jesus' ministry, of the end-time kingdom. *For a man who plays a multifaceted scriptural role, on this eschatological and salvation-historical stage, the expression "one like a son of man" can hardly mean not very much at all.* This wider context of the Gospels is very well known, but its importance for the "Son of Man problem" has mostly gone unnoticed. And several aspects of this bigger Gospel picture should be highlighted as we get our bearings on the Son of Man problem.

The "kingdom" has drawn near (Mark 1:15). Indeed, the "kingdom" is now manifest on earth already in Jesus' healings, exorcisms, and his teachings (e.g., Mark 4:1–32 and pars.; Luke 11:20 and par.; Luke 17:20). Whatever we may make of an earlier version of the material that is now in the Gospels, in Matthew, Mark, Luke, and John "kingdom of God" is a thoroughly biblical expression. Jesus' constant talk of the kingdom evokes the overarching biblical story, reaching back all the way *to the bestowal of royal authority* on Adam in Gen 1:26–28.[104] Jesus' kingdom of God announcement picks up all the key features of a biblical vision of the completion of God's purposes for humanity and the cosmos (in the fulfillment of prophecy and as the manifestation of true wisdom and justice, with the final defeat of evil, the return of the land to its God-intended Edenic bounty, and a completion of Israel's political and economic destiny in the service of the whole world). So, for Jesus to enact and announce the inauguration of God's kingdom means, in part, that humanity is now, at last, fulfilling its original purpose in manifesting God's own royal authority. In Jesus there is one who exercises the dominion in creation originally expected of Adam.

With the Gospels' Christology Jesus is portrayed as one who fulfills multiple images, types, and prophetic expectations in Israel's Bible. He is a new Adam (especially in the Markan temptation story, for example), he is the whole people of God, a new Israel (at Matt 2:15 and in the baptism story that reenacts Israel's crossing from the wilderness to the promised land), he is a

---

104. See esp. Beale, *Biblical Theology*, and cf. Wright, *Jesus*, 198–474, and Watts, "Restoration of the Image of God."

new Moses (in the Galilean wilderness wanderings, at the transfiguration, and in Matthew's Gospel as a whole), he is the Davidic messiah (in Peter's confession at Caesarea Philippi, to blind Bartimaeus, at the triumphal entry, and to the crowds in the wilderness in John 6) and a new Solomon (a teacher of wisdom who is endowed with a unique authority over demons). He is a healing prophet like Elijah and Elisha (especially in Luke, e.g., 4:25–28), a new Jonah (Luke 11:29–30 and par.), and one who teaches strange, politically subversive parables like the prophets of old. Probably at his baptism he is a new Isaac, the "beloved son" (Mark 1:11, cf. Gen 22:2, 12, 16). In his betrayal at the hands of his own brothers and his remarkable exaltation over them at the resurrection, he is a new Joseph. It is hard to think of a major Old Testament figure (aside from the notorious) who does not appear somewhere in the Gospels' portrayal of Jesus.

Interpreting the precise function of all this biblical imagery and language in the Gospels' Christology is a subindustry of New Testament scholarship in its own right. This is not the place to enter into the fascinating and intricate issues it raises. Probably, with Richard Hays, we should now recognize a two-way conversation between Old and New Testaments with each providing new meaning to the other.[105] Certainly, the Gospel writers are not simply proof texting when they describe Jesus in ways that evoke the lives of his forbears. The complex web of allusions and echoes to biblical passages mean that whenever Jesus is labeled with some title or office there is far more than just a simple denotation at work. The Old Testament language always *adds to* our understanding of Jesus' identity as a man who might otherwise seem to be a simple first-century carpenter with strange powers and precocious ambitions to be leader of the nation. Biblical language always supports his leadership by bestowing upon him something of the identity, the virtue, glory, and honor of his forbears and of divinely sanctioned offices. The kingdom is being inaugurated because *in this one man* the promises of old, of the covenant and of Scripture, are being fulfilled. The "what" of the kingdom is predicated on the "who" that is Jesus.

To be sure, it is never easy to determine too precisely or rigidly what is added to his identity in any given case. But given the intensely biblical texture of the Gospel stories, to say that Jesus is a "prophet" (Mark 6:4, 15; Matt 11:9; 14:5; Luke 24:19; John 6:14; 7:40; 9:17), the "messiah," God's "son," or "the Lord" always conjures up a whole web of intertextual connotations, with some more immediately relevant in each case than others. Often actors who speak of, or address, Jesus mean more than they think they mean. When Jesus affirms the truth of Caiaphas's question, "are you the son

---

105. See Hays, *Reading Backwards*.

of the Blessed?" (Mark 14:61-62), *we* the readers know (in the light of the baptism, transfiguration, encounters with demons who recognize Jesus, and the Parable of the Tenants) that Jesus assents to far more than the simple royal messianic claim that the high priest is worried over.[106] We should emphasize, with Hurtado and others who take his approach, as earlier generations mostly failed to see, that the narrative of Jesus' life itself gives content and meaning to the expressions and titles used of him. But, equally, to ignore the connative force of the biblical (and biblically based) titles and epithets for him would be to unnecessarily play off one aspect of the Gospels against another.

Jesus never categorically rejects the suggestion that he is the fulfillment of the many figures and types presented in Israel's Scriptures. On his steady march towards the cross he happily gathers up in his train the full weight of Israel's hopes for a new prophet and leader like the ones who had brought wisdom, healing, and salvation of old. Along the way he often challenges misunderstandings of him that arise when he is viewed through the lens of a particular biblical character or passage. (A fine example is his stance on some hostile Samaritan villages in Luke 9:51-56, whose behavior recalls the similar hostility Elijah experienced in 2 Kgs 1. Jesus is at pains to challenge his disciples' assumption that because he has, in so many ways, behaved like Elijah and Elisha in his healing works, he will not act like Elijah in calling down fire from heaven to destroy the Samaritans who oppose his emissaries.) But even where there is constant *redefinition*, not just affirmation, of messianic and prophetic hopes, one clear message that the Gospels proclaim loudly and clearly is that *in this one man the lives of all the nation's heroes meet*.

Hurtado's way of understanding the expression "the S/son of M/man" is really hard to accept in the light of these features of the Gospels. Although Dan 7 is a vivid and memorable description of God's eschatological judgment on his enemies—that also describes an apparently definitive removal of evil and a dramatic vindication of God's people—for Hurtado, it apparently plays no role in the Gospels' presentation of Jesus' understanding of his purposes. Daniel 7:13-14 is a clear example of Old Testament prophecy that combines talk of a divinely bestowed (and eternal) "kingdom" (*basileia*—v. 14) with the arrival on the scene of history of a divinely authorized figure and agent of divine rule—*whom all known Jewish interpreters at the time took to be a messiah* (according to the evidence of *1 En.* 37-71 and *4 Ezra* 13). Daniel 7:13-14, in other words, is one really clear example—perhaps *the clearest example*—of a biblical text that has a twin focus like the one we

---

106. The way the narrator and Jesus himself have a fuller understanding of the words and actions of individual actors in the Gospel story is particularly important for the Lukan portrayal of Jesus as "the Lord" (on which see Rowe, *Narrative Christology*).

find in the Gospels: a focus on the eschatological arrival of the kingdom of God (v. 14) combined with a focus on the arrival of a divinely sanctioned and empowered representative of God (a messiah) (v. 13). But for Hurtado, Dan 7 plays *no* role in the shaping the Christology of the Gospels! This is as extraordinary an approach to the Gospels as it is improbable.

He accepts that there are "likely allusions" to Dan 7:13 in Mark 13:26 and 14:62, but, as far as I can tell, for Hurtado Dan 7 makes no significant contribution to Jesus' self-claims and the development of the Gospel plot, even in those two passages. For Hurtado, the expression *ho huios tou anthrōpou* in those verses makes clear that Jesus is talking about himself (it *denotes* Jesus). But insofar as *ho huios tou anthrōpou* also refers in those verses to the "one like a son of man" who comes on clouds in Dan 7:13, the language of that OT verse is nothing more than simply a convenient proof text for Jesus' imminent cloud-borne exaltation (cf. Acts 1:9–11) and/or his return on clouds at the parousia (Mark 13:26).[107] By contrast, for Hurtado, the citation of Ps 110:1 (with which Dan 7:13 is combined) in Mark 14:62 both denotes and connotes: it implicitly denotes Jesus and it evokes a whole set of royal messianic texts and expectations. Jesus' citation of Dan 7:13 at his trial, on the other hand, *connotes* nothing.

So, Hurtado's understanding of the non-significance of Dan 7:13 for the Gospels is doubly odd. In two ways, given that every other major figure and prophetic type in the Old Testament lends Jesus their garb, it is surprising that Dan 7:13 makes no substantive contribution to his identity. On the one hand, given the literary and theological significance of Dan 7:13 we expect it to figure somewhere in the Gospels' portrayal of Jesus. If Dan 7:13 were some anodyne verse tucked away in a chapter not much studied of a book not overly cherished (of Ecclesiastes or Esther, let's say), then Hurtado's treatment of Mark 13:26 and Mark 14:62 would make sense. But Daniel is a mainstream biblical text where the rivers of older prophetic and Wisdom literature meet in the creative fusion that is the emergence of a new genre (that modern scholarship has labeled "apocalyptic"); a generic form that flows widely down through the centuries of Second Temple Judaism. Daniel 7 is literarily a pivotal chapter in the book (that binds together themes of the first six chapters to the visionary form of chapters 8–12). Even

---

107. Hurtado, *Lord Jesus Christ*, 297, says that in 14:62 *ho huios tou anthrōpou* is a "literary device" that registers the claim that Jesus is the figure of Dan 7:13. But because Hurtado thinks there was no first-century Jewish interest in Dan 7:13—certainly not a well-established understanding of the manlike figure that went beyond the bare statement of Dan 7:13 itself—it is hard to see what point there can possibly be to an identification of Jesus as "the figure of that passage" (ibid.) in the climactic scene of the Gospel narrative.

if we were to date the *Similitudes of Enoch* to the late first century AD we are still faced with solid evidence that Jews in the first century AD were fascinated by the meaning of Dan 7:13, that they interpreted it messianically and that some/many(?) eagerly awaited its fulfillment.[108] So if the Jesus of the Gospels is not, as Hurtado alleges, somehow defined by the prophecy of Dan 7:13—and he did not share assumptions with his contemporaries about its meaning—that would be a rather striking anomaly in their portrayal of him. Secondly, if Dan 7:13 appears just two times—in passages of great import within the Synoptic plot line—but it conveys no additional meaning to the portrayal of Jesus of Nazareth that also would be odd, given the way scriptural texts function Christologically throughout the Gospels.

The way that Dan 7:13 must in fact have functioned, for the Gospel writers and readers, as a scriptural text that carried definite meaning in its depiction of the "one like a son of man," can be illustrated through some reflections on Mark 2:1–10. A reference to Dan 7:13 is nothing like as obvious in Mark 2:10 as it is in Mark 13:26 and 14:62. However, as we have seen, first-century Jewish readers could well have heard in the talk of the Son of Man's "authority" to forgive sins an interpretation of the "authority" bestowed in Dan 7:14. In a later volume I will present my own reasons for thinking that Dan 7:13 is, without a shadow of a doubt, in the mind of Mark and of Mark's Jesus at this point. But for now, let us consider what a reading of Mark 2:10 that sees no reference to Dan 7:13–14 actually means.

For Hurtado, Mark 2:10a might just as well be translated:

> "But that you may know that *I* have authority on earth to forgive sins."[109]

Jesus could have apologized for his earlier declaration that the paralytic's sins are forgiven (2:5) by explaining that he had only delivered the message that God himself had forgiven the man. But instead of avoiding the charge of blasphemy (2:6) that way, Jesus ups the ante: "Be in no doubt, yes, I myself have forgiven this man's sins."

There are problems with this interpretation of Jesus' climactic statement. It is barely *historically* plausible that a first-century Jew—even a first-century Jew who believed he was a prophet and the messiah—would make such a bold claim. And that means that it is barely historically plausible

---

108. Besides the evidence of the *Similitudes* and *4 Ezra*, see N. T. Wright's discussion of the evidence for an interest in Daniel amongst Jewish messianic and revolutionary movements (in his *New Testament*, 304).

109. Hurtado's discussion of this passage in his *Mark* commentary (1984 [1995]) takes *ho huios tou anthrōpou* to be a title, so what follows is based upon his more recent rejection of the titular approach.

that Jesus' *followers would both stick with him and, indeed, would grow in numbers,* as Mark says they did. My concern here is not, in the first instance, with the historical Jesus, but with Mark's portrayal of Jesus and the historical plausibility of that portrayal within the narrative world of Mark.

The laws of Moses are clear. They provide a covenantal framework, grounded in the relationship between the one God and all of creation, that defines God's relationship to the world and with his people: *he* forgives sins, and first-century carpenters do not. The scribes who "puzzle" at Jesus' pronouncement of sins (2:6) are not grumbling, whining casuists. They are not troubled that Jesus is a threat to their own development of the laws of Moses (unlike the Pharisees of Mark 7:1–13). They are the guardians of Torah and their bemused questioning to themselves is understandable and commendable: Jesus' initial declaration is dangerous since it could be taken to mean that he, an ordinary man, now claims to do what only God himself can do. If Jesus then just boldly asserts his authority—"well yes, actually I can, just watch me!"—with no recourse to scriptural or covenantal precedent then yes, indeed, the scribes had good reason to be worried. And they have every reason to conclude that the healing he effects is the work of some foreign god or demon (cf. Mark 3:22). That would be a Marcionite Jesus, who bypasses the OT and its account of God's relationship with the world and with his people; a Jesus who would be unintelligible to his fellow Jews, perhaps marveled at for his wonder-working powers by the less well-versed in Torah, but derided as a fool with not even a basic grounding in Moses and the prophets by most.

If Mark thinks that Jesus simply claims "I can forgive sins" in 2:10 then Mark does not understand Jesus' first-century context. He is a poor historian. This reading would also be out of keeping with his literary technique, which is now universally reckoned to be thoughtful and artful. The first eight chapters of Mark are full of Christological possibility. Through multiple scriptural allusions the attentive reader works out that Jesus has a complex, scripturally informed identity. But Christology is never discussed openly until a private conversation with the disciples in 8:27–38. The demons evidently know who Jesus is, but Jesus himself is keen to avoid open discussion, much less an open declaration, about his identity during this phase of his ministry. If Jesus says, as Hurtado's approach to the s/Son of m/Man problem takes it, "I have authority to forgive sins," then such a bold, public declaration of what is, in effect, a claim to a divine identity, would be wholly out of keeping with Mark's way of handling Jesus' self-consciousness and purpose.[110]

---

110. I also think his words would be taken as a direct challenge to the Temple and the priesthood, but we can leave on one side, for now, that aspect of the story for the sake of conceptual simplicity.

On the other hand, putting aside Hurtado's model, if Mark 2:10 does in fact use an expression with titular force and one that is meant to evoke a particular scriptural text—namely Dan 7:13—then the verse fits Mark's overarching literary technique and it accords well with other indications that he has a good grasp of basic first-century Jewish religious, political, and cultural realities. On other grounds, Mark, I take it, knew what it meant to write an historically plausible presentation of Jesus' interaction with the authorities and institutions of his day.

Entering his narrative world on that basis, it helps to put ourselves in Jesus' shoes. Jesus believes he has the authority and power to forgive and heal. He naturally submits to the authority of Scripture: to the God-given laws of Moses and the revelation of the divine identity therein (e.g., Mark 1:44; 7:10). He wants to keep the followers he has gained (Mark 1:16–20) and he is looking to take on more: he is setting about the creation of a new, restored Israel (Mark 1:14–15; 3:13–19). At this early stage of the start-up he does not want to burn what little social capital he has already created. *So he could not possibly just declare "I can forgive sins." He must, rather, base his self-claims on the scriptural revelation.* If Mark 2:10 refers to Dan 7:13 and an interpretation of the "authority" given *by God* to the son of man figure in Dan 7:14 then no one can accuse Jesus of apostasy. Genius. His interpretation of Daniel might be wrong and his claim to be the one that Daniel saw on the clouds is bold and risky. But Jesus is no apostate leading the people astray after the worship of strange gods. He has not undergone epispasm. He does not put himself forward as a rival god to the one God. He speaks and acts from within a scripturally defined framework. And if there is to be an argument, he has staked the ground on which it should be fought (the interpretation of Scripture in relation to his own claim to both fulfill and define the meaning of Dan 7:13–14).

If Jesus thinks of Dan 7:13–14 in Mark 2:10 then the story is also in keeping with Mark's understanding of his Christological reserve. This is the first time the expression *ho huios tou anthrōpou* is used. For a Greek speaker who hears Mark for the first time, the phrase is odd, even barbaric. Jesus does not say "I am *'the one like a son of man'* that Daniel saw," and "I have been *'given authority'* (Dan 7:14) to forgive sins." Everything happens quickly. The man is lowered through the roof. Dust and shards of broken tiles fly. Jesus pronounces the man's sins forgiven. The scribes are outwardly silent, but Jesus turns and challenges them directly. He says something about "the son of the man," and moments later the paralytic is up and about, his stretcher in hand. The miracle is plain for all to see, and glorious and terrifying (see Matt 9:8); the strange talk of a "son of the man" is hardly a crystal-clear self-claim. Was that Daniel's "one like a son of man" he was talking about? It must have been, because he appealed to his God-given "authority." But did Jesus actually say that he himself is the one Daniel saw? Before the dust has settled proceedings have moved on.

Mark 2:10 is best taken as a titular Son of Man saying, but one governed by Mark's understanding of Jesus' riddling teaching strategy (see esp. 4:10–12). (The same goes for Mark 2:28.) Nothing is immediately obvious. Everything will be made clear for those with ears to hear, to those who stay with Jesus on his journey to the cross. And in the end the light will dispel confusion (4:21–23). For the time being, the healings and signs give the disciples much else to be excited about. So it is understandable that no one immediately proclaims Jesus as "the Son of Man" when he puts them on the spot at Caesarea Philippi. He has never explicitly said "I am the Son of Man of Daniel's vision."

In short, if Jesus has in mind Dan 7:13–14 in Mark 2:10 the story fits well in its first-century Jewish context and in Mark's telling of the unfolding mystery of the kingdom. If, with Hurtado (and others), there is no reference in that verse to Dan 7, then the passage is odd historically, literarily, and, we might add, that theologically it makes Jesus out to be a strange kind of Jew; one ignorant of first-century Jewish mores, but remarkably compelling nonetheless.

Whatever we make of Mark 2:1–10 at the historical Jesus level of the tradition, a riddling but deliberate reference to Dan 7:13–14 in Mark 2:10 coheres well with Mark's presentation of Jesus' extraordinary ministry. And it renders Jesus an historically plausible first-century Jew in a way that a no-reference reading to Dan 7:13–14 does not. When I get to the new paradigm I will offer a comprehensive explanation of the Son of Man title and attempt to show that these observations on just one passage are similar to those that should be made for the role of the Son of Man in the Synoptics as a whole. If "the son of man" is just Jesus' way of saying "I" then much in the Synoptics remains inexplicable and implausible. When, on the other hand, we get to the heart of the (apocalyptic) significance of the Son of Man title, much else that is mysterious becomes intelligible.

V: A Nontitular Expression?

On points 2, 5, and 6, Hurtado's view that the Greek *ho huios tou anthrōpou* in the Gospels is not a title is unusual. If there were no clear links to Dan 7:13, nor to a traditional interpretation of that OT passage, then his theory might just work. But the vast majority of modern commentators rightly recognize that the particularizing force of the Greek—(literally) "*the* Son of *the* man"—makes it titular. Indeed, we have already noted the ambiguity in Hurtado's own view on this matter; he ends up not very far from the admission that in fact the son of man expression both *refers* to Jesus and that it *characterizes* him as "*the* man" or "this man." And as we shall see, if the expression in effect means Jesus is "the man" then it is highly likely that, in a first-century Jewish context, it does in fact have a very specific titular force.

We may grant that it is not an official "title" *tout simple* (as with "The President" or "The Prime Minister"), but it nevertheless has a titular force (as with "The Boss" for a Managing Director or CEO, or for Bruce Springsteen), because it conveys a whole set of meanings that are otherwise not obviously present in the individual person to whom it is ascribed (as with "Superman" to Clark Kent). This state of affairs, and the fact that it was not a widely used confessional title in the early church is hardly surprising given Hurtado's first point (in my summary above): the Son of Man was a definite figure of Jewish hope, *but not a title,* so it is hardly surprising that it did not take hold *as a title* in the early church. (By contrast, of course, there is plenty of evidence that "Son of God" and "Messiah" and "Lord" had currency as titles in the first century.)

Furthermore, the lack of evidence for a Son of Man title in pre-Christian Judaism has fundamentally to do with the genre of literature in which the figure first appears. There is no title in Dan 7:13 either. The passage is a vision, where allegory, similitude, and metaphor point to realities beyond ordinary human telling. (God is "the Ancient of Days" in v. 9—an expression that did not gain titular force in Second Temple Judaism). It may well be that the implied reader of Dan 7 is meant to immediately figure out the identity of the manlike figure. But it is fitting that, for Daniel's *night* vision (see v. 2), what he sees is hazy and indefinite. (And that indefiniteness, both in Daniel itself and then in the *Similitudes* and *4 Ezra,* likely made a crucial contribution to the Son of Man texts' effectiveness as subversive political tracts that motivated Jews to resist the dominating oppressive forces under which they suffered.) In faithfulness to the limitations of the apocalyptic (that is *visionary*) genre, it is not surprising to find that in Rev 1:13 there is absolutely nothing titular to the description of Jesus as "one like a son of man" in the midst of the lampstands. So for these reasons we should not be surprised to find that although Jesus was believed to fulfill a specific apocalyptic hope grounded in Dan 7:13, the Son of Man did not function as a confessional *title* for him.

But even on this point caution is needed, since in his dying words Stephen uses the expression "the Son of Man" to refer to Jesus in a way that most naturally suggests the expression *was* a title well-known to the audience. As we have seen, in the previous session, Acts 7:56 is best taken as a reference all the way back to Dan 7 itself (via texts such as Luke 21:27 and 22:69). Stephen proclaims that *Jesus of Nazareth* is the one that Daniel saw only dimly. So in this text "Son of Man" is a definite figure—the figure of Danielic hope—and Acts 7:56 cannot simply be rewritten ". . . I see the heavens opened, and Jesus standing at the right hand of God." And in that case, Acts 7:56 could very well be precious testimony to the way the earliest Christian believers in Jerusalem *did* sometimes speak of Jesus as *the Son of Man* (a title). Jesus was, for them, *the Son of Man* figure whom Daniel also saw. Hurtado has not shown why that construal of the Acts 7 evidence is not the most likely.

Hurtado does not adduce any clear parallel for his proposal that the expression is simply one aspect of Jesus' distinctive idiolect. Who else in (Jewish) antiquity adopted such a distinctive, self-referential neologism? Of course, with so little first-person reported speech from Jewish antiquity preserved to posterity this is a question that will likely never be answered. But the textual base we do have probably falsifies the theory. We have already seen how in Mark 2:10 there are really serious problems if *ho huios tou anthrōpou* means, in effect, "I." There are two texts in John where it is really hard to see how *ho huios tou anthrōpou* can be simply replaced with the personal pronoun ("I"/"me"). It makes no sense to rewrite John 5:27 as God "has given him (the Son) authority to execute judgment, because he is *me*." "The Son of Man" *must* have a titular, connotative force in that verse. And the same goes for the expression in John 9:35–38. In other passages, the fact that Jesus does not use a first person pronoun helps make sense of the Son of Man saying and its context. In the three passion prediction sayings (Mark 8:31–38; 9:30–32; 10:32–34 and pars.), the hostile and bewildered reaction of the disciples makes excellent sense if the Son of Man is a well-known figure. It is not just that they are offended because Jesus thinks he is going to have to suffer a horrible death; they are baffled at the way he also seems to subvert well-established expectations about Daniel's Son of Man figure.

In later volumes, in Parts 5–6, I will explain why the nontitular solution is a theory of which we have no need. There is a way to understand Dan 7, the *Similitudes,* and the New Testament Son of Man sayings that gives conceptual coherence to the diversity of Gospel sayings. In all but a few texts either Dan 7:13 and/or the well-attested Jewish tradition that is connected to it are clearly in view. I will offer an explanation that also takes seriously the data that leads Hurtado to reject the titular approach. An approach, that is, that explains why it is that Jesus would speak, in an admittedly strange way, about the Son of Man in the third person, but that no one else addressed him as such. I will also explain (more fully than the brief comments above) why it is that as a reference to a definite well-known Jewish figure (with titular force) the expression does not appear more frequently outside the Gospels.

But for now we can conclude that Hurtado's arguments about the titular or nontitular use of the Son of Man expression are unconvincing. He has not shown that "Son of Man" has no titular force in the Gospels (and in Acts 7:56), and he has not provided reasonable grounds to doubt that the Son of Man expression functions linguistically to ascribe to Jesus (to connote) a set of known pre-Christian hopes surrounding the figure who first appears in Dan 7:13.

Indeed, the outcome of his own argument points ultimately in the direction I will go in the new paradigm. He says that the expression means something like "the man" or "this man" and the "semantic force of the expression is an emphatic reference to Jesus as human being, *the* human being/descendent."[111] Indeed. Ecce homo! For Hurtado this presumably has little, or no, connotative force because talk of "*the* man" would not evoke any specific identity or eschatological figure for first-century Jews. However, that judgment is only tenable if Jesus' contemporaries had neither any real interest in Adam, nor Adam's relation to the messiah and eschatological salvation.

However, in chapter 7, and then again in Part 5, I will lay out the evidence for thinking that if Jesus means by his talk of *ho huios tou anthrōpou* that he is "the man" or "*the* human being" then that expression must evoke a whole set of well-known expectations and hopes surrounding the expectation that, in the end of days, there would appear a new, perfect Adam. That expectation is what Dan 7:13 is all about. If, with Hurtado, Jesus' idiomatic use of *ho huios tou anthrōpou* "is an emphatic reference to Jesus as human being, *the* human being/descendent" then Jesus claims to be *the* man, the truly human one; *he is the one who truly is what Adam was created to be*. Far from meaning not very much at all, in the context of the overarching shape of the biblical metanarrative this is a specific, and astounding, claim that warrants the titular force of the peculiar Greek expression. It is also a claim that takes us to the epicenter of the explosion that was Christological origins.

VI: Conclusion: the Emerging Consensus on the Son of Man

The emerging consensus has not satisfactorily explained the peculiar expression *ho huios tou anthrōpou* in the Gospels. Its leading voices have done insufficient justice to the expression's titular force and the ways it defines the shape of the Christology of the Gospels.[112] More thought needs to be given to the pos-

---

111. Hurtado, *Lord Jesus Christ*, 305–6.

112. Thirty years ago Bauckham wrote a brief article on the Son of Man ("Son of

sibility that with the Son of Man title the Christology of the Gospels is much closer to that of Paul and other NT texts. In particular, there are grounds for thinking that the incarnational elements of "Christological monotheism" are consistent with those Son of Man sayings that indicate that Jesus had come, from heavenly preexistence, in his earthly life. These points of conceptual connection between the Son of Man Christology of the Gospels and the early post-Easter faith obviously have implications also for the historical question: where did Paul's "Christological monotheism" come from?

Man"—1985, reprinted in his *Jewish World*, 93–102). That article anticipates Hurtado's view that, because "Son of Man" was not a recognized title for a messiah or redeemer figure in pre-Christian Judaism the expression in the Gospels does not automatically refer to an existing tradition of Jewish interpretation of Daniel 7 or to a well-known "apocalyptic figure" (see p. 27). As far as I can tell other major issues in the Son of Man debate have not received Bauckham's attention, especially in the light of his more recent and seminal work (in his *Jesus*).

CHAPTER 4

The *Origins* of NT Christology

Questions and Problematic Arguments

WHILST THERE IS GROWING agreement among NT scholars that there is both a genuine worship of Jesus in the earliest datable Christian material and also a "Christological monotheism," there is much less agreement as to how this remarkable situation came about. There are several discrete questions that have yet to be answered in a way that could command common assent and my aim here is to show that there are weaknesses to the approaches that Hurtado and Bauckham each take that have left the emerging consensus open to continued criticism.[1]

This chapter considers aspects of the *origins* problem. For the most part, I shine the spotlight on Hurtado's argument that Christ devotion has its origins in certain religious experiences of the first Christians. But we begin with a consideration of some objections to broader, shared perspectives within the emerging consensus and some comments on the challenge now facing any plausible account of the origins of "Christological monotheism."

1: No Precedent in Pre-Christian Judaism for "Christological Monotheism"?

Hurtado and Bauckham both think that the high Christology of the NT had no real precedent in pre-Christian Judaism. Jews did not treat God's designated rulers or agents (prophets, priests, and kings, for example) the way that the earliest Christians treated Jesus. There was no inclusion of a second figure in the divine identity in pre-Christian Judaism. Early Christian

---

1. Gordon Fee (*Pauline Christology*, 552–54) and Chris Tilling (*Christology*, 259–63) both conclude their recent monographs with a recognition that it is hard to explain the origins of Paul's divine Christology.

beliefs about Jesus and the treatment of him as a divine figure are unique and unprecedented.

There can be no denying that the complete pattern that goes to make up the "Christological monotheism" and the Christ devotion of the NT is unique and in that sense unprecedented. But there are real problems with the way that Hurtado and Bauckham rule out all the possible evidence for any kind of precedent in the biblical and Jewish tradition. And this is probably the issue on which there is now most disagreement, including among those who are persuaded of some of the key findings of the emerging consensus.[2]

In the last half century there has steadily accumulated a wealth of possible evidence that pre-Christian Judaism already thought about messianic and mediatorial figures in ways that anticipated the early Christian beliefs about Jesus (and the treatment of him as a divine figure). Much of that evidence is certainly pre-Christian. Some of it is post-Christian, or *possibly* post-Christian, but of an uncertain date, though a good case has been made that it reflects pre-Christian Jewish piety. A venerable line-up of specialists has seen considerable continuity between NT Christology and this Jewish material, where Hurtado and Bauckham see either none or not much of any real significance.[3]

In the rest of this study, I will argue that in "Christological monotheism" there is indeed some continuity (though also radical discontinuity) with Jewish and biblical theological categories and devotional patterns; far more continuity than the emerging consensus as a whole, and Hurtado and Bauckham in particular, recognize. (I will also argue that recognizing that continuity helps us see with greater clarity the ways in which there is radical novelty in earliest Christian beliefs about God and his messiah.) At this juncture I flag up two problems with the way they handle this aspect of the historical investigation.

2. Andrew Chester, for example, agrees that there is very early evidence for a full Christology of divine identity (and even that Hurtado's religious experience hypothesis is on the mark), but he also finds considerable continuity between an early high Christology and Jewish mediatorial speculation (see his *Messiah*). Daniel Boyarin (in his *Border Lines* and *Jewish Gospels*) goes even further: there was a binitarian strand of Jewish theology already in pre-Christian Judaism (attested especially in Dan 7 and the *Similitudes of Enoch*).

3. The leading voices for the case for continuity are Christopher Rowland (see his *Open Heaven* (1982), "Apocalyptic Visions" (1983), *Christian Origins* (1985), "Man Clothed in Linen" (1985)), Jarl Fossum (in *Name of God* (1985) and *Image of the Invisible God* (1995)); Andrew Chester (esp. "Jewish Messianic Expectations" (1991) and *Messiah* (2007)); Alan F. Segal (e.g., *Paul the Convert* (1990), "Risen Christ" (1992)); Adela Yarbro Collins (in, e.g., Collins and Collins, *King*, 2008), Samuel Vollenweider, *Horizonte neutestamentlicher Christologie* (2002). Martin Hengel saw more continuity than do the heirs to much of his work, Hurtado and Bauckham.

Firstly, there are problems with the ways they handle the relevant Jewish texts. Quite often they take a minority or idiosyncratic position on possible examples of a precedent for some NT text or Christological theme. And sometimes they provide a brief discussion of a non-Christian text that leads to strong claims about its meaning and historical position where a fuller analysis would really be needed to sustain their case. In several instances, the most recent specialist treatment of Jewish material counts strongly against their judgments. In the next three chapters I offer case studies — in the evidence for a Jewish belief in a "divine" messiah (chapter 5), an openness already in pre-Christian Judaism to the patterns of the Greco-Roman Ruler Cult (chapter 6), and a tradition in which the angels offer *proskynesis* to Adam (chapter 7) — of Jewish material that illustrates this weakness in the Hurtado and Bauckham treatment of the sources.[4] In Parts 5 and 6, I will then present the case for substantial continuity between the "Christological monotheism" we find in the NT and patterns of biblically grounded Jewish practice and belief surrounding the high priest, drawing on material that so far has not yet received the attention it deserves. This will include a treatment of texts that we have known about for quite some time, and that some of us have discussed in other places, but that Hurtado and Bauckham have so far barely considered.[5]

Secondly, there is a problem in the way that Hurtado considers the case for pre-Christian "precedents" for NT Christology. *There is no doubt that the full and precise shape of "Christological monotheism" is unprecedented.* It has no exact parallel anywhere in antiquity, and the biblical tradition does not explicitly predict it. (Though the NT can, without distortion of the biblical text, claim that "Christological monotheism" does not conflict with the revelation given to Israel before Jesus' arrival.) Hurtado recognizes the role of, what he calls, the Jewish "divine agents" tradition. However, when it comes to the cultic devotion to Jesus and the binitarian shape of NT

---

4. Bauckham's work in this area is more recent than Hurtado's (which is mostly to be found in his 1988 book *One God, One Lord*). Besides the Jewish texts I will discuss in chapters 4, 5, and 6, Bauckham's treatment of the angel Iaoel in the *Apocalypse of Abraham* (in *God of Israel*, 224-28) is not really convincing, especially in its failure to discuss the fact that Iaoel is a name of the God that Abraham hymns in 17:13.

5. I think especially of Ben Sira/Sirach 50:1-21, the XIIIth of the *Songs of the Sabbath Sacrifice* (4Q405 23 ii), and the story of Alexander the Great's Worship of the High Priest (Josephus *Ant.* 11:326-38 and pars.). Hurtado has commented briefly on two of these (and texts that I have argued are related to them) in his *Lord Jesus Christ* (40-42), but not on any of my detailed discussions of them (in Fletcher-Louis, "Cosmology of P"; *All the Glory of Adam*, 356-94; "Alexander the Great") or my treatment of some other related texts (in, for example, Fletcher-Louis, "God's Image," "Humanity and the Idols," and "2 Enoch").

theology, he demands too much of the Jewish material for it ever to hope to gain a proper hearing as a factor in explaining the phenomenon attested in the NT. "Precedent" does not have to mean that everything that is predicated of Jesus has already been predicated of another figure, nor that the full pattern of devotion accorded to Christ was already in place or expected in the future for some eschatological figure.[6] Precisely because, as Hurtado has so persuasively argued, Christ devotion entails a complex pattern made up of several discrete elements (set out in chapter 1 §1.III), the historian's quest to understand the origins of that pattern should consider the possibility that there are precedents here and there to parts, if not the whole. And the existence of precedents for aspects of Christ devotion need in no way threaten the historical (and theological) uniqueness of early beliefs about Jesus. Indeed, it may well be that it is through a consideration of its relationship to its Jewish precedents that we are truly able to discern the particular, and unique, character of "Christological monotheism."

This, after all, is the way historical precedent works. The Dominican friar Girolamo Savonarola (1452-98) is generally reckoned to have anticipated Luther's German Reformation with an uprising against the power of the clergy in Renaissance Florence. But the full flowering of a theological and ecclesial revolution was only seen several decades later the other side of the Alps in Germany (and Switzerland). Savonarola was an historical precedent for Luther, but by no means did his attempted reformation have all the elements of the theological, ecclesial, and political revolution that would spread from Germany. For the waves of Pentecostal and Charismatic renewal and revival that have overtaken parts of the church in the twentieth century there is precedent in pietistic and popular movements, some of which were focused on visionary and "Spirit" experiences, in the medieval church. But, in many ways modern Pentecostalism is theologically (and sociologically) quite peculiar to the twentieth century. Such is the stuff of historical precedent. And sometimes precedent entails a degree of historical causality (Savonarola inspired Luther and influenced his theology), but sometimes it only offers an intriguing comparison from another, separate historical context (modern Pentecostal movements usually spring up with no direct influence from pre-twentieth-century church history, but then may subsequently appeal to it to explain themselves). But all agree that we understand Luther's Reformation and modern Pentecostalism best when we consider their continuities, as well as discontinuities with their historical precedents.

---

6. As Hurtado insists is the criterion for the assessment of any would-be Jewish precedent in his *Lord Jesus Christ*, 40.

The issue with Christ devotion and Christological monotheism, then, is not whether there ever was in pre-Christian Judaism or the Greco-Roman world "a full *pattern of religious behavior*" of the kind practiced in early Christianity.[7] The issue is whether Jewish texts (or indeed biblical ones) in fact show that parts of that full pattern were anticipated in ways that can help explain, as one or more of a set of factors and forces, the appearance of Christ devotion and "Christological monotheism." At one level, this is surely to state the obvious. The appearance in the late Second Temple period of would-be "messiahs" and the hope for a variety of Jewish redeemers or mediatorial figures is obviously *precedent* for the treatment of Jesus *as the Messiah* and a mediator between God and man. And the possibility that *some such figures were the focus of devotional behavior* (whether in theological theory or even in first-century practice) does not need to threaten the historical uniqueness of Christ devotion. Indeed, it may well sharpen up our understanding of the ways in which beliefs about *this particular messiah* (the Messiah *Jesus*) and the *peculiar kind of devotion* of which he was deemed worthy, set him apart as a unique individual figure within a distinctive theological framework. Steve Jobs was a remarkable man. The better I understand the species "entrepreneur" and the many among his contemporaries who have made history in the realms of business, technology, and design, the more Jobs's *unique* achievement and personal genius comes to the fore. Similarly, I will argue in Parts 5 and 6 that to know the Jesus of Christ devotion is to know him by comparison with his precedents and his peers, some of whom also received their own kind of cultic devotion.

2: Lack of Opposition to Early Christology

James Dunn, Maurice Casey, and James McGrath have all objected to the emerging consensus claims for an early high Christology on the grounds that there is no real evidence of opposition to early Christian attitudes towards Jesus from non-Christian Judaism. As McGrath puts it, a lack of opposition to early Christology is the proverbial dog that did not bark: if the early Christians really did treat Jesus the way that Hurtado and Bauckham claim they did then we would expect to see evidence of a vociferous opposition to early Christianity from Jews for whom there was a strict adherence to a belief in one God.[8]

---

7. The criterion of historical investigation laid down in Hurtado, *Lord Jesus Christ*, 40.

8. McGrath, "Intertextual Echoes," 77. See further Casey, "Christological Development," 224, 231; Dunn, "How Controversial?"; *Theology of Paul*, 257–60; *Worship*,

It is true that opposition has often been discerned behind the pages of John's Gospel, where Jesus is repeatedly attacked for his elevated self-claims. Such passages have been judged a reflection of struggles between the church and local synagogues, as Christological development supposedly pushed Jesus up the ontological ladder towards a fully divine position. However, the chief witness for the emerging consensus case for an early high Christology is Paul, not John, and Dunn, Casey, and McGrath all point to a lack of evidence of conflict around Christology in Pauline texts. For these scholars then, a fully divine high Christology cannot in fact have been present as early as Hurtado and Bauckham allege: the emerging consensus misconstrues the *shape* of Pauline Christology (as we saw in our review of Dunn, Casey, and McGrath in chapter 2) and it works with an implausibly early *date* for the eventual emergence of such a genuine worship of Jesus and a "binitarian" monotheism.

In several publications Hurtado has tried to respond to this objection by collecting evidence that there was in fact plenty of opposition to early Christians for their Christ devotion.[9] However, Dunn and McGrath remain unconvinced. Whilst I do not draw the same conclusions that Dunn, McGrath, and Casey have drawn from their critique of Hurtado at this point, I have offered my own discussion of his position to which he, in turn, has replied.[10] His reply has not dissuaded me of the essential substance of my critique and, as I see it, the implausibility of Hurtado's model on this issue can be summarized in the following four points.

1. On careful consideration of the texts adduced for the case, the argument for a non-Christian Jewish opposition to Christ devotion is "surprisingly weak."[11] In part, the issue here is simply that explicit evidence of opposition to Christ devotion does not appear where we would expect it if it had been the issue Hurtado alleges it was. It is nowhere explicit in any of Paul's letters and we would certainly expect it to be "reflected in the letters (Galatians, Romans) where Paul engages most directly and sharply with traditional Jewish beliefs as they impinge on his mission."[12] At key points in Romans Paul is evidently sensitive to Jewish accusations against his gospel (see, e.g., Rom 3:1-8), but he seems unaware of any opposition specifically to a worshipful treatment of Jesus as divine.

113-16; McGrath, *Only True God*, 47, 54, 68, 80, and my discussion of this issue in Fletcher-Louis, "A Review," 171-76.

9. Hurtado, *How on Earth?*, 68-70, 152-78 (a slightly revised version of "Jewish Opposition").

10. Fletcher-Louis, "A Review," 171-76, and Hurtado "Response," 17-18.

11. To quote the words of Dunn, *Worship*, 113.

12. Ibid., 116.

In Acts Luke records a variety of non-Christian Jewish responses to the early Christians, but in no case are the earliest believers charged with idolatry in worshipping Jesus. There is plenty of opposition to the new movement, but it is never clearly targeted against Christ devotion. There is antagonism to the Christian belief that Jesus had risen from the dead (Acts 4:2; 23:6–10; 24:15, 21; 25:19; 26:6–26) and opposition to the early Christian appeal to Jesus as a legitimate source of divine power and authority (4:7, cf. 5:28, 40). Luke claims the Jews are often jealous of the disciples' influence and power amongst the wider population (5:17; 13:45; 17:5). Christians can be accused of slandering or blaspheming God and Moses (6:11, cf. 15:5), and there is a fear that Jesus is going to destroy the Temple and change the Mosaic laws (6:14, cf. 18:13; 21:28; 24:6). So, here is plenty of evidence of a Jewish opposition that had nothing to do with the peculiar shape of an early Christian binitarianism (see also Acts 12:1–4; 13:5–11). And Paul's claim that he has been sent with good news to the Gentiles was apparently provocative (22:21–22). But there is no specific opposition against a worship of Jesus.

Even though Paul in Galatians and Romans is primarily addressing the stance of *some Jewish-Christians*, not non-Christian Jews per se, if Christ devotion was a live issue for the latter we would expect it to figure in Paul's interaction with the former. Even if he and his fellow Jewish Christians were all united against the (alleged) opposition to Christ devotion, why then does Paul never appeal to that solidarity in his argument over the works of the law? Why do we not hear him say to the Judaizers, "we are united on the worship of Jesus against our persecutors, neither should we flinch on our freedom from Torah"?

Hurtado's attempt to find evidence of opposition to Christians for their Christ devotion relies on dubious interpretations of several key NT texts. For example, it is a non sequitur to say that because Jews pronounced a curse on Jesus (as 1 Cor 12:3 shows some did) that they were opposed specifically to Christ devotion.[13] Non-Christian Jews would have plenty of reason to curse Jesus and we cannot assume that it was a worship of him that provoked them. Again, the fact that there are Gospel texts where Jesus can speak of his followers being persecuted "for my name's sake" and "on account of me" (Mark 13:13; Matt 5:11) cannot simply be assumed to be evidence of early Christ devotion.[14] Such statements appear in the context of the Gospel story where no worship of Christ is in view. They can make sense simply as statements that those who follow Jesus as Israel's chosen messiah (whether or not, at some future point, they *worship* him), will be persecuted.

---

13. As Hurtado claims in *How on Earth?*, 176.
14. See Hurtado, "Response," 18, where he also notes John 9:22; 12:42.

The Qumran covenanters showed a similar loyalty to the Teacher of Righteousness (1QpHab 7:10–8:3; 9:9–10; 11:4–8). To take these texts the way Hurtado does is to wrench them from their Gospel contexts.

2. In extracting these and other Gospel texts from their narrative context—the Gospels' account of Jesus' earthly life—Hurtado's argument reflects the form critical paradigm that uses Gospel passages to reconstruct the life of the early church, rather than as trustworthy testimony to the life of Jesus. For example, for Hurtado, the accusation that Jesus is guilty of blasphemy in his forgiveness of sins (see Mark 2:7) reflects later Christian Christ-devotion. So too, the blasphemy charge at Jesus' trial "dramatizes the theological issue dividing Jews and Christians" at the time Mark was written and "reflects the actual experiences of Jewish Christians" when they were "called to account before Jewish authorities for their devotion to Christ and charged with blasphemy."[15] The evidence of John is treated in a similar way: texts that purport to describe what actually happened during Jesus' life are judged indirect evidence of early Christian practices.[16] Theoretically, such an interpretative procedure is legitimate, but in the absence of concrete external evidence for an early (pre-Johannine) persecution from outside the Gospels the use of such passages this way simply begs the question. It also fails to reckon with the major challenge to the form-critical paradigm that has now been launched by Bauckham, who has made a persuasive case that the Gospels are eyewitness testimony of Jesus' life, not thinly veiled testimony to the creative theological developments and struggles within the early church and its diverse factions.[17]

3. There is plenty of evidence that some Jews opposed and persecuted the new movement we call Christianity. That evidence is best explained as a reaction to early Christian beliefs and practices that were viewed as a threat to traditional Jewish attitudes towards the Torah (especially the Pharisaic interpretation of it), the Temple, and the hope of national restoration in which one or more messianic figures would play a leading role. For example, Stephen is tried and killed in Acts, not because he worships or prays to Jesus, but because he speaks words against the Temple and Torah (Acts 6:14), and because in his speech to the Sanhedrin he implies that the Jerusalem Temple has become an idol, a "work of human hands" (7:48, cf. 7:41–43), and because he implies that the authorities are murderous, stiff-necked, idolaters (7:51–52, cf. Exod 33:3, 5; 34:9; Deut 9:6, 13; Ezek 44:7–9).

15. Hurtado, *How on Earth?*, 166–67.

16. For Hurtado's treatment of the Johannine evidence (John 5:18–23; 9:22; 10:31–33, 36; 12:42; 19:7) see Hurtado, *Lord Jesus Christ*, 352–54; *How on Earth?*, 70–71, 152–53; "Response," 18.

17. Bauckham, *The Gospels* (1998) and *Eyewitnesses* (2003).

Paul himself implies that he was a persecutor of the church because he was "zealous" for the legal "traditions of the fathers," a phrase that has in mind in particular Pharisaic traditions (*halakhot*) designed to protect the Torah from the kind of infringement the Gospels say Jesus was accused of by the Pharisees (Gal 1:13–14, cf. Mark 7:3, 5, 8–13 par. Matt 15:2–6; Col 2:8). If the issue for Saul the Pharisee had been a jealous desire to protect the one God from a binitarian mutation he would more likely have spoken not of his "zeal for the traditions of the Fathers," but of his "zeal for (the one) God" (cf. Acts 22:3; Rom 10:2 and 2 Kgs 10:16 "zeal for the LORD"). And Paul believes Christians were persecuted not "*for the throne* of Christ"—as if his fellow Jews were unhappy that he gave his messiah such an exalted, divine identity—but "*for the cross* of Christ" (Gal 6:12). Here, and throughout the Pauline corpus then, there is evidence that many Jews found the claim that the long-awaited messiah had in fact died, accursed (Gal 3:13), on a Roman cross deeply offensive and so they persecuted their fellow Jews who treated Jesus, nevertheless, as the messiah.

4. There is a notable lack of considered, theological, and scriptural apologetic for Christ devotion in the NT. For the emerging consensus model this is surprising. Time and again, Paul appeals to Christological tradition and established, formulaic language in a way that suggests most, if not all, Christians everywhere shared a common Christology.

Hurtado says that historically the worship of Jesus by first-century Christians happened despite the fact that it must have incurred the charge of idolatry from non-Christian Jews.[18] Why then is there no evidence of the early Christians wrestling with the issue of idolatry and the formulation of scriptural and theological arguments to explain why they believed they were not guilty as charged?

Given all we now know about the nature of that Christology, Hurtado's model would lead us to expect that the first Christians created and regularly produced arguments to justify the fact that they remained biblically faithful monotheists. Hurtado seems to agree, and he adduces a couple of texts that he thinks represent a Christian apologia for Christ devotion.[19] John 5:19–23—where Jesus rebuts the charge that he has made himself equal to God by claiming his status and authority has been given to him by the Father—could theoretically have functioned as such an apology. But on Hurtado's reading of the NT it is a late text and, in any case, recourse to Gospel material as indirect evidence for early Christian life outside the Gospels simply begs the question. For the Pauline (and pre-Pauline) mate-

18. Hurtado, *How on Earth?*, 155–56.
19. See Hurtado, "Response," 18.

rial, Hurtado's appeal to the use of Isa 45:22-25 in Phil 2:9-11 is hardly compelling. The fact that somebody penned a prose hymn in which Jesus is slotted into the position occupied by *Yhwh-Kyrios* in one of the most monotheistic passages in the OT only accentuates the problematic nature of the question at hand: Phil 2:9-11 functions powerfully as Christological proclamation, but it is hard to see how any first-century Jew would deem it a persuasive defense of that proclamation. And certainly it is not used that way by Paul in his letter to the Philippians. Even if a non-Christian Jew were to agree that Jesus somehow lived beyond death and was exalted to a post-mortem heavenly existence (as the Pharisees were evidently willing to do in Acts 23:9) they would, on Hurtado's model of Christological origins, be utterly incredulous of the suggestion that this divine exaltation gave Jesus a position as *Yhwh-Kyrios*.

Confessionally orthodox Christians in the twentieth century have sometimes been maligned by fellow Christians who have drunk deeply from the philosophical wellsprings of modernity, but there is precious little evidence that Christology led to an analogous first-century Jewish persecution of Jesus-worshipping Jews. In the final analysis, the lack of evidence for Jewish opposition to Christ devotion and "Christological monotheism" leaves us on the horns of a dilemma. The evidence gathered by the emerging consensus is too strong to allow us to conclude (as do Dunn, Casey, and McGrath) that in fact we have been wrong all along in what we have said about Christ devotion. Nevertheless, the lack of Jewish opposition to that devotion is as puzzling as the fact of that devotion was clearly an historical reality.

So we are bound to wonder whether another explanation of the two sets of evidence (Christ devotion but no Jewish opposition) can be found. If Paul did not think his devotion to Christ was controversial, perhaps this was because first-century Jewish monotheism (and, indeed, biblical theology itself) was already prepared for the kind of treatment that Paul and others gave their new-found messiah. Indeed, this is the proposal I will lay out in the following chapters. Although such a proposal will inevitably challenge some conceptual and exegetical judgments of the leading voices in the emerging consensus, it will also answer some of the objections of its detractors and therefore, I hope, provide more solid historical grounds for accepting its main findings.

3: Psalm 110 and the Identification of Christ with *Yhwh-Kyrios*

Despite so many persuasive arguments from Bauckham and others, some remain steadfast in their objection to the "Christological monotheism" case.[20] One reason for this seems to be a reluctance to believe that Paul could possibly maintain his commitment to the one God of Israel and now speak of God in a way that implied a two-ness within the divine identity. This is an important issue which cannot be quickly passed over: if Paul remained firmly committed to Jewish monotheism we need to explain how he could possibly adopt the kind of "Christological monotheism" present in the confession in 1 Cor 8:6.

The sharp end of this problem is the fact that, as Bauckham has stressed, Jesus is identified with the *Yhwh-Kyrios* of Israel's Scriptures. Where did this identification come from? What gave the early Christians license to adopt creative Christological readings of biblical *Yhwh-Kyrios* texts? To date, as far as I am aware, no one has offered a convincing explanation of the origins of this remarkable phenomenon. No one in the emerging consensus appeals, for example, to Son of Man texts that might imply that behind the *Yhwh-Kyrios* Christology of 1 Cor 8:6 and Rom 10:9–13 there stood a Gospel tradition that the historical Jesus identified himself, as the Son of Man, with the *Yhwh-Kyrios* of the biblical theophany tradition. As we have seen, Hurtado and Bauckham are leery of any recourse to the Gospel Son of Man expression and Bauckham focuses instead on the NT use of Ps 110:1. He thinks that it is the Christological reading of Ps 110:1, which goes back to Jesus' own interpretation of the psalm, that was largely responsible for the NT Christology of divine identity.[21] He argues that the Christological application of Ps 110:1 puts Jesus next to God on the divine throne and therefore squarely within the divine identity. And he thinks that Ps 110 probably provided the *earliest* expression of a divine identity Christology.[22]

There is no doubt that Ps 110, the most cited OT passage in the NT, was of great significance to the first Christians.[23] However, there are real

20. See Dunn, *Worship* (2010); McGrath, *Only True God* (2009); "Intertextual Echoes" (2013).

21. Bauckham, *God of Israel*, 22, 173–75; *Short Introduction*, 89, cf. Hengel, *Studies*, 119–26; Hannah, "Throne," 71–81, and Fee, *Pauline Christology*, 560–61.

22. Bauckham, "Hebrews," 17.

23. Outside of the Gospels in: Acts 2:33–35 cf. 5:31; 1 Cor 15:25; Rom 8:34; Col 3:1; Eph 1:20; Heb 1:3, 13; 8:1; 10:12–13; 12:2; 1 Pet 3:22; Rev 3:21. See also *Asc. Isa.* 10:14; 11:32–33; *1 Clem* 36:5; Polycarp *Phil* 2:1; *Barn.* 12:10; Mark 16:19; *Apoc. Pet.* 6:1. Against the view of some (e.g., Hannah, "Elect Son of Man," 72, cf. Hengel, *Studies*, 133) I do not count Acts 7:55–56 as an allusion to Ps 110:1.

problems with an appeal to the use of Ps 110:1 for an explanation of the origins of "Christological monotheism." Creative scriptural interpretation, as the use of Deut 6:4 in 1 Cor 8:6 and Isa 45:21–23 in Phil 2:9–11 beautifully demonstrate, contributed greatly to the ways the first Christians came to express their new faith. But such examples of the early Christian interpretation of Scripture cannot straightforwardly be used to explain the *origins* of the *Yhwh-Kyrios* Christology that they presume. There is no evidence, for example, that the historical Jesus claimed to fulfill Isa 45:21–23 in a way that would then explain the remarkable application of that text to him in Phil 2:10–11. At first blush, Ps 110:1 might seem to offer what such Pauline passages cannot offer: an interpretation of a biblical text that goes back to Jesus himself and that expresses a high Christology. However, on reflection, the case for thinking Scripture interpretation was *generative* of "Christological monotheism" flounders on the pivotal role that Ps 110:1 evidently played.[24]

The early Christians believed that their interpretation of Ps 110:1 was grounded in Jesus' own use of that psalm to describe himself. However, in the Gospels Jesus is identified, according to his own argumentation (Mark 12:35–37 and pars.), *with the second kyrios of the words in Ps 110:1 (= LXX Ps 109:1)*: "The *Kyrios* said to my *kyrios*, 'Sit at my right hand....'" The first *Kyrios* is a Greek substitute for the Tetragrammaton, but the second simply translates the Hebrew word *'adon* and the distinction between the two is a presupposition of Jesus' interpretation. There, his argument goes: according to David in Ps 110, *Yhwh-Kyrios* says to his, that is to David's, Lord (*'adon-kyrios*), "Sit at my right hand." So if David's Lord (*'adon-kyrios*) is addressed this way by *Yhwh-Kyrios* how then can David's Lord be David's own "son"?! This (messianic) *'adon-kyrios* is David's senior, not his junior (as the expression "Son of David" would imply). This is all obvious to the biblically literate reader of the Greek accounts of Jesus' appeal to Ps 110. It would have been even more obvious at a Hebrew or Aramaic speaking stage of the tradition where we can assume that a clear linguistic distinction between the two figures in Ps 110:1 would have been made.

In various ways the psalm stresses the subordination of the "messianic" *kyrios* to the divine "*Kyrios*": the latter is the acting subject in vv. 1, 2, 4, and the one who empowers and installs the messianic *kyrios* in his royal and military office. It is true that the messianic *kyrios* has a position of exalted and universal authority (vv. 1–2, 5–6), acting on behalf of *Yhwh-Kyrios,* but at no point in the psalm is there any suggestion that the divine

---

24. Compare Chester, *Messiah,* 107 for criticism of the role of Scripture interpretation in Bauckham's model.

name—*Yhwh*—is given to the messianic *'adon-kyrios*.[25] Indeed, we should perhaps not assume that at first anyone thought Jesus was seated *on Yhwh-Kyrios' own throne*. That is certainly the way Jesus' fulfillment of Ps 110:1 came to be understood (see esp. Rev 3:21; 4–5). However, in and of itself, Ps 110:1 can be taken to mean that the messianic *'adon-kyrios* sits next to *Yhwh-Kyrios on his own throne that is smaller and placed in a clearly subordinate position to the divine throne*. The fact that Jesus is remembered to have combined Ps 110:1 with Dan 7:13 would encourage that notion, since the intertext of Dan 7:13 includes a reference to *multiple* thrones in heaven (Dan 7:9). This would surely have encouraged the view amongst Jesus' first followers after his death that his appeal to Ps 110 implied a somewhat subordinationist Christology.

Certainly then, there are multiple reasons to conclude that it was quite a step from seeing Jesus as the second *kyrios* of Ps 110:1 to seeing him as, in effect, the *first Kyrios* of Ps 110:1 (that is *Yhwh* himself). Bauckham and others have not yet explained where or how that referential shift took place. As it is, the fact that Ps 110:1 is often combined in NT texts with Ps 8:6—a text describing the exaltation of *humanity*—places a further question mark against the assumption that the early Christians were focused on Ps 110:1 as the *source* of their conviction that Jesus Christ should be identified with *Yhwh-Kyrios*.[26]

The fact that the early Christians imagine Jesus seated at God's right hand with specific reliance on Ps 110 along with the memory of Jesus' claim to fulfill that text also tells against appeal to religious experience to explain the earliest high Christology. If the earliest Christians saw Jesus seated in heaven—even on God's own throne—in visions, were they not bound to conclude simply that he was (or had become) the messianic *'adon-kyrios* of which Ps 110:1 spoke? Why did the widespread, even dominant, role of Ps 110:1 on the early believers' imagination not exercise a constraint against overblown Christological claims? Or, to put the matter more positively, we are bound to wonder why the earliest *Jewish* believers in Jesus did not appeal to Ps 110:1 to justify their belief in Jesus' exaltation to the highest position in heaven without that position in fact threatening the unique, singular, and undifferentiated identity of the one God. With Ps 110:1 they could both have their newfound Christological cake and still have eaten

---

25. As David Litwa, *Iesus Deus*, 194, has now pointed out in a similar treatment of Ps 110 to my own here (and with reference to wider scholarly discussion of the psalm).

26. For Ps 110:1 combined with Ps 8:6 see Rom 8:32–34; 1 Cor 15:25–27; Eph 1:20–22; Heb 1–2 and note the way the Greek word "*hypokatō*" ("under"), that is lacking in the LXX of Ps 110:1, seems to have entered the text of Matt 22:37 and Mark 12:37 from Ps 8:7 (contrast Luke 20:43).

a simple, unitarian, monotheistic faith with their messiah in a properly subordinate position next to God. If the earliest high Christology was precipitated by powerful religious experiences, why did Ps 110:1 not provide the hermeneutical grid through which those experiences were interpreted such that full-blown Christ devotion and "Christological monotheism" was prevented: Christ was *only* the messianic Lord (*'adon-kyrios*), *not* also the *Yhwh-Kyrios*? Conversely, and in response to Bauckham's emphasis on the role of Ps 110:1 in the creation of "Christological monotheism," does not the absence of allusion to Ps 110:1 in the earliest classic texts that contain a clear identification of Jesus Christ with *Yhwh-Kyrios* (e.g., 1 Cor 8:6; Phil 2:9–11) suggest that the memory of Jesus' use of that psalm was only incidental to the emergence of a full "Christological monotheism"?

In Parts 5 and 6 I will offer answers to these questions from within a paradigm that explains why Jesus' use of Psalm 110:1 *did* in fact contribute significantly to the early Christian identification of him with *Yhwh-Kyrios*. But for the time being, taking the case for the impact of Psalm 110 on the terms set out by Bauckham and others, we are left with a puzzle: how to explain that early Christian identification of Christ with *Yhwh-Kyrios*. Since, as we shall see (below), the visionary religious experience hypothesis (advocated by Hurtado) does not explain the origins of the *Yhwh-Kyrios* Christology, and the Scripture interpretation and debt to Jesus' use of Ps 110 approach cannot bear the weight of an historical explanation that Bauckham asks of it, we have a phenomenon at the heart of NT Christology that the emerging consensus has not yet explained.

4: The Origin of a Belief in Christ's Role as Agent of Creation

The fact that so many texts give Christ a personal role in the work of creation also lacks adequate explanation in the work of the emerging consensus. This aspect of the early high Christology texts has not received much analysis in its own right, but it is another major achievement of the emerging consensus that a spotlight should now fall on its central importance. Its origin needs to be explained.

In the past, scholarship has, as with so much "high" Christological material in the NT, argued that Jesus' *Schöpfungsmittlerschaft* comes from the influence of Hellenism.[27] Certainly, it is true that the prepositional language in which it is expressed in 1 Cor 8:6 ("*through whom* all things"), in Col 1:15–16 ("*in him* was created . . . all things *through him* . . ."), and the Logos

---

27. See the review in McDonough, *Creator*, 4–5.

theology of John 1, all reflect the language and thought forms of the wider Greco-Roman world. But several factors count strongly against the generative influence of Hellenism and suggest that the *substance* (if not the *form*) of this aspect of Christology took shape as an essential component of the earliest Christology amongst Jesus' Jewish followers soon after their master's death. In any case, judging by its appearance elsewhere in Paul (Rom 11:36) and in non-Christian Jewish literature (Josephus *J.W.* 5.218; Philo *Cherubim* 127) the "from him," "through him," and "to/for him" language for God's creative work was probably already traditional for Greek-speaking Jews.

The whole question has been helpfully reopened in a recent study by one of Bauckham's students, Sean McDonough.[28] There are principally three arguments against the influence from Hellenism thesis. The Christ as agent of creation Christology appears in thoroughly Jewish contexts, such as the reworking of the quintessentially biblical Shema in 1 Cor 8:6. There is no NT example to the contrary: there are no places where Christ's creative agency is expressed in unavoidably non-Jewish, Greco-Roman context and terms. Secondly, this aspect of Christology that appears in several strands of NT literature (Pauline texts, John, and Hebrews) is never justified. In every case it appears as an unquestioned presupposition of the faith once for all delivered to the church. So it most likely arose within the earliest, Palestinian Jewish phase of the movement's development. That seems to be the inevitable conclusion of its presence in 1 Cor 8:6 where we have now found concrete evidence of a confession of the earliest, Jerusalem-based church (in our analysis of the verse's numerical structure). In any case, thirdly, there are significant differences between the way commonplace language for mediation is used in the wider Greco-Roman world and the way that language is used in the NT. In particular, Hellenism offers no real precedent for the peculiar notion that the individual human *person* Jesus Christ was actually an agent of the original creation of the world.[29]

Bauckham argues that this aspect of Christological monotheism should be understood as a case of thoroughgoing theological consistency:

> If Jesus is no mere servant of God but participates in the unique divine sovereignty and is therefore intrinsic to the unique divine identity, he must be so eternally. The participation of Christ in the creative work of God is necessary, in Jewish monotheistic terms, to complete the otherwise incomplete inclusion of him in the divine identity. It also makes it even clearer that the intention of this early Christology is to include him in the unique

28. Ibid.
29. See ibid., 97–134.

divine identity, since in the creative work of God there was for Jewish monotheists no room even for servants of God to carry out his work at his command.[30]

This is a conceptually plausible explanation. However, it suffers three problems. First, as far as I can tell, there is no direct textual evidence for it. Secondly, it probably relies on mistaken judgments about the nature of Jewish monotheism. Thirdly, comparative Jewish evidence counts against the earliest believers in Jesus taking such logically consistent theological steps.

I will come to the second point after first commenting on the third. As we will discover in the next chapter, the *Similitudes of Enoch* (*1 En.* 37–71) provides a partial parallel to the inclusion of a messianic figure in the divine identity (as Bauckham himself has admitted). In the *Similitudes* the transcendent messiah who shares God's throne, receives worship, and who appears as end-time judge takes over the position of *Yhwh* in biblical theophany texts. He is even given a preexistent, premundane origin and it is striking that it is nowhere said that he is a creature. Bauckham thinks there is a partial inclusion of the Enochic Son of Man-Messiah in the divine identity.[31] If that is the case, *the Enochic Son of Man-Messiah is nevertheless not said to be an agent of creation.*

Several of us have argued that in *1 En.* 48 the Son of Man-Messiah is given, or closely identified with, the name of God.[32] Although the identification between the two is not as complete as it is in the case of Jesus Christ, it is also significant that in *1 En.* 69:13–25 the name of God is part of an oath with which the world was originally created. The name of God, in other words, is treated as a distinct entity in its own right. Judging by its presence in other Jewish texts, the idea that God's name (or "Name") had creative potency from the beginning of the world was well-established in the pre-Christian period (*Jub.* 36:7; *Pr. Man.* 3; *L.A.B.* 60:2, cf. Philo *Migration* 103).[33] So, in *1 En.* 37–71 the Son of Man-Messiah is closely identified with, or possesses, the divine name by which the world is created. And this, as we shall see, reflects the text's willingness to ascribe biblical *Yhwh* language to the same figure. But, crucially, *1 En. 37–71 does not make the Son of Man-Messiah himself the agent of creation.* It nowhere provides parallels for

---

30. Bauckham, *God Crucified*, 36 (= *God of Israel*, 26), cf. Hurtado, *Lord Jesus Christ*, 124-25; *How on Earth?*, 102, Hengel, *Son of God*, 67-76; Habermann, *Präexistenzaussagen*, 421-22; McDonough, *Creator*, 48.

31. Bauckham, *God of Israel*, 16.

32. Fletcher-Louis, "Divine Humanity," 114; Barker, *Great High Priest*, 65-66, 82; Gieschen, "Name of the Son of Man"; Waddell, *Messiah*, 72-75, 101-2, 168-69.

33. See further Fossum, *Name*, 76-84, 245-56 on later material.

the "in him" and "through him" language used for Jesus Christ in the NT. Indeed, it seems careful *not* to say that the Son of Man himself was an agent of creation in the way that he receives the name, but remains a distinct entity from the name.

So the *Similitudes* functions as a control that tells against Bauckham's argument: *for the authors of this pre-Christian Jewish text*—and to reframe Bauckham's own statement of the argument—*the participation of the messiah in the creative work of God was not necessary . . . to complete an otherwise incomplete inclusion of him in the divine identity.* Comparison with the *Similitudes,* in other words, suggests that it must have been more than just a desire for theological consistency that precipitated Christ's inclusion in the work of creation. Other Jewish texts written after AD 70 that we will consider briefly in later chapters (*4 Ezra, Sib. Or.* 5 and compare *3 En.*) suggest that the *Similitudes* was by no means exceptional in allowing a messianic figure a partial inclusion in the divine identity. Those texts also lack the kind of personal participation in the work of creation that we find for the messiah in the NT. Indeed, we will also find in chapter 7 that a Jewish story (the Worship of Adam Story) in which Adam is worshipped by the angels provides another control by which to test Bauckham's hypothesis. In that case, I will argue, Adam carries or expresses the divine identity in a way that warrants the angelic worship of him. But in all the diverse witnesses to the story there is no suggestion that Adam should be included in the creative work of God. No one felt the need to tidy up the story's theology in the way that Bauckham argues Christians thought it necessary to ensure their Christology was systematically tidy. And this, we should note, cannot simply be because the biblical text makes crystal clear that Adam was the last of the works of creation so could not possibly be an agent of creation. There is other evidence that, particularly in reliance on Ezek 1:26 and the Septuagint translation of Gen 1:26—to which we shall come in later chapters—that Jews could conceive of a heavenly "adam" who transcended the work of creation, including the creation of the earthly Adam on the sixth day. But no attempt is made to identify the Adam worshipped by the angels with that heavenly Adam and include him in the work of creation.

All these comparative texts as near as falsify Bauckham's explanation of the way Jesus Christ is treated as a divine agent. And they strongly suggest that Bauckham's hypothesis partly misconstrues the nature of Jewish monotheism. It is by no means obvious that a participation in God's divine sovereignty would need also to go with an inclusion in his identity as the Creator. I see no reason why Jews could not happily believe that God would delegate to an individual figure a universal, cosmic power and authority without God also including that figure in his own identity as Creator or, even and more simply, in his sharing with that figure the divine work of creation. It may well be that there are theological and other advantages to such a "complete" inclusion in the divine identity. But I am unpersuaded that Jewish monotheism entailed the kind of neat "in" or "out" line of distinction between inclusion in the divine identity (that allowed the carrying out of divine functions) or exclusion from the divine identity (with no sharing or delegation of divine functions) that Bauckham describes. It is not straightforwardly the case that, as Bauckham says (in the quote above), "there was for Jewish monotheists no room even for servants of God to carry out his work at his command." Already in Gen 1, God delegates to parts of creation a creative role in the making of the cosmos. God commands the earth and the waters to create and they do so, on three occasions (vv. 11, 20, 24). This and other features of OT creation traditions lead a growing number to speak now of a creaturely co-creativity in biblical theology.[34] And that notion has left its mark in various ways on postbiblical literature. For example, Josephus's statement that Moses was a "divine man" (*theios anēr*) is predicated on the claim that what the lawgiver does in setting up the tabernacle is to create a minicosmos (*Ant.* 3:180-86). Josephus's language there has puzzled modern commentators.[35] But Josephus's description of Moses simply reflects Priestly material in the Pentateuch (now much discussed by OT scholars) in which the description of Moses's work in setting up the tabernacle is viewed as an imitation, recapitulation, or extension of the work of the Creator in Gen 1 (cf. Exod 39:32, 43; 40:33 with Gen 1:28; 2:1-3). Josephus's evidence suggests then that first-century Jews could comfortably use "divine" language for "servants of God" who carry out his commands to undertake distinctively *creative* work of the kind described in Genesis. More strongly still, there are texts that assign Wisdom a role in the work of creation without Wisdom thereby taking on a distinct identity as one included in the divine identity.[36]

So, the early Christian belief that *this particular messiah, Jesus* Christ, belongs fully within the divine identity, even with a *personal* role in the work of creation from its very beginning, was exceptional. And that inclusion is not readily explained by a desire for a systematic or tidy theology. On the one hand, Jews could ascribe creative agency to entities that were *not* fully included in the divine identity and, on the other hand, they could ascribe a (limited) "divine" identity to messianic and other figures *without the need*

---

34. See e.g., Elnes, "Creation and Tabernacle," 151; Garr, *In His Own Image*, 175; W. P. Brown, *Seven Pillars*, 44-46.

35. E.g. C. R. Holladay (*Theios Aner*, 47-102) struggles to make sense of it and is unaware of the OT tradition of a Tabernacle and Temple cosmology.

36. For Wisdom as Creator in Sir 24 see Sheppard, *Wisdom*, 25-26; Fletcher-Louis, "Cosmology of P," 80-94 and compare Prov 8:22-30; Wis 7:22; 8:5-6.

to give them the kind of full, personal role in work of creation that we find in NT Christology. The exceptional character of this aspect of "Christological monotheism," which is fully appreciated through a consideration of both the continuities and discontinuities with (partial) Jewish "precedents," still has to be explained.

Others have argued that Christ's creative agency is a reflection of the identification of him with preexistent Wisdom who plays a similar role in several Jewish texts (Prov 8; Sir 24; Wis 7:22). Again, whilst parallels between several of the key NT passages and Jewish texts can be adduced, and one Pauline text might possibly identify Jesus with Wisdom (1 Cor 1:24), the case is actually much weaker than has sometimes been claimed, as several recent studies have noted.[37] Jesus *has* wisdom and is often depicted as a sage. However, no Gospel passage clearly claims that Jesus *is* Wisdom, let alone that Wisdom or Jesus-as-Wisdom was an agent of creation (although the first of these ideas is perhaps implicit in Matt 11:19 par. Luke 7:35 and in Matt 23:34, cf. Luke 11:49). Neither has anyone adduced evidence that Israel's royal messiah was identified with Wisdom (in a way that would lend itself to the idea that the royal messiah had a place in the work of creation). In any case, the role of Wisdom language in the Christ-as-Creator passages has perhaps been overplayed. For example, Christ's role as creative agent in Heb 1:2-3 has been compared with the depiction of Wisdom in Wis 7:22-27. It is true that the two passages have several words in common, but none of them (*apaugasma*—"radiance, reflection"; *doxa*—"glory"; and *dynamis*—"power") are particularly unusual, nor are they distinctive of the Wisdom tradition, and the rest of Hebrews shows no interest in either wisdom in general, Lady Wisdom in particular, let alone the book of Wisdom.[38]

In any case, what Wisdom contours there may be to the characterization of Jesus—as preexistent one and agent of creation in some NT passages—would only go to accentuate the puzzle: how come the earliest Christians identified the transhistorical Lady Wisdom with the individual man Jesus Christ? If Christ's role in the work of creation were due to his identification with Wisdom we would expect the primary NT texts to place much less stress on Christ's distinct *personal* identity as an agent of creation.

---

37. For criticism of the role of Wisdom in the formation of a Christology of preexistence see Fee, *Pauline Christology*, 93, 96-97, 317-25, 595-619; Gathercole, *Preexistent Son*, 193-208; McDonough, *Creator*, 37-40, 78-85.

38. Cf. McDonough, *Creator*, 196-99. Philo uses the word *apaugasma* in *Creation* 146; *Planting* 50 and *Spec. Laws* 4:123 with no technical sense nor with any association with Wisdom. See also *T. Abr.* 16:8 and the use of the verbal cognate in Philo *Abraham* 119; *Let. Arist.* 76 and 97-98 (in association with *doxa* but not Wisdom).

Resorting to Wisdom to explain Christ's role as co-Creator simply raises new questions.

In his recent study, McDonough mounts a more multifaceted case for the origins of the belief in Christ's *Schöpfungsmittlerschaft* in the Jewish phase of the early Christian movement. He is reluctant to pronounce on the details of the process. But he thinks this aspect of Christology was formed out of the catalyst of the memories of Jesus in the Gospels, with preexisting biblical and Jewish traditions surrounding the (royal) messiah serving as an organizing principle, and contemporary Greco-Roman language and allusions to Wisdom traditions variously used to express the idea. He helpfully stresses the tight conceptual interconnections between the work of creation and the work of salvation in biblical theology and highlights the presence of explicit creation language in the Gospels that is often overlooked in discussions of their Christology. This serves to bolster, through recourse to the primary texts, the logic of Bauckham's argument: his followers believed that already in his life and death there was present the work of the Creator, since the inauguration of the new kingdom evokes the renewal of creation (especially in nature miracles and healings). So it will have been only a small conceptual step to take Jesus' role in creation back from new creation to the original creation.

As we shall see in the coming chapters some of McDonough's arguments are persuasive and his recourse to important recent work on the ancient Near Eastern and Israelite understanding of creation, divine deliverance, and the role of the king is highly suggestive. However, the evidence he is able to adduce for a connection between the king and the work of creation in biblical and Jewish traditions is meager and the comparative control case of the *Similitudes* and the Worship of Adam Story makes his model problematic as much as it does Bauckham's. Clearly, wherever belief in Christ's role as co-Creator appears in the NT, it is connected to the conviction that his salvific work is a new creation (which was an ongoing experience for the early Christians), but as discussion in later chapters will show, belief that Jesus was himself, *personally*, present and active in creation remains hard to explain from within the emerging consensus conceptual framework.

5: Problems with Hurtado's Explanation of the Christ Cult

Hurtado's theory that the decisive factor leading to Christ devotion was powerful religious experiences in which God directed such worship is innovative and has been welcomed in some quarters (for example, by Andrew Chester).[39] It is, however, problematic and on careful examination,

39. Chester, *Messiah*, 80–105, 119–21, 189–90; "High Christology," 47–50.

is not supported by the primary texts. I have provided a detailed critique of this part of Hurtado's model for Christological origins elsewhere, to which he has also responded.[40] To my mind, his response has not answered the objections, and others also seem less persuaded by this part of his model.

His theory suffers three problems which are worth reviewing because at several points they also illustrate the ways in which Hurtado's model downplays the significance of Jesus' life and the early Christian understanding of it in incarnational terms. Careful consideration of his case also helps us appreciate the nature of the historical data that must be satisfactorily explained if any account of the origins of an early high Christology is to be persuasive.

I: Lack of Textual Support for the Theory

First, on close examination, the NT texts to which Hurtado appeals for evidence that visions of the risen and exalted Jesus in glory provided the decisive stimulus for early Christian Christ-devotion,[41] do not provide direct evidence for what Hurtado supposes took place.

It is possible that in 2 Cor 3:7—4:6 Paul draws Christological lessons from his original Damascus Road experience. But the earliest Christians had already adopted a full-blooded Christ devotion before Paul's conversion and, in any case, neither in 2 Corinthians nor anywhere else in Paul, is there any direct, tangible evidence for thinking that visionary (and related) experiences actually *caused* Jesus' followers to worship him in the first place.[42] The earliest Christians prized the presence of God's Spirit in their midst and believed that by that Spirit Christ continued to work wonders. This Spirit guided individuals and communities in the processes of decision-making (Gal 2:2, cf. 1 Cor 14:26; Acts 10:19; 11:12; 13:2, 4). Having a direct personal encounter with the risen Lord also seems to have validated the position of apostles (1 Cor 9:1; Gal 1:11-12). But I see no evidence of a "microculture" in which visions

---

40. Fletcher-Louis, "A Review," and Hurtado, "Origins."

41. Hurtado, *One God*, 117-22; *Lord Jesus Christ*, 70-74, 176; *How on Earth?*, 192-204.

42. As Gordon Fee, who is sympathetic to Hurtado's explanation of the origins of Christ devotion, points out (*Pauline Christology*, 553). Hurtado (*How on Earth?*, 170) and Chester ("High Christology," 48) also take Gal 1:16 as evidence of the importance of visions for Paul. However, that verse is much more likely to refer to Paul's own conformity to Christ who is then revealed "in (*en*)" Paul, not "to" him (see Fee, *Pauline Christology*, 220-22, 553).

and revelations guided the earliest believers in matters of faith and order *of the kind* that Hurtado thinks happened with Christ devotion.[43]

There is no evidence in any other visionary passage in Acts, or elsewhere in the NT, that the earliest followers' visions of the risen and exalted Jesus were the context within which Christ devotion first came about. As noted above, in the account of the death of Stephen (Acts 7), the Sanhedrin are enraged because Stephen accuses the authorities of being murderous, Torah-breaking idolaters. Stephen's vision of the risen Christ (Acts 7:55-56) perhaps compounds their rage because hereby he claims to have access to God's throne room (through an open heaven) that bypasses the Sanhedrin's position of authority (and the God-sanctioned role of priestly mediation). However, there is no focus in that vision on a specifically high Christology. Jesus *stands* at God's right hand. He does not sit on God's throne as we might expect if the point was that Jesus was now included in the divine identity. And, whilst it is true that Stephen prays to Jesus in a way that reflects the early church's devotion to him (vv. 59-60), that only happens *after* the Sanhedrin have determined to kill him. This passage therefore provides no evidence that Christ devotion was itself the reason for a Jewish persecution of Christians or that radical new ideas about Jesus' position in heaven were nurtured by visions.

So it is going well beyond the evidence to ascribe the innovation in Christ devotion to experiences of the risen and glorified Christ.[44] The same judgment goes for Hurtado's appeal to material in John's Gospel (esp. John 14-16), which he alleges testifies to a Spirit-inspired charismatic exegesis that helped produce new Christological insights (some of which were then included in John's Gospel itself). The Spirit's role in John is, inter alia, to *remind* his disciples (14:26-27) of the things Jesus said, not to inspire "newly perceived truths about Jesus . . . apprehended as disclosures given by God."[45]

II: Opposition to the Role of Visions in Some Parts of Early Christian Life

Whilst Hurtado's insistence that we take early Christian religious experience seriously is welcome, he does not interact much with wider scholarship on the role of "mystical" (visionary and related) experiences in the Second Temple period. He anachronistically divorces spontaneous Spirit-led experiences,

---

43. Despite Hurtado's claims in *How on Earth?*, 197.

44. See esp. ibid., 192-204.

45. As Hurtado (in *Lord Jesus Christ*, 378) claims. See also his article "Remembering," esp. 202-13.

that today we might associate with a Charismatic or Pentecostal form of Christianity, from a more sober, theologically rigorous spirituality. And he does not consider the possibility that for the early church religious experience was a complex phenomenon, in which there was careful differentiation between the constructive and the harmful or prohibited, which would mitigate the role of such experiences in the eruption of a new Christology.

In particular, he does not take account of the rather widespread evidence that in some quarters visionary experience was contrasted with, or set in opposition to, the experience of the (incarnate) earthly Jesus. For example, in John's Gospel, as Christopher Rowland has argued, there are texts that deny the need for a visionary ascent to heaven (3:13; 6:46; 12:45) because, as other texts claim (1:51; 1:14–18; 14:9), in Jesus the disclosure of heavenly revelation, indeed the vision of God himself, is available on earth. As Rowland explains, divine revelation

> . . . is not found in the visions of the mystics and in the disclosures which they offer of the world beyond, but in the earthly life of Jesus Christ. There is in the gospel narrative and its incarnational direction a definite attempt to stress that revelation is found in this human story.[46]

This *antipathy to mystical experiences because they distract from the Incarnation as the locus of revelation* probably also explains a polemic against visions in Colossians. Jews in the apocalyptic and mystical tradition sought out the treasures of wisdom and knowledge through visions, accounts of other peoples' ascents to heaven, and through a heavenly liturgy. But, for Paul, the Colossian Christians need to fully appreciate that "all the treasures of wisdom and knowledge are hid" *in Jesus Christ* (2:3). Indeed, the Colossian Christians are warned that they should not be distracted by the claims of those who have visions and encounters with the heavenly, angelic realm (2:18) that can be a distraction from the true life lived in intimate communion with Jesus Christ, the head, who has already been revealed, in the Incarnation, as the one in whom "all the fullness was pleased to dwell" (1:19).[47]

If we follow Paula Gooder's recent analysis, Paul quite likely adopts a similar stance on the unimportance and dangers of visionary experiences in 2 Cor 12.[48] She persuasively argues that Paul here lampoons himself as a failed mystic with paltry "visions and revelations of the Lord": he boasts of

---

46. Rowland, "Apocalyptic," 426, cf. Rowland in Rowland and Morray-Jones, *Mystery*, 123–31 and, most recently, Gieschen, "Descending Son of Man."

47. See the fuller discussion of Colossians and its relationship to Jewish mysticism in Fletcher-Louis, "Jewish Mysticism."

48. Gooder, *Third Heaven?*

an occasion when he *only* ascended to the third, not to the seventh heaven. Paul records no actual vision of the Lord in the highest heaven, only "unutterable words" (v. 4). The super-apostles who have disturbed the Corinthian Christians rely on visions and revelations of the Lord; Paul does not (2 Cor 12:1, cf. Gal 1:8). On this reading of the evidence, the only thing that Paul learns from this ascent to heaven—that Christ's power in him is made perfect in weakness (v. 9)—is a truth that stands at the very heart of the gospel message, that one learns *from the cruciform character of Jesus' life and ministry*, and that Paul embraced when he first became a follower of Jesus. Paul did not need to ascend to heaven to learn this and so his parody of an ascent to heaven for a vision of Christ sends him (and his Corinthian readers) back to the basic, core content of the gospel, which is the crucifixion at the climax of Jesus' life of weakness and vulnerability.

Material in Luke-Acts adds to the impression that there was a widespread concern to distance Christian life and spirituality from those in the wider religious environment who looked to visions and similar religious experiences as a source of revelation. The Lukan account of Jesus' baptism, more clearly than the one in Mark and Matthew, excludes any suggestion that Jesus merely has a (subjective, personal, inward) vision. The Spirit came not "into" (*eis*) him (Mark 1:10), but "on" (*epi*) him, and it did so "bodily" (*sōmatikos*) (Luke 3:22), in full public view. At the transfiguration, Luke alone tells us that "the disciples were heavy with sleep, *but when they became fully awake*, they saw his glory" (9:32).[49] Along with features of the story that reflect Luke's penchant for realism—Jesus is praying (9:29) and conversing with Moses and Elijah (9:31)—the arousal-from-sleep element is best explained if Luke is keen to avoid any suggestion that the disciples merely had a subjective vision of Jesus in glory. Luke's postresurrection narratives make much the same point. In the upper room, Jesus stands in the midst of the disciples, but he is no mere "spirit" and they are not hallucinating: he has hands and feet, and he can eat (Luke 24:36-43).

So, there is plenty of evidence that challenges Hurtado's thesis that there was a widespread early Christian confidence in the place for powerful revelatory experiences in matters of religious life and thought that made the creation of new theological content and practice possible. Hurtado is right that visionary activity was widely accepted and, for some purposes, much encouraged (Acts 2:17-21; 1 Cor 12, 14; 1 Thess 5:19-22). Nowhere are visions, prophetic oracles, and Spirit-inspired exegesis deemed inappropriate *per se*: the Johannine Christians are to "test the spirits," not to deny

---

49. For the Greek here meaning "become fully awake" see, e.g., Heil, *Transfiguration*, 263 and LSJ 392.

the existence of the spirit-realm (1 John 4:1-6). But, as a movement that wanted to remain faithful to Israel's own legislation on such matters, diverse sections of the early church strictly avoided giving quarter to any powerful revelatory experiences that challenged their received understanding of the identity of the one God which they believed, from their experience of him, *from the beginning* (1 John 1:1), now included Jesus Christ. Judging by the language in Matthew, Mark, and John, "the beginning" that the author of 1 John speaks of as the point of departure for Christological understanding is the life and ministry of Jesus, not visions at the beginning of the life of the early church after his death (cf. Matt 1:1; Mark 1:1; John 1:1-18). In any case, in avoiding giving authority to visionary revelation after Jesus' death and resurrection they followed OT warnings against being led astray by false prophets (see Deut 13:1-5). And they were probably mindful of a keen interest in visions and revelations (including perhaps ascents to heaven) in the non-Christian Jewish world where people looked to such powerful religious experiences for guidance and inspiration ahead of the eschatological dénouement (see e.g., 1QM 10:10-12; Josephus *J.W.* 6:284-300).

Johannine, Pauline, and Lukan traditions all subordinate visionary revelation to the historical actuality of Jesus the Messiah as the definitive content and source of all that visions might otherwise offer. And so it is not surprising that the NT as a whole lacks actual evidence for the thesis for which Hurtado argues. As it is, the NT has quite a lot to say about Jesus' own religious experience; his visions and his sense of a peculiar intimacy with his heavenly "Father" (esp. at the baptism and transfiguration, and see Luke 10:18, 21-22 and par.). When I come in Part 6 to unpack the NT evidence for the new paradigm, I will argue that any consideration of the role of religious experiences in explaining Christological origins should start where the NT itself invites us to start, not with putative experiences of Christians in the post-Easter church, but with Jesus himself, his experiences, and the apocalyptic, visionary atmosphere in his own family—as described in the Matthean and Lukan infancy narratives.

III: Social Scientific Studies and Innovations in Early Christianity

Finally, consideration of the way new religious ideas emerge and new movements are created, along with the evidence we have for Christianity's emergence as a movement from within Judaism, tells decisively against Hurtado's theory. The interpretation of religious experience is always socially framed or conditioned. On Hurtado's understanding of Jewish monotheism, we would expect visions of the risen Jesus to lead to his first followers treating him as a peculiarly exalted divine mediator, not one who should actually be worshipped. When they beheld him exalted in glory they would be bound to interpret him through the grid of the Jewish divine mediators tradition, not treat him as one worthy of worship.[50]

Hurtado has countered this objection by an appeal to social scientific studies that show that powerful religious experiences can in fact, on occasion, lead to radically new ideas and beliefs.[51] However, on careful examination, such studies do not support the specifics of this historical case.

All the evidence we have speaks of a unanimous adoption of Christ devotion by Jesus' followers in the earliest years after his death. There was no division on this point between the Jerusalem-based Aramaic-speaking churches and the later Greek-speaking, and especially Pauline, churches. *All* the key leaders of the movement supported it. There is no evidence of dissenting individuals or communities. On Hurtado's model, during his life, Jesus did not speak or act in ways that would have caused his disciples to worship him. Nevertheless, Hurtado believes powerful religious experiences of multiple individuals and communities were enough to transform the most basic theological convictions and practices of all these people who had grown up with a shared Jewish faith, and were now united in their experience of Jesus during his (recent) earthly life (kept alive, by the twelve apostles, and by others—e.g., Acts 4:2; 10:34–43). The social-scientific studies to which Hurtado appeals do not provide clear analogies for this historical pattern and in the light of my criticism of his recourse to social scientific study Hurtado appears now to have conceded that what happened in early Christianity "appears not to fit the typical pattern of religious innovation."[52]

Perhaps he will argue, nevertheless, that history includes the unprecedented. That may be, and the NT texts do indeed claim much for early Christianity that is unprecedented. However, the lack of a social scientific analogy to the religious experience explanation of Christological origins is not the only reason to doubt its historical plausibility. Two control studies—innovative Jewish Christian beliefs about the resurrection and the role of Torah in the new movement—show that if the innovation in Christology happened the way Hurtado supposes then the NT would contain stories of surprised believers and of conflict within the new movement around Christ devotion.

---

50. A point that others (e.g., Allison, *Constructing*, 250; Boyarin, "Enoch, Ezra," 355–56) have made.

51. Hurtado, *Lord Jesus Christ*, 66–70, and *How on Earth?*, 179–203.

52. Hurtado, "Response," 14.

Firstly, there is the case of the resurrection. First-century Jews (with the notable exception of the Sadducees) were looking forward to a general resurrection of the dead at the end of days. His followers remembered Jesus endorsing that hope (Mark 12:18–27 and pars.). After his death, the earliest Christians radically reconfigured their belief in a general resurrection in the eschaton, in a way not dissimilar to the reconfiguration of Jewish monotheism to include Jesus within the divine identity. Now, they concluded, the one man Jesus, who had died accursed on a cross, had been raised from the dead ahead of the rest of God's people. This "mutation," to use Hurtado's language, in Jewish eschatological expectation happened, according to the NT documents, to all of Jesus' followers and it happened because the earliest believers (as individuals and in groups) had direct encounters with the risen Jesus. This was such a startling innovation, requiring *evidence* for all the key followers, that the writers of various NT documents saw fit to record the way it was remembered to have happened. It was not just enough to record an empty tomb. So, *why do we not have a similar record of religious experiences leading to Christ devotion on various occasions—to groups and to individuals—given that the reworking of the shape of Jewish monotheism was just as much, if not more so, a startling feature of what became universal Christian belief?* The Gospels describe how those various resurrection appearances led to an agreed stance on the empty tomb and resurrection, in the face of some initial skepticism from some (Matt 28:17; John 20:24–29). Why do the NT texts not, in a similar way, describe the process that the first followers had to go through, individually and collectively, to agree that Jesus now should be worshipped? On Hurtado's model, we expect, at the very least, stories of doubters being convinced through their own powerful revelatory experiences.

We come to a similar conclusion if we compare the history of the early church's position on Torah and the inclusion of Gentiles in the new movement. The first Christians spent many long hours in heated argument (and passionate letter writing) to try to achieve a practical consensus on the status of Torah, especially for gentile believers. According to Acts, Peter's position changed, at least for a period, *because he had a vision* (Acts 10). This at least supports the basic premise of Hurtado's theory: visionary experiences can precipitate changes in belief and practice. But then again, the case of Peter's vision and his stance on Torah compliance actually tells against Hurtado's theory. For one thing, it shows that a vision itself is not enough. The vision only prepared Peter for *a concrete, objective-not-visionary communal experience* in which the Spirit was poured out on a group of Gentiles without their first becoming circumcised and Torah-observant (10:44–48). Secondly, these events led to meetings of the new movement's leaders (Acts 11 and 15) in order to determine policies. Other passages in Acts and in Paul's letters show that the argument about Torah and the status of the Gentiles persisted with some variety of views amongst Jesus' followers, causing ongoing disagreement. *Why do we have nothing quite like this material in Acts—and in cognate passages in Paul—for the radical innovation that was Christ devotion? Hurtado's model leads us to expect that evidence of a theological firefight, provoked by the desire of some to include devotion to the risen Jesus alongside their devotion given to the one God. If not direct evidence, we expect smoking guns; strained relationships and ongoing invective. But there is none.* Why is there no evidence that followers of Jesus from the period of his ministry, remembering his own faithfulness to Jewish monotheism, resisted the innovations in Christ devotion initiated by some in the new movement?

Hurtado's response to this argument seems to be twofold.[53] Firstly, he minimizes the impact of Jesus' own life on his followers. Although he thinks Jesus' own life did not provide his followers with cause to worship him, he rejects the suggestion that loyalty to Jesus' ministry would have caused some to argue strongly against worship. Even if "Jesus' ministry lasted as long as four years, that would be a very short time for a new tradition to have developed" such that some would have felt that Jesus' own teaching and behavior was dishonored by the innovation.[54] Whether that is a fair judgment on the historical Jesus and his "movement" will depend on our evaluation of the content and historicity of the Gospel material. The account in Acts of the way that being with Jesus throughout his ministry was a criterion of selection for leadership in the post-Easter community (according to Acts 1:15–26, cf. 10:39–41) would suggest that there was in fact a well-defined, authoritative "tradition," that the earliest believers were not willing to challenge.[55] Be that as it may, Hurtado's judgment on this point exemplifies his tendency to play down Jesus' own role in the formation of NT Christology that we reviewed earlier in the last chapter.

Secondly, he says we actually have little evidence for the earliest years of the new movement so we should not read too much into the lack of reference to controversy in the sources. But the two control studies just reviewed—innovative beliefs about (a) the role of Torah for this form of messianic Judaism and (b) the resurrection—show that when issues were contentious or when beliefs changed dramatically, the NT writers recorded the events and some of the processes that led to the change. The lack of

53. Judging especially by Hurtado's "Response" (15–16) to my review.
54. Ibid., "Origins," 15.
55. See further Bauckham's well-argued case for a stable and authoritative Jesus tradition in the early years, before the writing down of the Gospels (*Eyewitnesses*).

evidence for controversy around the innovation Hurtado imagines remains a puzzling feature of the textual record that tells against his theory.

6: Conclusion: In Search of an Explanation of the Origins of Christ Devotion

Hurtado's explanation of the origins of Christ devotion is unconvincing. Another explanation is now needed. One strength of his theory, however, cannot be ignored. He rightly points out that, according to the primary sources, during Jesus' life there was no Christ devotion. It began only after his death and resurrection. Strikingly, this is also the case with John's Gospel where, even though Jesus is so explicit in making claims for his own divine identity—at one point even implying that he should be worshipped (John 5:22–23) and in another instructing the disciples to pray to him and in his name (14:13–14)—the disciples never set about worshipping him in the way they would after his death.[56] (The brief, spontaneous worship of him by the healed blind man in John 9:35–38 is only a partial exception to the rule.)

What is now needed is an explanation of the origins of Christ devotion—and the beliefs that precipitated it—that accounts for all the evidence for the beliefs, behaviors, and history of the early Christian movement. Such an account would have to explain, for example, the fact that there is no evidence of either conflict within the new movement over this innovation or, even, surprise amongst its earliest adopters. In chapters 5, 6, and 7 we will consider the possibility that there were pre-Christian Jewish traditions that prepared the ground for Christ devotion in a way that helps to explain the lack of opposition to it. Our discussion of those traditions will help to prepare the way for a more comprehensive set of proposals that explains the origins and shape of "Christological monotheism." The early Christians' distinctive religious experience will play a part in that model, but not quite the one Hurtado proposes.

7: Conclusion to Chapters 3 and 4

In this and the last chapter we have reviewed some serious weaknesses in the emerging consensus model of Christological origins. In chapter 3 we considered the ways in which the emerging consensus model does insufficient justice to the shape of NT Christology. We drew attention to some ways in

---

56. This point is forcefully and perceptively made in Hurtado, "Remembering," 196–200.

which it seems to miss the fully incarnational shape of the earliest Christology. Secondly, we saw that it pays insufficient attention to the discrete identities of God the Father and the Lord Jesus Christ, the Son. And thirdly we pointed to inadequacies in its treatment of the Son of Man expression.

In Parts 5 and 6, when we lay out the new paradigm, we will argue that the distinct identities of the Father and the Son and the thoroughly incarnational character of Jesus' biography are conceptually intertwined. I will also argue that when we focus on these two features of the shape of Christology we see more clearly their inextricable relationship to the decisive factor at the historical *origins* of Christology: the life, death, and resurrection of Jesus. In attending fully to these aspects of the shape of Christology it will be possible to provide a fully rounded model of Christological origins that more satisfactorily explains all the primary source data.

We turn in the next three chapters to a fresh consideration of some Jewish (and biblical) material that others have adduced as evidence for an historical precedent for Christ devotion. Then in chapters 8 and 9 (that make up Part 4) we will return to the New Testament to consider again its Christological material in the light of Part 3. Both Parts 3 and 4 will introduce concepts and primary sources that will clear the ground for the full unveiling of the new paradigm in Parts 5 and 6.

EXCURSUS A

Theological Problems Posed by the Emerging Consensus

THE LAST TWO CHAPTERS have been concerned with strictly historical questions: what exactly the earliest Christians believed about Jesus and how they treated him in their devotion (shape), and where their innovative beliefs and practices came from (origins). I turn now to some issues of hermeneutics and Christian theology. For many of us, including the leading voices of the emerging consensus, the quest for Christological origins is a pressing concern because we are practicing, confessing Christians. And for the vast majority of us (whatever our particular tradition) being a Christian means we regularly engage in a variety of expressions of devotion to Jesus Christ. The nature of a (scripturally faithful) Christian life calls for a theological warrant for our behavior. Are we in fact required, as his followers, to "worship" Jesus? If we are, then how should we worship him? What, in other words, really is this "worship" of Jesus that we are called to? Is it possible, given the nature (the shape and the origins) of Christ devotion, to discriminate between appropriate and inappropriate—between a faithful and a sinful or idolatrous—worship of Jesus? How do we now, within the framework of a Christ-centered theology and spirituality, discern what the rabbis called "strange worship" (*avodah zarah*)—forms of worship that are in fact heterodox and idolatrous? How does a healthy, theologically disciplined worship affect our relationships one with another, our ongoing whole-life discipleship, our ecclesiology, political theology, and our missiology?

Also, given the plethora of views about the essentials of Christian theology that form diverse Christian traditions—and recently developed and evolving new theological positions—all vying for the claim to "orthodoxy," what can the findings of the emerging consensus now say definitively about the nature of the Jesus we worship (in relation to God, humanity, the world, history, and so forth)? What, if any, are the implications from the recent advances in our understandings of early Christ devotion for *how* we should Worship

This is not the place to address all these questions and others like them. (What, for example, the origins and shape of the earliest Christology means for an honest-to-Jesus theology for politics, the environment, and business.) For the most part, as my argument progresses, what I have to say about them will be implicit, not explicit. Though towards the end of my unpacking of the new paradigm we will inevitably have to address them directly.

For now, at the end of Part 2, it is appropriate, with these big picture theological concerns in mind, that we pose some questions in particular of Hurtado's model. Hurtado does not claim his work is a theological enterprise, but he is open about his own Christian commitments and, throughout, an implicit purpose of his enterprise seems to be to provide a secure historical basis for an orthodox Christology. And certainly others have made use of his work to that end.[1] So, although he does not ask that his work be judged for its theological implications, it is as well that we consider these here. There are two interrelated theological problems posed by his model that I would like to highlight.

I: Religious Experience and Revelation

To begin with, there is Hurtado's appeal to religious experience as the origin of Christ devotion. An early origin of Christ devotion has the appeal of historical simplicity, but why should Christians follow the example of the earliest Christians in their worship of Jesus if it is simply based on powerful religious experiences? Visions, dreams, and other similar experiences are a notoriously shaky foundation for religious belief. Bousset, Hurtado's hero and nemesis, in his own way anticipated Hurtado's religious experience hypothesis by arguing that the high Christology of the earliest Palestinian community was created by a psychological resolution of the crisis of faith caused by the death of Jesus.[2] If Hurtado is right that religious experiences fostered or created an early high Christology, how can we be sure that in fact those experiences were not a communal delusion that dealt with the cognitive dissonance caused by Jesus' crucifixion? The scenario is not hard to imagine for anyone who has studied the psychology of religion: led by his

---

1. See, for example, the appeal to it in O. Crisp, *Divinity*, 164–65, and see Hurtado's own brief comments on the implications of his work for systematic theology in his *God*, 112–13.

2. Bousset, *Kyrios Christos*, 31–32.

principal followers, after his death, the Jesus movement misinterpreted their own grief-generated religious experiences to mean that Jesus was now to be worshipped as a unique, unprecedented manifestation of the one God?[3]

Christian theology has usually claimed that at its heart there is a revelation not given through powerful religious experiences (dreams, visions, and the like) but through historical events; namely, the Incarnation and resurrection. Hurtado's model eschews a focus on the life of Jesus as the source of revelation as to Christ's identity. As we will see in the chapters that follow, this decision affects his understanding of the shape of the Christology that he discerns within and behind the pages of the NT. And in the rest of this study I hope to show that a model that misses the origins of the earliest Christology in the Incarnation, fails to appreciate the essentially incarnational shape of early Christian theology. That too has important implications for the nature of Christian life and discipleship.

II: The Worship of Jesus and Idolatry

Secondly, in his recent book-length review of the work of the emerging consensus, James Dunn warns that a worship of Jesus that fixes attention on Jesus risks an idolatry of him.[4] Dunn's point is a theological and pastoral one. Hurtado himself says that historically the worship of Jesus by first-century Christians happened despite the fact that it must have incurred the charge of idolatry from non-Christian Jews. If that is the case, should we not agree with Dunn's warning? Why is an "orthodox" Christ devotion not in fact idolatry (as many down the centuries from the other historic biblical faiths and, in recent years, enlightened philosophical critics of Christianity have charged us)?[5] Hurtado does not tell us why Jesus' followers today are immune to the charge of idolatry if we worship Jesus. As far as I can tell, he does not see first-century Christians coming up with any other theological justification than that they believed God had told them to worship Jesus (in their individual and corporate religious experiences) and because they saw, or encountered, a transformed, glorious, and exalted Jesus. So, presumably, on this model, Christians today should also worship Jesus because we give authority to the New Testament description of the life and experiences of its authors and the first Christians; because, in other words, we trust the

---

3. Compare Gerd Theissen's explanation of Christ devotion in his *Theory*, 41–47.
4. Dunn, *Worship*, 147–48.
5. C. K. Rowe has pressed a similar point in criticism of the emerging consensus ("Romans 10:13," 171–72).

earliest followers that they heard "God" right and that the saw or heard the "risen" Jesus right.

Any Christian theology that accords authority to the NT entails a degree of trust in the earliest believers, especially in the testimony and theological reflection on that testimony of the writers and collectors of the New Testament texts. But probably most will be skeptical that, for so weighty a matter as the worship of Jesus, theological warrant can simply be found in the visions and other powerful religious experiences of the post-Easter church. For one thing, it is hard to get past the problem that the New Testament does not itself ask that Jesus' divine identity be accepted on that basis. Hurtado reads between the lines to find an historical explanation for the origins of Christ devotion which is not explicit anywhere in the primary texts. And that surely creates the suspicion that, if Hurtado's historical explanation is to be believed, the NT writers had some reason to suppress the actual origins of Christ devotion. In place of a straightforward trust in what the NT authors themselves claim, Hurtado asks that we trust his own new and additional disclosure of historical realities for which there are no direct and explicit primary source witnesses. (And, I will argue in Part 6, Hurtado's model ignores the straightforward and clear explanation of the origins of Christ devotion that the NT itself gives.)

Neither is it obvious how one might discern the difference between a genuine, healthy, and theologically valid form of worship of Jesus and one that is heterodox, dysfunctional, or even "idolatrous." As far as I can tell, this is not a question that has thus far concerned Hurtado. It is, of course, a question that has dominated theological debate down through church history. *The idolatry question is a pressing one for the emerging consensus because, at least on Hurtado's model, the behavior of the earliest Christians has the structural hallmarks of an idolatrous worship of Jesus.* This is not an issue that, as far I am aware, anyone else has raised and it is only evident once we reflect a little on the structure of idolatry and the biblical critique of it.

To the discerning eye of the biblical writers, the idol maker and worshippers of idols make or treat something as divine that is not. The idol is feared as an object that is believed to have a power that it does not really have (Jer 10:5; Bar 6:4-5, 16, 29, 69), to be able to reveal and teach even though it is dead (Jer 10:8). Idols are believed to be living beings that reveal higher, divine truths; to their priests and their devotees. Sometimes, that "revelation" was believed to take place through the routinized rituals of mantic divination in the presence of the idol (through haruspicy, lecanomancy, and dream incubation, for example). At other times, revelation was sought through ecstatic, altered states of consciousness, and prophecy (see Wis 14:28; the longer text at *Jos. Asen.* 12:9; Athenagoras, *Leg.* 27:1, cf. Wis

14:23; Bar 6:32). The reality of the religious experiences surrounding the worship of idols meant that for first-century Jews it was not possible altogether to deny them a spiritual reality. For Paul, for example, idols are not utterly dead and lifeless, they can be inhabited by demons (1 Cor 10:20). They have power and life insofar as it is given to them by their worshippers and by those who fear them (even if those who fear them do not worship them). But for the biblical authors and for the Jewish tradition anything that an idol might be believed to reveal is a lie (Wis 14:28; Bar 6:47); it cannot truly teach (Jer 10:8; Hab 2:19).

In the biblical and postbiblical tradition there is a double-edged critique of idolatry. On the one hand, idolatry entails an intellectual act of "stupidity and ignorance" (*Apoc. Abr.* 6:3, cf. Rom 1:21-23): a failure to recognize that God is the one who causes everything to be and that the idol is really nothing at all. On the other hand, idolatry entails a "putting on" (Wis 14:21) to an object a divine identity that does not belong to that object. The idols are what the artisans wish them to be (Bar 6:45). They are made "with the stamp of the artisan and the imagination of a man" (Acts 17:29); the "inventive work" of human creativity (Wis 15:4), made to serve human needs and desires. In the modern period, with an eye to the critique of religion in Feuerbach, Nietzsche, and Freud, this second aspect of the biblical analysis of idolatry has come to be known as a "projection" through which ideas, hopes, and fears are placed onto the object, even though they do not inherently belong to it.[6] The idol of the goddess Ishtar is accorded military power and forces that are believed to guarantee fertility. But in reality "she" is a dead lump of stone and precious metals.

Some of us have grown in our understanding of the dynamics of "projection" through the insights of modern psychological and sociological research that have shed new light on the ways human beings are prone to project both positive and negative values, feelings, and expectations onto other objects and people. And we have become sensitized to the dangers of such projection in the religious sphere, even in the church context where charismatic individuals or traditionally defined authority figures (the "clergy," "elders," "the pastor," "the apostle," or "evangelist") easily attract the powerful forces of idolatrous projection that can lead to dysfunctional and abusive relationships.

How do we know that the early Christian exaltation of Jesus and worship of him was not just another case of this kind of projection; a projection fully endorsed by a consciously constructed religious system of worshipful

---

6. For idolatry as projection see Halbertal and Margalit, *Idolatry*, 2-3, 115, 128-30, 238.

practices? Jesus is powerful—even to be feared as the end-time judge—and as the "sinless one" he is believed to be free of the corruptions that afflict ordinary human beings. Why is this not a classic and obvious case of idealizing projection in which his followers empty themselves of their own significance and value as they ascribe their greatest ideals to their former master? His devotees believe that he can appear and speak to them, even in dreams and visions, just as idols were believed to speak to their priests and pilgrims. The priestess of the oracle at Delphi entered a trance possessed by the god Apollo and prophesied for pilgrims from far and wide. Political decisions were made on her guidance. Why is the process of religious decision making in the earliest Christianity that Hurtado imagines no different?

This question becomes pressing if we follow Hurtado's account of Christological origins since that too is structurally not unlike the way idols are treated in ancient paganism. Hurtado's account of things inevitably raises the possibility that the earliest Christians simply projected onto the man Jesus (albeit in his postresurrection "exalted and glorified" state) a set of "divine" attributes (creative and salvific power, divine glory, life, wisdom, sinlessness, universal authority, and so forth) that did not in reality belong to him? According to Hurtado, the historical Jesus did not set himself forth as one possessing these attributes. So we are left with the unavoidable suspicion that the earliest disciples' worship of the exalted Christ in fact came about because they projected onto Jesus their own transcendental ideals after his death. How, in effect, is Christ devotion any different to the worship of the Roman emperor (that Jews and Christians both judged idolatrous) or the not explicitly religious modern idealization of A-list celebrities, sports stars, and political dictators? Hurtado might counter that the Christians worshipped Jesus because they believed "God instructed them to do so" in their visions. That would make the religious experience of the first Christians *the* historical event that carries the weight of two thousand years of Christian orthodoxy. What warrant is there for placing the weight of two thousand years of Christian life and practice on such a subjective experience (albeit a subjective *group* experience)? Israel's Mesopotamian neighbors also believed that the making and worship of idols was commanded by their gods.[7] How can we be sure that Bousset was not right to argue that the exaltation of Jesus was partly the result of visions occurring in the context of the psychological dissonance between their "most ardent hopes" and "the unexpected defeat and failure of their hero"?[8] By singing songs to him

---

7. See, for example, lines 2, 14–16, 24–27 of the Assyrian text describing the making or renewal of the idols in Dick, *Born in Heaven*, 64–66.

8. Bousset, *Kyrios Christos*, 50–51.

that recounted his life, by telling, writing down, and creatively adding new stories to his memory, or rewriting old ones, and by confessing their belief that he belonged within the divine identity, the earliest Christians attempted to overcome their grief at his loss: to make the absent reality present once again (in a way that is typical of idolatry—see Exod 32 and Wis 14:17).

Idolatry is essentially a matter of claims for an identity that are not intrinsic to an entity or person; a transcendent presence that is in fact absent. A lie. (Lies that are adopted in the deluded conviction that the divine reality that is worshipped can act for the worshipping individuals and communities.) Idolatry, for the biblical authors, is partly then discerned by a consideration of the origins of the entity that is worshipped. The discernment of idolatry is a kind of science; a ruthless commitment to objectivity. "Look, it is made from wood from a felled tree; from wood that is used to make a fire. The human hands that made it are superior in the chain of causality to the thing itself. Both, in fact, are made by the Creator (the ultimate cause of all reality). It has no breath, it is dead, despite the worshippers' claims that it has actually come to life and that the god has been born in it" (see e.g., Jer 10:3-15; Isa 44:9-22; *Apoc. Abr.* 1-7).[9]

The emerging consensus view of Christological origins is appealing because it offers a far more historically simple and straightforward account of how and why the worship of Jesus began. Compared to the complex, densely footnoted and often inconclusive arguments of older publications on Christology, Hurtado's *Lord Jesus Christ* is a much-needed breath of fresh air. For all the reasons I laid out in chapters 1 and 2, there is now, in my view, no going back to some of the old complexities. For example, I judge that the arguments for a very early date for the birth of Christ devotion are unassailable. They are also, for the historian, attractive by virtue of their simplicity: it is much better to trust the New Testament texts' own witness to an early, taken-for-granted "Christological monotheism" if there are good reasons for doing so, than to spill unnecessary ink on complex theories of development. Others will also, no doubt, find the arguments for a very early high Christology *theologically* attractive. I agree they are theologically attractive insofar as they help us live with intellectual integrity within a realm that gives a basic and all-encompassing assent to the authority of Scripture: "look, the New Testament texts' claim for an early worship of Jesus *is* historically plausible." However, on the issue of idolatry and the worship of Jesus, Hurtado's arguments are not so helpful. For all the reasons laid out in this excursus, if we are to satisfactorily answer the question "Is Christ devotion

---

9. For the prophetic critique of idolatry against its ancient Near Eastern background see now the essays in Dick, *Born in Heaven*, esp. 1-53 and my discussion of Gen 1:26-27 in Part 5.

idolatrous?" it really does not matter whether the phenomenon Hurtado has described is late or early, or, for that matter, whether it was universal or just adopted by one wing of the new movement. The early appearance of Christ devotion *arising from powerful religious experiences* could be nothing more than a case of a communal delusion.

Bauckham and other leading voices in the emerging consensus have not yet offered us a carefully worked out explanation of the origins of "Christological monotheism" as has Hurtado. Bauckham is very much interested in Christian theology and the role of the New Testament as authoritative Scripture for Christian practice and belief. So he and all theologically committed voices in the emerging consensus now surely need to explain what theological or philosophical warrant there is for believing that the historical origin of "Christological monotheism" does not, in the end, rest on our accepting the subjective and potentially unreliable and self-serving testimony of a group of Jewish visionaries? How can we be sure that, if we ourselves practice some kind of "Christ devotion," we are not also unavoidably colluding in a first-century idolatrous deification of the historical Jesus. It may be that we will conclude that there is a worship of the Lord Jesus Christ that is a faithful recognition of who he was and is: that once we assent to the framework of a biblical understanding of the reality of "God" (and specifically therefore of *Yhwh* God) we are bound now to worship Christ as a fitting and proper expression of our worship of the God first revealed to Israel and through the Old Testament (or Hebrew Bible). In that case are we not also bound, through a ruthlessly honest, submissive, study of the New Testament, and listening for the voice of God's Spirit, to try to discern the difference between a healthy worship of Christ and an unhealthily idolatrous one?

PART 3

WE SAW IN CHAPTERS 3 and 4 that the emerging consensus is not yet able to answer some critical questions in the historical study of Christological origins. In particular, it has not yet offered a satisfactory explanation of the origins of Christ devotion and "Christological monotheism." Hurtado's appeal to the role of powerful religious experiences in bringing about a decisive shift from a pre-Christian monotheism to a "binitarian" or "dyadic" monotheism that included the worship of Jesus does not, on several counts, fit the historical evidence. Bauckham has not yet addressed the historical origins question in a comprehensive way and aspects of his own model—that he has begun to unpack—are problematic.

Bauckham and Hurtado agree that Christ devotion and the theology it presumes is without real precedent in pre-Christian Judaism or the Greco-Roman world: there is radical *discontinuity* between Jewish monotheism before Christianity and the "*Christological* monotheism" we encounter in the NT. This view is distinctive of their work, and others in the last half-century have argued for greater *continuity* between pre-Christian Judaism and "Christological monotheism." There are quite a few specialists who share the emerging consensus view that the "high" Christology of the NT is essentially Jewish, but they have argued that a treatment of Jesus in exalted, transcendent, or even "divine" terms can be explained in large part by the presence within pre-Christian Judaism of existing categories and expectations. Hardly anyone has argued his followers simply slotted Jesus into a pre-Christian package. But individual texts and themes in NT Christology have been explained through recourse to extrabiblical, late Second Temple material. In particular, over the last thirty years a number of texts have been cited as evidence that Jews were willing, or that they expected, to worship divinely sanctioned figures alongside God himself.

In chapters 5, 6, and 7 we take three case studies for the *continuity* perspective; three textual traditions or themes that have been put forward as evidence to suggest that in some ways the treatment of Jesus as a divine figure, and specifically the *worship* of him, had historical precedent in older Jewish beliefs and practices. A comprehensive consideration of the *continuity* case could range more widely since there is other material that some of us still believe is more relevant to Christological origins than the leading voices in the emerging consensus allow. However, my purpose in Part 3 is simply to consider case studies that will help prepare the ground for a more comprehensive set of proposals (which will accommodate all the possible evidence for continuity, not just the three primary test cases considered here).[1]

The outcome of these three case studies will be two-sided. On the one side, we will find plenty of evidence to challenge the *discontinuity* perspective. With the *Similitudes of Enoch* and related texts (chapter 5) we argue that there *was* a lively interest in a messiah who manifests, or shares in, the divine identity. Specifically, in some quarters there were messianic expectations surrounding a preexistent and "divine" *Son of Man* figure that is of the utmost importance for the study of the Gospels. Similarly, a story in which Adam is worshipped by the angels (examined in chapter 7) strongly suggests that in their understanding of Jewish monotheism Hurtado and Bauckham have missed some ways in which the worship of the man Jesus could have been seen as the fulfillment of a distinctive, biblically grounded, theological anthropology. In chapter 6 we find firm grounds for accepting the central thrust of William Horbury's argument that the worship of Jesus was anticipated by a Jewish accommodation of aspects of the Greek

---

1. In the 1990s there was a flurry of studies examining the possibility that angelic or "angelomorphic" traditions contributed to Christological origins. My own doctoral dissertation (published as Fletcher-Louis, *Luke-Acts: Angels, Christology and Soteriology*, 1997) argued that in places Luke-Acts articulates a Christology in dialogue with angelic and angelomorphic categories. See also the important studies by Loren T. Stuckenbruck, *Angel Veneration* (1995), and "'Angels' and 'God'" (2004); Charles A. Gieschen, *Angelomorphic Christology* (1998); Darrell D. Hannah, *Michael and Christ* (1999). In later chapters I will occasionally suggest that angelic traditions helped shape the earliest beliefs about Jesus (and indeed Jesus' own language of himself). However, when we consider all the sources and evidence, angelic categories are not nearly as historically important as one might judge from my *Luke-Acts*. Where they do figure prominently, they are a subsidiary and component part of larger, more widespread categories. (For an important critique of the angel Christology approach, see now Bauckham, "Devotion to Jesus Christ," 182-85.)

and Roman veneration of divine rulers. The positive findings of each of these three case studies will be taken up in Part 4 (Volume 2) when we return to the New Testament to consider their relevance for the Christology of Phil 2:6–11. They will then reappear in our presentation of the new paradigm in Part 5.

On the other side, however, one outcome of Part 3 will be to show that none of the material examined in these three case studies provides a straightforward line from pre-Christian Jewish practices and theology to Christ devotion and "Christological monotheism." Above all, the way Jesus is *included* in the divine identity finds no precise parallel in the pre-Christian Jewish traditions surrounding figures that are uniquely set apart to *manifest*, or *share in*, the divine identity.

The traditions examined in the next three chapters raise questions of their own: how could Jews write and cherish texts that apparently ascribe a "divine" identity to a figure such as Adam, a messianic "Son of Man," or even to individuals such as Daniel (Dan 2:46), given the shape of biblical theology? Our study of the Worship of Adam Story will offer a preliminary answer to that question. And we make some suggestions about the relationship between God as Creator and the rest of reality that speaks to the issue in a separate excursus (Excursus B) at the end of Part 3. However, one outcome of these case studies will be the need for a fuller investigation of the relationship between traditions that have been inadequately treated by Bauckham and Hurtado and Israel's Scriptures. Equally, although we will make some suggestions about the social setting of each of the traditions considered in the next three chapters, greater confidence and clarity about their life setting—especially their place in relation to mainstream Temple and Torah piety and parties—would help us to better assess their likely significance for Christological origins.

The new paradigm will offer a set of proposals and fresh evidence for the view that the Jewish material examined in chapters 5, 6, and 7 is by no means "heterodox." The material will be gathered up within, and called upon to speak for, a comprehensive vision of the route from Old Testament theology to the "Christological monotheism" that we find in the New Testament. But before we get to the new paradigm, in Volume 2 we will take the findings of Part 3 and apply them to one key New Testament passage: Phil 2:6–11. That close-up exegetical study will illustrate the importance of the *continuity* perspective for a proper understanding of the precise shape of "Christological monotheism." Philippians 2:6–11, and the use Paul makes of it in his letter to the Philippian Christians, makes best sense against a background that includes the kind of material covered in Part 3. That case study will also confirm the impression gained in Part 3 that the earliest

Christology cannot be explained as a simple outgrowth of pre-Christian Jewish traditions. Reading Phil 2:6–11 with the material of chapters 5, 6, and 7 fresh in our minds will deepen the historical problem that is the quest for Christological *origins*.

CHAPTER 5

The *Similitudes of Enoch* and a Jewish "Divine" Messiah

THE TEXTS THAT PUT Jesus squarely within the divine identity call him the "Christ" (1 Cor 8:6; Phil 2:5, 11; Col 1:15). Many in the twentieth century have thought that by the time we get to Paul and his letters this word is little more than a proper name. However, N. T. Wright and others have argued that for Paul there remained a strong sense that Jesus was Israel's *messiah* and so "Christ" has titular force.[1] Certainly, in the Gospel tradition the word "Christ" is simply a Greek translation of a Hebrew or Aramaic "messiah" (e.g., Matt 1:1, 17; Mark 8:29; 14:61; Luke 2:26). Even when the word "Christ" is not present, other expressions, such as "son (of God)," likely include reference to biblical language for the (royal) messiah (e.g., Col 1:13; Heb 1:1). The whole argument of Hebrews—that Jesus is priest, not just king (after the order of Melchizedek)—is predicated on the assumption that Jesus' *royal* messianic identity was well-known and not at issue (see esp. Heb 7:14). And in Revelation Jesus is the "lion of the tribe of Judah, the root of David" (5:5). So there are, at the outset, solid grounds for thinking that so-called "*Christ*ological monotheism" and "*Christ* devotion" should be explained against the background of Jewish expectations for a coming messiah.

However, there is a well-established view in NT scholarship today that, in the words of Richard Hays, "nowhere in pre-Christian sources is there any suggestion that the messiah was expected to be a supernatural or divine figure."[2] If that is the case, then the identification of Jesus with Israel's messiah

---

1. Wright, *Climax*, esp. 18–55; "Romans," 416–19; *Resurrection*, 333–38, 394–98, 553–84, *Paul*, 517–36, 734f, 816–24, "Messiahship in Galatians." cf. Hays, *Conversion*, 101–18 and now see esp. Novenson, *Christ*.

2. Hays, *Moral Vision*, 78, cf. N. T. Wright, *People of God*, xiv and his *Paul*, 646: "Judaism did not have a belief in a 'divine messiah' or anything remotely like it."

was a *presupposition* of "Christological monotheism," but it can hardly have been its cause: Jesus' fulfillment of Israel's messianic hope helps us understand an aspect of the *shape* of "Christological monotheism," but could never explain its *origins*. However, this view of Jewish messianism is not shared by all, and two arguments in recent scholarship (from different quarters) have made a strong case for a Jewish, pre-Christian understanding of the messiah that might explain, or *help to* explain, the origins of "Christological monotheism" and Christ devotion. In this and the next chapter we consider those two arguments. Firstly, in this chapter, we consider the possibility that the *Similitudes of Enoch* and related texts evince a pre-Christian Son of Man expectation that prepared the way for a high and fully divine Christology.

1: The Enochic Son of Man, Christology, and the Enoch Seminar

As we have seen, in the Gospels the primary Christological focus is the Son of Man expression or title. In the past, scholarship placed considerable weight on the Son of Man title in the development of Christological origins. In particular, it was thought that in using the expression Son of Man Jesus or the Gospel writers had in mind an existing "Son of Man" tradition and a well-defined set of Jewish expectations that are attested already in Dan 7 and that were also presumed in the Jewish texts that elaborated on the Danielic vision of "one like a son of man" coming on clouds; namely the *Similitudes of Enoch* (*1 En.* 37–71, also sometimes called "the Book of Parables") and *4 Ezra* 13.[3] These texts also know a preexistent Son of Man figure who is at the very least heavenly or "transcendent," if not actually "divine" in some sense.[4] He comes at the eschaton as judge of the wicked and savior of the righteous. In the *Similitudes* he is seated on a throne of divine glory and seems even to receive human worship (46:5; 48:5; 62:6, 9, cf. 92:1). In both texts the Son of Man figure is called "messiah" (*1 En.* 48:10; 53:4; *4 Ezra* 13:25, cf. 12:31–34; 7:28).

Whilst there are differences between those two texts, there are also striking similarities, and most have thought there are multiple points of contact between the *Similitudes* and some Gospel Son of Man sayings,

3. E.g. Bousset, *Kyrios Christos*, 31–32. For the *Similitudes,* the best English translation is the one with critical notes in Nickelsburg and VanderKam, *1 Enoch 2*, but readers might also refer to the translation in D. Olson and M. Workeneh, *Enoch,* and the E. Isaac translation in *OTP* vol. 1, 29–50.

4. I do not attempt a definition of "divine" at this point. In the course of the discussion that follows in this and subsequent chapters, and in the excursus at the end of Part 2, I hope it will, albeit slowly, become clear what exactly I mean by the word.

especially in Matthew. *4 Ezra* is a Jewish text from around 100 AD, however for most of the modern period the *Similitudes* has long been judged pre-Christian. There are other Jewish texts from the end of the first century AD that lack a reference to Dan 7:13 but that nevertheless share an interest in a heavenly redeemer figure with characteristics similar to those of the figure in Dan 7:13, the *Similitudes,* and *4 Ezra* 13 (esp. *Sib. Or.* 5:414-33, cf. *2 Bar.* 29:1—30:5; 39:7; *Apoc. Abr.* 31:1). So it is easy to understand why scholars have in the past posited a pre-Christian belief in a heavenly, transcendent messiah, and categorized diverse texts that await such a figure under the "Son of Man" heading.[5] In turn, this Jewish background has helped explain the origins of a high Christology; with Jesus at some point in the development of the tradition about him (if not even in his own self-consciousness) identified with the Son of Man who comes from preexistence in heaven to earth. The Jesus of the Gospels and of other NT texts is clearly *more than* the Son of Man of the *Similitudes*, not least in his suffering unto death on the cross, but there is much in this Jewish material that anticipates aspects of "Christological monotheism."

So the lack of interest in the Jewish Son of Man texts among those championing the early high Christology emerging consensus is striking. Hurtado engages only briefly with the *Similitudes* and *4 Ezra* (but not with *Sib. Or.* 5:414-33), denying the existence of a clearly defined pre-Christian Son of Man expectation and dismissing the existence of an early Christian heavenly "Son of Man" Christology that could be judged to have played a key role in the origins (and shape) of Christ devotion.[6] He rejects the presence of any "worship" of a clearly defined Son of Man figure in the *Similitudes,* and cites that text to illustrate the *lack* of Jewish precedent for the central position of Jesus Christ's *name—the Lord—*in early Christian devotion.[7] And in a more recent book on the Son of Man, subtitled *The Latest Scholarship on a Puzzling Expression of the Historical Jesus*, of which Hurtado is a joint editor, the *Similitudes'* role is marginal.[8]

---

5. See, e.g., Bousset, *Kyrios Christos*, 35-56.

6. See Hurtado, *Lord Jesus Christ,* 295-98, cf. *One God,* xi, and, most recently, his comments in "Fashions," 307-13, where he strongly, and rightly, criticizes the history of religions schools' identification of a "Son of Man concept" that exemplified a wider oriental Anthropos, or *Urmensch,* myth.

7. Hurtado, *Lord Jesus Christ,* 38-39, 143.

8. Hurtado and Owen, *Son of Man* (2011). Brief discussion of the *Similitudes* appears on pp. 46-47, 84-85. In the penultimate essay D. D. Hannah considers the relationship between the Son of Man in the *Similitudes* and the Christology of the book of Revelation ("Elect Son of Man").

Bauckham has made some important contributions to our understanding of the *Similitudes* (see below), but also seems disinclined to give a prominent role to a pre-Christian Son of Man expectation in his account of Christological origins.[9] Other recent contributors to the quest for Christological origins (such as N. T. Wright, A. Chester, and W. Horbury) are equally shy of these Son of Man texts.[10] Wright stands at the furthest extreme. He confesses his "puzzlement" at the "rambling and convoluted details of 1 *Enoch*," struggles to see a clear reuse of Dan 7 in the *Similitudes* (even though there is now a consensus that Dan 7 informs 1 *En.* 46–47), and completely ignores the *Similitudes* in his most recent discussion of Pauline Christology.[11]

This neglect of the *Similitudes* exemplifies a distinctively British aversion to theories that flourished in German scholarship in the last century.[12] But a quirk of the parochial nature of the modern history of NT scholarship is by no means the only reason for the avoidance. The scholarship leading to the emerging consensus has all happened after the announcement (in 1951) by the official editors of the Dead Sea Scrolls that copies containing *all* parts of 1 *Enoch* (in its original Aramaic) *except* the *Similitudes* are among the documents preserved in the library of the Qumran community.[13] In time, that announcement precipitated the widespread view, that can be seen especially in J. D. G. Dunn's seminal 1980 book on Christology, that probably the *Similitudes* are post-Christian and may even represent a Jewish *response to* late-first-century Christian beliefs about Jesus.[14] With that announcement, and with a careful study of the differences between the various discrete texts that had previously been lumped together, the theory of a pre-Christian Son of Man concept suddenly seemed like the building of castles in the air. Much

9. See his older study, Bauckham, "The Son of Man" (1985), reprinted in his *Jewish World* (2008), 93–102.

10. For Chester's brief comments on the *Similitudes* see *Messiah*, 344–45, 374–75. Horbury offers his own theory to explain the worship of the Son of Man in 1 *Enoch* (see below), but does not engage with the text in any detail.

11. I quote from N. T. Wright, *People of God*, 317, and refer to his *Paul*, 693, where at least a brief mention of 1 *En.* 37–71 surely belongs.

12. Hurtado is an American, but has had a long association with the UK (even prior to his occupancy of a chair at the University of Edinburgh from 1996–2011). Wright, Bauckham, Chester, and Horbury are all, each in their own way, quintessentially English scholars. A British resistance to the Son of Man hypothesis is also evident in the work of J. D. G. Dunn (a Scot) and the late P. M. Casey (an Englishman).

13. On that announcement and the period that followed (up until and beyond publication of the Qumran Enochic texts in 1976), and its effect on scholarship on the *Similitudes*, see G. Boccaccini, "Enoch Seminar," 13–14.

14. See Dunn, *Christology*, 77–82, and continued skepticism about the date of the *Similitudes* in recent books by Hurtado (*Lord Jesus Christ*, 296) and Tilling (*Christology*, 214–15).

was made, also, of the fact that in the Jewish sources there is no Son of Man "title"; at most only a distinct *figure*.

But whilst the emerging consensus scholars (based especially in the UK) have been working towards an argument for an early high Christology, others in Europe and North America have been steadily building the case for a rehabilitation of the *Similitudes* as an important Jewish text that is certainly not a reaction to Christian beliefs about Jesus, but one most likely written before Jesus' ministry. That case has come to its fullest expression in the work of the biannual Enoch Seminar (founded by Gabriele Boccaccini) which devoted its third meeting (in 2005) to the study of the "Parables" (as the Seminar calls *1 En.* 37–71).[15] The overwhelming conclusion of that conference (of forty-three international specialists) was that the *Similitudes* is a pre-Christian Jewish document (with many arguing for a late-first-century BC date).[16] Furthermore, several contributors stressed the importance of the *Similitudes* as testimony to a messianic hope quite unlike the one scholars have long recognized was attached to an earthly Davidic, militaristic savior that many late Second Temple Jews believed would be an agent of national restoration. In the *Similitudes* and several other pre-Christian texts now known from Qumran (e.g., 11QMelch, and 4Q491c) there is what one seminar participant, Helge Kvanvig, labels a "high" messianic eschatology clearly distinct from the messianism of traditional earthly Davidic hope.[17]

So, in his introduction to the conference volume, Boccaccini triumphantly announces that "from their unfortunate exile, the Parables are back!"[18] And although these scholars are not asking for a simple reinstatement of the theory that there was an entirely coherent, well-defined apocalyptic "Son of Man" messianism (as previous generations of scholars believed), their work forces us to look once again at the evidence for a pre-Christian belief in a transcendent or even "divine" messiah anchored especially in Dan 7:13. Two doctoral monographs arguing for the influence of the *Similitudes* on NT Christology—one by James M. Waddell on Pauline Christology (2011) and one by Leslie W. Walck on Matthew's Gospel (2011)—build on the findings of the Enoch Seminar. And contributions since the 2005 meeting of the Seminar have continued to argue for some kind of well-established "Jewish

---

15. The conference papers were published in Boccaccini, *Book of Parables* (2007). The 2013 meeting was also devoted to "Enochic Influences on the Synoptic Gospels."

16. See the report in Boccaccini, "Enoch Seminar," 15, and compare Olson and Workeneh, *Enoch*, 12, and Nickelsburg and VanderKam, *1 Enoch 2*, 58–64.

17. See Kvanvig, "Parables of Enoch," 192, and compare in the same volume J. J. Collins, "A Response," 220, and Koch, "Questions," 228. See also now Nickelsburg and VanderKam, *1 Enoch 2*, 79–80.

18. Boccaccini, "Enoch Seminar," 16.

Son of Man tradition,"[19] that is, something that could be called a "messianic concept" in which there is "an exalted human figure, given a heavenly *locus*, accorded the role of Eschatological Judge and/or Prosecutor, and possessing a redemptive- or salvific-outcome function."[20]

Not all in the household of NT scholarship have joined the feasting to celebrate the return of the prodigal. Many seem either to have not noticed or would rather not acknowledge the *Similitudes*' return.[21] Certainly, they see no reason for feasting. Whether the *Similitudes* is avoided because it is a difficult, sometimes rambling, text surviving in Ethiopic (which most of us cannot read), or because its Son of Man theology threatens the uniqueness and historicity of an "orthodox" NT Christology, is hard to tell.

From the other side—from the Enoch specialists—there has been a little implicit, but no direct, engagement with the work of the emerging consensus. In a recent article, Boccaccini has sketched a reconstruction of Christological origins that echoes the work of Hurtado on the *date* of the earliest NT Christology with the claim that "there never was in Christianity something like a 'low Christology,' centered on the view of Jesus as a human Messiah."[22] However, for Boccaccini, the origin and shape of the earliest Christology is quite unlike that described by Hurtado: from the beginning, Christianity had "its roots in Enochic Judaism" where it found Christological "cohesion in the belief of Jesus as the 'Son of Man,' an exalted heavenly Messiah, the forgiver on earth and the would-be eschatological Judge." Echoing in some ways the older approach of Bousset, Boccaccini thinks the first Christology was not a low Christology, but neither was it a fully *high* Christology, with the *Similitudes* demonstrating that it was possible to worship Jesus without giving him the kind of full divine status that appears only later in the book of John.[23]

For the most part, the Enoch Seminar—which has considerably advanced our understanding of the *Similitudes*—and those who have created the early high Christology "emerging consensus" have worked independently of each other. Boccaccini and his colleagues have offered little engagement with the overwhelming NT evidence for "Christological monotheism." Hurtado and Bauckham and their colleagues have not yet

19. As J. Harold Ellens, "11QMelch," 341, calls it.

20. Ibid., 345–46.

21. In his latest discussion of the (lack of) evidence for a Son of Man concept in pre-Christian Judaism, Hurtado does not engage the work of the Enoch Seminar and the results of its 2005 meeting (Hurtado, "Fashions").

22. Boccaccini, "Jesus the Messiah," 214.

23. Ibid., 214–15. His position is similar to the one laid out in Collins and Collins, *King and Messiah,* and the treatment of Pauline Christology in Waddell, *Messiah.*

responded to the important findings of the Enoch Seminar. With so much achieved by both groups of specialists it is surely time for dialogue. The new consensus that the *Similitudes* is pre-Christian means no historical discussion of Christological origins can now afford to ignore it. On the other hand, it is unlikely (not least in view of all that we have already laid out in this book) that the Enochic tradition explains the church's earliest Christology as neatly as Boccaccini imagines. So, to a more detailed consideration (but not full analysis) of the *Similitudes* and its relationship to "Christological monotheism" we now turn.

The *Similitudes* describes a human—or human-*like*—figure who is twice called "the messiah" (48:10; 53:4), twice the "Righteous One" (38:2; 53:6), more frequently "the Chosen/Elect One" (e.g., 39:6; 40:5) and the "Son of Man" (seventeen times, e.g., 46:1–2, 4; 48:2).[24] With the introduction of the "Son of Man" expression in 46:1–2, it is clear that a reference to Daniel's "one like a son of man" is intended, since chapters 46–47 as a whole interpret Dan 7:9–14.[25]

Throughout, the Chosen One-Son of Man has a highly exalted position in the heavenly realm. He has a premundane preexistence (48:2–3, 6–7, cf. 46:3; 39:4–8; 62:7), is ascribed glory (49:2, cf. 51:3), and is seated on God's own throne of divine glory (45:3; 51:3; 55:4; 61:8; 62:2–3, 5). He acts as an agent of revelation (46:3), as a savior (48:4–6), and as the end-time judge of sinners and fallen angels (55:4), though his own countenance also recalls that of the holy angels (46:1). Several passages are normally taken to mean he is worthy of worship (46:5; 48:5; 62:6, 9).

At the same time there are aspects of his characterization which distinguish him from God and that point to his earthly or human identity. Underlying some of the expressions in the Ethiopic manuscripts that we translate "Son of Man," Helge Kvanvig argues for allusions to Adam: the Enochic Son of Man is a kind of second Adam figure.[26] Mysteriously, in 71:13–17, Enoch, the seventh descendent from Adam (60:8, cf. Gen 5:1–24), is himself identified with the variously named figure of the preceding visions. Scholars are divided on the relationship between chapter 71 and the rest of the text. Some see it as an appendix—bolted on at a later stage of the text's

---

24. For a fuller discussion, especially of the difficulties surrounding the original language behind the different Ethiopic expressions that have traditionally been translated in modern versions with the one expression "Son of Man," see: the various essays in Boccaccini, *Book of Parables*; Waddell, *Messiah*, 48–103; and the commentary of Nickelsburg and VanderKam, *1 Enoch 2*.

25. See esp. VanderKam, "Daniel 7," and Nickelsburg & VanderKam, *1 Enoch 2*, 113–16, 154–69.

26. Kvanvig, "Son of Man," 193–95.

development—that does not reflect the view of the Son of Man figure of the preceding visions.[27] Others have argued that some kind of identification of Enoch and the heavenly, enthroned Son of Man was intended throughout.[28]

Given the nature of some NT "Son of Man" sayings there is much here that might help explain the origins of early Christian beliefs about Jesus. The glorious, transcendent, or, we might say, "divine" aspects of some Son of Man texts have a clear analogy in the *Similitudes*' interpretation of Dan 7:13. Indeed, the paradoxical relationship between Enoch and the Son of Man in the final form of the text (that comes to a climax with the identification of the two in the last chapter—ch. 71) might be a valuable parallel to the paradoxical relationship between Jesus and the Son of Man (who is always spoken of as if he is somebody other than Jesus himself, but with whom Jesus is identified, especially at the trial scene at the climax of the Gospels).[29]

However, a confident recourse to the *Similitudes* to help explain the meaning (or origin) of the NT identification of Jesus as "the Son of Man" has been hampered by the complex literary and conceptual structure to the Jewish text. There are places where there are clear interpolations (though none discernibly Christian in character). The identification of Enoch with the Son of Man-Messiah in the last chapter comes somewhat unexpectedly and is hard to square with the fact that the Son of Man is a figure of premundane preexistence whom Enoch himself sees as another person in his visions. It is likely, but not absolutely certain, that in the Greek or Aramaic (or Hebrew) original there was one consistently used expression behind the several different Ethiopic expressions that modern translations usually render "Son of Man." In any case, in its extant form a definite Son of Man figure (even if not a Son of Man *title*) is in view.[30] Leaving aside these important questions for now, we can still give careful consideration to the possibility that the Enochic Son of Man provides an historical precedent for the inclusion of Jesus in the divine identity.

---

27. E.g., Nickelsburg (in Nickelsburg and VanderKam, *1 Enoch 2*, 330–32).

28. See esp. Kvanvig, "Son of Man"; compare VanderKam, "Righteous One," and see now Fletcher-Louis, "*Similitudes*" for new proposals to support this line of interpretation.

29. On this paradox see Kvanvig, "Son of Man," 213–14.

30. See Waddell, *Messiah*, 76–85; Nickelsburg and VanderKam, *1 Enoch 2*, 113–16.

2: Hurtado: No Precedent for Christ Devotion in the *Similitudes*

Hurtado has claimed that there really is no evidence for a divine Son of Man-Messiah figure in *1 Enoch* and that the obeisance referred to in a few texts does not amount to "worship" of a second figure alongside God.[31] This is an idiosyncratic view and it would be tempting to dismiss it as a rather convenient way of ensuring the unprecedented uniqueness of Christ devotion. However his reasoning raises important questions, the consideration of which helps to clarify what exactly the rest of us mean when we say there is "worship" given to the Enochic Son of Man-Messiah and how that "worship" may or may not anticipate the worship of Jesus.

Hurtado interprets three of the passages describing obeisance to the Son of Man figure (48:5; 62:6, 9) with reference to texts in Isaiah that describe obeisance, *but not worship*, to Israel and to the Servant of the Lord (Isa 45:14; 49:7, 23; 60:14). Secondly, he points out that the obeisance to the Son of Man figure is a future expectation and from this concludes there is no evidence in the *Similitudes* of a pre-Christian community of Jews who were already worshipping a figure alongside God. Thirdly, he has tried to counter the claim that what the Son of Man receives must be *worship* because he is *enthroned* in heaven. Against the apparent logic of that view, he insists that the "obeisance" texts describe the Son of Man sitting on an ordinary throne *on earth*, not in heaven, so genuine worship is not intended.

Each of these points really lacks the force Hurtado gives it. There is, indeed, an Isaianic background to chapter 48, but in other ways the context of 48:5 also goes beyond that background. Instead of being "called" and "remembered" in his mother's womb (Isa 49:1), the Son of Man is "named, chosen," and "hidden" before all creation. So, it is quite appropriate that in this context the "obeisance" be something greater than that given to Israel and the Isaianic servant. Equally, the Son of Man is not simply seated on his *own* throne, a throne of his *own* glory or one like David's. He is seated on God's throne and so has God's own divine glory (45:3; 51:3; 55:4; 61:8; 62:2–3, 5; 69:29, cf. 49:1–2).[32] Other aspects of the text, to which we shall come shortly, show that he is *partially* included in, or that he clearly manifests, the divine identity.

In response to Hurtado's third argument, it is not actually stated that the throne is only on earth. The Son of Man's scope of judgment extends

---

31. See Hurtado, *One God* (2nd ed.), xi, 54, and *Lord Jesus Christ*, 38–39.

32. See the careful study of these portions of the *Similitudes* by Darrell Hannah (Hannah, "Throne").

well beyond the confines of the earthly sphere to include spiritual beings and the heavenly realm (55:4; 61:8, cf. 62:6 and 69:25–29 with 69:16–25). It is the enemies of God's people whose rule is confined (for a time until their punishment) to the earthly sphere (62:9, cf. 46:7; 55:4). In any case, whilst a heavenly location would certainly indicate that obeisance was genuinely worship, it can hardly be the case in the Jewish context that obeisance on earth cannot be an expression of worship since Israel regularly offers worshipful prostration to the living God *on earth* (e.g., Exod 4:31; 24:1; 34:8; 2 Chr 29:28–30). In any case, the texts speak of far more than mere *proskynesis* to the Son of Man: there is praise, blessing, glorifying, and exalting (46:5; 62:6). And as James Waddell has now pointed out, in every respect the language used for what is done to the Son of Man in these texts is language that in other portions of the *Similitudes* is used for worship of God himself (the one whom the *Similitudes* calls "the Lord of Spirits").[33]

Because the *Similitudes* almost certainly come from the Roman period (see below) such language also has to be understood in relation to the conventions of the Hellenistic Ruler Cult and emperor worship where the ruler has a divine status (see chapter 6). In that context, the language of supplication and petition (62:9) would be seen as part and parcel of a worship befitting a divine ruler.[34]

Thirdly, whilst it is true that the worship of the Enochic Son of Man is a future, not a present reality, that is nevertheless of inestimable significance for the understanding of both the *origins* and the *shape* of "Christological monotheism." On the matter of origins, it offers an obvious and straightforward explanation of Christ devotion: the earliest Jewish believers worshipped Jesus because they believed he truly was, as he had claimed to be, the (preexistent) Son of Man they had been waiting for.

I: Jesus the Son of Man and the Origins of Christ Devotion

Returning briefly to the New Testament we find evidence to suggest that the *Similitudes* provides a golden key to unlock the puzzle that is the origins of Christ devotion. Three texts suggest that the earliest acts of cultic devotion to Christ were based on the conviction that he was the Son of Man. That in turn suggests that the earliest Christians believed Jesus was the one the *Similitudes* predicted and that they worshipped him just as that Jewish text said they should.

33. Waddell, *Messiah*, 92, 96–100.
34. Though ultimately the worship of the Son of Man is presented as of a different, superior, kind to that of human pagan rulers (see Fletcher-Louis, "*Similitudes*").

In John 9, the one clear case of a worship of Jesus in John's Gospel is based on a Son of Man Christology. The blind man whom Jesus has healed offers Jesus *proskynesis* because he comes to the conclusion that Jesus is the Son of Man (9:35-38).

Secondly, Acts 7 describes an event from the early years of the Christian community living in Jerusalem. Stephen is accused before the Sanhedrin, found guilty, and stoned to death. He has a vision in which he sees Jesus as the Son of Man standing at God's right hand (v. 56). He then prays to Jesus that he might receive his spirit and intercedes on behalf of his assailants that Jesus might forgive their sins. And in so praying he exemplifies the multifaceted phenomenon that is early Christian devotion to Christ. This is not the first such act in the history of the church that Luke describes, but it is striking that a Son of Man Christology is central to the story.

Thirdly, in Matthew 28 we are told that the disciples worship Jesus immediately after his resurrection. The women do that when they meet Jesus (28:9) and so do the eleven when they join him on a mountain in the Galilee (28:16-20). That worship of him is endorsed with Jesus' command to go out into the world and baptise believers in the "name of the Father, of the Son, and of the Holy Spirit." Here, says Matthew, was the beginning of the Christ devotion that later Christians took for granted. And although there is no explicit reference to the Son of Man title, it is generally reckoned that the closing scene alludes to and fulfills the one in Dan 7:13-14. Numerous points of connection have been made.[35] We only need note the most obvious. The mountain top scene evokes the exalted, heavenly position of the one like a son of man in Dan 7:13-14. There is a clear linguistic echo of Dan 7:14—"*kai edothē autō exousia*" ("and authority was given to him") in Matt 28:18—*edothē moi pasa exousia* ("and all authority has been given to me"). (A similar linguistic echo of Dan 7:14 is present in the Son of Man saying in John 5:27). The Greek of Dan 7:14 twice uses the word "all"—"*all the nations* (*panta ta ethnē*) of the earth . . . and *all* glory ") to describe the comprehensive scope of the authority and glory given to the "one like a son of man." In the same way, in Matt 28:18-19 Jesus has "*all* authority" over "*all the nations*" (*panta ta ethnē*) and he will remain with the disciples for "all" days (v. 20).

So, given these echoes of Dan 7:13-14, when it says in Matt 28:17 that the disciples worship Jesus, as historians we are bound to think of the worship rendered to the Son of Man figure in the *Similitudes*. And we are bound to wonder whether Matthew faithfully preserves the memory that it was *as the Danielic Son of Man* that Jesus was first worshipped because he was

---

35. For a detailed comparison, see Davies and Allison, *Matthew*, vol. 3, 682-83, 688.

deemed the one who fulfilled the kind of eschatological expectation laid out in the *Similitudes of Enoch*.

3: Bauckham: The *Similitudes* as a Partial Precedent for "Christological Monotheism"

Neither Hurtado nor Bauckham discusses the possibility that the *Similitudes* connects so directly to texts wherein worship is given to Jesus as the Son of Man. However, Bauckham has offered a fuller and more nuanced assessment of the position of the Enochic Son of Man in relation to the one God, recognizing in particular indications that in the *Similitudes* the divine identity is extended to include this separate figure.[36] At the same time, he has also offered an account of the relationship between the Son of Man in the *Similitudes* and Christ in the NT that respects subtle but important differences without rushing to adopt a position only of black and white contrast.

To begin with, scriptural *Yhwh* texts are applied to the Enochic Son of Man in a way that parallels or anticipates what early Christians did to Jesus.[37] In *1 En.* 52:6 and 53:7 theophany texts that describe mountains melting like wax before *Yhwh* (Mic 1:3–4; Pss 97:4–5; 68:2 and see also *1 En.* 1:6) are applied to the "Chosen One." Similarly, the statement in *1 En.* 46:4 that the Son of Man will "crush the teeth of the sinners" ascribes to him language for God in Pss 3:7 and 58:6.[38] And to those three texts we can add *1 En.* 61:5 where the biblical Day of *Yhwh* seems to become the "Day *of the Chosen One*."[39] The Son of Man is a divine warrior appearing as *Yhwh* himself on the great day of his (end-time) theophany. Indeed, in the later apocalypse *4 Ezra*, Daniel's Son of Man figure similarly appears as the divine warrior where it is also said that he causes the trembling and the melting of those who hear his voice "as wax melts when it feels the fire" (13:3–4).[40] In

---

36. See Bauckham, *God of Israel*, 170–71, cf. Nickelsburg and VanderKam, *1 Enoch 2*, 172, 265. Although he tells me that he has now changed his mind on the *Similitudes*, Bauckham's publications thus far have been instructive and I interact with them here at face value.

37. See Bauckham, *God of Israel*, 228–32 (who does not think this is any kind of historical precedent for what Christians did with Jesus), following up Horbury, *Jewish Messianism*, 103 (who does see precedent for NT Christology).

38. The role of *Yhwh* in supporting the righteous lest they fall may be evoked in the description of the Son of Man in *1 En.* 48:4.

39. See further the observations of Burkett, *Son of Man Debate*, 100, on Isa 24:21–23 behind *1 En.* 55:3–4.

40. Burkett, *Son of Man Debate*, 105, rightly compares the characterization of the man figure in *4 Ezra* with *Yhwh* in Ps 104:32; Hab 3:6; Isa 66:15–21.

5. THE *SIMILITUDES OF ENOCH* & A JEWISH "DIVINE" MESSIAH

view of this material, Bauckham accepts that the *Similitudes* and *4 Ezra* do tend in the direction of more than just a functional overlap between God and messiah towards an identification of God and his agent.

But he also points out that "they stop far short of the kind of identification of God and Jesus Christ that we find in Paul and other early Christian literature."[41] In Paul, there are numerous divine prerogatives ascribed to Jesus Christ, including creative agency, salvation of the world, and cosmic rule. In the *Similitudes*, the Son of Man's role is limited to that of judgment. Bauckham also insists—quite rightly I think, and against most recent scholarship—that in the *Similitudes* there is actually no recourse to the description of a messianic Lord seated next to *Yhwh* himself in Ps 110:1 to give scriptural justification for the exalted position of the Son of Man-Messiah. Although many have reached for that biblical text to explain the remarkable enthronement of the Enochic Son of Man on God's own throne of glory, Bauckham points out that there really is no linguistic connection to that particular psalm.[42]

The contrast between what is said of the Enochic Son of Man and New Testament Christology has further been strengthened by the recent study of C. Tilling.[43] Tilling accepts that, up to a point, the relationship between the Son of Man-Messiah and the righteous anticipates the relationship between Christ and the world in Paul. For example, the righteous hope in, and depend on, the Enochic Son of Man (*1 En.* 48:4-6). Denial of the Lord of Spirits is joined to denial of the Anointed One (48:10), and the spirit of those who have fallen asleep indwells the Son of Man (49:3). There is even a passage that suggests prayer to Enoch (65:3).

Nevertheless, Tilling highlights ways in which the devotion to Christ in the NT is *personal* and *all encompassing*, with the full range of language for Israel's and the world's relationship to God (not just the language of cultic rituals) now applied to believers' and the world's relationship to Christ. By contrast, within the *Similitudes*, the Son of Man-Messiah does not fully participate in the relationship between creation and God (who is called "The Lord of Spirits"). Tilling points out that in some ways it is the relationship between the Lord of Spirits and the rest of reality in the *Similitudes* that is a better comparison for the relation between Christ and the rest of reality in Paul.[44]

---

41. Bauckham, *God of Israel*, 231, cf. 16.

42. Ibid., 170-71. For a recent presentation of the case for the use of Ps 110, see Kvanvig, "Son of Man," 189-93.

43. Tilling, *Christology*, 206-30.

44. See ibid., 212-28. As with so much of the work of Hurtado and Bauckham, Tilling seems overly concerned to ensure that the *Similitudes* do not provide any kind

In one place, Bauckham helpfully summarizes the contrast between the *Similitudes* and the NT by saying there is only "functional overlap" between God and the Enochic Son of Man, as opposed to a "personal identification" between God and Christ in Pauline literature.[45] Certainly, because the Enochic Son of Man has no biography or earthly career it cannot be said that he is a distinct "person" in the way that is true of the Son's relationship to the Father in "Christological monotheism."[46] However, it is a mistake to limit the relationship between the Enochic Son of Man and the Lord of Spirits solely to shared *functions*. Bauckham has also stressed the importance of the fact that the Son of Man figure is seated on God's own throne (of glory) and that he is said to be the one who "rules over all" (62:6).[47] This means, for Bauckham, that the Enochic Son of Man is unique in Second Temple Jewish literature: "Because he participates in a key aspect of the unique identity of God—rule over all things—he receives the recognition which, in Second Temple Judaism, is restricted to that unique identity: worship."[48] "His inclusion in the divine identity is *partial* . . . ."[49]

Indeed, to these points there should be added several others which reinforce the conclusion that in this case a shared divine function means also (a limited) shared divine identity. Many modern commentators have discerned allusion to Ezek 1:26–28 in the passage where the Son of Man figure is first introduced (ch. 46).[50] Ezekiel 1:26–28 is the climax of the famous throne vision in which prophet in Babylon sees God with something like a human form above the four living creatures; a form that is called "the likeness of the glory (*kavod*) of *Yhwh*" (1:28). For many of us, when *1 En.* 46:1 says that with the "one who had a head of days" there was another

---

of precedent for Pauline Christology and he slightly tips the balance towards contrast between the two instead of similarity and continuity.

45. Bauckham, *God of Israel*, 232. See also Hurtado, *One God*, 53–54: the Son of Man figure in *1 En.* 46 does not rival God or become a second god, rather "he is seen as performing the eschatological functions associated with God and is therefore God's chief agent, linked with God's work to a specially intense degree."

46. So D. Boyarin's claim that the Enochic Son of Man is a "divine person," and "a Son alongside the Ancient of Days, whom we might begin to think of as the Father" (*Jewish Gospels*, 77) is misguided. For further observations on the Enochic Son of Man's lack of personality, see Fletcher-Louis, "*Similitudes*," 77–78.

47. Bauckham, *God of Israel*, 176, says this is a universal rule *on earth*. But that is not explicit in the text and other passages in the *Similitudes* envisage the Son of Man figure's authority extending well beyond the earthly realm (55:4; 69:28; 61:8–9).

48. Ibid., 171.

49. Ibid., 16 (italics added).

50. See, e.g., Black, *Enoch*, 206; VanderKam, "Daniel 7," 197; Kvanvig, "Throne"; and Waddell, *Messiah*, 61, 80–85.

"whose face was like the appearance of a man" (that is, the Son of Man) this is an obvious allusion to Ezek 1:26—where Ezekiel sees this glorious likeness of *Yhwh* as "a likeness as the appearance of a man" on God's throne. An allusion to the Ezekiel text at that juncture is fitting given that the Son of Man-Chosen One later appears on "the throne of (divine) glory"; a phrase that must have in mind God's throne as it is described, for example, in the vision in Ezek 1.[51]

Secondly, it is possible that, as we noted in chapter 4, in the original text of *1 En.* 48:1-7 the secret name of God (*Yhwh*) becomes the possession of the Son of Man. There is not complete identification of the Son of Man with God's name, but several of us have pointed to the close association of the two.[52] In *1 En.* 46:4-6 and 48:5 the two are treated in parallel, as if they are one and the same, and it is possible that behind the extant Ethiopic text of 48:2 the original said that the name with which the Son of Man is named is God's own name. The close association is important because in 69:13-25 the name is part of an oath with which the world was created.[53] Indeed, immediately after that passage there is an account of creation rejoicing at the revelation of the Son of Man's name (69:26), once again suggesting a close association. So, although the Son of Man is not *personally* identified as an agent of creation, he is closely identified with one that is. Indeed, a similar association appears in the later, but related, depiction of the enthroned Enoch in *3 En.* 12-13 (see below).

Whether the *Similitudes* is really the exception that proves Bauckham's rule that Jewish theology did not permit a sharing of the divine identity with others is a matter to which we shall return. His own discussion of the theophany material in *4 Ezra* perhaps qualifies that claim (even though the Son of Man figure in *4 Ezra* does *not* share God's throne and is *not* worshipped). For reasons that will become clear when I lay out the new paradigm—and in view of our discussion above—it is best to say that the Son of Man-Messiah in the *Similitudes* "expresses," and "shares in" or "participates in" the divine identity. It is unwise to speak of an "inclusion" in the divine identity (even a "*partial*" inclusion). In the NT there is a *full inclusion* of Jesus in the divine identity (as preexistent, premundane co-*Creator*, ruler over all, and end-time judge), whereas in the *Similitudes* the messiah figure *expresses* and *partially shares in* the divine identity (as one who has

---

51. It will also, of course, have in mind the vision of God's throne in Isa 6, a passage that has contributed to the creation of a partial throne theophany in *1 En.* 39:12-14.

52. Fletcher-Louis, "Divine Humanity," 114; Barker, *Great High Priest*, 65-66, 82; Gieschen, "The Name"; and Waddell, *Messiah*, 62, 72-75, 101-2, 168-69.

53. For the name of God as an effective agent of creation see also *Jub.* 36:7; *Pr. Man.* 1:2-4; *L.A.B.* 60:2, cf. Philo *Migration* 103.

premundane preexistence, occupancy of God's own throne, rulership over all with responsibility for end-time judgment, and identification with God's own divine glory).

I: Jesus the Son of Man and the Origins of "Christological Monotheism"

Bauckham has so far not given us his view of the dating of the *Similitudes*, however, judging by other comments, he does not think it played any role in the origins of "Christological monotheism." In his most recent article on the topic he says that the "lavish application to Jesus of texts about YHWH from the Hebrew Bible is another completely unprecedented feature of earliest Christianity."[54]

However, in view of the work of the Enoch seminar we are bound now to consider the possibility that the messianism of the *Similitudes of Enoch* prepared the way for the worship of Jesus and his full inclusion in the divine identity. In chapter 3 we noted a number of ways in which the Gospels' Son of Man texts convey the sense that Jesus is uniquely endowed with divine attributes (with divine glory, clouds as a means of transport, a heavenly throne, a position over the angels, and authority to exercise divine judgment, for example). And despite Bauckham's recent comments (above), it obviously does present a rather clear precedent for the application to Jesus of texts about *Yhwh* in the Hebrew Bible. And in the light of the ways that the *Similitudes* (and *4 Ezra*) transfer the language and image of *Yhwh*'s theophany specifically to *the son of man figure of Dan 7:13–14*, we are bound now to consider more carefully the portrayal of the Son of Man in the Gospels.

As we have seen, Hurtado, and more especially Bauckham, have demonstrated that at the heart of Pauline (and other witnesses to the earliest) Christology there is an identification of Jesus Christ with the *Yhwh-Kyrios* of Israel's Scriptures. So it is of the very greatest significance for an understanding of the origins (and shape) of that Christology that from among the various Gospel expressions for Jesus it is, above all, with the Gospels' Son of Man title that there is a parallel or *precedent* for such a Christological reading of Scripture. There are at least two Son of Man sayings, or constellations of sayings, that claim or imply an identification of Jesus with the *Yhwh-Kyrios* of Israel's Scriptures.

As Edward Adams has recently demonstrated, the coming of the Son of Man with (his/holy) angels in Mark 8:38, 13:26 (and pars.) and Matt 25:31 "combines Dan. 7:13 with Zech. 14.5," a text, that like others in the OT,

---

54. Bauckham, "Devotion to Jesus Christ," 194.

describes how "*Yhwh* (LXX *Kyrios*) my God will come, and all the holy ones with him" to judge the peoples. Adams calls this a "Christological specification of the Old Testament and Jewish expectation of God's end-time coming/descent to earth."[55] We may be more precise and say that is a clear instance—albeit more allusive than some of the instances in Paul's letters—of a Christological interpretation of a *Yhwh-Kyrios* text. It is allusive—so not a straight quotation of Zech 14:5—because in Mark 8:38 and, even more so in Mark 13:26, the Son of Man's inclusion in the divine theophany evokes a number of biblical (and extrabiblical) coming-of-*Yhwh* God texts.[56] In addition, in the immediate context of Mark 13:26 there is other language—of the sun, moon, and stars failing (in Mark 13:24–25)—that represents a conflation of biblical texts that describe the awesome and terrible effect of the coming "Day of *Yhwh-Kyrios*" (Joel 2:10; 4:14–15 LXX; Isa 13:9–10, cf. Isa 34:4).

We have seen how in *1 En*. 61:5 the biblical "Day of *Yhwh*" becomes the Day of the *Chosen One*" (who is also the Son of Man). So Mark 13:24–27 as a whole perhaps knows the Son of Man-theophany material in the *Similitudes*. Indeed, it is striking how in another Gospel Son of Man passage the same scriptural *Yhwh* text that is applied to the Enochic Son of Man informs Jesus' depiction of the Son of Man. The prediction that at his coming the Son of Man will be like lightning that lights up the whole world (in Matt 24:27) or the whole sky (in the parallel Luke 17:24) is particularly reminiscent of Ps 97:4: "His (*Yhwh*'s—vv. 1, 9, 12) lightnings light up the world, the earth sees and trembles" (see also Pss 18:13–14; 144:6; Zech 9:14). The next verse of Ps 97—"the mountains melt like wax before *Yhwh*, before the Lord of all the earth"—is one of those biblical verses that is taken up in the *Similitudes of Enoch* (*1 En*. 52:6; 53:7) and *4 Ezra* (13:3–4) where biblical theophany language is given to the Son of Man figure in his role as the end-time judge.[57]

In chapter 9 I will present more evidence for this Christological interpretation of scriptural *Yhwh* texts by means of the Son of Man title in other parts of Luke 17:22–30. For now it is enough that we register this rather strong circumstantial evidence for a line of continuity between the *Similitudes* (and *4 Ezra*), the Gospel Son of Man texts, and a central component

---

55. Adams, *Stars Will Fall*, 150 (cf. 149–53).

56. For full biblical references see ibid., 150–52. We might note in particular *1 En*. 1:3–9 (cited in Jude 14–15) and Isa 66:18, which combines the coming of *Yhwh-Kyrios* with a *gathering* of peoples in a way that anticipates Mark 13:26–27; Matt 25:31–32. The *Yhwh-Kyrios* Christology is even clearer in Matt 16:27–28, the Matthean parallel to Mark 8:38—9:1. In Matt 16:27–28, where the angels are the Son of Man's, the language of divine judgment from Pss 28:4; 62:12 and Prov 24:12 is applied to the Son of Man (cf. Sir 35:24; Rom 2:6; Rev 22:12) and the "kingdom" is *his*, not simply God's.

57. See Bauckham, *God of Israel*, 229–31, following up the observations of Horbury, *Jewish Messianism*, 103–4. Compare Tilling, *Christology*, 210.

feature of the "Christological monotheism" attested in Paul's letters. In all three, scriptural *Yhwh-Kyrios* texts are applied to a messianic figure. In the first two, that figure is Daniel's "one like a son of man."

So evidence that it was specifically *as the Son of Man* that Jesus was first identified with *Yhwh-Kyrios* is surely of the utmost importance for the quest for the origins of "Christological monotheism." It is not just that there are texts in both the Gospels and in Paul where Jesus (either as Son of Man or as the exalted Lord) is identified with *Yhwh-Kyrios*. It is also that specific texts outside the Gospels in which the exalted Jesus is identified with *Yhwh-Kyrios* have an obvious basis in a Gospel Son of Man text. This is the case with the Son of Man thief saying in Luke 12:39–40 (= Matt 24:43–44). There is surely some kind of conceptual or tradition-historical connection between the statement there that the Son of Man comes as a thief in the night and passages in Paul that describe the Day of the Lord (*Kyrios*) Jesus Christ as a thief (1 Thess 5:2, 4; cf. 2 Pet 3:10; Rev 3:3; 16:15).[58]

What is remarkable about all these Gospel texts is the fact that *it is only with the Son of Man title that we have a clear citation or allusion to a scriptural Yhwh text in the service of a Yhwh-Kyrios Christology*. We never find Jesus connected in this way to scriptural *Yhwh-Kyrios* texts through his identity as a prophet, the messiah (*christos*), a son of David, the Son of God title, or even the word "Lord."[59] So, given the overwhelming evidence (agreed upon by most New Testament scholars) that the Son of Man expression has titular force in the Gospels (whether or not it had titular force for Jesus himself), there is an a priori case for thinking that the *identification of the exalted Jesus with Yhwh-Kyrios,* which is so well attested in Pauline and other New Testament texts, has its historical basis in the Gospel Son of Man tradition.

In its simplest—or crudest—terms, there is a case now for thinking that the historical Jesus claimed he was "the Son of Man" of one strand of contemporary Jewish messianic expectation, that is now attested in the *Similitudes* and *4 Ezra*. In so doing, he also claimed an identification with *Yhwh-Kyrios* (as the memory of his words in the texts just reviewed demonstrate). Paul, and others, then took that *Yhwh-Kyrios*-Son of Man Christology for granted when they applied scriptural *Yhwh* texts to him. And the earliest believers worshipped Jesus precisely because they came to

---

58. For the possibility that the Son of Man thief saying is indebted to the story (and contemporary Jewish interpretation) of the Israelites *plundering* of the Egyptians (Exod 12:36) when they escape from Egypt and are led by the Angel *Yhwh* see Fletcher-Louis, "Thief Saying."

59. Though a similar *Yhwh-Kyrios* Christology does appear in the Gospels' storm-stilling stories (that I discuss in chapter 9), there is no Christological title or epithet to attach Jesus to *Yhwh-Kyrios* in those passages.

believe that Jesus was, indeed, the Son of Man figure of contemporary Jewish hope (as John 9:35–38; Acts 7:54–60, and Matt 28:16–20 indicates was the case at the earliest phase of Christological origins). The leading voices of the emerging consensus have not told us why this scenario—or something like it—is historically implausible, even though with Bauckham's work the way that the *Similitudes* applies scriptural *Yhwh* texts to the Messiah-Son of Man has come to the fore.[60] Because the thoroughgoing rejection of the apocalyptic Son of Man theory (advocated by Hurtado) is unworkable, it is surely time to return to consider afresh the possibility that the Son of Man provides a (or *the*) missing key to unlock the mysteries of the origins of "Christological monotheism." And surely NT scholarship can no longer avoid careful consideration of the role of *1 En.* 37–71 in the formation of NT Christology.

4: The Enoch Seminar: Continuity between the "Parables" and NT Christology

Some have followed Bauckham in accepting that the *Similitudes* does to some extent anticipate NT Christology, whilst nevertheless stressing that this text is a *unique* special case.[61] Bauckham thinks the *Similitudes* is a parallel case to early Christology inasmuch as the *Similitudes* illustrates the direction scriptural exegesis *could* go and that Christians *did* in fact go with their Christ language.

But the *communio opinionis* of the Enoch Seminar is that there is some kind of *genetic* relationship between the *Similitudes* and NT Christology. For example, as a leading member of the Seminar, George Nickelsburg claims that "there is some consensus that the author of Matthew knew the "Parables" and there are perhaps five passages that assume knowledge of the *Similitudes* (Matt 13:36–43; 16:27–28; 19:28; 24:30–31; 25:31–46).[62] Matthew 19:28 and 25:31–46 are the most celebrated instances of likely knowledge of the *Similitudes*, since in both passages the Synoptic Son of Man sits, with judicial authority, on a "throne of glory," as does the Enochic Son of Man. On careful examination, the two texts certainly have much in common and Nickelsburg argues that the *Similitudes* are also presumed in the Markan,

---

60. For puzzlement at Bauckham's failure to follow through on the implications of his treatment of the *Similitudes* for Christological origins, see the important comments in Boyarin, *Jewish Gospels*, 178 n. 27.

61. Hannah, "Throne," 68, 88–89; Tilling, *Christology*, 206, 212–28.

62. Nickelsburg and VanderKam, *1 Enoch 2*, 72. Cf. esp. the essay by Leslie W. Walck, "Son of Man" (in Boccaccini, *Book of Parables*) and Walck, *Son of Man*.

Lukan, Johannine, and Q Son of Man sayings, and that this relationship also stands behind some of Paul's Christological material.[63] In particular, he stresses the ways in which both the Gospel tradition and the *Similitudes* go beyond Dan 7:13 in focusing on the Son of Man's role as eschatological judge.[64] Indeed, his point could be sharpened up by the observation that the *Similitudes* and the Gospels share a belief that Daniel's Son of Man figure takes the place of *Yhwh(-Kyrios)* in the divine theophany.

Nickelsburg is overhasty in claiming a "consensus" that the *Similitudes* is known to the author of Matthew, since the possibility of a relationship is barely considered by the scholars who have created the "emerging consensus" on Christological origins.[65] And more thought ought to be given to the possibility that in their references to Daniel's "one like a son of man" Matthew and the *Similitudes* simply share a common interpretative tradition, not that Matthew actually knows the *Similitudes*. Certainly we now need to explain the striking parallels between the two and the fact that both look back to—but go beyond—what is explicitly said in Dan 7 itself. In Part 4, when I come to lay out a new paradigm for Christological origins, I will explain my own view of this matter, offering a new explanation of the relationship between the *Similitudes* and the NT. For now I simply flag up the key issues that make the question both fascinating and vexing.

Firstly, if there are simply parallel lines of exegetical development then we are bound to wonder what motivated the communities behind the *Similitudes* and the NT to come to such similar portrayals of a second figure who sits *alongside*, but who also, each in his own way, *shares* the divine identity? Secondly, why is it that, both in the Gospels and in the *Similitudes*, this development is attached in particular to the Danielic Son of Man figure, who appears, once again, in a later text—*4 Ezra* 13—with the same kind of theophanic character that is encountered in the Jesus tradition and the Enochic material? Thirdly, why also, then, is there a less strongly "divine" portrayal of the Son of Man in *4 Ezra* 13 (with no glorious enthronement and worship)? Fourthly, we might ask why it also seems to be the case that there is similarity of Son of Man language so strongly in just one of the Gospels (Matthew), but not in the others? Fifthly, why did the Jesus tradition fix on the enthronement of Ps 110:1, combining it with Dan 7:13, but the *Similitudes* makes no explicit use of that Psalm?

---

63. See esp. Nickelsburg, "Son of Man," and compare the work of Walck ("Son of Man" and *Son of Man*) and James Waddell (*Messiah*).

64. See Nickelsburg and VanderKam, *1 Enoch 2*, 70–76.

65. Bauckham dismisses this possibility briefly in *God of Israel*, 172 n. 46.

Sixthly, if, as many others suppose, the relationship was not *parallel* exegetical development (as Bauckham imagines) but a genetic conceptual and textual influence (the Synoptics indebted to the Enochic Son of Man), then how did that come about? Did a Jewish contingent within the earliest Christian movement, perhaps in a distinct community responsible for Matthew's Gospel, cherish the *Similitudes,* or was Jesus himself inspired by this strange Enochic vision? If the connection goes back to Jesus, then why was it (only or primarily) Matthew who included those parts of Jesus' teaching that alluded to the Enochic Son of Man expectation?

5: Provenance: A Marginal, Sectarian Text?

The possibility of a genetic, textual relationship between the *Similitudes* and the Gospels implies a shared or overlapping social location (Jews and Christians could not surf a first-century internet for books that might support their views). But consideration of that issue raises many questions. We know that other parts of *1 Enoch* were in wide enough first-century circulation for some Christians to use them and treat the tradition as authoritative (e.g., Jude 14–15, cf. *Barn.* 16:5–6). The use of *1 Enoch* in the letter of Jude even suggests that Jesus' own family had a particular interest in the Enochic tradition. In any case, those Christians who quote from *1 Enoch* use its oldest, best known portions (Jude 14–15 cites the opening chapter: *1 En.* 1:9). But the *Similitudes* was several centuries younger than the *Book of Watchers* (*1 En.* 1–36) and, judging by the remains of the inventory of the Qumran Library, it was not included in the Essene version of the Enochic "canon." So whose Enochic canon *did* it belong to and why did the Qumran community not include it? Why did the early Christians come to believe that their Jesus-the-Messiah fulfilled Daniel's vision and that Enoch did not (against *1 En.* 71)? Answering these key questions could lead to a much clearer and deeper understanding of the origins (and meaning) of Gospel Son of Man sayings, and of NT Christology as a whole.

Probably one reason that NT scholars have been leery of the possibility of influence from the *Similitudes* to early Christology is the usual view that apocalyptic literature in general—and the Enochic tradition in particular—is marginal and sectarian. If, like the apocalyptic book of Daniel, *1 Enoch,* including the *Similitudes,* had been part of the first-century Jewish Bible for all Jews, reflecting the piety of the Temple and an unquestioning commitment to the Mosaic Torah, it would be easier to credit it with an influence on some of Jesus' Son of Man sayings. However, for most scholars—including leading voices in the Enoch Seminar—*1 Enoch* has exemplified a world-ending "apocalyptic" eschatology that belongs outside the mainstream world of Temple and Torah piety; most have thought that the apocalypticism of which *1 Enoch* is an example represents a breakaway movement that rejected or ignored much in the religion of Moses and the Pentateuch.[66]

Indeed, the "high" messianic hope of the *Similitudes* has regularly been viewed as one key piece of evidence confirming this marginal, sectarian view of the text. Its messianism seems so different to Israel's hope for a royal, Davidic ruler who will serve as God's appointed leader of an end-time national restoration. In fact, among the various expressions for the composite figure that we label the (Enochic) Son of Man, the word "messiah" only occurs twice and other expressions or titles predominate. It is true that, besides the two references to the Son of Man as "messiah" (48:10; 52:4), there are other passages where language from the famous messianic prophecy in Isa 11:2-4 is applied to him (49:3-4; 51:3; 62:2-3).[67] However, there is nothing to suggest Davidic lineage or the kind of career that would be expected of an earthly ruler, as is found, for example, in the messianic prophecies of the near contemporary *Psalms of Solomon* (17 and 18). Indeed, it has been hard to see how the description of this heavenly Son of Man has any connection to the various (royal) messianic figures that appear in the historical accounts of Roman-period protest and revolution. For some Enoch specialists, this all goes to suggest that the messianism of the *Similitudes* reflects the *diversity* of Second Temple messianic hope and the distinctive, sectarian views of one particular group.

But if the *Similitudes* are an ultrasectarian text of a wider sectarian movement, it is hard to see how they can have influenced Jesus or his earliest followers, since the NT never refers to a group or movement of Enochians (and only once quotes from *1 Enoch*—in Jude 14-15).[68] Judging by the Gospels, Acts, and Paul's letters, Jesus and his disciples carefully positioned themselves in a *close* (and also competitive) relationship to the rest of the nation of Israel that continued to define itself by its central institutions (Temple and Torah), and to those parties based in and around Jerusalem.

66. For a fuller account of the standard view of Jewish apocalyptic(ism), see Fletcher-Louis, "Jewish Apocalyptic."

67. Ps 2:2 has probably also influenced *1 En.* 48:8, 10.

68. In his recent commentary (Nickelsburg and VanderKam, *1 Enoch 2*), Nickelsburg describes a strange scenario in which, in his view, the *Similitudes* is reflected in all four Gospels (and in the hypothetical Gospel source Q), but it emanates from a distinct community that is neither Essene, Sadducean, nor Pharisaic, but that shared a common milieu with "one branch of the early Jesus movement" (*1 Enoch 2*, 66). Of the existence of such a first-century Jewish milieu all the available primary texts (and the archeological record) are silent.

There is little to suggest that the Jesus movement ever thought of itself as a new manifestation of a much older sectarian tradition that had long ago retreated from the Jerusalem temple and from a Mosaic Torah to some spiritual oasis in the Judaean wilderness.

The evidence of the NT and its connections to the Enochic literature could mean in fact that the sectarian model is misguided. Indeed, there are other considerations that suggest 1 *Enoch* and the *Similitudes* reflect mainstream and broadly shared messianic beliefs which then point us to a more historically believable explanation of the relationship between Jesus the Son of Man and the Enochic Son of Man in the *Similitudes*. I simply note these here, without full discussion, simply because they add further weight to my contention that the study of New Testament Christology now needs to pay renewed attention to this important Jewish tradition. A proper understanding of the relationship between the *Similitudes* and the NT will also make a small, but important, contribution to the new paradigm of Christological origins (in Parts 5 and 6).

I: Related Texts Describing a "Transcendent" Messiah or Figure

There are, as we have seen, intriguing connections between the Son of Man portrayal of the *Similitudes* and the Son of Man figure in *4 Ezra*. In the past, *4 Ezra* 13 has all too easily been dismissed as simply evidence of a late-first-century messianic development (perhaps one influenced by early Christian beliefs about Jesus). However, a good case can be made for thinking that chapter 13 of *4 Ezra* contains an older tradition modified and reused in the late first century.[69] In any case, to those texts from the end of the first century that evince a preexistent, heavenly messiah (*Sib. Or.* 5:414-33, *2 Bar.* 29:1—30:5; 39:7; *Apoc. Abr.* 31:1) we should now add the evidence of various texts that suggest for the *pre-Christian* period the *Similitudes* was by no means unique in its "high" messianic eschatological expectation.

In the (probably) second-century BC third book of the *Sibylline Oracles* there is brief mention of a king whom God will "send from heaven" (3:286) with responsibility for judgment of each man "in blood and beams of fire."[70] A few biblical psalms (discussed below), especially in their Greek translation, reflect belief in a preexistent messiah.

---

69. See, e.g., Stone, "Enoch's Date," 448-49.

70. This text has suffered neglect due to an error in the standard edition of the Greek, which all but removes any suggestion that the king is a preexistent being with the words "*the heavenly God* will send" at line 286 (as in, for example, *OTP* vol 1, 368).

In his 2007 Enoch Seminar piece dedicated to the *Similitudes*, Helge Kvanvig drew attention to the parallels between the enthroned Son of Man and the text of a now much-discussed Qumran hymn in which the speaker describes himself seated in the heavens with incomparable glory.[71] The most important portion of 4Q491c (formerly labeled 4Q491 11 i) reads:[72]

> 5 . . . a mighty throne in the congregation of the gods upon which none of the kings of the East shall sit, and their nobles [shall] not [. . . there are no]ne comparable 6 to me in]my glory and besides me no-one is exalted, nor comes to me, for I sit in [. . . hea]ven and there is no 7 [. . .] I am counted among the gods and my dwelling is in the holy congregation; [my] des[ire] is not according to flesh, [rather] my [por]tion lies in the glory of . . . .

It is likely that the speaker of this hymn is the priest who served as the leader of the Qumran community.[73] Perhaps these are the words of the one known at Qumran as the Teacher of Righteousness. Some have argued that the position of the speaker is simply what will be expected for the messiah in the eschaton.[74] However, it is more likely that the hymn was already in use in a liturgical setting where somebody in the community actually spoke the words cited above. There is nothing in the text itself that means it has to be a description of what the messiah *will say in some eschatological future* and the hymn obviously provides the words for somebody in the present. Furthermore, we now know that one version of this hymnic form was a part of the Qumran community's book of *Thanksgiving Hymns* (see 1QH^a XXVI 6–16 and 4Q427 frag. 7 i–ii, cf. 4Q471b), which certainly contains texts to be used by the community already in its present liturgical life.[75]

Whether or not the text was used straightforwardly in the present or it was reserved for use by a future messiah, the position of the speaker, who must be a human being, is remarkable. The language of *enthronement* in the heavenly realm and of *(divine) glory* is strikingly reminiscent of the characterization of the Enochic Son of Man (although there is no indication

---

For the correction, see now Buitenwerf, *Sibylline Oracles*, 207.

71. Kvanvig, "Parables of Enoch," 191–92, cf. J. J. Collins, "A Response," 219–20.

72. On this text see Fletcher-Louis, *Glory of Adam*, 199–216; Alexander, *Mystical Texts*, 85–91; J. Angel, "Liturgical-Eschatological Priest," and *Eschatological Priesthood*, 132–46.

73. The fact that the speaker of the hymn in 4Q427 frag. 7 i + 9 line 12 promises not to crown himself suggests, as a priest, he disavows the Hasmonean claim to the combination of royal and priestly offices.

74. See, e.g., Chester, *Messiah*, 244, and the review of that view in Fletcher-Louis, *All the Glory*, 205–12.

75. For a discussion of the texts, see, e.g., Alexander, *Mystical Texts*, 85–91.

that the speaker occupies God's *own* throne). The speaker is not explicitly praised or worshipped by others, though in a sense he praises himself. And in one portion of the same (or a related but distinct) Self-Glorification Hymn the psalmist boasts of his superiority to all the angels or "gods" ("*elim*") (see 4Q471b 1-3 5).

Kvanvig also draws 11QMelchizedek into the discussion of the *Similitudes*. In that text, Melchizedek (who appears as a priest-king in Gen 14:18-20 and Ps 110:4) is a divine warrior and judge who is identified with the "god" (*elohim*) of Ps 82:1 and then with the *Yhwh* of Isa 61:2: "the year of *Yhwh*'s favor" becomes "the year of Melchizedek's favor" (11QMelch 2:9). The point is then reinforced with the word "god" (*el*) as a reference again to Melchizedek, substituting for the Tetragrammaton of Ps 7:8b-9a [Eng. 7b-8a]: "over it [i.e., the assembly of the peoples] return to the height, *god* [i.e. Melchizedek, where MT has *Yhwh*] will judge the peoples" (11QMelch 2:10-11). At one point it is possible that "*Yhwh*'s inheritance" becomes "Melchizedek's inheritance" (2:5, cf. Deut 32:9).

In the past the Melchizedek of this text has been viewed as an angel, perhaps even Michael. However, there are no reasons to detach this Melchizedek from the historical and human (but also mysterious) Melchizedek of Gen 14 and Ps 110. The appearance of the "god" Melchizedek as end-time judge in 11Q Melch takes place at the Day of Atonement of the climactic year of jubilee and there are plenty of reasons to assume that the text describes one who is both "divine," but also a recognizably human priest-king.[76] It is possible that Melchizedek is identified with the "anointed one" (the *priestly* messiah) of Dan 9:25-26, who is also seen as the "anointed of the spirit" in Isa 61:1 (11QMelch 2:18). In any case, it is remarkable, given the way in which Melchizedek replaces both the Tetragrammaton and the word "god" (*elohim*) of biblical passages, that this Qumran text has figured so little in recent discussion of the origins of "Christological monotheism."[77]

II: The Old Greek Translation of Daniel 7:13

Evidence that the *Similitudes* reflects wider currents in the Second Temple period and an established, but not completely uniform, tradition of interpretation of Dan 7:9-14, comes from one of the Greek translations of Dan

---

76. For a fuller discussion of 11QMelchizedek (11Q13), see Fletcher-Louis, *Glory of Adam*, 216-21, cf. Chester, *Messiah*, 260-61, and van der Water, "Michael or Yhwh?"

77. Bauckham's claim (*God of Israel*, 222-23) that 11QMelch does not place Melchizedek in the position occupied by *Yhwh* in Ps 7:8 [Heb 7:9] is unconvincing given the application of Isa 61:2 to Melchizedek (which Bauckham does not mention).

7. We have two ancient Greek translations of Daniel; the Old Greek (OG) and Theodotion. The latter faithfully translates the Aramaic known to us at Dan 7:13.

However, the OG, which is generally reckoned to be the older of the two translations, has something quite different and remarkable:

> **13** I was watching in a vision of the night and lo on the clouds of heaven one as a son of man came and as the Ancient of Days (*hōs palaios hēmerōn*) he was present and those standing by were present with him. **14** And to him was given authority and all the nations of the earth according to their kind and all glory was offering him service (*latreuousa*) . . .

This Greek version is certainly pre-Christian because it is reflected in several NT Son of Man texts.[78] Once again we have a text that interprets the original, Aramaic version of Dan 7:13 to mean that the "one like a son of man" figure is somehow *identified with*, expresses, or *shares in* the divine identity. And so the OG supplies another valuable witness to a wider stream of (pre-Christian) interpretation of Dan 7:13–14 where it is assumed that the man figure has some kind of divine identity. There are at least three, perhaps five, considerations that lead to that conclusion.

Firstly, it shares with the *Similitudes* the belief that Daniel's "son of man" figure will be manifest in the position of Israel's God—of *Yhwh*. Where the Aramaic and Theodotian have the "one like a son of man" coming *to* the Ancient of Days, in the OG he will be present *as* the Ancient of Days. So too, in the *Similitudes* the Son of Man-Messiah appears, or "comes" so to speak, as *Yhwh* in his theophany.

Secondly, there is evidence that ties the OG closely to the *Similitudes*' interpretation of Dan 7. Hitherto unnoticed by commentators, there is a likely conceptual connection between one part of Dan 7:14 OG and *1 En.* 46 (the chapter of the *Similitudes* that introduces the Son of Man figure through an interpretation of Dan 7:9–14). Daniel 7:14 OG says that "all the nations of the earth according to their kind" are *"given to"* the man figure.[79] *1 Enoch*

---

78. Matt 24:30; 26:64; Rev 14:14–16 all have the Son of Man *on* clouds, as in the OG of Dan 7:13 (unlike the Aramaic, Theodotian, and some Synoptic Son of Man texts that have the man figure *"with* clouds"). Revelation 1:13–16 depicts the Son of Man *as* the Ancient of Days. And those Synoptic texts that place the Son of Man on a heavenly throne and have him coming with angels suggest a reading of the OG in which the attributes of the Ancient of Days in Dan 7:9 are assigned to the man figure of Dan 7:13. (See L. T. Stuckenbruck, "Old Greek Recension" and Aune, *Revelation*, vol. 1, 91–92, for discussion). Reynolds, *Apocalyptic Son of Man*, 138–46, shows that John 5:27 reflects the OG, not Theodotion at Dan 7:13–14.

79. I take the neuter plural phrase "all the nations of the earth . . ." (*panta ta ethnē*

46:4-5 seems to assume such a reading of Dan 7:14 when it says the Son of Man will have authority over the kings and the mighty ones (vv. 4-5a) and that he is the one who is the source of their kingship (v. 5c). Neither of the Aramaic nor the Theodotian Greek translations ascribes to the Danielic man figure this degree of authority over other kingdoms.

Thirdly, whatever we make of the literary relationship between the OG of Dan 7:14 and 1 En. 46, *the OG of Dan 7 agrees with the Similitudes that the man figure is the rightful recipient of worship*. In the OG of Dan 7:14, since the man figure comes "*as* the Ancient of Days" the way he receives service (*latreuō*) is best treated as a simple case of a worship appropriate to a genuinely divine being. In the OG of Dan 7:14, the verb *latreuō* picks up the use of the same verb in earlier passages. In its *eight* previous occurrences that verb in Daniel always refers either to a legitimate worship given to God or to an illegitimate worship of the pagan gods and their idols (see Dan 3:12, 14, 18, 95; 4:37; 6:17, 21, 27).[80] It is really hard to explain the use of the *latreuō* in Dan 7:14 if the OG translator does not think that the kind of worship that is normally owed to God will soon rightfully be given to this man figure. And, of course, there are aspects of the original Aramaic text that fit that interpretation too. The man figure has a specifically divine prerogative in his travelling on clouds. He has a universal authority and the statement that "all glory" offers him service seems to be a statement of total, cosmic authority; not just authority in the earthly sphere. So, for several reasons, it is best to conclude that what is done to this figure in the OG of Dan 7:14 is done *in respect of his identity*: he is worshipped *because he manifests and expresses the divine identity, and because he possesses (delegated) divine prerogatives*.

The Aramaic at Dan 7:14 might itself intend a worship of the man figure since the verb usually translated "serve" (*pelakh*) is used repeatedly in the previous chapters of Aramaic Daniel for full-blown cultic worship (Dan 3:12, 14, 17-18, 95; 6:17, 21, cf. 7:27).[81] It is true that Theodotian has *perhaps* tried to avoid giving the reader the impression that the man figure is treated the way God is to be treated by using of a different verb that might, but does not have to, denote worship (*douleuō*). But that explanation of Theodotian's

---

tēs gēs) with the first verb (*edothē*). That is grammatically more likely than the NETS translation (Pietersma and Wright, *New English Translation*, 1012), which has the neuter plural "all the nations of the earth" as a subject of the feminine singular participle, "serving" (*latreuousa*).

80. For the OG of Dan 7:14 as a statement of cultic worship, see now Reynolds, "Old Greek of Daniel," 75-76; *Apocalyptic Son of Man*, 36-37.

81. So, most recently, Reynolds, *Apocalyptic Son of Man*, 30, who notes this is consistent with the man figure's movement with the clouds in a way reserved in the OT for God himself.

use of a different verb would add yet another reason to think that worship really is in mind in the OG of Dan 7:14: Theodotian, on this reading, wants to distance himself from the theology of the OG. However, Theodotian itself may simply have chosen a verb that has a wider scope. His use of *douleuō* could have in view *both* cultic devotion *and* political service. In any case, the OG (along perhaps with the Aramaic itself) presents a manlike figure on the clouds who is the rightful recipient of cosmic worship. How a Jewish author could think that way and remain faithful to Israel's Scripture is not yet clear and is a matter to which we shall have to return.

For now it is enough to note that unless the OG translation of Daniel was written by members of the distinct, hypothetical community responsible for the *Similitudes, this Greek version of Daniel shows that others were reading Dan 7:13 the way the authors of that Enochic text read it.* That impression is reinforced by the intriguing change from the Aramaic statement that the man figure comes *"with* the clouds" (cf. Theodotian) to the OG translation that has him come *"on* the clouds." This subtle change is perhaps intended to evoke the OT image of God riding as divine warrior and judge *on* the clouds (Isa 19:1, cf. Ps 104:3).[82] Such an image would reinforce the impression of the Aramaic original, that is then picked up also in the *Similitudes,* that the "one like a son of man" plays the role of *Yhwh* as a divine warrior in a theophany (see the discussion of *1 En.* 46:4; 52:6; 53:7; 60:5; *4 Ezra* 13:3-4 above).[83]

The lack of discussion of the Greek translations of Dan 7:13-14 in all the heated scholarly discussion around the Son of Man expression in the Gospels is puzzling and unfortunate.[84] Presumably, the neglect is partly because scholars struggle to make sense of a statement that Daniel's man figure comes *"as* the Ancient of Days." The OG of Dan 7:13 is a witness for neither of the principal positions on the much argued over meaning of Dan 7:13: that the one like a son of man is an angel (Michael, for example), or that he is a literary symbol of the exalted and vindicated Israel. If we follow those, especially in British scholarship, who believe the man figure is a symbol for Israel,

---

82. Cf. Meadowcroft, *Aramaic Daniel,* 227-28.

83. For Daniel's one like a son of man as a divine warrior who behaves like the West Semitic storm god Baal, see J. J. Collins, *Daniel,* 286-94; Angel, *Chaos,* 99-110.

84. The recent study of John's Son of Man sayings by B. E. Reynolds (*Apocalyptic Son of Man*) is a welcome exception (see esp. 34-40). The OG certainly does not intend a "comparison between" the son of man figure and the Ancient of Days and it is most definitely incompatible with the view that the one like a son of man is a symbol for Israel (*pace* M. Casey, *Interpretation and Influence,* 132). Neither can it be treated as a scribal error (as ibid., and J. J. Collins, *Daniel,* 275, 311, claim, and as the NETS translation at Pietersma and Wright, *New English Translation,* 1012 seems to assume): see Stuckenbruck, "Old Greek Recension," 270-73.

it makes little sense to say that Israel came or was present *"as the Ancient of Days."* But neither does it make much sense to say that the "one like a son of man" is a principal angel, like Michael, and that he comes *as* the Ancient of Days. In contemporary Jewish texts principal angels often appear with divine authority, but they do not typically come *as God himself.* The OG of Dan 7:13-14 suggests the first readers of Daniel, and the original author himself, would not have agreed with either of these two modern interpretations.

So the OG has been left, bleating feebly, on the sidelines of one of the most heated debates in modern biblical discussion. Conceivably it might make sense for the OG to have in mind *the* Angel of the LORD coming "*as* the Ancient of Days," but then other aspects of the text—such as the clouds as a means of transport—do not fit that interpretation. (The Angel of the LORD never moves about on clouds.) The OG has seemed to be an irrelevant witness. But perhaps, in view of its agreement with the perspective on Daniel's "one like a son of man" in the *Similitudes,* its time to stand up and be heard has now come.

III: The *Similitudes* and Enoch's Transformation in 2 *Enoch* and 3 *Enoch*

In its current form, the *Similitudes* claims that Enoch himself somehow becomes, or always was, the Son of Man figure who is enthroned in divine glory (1 *En.* 71:13-17). What that means, and how it could be, has been the subject of much discussion. But it is highly unlikely that the identification was made only after the text entered the Christian environment. So, bearing in mind that identification, all scholars also recognize some kind of connection between the *Similitudes* and two other Enochic texts—2 *Enoch* (formerly known as *Slavonic Enoch*, but now also attested in Coptic fragments) and 3 *Enoch* (that is attested only in Hebrew). Both of these have significant and multiple points of contact to the *Similitudes* and because they each belong in their own ways to quite distinct literary and theological milieus they provide further evidence that the *Similitudes* and its Son of Man-messianism was neither idiosyncratic, marginal, nor confined to a particular group in the Jewish world.

Neither text refers to Daniel's "one like a son of man," but both ascribe to Enoch an exalted position like the one given to the Son of Man in the *Similitudes*. In 2 *Enoch,* Enoch is transformed by investiture with radiant, heavenly garments *of God's own glory* in the highest heaven before God's throne (22:8-10). The longer (and perhaps original) text at 24:1 says that God then seated Enoch at his left-hand side. In any case, after his journey to heaven and transformation to a new heavenly identity, Enoch receives obeisance from his fellow humans in a way that is best taken as a kind of worship of him (chs. 57 and 64). The date and origin of 2 Enoch is uncertain, though it was most likely written sometime before the end of the first century AD

3 Enoch is certainly post-Christian and took its present form probably several centuries later than 2 Enoch (no earlier than the fifth century AD?). Nevertheless, it is clearly continuous with material in both 1 and 2 Enoch. In this Hebrew text, Enoch experiences a transformation that recalls the one Enoch had in 1 En. 71:11–12. He is enlarged and becomes coextensive with the world—reflecting God's glory that fills the earth in Isa 6:3 (see 3 En. 9:1–5)—and he is turned into fire so that his presence recalls biblical accounts of *Yhwh's* storm theophany (3 En. 15:1–2; cf. Ezek 1:4, 13–14, 24; Ps 18:7–15) in a way that parallels the application of divine warrior imagery for the Son of Man in the *Similitudes* and 4 Ezra (1 En. 52:6, 53:7; 4 Ezra 13:2–13).

He is given the glorious robe and crown of the priesthood (12:1–4; cf. 13:1–2; 14:5), becomes the angel Metatron, is called by God "the lesser *Yhwh*," and is identified with the name-of-God-bearing angel of Exod 23:20–22. The name of God containing the letters by which the world was created is written on his crown (13:1–2; cf. Exod 28:36). Angels fall prostrate before him because of the crown on his head and he is installed as judge over the angels (16:1), on a throne like the throne of glory (10:1) at the door of the seventh heavenly palace (10:2).

Some kind of relationship between the Enoch-Metatron of this rabbinic-era text and the Son of Man-Messiah cannot be denied. There are clear points of connection that suggest 3 Enoch has grown out of the *Similitudes*. For example, in God specially *choosing* him (4:8, cf. 6:3) there is perhaps a recollection of one of the names of the Enochic Son of Man (e.g., 1 En. 39:6, 40:5; 45:3). However, much that makes up the character of that figure in the *Similitudes* is missing. So it is equally likely that 3 Enoch and the *Similitudes* represent separate branches of a more widely known tradition of speculation about Enoch as a human being with whom God shared something of his own identity.

The evidence of 3 Enoch (and also of 2 Enoch) for an assessment of the date and location of the *Similitudes* is also tied up with complex historical questions around the origins of Jewish mysticism. 3 Enoch is an important text for *merkabah* and *hekhalot mysticism*, a phenomenon that is well-attested for the rabbinic period, where the angel Metatron also figures prominently.[85] After years of skepticism about the possibility that rabbinic-

---

85. For an introduction to that later mystical tradition see C. Morray-Jones in Rowland and Morray-Jones, *Mystery*, 219–64, and for the primary texts see now Davila, *Hekhalot Literature*.

era mystical texts have their roots in the Second Temple period, there is now growing recognition that a mystical tradition existed before AD 70 and that the later material is somehow related to it.[86] That judgment adds further weight to the view that the account of Enoch's visions (37:1; 57:1) and transformation (71:11-12) in the *Similitudes* attests a widely known literary tradition of which the *Similitudes* was but one, not unrepresentative, example.[87] Of course, this issue relates to wider questions about the nature and shape of Second Temple theology and spirituality, and also the origins and character of later rabbinic spirituality and theology. Those questions become sharply focused also on the nature and origins of a Two Powers in heaven heresy that crops up in later rabbinic texts. Rabbinic references to a Two Powers in heaven heresy have in their cross hairs both the kind of "Christological monotheism" attested in the NT and the Son of Man-messianism of the *Similitudes*, even though there is no explicit evidence to suggest they actually encountered the *Similitudes* itself.[88]

6: The *Similitudes* a Mainstream Second Temple Text

Finally, the usual view that the *Similitudes* is a sectarian work has been forcefully challenged by Pierlugi Piovanelli.[89] He has highlighted the text's positive attitude to both Jerusalem, the land around it, and some among the nations outside of God's chosen people. The kind of criticism of the Second Temple and its official clergy that crops up in other parts of *1 Enoch* (e.g., 89:73-74; 93:9) is lacking. By comparison, for example, with Qumran literature, references to the righteous are general, not community specific, and the wicked are the "kings and the mighty ones (and the exalted)" (mentioned fifteen times from 38:4-5 onwards), who are repeatedly said to "possess/rule the land" (38:4; 48:8; 61:1, 3; 62:6; 62:9; 63:1, 12; 67:12).[90] Following Piovanelli, and with further support from a couple of studies by

---

86. For the view that the Dead Sea Scrolls show that later Jewish mysticism has its roots in Second Temple spirituality, see now the important study by Philip Alexander, *Mystical Texts* (2006).

87. For actual visionary practice attested in the Jewish apocalypses, see Fletcher-Louis, "Religious Experience" and my discussion of apocalyptic in Part 5 (below).

88. On all this, see the seminal study of the late A. F. Segal, *Two Powers* and compare D. Boyarin, *Border Lines*; "Two Powers," and "Beyond Judaisms".

89. Piovanelli, "Testimony for the Kings" (2007).

90. Apparently in the light of Piovanelli's argument, G. W. E. Nickelsburg now rejects the view that the text is sectarian, though he still hangs on to the old idea that it belongs to a distinct community separate from other known forms of Judaism (*1 Enoch* 2, 83, cf. 104, 62-63).

James H. Charlesworth, there is perhaps now an emerging consensus that the enemies of the people of God are most likely the "Roman rulers of Palestine and/or their clients in the Herodian house."[91] That means that the *Similitudes*' intended audience is "the ensemble of the Jewish people fallen under the domination of a new and merciless dynasty."[92] This new view is then further supported by Leslie Walck's social-scientific study that suggests the author most likely belongs to a class of religious leaders who have lately been removed from office by the incursion of a new ruling power.[93]

This assessment fits very well with the view of a growing number that the *Similitudes* comes from the second half of the first century BC and that it reflects the plight of the Jews under the rule of Herod (and his Roman overlords).[94] If the text is not sectarian, and the author believes he speaks for the whole Jewish people, then it is not surprising that there are so many parallels and connections to the *Similitudes* in other texts. In particular, this would help explain the parallels to the *Similitudes* in the Gospel Son of Man sayings. Either the Gospel Son of Man sayings reveal knowledge of a well-known, mainstream Jewish text to which Jesus or the Gospel writers after him could allude or refer, knowing that their audience would hear and appreciate the reference, or, as a mainstream text, the *Similitudes* attests a standard first-century interpretation of Dan 7 shared by others.

Whilst a conclusion along these lines would solve the enigma of the text's relationship to other Jewish and early Christian texts, it creates a new puzzle. If the *Similitudes* is a witness to a common Judaism that rejected the Herodian settlement with Rome, and it shows no evidence of a distinct community with a sectarian base outside of Israel's central institutions, then where exactly does it belong on the map of Jewish communities known to us? Since it is not Essene and cannot be Sadducean because it expects a coming resurrection (51:1, cf. 61:5), the one obvious alternative is that it speaks for the piety and eschatological hopes of (some in) the growing Pharisaic movement. That, of course, would have far reaching implications for our understanding of the shape of mainstream Jewish monotheism at the turn of the eras. It is a possibility to which we will return in a later volume.

---

91. Nickelsburg, *1 Enoch 2*, 63, cf. 47. See also Charlesworth, "Composition Date" and "The Date and Provenance."

92. Piovanelli, "Testimony for the Kings," 374–75.

93. See Walck, *Parables of Enoch*, 30–49, and "Social Setting."

94. For further arguments to support this date and setting see Fletcher-Louis, "*Similitudes*."

7: Conclusion

In the *Similitudes of Enoch*, the Son of Man-Messiah *expresses* and *participates in* the divine identity. There are good reasons for thinking that this fascinating text represents mainstream first-century Jewish beliefs. It witnesses to a living and more widely attested tradition of interpretation of Dan 7:13 in which it was believed that, when he appeared, the "one like a son of man" figure would manifest the divine identity of Israel's one God. Its interpretation of Dan 7 is remarkably close, in particular, to the one put forward by the Old Greek translation of that text. There are also clear lines of continuity with the way the Son of Man expression is used in the New Testament and in the later text from the end of the first century, *4 Ezra*. There is, then, rather more uniformity to the first-century interpretation of Dan 7:13 than has sometimes been alleged by New Testament scholars.[95]

So we are now in a position to confidently answer the questions that I laid out when we reviewed the emerging consensus approach to the Son of Man problem (in chapter 3 §3.III). Yes, there were Jews before Jesus who eagerly read Dan 7 and hoped and prayed for "the coming of the one like a son of man" of Dan 7:13. Yes, those Jews went beyond the simple plain sense of Dan 7 and agreed amongst themselves on some distinctive characteristics of the figure who would come. And yes, if there was talk, in Jewish Christian Greek texts, of *ho huios tou anthrōpou* that could readily be taken as a reference to both Dan 7:13 and to a constellation of expectations circulating (some fixed, some floating in the realms of debate) around that visionary text.

So it is hard to deny that the distinctive "messianic" hope of the *Similitudes* must have something to do with the Gospels' portrayal of Jesus as the "Son of Man." The *Similitudes* help explain why Jesus is remembered to have used the expression Son of Man as if it referred to a known messianic figure. It also helps explain some striking aspects of the Son of Man's characterization in the Gospels (such as his association with divine glory and his enthronement in heaven) that are not spelt out in Dan 7 itself. It may also help explain the origins of "Christological monotheism" and Christ devotion, since the way the Enochic Son of Man is worshipped—as one who expresses or shares in the divine identity—goes some way towards Jesus' position in the NT.

But the connections between the Gospels' Son of Man title and the *Similitudes* also raise other questions. Firstly, why does Jesus prefer this title to other messianic titles? Secondly, why does no one else recognize him or acclaim him as the Son of Man? Thirdly, why does the expression apparently

---

95. D. Burkett, for example, exaggerates the lack of connections between the sources in his *Son of Man Debate*, 74, 110–14, 119–21.

play a critical role at his trial and condemnation (Mark 14:62 and pars.)? Fourthly, why does the post-Easter church refrain from confessing Jesus as the Son of Man? Why, in other words, does it not figure as a Christological title outside the Gospels (apart from the one likely titular occurrence in Acts 7:56)? Fifthly, if the Gospels are indeed dependent on the *Similitudes*, why do they never mention Enoch, nor refer explicitly to his writings (we never have "this was to fulfill what was written in the prophet Enoch"). The more strongly we tie the New Testament Son of Man sayings to a preexisting Jewish tradition of the kind now extant in the *Similitudes* the harder many of these questions—specifically the second, the fourth, and the fifth—are to answer.

Even more importantly, the *Similitudes* and related texts raise important questions for our understanding of Jewish monotheism and the origins of "Christological monotheism." How could first-century-BC Jews compose such a text from within a biblically faithful theological framework? Why is it that with the *Son of Man*-Messiah, but not in other messianic texts, we have such a clear identification with *Yhwh-Kyrios*? And why, if there are continuities between the (expectation of the) coming glorious messiah in the *Similitudes* and (the experienced reality of) Jesus as a glorious, enthroned-in-heaven messiah, are there also significant discontinuities? Jesus is more fully *included* in the divine identity in a way that is nowhere true of a Son of Man figure in pre-Christian tradition. If the *Similitudes* is to play any role in our understanding of Christological origins these differences need explaining every bit as much as do the continuities. Why do the classic texts witnessing to "Christological monotheism," especially the rather early material in 1 Cor 8:6 and Phil 2:6–11, go way beyond the Son of Man's *expression of,* and only partial *sharing in,* the divine identity in the *Similitudes*? Why, again, do the classic texts witnessing to "Christological monotheism" neither include the Son of Man title nor show any wider interest in the language and imagery of Daniel 7?[96]

We still need a better understanding of the place of the *Similitudes* in Second Temple Jewish life and, above all, its relationship to biblical theology. With a clearer view of the text's life setting we would also be able to be more decisive in our estimation of its role in the origins and shape of early Christology. But probably the primary reason so many commentators, especially those with a primary expertise in New Testament studies, have lately been disinclined to give much space to the *Similitudes* in the quest to

---

96. There are, of course, notable exceptions to that statement: Matt 28:18–20 witnesses to "Christological monotheism" and many commentators think it alludes to Dan 7. Revelation 1:13–16 explicitly refers to Dan 7:13 and is a key passage for the fully divine Christology of the book of Revelation.

understand Christological origins is the fact that it seems so much at odds with OT theology.

In the next two chapters—and in the excursus that follows—I will present more evidence that the *Similitudes*' theology is by no means unusual. Quite a few primary texts invite a fresh approach to the basic shape of biblical theology. And with those texts too we will find reasons to reject any hasty judgment that really they represent an idiosyncratic and heterodox Judaism that had moved away from the basics of the faith revealed in Israel's Scriptures. Rather, along with the *Similitudes*, they emanate from somewhere within the broad parameters of normative Jewish practice and belief, and so they invite us to rethink some of our assumptions about the nature of OT theology. Ultimately, in Parts 5 and 6, we will also find that it is in only in combination with those other texts (and many more besides) that the *Similitudes* can make a vital contribution to a full and satisfactory explanation of Christological origins.

CHAPTER 6

The King, the Messiah, and the Ruler Cult

WILHELM BOUSSET ARGUED THAT Greco-Roman religiosity influenced the early church's views about Jesus as it moved beyond its Jewish Palestinian beginnings. The emerging consensus has demonstrated the historical implausibility of this explanation of Christ devotion.[1] Indeed, a distinctive feature of the emerging consensus is an aversion to the possibility that religious patterns in the Greco-Roman world played any constructive role in the formation of the Christological material in the New Testament. Christ devotion was birthed in a Palestinian Jewish context hermetically sealed off, theologically and experientially, from the patterns of worship that pagans in the wider Mediterranean took for granted. If there is ever any interaction with Greco-Roman religion in the New Testament—with the cult of the divine emperor, for example—it is simply to challenge polytheistic and idolatrous religion with the worship of the one God, now revealed in and through the exalted Messiah Jesus.

From an altogether different perspective, William Horbury has offered an explanation of the worship of Jesus echoing Bousset's recourse to Greco-Roman religion that nevertheless challenges its developmental approach and the assumption that Christ devotion must have started outside the Jewish context of earliest Christianity.[2] Horbury proposes that, instead of an influence on the development of the early church from Greco-Roman religion, *already, before Jesus, Judaism in the Hellenistic and Roman periods had been significantly impacted by the encounter with Greco-Roman religious life and thought in a way that—together with the continued influence of*

---

1. Its implausibility is laid out emphatically in Frey, "Eine neue religionsgeschichtliche Perspektive."

2. Esp. Horbury, *Jewish Messianism* (1998) and "Early Christology" (2005), along with the essays collected in *Jews and Christians* (2003).

older, traditional, biblical piety—prepared the way for the worship of Jesus as Israel's messiah.

Horbury's work deserves more careful consideration than it has so far received and for several reasons it merits a whole chapter on our journey towards a new paradigm for Christological origins. In part it has been marginalized because his thesis strikes at the very heart of the emerging consensus view that the earliest and fullest Christology was formed in a Jewish environment that was theologically hermetically sealed off from the wider Greco-Roman pagan environment. Nevertheless, Horbury is one of a number of voices, especially in North America and Germany, who have lately argued that Greco-Roman traditions had a far greater importance for first-century Judaism and the earliest phases of church life and thought, even in Palestine, than the emerging consensus scholars have recognized.[3] I consider Horbury's work here in detail, not just because it is a representative example of a minority stance, but also because critical dialogue with it will highlight some problems in the study of Christological origins that are present more widely in recent scholarship. Consideration of his work also forces us to engage with primary texts that will sharpen up our thinking about Christological issues in later chapters. We will cash in some of the findings from this chapter in our examination of Phil 2:6–11 in chapter 8. But most importantly of all, aspects of Horbury's argument will make a small, but vital, contribution to the new paradigm that I will lay out in Parts 5 and 6.

1: William Horbury: Jewish Messianism, Ruler Cult, and Christ Devotion

Horbury's argument has several parts.[4] We can start with his insistence that it is a mistake to distinguish too sharply between the belief in an ordinary human, earthly king and texts that describe a heavenly and preexistent messiah. Whilst it is generally accepted that there are several texts (such as the

---

3. For Americans who give the Greco-Roman material a high profile, see the work of Adela Yarbro Collins (in e.g., Collins and Collins, *King*), the provocative book by Peppard, *Son of God* (2012), and D. Litwa's recent work (in his two books *Being Transformed* and *Iesus Deus*—2012 and 2014). On the German side, see especially the work of Samuel Vollenweider (e.g., his seminal article on Phil 2:6–11—"'Raub'"—and his "Metamorphose") and Dieter Zeller (in for example his "Menschwerdung des Sohnes Gottes" and "New Testament Christology"). These scholars can all appeal to the widely accepted thesis that there was creative interaction between Jewish and Greek worlds in Martin Hengel's classic study *Judaism and Hellenism* (see, for example, the discussion of Hengel's work in Litwa, *Iesus Deus*, 6–18).

4. A succinct summary is laid out in Horbury, "Early Christology."

Similitudes, *4 Ezra* 13 and, the late-first-century-AD *Sib. Or.* 5:414–33) that accentuate the messiah's heavenly and superhuman characteristics, nevertheless Horbury points out that other texts that scholars in the past have placed in another messianic category also highlight his spiritual and supernatural aspects (e.g., *Ps. Sol.* 17:23, 47; 18:18). Thus, it is possible to speak of a "coherent" Jewish belief in a "spiritual messianism" that invariably thought of the coming messiah as an embodied and divine spirit.

Furthermore, Jewish texts derive these ideas from the OT where in psalms and oracles the present and future king invariably has an exalted, god-like form. For example, in Isa 11:1–4 he has a divine spirit. In Num 24:17 (a verse that was widely influential in the Second Temple period) he is described as a "star." A couple of biblical texts suggest the coming king will be preexistent (Mic 5:2; LXX Ps 109:3 [Eng. Ps 110:3]). Some are happy to have praise and *proskynesis* directed to the ruler in ways that suggest more than just honor paid to a superior. For example, in 1 Chr 29:20 the people bow "before *Yhwh-Kyrios and the king*"; a king, that is, who a few verses later sits on the "throne of *Yhwh-Kyrios*" (v. 23).[5] In Ps 45 the king is a "god" (*'elohim*) praised for his beauty and power, and other psalms voice similar praise that includes the ruler (Pss 2, 110). In Isaiah's famous prophecy, the coming king will be called "Wonderful Counselor, Mighty God (*'el gibbor*), Everlasting Father, Prince of Peace" (Isa 9:6), language that in other texts is specifically used for *Yhwh* himself (see Isa 10:21 and Jer 32:18). Greek translations, the Aramaic targums, and other Jewish texts retain and develop the language of such passages in the Hebrew Bible, Horbury argues. The language of *proskynesis* to the king is clear in Greek translations of the Psalms (LXX Ps 71:11 [Heb. 72:11]), even where a prostration that could be construed as worshipful is lacking in the underlying Hebrew text (LXX Ps 45:13). Equally, the Greek translation of Isa 9 retains a sense of the coming king's transcendent identity with the statement he will be called "*Angel* of Great Counsel" (LXX Isa 9:5).

Many have recognized traces of a wider ancient Near Eastern view that the king is "divine" in parts of the Hebrew Bible.[6] But most have then claimed that in the postexilic period, with the rise of monotheism and after the reforms represented by the books of Deuteronomy and Isaiah, it really becomes impossible to speak of a "divine" king, in a way that might have been possible in some preexilic circles (and certainly was the case for the kings of Israel's neighbors). Whilst Horbury does not engage that histori-

---

5. M. Barker also makes much of this text in Barker, "High Priest."
6. For a recent discussion of the relevant evidence see e.g., Collins and Collins, *King*, 1–47.

cal reconstruction of the development of Israel's kingship theology directly, he argues nonetheless that it is a mistake to see older Israelite kingship traditions disappearing altogether. At least those older traditions are *comparable* to the view that the ruler is transcendent in diverse sources in the late Second Temple period.

To some extent, *the flowering of a transcendental messianism in the Hasmonean and Herodian periods can be explained,* he argues, *as a positive response to the Hellenistic Ruler Cult and the Roman emperor cult.*[7] Whilst Jews by no means bought into all parts of the ruler worship pattern that was promulgated by their neighbors, they emulated it in some ways. To varying degrees they took up the language of praise and honor for their own rulers and allowed some of the practices of the contemporary Ruler Cult to color their portrayal of the coming royal messiah. In particular, they were willing to render their own ruler acclamation, praise, *proskynesis*, petition, and prayers for his well-being. The influence of this constellation of themes can be seen, for example, in the depiction of the Son of Man-Messiah in the *Similitudes of Enoch* (1 *En.* 37–71), that Horbury dates to the Herodian period.[8] Reigning kings, such as those of the later years of the Hasmonean dynasty and the Herodian household, were in turn expected to behave as true quasidivine rulers; taking on some of the pomp and circumstance of contemporary royal ceremony. In short, whilst Jewish messianism before Christianity is deeply indebted to *biblical* language, for Horbury Jewish monotheism at this time is very much an "*inclusive* monotheism" that is open to creative and sometimes accommodating dialogue with the wider Greco-Roman worlds.

From this reconstruction of Jewish messianism Horbury concludes that:

> Messianism is then likely to have been a major factor in creating the cult of Christ among Christians and their corresponding christological affirmations. Recognition of Christ as the messianic king, which began during the period of Jesus' ministry and pervaded the early Christian community, would lead to titles, acclamations, and hymnody reflected in the New Testament.[9]

Horbury's impressive work on Jewish messianism makes a vital contribution to the study of Christian origins (and Judaism in antiquity). He

---

7. Horbury, *Jewish Messianism*, 68–77, 127–40; "Early Christology" 18, 21–23. In the Bousset era of scholarship the role of emperor worship in the formative context of Christian origins was not taken as seriously as it is now (see Peppard, *Son of God*, 16).

8. For Horbury on the *Similitudes* see esp. his *Jewish Messianism*, 58, 89, 113, 125.

9. Horbury, "Early Christology," 22, cf. *Jewish Messianism*, 109–52.

has mounted a strong case for the prevalence of royal messianism at the turn of the eras and has effectively challenged a recent tendency to divide and separate texts that really are interconnected in a coherent tapestry of biblical echoes and interpretations. His argument, that because late Second Temple Judaism is *Hellenistic* Judaism it was therefore very much open to the patterns of thought and behavior surrounding the cult of the ruler, is both cogent and illuminating.[10] There are serious problems with his argument that we shall come to presently. But first, there are at least four points that mean it should be taken seriously as a potentially plausible historical explanation of the origins of Christ devotion.

Firstly, Horbury has shown that Israel's Scriptures contain plenty of material that would support a late Second Temple accommodation to Greco-Roman patterns of ruler worship. Too often that material is ignored by historians who assume that the theology of the Deuteronomist and of the later chapters of Isaiah purged biblical faith of every hint of an older veneration of the king as an exalted or even "divine" being. *It is an unavoidable fact—that itself needs to be explained in any account of Old Testament theology—that its authors and editors did not exclude all "god" language for kings and rulers from the final form of the Hebrew Bible.* Either the theology we find in Deuteronomy and Isaiah did not become the absolute norm or, perhaps, we have misunderstood those two biblical texts and their theology.

Secondly, Horbury's thesis is supported by other recent studies that have reminded us that Judaism was by no means hermetically sealed off from Hellenistic influence and that there was a spectrum of Jewish responses to Greco-Roman cults of the divine human ruler.[11] To be sure, there is plenty of evidence that many reacted with whole-hearted antipathy to both the worship of divine rulers in general and of the emperor in particular. Obviously, that antipathy fuelled the Maccabean uprising and it was one factor among the many that led to revolt in AD 66. However, it is not the case that those pagan patterns were always greeted with the kind of hostility that prevented any positive influence on Jewish ways of thinking about rulers. One only has to read Philo's glowing account of the reign of Augustus to appreciate that many Jews had every reason to be thankful to the best of Rome's rulers, even if that meant some acceptance of the essentials of emperor worship (see Philo *Embassy,* 143–50). Herod, his family, and court managed to be both self-consciously Jewish and to embrace much

---

10. For recent studies indebted to its central thesis, see J. J. Collins "Son of God," esp. 301–5, and C. Leonhard, "'Herod's Days.'"

11. See Bernett, *Kaisercult,* and "Imperial Cult"; Peppard, *Son of God,* 92–93, and note now the arguments for an early Christian openness to patterns of Ruler Cult in Litwa, *Iesus Deus,* 181–224.

of the politics and religion of the empire. In an earlier period there is even evidence that the Hasmoneans eventually adopted a tempered openness to aspects of the new Hellenistic Ruler Cult.

A particularly important example of that openness is provided by 1 Maccabees and its poems in praise of Judas and Simon Maccabeus (in 1 Macc 3:3–9 and 14:4–15). These both bear comparison with the court theology of Hellenistic kingdoms and offer a precedent for aspects of the cult of Christ.[12] Judas and Simon are praised for their deeds and benefactions for the sake of Israel's well-being in a way that echoes the ascription of divine honors to heroes and rulers in Greco-Roman texts. Indeed, J. W. van Henten has now demonstrated that these passages in 1 Maccabees are generically similar to honorific decrees that legitimate near-contemporary Hellenistic divine rulers in Egypt.[13] Those decrees established the new cult of a ruler and were deposited in writing in temples. 1 Maccabees 3:3–9 and 14:4–14 echo very precisely the encomiastic form and much of the content of those decrees, that also focus on the personal achievements and benefactions of the rulers as a basis for cultic devotion to them. And it is striking that the practice of depositing the honorific decree in the temple is emulated also in 1 Macc 14:25–49 where a decree that grants Simon an exclusive position at the head of the nation—whilst celebrating his achievements and services to his country—is also written up on bronze tablets and deposited "in a conspicuous place" (v. 48) in the Jerusalem Temple complex. So, as a form of praise of Israel's own rulers that incorporates elements of the cultic procedures of the Hellenistic Ruler Cult, these texts demonstrate a remarkable openness to non-Jewish religious and political conventions in a way that endorses the heart of Horbury's proposals.[14]

Thirdly, there is one now very well known Qumran text that likely reveals a conscious interaction with pagan patterns of divine kingship. In

12. The texts are briefly mentioned in Horbury, *Jewish Messianism*, 133.

13. Van Henten, "Honorary Degree" and "Royal Ideology." E. Krentz shows that van Henten's focus on Egyptian parallels must be widened to include the parallels of Asia Minor and Syria (Krentz, "Simon the Maccabee"). See also Gardner, "Jewish Leadership," 332–37, on conventions of the benefactor in 1 Macc 14. The fact that Simon was called "the Benefactor" (*ho Euergetēs*) (according to Josephus *Ant.* 13:214) should be compared with the use of similar titles and language for Hellenistic divine rulers (such as Ptolemy III Euergetes who reigned 246–222 BC and Ptolemy VIII Euergetes 170–116 BC), especially the Seleucid Antiochus "the god, Epiphanes . . . Benefactor and Savior" (in Josephus *Ant.* 12:258–61).

14. For the accommodation to Hellenism in the portrayal of Judas and Simon, see Himmelfarb "1 Maccabees," 241–47, and for other ways that 1 Macc 14 reveals accommodation to Hellenistic culture see Fine, *Art*, 61–65. For a more complex example of a Jewish accommodation to the conventions of Ruler Cult see Fletcher-Louis, "Alexander the Great."

the previous chapter we brought the Qumran Self-Glorification Hymn to the witness stand in the case for a widespread interest in a "divine" messiah in late Second Temple Judaism. One feature of the 4Q491c version of that Qumran hymn has until now been overlooked. In 4Q491c frag. 1, lines 5–6 the speaker boasts of his throne in heaven, which he says is:

> 5 . . . a mighty throne in the congregation of the gods upon which none of the kings of the East shall sit, and their nobles [shall] not [. . . there are no]ne comparable **6** to me in]my glory

In comparing himself—his glory and his throne "in the congregation of the gods"—*with the kings of the East,* the speaker must have in view the claims of the rulers of Israel's neighbors to a divine kingship.[15] Specifically, he must have in mind the oriental blend of traditions and motifs that became such a well-known feature of theopolitical life in the Near Eastern territories at the end of the Mediterranean world in the Hellenistic age. He boasts of his "divine" status over against the likes of Antiochus IV Epiphanes (and the more than twenty Seleucid rulers that followed him). He contrasts his apparently "divine" identity with the self-claims of the new Pharaohs in Ptolemaic and imperial Egypt. Local rivals in near by Nabatea are also in his sights.

That the speaker should be conscious of these rivals is hardly surprising given the claims he makes for himself.[16] But what is remarkable is the way the text so brazenly exalts the Jewish speaker over these rival kings. The text does not rebuke those kings the way Isaiah rebuked the king of Babylon for his pretensions to a divine position above the Most High (in Isa 14:4-20). On the contrary, by claiming to belong to the "congregation of the gods (*elim*)" the speaker imitates the language used for Hellenistic and later Roman rulers who were added to the Greek and Roman pantheons, as new demigods and Olympiads (see, e.g., Horace *Odes* 3:3:9-12, where Augustus is "couched at ease" among the demigods Pollux and Hercules on "heaven's proud steep" and Suetonius *Div. Jul.* 88:1 where Julius Caesar is said to have been "numbered among the gods").[17] Some kind of competitive emulation of the conventions of the pagan Ruler Cult seems to be at work in this remarkable Qumran hymn.

15. All four witnesses to the hymn (4Q491c, 4Q471b, 4Q427 7 i and 1QH^a XXVI) are dated on paleographical grounds to the late Hasmonean-early Herodian period.

16. The prominence of an oriental divine kingship in the Hellenistic period means it really is highly unlikely that the Hebrew of the crucial phrase in line 5 should be translated "a mighty throne . . . upon which none of *the ancient kings* (*mlky qdm*) shall sit" as some have proposed.

17. For Alexander the Great as a "thirteenth" god added to the twelve gods of the Olympian pantheon see Aelian *Var. Hist.* 5:12 (cf. Long, *Twelve Gods,* 71–72, 84, 118–20, 187–89).

The fourth point in support of Hobury's thesis requires a summary of one aspect of Phil 2:6–11 that we will discuss in chapter 8. There we will find that, as a consensus of commentators have come to see in the years since Horbury's own research, Christ is portrayed as *the ideal divine human ruler*. Picking up older Hellenistic Ruler Cult traditions, but more importantly echoing contemporary first-century language and ideas surrounding the ideal Roman emperor, "Christ is presented as becoming emperor of the universe."[18] To an extent, the Christ hymn is a conscious emulation of the kind of poetry, hymns, and songs that were directed to Augustus and his successors. This is a little surprising if "Christological monotheism" was formulated in an essentially Jewish context that only ever took a hostile view of the (idolatrous) worship of the emperor and divine human rulers in the Hellenistic world. We know, of course, that many Jews did take an entirely negative view of the cult of the ruler. Indeed, some Jews seem to have rejected the need for any kind of human ruler at all, perhaps largely as a reaction to the role played by the emperor in the Roman political system (see, e.g., Josephus *Ant.* 18:23).

But the fact that Phil 2:6–11 so comprehensively portrays Jesus as the ideal divine ruler—as the true emperor—is much easier to explain if, as Horbury argues, there was already in some pre-Christian Jewish circles an openness to the patterns of the Ruler Cult. What we might call an "imperial Christology" is understandable if, in line with the Jewish material that Horbury discusses, some first-century Jews were looking forward to the revelation of a messiah who would be Israel's own heaven-sent answer to Caesar; a messiah who would outdo Caesar by being the best that Caesar could ever be as benefactor and savior (and much more besides). The *worship* of Jesus Christ as the true imperial "Lord" over all (see Phil 2:10–11) would then represent the Christian claim that in *this* messiah—in *Jesus*—Israel's long awaited divine human ruler had now arrived. It would mean that the praise of him in Phil 2 builds on the precedent set by praise to Jewish rulers of the kind now preserved in 1 Maccabees. And both Phil 2 and 1 Maccabees would look back, ultimately, to the kind of praise given to Israel's king as a "divine" figure in the Hebrew Bible (in, e.g., Ps 45:6).

For these and other reasons that I will come to, Horbury's basic insight that the Ruler Cult could have a *positive* influence on Second Temple messianism will make a small, but vital, contribution to the shape of the new paradigm that I will outline in Parts 5 and 6. However, there are also problems with Horbury's reconstruction of Jewish messianism and, whilst it is undoubtedly the case that the material and patterns of belief he lays out

---

18. Oakes, "Re-mapping," 318.

contributed to the formulation of early Christology, it does not provide a satisfactory explanation of the shape and origins of "Christological monotheism," as several reviewers have pointed out.[19]

2: Some Weaknesses of Horbury's Model

It is true that there are passages where elements from the constellation of verbal and ritual actions of the Ruler Cult are accorded to the Jewish king or to other righteous Israelites. And this must qualify any claim, following the recent work of Hurtado in particular, that worship of Jesus is wholly without precedent in the Jewish context. However, Hurtado is right to object that what we have with Jesus and the early church is "an *emphasis* on Jesus in early Christian songs [that] is unprecedented, and constitutes at the least a significant degree of difference from the liturgical practices and pattern characteristic of Jewish groups of the period."[20] *If there is some kind of application of the patterns of Ruler Cult to the Jewish king it is quite unlike the full pattern of cultic devotion that we find accorded Jesus Christ.*[21] In particular, following our survey of the evidence for so-called "Christological monotheism," the material Horbury gathers does not explain either the way in which Jesus is identified with *Yhwh-Kyrios* or, to use Bauckham's language, the fact that he is fully included in the divine identity.[22]

It is possible that the worship of the Son of Man-Messiah in the *Similitudes* is partly indebted to biblical texts that describe obeisance to Israel's king. However, the key biblical texts that would justify worshipful prostration to a messiah (noted above) do not figure in the *Similitudes*.[23] Furthermore, the *Similitudes*' debt specifically to the patterns of a non-Jewish Ruler Cult is unlikely. Horbury has not demonstrated any firm connections between the way the Son of Man is described and specifically Greco-Roman

---

19. See responses to various aspects of Horbury's work in Hurtado, *Lord Jesus Christ*, 28 n. 2; *How on Earth?*, 20–22; Bauckham, *God of Israel*, 107–26; 228–32; Chester, "High Christology," 26–27, 46; Knibb, "Septuagint and Messianism," 360–61; Tilling, *Christology*, 230–32.

20. Hurtado, *Lord Jesus Christ*, 149 (my italics).

21. But that does not warrant a wholesale dismissal of Horbury's case on the grounds that it does not provide evidence for an *established* Jewish cult of the ruler or the messiah that matches the Christ cult *in all its parts* (as Hurtado does in *How on Earth?*, 20–22). Tilling's view, in "Problems," 209, that Bauckham's response to Horbury is "devastating" is also an overstatement.

22. A point expressed in different language in Hurtado, *How on Earth?*, 21.

23. The one possible exception is an allusion to Ps 2 in *1 En.* 48:8, 10 (in the context of a description of worship offered to the Son of Man figure in 48:5).

conventions. We may say there is competition between the text's messianic ruler and the Ruler Cult. Certainly, *it is likely that the depiction of the Son of Man as a royal figure with premundane preexistence, who is seated on God's own throne of glory, is intended as a theological and political polemic against the claims of Roman rulers and their client kings.*[24] But the fact that the *Similitudes* polemicizes so trenchantly against the "kings and mighty ones who possess (or 'seize') the land/earth" and their idolatry (46:7), the probable setting in a context of Herodian and Roman rule, and the absence of language and imagery from the Ruler Cult and emperor worship means the *Similitudes* is unlikely to be consciously emulating or borrowing from the (idolatrous) practices of a non-Jewish Ruler Cult. If there is *worship* of the Son of Man-Messiah as a being who manifests God's own divine identity then the author most likely believes such a messianic hope is justifiable because he derives its contours from his own *biblical* tradition, not from the pagan world that now oppresses him. The Son of Man and the worship of him is introduced (in *1 En.* 46–48) through an interpretative expansion on Dan 7, drawing also on texts from Isaiah and the Psalms, not with recourse to the conventions or linguistic patterns of the non-Jewish Ruler Cult. In the midst of that introduction, the evocation of Isaiah's taunt against the king of Babylon who exalts himself to heaven as a rival to the Most High (Isa 14:4–20) in the castigation of the kings and the mighty in *1 En.* 46:7 shows that the author believes he is setting a biblical vision of delegated messianic rule over against the pretensions of pagan rulers and their self-exalting claims. God's own delegation to the Son of Man-Messiah *in heavenly preexistence* is set over against a pagan pattern of earthly self-exaltation within history.

Similarly, when reviewing Horbury's work, Chester questions whether (royal) messianism is really strongly present in the hymn to Christ in Phil 2.[25] To be sure, both the hymn in Phil 2 and the little piece in Phil 3:20–21 that goes with it have strong parallels with the traditions surrounding good and bad "divine" human rulers in the pagan world. Also, Phil 2:6–11 is generally reckoned to have an encomiastic form and so it bears comparison with the encomia to Judas and Simon in 1 Maccabees. But there is no explicit reference in Phil 2:6–11 (or its wider literary context) to biblical kingship texts. And, in any case, Phil 2:6–11 goes way beyond what we have

---

24. For a detailed argument for this explanation of the text's distinctive portrayal of the Son of Man-Messiah see Fletcher-Louis, "*Similitudes,*" 67–71. And see Piovanelli, "Testimony for the Kings," 376–77, for a contrast between the *Similitudes* and contemporary, Roman era, expectations for a divine ruler (in Virgil's *Fourth Eclogue* and his *Aeneid* 6:791–93).

25. Chester, "Christ of Paul," 115–16. For Jewish messianism and Phil 2 see Horbury, *Jewish Messianism,* 109–11, 113, 115.

in 1 Maccabees since it treats Jesus as one who is a fully divine being, who possesses (or shares) the name of God *Yhwh-Kyrios*. The word "*kyrios*" for Jesus in Phil 2:11 might have in view a royal or imperial "lordship," but its primary function seems, in the context, to be the identification of Christ with *Yhwh-Kyrios*. Nothing in 1 Maccabees comes close to this extraordinary claim for Christ; nor to its presentation of his story as one that begins in heavenly preexistence. So, although there is an "imperial Christology" in Phil 2:6–11, its peculiar *incarnational* shape (that we will explore in full in chapter 8) cannot be straightforwardly derived from a pre-Christian royal messiah tradition that had been formed under the influence of Greek and Roman divine ruler motifs.

The confession in 1 Cor 8:6, and all the other related material in the NT that we have already touched on, suggests that the earliest expressions of "Christological monotheism" were formulated without specific interest in the kind of messianic notions discussed by Horbury. There is some slight evidence for a connection between (royal) messianic categories and devotion to Christ in other passages, but not much, and not much in the early evidence of Paul's letters. If Christ is "God" in Rom 9:5 then that verse *might* allude to Ps 45:6. There is kingship language in Heb 1 (esp. vv. 5, 8, cf. v. 3e), but the catena of biblical texts applied to Christ follows an opening Christological statement (in vv. 2–3) that has no basis in biblical or extrabiblical royal messianic texts. Insofar as Hebrews' Christology is a fully divine one, there is no evidence that it is indebted to a Jewish royal messianic hope. Horbury's claim (in the quotation above) that a view of Jesus as "messianic king . . . pervaded" early Christianity is also problematic. Whilst there is royal messianism throughout the NT, it is also, time and again, subjected to subtle and explicit critique and ultimately the real focus is on Jesus' inclusion within the divine identity in a way that goes far beyond the Israelite view of the king.

If Jewish royal messianism had had the role in the origins of Christ devotion that Horbury proposes the language that is used to ascribe divinity to Jesus would surely be different. Given that there are, it is true, OT texts where the king is "god" (Ps 45:7; Isa 9:5) we might have expected the grammar of Christological monotheism to have created a different reworking of the Shema at 1 Cor 8:6: something like,

> For us there is
>
> > one *Kyrios* (i.e. *Yhwh*), the Father from whom . . .
> > and one *god*, Jesus Christ (i.e. the *messiah*) through whom
> > . . .

There are few places where the word "god/God" is used for Christ (John 1:1, 18; 20:28; 1 John 5:20; Rom 9:5; Titus 2:13; 2 Pet 1:1; Heb 1:8). But if Horbury were right about the earliest Christology's debt to Greco-Roman kingship traditions we would expect these to be more numerous. The fact that they are relatively few in number, and also marginal to the theological language of the Pauline corpus, might in fact be because some in the early church wanted to avoid the suggestion that Jesus' divine identity could be compared with—or *limited to* a comparison with—the divine Caesar (who was sometimes spoken of as a "god" and "equal to the gods").

It is unlikely that "Christ Jesus being *in the form of God*" in Phil 2:6 is in any way derived from Jewish kingship or royal messiah traditions, since they provide no clear linguistic precedent for Jesus being *en morphē theou*.[26] It is more likely that, for Paul (and for his Christian predecessors), because Jesus Christ is "in the form of God" in preexistence (v. 6), he always was what God made him publicly to be after his death (vv. 9–11): one who is *highly exalted above* all earthly rulers (see further chapter 8).

One real strength of Horbury's work is his ability to see the connections between diverse texts and traditions. However, sometimes a focus on connections and similarities needs to be combined with recognition of the texts' particularities and differences. Even when Jewish material affirms aspects of a non-Jewish Ruler Cult there are also ways that they resist the wholesale adoption of non-Jewish cultic conventions.[27] For example, there are obvious differences between the 1 Maccabees passages reviewed above and contemporary Hellenistic honorific decrees. Whilst the encomiastic *form* and the focus on Hasmonean *personal achievements* and "glory" or "honor" (1 Macc 3:3; 14:4–5, 9–10, 21, 29, 35, 39) is precisely what we would expect for the veneration of a divine ruler in the Hellenistic environment, the praise they offer is really quite muted in comparison both to the devotion offered to Christ and the language used for Hellenistic rulers. In the non-Jewish honorific decrees "god" language is freely used of human rulers. For example, in the Rosetta stone inscription (that was deposited at a temple in Memphis) Ptolemy V is the "living image (*eikōn*) of Zeus" (line 3) and his principal title is "(The Everliving, Beloved of Ptah,) God epiphanes eucharistos (*Theos Epiphanēs Eucharistos*)" (lines 9, 37, 38, 49, 51).[28] This and other decrees like it stipulate the creation of a cult statue of the king

---

26. A. Y. Collins (in Collins and Collins, *King,* 208) sees in Phil 2:6 a claim that Jesus is the preexistent heavenly messiah, but without clear support from Jewish texts for such an understanding of the phrase "in the form of God."

27. A point helpfully explored in Gardner, "Jewish Leadership."

28. *OGIS* 90 (W. Dittenberger, *Orientis,* vol. 1, 140–66). For a translation see, e.g., Danker, *Benefactor,* 206–12.

and they make provision for the wider population to fully participate in the new cult through processions, festivals, the singing of songs, and the making of more images for the citizens' own personal use. These features are mostly lacking in 1 Maccabees. 1 Maccabees 3:3–9 and 14:4–15 are encomia to Hasmonean rulers in a way that is striking and without precise precedent in the biblical tradition. They represent a quite different—open and accommodating—stance towards pagan culture to the one that we find in the *Similitudes of Enoch*. But in terms of form and content they are encomia, not hymns. They do not, that is, praise Israel's rulers as divine beings.[29] Although they are happy to use the prevalent Hellenistic language of benefaction to describe Judas and Simon,[30] they also clearly avoid speaking of Israel's rulers as "saviors." In the Hellenistic world a divine ruler is a "savior (*sōtēr*)," but in 1 Maccabees it is God himself who is praised as the "savior" (1 Macc 4:30). So, whilst 1 Maccabees vindicates Horbury's claim that Hellenstic-era Judaism knew very well and interacted creatively with the patterns of Ruler Cult in the east-Mediterranean world, it also helps us appreciate the ways Jews *rejected* specific elements within that Ruler Cult; especially, for example, the making of cult statues and the appropriation of "God" language for the human ruler.

Equally, such Hasmonean-era praise of Jewish rulers lacks both the incarnational shape and divine-identity language that the NT ascribes to Jesus. There is no evidence that any Jew claimed that a Hasmonean "king" or Herodian ruler had personally come from preexistence, as "the form of God" taking up human flesh; as *Yhwh-Kyrios* incarnate.

What the study of such traditions does show, however, is how far the early Christian treatment of Jesus is more like the Hellenistic treatment of rulers than it is like anything that went on in pre-Christian Judaism. On careful reflection, *the full pattern of Christ devotion in early Christianity looks in some ways much closer to what Ptolemaic priests and native populations in Hellenistic kingdoms did to their rulers than what we find in Hasmonean propaganda.* That is, the earliest Christian and Hellenistic devotees of the cult of the ruler focus strongly on the *personality* of the ruler and his *achievements* (that are celebrated in early Christianity, above all, in the Gospels and also in hymns of praise to him such as those in Phil 2:5–11 and Col 1:15–20). Both, then, provide for a pattern of ritual actions in honor of the divine ruler (with Christians feasting in memory of Jesus' life, death, and resurrection at the regular eating of the "Lord's Dinner"). It is true, of

---

29. For the distinction between an encomium (praise of a mortal) and a hymn (praise of a God) see Plato *Rep.* 10:607a and the discussion in Vollenweider, "Hymnus," 212–13.

30. See esp. Gardner, "Jewish Leadership," 332–37.

course, that there are fundamental differences too; with the early Christians not *adding* the cult of Christ to that of Israel's one God and their being no cult statues set up in shrines in his honor. Nevertheless, the similarities between the Christ cult and the non-Jewish Ruler Cult helps us to appreciate the lack of precedent for Christ devotion in the pre-Christian Jewish materials. But the similarities between the Greco-Roman treatment of rulers and the early Christian devotion to Jesus Christ merits further reflection. It is a subject which we shall return to in Part 6.

For now it is enough to stress that, whilst Jewish traditions expressing praise of a ruler offer a limited precedent for what Christians did to Jesus of Nazareth, it is not at all clear that once Jesus was recognized as messianic king that those Jewish traditions would lead "directly to the scenes of acclamation and obeisance" and to the very specific kinds of "hymns and the titles preserved in the New Testament" for Jesus (as Horbury proposed).[31] Neither, of course, is it now possible to argue, in the light of all that has been achieved by the likes of Hurtado and Bauckham, that "Christological monotheism" and its accompanying Christ devotion is the result of a competitive response to emperor worship. Early Christian competition with Roman religion would not have turned a "low" view of Jesus into one in which he is included in the identity of the one God. And in any case, all the signs are that "Christological monotheism" was birthed long before the early church was forced to reckon with Gentile claims for the emperor. Something else must have caused Jesus to be included fully within the divine identity in a way that is, nevertheless, comparable with, but that also goes beyond, what Greco-Roman communities accorded their rulers. So, the implausibility of Horbury's proposal that Jewish messianism (and Jesus' identification as the royal messiah) led *inevitably* to the Christ cult leaves us still in search of an explanation of Christological origins.

But we should not leave his work there. Some critical observations on other aspects of Horbury's work helps to orient us towards aspects of Jewish messianism, and recent work on it, that will ultimately lead to a more historically viable account for the birth of the earliest Christology.

3: High Priestly and Royal Messianism

Horbury works hard to counter the views of messianic minimalists who, in recent decades, have argued that there really is very little messianic hope in the pre-Christian world.[32] He argues both for the prevalence and continuity,

31. Horbury, *Jewish Messianism*, 150.
32. For a discussion of such voices, see Horbury, *Jewish Messianism*, 36–37; "Early

throughout the Second Temple period, of a Jewish hope for a coming royal messiah. His efforts certainly help to tip the balance back towards the traditional view that many or most Jews in the first century were hoping for a coming messiah. However, he overstates the extent of a *royal* messianic hope.[33]

One secure finding of the recent study of postexilic and Second Temple Judaism is the conclusion of the overwhelming majority of specialists that Jewish messianism was far more variegated than used to be thought (and than still seems to be assumed by some New Testament scholars). Biblical and extrabiblical texts, emanating from a variety of contexts and periods, look forward to royal, priestly, and prophetic "messiahs" and redeemer figures with "messianic" characteristics. The precise shape of those expectations varied from one period to another and, with the discovery and full publication of the Dead Sea Scrolls there is solid evidence that the shape of the messianic hope was a cause of party division. And beneath that variety of expectations for a coming ruler or redeemer there was a variety of positions on the more fundamental question: how should the nation be governed, now and in the eschatological future? Some Jews advocated leadership by a high priest who is also a royal ruler, whether a "king" in name or not was debated (see below), whilst others espoused a diarchic leadership by separate royal and priestly figures. There is very little evidence that anyone thought the nation's government should not include, somewhere in the picture, a high priest. By contrast, it has become increasingly clear in the last few decades that "there existed in early Judaism no continuous, widespread, or dominant expectation for a davidic messiah" (or for a royal, but not Davidic, messiah).[34]

There are a few texts where a Davidic and royal messiah is explicitly present, especially for the period after the first century BC when there was growing dissatisfaction with the Hasmonean royal priesthood and a new Roman and Herodian rule brought a painful change in political and religious circumstances (e.g., *Pss. Sol.* 17-18; 4Q174; 11QTS 56:12—59:21). But many primary sources, especially from the period before Roman rule, show no interest in a Davidic, royal messiah in a way that is quite surprising if we had reconstructed Jewish theology and hope entirely from the

---

Christology," 4-7; Chester, *Messiah*, 191-230, 276-97.

33. See the critical, but also appreciative, assessment of the details of Horbury's reconstruction in Chester, *Messiah*, 216-21, 277-84 (esp. 279-82).

34. Pomykala, *Davidic Dynasty*, 270. Cf. e.g., Pomykala, "Messianism," 939; Himmelfarb, *Kingdom of Priests*, 195 n. 86: a lack of "clear evidence for the expectation of a Davidic messiah in texts of the Second Temple period." For the absence see further Knibb, "Septuagint and Messianism"; J. J. Collins, "Messianism and Exegetical Tradition"; "Son of God," 305; Regev, *Hasmoneans*, 142-50.

evidence provided by the New Testament. In the face of this *lack* of evidence, Horbury's dogged insistence that there was a *consistent* and pervasive messianic hope partly has to do with assumptions he brings to the sources. In particular, he tends to assume (as have almost all parties in the ongoing debate around Christological origins) that "messianism" must mean *royal* messianism; the hope for a coming *king*.

Alongside the growing recognition that there is actually much less evidence of an interest in a *king* messiah in Second Temple Judaisms than it was previously thought there has been, simultaneously, an increased awareness of the importance of the priesthood both for postexilic political theology and for messianic expectations for a future, final deliverance. *Time and again we find that, on close examination, both Israel's Scriptures and the historical data that describe facts on the ground, it is the priesthood, especially the high priest, that governs the nation (either without or alongside a separate king).*[35] The high priest is an "anointed one," a *messiah* (e.g., Exod 28:41; Lev 4:5; 1 Chr 29:22; Sir 45:15, cf. e.g., 1QS 9:11; *m. Hor.* 2:2, 3, 7; 3:4; *2 En.* 22:8-10), and indeed has strongly royal characteristics. This, in turn, partly explains the absence of a belief in an independent royal household or hope for a coming king for much of the Second Temple period.

The priestly framers of the Pentateuch put the priesthood at the head of the nation in all spheres of life.[36] Israel are *allowed* a king (Deut 17:14-20), but only *required* to have a high priest, and throughout the Second Temple period, with the partial exception of the Herodian age, the nation was led by the high priest and his colleagues. From Aristobulus I (104-103 BC) onwards, the Hasmonean high priests claimed the title "king" and wore its symbol—a diadem (*J.W.* 1:70, cf. *Ant* 13:301; 20:241). Earlier Hasmonean high priests claimed to fulfill many of the roles of Israel's kings (see, for example, the evocation of biblical kingship passages in the descriptions of Judas and Simon in 1 Macc 3 and 14). Their incorporation of royal functions alongside or under the umbrella of their priestly office was not a novelty. Neither was it some kind of theological aberration. The Hasmoneans rose to power because they were the archdefenders of the faith, fighting for Torah and Temple against forces that could have subsumed the nation in

---

35. See e.g., E. P. Sanders, *Judaism*; Grabbe, *Judaic Religion*, 38, 53, 57-58, 136, 146-49; *First Century Judaism*, 29-36; the series of important articles by Arie van der Kooij ("Exod 19:6"; "Moses"; "Royal Priesthood"; "LXX Exod 23"; "Isaiah 9:6-7"); VanderKam, *Joshua to Caiaphas*; J. Angel, "Traditional Roots," esp. 53, and *Eschatological Priesthood*, 257-95.

36. As Horbury recognized in an important study ("Aaronic Priesthood"), which stands somewhat apart from his more recent work that has focused so exclusively on the king messiah.

a pan-Hellenic religious and political multiculturalism. And there is now plenty of evidence that their predilection for a *royal* high priesthood was essentially faithful to an older, traditional, Jewish political theology, and one firmly grounded in Scripture.

There is now plenty of evidence that a *royal*-priesthood model of governance was the preferred form of government for most of the preceding centuries of the postexilic period. This is one clear conclusion of the recent careful study of the history of the high priesthood by James C. VanderKam.[37] VanderKam shows that after the exile and return, all the way down through the pre-Maccabean period, Israel was governed by a high priesthood that wielded civic, not just cultic, authority.

His historical study correlates to the theology of several texts that show political realities in the pre-Maccabean period cannot simply be explained away as a reflection of what was possible under the constraining hand of Persian rule. It was not that Judea was simply forced to accept priestly rule because international relations prevented them having their own king. Recently published Dead Sea Scroll material, such as the third- or fourth- (or possibly second-) century BC *Aramaic Levi Document,* and studies of the important pre-Maccabean Hebrew Wisdom text Ben Sira show that for many Jews a royal priesthood was the *ideal,* not merely a reluctant accommodation to political realities.[38] In Ben Sira, the covenant with David is fulfilled not through a coming king, *but in the office of high priest* (see esp. 45:24–25). There is no hope for a future king in the one clear passage that looks forward to God's future work of salvation (36:1–22) and Simon, the high priest of the author's own day, acts to protect the nation in the way Israel's king had once done (compare 50:1–4 with 48:17–22; 49:11–13).[39] In the *Aramaic Levi Document,* the language of biblical royal oracles is even applied to the priesthood (see Isa 11:2 in *A.L.D.* 1 viii and Gen 49:10 in *A.L.D.* 67),[40] in a way that is still visible in the later Greek *Testament of Levi*

---

37. VanderKam, *Joshua to Caiaphas* (2004). His study does not include the evidence of the early Enoch literature and *Aramaic Levi Document,* which further strengthen the point.

38. For the pre-Maccabean crisis dating of *A.L.D.* see H. Drawnel, *Aramaic Wisdom Text,* 63–75; Greenfield, Stone, and Eshel, *Aramaic Levi Document,* 19–22.

39. See already Mack, *Hebrew Epic,* 35–36, 84–87, 167–71, and numerous more recent studies (e.g., Himmelfarb, "Ben Sira"; *Kingdom of Priests,* 34–38; Hayward, *Temple,* 47–49; 51, 70–71; Pomykala, *Davidic Dynasty,* 133–42; Knibb, "Septuagint and Messianism," 360, and van der Kooij, "Royal Priesthood," 260).

40. *A.L.D.* references follow the division of the text in R. Bauckham, J. R. Davila, and A. Panayotov, *Old Testament Pseudepigrapha: More Non-Canonical Scriptures,* (= *MOTP*).

(*T. Levi* 2:3; 4:5).[41] In other words *A.L.D.* does not need to look for a future coming king *because, it claims, classic biblical prophecies predicting a future "royal messiah" are fulfilled in and through the high priesthood.* In such texts, king*ship* remains—in faithfulness to Scripture—an integral part of a messianic hope, but *the king* does not. The priesthood takes up kingship in the place of a separate king. Horbury mistakenly claims that Ben Sira believes in a dual constitution (of king and priest) and he does not engage with the evidence of the *Aramaic Levi Document*.[42]

The earliest portions of the Enochic corpus that date from at least the third century BC and that were widely influential thereafter should probably be added to this evidence of Ben Sira and the *Aramaic Levi Document*. In the *Book of Watchers* (1 *En.* 1–36), stories of primeval sacral *kingship* in the Mesopotamian world (and perhaps in preexilic Israel) are transferred to Enoch, who is portrayed as a proto-high priest. Enoch is the Jewish answer to the antediluvian priest-king Enmeduranki of much older Akkadian texts, but his activities in this Jewish apocalypse are thoroughly priestly and the text has no interest in a separate royal figure.[43]

In the past, scholarship has tended to assume that Second Temple political theology cherished a separation of political and religious (cultic) spheres, viewing the involvement of the high priesthood in political affairs in the decades before the Great Revolt a lamentable departure from the biblical ideal.[44] But this is probably an anachronistic modern judgment borne of a "Two Kingdoms" political theology and the legacy of the Reformation that protested against the power of the priesthood in the Catholic Church. The evidence of the Hasmonean model of government, its continuity with the structure that prevailed in the pre-Maccabean era and texts that show

---

41. For Gen 49:10 in *A.L.D.* 67, see Drawnel, *Aramaic Wisdom Text*, 307–8 and Stone, Greenfield, and Eshel, *Aramaic Levi*, 35, 184–88 (= 11:6 in their division of the text).

42. Horbury, *Jewish Messianism*, 57. Chester, *Messiah*, who also puts much store by messianic texts, tends to exaggerate their *royal* character at the expense of evidence for priestly messianism (in, for example, his discussion of Qumran literature—*Messiah*, 69–71, 276), and he does not engage with the *Aramaic Levi Document*, recent work on Ben Sira, and VanderKam's important book on the high priesthood. John J. Collins discussed the application of biblical kingship texts to the priesthood in *A.L.D.* and *T. Levi* 18 in his important 1994 study of Jewish messianic expectation (*Scepter*, 86–89), but, without any real argumentation, played down the way these texts make the high priest a royal figure.

43. For Enoch's priestly characteristics in the *Book of Watchers* (and in other texts) see Fletcher-Louis, *All the Glory*, 20–27; Orlov, "Roles and Titles," 118–24. It is a mistake to say that in the *Book of Watchers* there is no messianism (so e.g., Kvanvig, "Son of Man," 200). There *is* messianism: it is *priestly* messianism.

44. See, e.g., Jeremias, *Jerusalem*, 149, 151, 158; cf. Rooke, *Zadok's Heirs*, and Bond, *Caiaphas*, 33–34.

how far a royal priesthood had become a theological ideal all point to a very different political theology to the one that has prevailed in the western Christian tradition.

This is not to deny that a hope for a royal messiah set apart from the high priest was not a live option for Jews. We know it was and it was bound to have been a live option because the Bible contains a covenant with David and prophecies of a future coming king. Sometimes in recent decades the case for a lack of interest in a *royal* messiah has been greatly overstated, as for example when E. P. Sanders argued that there is no royal messiah in the Qumran *War Scroll*.[45] But the existence of texts that give pride of place to the high priesthood or a high priestly figure (with no king or a subordinate royal figure) cannot be doubted (in addition to those above see e.g., *T. Mos.* 10:2; 4Q541 frag. 9; 1QSb 4–5; 11QTS 56:12—59:21). And it is not at all surprising that such texts exist: they correspond to what we know of Jewish political theology from the facts on the ground for most of the Second Temple period.

Furthermore, *the Second Temple belief that the high priest takes up the role and identity that was at one time played by the king is biblical.* The laws of Moses view the high priest as a royal figure in a way that would mean it was natural to conclude that a separate king was not necessary for an Israel organized in accordance with Torah (so Exod 28–29 should be read alongside Zech 3–6 where the postexilic constitution makes do without a king).[46] Some aspects of Aaron's garments are *distinctively* royal (the *mitsnefet*—the "turban" of Exod 28:4, 39, cf. Ezek 21:31 (Heb. = Eng. 21:26) and Isa 62:3; the *nezer* of Exod 29:6, cf. 2 Sam 1:10; 2 Kgs 11:12; Pss 89:40 (Heb. = Eng. 89:40); 132:18; 2 Chr 23:11), whilst others (the multicolored, bejewelled breastpiece and ephod) are *fitting* for a king (though not his sole prerogative). So it is not surprising that many postexilic texts say the (high) priest wore *royal* clothing. Many say he wore a crown (Heb. *'atarah, kalil, keter*; Gk. *stephanos*—Zech 6:11;[47] Ben Sira/Sirach 45:12; Josephus *J.W.* 5:235; *Ant.* 3:172, 187; 20:12; Philo *Moses* 2:114, *T. Levi* 8:2, 9, *3 En.* 1:3; 2:3, cf. Ezek 28:12; 1QSb 4:2–3; 11Q18 14 ii 2–5; 4Q405 23 i 6; *Let. Arist.* 98; *3 En.* 12:3).[48] In three he wears a *royal* "diadem" (Wis 18:24; Philo, *Flight* 111;

---

45. E. P. Sanders, *Practice and Belief,* 296. For the royal messiah in the *War Scroll* see 1QM 5:1 and 11:6–7 (discussed in Fletcher-Louis, *All the Glory,* 412–19).

46. See the recent treatments of the biblical Aaron in Davies, *Royal Priesthood,* 157–61, and Propp, *Exodus 19–40,* 524–25, 732.

47. Actually multiple crowns in both the Greek and Hebrew of Zech 6:11.

48. This tradition is also represented in the rabbinic-era Avodah *piyyutim*: see *Atah Konanta 'olam me-rosh* (in Swartz and Yahlom, *Avodah,* 72–73); and *Azkir gevurot elohah* 161 (ibid., 262–63); *Atah konanta 'olam be-rov ḥesed* 101 (ibid., *Avodah,* 318–19).

T. Levi 8:10; cf. Philo *Flight* 118; *Moses* 2:116, 131; Josephus *Ant.* 20:241, 244; *J.W.* 1:70).

In keeping with these interpretations of his garments in royal terms, a (high) priest can be placed on a throne. This is clear in the Hebrew of Zech 6:13 and the figure enthroned in heaven in 4Q491c frag. 1, 5-6 is almost certainly a priest (cf. thrones for priestly figures in Ps 110:1, 4; *2 En.* 24:1). Furthermore, functions that at one time would have been regarded distinctive prerogatives of the king are also given to the priesthood in the biblical and postbiblical texts. Historically, Israel's king had, at one time, acted as judge (2 Sam 8:15; 1 Kgs 3:9-28; 10:9, cf. Jer 22:3; 23:5), as was usual for ancient Near Eastern kings. But in the Pentateuch and in other biblical and extrabiblical sources it is the priesthood (along with Levites and a wider body of lay elders) who hold judicial responsibility (Deut 17:8-9; 21:5; Ezek 44:24; 2 Chr 19:8-11; Zech 3:7, cf. e.g., Hecataeus of Abdera XL.3.5; *A.L.D.* 14-15, 99;[49] Ben Sira 45:17; *Jub.* 30:18-21; 31:15; *T. Levi* 8:17; 1QSb 3:26-28; Josephus *Ant.* 4:218; *Ag. Ap.* 2:187). Aaron's "breastpiece of judgment" (Exod 28:15, 29-30) also functioned as a war oracle, revealing to the people when and when not to go forth against an enemy (Num 27:21). Already in the Pentateuch (Gen 34; Exod 32:27-29; Num 25), and all the way down through the postexilic period—not just under the Hasmoneans—priests are warriors, agents of God's judgment with the sword, the nation's leaders in battle; both spiritually and physically (Num 27:21; Deut 20:2-4; 2 Macc 15:12-16; *T. Levi* 5-6; the Qumran *War Scroll*—1QM, esp. 10:2-5;[50] Josephus *Ant.* 13:282-83; *Jos. Asen.* 23:14-17; 26:6; 27:6; *T. Mos.* 10:2; 11QMelch ii 9-14, cf. *Ant.* 13:284-87; *T. Reub.* 6:10-12). So, it is unsurprising that under Roman rule the high priest's garments, which evidently symbolized kingship and that could function as a war oracle, were, for the most part, kept under Roman (or Herodian) control, under lock and key in the Antonia Fortress, except for use at festivals (Josephus *Ant.* 15:404-8; 18:90-93; 20:5-12).[51] We have no hard evidence, but we can reasonably assume that they were protected in this way because they easily became the focus of "messianic" hope; the high priest who wore them might attempt to lead the nation in a

---

49. The translation of *A.L.D.* 14-15, in *MOTP* (p. 136) does not convey the judicial force of the Greek and Aramaic. For *A.L.D.* 14-15, 99 see the text and commentary in Drawnel, *Aramaic Wisdom Text*, 118-19; 164-65; 263-64, 343, 360-61, 372-73.

50. For the priesthood's role in the Qumran eschatological war, see Fletcher-Louis, *All the Glory*, 403-412, 423-475.

51. Jeremias's view that "the campaign over the high priest's vesture was for Jewry a religious campaign" (*Jerusalem*, 149) typifies his assumption that the priesthood was set up to be carefully separated from the political sphere.

revolt, whether by claiming himself to be a king or simply as a representative on earth of God, the King (with or without a separate royal messiah figure).

This evidence for a political theology that gives pride of place to a *royal priest* (a priest who is royal, not a king who is priestly), which has come to the fore only in the last couple of decades, is of inestimable significance for an understanding of Christian origins. The fact that, in the later years of the Second Temple period, some groups (such as the Qumran community) espoused a dual messianism is well known.[52] That separation of priesthood and kingship was likely a reaction to the perception that the combination of the two in one individual had led, with the Hasmoneans, to a corruption of power. However, Scripture and the relevant later Jewish texts such as those found in the Qumran caves are clear that for such a political settlement to work, the king nevertheless must remain *subordinate to* the priesthood that is entrusted with Torah instruction and leadership in the cultic sphere.

In all such matters the Pentateuchal laws are paramount. Deuteronomy *allows* the nation to have a king. But he has no positive function and his position is hedged about with warnings and regulations that anticipate the failures of Solomon and his successors (Deut 17:14–20, cf. 33:7). (The passage is most likely hostile to kingship in principle, but carefully composed to reflect the historical facts of the Israelite monarchy in the preexilic period.)[53] It is the priest who has supreme legal authority, not just in the cultic sphere (Deut 17:8–13, cf. 1 Kgs 3:16–28), and the Levites receive the fullest dose of Moses's blessing as the nation's teachers and ministers before the LORD (Deut

---

52. For the belief in a diarchic government outside Qumran see: (a) material in the *Testament of the Twelve Patriarchs,* which is likely to be a pre-Christian reaction to the Hasmonean combination of kingship and priesthood (*T. Jud.* 21:1–5; *T. Sim.* 7:1; *T. Jos.* 19:11, cf. *T. Reub.* 6:7–8; *T. Dan* 5:4; *T. Gad* 8:1); (b) perhaps the evidence of Pseudo-Philo (*L.A.B.* 48:2; 51:6–7); (c) the leadership of the movement Josephus called the "Fourth Philosophy" (Josephus *Ant.* 18:4), that was co-led by Zadok (who was surely a priest) and one named "Judas," or "Judah" (who was surely from the royal tribe); (d) and the Bar Kochba revolt (led by the would-be royal messiah Simon and the priest Eleazer). Given the political significance of Qumran and Essenism, of the Fourth Philosophy and of the Bar Kochba revolutionaries, it is likely that dual messianism became, in the first century AD, *the* alternative to the older royal-priestly model of governance. Perhaps it was the preferred view among some of the Pharisees and the masses (whilst the Sadducean aristocracy held on to the older view that the high priest was royal). Luke 1–2 suggests that at one time a John-the-Baptist–Jesus-of-Nazareth movement attracted the hope for a messianic restoration jointly led by a king and a priest. At any rate, Luke's historical note on messianic expectations gathering around (the *priest*) John the Baptist (Luke 3:15) is unsurprising testimony to the popular hope for a true priest messiah. In all this, of course, I mean by "messiah" or "messianic" far more than a narrow focus on eschatological redemption (as, for example in Chester, *Messiah*).

53. See now the important study of Deut 17:14–20 in Nicholson, *Deuteronomy,* 101–16.

33:8–11). So it is hardly surprising that when Second Temple texts envisage a joint messianic rule, in accordance with that Deuteronomic framework, the priest's superior position and responsibilities are clearly set out (see, e.g., *Jub.* 31:11–20; 1QSb 4–5; 4Q161 frags. 8–10 iii 17–24). This Deuteronomic pattern is vividly and emphatically elaborated in the vision of the eschatological future laid out in the Temple Scroll (11QTS 56:12—59:21).

The Pentateuch, it should be remembered, contains the laws of Moses, which according to the scriptural account of things are older than Israelite kingship, which, in any case, God gave to his people somewhat begrudgingly (1 Sam 8–13). In the ancient world generally—and this was no less true for Second Temple Judaism—*what is old is superior to the new.* That means Jews in antiquity would have reason to believe that the Pentateuchal constitution was preferable to the Davidic, Solomonic, and later preexilic model in which the priesthood is both separate from, and was sometimes subordinate to, the king.[54] That prioritizing of Torah (and priesthood) over kingship is, of course, consistent with the way in which the former is given to Israel through revelation at Sinai, whereas the latter is a human institution modeled on the royal rule amongst Israel's neighbors (1 Sam 8:5, 10–20). This, of course, is the other way around to the way history has worked in the Protestant West, where the Reformation and the waves of political and religious protest it spawned (including a tradition of protest from within the Catholic Church itself) have consistently proclaimed the new over against the old of the medieval world and its ongoing legacy. In the story we moderns tell ourselves the new (the "modern") is better than the old.

Furthermore, Protestant and modern secular metanarratives have long told us that it is the role of the king and secular authorities—the guardians of true religious liberty and protest—to set the people free from the oppressive powers of anachronistic institutions, especially the (Catholic) Church—the new Babylon—and its priests. Successive waves of protest, reform, and pioneering ventures in the religious and political spheres over the last four centuries have brought us many blessings, not least the freedom to subject Scripture, and traditional interpretations of it, to rigorous historical analysis. But latterly it has also had one lamentable consequence: we have developed a blind spot to some basic assumptions of ancient Jewish *and biblical* political theologies. *There is no evidence that Jews in the late Second Temple period thought about the relationship between kings and priests in the way that most of us have in the West for the last four hundred years.* Indeed,

---

54. For the correlation old-or-ancient equals true-and-reliable see, e.g., Josephus *C. Ap.* 1:59.

it is likely that matters were the other way around to the way they have been since the sixteenth century.

The Old Testament has some rather obvious and prominent passages that are strongly critical of kingship and the nation's desire for a king (esp. 1 Sam 8–13; 1 Kgs 9–12; Hos 8:4).[55] These stand alongside a clear preference for priestly and Levitical authority and leadership in the Pentateuch and other postexilic texts. Why it should be the case that the Bible has a bias to the priesthood and only a qualified support for kingship in its own right is a matter to which I will return in Part 5. In the new paradigm I will lay out some evidence for thinking that, inter alia, the Pentateuch and Primary History (Genesis–2 Kings) gives to priests a God-sanctioned supreme authority precisely because it was the priestly office that was designed to protect the nation from the destructive, abusive, and rebellious behavior of kings. The primacy of priesthood in the Hebrew Bible (and the Septuagint) articulates both profound theological reflection on the nature of leadership in God's people and also an urgent political pragmatism. Be that as it may, the traditional, pre-Hasmonean, king-free (royal-)priesthood constitution, that has a firm basis in the laws of Moses, seems to have been the established default model of both present and future ("messianic") governments throughout the Second Temple period. There certainly are texts that pick up the biblical promises to David and look forward to a coming royal messiah, and these become a particular feature of late-first-century BC and first-century AD Jewish hope. Christianity is the most obvious, undeniable, evidence for the presence of a well-developed and deeply held hope for a royal messiah in first-century Judaism.

But there is really no evidence that any Jewish movements imagined that the nation could be led by a king *and a king alone*. That lack of evidence is unsurprising. Such a scenario would run directly counter to the laws of Moses, which insist on the need for an anointed priest at the head of the nation, whether or not he governed the nation alongside and over and above a separate royal figure. The dual messianism that springs up in the late Second Temple period should perhaps be seen primarily as a response to the failures

---

55. Ben Sira offers a clear example of the kind of political theology that justified the priestly hegemony of the Second Temple period. In the praise of the fathers, it is kings who manifest the problem of sin (see Ben Sira/Sir 47:11, 19–21, 23–25; 49:4–5 and Mack, *Hebrew Epic*, 29). On the other hand, the way that the biblical promises to the king are transferred to the priesthood in 45:24–25 goes with an overarching biblical narrative that takes the high priest back to Adam (see esp. 49:16—50:1), through the priestly Enoch (44:16; 49:14). Arguably, Ben Sira is simply a good reader of Israel's Primary History (Genesis–2 Kings) and its political theology. In any case, in his prioritizing of Aaron and Moses and Adam's original glory over her kings he exemplifies the typical ancient conviction that the best constitution has the prestige of primeval origins.

6. THE KING, THE MESSIAH & THE RULER CULT

of the Hasmonean version of the model where the high priest's royalty was allowed to extend to the point that he claimed the actual title "king." In that case, the fact that diarchy was the preserve of marginal movements, such as the one based at Khirbet Qumran, suggests that *in the first century AD the traditional, historic, and biblically preferable model—the older alternative to dual messianism—was still royal priesthood.* The active involvement of the Saducean high priesthood in the early stages of the revolt against Rome in AD 66 shows that they (and many among the wider populous) still clung to the belief that the nation should be led by a (royal) high priest.[56]

Once we recognize the strong priestly dimension of Second Temple political theology, features of the primary sources that are otherwise obscured come to the fore. Throughout the modern period scholarship has observed and attempted to explain the fact that there are different kinds of messianism in the primary sources that have come down to us. As we have seen, attention has focused, in particular, on the impression that some texts speak of a transcendent, heavenly, or even "divine" messiah (in, for example, the Enochic *Similitudes* and *4 Ezra* 13), whilst others envisage the kind of earthly, Davidic (or David-like) ruler that crops up in accounts of messianic movements of revolt in Josephus and other sources (e.g., *Pss. Sol.* 17–18; 1QM 11; Josephus *J.W.* 2:57–59; *Ant.* 17:273–84; 18:1–10 and texts describing the leader of the revolt—Simon ben Kosiba—in AD 132–135). What has largely escaped NT scholars' attention is the likelihood that alongside a *variety* of perspectives on the human-or-transcendent identity (or the nature or "ontology") of the messiah, *there is important evidence for a thoughtful and passionate debate around the relationship between a royal, Davidic messiah on the one hand, and a high priestly messiah on the other.* We can be confident that there was such a debate because, for one thing, Israel's Scriptures are equivocal on the question of the ideal, God-intended model of national governance. Within the Pentateuch itself, some texts (that modern scholars attribute to the priestly author) advocate a (royal) high priest, after the model of Aaron, with no apparent need for a king (see, e.g., Exod 28–29, cf. Deut 17:8–13). Others, such as Deut 17:14–20 (cf. Num 24:17), do allow—or envisage a role for—a king (alongside and in submission to the priesthood). *Scripture itself does not tell the first-century reader how to reconcile these alternative models: it invites creative, thoughtful interpretation and debate.* We should assume that many Jews were waiting for God's final acts in history to make clear the way royal and priestly functions would be fulfilled in the new age.

---

56. For an investigation of the role of the priestly aristocracy in the leadership of the revolt (that overstates the case for a lack of involvement of other parties), see Goodman, *Ruling Class.*

The fact that Jews must have been acutely aware of the differences between royal and priestly positions, and the variety of possible models for the relationship between the king and priest in the ideal, eschatological age bears directly on some of the evidence that Horbury (and others) bring to the discussion of Christological origins. In the rest of this chapter I identify three weaknesses in Horbury's assessment of the primary sources. Discussion of these will help prepare for the new paradigm that I will lay out in Parts 5 and 6. In particular, an awareness of the biblical preference for the priesthood alongside a critique of kingship, which figures too little in Horbury's assessment of things, brings into focus the ways in which a Jewish engagement with the Greco-Roman belief that special individuals had a "divine" status was tied to distinctively Jewish beliefs about the identity of humanity as a whole.

I: The Divine "Glory" of the (High Priestly) Messiah

First, then, it is worth reflecting on Horbury's use of the word *"glorious"* to sum up the Jewish hope for a "spiritual messiah" who is more than human and, in some cases, very much "divine."[57] There is no doubt that "glory" is an appropriate word to describe some language for the royal messiah in Jewish texts. It helps Horbury establish genuine connections to the ways in which rulers appear in the context of the Greco-Roman Ruler Cult and it prepares for his claim that Jewish messianism explains an early high Christology, since the "glory" (*doxa*) of Christ figures prominently in NT texts. It is one of the ways that he attempted to demonstrate coherence where others have lately argued for a not-so-coherent variety of messianic expectations. But the use of the language of "glory" in the Jewish material needs to be examined carefully, not least because the English word can all-too-easily betray subtle distinctions in the Jewish primary texts.

Hebrew and Greek words behind the English "glory" are often used to describe messianic figures who are, without a shadow of a doubt, royal (see below). However, the Jewish sources distinguish between the use of such terminology to describe something that is properly *God's* (and that God bestows on others) and something that properly belongs to human beings (that might be better translated "honor"). In Hebrew texts, God has

---

57. E.g., Horbury, "Early Christology," 20, 23; *Jews and Christians*, 148 (on Isa 32:2); "Monotheism" 40. My comments on the relative importance of royal and priestly categories apply also to S. M. McDonough's attempt to connect divine glory to Israel's *royal* messiah as an inspiration for the early Christian belief in Christ as Creator (*Christ as Creator*, 86–94).

hod, hadar, and *kavod.* All these could be translated "glory," though the first two words are often more helpfully translated with similar words such as "splendor" and "majesty." The Hebrew *"kavod"* has a particular history as *the* word for the tangible, physical aura around God and for the anthropomorphic form of God on the heavenly throne in both biblical texts (Isa 6:3; Ezek 1:28) and extrabiblical ones (see *1 En.* 14:20 and *T. Levi* 3:4, where God is "the Great Glory").

There are texts where the king has *hod* and *hadar* (e.g., Heb. Pss 21:6 [Eng. 21:5]; 45:3-4 [Eng. 45:2-3], cf. 110:3). There are others, that stem in particular from 1 Kgs 3:13-14, where God promises to give Solomon *kavod* (*doxa* in the Greek—cf. 1 Chr 29:28; 2 Chr 1:11-12; 32:27). But in some texts it is clear that this royal *kavod* comes *from below*—from the king's achievements and *the honor given to him by others* (Isa 22:23-24; Prov 25:2, cf. 1 Macc 14:10, 39). There are no biblical texts where the king's *kavod* or *doxa* clearly comes from above *and is God's own divine glory (that is occasionally seen on or in close proximity to his heavenly throne).* And in the account of Solomon's reign that follows the divine promise in 1 Kgs 3, the choreography of the Temple dedication is careful to ensure that Solomon himself is separated from the divine glory that fills the sanctuary (1 Kgs 8, esp. vv. 6-14). After the disaster of the exile and the failures of Israel's kings, there is some hope for a new king, but it is striking that in Zech 6:13 the most that can be said is that the coming king will bear "splendor" (*hod,* translated "virtue" in the Greek, cf. 10:3).[58] In the biblical texts where Horbury rightly points out there is exalted, even "divine" language for the king (e.g., Pss 2, 45, 72, 89), any notion of the king possessing *God's own* glory is consistently avoided (see esp. Ps 72:18-19). This pattern continues in postbiblical literature.[59]

So, for example, with Ben Sira's careful use of glory language for the priesthood (45:7, 20, 23; 50:7, 11, 13), but not for Israel's kings, it "is hard to escape the conclusion that for Ben Sira the truly glorious institution, the institution whose occupants were worthy of it, was priesthood, not kingship."[60] The Qumran *Scroll of Blessings* (1QSb) carefully distinguishes

---

58. Cf. Zech 10:3, where *Yhwh-Kyrios* makes the house of Judah "like *his majestic* war horse (*sus hodo*)".

59. I agree with Bauckham (*God of Israel,* 228-29) that *Ps. Sol.* 17:31 does not refer to the glory of the coming royal messiah as the glory of *Yhwh-Kyrios* (*pace* Horbury, *Jewish Messianism,* 103). The context and other references to the glory of Jerusalem (in *Pss. Sol.* 2:19, 21; 11:7) show that the reference is to the glory of the restored holy city. The "man of glory" in 1QM 12:8 is a possible, but by no means certain, reference to a royal human figure with divine glory (see Fletcher-Louis, *All the Glory,* 442-45).

60. Himmelfarb, *Between Temple and Torah,* 251.

between the *kavod* given to a high priest (1QSb 4:28; cf. 3:25) and the exalted, *but glory-free*, identity of the "Prince of the Congregation" (1QSb 5:20–29). Indeed, there is an explicit promise that the *kavod* that belongs to the high priestly office will never be given to another (5:18). There is a similar contrast between Levi and Judah in the blessings of *Jubilees* 31.[61]

So, *both the biblical and postbiblical tradition avoids glory language for the king and royal messiah*, especially if there is any suggestion that a *divine* glory (or "the Glory"—*ha-kavod*) is in view.[62] On the other hand, the priest's *kavod* in 1QSb 4:28 and 5:18 (cf. 3:25) reflects the biblical command that Moses give to Aaron garments "for beauty and for *glory* (*kavod*, *doxa*)" (Exod 28:2, 40). Numerous texts from the Second Temple period have *kavod* and *doxa* (and related words) for the priesthood. In some texts this language is explicitly tied to the high priest's gold and jewel-studded garments, especially the headdress, which carries the four-lettered name of God.[63] To speak of *this* messiah as "glorious" was natural: *the high priest is Mr. Bling*. Torah's sartorial regulations for the nation's leadership make clear that glory belongs to the priesthood, but not to a separate king (who is not allowed to wear the distinctive glorious garments of the priest—Sir 45:13; cf. Lev 19:19; Deut 22:11; Josephus *Ant*. 4:208; *m. Kil*. 9:1) and for whom no special gold and jewel-studded radiant garments are stipulated. *Some of the texts that speak of priestly "glory" also indicate that God's own divine Glory is meant* (the Hebrew text of Ben Sira 45:7–8, 20; both Hebrew Ben Sira and Greek Sirach 50:7, 11; *Let. Arist*. 98; 4Q408 3 + 3a line 5; 4Q405 23 ii 3, 8–9, cf. 1QSb 4:28).[64]

---

61. Macaskill's claim (*Union with Christ*, 113) that there are "numerous examples" of texts where the (royal) messiah is "glorious" is not borne out by the texts. As Macaskill points out, David has a *"throne* of glory" (or "glorious throne" in Sir 47:11). But when it comes to glory and the human being, for Ben Sira/Sirach it is the high priest, not the king, who has divine glory.

62. Judas and Simon Maccabeus are ascribed "glory" (*doxa*) in 1 Macc 14:4–5; 15:32, 36. But this is the personal glory (or "honor") of achievements and fame, and the honor rendered by others, not God's own divine "glory." English translations sometimes obscure the way the Hebrew Bible avoids glory language for the king, but gives it to the high priest. For example, at 2 Sam 1:19 the NRSV and ESV refer to the king as the "glory" of Israel, but the word in the Hebrew is *tsevi* ("beauty"), not *kavod* (cf. translators at Zech 12:7). Meanwhile, in the NRSV the *"doxa"*—which is most certainly divine glory—of Simon the high priest in Sir 50:7, 11, 13 is translated "splendor," "splendid."

63. Ben Sira 45:7, 12; 50:7, 11; *Let. Arist*. 96, 98; 1QSb 4:28; 4Q408 3 + 3a line 5; 4Q405 23 ii 3, 8–9, cf. Josephus *Ant*. 3:187. The Qumran texts are discussed in Fletcher-Louis, *All the Glory*, 374–81.

64. I discuss these texts in my *All the Glory* and some of them will be considered in detail in Volume 3 of this book.

There are NT texts that ascribe divine glory to Jesus and such language contributes significantly to the worship of him (his "glorification") (e.g., Heb 1:3; Rev 5:12–13; cf. Phil 3:21). So, if there is a well-established tradition that the priest has God's own glory, this may well provide an important background to some of the language that goes to make up "Christological monotheism." In this case we might have a messianism that was genuinely the kind of "divine" messianism that prepared the way for Christ devotion; the kind of "divine" messianism for which Horbury has searched with only partial success in the texts witnessing to the veneration of a royal ruler or the expectation of a coming king.

However, the possibility that *priestly* messianism has any role to play in the creation of NT Christology has barely figured in modern scholarship. Obviously, such Jewish traditions would have some relevance for the Christology of Hebrews (where "glory" language figures prominently—Heb 1:3, 2:7, 9; 3:3; 13:21). But Hebrews is usually regarded as a marginal early Christian text and it has been hard to see how the possibility that some Jews believed in an exalted, let alone a glorious and "divine," priesthood has any direct bearing on other mainstream NT texts.

II: A Dubious Royal Interpretation of Dan 7:13 and Ps 110

The recent work of specialists in the Jewish and late biblical material highlighting the importance of the priesthood now invites reflection on the possibility that many of us, especially New Testament scholars, have been reading some key primary texts with royal-messiah-tinted spectacles. This is a question that could be put to several recent studies by NT scholars, and Horbury's treatment of Dan 7:13 and Ps 110 provides a particularly clear illustration of the problem.[65]

Horbury rolls up into one coherent, and undifferentiated, royal messianic identity evidence surrounding the Danielic son of man figure and the enthroned messianic Lord of Ps 110. His claim that Daniel's "one like a son of man" was widely taken in Jewish, pre-Christian interpretation as a royal messianic figure stretches the evidence.[66] There is some slight evidence for a *royal* figure in Dan 7:13. But not much. It is true that he receives

---

65. As would his treatment of the transfiguration story (Horbury, *Messianism*, 134).

66. See Horbury, *Jews and Christians*, 125–55. He is criticized by Chester (*Messiah*, 221) for his treatment of this material. Though Chester is equally unbalanced in his focus on royal, not priestly, messianism in other places. This kind of kingship bias is also a feature of N. T. Wright's work, e.g., in *Paul*, 97–139.

"kingship" or a "kingdom" (v. 14) and that he is set over against great beasts who symbolise the kings of the nations that oppress Israel (vv. 3–8, 17). But the really obvious and striking features of the man figure are hardly royal. If he is a king then why describe him as *"one like a son of man"*? That is hardly biblical kingship language. And the king is never described coming (whether to God or from God) on clouds. Indeed, if these are the clouds of God's glorious presence, it is surely not insignificant that Solomon, who for a period embodied the height and greatness of Israel's kingship (1 Kgs 3–8), is separated from such clouds as they filled the sanctuary at the Temple's dedication (1 Kgs 8, esp. vv. 1–22). If there is an Israelite king in the highly symbolic drama that is Dan 7, then where are the biblical symbols of kingship: a scepter, a rod, a mule, a branch, comparison to a lion (Gen 49:9, cf. 4 Ezra 11:37; 12:1, 31–32), or "son of God" language? *None of the classic kingship and royal messiah texts or motifs is evoked in the description of the man figure.* There is nothing else in the rest of Daniel to suggest the author looks for a coming king and so, quite rightly, the majority of commentators in the modern period have looked to other explanations of the mysterious "one like a son of man."

As we have seen, in the *Similitudes of Enoch* there is some, albeit limited, royal language used to interpret Daniel's "one like a son of man," but it is generally reckoned also that the composite Son of Man-Messiah of the *Similitudes* is *not* a royal messiah with the kind of earthly career we would expect of a king like David and Solomon. In the *Similitudes* there is an assiduous avoidance of biblical texts that describe the king doing the things that kings typically do during their earthly reign. He does not march out against his enemies, lead the nation's restoration and territorial expansion, or (re)build the Temple (as in Gen 49:8–12; Pss 45; 72; 110:2–3, cf. *Ps. Sol.* 17, 18; 1QM 11; *Sib. Or.* 3:286–94; 5:414–33). Avoidance of any account of the Son of Man's *deeds* and of his accomplishments on behalf of Israel (his *benefactions*) should probably be seen as an indication that the text is written as polemic against Greco-Roman attitudes towards the ideal ruler.[67] At any rate, it shows that *for the Enochic tradition Daniel's "one like a son of man" is royal in only a highly qualified sense.*

As for Dan 7 itself, the fact that the man figure receives "glory" (Aramaic: *yeqar*) from God in Dan 7:14 suggests that he is just as likely to be a high priest as he is a king messiah. Given the way the high priest is given royal garments and biblical kingship prophecies were fulfilled in the priesthood in contemporary Jewish texts, such royal language and imagery as there is in Dan 7:13–14 could just as well be part of a description of a figure

---

67. See Fletcher-Louis, "Similitudes," 67–71.

who is a *royal* high priest. There are also biblical texts that put the high priest in closer proximity to the clouds of God's presence than was possible for Israel's kings (see Exod 40:16-38; Lev 16:2, cf. 1 Kgs 8:10-11).

Equally, Horbury's argument that Ps 110 was already, in pre-Christian Judaism, linked to Dan 7:13 is not really convincing.[68] There is nothing very obvious that would suggest a close connection between Ps 110 and Dan 7. Although Dan 7 is clearly in view in the *Similitudes* (esp. in *1 En.* 46-48), Ps 110 is conspicuous by its absence.[69] It is possible, but hardly obvious, that Ps 110 explains the enthronement of Moses in Ezekiel the Tragedian's *Exagoge* 68-82, which, again, has no real linguistic connection to either Dan 7 or Ps 110.

There is one text where, beyond doubt, there is a parallel to the cloud-borne coming of Daniel's "one like a son of man" (Dan 7:13). That is the passage in the third- or fourth-century BC *Book of Watchers* that describes how Enoch is carried up to God's throne room by the clouds (*1 En.* 14:8—15:1). In the context, Enoch is described in language that suggests he is an Adamic figure (*1 En.* 14:2; cf. Gen 2:7, 21-24);[70] one, you might say, who is "like a son of man." He is, after all, the seventh from Adam (Gen 5:1-24). Horbury does not discuss this passage; a striking and unfortunate omission. There is nothing in the context of *1 En.* 14 to suggest that its obvious parallels to Dan 7 supports a royal messianic reading of Dan 7:13. The parallel between the two passages does, however, point to the priestly identity of Daniel's man figure, because Enoch is a proto-priest in the *Book of Watchers* and his coming to God with clouds in *1 En.* reflects the high priest's coming to God in the Holy of Holies on the Day of Atonement (Lev 16:2, 12-13).

It is understandable that modern scholars, in particular those who live and breathe NT texts, have turned to Ps 110:1 in an attempt to explain the enthronement of the Enochic Son of Man in the *Similitudes*. But it should be remembered that Ps 110 describes a figure who is first a king, and then a priest, after the order of Melchizedek (v. 4, cf. Gen 14:18-20). Psalm 110 represents the political model of the old Canaanite city-states that allowed the king to function as a priest (sacral kingship). That Canaanite view that the ruler can, or should, serve as priest in the state cult is a political model

---

68. Horbury, *Jews and Christians*, 137-42. He is indebted, in part, to the older study of Theisohn, *Der auserwählte Richter*. This is one aspect of Horbury's work that seems to have been particularly attractive to some NT scholars (e.g., Gathercole, *Preexistent Son*, 232-33).

69. Here I follow Bauckham, *God of Israel*, 170-71.

70. In the Greek at 15:1, at the climax of his ascent to heaven, Enoch is addressed as "the true man" and "man of truth." See further Fletcher-Louis, "Religious Experience," 138.

quite similar to the one adopted by the Roman emperors after Augustus was granted the office of Pontifex Maximus in 13 BC. It is emphatically *not* the model given to Israel in the laws of Moses (even though there is some evidence that it was a model that was sometimes adopted in preexilic Israel).

It is true, of course, that according to the Gospels Jesus connected Dan 7:13 and Ps 110:1 and so we are bound to wonder whether the connection was there already in pre-Christian Judaism. But there is nothing in the NT to suggest that the Jesus of the Synoptic trial story appeals to an existing tradition when he combined those two texts. And the charge of blasphemy that it provokes could be taken to mean this was in fact a shocking novelty. As it is, *the lack of explicit reference or allusion to Ps 110 in the Similitudes of Enoch is best taken as evidence that Dan 7:13 describes a different kind of figure to the one in view in that biblical psalm.*

Horbury attempts to consolidate his case for a pre-Christian (royal) messianic interpretation of Dan 7 by appeal to evidence that in this period Jews could speak of the coming king as "a/the *man*."[71] There is some limited evidence for this, though much of it comes from the period after AD 70. It is true that in the Hebrew Bible the king can be associated with Adam or the true human being as God's image (esp. in 1 Kgs 3–4, cf. Ezek 28:12–16).[72] However, *for the Jewish sources that are pre-Christian, the evidence suggests "a/the man" language would refer to the high priest set apart as the true human, or to a wider collective true humanity, represented above all by righteous Israelites*. Besides Gen 1:26–28, the most important biblical text for an interest in "man" is Ps 8; a biblical psalm that applies royal language to *humanity as a whole* (vv. 5–8). In the first century, Jesus' followers used Ps 8 (in combination with Ps 110:1) to interpret Jesus Christ's identity (e.g., 1 Cor 15:27; Eph 1:22; Heb 2:6–8). So if there was a well-established pre-Christian expectation that the royal messiah would be "a man" it is surprising that Horbury is not able to adduce any evidence for a contemporary Jewish royal messianic reading of that psalm.[73] There *is* evidence that some Jews interpreted Ps 8 messianically; but only in the sense that *the Psalm's vision of God putting "all things" under humanity's feet was fulfilled in the high priest*, who is the true Adam. In Ben Sira 49:16—50:13, it is the high priest Simon who

---

71. See Horbury, *Jews and Christians*, 144–51.

72. The Adamic character of the king of Tyre in Ezek 28 is the most obvious example. On Solomon in 1 Kgs 3–4 as an Adamic figure and God's image see, e.g., Leithart, *1 & 2 Kings*, 49–52; Beale, *Biblical Theology*, 65–73.

73. See also the criticism of Horbury's interpretation of the evidence he adduces in the Septuagint by Knibb, "Septuagint and Messianism," 360–61.

takes up the beauty of Adam, fulfilling, in turn, the vision of "man . . . the son of man" in Ps 8:4–8.[74]

III: Dan 2:46, 7:13–14, and the True Humanity Receiving Worship

This evidence of a close relationship between the high priest (who is a "messiah") and *the (true) man* takes us to one more observation on Horbury's tendency to see everything through the royal messiah lens. *The modern discussion of Jewish messianic hopes has generally failed to take account of the fact that, in its canonical form, the Hebrew Bible makes a decisive declaration that qualifies all hope for a royal ruler or redeemer.* Genesis 1:26–28 says, as Old Testament scholars have long agreed, that *the rights and responsibilities of the king in ancient Near Eastern political ideology were originally given by God to humanity as a species.* Whereas Egyptian and Assyrian kings are referred to as God's "image" (as also, for example, in the Hellenistic-era decree honoring Ptolemy V on the Rosetta Stone, cited above), the Hebrew Bible *democratizes* that privileged royal identity by ascribing it to all humanity (without any distinction of class or status within society). Psalm 8 does much the same thing with royal language applied to all human beings in their position of authority over all creation.[75]

So the Hebrew Bible draws attention away from a singular focus on a *royal* messiah and asks that God's people consider the call to *all humanity* to live the royal life. And at this point we should reflect on the way a seminal piece by N. T. Wright on the interconnectedness between "Adam, Israel, and the Messiah" bears on the nature of Jewish messianism. In his 1991 study of Pauline theology, Wright drew attention to texts in Genesis and other parts of the Hebrew Bible that evoke the language used in Gen 1:26–28 to describe God's original intention for Adam—blessed, multiplying, filling, subduing, and ruling in the earth (Gen 1:26–28).[76] The point is clear and

---

74. For Ps 8 in Ben Sira 49:16 and 50:11–13, see Aitken, "Semantics of 'Glory,'" 10; Fletcher-Louis, "Cosmology of P," 107. For the high priest and Adam see Hayward, *Jewish Temple*, 44–47. Psalm 8:5–7 [Heb.] is probably also evoked in the description of the priestly figure in 4Q418 81 lines 2–5. I discussed that passage in my *All the Glory*, 176–87, but missed the echoes of Ps 8.

75. For a recent thorough exploration of this aspect of Genesis 1 and related texts see Middleton, *Liberating Image*.

76. N. T. Wright, *Climax*, 21–26. The language of Gen 1:26–28 is evoked, for example, in Gen 12:1–3; 16:10; 17:6; 26:4; 28:3; 35:11–12; Exod 1:7; Josh 18:1. See further detailed discussion in Beale, *Biblical Theology*, 46–52. See also Wright "Romans," 416–19; *Resurrection*, 248, 333–38, 395, 582, 655.

now widely acknowledged: Israel is called to be what Adam was called to be as God's image and likeness.

Wright also argued that Israel's king and the coming royal messiah is a representative of the nation (that in turn recapitulates the original pre-fall Adam). This, he has claimed, is a key to understanding the meaning of Paul's use of the title Christ: Jesus *Christ* is Israel's representative true king; his exaltation is his people's exaltation; his faith, their faith, and so on. On this second point his argument has not won many adherents: there is scant evidence, especially in Second Temple Judaism, that royal messiah language carried the representative connotations he alleged. There are clearly places in Paul where "*christos*" is incorporative (in the frequent phrase "in Christ," for example) and others where a representative sense of the word is natural, but it is hard to find evidence that Jews would think of the *royal* messiah as representative of his people, let alone that Jews would naturally think themselves "*in* the king."[77]

But *the evidence that Israel is the true Adam is widespread, both in the Hebrew Bible and in postbiblical literature.* Gregory Beale makes this a conceptual pillar of his *New Testament Biblical Theology* and uses it with good effect in his discussion of NT Christological texts.[78] But it has figured not at all in the work of the leading voices of the Christological origins "emerging consensus."

The issue of the correlation between a ruler—a *messiah*—and Adam and Israel will be a primary focus of the new paradigm in Parts 5 and 6. It will also figure in our discussion of Phil 2:6–11 in chapter 8. Suffice it to say, at this point, that whilst Wright's unconvincing focus on the *royal* messiah probably illustrates the problem of NT scholarship's overemphasis on kingship, *his seminal argument for a story line that takes Israel's own national and covenantal identity back to Adam does help explain the shape of Jewish monotheism and the ways in which Ruler Cult traditions are used in Greco-Roman-period Judaism.* Genesis 1 echoes the language and ideology of ancient Near Eastern kingship to argue that what the nations claimed for the guy at the top, the one true God originally gave to all humanity. Adam has the privileged position as God's image that was reserved for kings in Egypt and Mesopotamia. Since Israel is the true Adam (following Wright), we are not at all surprised to find equally that there are texts that do for Israel, or for individual Israelites, what Gen 1 does for humanity. In the Pentateuch, for example, the expression "son of God" is not used for a king but for the

77. See e.g., the criticism in Chester, "Christ of Paul," though for a recent voice in Wright's support see Novenson, *Christ*, 26–28, 66, 117–19, 124–29, 131, with reference to 1 Kgs 12:16; 2 Sam 19:44 [MT & LXX: 19:43]; 20:1 (cf. Wright, *Paul*, 828–30).

78. Beale, *Biblical Theology*, 46–52, cf. McDonough, *Creator*, 86–89.

6. THE KING, THE MESSIAH & THE RULER CULT

nation as a whole (Exod 4:22; cf. Deut 14:1). Israel the people has the privileges and position in relation to the one true God that Pharaoh claimed in relation to his gods (as their "son"). There has been a "nationalisation of the royal ideology" that is everywhere else assumed in the ancient Near East.[79] This theme has been much discussed in OT scholarship, but seems generally to have been overlooked by scholars focused on NT history and theology.

Indeed, the phenomenon has largely gone unnoticed in the discussion of Jewish messianic hope outside the NT. It is generally acknowledged that "son of God" language is not as prominently connected to a royal messianic figure in Second Temple texts as we might expect it to be. And the fact that divine sonship language is used for the righteous in general in some texts (*Sib. Or.* 3:702; *Jos. Asen.* 6:3, 5; *Ps. Sol.* 17:27; Wis 2:18; 5:5) is hardly surprising given the way that in the OT the "son of God" expression was taken from the king and given to all God's people. Similarly, in the Hellenistic and Roman imperial periods, Jewish talk of the righteous in general as God's "sons" would be heard against the backdrop of divine rulers and deified emperors' claiming to be the "son of a god." There was, in effect, a strongly *republican* spirit in Second Temple Judaism that was firmly grounded in a distinctively biblical theological anthropology. So it is not at all surprising to find—but certainly surprising that scholars have missed the significance of—a statement in 1 Macc 8:14–15 praising the Roman model of government that rejected the need for a king in favor an elected ruler and senate.

Coupled with Wright's work on the relationship between Adam and Israel, the way that royal themes are applied to the whole people of God in the biblical tradition takes us back to another weakness in Horbury's analysis of the primary texts. On careful examination, some of Horbury's evidence for a Jewish sympathy for aspects of the Greco-Roman Ruler Cult actually reflects a Jewish interest in *the privileged, exalted identity of the people of God as a whole, not a king in particular*. One case study illustrates the point well and will arm us with primary source data that will equip us for the exegetical task in later chapters.

Horbury appeals to an important study of Dan 2:46 by Brian A. Mastin as evidence for a Jewish messianism that has accommodated the patterns of Ruler Cult.[80] Something very important happens in this verse, but is not quite what Horbury thinks. In Dan 2, Daniel discloses and interprets King Nebuchadnezzar's dream. In response the Babylonian king

---

79. The expression is Bernard M. Levinson's (see his "Kingship in Deuteronomy," 531).
80. Mastin, "Daniel 2:46; Horbury, *Jewish Messianism*, 75, 133."

fell on his face, worshipped Daniel, and commanded that a grain offering and incense be offered to him. (2:46)

The fact that Daniel does not reject this behavior and that he goes on to receive from the king gifts and an exalted position in Babylon (2:48–49) has long puzzled commentators. There is no substantial difference in either of the two Greek translations of the verse (LXX and Theodotian): both faithfully convey the meaning of the Aramaic. Mastin shows, through a careful analysis of the language, that there is no escaping the conclusion that, at least from the Hellenistic perspective, what the king renders to Daniel is worship and that the treatment of Daniel reflects the way divine benefactors—both the gods and divine men—were treated in the Hellenistic world.[81]

The story is a nice example of the truth of Horbury's claim that Jews in the pre-Christian era sometimes interacted positively or "inclusively" with Greco-Roman patterns of cult. However, on one point Horbury's treatment of this verse is certainly misguided: we cannot rush to the conclusion that this passage provides evidence of a Jewish *messianism* that accommodated such patterns. The main outcome of Mastin's original argument is that Daniel is treated as a divine benefactor would be treated. But in the Hellenistic environment, the Ruler Cult was one particular manifestation of the conviction that all sorts of benefactors, not just kings, should receive divine honors. Rulers were not the only ones to achieve great things for their communities. Besides the gods themselves, philosophers, miracle workers, culture heroes, and founders of city-states could also receive cultic honors in gratitude for their ("divine") works of service to society (their *benefactions*).[82] And for various reasons it is most likely that it is simply as a benefactor who is uniquely in touch with the divine realm that Daniel receives acts of cultic veneration.

Daniel in this passage is "the representative of Israelite wisdom,"[83] a "lover of wisdom" (a "philosopher," if you like), and has just demonstrated his privileged position as one who has access to the true God who is the "revealer of mysteries" (2:47, cf. vv. 20–23). He is one of those who is "skillful in all wisdom, endowed with knowledge, understanding learning" (1:4,

---

81. Ibid., 80–82; cf. J. J. Collins, *Daniel*, 171. The argument of Millard ("Incense") that there is no treatment of Daniel as divine is unconvincing. Millard ignores the text's Hellenistic context and his own lexical data shows that, taken together, the various terms used in Dan 2:46 must mean that Daniel receives worship as one with a divine status or identity.

82. See, for example, the description of the "divine" Moses as bestower of benefits on the Egyptians in *Artapanus* frag. 3:4 (Eusebius's *Praep. Evang.* 9.27.4 "as a grown man he bestowed many useful benefits on mankind" (*polla tois anthrōpois euchrēsta paradounai*).

83. Mastin, "Daniel 2:46," 89.

cf. 1:17, 20). So as a Jewish wise man, the cultic veneration of him reminds us of the way Greece's philosophers—who were thought of as mediators between the gods and men, and in the case of Pythogoras and Empedocles who were believed to have performed extraordinary miracles—were treated as divine men.[84] Of course, in Daniel's case his wisdom is a share in God's own wisdom; the one "to whom belongs wisdom and might" (2:20–23). But that only reinforces the point: Nebuchadnezzar responds to Daniel's personal or professional character, his skill, that sets him apart as one peculiarly close to the divine.

Although he is introduced in Dan 1:3 as a member of Israel's royal family, and *after* Nebuchadnezzar's worship of him in 2:46 he is exalted to a position as ruler of the province of Babylon (2:48), there is no real reason to think that the honors he receives are specifically a reflection of the Ruler Cult. *Daniel is a foreign courtier who is exalted because Nebuchadnezzar concludes from his wisdom and evident proximity to the gods, and from the service he is able to render to his own reign as king of Babylon, that he is worthy of honors befitting a god; he is worshipped as a divine benefactor, and one peculiarly intimate with the realm of the gods, but not specifically as a ruler.* His exaltation to a position as a provincial ruler gives him a function he did not have before. On the other hand, his simultaneous exaltation to a position as *"leader of all the wise men* of Babylon" (2:48) recognizes the superior wisdom he already has.

Josephus' retelling of the passage is instructive. In his *Jewish Antiquities* he explains that:

> When Nebuchadnezzar heard these things and recollected the dream, he was amazed at the nature (*physis*) of Daniel and falling on his face, he acclaimed Daniel in the manner that men worship (or "offer *proskynesis* to") God (*ton theon proskynousi*), and commanded that there be sacrifice to him as to a god (*thyein de hōs theō*) (*Ant.* 10:211–12, cf. 10:268).

For Josephus, the king treats Daniel as one worthy of the same kind of honor, that is *"worship,"* that is normally reserved for God himself. (I take it that Josephus means that Nebuchadnezzar worshipped Daniel the way Jews would worship their one God, though conceivably Josephus means that the king accorded Daniel the same kind of "worship" that would ordinarily be given to pagan gods.)

---

84. On Pythagoras and Empedocles, see Blackburn, *Miracle Traditions*, 37–53; Cotter, *Miracles*, 37–39, 143–44, 151, 189. On the divinity of the philosophers of the Hellenistic age, see Lenz, "Deification of the Philosopher."

There is no obvious reason for thinking that Josephus' interpretation distorts the biblical text. However, there is an emphasis in the biblical Daniel that Josephus probably misses: Daniel the individual epitomizes the identity (or "nature"—so Josephus) of all God's people, who, in turn, reflect the original intention for humanity.[85] Daniel is introduced as a paragon of Israelite virtue (Dan 1:3-4, 8-20) and Torah piety. Later in chapter 2 we are told that in addition to his wisdom he has the divine spirit (or "spirit of God"—*ruah 'elahin*) dwelling within him (Aramaic Dan 4:5, 6, 15 [Eng. 4:8, 9, 18]; 5:11, 14). This echoes the original creation of Adam (Gen 2:7), and Daniel's exaltation to a position of rulership over Babylon (2:48)—after he receives cultic honors—partly has in view, then, the rulership originally given to Adam in Gen 1:26-28. So Daniel is presented in these early chapters as the true Israelite and, as the true Israelite, he is what Adam was created to be.

So, on one level, these early chapters of Daniel confirm the importance of the evidence gathered by Wright in his 1991 discussion of the relationship between Adam and Israel. And those connections raise further questions about the nature of the cultic devotion given to Daniel because they anticipate the "worship" of the "one like a son of man" in Dan 7:13-14. Although it has not received the attention it deserves in Daniel scholarship, there is an obvious literary and theological relationship between Dan 2:46 and Dan 7:13-14.

In both texts a human (or humanlike) figure receives worship. Daniel is presented as a representative Israelite and his peculiarly wise and spirit-filled identity somehow makes him what Adam was created to be. The man-figure in Dan 7:13 is also often seen as a kind of true Adam. He is depicted as the truly human one over against the bestial nations and chapter 7's plot line recalls Gen 1; with the winds of heaven stirring up the sea at the start (v. 2; cf. Gen 1:2), the human figure appearing at the climax (vv. 13-14), with beasts in between (vv. 3-8, cf. Gen 1:20-25). He is also aligned closely with Israel, the "(people of) the holy ones of the Most High" (Dan 7:18-27). The divine gift of kingdom and dominion that he receives, they receive (vv. 14, 22, 27). So what he receives means the restoration to the nation of the position that was originally given to Adam (Gen 1:26, 28). Within the overarching sweep of Dan 1-7, the appearance of the "one like a son of man" gives to all the people of God something of the position and status that Daniel the wise courtier receives in 2:46-48. These points of correspondence are part of a wider set of literary parallels between Dan 2 and 7 that together

---

85. We could compare the way Moses is judged "worthy of god-like honor" (*isotheos timē*) by the Egyptians in *Artapanus* (9.27.6) (see further Barclay, *Jews*, 127-32) and the way Philo makes clear that "god" language is appropriate for Moses because he is an example to be imitated by others, i.e., by the whole nation of Israel (*Moses* 1:158).

comprise the outer bracket of a chiastic structure through the whole of Dan 2–7.[86]

There are some important interpretative conclusions that arise from the way Dan 7:13-14 reprises 2:46-48. Above all, it intensifies the case for thinking that what happens to Daniel in the first passage is somehow an acceptable expression of cultic honors. Whatever we say about Dan 7:13-14 has implications for our evaluation of 2:46-48. And the former passage tells against an argument that Daniel does not actually accept the misguided behavior of an ignorant Gentile. Although it is true that the drama of Dan 2 is played out on a Gentile stage, where actors behave according to the conventions of a pagan religious environment, in Dan 7 the stage is more obviously biblical. The appearance of the beasts from the sea and God's judgment of them (7:3-12) evokes the language of an older Israelite theme of God's battle with the forces of chaos (see, e.g., Pss 74:13-14; 89:8-10 [Eng.]). The one true God takes his seat on a throne surrounded by angelic courtiers; a familiar scene in emerging Jewish apocalyptic literature (cf. *1 En.* 14:18-23). There is no polytheism here, just the distinctive Jewish monotheism that celebrates the supreme position of the one God in the midst of an angelic throng. No one has suggested that the "worship" given to the "one like a son of man" (if that is what it is) is a case of a Jewish accommodation to the Hellenistic Ruler Cult. If there are nonbiblical elements to Dan 7 they are echoes of older Canaanite traditions (in the "Ancient of Days" and the portrayal of the man-figure as a Baal-like rider of the clouds), not later Hellenistic ones. So if the man-figure, who has Adam-like characteristics and is somehow a representative of all God's people, can receive a legitimate "worship" in a thoroughly biblical scene, we are surely invited to conclude that the "worship" of a similar figure in Dan 2:46 is also, in some sense, legitimate. At least, the way Dan 2:46 anticipates Dan 7:13-14 invites the implied reader to conclude that what Nebuchadnezzar does is a partially acceptable foreshadowing, from a Gentile who does not truly understand the meaning of his actions, of the worship of the "one like a son of man" by all the nations in the eschatological future (see Dan 7:14).

In bringing Dan 2:46 to our attention and including it within a larger hypothesis about the nature of pre-Christian Judaism, Horbury has done us a great service. Daniel 2:46 is certainly evidence of something along the lines for which he argues. But these brief observations on the verse *in its immediate literary and theological context* show that it is not quite as straightforwardly evidence for the phenomenon Horbury describes as he imagines. According to Dan 2:46 (and perhaps also Dan 7:13-14), for Jews

---

86. First laid out by Lenglet, "Daniel 2–7"; cf. J. J. Collins, *Apocalyptic Vision*, 11-14.

in pre-Christian antiquity, the Hellenistic view that powerful and virtuous individuals were worthy of cultic honors correlated to a vision for human beings as God originally created them; a vision that some Jews believed was realized already in history by some of God's people. It is not just Israel's ideal ruler that some Jews believed was worthy of cultic veneration—a view that is *possibly* reflected in Dan 7:13-14; it is the true human being who is able to be what Adam was created to be.

In any case, there is no avoiding the fact that, in texts such as these, Jewish authors show no embarrassment in using language that later Christians and modern scholars have often judged to be incompatible with Jewish monotheism. A nice parallel to Dan 2:46 (not discussed by Horbury) is provided by a passage in the near contemporary text *Jubilees,* a text that is well-known for its fiercely orthodox and Torah-pious perspective on Israelite identity. In *Jub.* 40:7 the brief and undeveloped mention of Egyptians being commanded to "kneel!" before Joseph in Gen 41:43 is expanded with a typical Hellenistic-era acclamation of him as "god, god, Mighty One of God."[87] Here, too, the notion that Joseph is the Israelite par excellence is likely to be just as important as the notion that he is specifically a "divine" *ruler* (as Pharaoh's second-in-command).

Horbury has done much to help us appreciate the extent to which Jews were willing to emulate the language and behavior of Greeks and Romans who treated rulers as "divine." Indeed, the fact that this phenomenon is much wider than just the emulation of the Ruler Cult, extending also to a wider concern for cultic honors to uniquely powerful individuals who are close to God and do good works for the wider community (as benefactors), only reinforces the truth of one key element of Horbury's thesis; Jewish monotheism sometimes had an open, accommodating attitude towards aspects of pagan piety.

But this is the point at which Horbury's approach to the origins of Christ devotion is also most vulnerable to criticism. Horbury's insistence that Jews were open to a Greco-Roman view of the human being (viz the *ruler*) contrasts sharply with the views of Hurtado and Bauckham who emphasize the evidence that Second Temple Judaism rejected non-Jewish, unbiblical attitudes towards the divine realm. Bauckham, in particular, has stressed the widespread evidence that theological commitments guide, undergird, and determine what Jews could say about, or do to, human beings and mediatorial

---

87. On *Jub.* 40:7 see VanderKam, *Book of Jubilees,* vol. 2, 265; Fletcher-Louis, *Luke-Acts,* 168, and see further my *Luke-Acts,* 165-73, for the wider tradition of Joseph's heavenly and "divine" identity that was quite independent of his specific position as ruler in Egypt. For a heavenly or "divine" Israel in DSS texts see my *All the Glory,* esp. 88-135.

figures: Jews of this period, he argues, are steeped in Scripture (as so many primary sources show) and so cannot possibly have allowed theological formulations or behavior that transgressed biblical monotheism.

Although there has been dialogue between Horbury and Bauckham, there seems now to be an impasse between these two approaches.[88] On the specific case for the influence of the Ruler Cult, Horbury, I think, has the better of the argument from textual evidence. At least, that is, there is plenty of evidence *in the texts*, especially those from the Hellenistic and pre-Roman period, that some Jews *did* accommodate non-Jewish attitudes that gave human beings a "divine" identity or status (especially, but not exclusively, in the case of rulers). At least, they rendered to human beings an identity that justified some of the cultic honors that were traditionally given to remarkable and "divine" individuals in the Greco-Roman world, and in doing so they deemed appropriate a behavior towards such individuals that would normally be reserved for God alone. The case of Dan 2:46 is supported by the use of divine benefactor language for others, especially Moses, in other near contemporary texts. It goes to show the importance of older scholarship on the role of Greco-Roman divine man traditions in the pre-Christian Jewish world.[89] As far as I can tell, neither Bauckham nor Hurtado has so far adequately treated all the evidence Horbury marshals for his case.

On the other hand, Bauckham has the better of the argument from theological principle: Jews were monotheists and as such were as interested as much in orthodoxy as they were in orthopraxy (something for which there is also plenty of textual evidence, as Bauckham has shown). Together, Scripture, daily prayer, and Temple worship provided a sacred canopy with clear theological boundaries. Those theological boundaries drew a clear line of distinction between God and the rest of creation, including humanity. Horbury claims that Hellenistic-era messianism stood in continuity with much older Israelite piety surrounding the king, but he really does not face squarely the theological question: *if Jews* (and their Israelite forbears of the biblical period) *accorded the (coming) king divine honors, how, given the shape*

---

88. For Bauckham on Horbury see Bauckham, *God of Israel*, 107–26, 228–32; for Horbury on Bauckham see Horbury, *Jews and Christians*, 12–15. Hurtado has not yet entered the debate directly, but judging by a recent article he does not think the kind of material Horbury discusses undermines his earlier work on Jewish monotheism (see Hurtado, "'Ancient Jewish Monotheism'").

89. On the "divine man" and early Christianity, see the review of literature in Klauck, *Religious Context*, 174–77, and the comments of Litwa, *Iesus Deus*, 21–23. There has been criticism of the way older scholarship lumped together diverse textual evidence into a unified "divine man" figure. But the evidence that Greeks and Romans could think of individual human beings in "divine" terms and render them cultic honors accordingly is plentiful.

of Jewish monotheism, did they justify that theologically? How does the author of *Jubilees* justify the description of the Egyptian acclamation of Joseph?

Indeed, in my own criticisms of Horbury in the preceding pages, I have highlighted other ways in which more needs to be said about the specific *theological* shape of Scripture than he has done so far (viz his handling of glory language for the king and priesthood). If any of Horbury's arguments for an "inclusive" monotheistic stance towards the pagan world are to be placed on a solid historical footing something needs to be said in response to the usual view that in the postbiblical period the monotheism of the Deuteronomist and of Second Isaiah removed or suppressed any older Israelite belief in the deity of the ruler. The evidence of Dan 2:46 and other texts reviewed here (and in the next chapter), and of our discussion of the *Similitudes of Enoch* in the last chapter, suggests the standard scholarly account of the development of Jewish monotheism is problematic. But how then should we read the Hebrew Bible and its overtly monotheistic statements? Or, more to the point, how did the Jewish authors of Dan 2:46, *Jub.* 40:7, the *Similitudes of Enoch*, and writers of similar texts read their Bibles?

For now, we have an impasse. Hurtado rejects the possibility that Nebuchadnezzar's "worship" of Daniel in Dan 2:46 is put forward as actually exemplary for Jewish readers of the text.[90] Given everything he has so far written, I assume Bauckham would agree: the constraint of Jewish monotheism must mean that, because Daniel does not share the divine identity in this text, he does not actually receive what Jews would call proper "worship." However, for the basic thrust of Dan 2:46 Horbury has the weight of historical and exegetical argument on his side: Dan 2:46 allows and celebrates the "worshipful" treatment of Daniel as a divine benefactor.

So, we are left on the horns of another dilemma: why does the book of Daniel—that in so many respects is a satire against the powerlessness of pagan idolatry and the arrogant pretensions of contemporary rulers—allow Daniel to be treated in a way that *according to the conceptual framework of contemporary Hellenistic religious life* means he was worshipped as a divine benefactor? The narrator provides no hint of a disparaging view of Nebuchadnezzar's actions. Is the implied reader simply supposed to sneer in disgust or groan inwardly, even though the text's protagonist—Daniel—goes along uncomplainingly to receive the honors paid to him?[91] And the connections between Dan 2:46 and 7:13 suggest that, for the author, the treatment of Daniel anticipates the fully legitimate worship of a coming "one like

---

90. In private conversation.

91. In other stories, the God-ordained protagonist makes clear that a pagan instinct to worship one who is not God himself is misguided (see, e.g., the angel in *Jos. Asen.* 15:11–12 and Peter in Acts 10:25–26).

a son of man." For an approach to Dan 2:46 in keeping with the arguments of Mastin and Horbury to stand *we would need a clearer understanding of the theological framework that could allow a Jewish author, who is in every other respect fully committed to scriptural revelation, to write what he has written.*

IV: Conclusion

So, at the end of this discussion of Horbury's work we have some positive conclusions and many unanswered questions. There were Jews in the Greco-Roman period who, to some extent, allowed rulers and others the kind of honorific praise that was normal in the wider ancient world for exalted (and *"divine"*) human beings. But what the early Christians did to Jesus by fully *including* him in the divine identity is certainly without precedent in the material examined by Horbury. There is no sense in which the Daniel of Dan 2:46 and the Joseph of *Jub.* 40:7 can be said to be "included" in the identity of the one God, the Creator and Ruler of all. So, even the word "divine" means something different in the case of these texts by comparison to its normal use to refer to Israel's one God. And so it is one thing for non-Jews to treat Daniel as if he were a "divine benefactor," or to hail Joseph "a god." It is quite another to say that Jesus Christ is so fully identified with the one God who created the world, with *Yhwh-Kyrios,* that he belongs firmly within a redefined confession of *that* divine identity.

If the two phenomena are quite discrete conceptually and in practice, more work needs to be done on the historical relationship between them, *if* there was any at all. But regardless of any role that a Jewish accommodation to the Ruler Cult might have had in the formation of early Christology, the pre-Christian texts we have studied in this chapter demand a better theological explanation in their own right. How did Jews of the period justify the adoption, or emulation, of Greco-Roman practices that gave "divine" human beings cultic honors? How were texts such as Dan 2:46 and *Jub.* 40:7 justified conceptually, *theologically*, within the constraints of biblically grounded Jewish monotheism? What is the relationship between Dan 2:46, where a non-Jewish "worship" of Daniel is accepted, and Dan 7:13–14, where the "worship" of the "one like a son of man" (if, indeed, "worship" is what it is) is framed in a thoroughly biblical literary and theological context?

Then there is the matter of Horbury's overemphasis on royal categories to the exclusion of the evidence that Jews gave ultimate authority to a high priest, who both represented a wider true humanity and who was sometimes given divine "glory." Some, no doubt, will balk at the presentation of evidence for a Jewish high priest with a "divine" glory that properly belongs to God himself, since it seems incompatible with the Isaianic proclamation that God does not share his own divine glory with another (Isa 42:8; 48:11). But the relevant texts ground their rhetoric of priestly glory in the biblical text itself (Exod 28:2, 40). So more thought needs to be given to the specific place of such ideas within a biblically faithful, theocentric theology. If, as I have argued, the high priest has a position of preeminence in Israel's political theology (or theolog*ies*) then more thought needs to be given to the reason for that. VanderKam and others have provided historical and textual evidence for the phenomenon. But what has it to do with the theological shape of Israel's Scripture? Why does the OT say that kings are either unnecessary or that they should rule from a position of submission to priests? And what has any of that to do with New Testament theology and Christological origins? On the face of it, it is hard to see how it can have anything very much to do with early Christian life and thought since, apart from the peculiar Christological perspective of the book of Hebrews, priestly ideas seem not to have been the least bit relevant to the early church. To all these questions we shall return with fresh observations and some answers in later volumes.

4: Conclusion to Chapters 5 and 6: Messianism and the Origins of "Christological Monotheism"

Here then, with the results of recent work on *1 En.* 37–71 (and related traditions) examined in chapter 5 and the undeniable truth to aspects of William Horbury's model of a pre-Christian Jewish appropriation of some of the conventions of Greco-Roman Ruler Cult (examined in this chapter), we have evidence that challenges one aspect of the work of Hurtado and Bauckham. That is, there is plenty of evidence that some Jewish messianic expectations and a willingness, in some quarters, to emulate the treatment of "divine" human beings in the wider Gentile world *do* offer likely precedents for *some aspects* of the worship of Jesus and his inclusion within the divine identity.

We still need a better understanding of the place of these traditions in Second Temple Judaism, especially in relation to Scripture; its understanding of God (theology) and its view(s) of a human (messianic) ruler in the divinely sanctioned order (political theology). With a clearer grasp of the place of the *Similititudes* in the development of Jewish practice and belief, and a better understanding of the evidence for a Jewish royal and priestly Ruler Cult, it might be possible to reach some confident judgments on the contribution of Jewish messianism to Christological origins. To that end, and in view of the evidence noted above for an interest in an exalted true humanity that is worthy of worship, we come in the next chapter to Jewish texts that exalt the pre-fall Adam.

CHAPTER 7

A "Divine" and Glorious Adam Worshipped in Pre-Christian Judaism?

OUR EXAMINATION OF JEWISH messianism in the last chapter pointed to the importance of Adam and the notion that the righteous were what Adam was created to be. We have seen that the kind of honors given to divine rulers and benefactors could be applied by Jews both to human leaders and to righteous, exemplary Israelites. I suggested that this phenomenon was grounded in the belief both that Adam was originally created with a peculiarly exalted position, equivalent to that of the kings of the ancient Near East and, following the work on Israel and Adam by N. T. Wright, that Israel as a nation was viewed in the Bible and in Jewish antiquity as a new, restored Adam.

There are aspects of the portrayal of the Son of Man-Messiah in the *Similitudes of Enoch* that also suggest a debt to ideas surrounding the original identity of Adam. The Enochic Son of Man's position on God's throne of divine glory somehow leads to the righteous receiving "glory and honor" (*1 En.* 50:1) and "garments of incorruptible glory" (62:15–16). With *his* end-time appearance *their* resurrection and exaltation will be, in part, a recovery of the death-free life like that of the angels that humanity possessed in the beginning (69:11). In their eschatological transcendence of their mortality they get to be what he has been since preexistence.

The modern study of the Enochic Son of Man has often marginalized the evidence for the enthroned figure's positive relationship to a wider righteous humanity. The identification of the preexistent messiah with Enoch, *the seventh from Adam*, has been particularly troubling for scholars, with many judging that identification (in the last chapter—ch. 71) a later addition that is at odds with the rest of the work. But there are good arguments for thinking that all along the *Similitudes* had in mind its climactic identification of Enoch with the heavenly Son of Man.[1] Be that as it may, a scholarly reluctance to admit the authenticity of the identification perhaps partly reflects the tendency of many modern readers to assume the biblical tradition has a wholly negative view of human nature. Much Christian scholarship and popular piety—at least in the Western tradition—has had a low view of human nature, nurtured, of course, by a rich seam of reflection on the human condition in Paul's letters.

But there are places in the Pauline corpus where Paul has a remarkably positive view of human life and destiny. For example, in Rom 2:6-7 he commends those who seek after glory and honor and immortality. According to Eph 2:6 he is happy to think the saints are already enthroned in the heavenlies in Christ (a position that, on Bauckham's reckoning, might imply their inclusion within the divine identity) (cf. Col 3:1-3). With such texts Paul (or the Pauline author of Ephesians) reflects well-established Jewish tradition that had a high view of Adam before his fall.

The early chapters of Daniel claim that it has been possible, through Torah faithfulness and God's own gift of the divine spirit and his wisdom, for some Israelites to recover the identity originally intended for Adam. The Qumran community thought that humanity is trapped in the realm of the flesh, but that, equally, *it is possible to recover, at least in certain ways and contexts, the lost identity of the prelapsarian, sinless, Adam*. Especially in the context of worship the community members believed they were transferred into a new Eden where they could experience the upper world of heaven in a true temple space. Glory (*kavod*) and associated words for honor, splendor, and beauty (*hadar, hod, tipheret*) decorate the poetry of the community's praise. And that language is not reserved solely for God and descriptions of his presence. The community tasted the eschatological recovery of "all the glory of Adam" (1QS 4:22-23; 1QH^a 4:14-15, cf. 4QpPsa (4Q171) 3:1-2).[2] There is much to suggest that for the Qumran community as a whole the recovery of the glory of Adam meant participation in the glory of God. At least there are some DSS texts where "high priestly clothing symbolizes the high priest's embodiment of the divine glory."[3]

Whilst the Qumran community had its own distinctive claims for a present experience of transformation and participation in the heavenly realm, in many respects its interest in Adam's glory was typical of ancient

1. See esp. Kvanvig, "Son of Man."

2. See Fletcher-Louis, *All the Glory of Adam*, the scholarship discussed there and, for example, J. L. Angel, *Eschatological Priesthood*.

3. J. L. Angel, *Eschatological Priesthood*, 120, cf. 165. See 1QSb 4:28; 4Q408 3 + 3a line 5; 4Q405 23 ii 3, 8-9, cf. 4Q418 81 5 and the discussion of those texts in Fletcher-Louis, *All the Glory*.

Judaism.[4] Although some have recently challenged the view that there was a widespread interest in Adam and a developed interpretative tradition (or traditions) surrounding Gen 1-3 and related texts (such as Ps 8) in late Second Temple Judaism, there remains plenty of evidence that that was indeed the case.[5] Several sources refer to texts that were (allegedly) written by Adam that are not included in the Bible.[6] We do not know exactly what these were (if they actually existed and are not just legendary). But we do know that there was a particular interest in Adam's original, glorious, and in some ways "divine," pre-fall identity.

Some texts speak of Adam's wondrous, divine beauty or splendor (*Sib. Or.* 1:24; cf. Ben Sira 49:16; *Apoc. Abr.* 23:5; *L.A.B.* 26:6-15). The scrolls and a passage in Philo attest a tradition well known in later literature that the works of creation were made *for Adam* (4Q392 1 4-6; Philo *Creation* 78-79, cf. *4 Ezra* 6:46, 8:44; *2 Bar.* 14:18; 73:6; Latin *L.A.E.* 8:1-3 = Greek *L.A.E.* 29:13-14). That tradition meant for many that he created it *for Israel*, because the nation was set apart to be a new corporate Adam (*T. Mos.* 1:12; *4 Ezra* 6:55; 8:1; 9:13; *2 Bar.* 14:19; 15:7; 21:24). In quite a few texts there is the notion that Adam was created with cosmic dimensions.[7] In *2 En.* 30:11 [J], he is created to be "a second angel, honored and great and glorious . . . incomparable" in all creation. Other texts envisage Adam possessing, or wearing, glory before his fall (Latin *L.A.E.* 11:3; 16:2; Greek *L.A.E.* 20:1-2; 21:2, 6; *3 Bar.* 4:16).[8] In the *Testament of Abraham A* 11:4-12, the first-formed Adam sits on a gilded throne at the gate of heaven, most marvellous and adorned with glory, with a form like that of God himself ("the Master").

A case can be made that each of *2 Enoch*, the *Life of Adam and Eve*, *3 Baruch*, and *Testament of Abraham* (or the relevant Adamic portions of each of these) are Christian. But it is unlikely that they all are and, time and again, what they say about Adam makes best sense as the work of a

---

4. See the discussion of wider evidence in, for example, Kim, *Origin*, 187-92.

5. Grant Macaskill's recent attempt to argue against the presence of a widespread pre-Christian Adam tradition that had a particular focus on his pre-fall glory (*Union with Christ*, 128-43) is highly problematic. His discussion of the primary texts is selective and limited, he strangely plays off different parts of the biblical story against each other, does not interact with any recent scholarship on the OT material, and fails to engage with recent studies that tell against his arguments for the origins and meaning of extrabiblical texts (such as Eldridge, *Dying Adam*; Levison, "Adam and Eve"; Fletcher-Louis, "Cosmology of P").

6. Josephus *Ant.* 1:69-71; *2 En.* 33:8-12 [J & A]; Latin *L.A.E.* 50:1-2, cf. *Jub.* 8:3.

7. E.g. *Apoc. Abr.* 23:5; *2 En.* 30:13, and see further the texts I refer to in Fletcher-Louis, *Luke-Acts*, 143-44. For the way such gigantism implies divinity in a Greco-Roman context see Litwa, *Iesus Deus*, 169-70.

8. For this notion in rabbinic texts see Anderson, *Genesis of Perfection*, 117-34.

Jewish author (even if Christian readers could later make good use of it). For example, what 2 *En.* 30:11 says about Adam (quoted above) draws on Ps 8 (esp. v. 5 [Heb. v. 6]). For such an application of Ps 8 to the creation of Adam we have a parallel from the second century BC in Ben Sira 49:16.[9] And Jewish texts say that Adam was angelic before his fall (1 *En.* 69:11; 4Q417 1 i 17). But the New Testament says that it is Jesus who fulfills Ps 8 (Heb 2:6-9, cf. Rom 8:32-34; 1 Cor 15:25-27; Eph 1:20-22). So, how likely is it that a Christian scribe would create that image of Adam?[10]

In any case, the other texts, especially the Dead Sea Scrolls, anchor the view that Adam had a glorious identity before he fell in pre-AD 70 Judaism. Some readers of these texts may be tempted to jump to the conclusion that they go far beyond the meaning and intention of the biblical text. Indeed, some speak pejoratively of an Adam "myth" as if such traditions are really theologically discontinuous with the biblical text itself.[11] They certainly challenge some modern Western Christian readings of the biblical Adam story. But to what extent they are actually unfaithful to the intention of the biblical text is an issue that now needs to be considered anew in the light of the latest scholarship on the OT texts themselves. For now, I offer a focused study of one particular postbiblical Adam tradition which will prepare the ground for some fresh proposals about the ways Jewish Adam traditions are continuous with the biblical text. I return to this question in more detail in Part 5.

None of the texts and traditions just noted can fully explain the radical moves made by the first Christians that led them to worship Jesus Christ. In various ways what they say about Adam before his sin and exit from Eden anticipates what the earliest Christians ascribed to Jesus, who is set apart from the rest of creation with incomparable glory and honor. But in these texts Adam is not included in the divine identity in the way that Christ was. However, there is one tradition that takes the exalted view of Adam to a point that seems to offer a quite specific precedent for the early Christian treatment of Jesus.

---

9. For Ps 8 in Ben Sira 49:16, see Fletcher-Louis, "Cosmology of P," 107. See also the incomparability of Israel in relation to the "form/construction of Adam" in 1QM 10:14.

10. It may be that, *in its present form*, other parts of the Adam section in 2 *En.* 30:8—33:2 (in the longer recension) are Christian (cf. Macaskill, "2 Enoch," 94-98). However, given the ways the text's view of Adam is integral to its overarching purpose and theology (see Fletcher-Louis, "2 Enoch"), it is likely that the "original" text included much of the substance of 2 *En.* 30:8—33:2.

11. So Macaskill (*Union with Christ*, esp. 131). Bauckham ("Genesis 1-3," 178) finds no support for the notion that the world is created for Adam in the biblical text itself.

In response to Hurtado's first monograph arguing for the importance of worship as a criterion that establishes the unprecedented treatment of Jesus as a divine being, David Steenburg drew attention to a story about Adam in the *Life of Adam and Eve* 12-16, which he argued provides a partial precedent for Christ devotion.[12] Here is a translation of the Latin version of this important text:[13]

> 12:1 And the devil sighed and said, "O Adam, all my enmity and envy and sorrow concern you, since because of you I am expelled and deprived of my glory which I had in the heavens in the midst of angels, and because of you I was cast onto the earth." 2 Adam answered, "What have I done to you, and what is my blame with you? Since you are neither harmed nor hurt by us, why do you pursue us?"
>
> 13:1 And the devil replied, "Adam, what are you telling me? It is because of you that I have been thrown out of there. 2 When you were created, I was cast out from the presence of God and was sent out from the fellowship of the angels. 3 When God blew into you *the breath of life* (Gen 2:7) and your countenance and *likeness* were made *in the image of God* (Gen 1:26), Michael brought you and made you worship in the sight of God, and the Lord God said, "Behold Adam! I have made you in our image (*imago*) and likeness (*similitudo*)."
>
> 14:1 And Michael went out and called all the angels, saying, "Worship (*adorate*) the image (*imago*) of the Lord God, as the Lord God has instructed. 2 And Michael himself worshipped first, and called me and said, "Worship the image (*imago*) of God, Jehova." 3 And I answered, "I do not worship Adam." And when Michael kept forcing me to worship, I said to him, "Why do you compel me? I will not worship one inferior and subsequent to me. I am prior to him in creation; before he was made, I was already made. He ought to worship me.
>
> 15:1 When they heard this, other angels who were under me refused to worship him. 2 And Michael asserted, Worship the image (*imago*) of God. But if now you will not worship, the Lord God will be angry with you." 3 And I said, "*If he be angry with me, I will set my throne above the stars of heaven and will be like the Most High.*" (Isa 14:13-14)
>
> 16:1 And the Lord God was angry with me and sent me with my angels out from our glory; and because of you we were

---

12. Steenburg, "Worship of Adam" (1990).
13. Following, with minor modifications, the translation in *OTP* 2:262.

expelled into this world from our dwellings and have been cast onto the earth.

For some of us this has seemed to be a straightforward case of God-ordained worship of a human being that anticipates the worship of Jesus Christ, albeit with many aspects of the full NT pattern of worship not present in this brief story. Of course, in the setting of this pseudepigraphical story Adam has not yet sinned. So the angelic worship of Adam provides a precedent for the worship of Jesus inasmuch as Jesus' followers also believed that Jesus was sinless (Rom 8:3; 2 Cor 5:21; 1 Pet 2:22; 1 John 3:5) and that as a new Adam he was obedient where Adam failed (Rom 5:12-21; 1 Cor 15:22, 45; Heb 2:5-18, cf. Luke 3:23—4:13). Following Steenburg, it has also been argued that the very same texts that can be taken as an expression of the worship of Christ work with an "Adam Christology." In particular, the obedience, suffering, and vindication through exaltation of Christ in the Phil 2:6-11 has been compared to the disobedience, suffering, and promised exaltation of Adam (in the Bible and postbiblical tradition). The Christ hymn in Colossians also begins with a possible reference to Gen 1:26 by saying he is "the image of the invisible God" (Col 1:15). If there was a Jewish belief that the true Adam who was God's image and likeness was worshipped by the angels then it is not at all surprising that Jesus would be worshipped—*as that true Adam*—by his followers.

Certainly there are significant differences between the earliest Christian beliefs about Jesus and what this (and other) Jewish traditions were willing to say about Adam. Nevertheless, the possibility that Adam is worshipped here gets to the very heart of several critical questions: what is first-century Jewish monotheism and in what ways did "Christological monotheism" carry over or reshape a pre-Christian monotheism that already accommodated (conceptually if not in actual practice) the worship of a human being who served as God's "image and likeness"? If this story is a pre-Christian anticipation of the worship of Jesus then it poses an important question for the nature of Christ devotion: namely, does the early Christian worship of the Lord Jesus Christ as one who belongs within the divine identity include, in any sense, the worship of the *human being* Jesus of Nazareth? If Jesus was considered a true Adam who recapitulated humanity's pre-fall identity then, at least in part, worship of him would surely be worship that reprised the angelic worship of Adam. Or, does the early Christian worship of the Lord Jesus Christ as one who contributed to the original work of creation exclude any notion that his identity was, for a time, constituted by a creaturely life on earth?

Discussion of this pseudepigraphical Adam story has tended to be woodenly reactive to the proposal that it explains Christ devotion. Dunn appeals to the story to support his claim that what was done to Jesus by the early Christians was not that surprising or radical.[14] On the other hand, Hurtado and Bauckham, as we shall see, both dismiss the text's relevance for the origins of the earliest Christology. I have written about the text and its relationship to Christology in three previous publications. I remain convinced that the preservation of this ancient story providentially provides a vital witness to a fresh and clearer understanding of the Bible's own theological anthropology and to one likely historical factor that led to "Christological monotheism." Pondering the subtleties of a possible relationship between a Jewish worship-of-Adam tradition and Christological origins also helps to tease out the contours of the *shape* of the earliest Christology. So in this chapter I offer a lengthy consideration of this extrabiblical tradition. Our findings will then be brought to bear on a detailed study of Phil 2:6–11 in chapter 8. They will also provide valuable evidence to support aspects of the new paradigm (in Parts 5 and 6).

1: Introduction to a Critical Study of the Worship of Adam Story

Gary Anderson has labeled the story in *L.A.E.* 12–16 the "Exaltation of Adam."[15] I prefer the label the Worship of Adam Story. It is true that, as Anderson argues, there are important parallels between the choice of Adam as the *last* of God's works over others created before him (including Satan) and the pattern of God choosing the younger son over the firstborn throughout Israel's history. Anderson has insightfully shown that the conflict between Adam and Satan is a reflection of one aspect of the biblical doctrine of election, wherein God chooses Israel over others who are often jealous of the favored, beloved, chosen one. And in classic examples of that pattern, God does, indeed, *exalt* the younger son; in the case, for example, of Jacob, Joseph, and David. But in our story, Adam *is not exalted*. He is simply created and God commands the worship of him *at the moment of his creation*. There never was a time when Adam was not, in God's view, entitled to receive worship. So "exaltation" is not in view here.

In the twentieth century, the story became accessible to scholarship through the publication of the Latin version of the *Life of Adam and Eve*, which most have taken to be a translation of a Jewish, and probably

---

14. Dunn, *Worship*, 88–89.
15. Anderson, "Exaltation of Adam."

pre-Christian, pseudepigraphon. As standard modern publications of the Latin *Vita* show, it has many parallels to a Greek Adam text that has long been *mislabeled* the *"Apocalypse of Moses."* And the last thirty years of scholarship has now exposed the frustratingly complex nature of the *Life of Adam* tradition, which is extant not just in a Latin and a Greek form, but also in Armenian, Georgian, Slavonic, and Coptic versions. The extant version of the Greek Adam book does not include the Worship of Adam Story that is preserved in chapters 12-16 of the Latin, although a brief comment in some manuscripts of the Greek text at 16:2 shows that scribes writing in Greek did know the full version of the Worship of Adam Story.[16]

Scholarship is now divided on the question of a Jewish or Christian provenance of the Adam traditions now preserved in these different linguistic manifestations of the "Primary Adam Books," with some specialists preferring tentative proposals over confident claims. It is generally reckoned that those portions of the Latin not present in the Greek derive from a now-lost Greek text which also stands behinds the Armenian and Georgian. But in places, the Armenian and Georgian also seem more reliable than the Latin. It is possible, in any case, that all versions ultimately go back to a lost Hebrew text (or to separate Hebrew traditions).

In what follows, I use the synopsis and translation of the Greek, Latin, Armenian, Georgian, and Slavonic texts, edited and translated by Gary Anderson and Michael Stone, which supersedes older editions and translations (= *Synopsis*).[17] This helpfully divides up the *Life of Adam and Eve* traditions into thirty-nine discrete pericopae (of which our story is *Synopsis* pericope §5).

2: Arguments against the Story's Relevance for Early Christology

Between them Hurtado and Bauckham lodge four objections to Steenburg's original case that *L.A.E.* 12-16 helps explain the emergence of Christ devotion.[18] First, they point out that the story is of uncertain date and claim it is quite possibly Christian. Secondly, in any case, "the scene is exceptional

---

16. Manuscripts ATLC (see Anderson and Stone, *Synopsis*, viii, 50; Dochhorn, *Apokalypse*, 308, and the discussion by Eldridge, *Dying Adam*, 96).

17. Anderson and Stone, *A Synopsis*, (2nd ed., 1999).

18. Hurtado, *One God*, (2nd ed.), x-xi; *Lord Jesus Christ*, 39-40; Bauckham, *God of Israel*, 203-4; "Devotion to Jesus," 185-86. For support for Steenburg's central thesis, see Chester, *Messiah*, 72-73, 113-15; Fletcher-Louis, *Luke-Acts*, 142-43; "Divine Humanity," 114-15, 127-28; *Glory of Adam*, 98-103; G. van Kooten, *Paul's Anthropology*, 27-32.

in the literature of Second Temple Judaism."[19] Thirdly, Bauckham argues Adam is not actually worshipped. Beneath the Latin *adorare* (which until now everyone else has translated "worship") there is a Greek *proskynein* ("to bow down, prostrate"), which means "worship" only in certain contexts. Here the context is the need for an appropriate recognition of Adam's superiority over the angels, and there is nothing else to indicate Adam's inclusion in the divine identity: "Adam does not occupy the divine throne."[20] Fourthly, Hurtado stresses the fact that the text is a literary piece with no correlation to contemporary Jewish cultic practice, which "is precisely what we need in order to have a real precedent for the worship of Jesus."[21]

On close examination, none of these objections carries much weight, and this opposition to Steenburg's case has in some ways not done justice to the current state of specialist analysis of this fascinating collection of Adam texts. However, careful consideration of these objections certainly helps clarify wider interpretative questions and theological issues in the quest for Christological origins. In my own research, the inspiration for the formulation of a new theological and historical paradigm to explain Christological origins (that will be laid out in Parts 5 and 6) came about in large measure as a result of my wrestling with this remarkable text and its interpretative possibilities in the light of recent scholarship on OT theological anthropology. As first steps towards a presentation of my own understanding of the Worship of Adam Story, I begin with a response to each of these objections. I will conclude that, in the final analysis, there are no grounds for thinking that there was a *direct* causal relationship between the *extrabiblical* Worship of Adam Story and "Christological monotheism." However, in this and then more fully in later chapters, I will show that this story does help explain the *shape* of "Christological monotheism" texts. I will also lay out an explanation of Christological origins for which the Worship of Adam Story provides invaluable confirmatory evidence. There are, cumulatively, rather strong grounds for thinking the story was pre-Christian and that it was *indirectly* a factor in the birth of Christ devotion.

3: A Pre-Christian Date for the Worship of Adam Story

In response to the first point, it is true that we do not know the date of the Latin version of the *Life of Adam and Eve*. It could be a Christian work. However, there is nothing specifically Christian about the story in chapters

---

19. Bauckham, *God of Israel*, 203.
20. Ibid., 204.
21. Hurtado, *Lord Jesus Christ*, 40; cf. *One God* (2nd ed.), xi.

12–16, which is a distinct literary unit within a larger (narratively coherent) collection of Adam traditions.[22] Then there are several considerations that cumulatively make an overwhelming case that this part of the *Life of Adam and Eve* is both pre-Christian and, in all likelihood, that it was known to the first Jewish followers of Jesus.

Besides its appearance in the Latin, Georgian, and Armenian versions of the *Life of Adam and Eve*, the Worship of Adam Story is attested in both Jewish and Christian sources in a way that suggests a nonsectarian provenance and wide circulation in the first century of the Christian era (if not earlier). In the Christian environment, the story is attested in diverse pseudepigraphical sources, but the church fathers themselves do not quote from it. Because their theology was Christocentric, not anthropocentric, it is unsurprising that they did not make direct use of it. This also means it is unlikely that early Christians created the story, even if they found it useful when appropriated through a Christological lens.[23] We know that the rabbis were aware of it because they preserve a similar story that says when the angels began to worship the first human being, God took steps to ensure that in future they would not mistake Adam for his Creator.[24] This is clearly designed to refute the Worship of Adam Story and is best taken as evidence that "certain people in the first centuries C.E. maintained that Adam, although created, was a divine or at least semidivine being who deserved to be worshipped, and the rabbis vehemently opposed such a 'heretical' idea."[25] It is possible that the rabbis are reacting to a story dear to Christians, but several considerations make this unlikely. At no point do the rabbinic texts explicitly polemicize against Christians for believing that Adam was worshipped as a divine being. And given the way the Adam story is marginalized in mainstream patristic

---

22. So it is not enough to dismiss importance of the Worship of Adam Story for Christological origins by simply asserting that the *Life of Adam and Eve* cannot be treated as a pre-Christian Jewish text (as does Bauckham in "Devotion to Jesus Christ," 185–86).

23. So Eldridge, "Dying Adam," 252–53, and Toepel, "Adamic Traditions," 310–11. An example of the story's practical use when refracted through a Christological framework may be illustrated by the way it likely underlies Gregory Nazianzen's advice to bapitzands (in a sermon in 381 AD) that to the devil when he demands their worship (as in Luke 4:5–8) they should say "I am the image of God myself. I have not been cast down from the glory above as you have: I have put on Christ; I have been transformed into Christ by Baptism; you worship me (*sy me proskynēson*)!" (*Oration* 40:11). I am grateful to Gabrielle Thomas for drawing my attention to this as a possible Christological reworking of the Worship of Adam Story.

24. *Gen. Rab.* 8:10; *Eccl. Rab.* 6:9:1 and *Pirqe R. El.* 11. Bauckham's statement that rabbinic texts say nothing about obeisance to or worship of Adam (Bauckham, *God of Israel*, 203 n. 47) is puzzling.

25. Schäfer, *Jesus*, 206 (cf. 203–13).

theology, it is more likely that the rabbis are reacting to a story that had been doing the rounds in their own *Jewish* environment.

It is not quite true that the story is unattested in the Greek version of the *Life*.[26] As we have noted already, some manuscripts at the Greek L.A.E. 16:2 explicitly refer to the story of the worship of Adam by the beasts and commentators agree that the "author of the Greek Life of Adam and Eve must have known it in some form, but he has chosen not to narrate it."[27] Because the story does not fit well with the belief that it is *Jesus Christ who is the image of God*, the fact that it is fully told in the Latin, Armenian, and Georgian, but not in the extant Greek and the Slavonic is best explained as textual evidence for its suppression in Christian transmission. Either the Greek and Slavonic tradents disapproved of the story altogether or they were concerned that it should only be handled with extreme care, and it should not be widely known among the uneducated or the laity, who might misunderstand it. The fact that some Greek manuscripts refer to the story, but do not lay it out fully, suggests this second explanation.

In any case, I will come shortly to evidence that the story is at home in a Jewish milieu (that had a quite sophisticated theology surrounding Adam's identity as God's image and likeness). That evidence also helps explain why, in the course of Christian history and with increasing distance from a Jewish theological framework, the story became puzzling and required either careful handling or suppression. In any case, a Greek version of the story is well attested in Christian sources outside of the church fathers.[28]

In the Latin (and Armenian and Georgian) versions of the *Vita* the Worship of Adam Story is included in a distinct literary block (*L.A.E.* 1–22) that Gary Anderson has labeled the "Penitence Narrative."[29] For the most part, the Penitence Narrative is missing in extant Greek manuscripts. But it is a unified literary block focused on the interpretation of Gen 3:14–19, which, unlike other parts of the *Life of Adam and Eve* material, demonstrates use of Jewish exegetical techniques and a reliance on the Hebrew text of Genesis. That adds to the impression that the Worship of Adam Story goes back to a Jewish (not a Christian) author. However, it is also raises a question to which we shall return: if the Penitence Narrative has been created through a creative exegetical engagement with the (Hebrew text of

---

26. Despite the impression given in Hurtado, *Lord Jesus Christ*, 39 n. 40, and Bauckham, *God of Israel*, 203.

27. J. Magliano-Tromp, "Adamic Traditions," 298.

28. See *Apoc. Sedr.* 5:1–2 and *Gos. Bart.* 4:52–55.

29. See Anderson, "Penitence Narrative," and the review in Eldridge, *Dying Adam*, 69–72; cf. 128.

the) first chapters of Genesis (and its problems), what scriptural basis does the Worship of Adam Story (that is part of that Penitence Narrative) have?

It is true that J. Tromp and M. de Jonge have argued that the extant Greek *L.A.E* is a Christian text.[30] But the fact that the Worship of Adam Story is part of a block of traditions (the Penitence Narrative) that is not present in some Greek manuscripts could very well mean that, along with the Penitence Narrative, it has a separate tradition history and a much older provenance than the extant Greek version of the *L.A.E.*[31] In any case, the Tromp and de Jonge view that the Greek is Christian has been challenged by Michael Eldridge, who has argued at length that the literary and theological purpose of the Greek version makes very little sense as a work created by a Christian.[32] Among many arguments for a Jewish origin for the *L.A.E*, Eldridge highlights the fact that the Worship of Adam Story pericope is unnatural in a Christian text that would be more likely to put the focus on Christ.[33] Jack Levison has also now argued, in the light of a careful comparison between the Greek *L.A.E* and Rom 1:18–25, that it is not implausible that "Paul used some form of this narrative—presumably written but possibly oral," and that Paul and the *L.A.E.* reflected a shared interpretative tradition.[34] So, for multiple reasons, it is simply no longer possible to refer, without further ado, to the view of de Jonge and Tromp that the Greek *L.A.E.* is Christian.[35]

30. See de Jonge and Tromp, *Life of Adam and Eve,* 65–78, and de Jonge, "Christian Origin".

31. Bauckham says—without argument or recognition of the important work of Anderson on the Penitence Narrative and the monograph by Eldridge—that the Latin, Armenian, and Georgian versions "represent later developments" (Bauckham, *God of Israel,* 203). However, for the possibility that the Armenian and Georgian (which both include the Worship of Adam Story) are closer to a Greek original than the Latin see Stone, *History,* 36–39, and Eldridge, *Dying Adam,* 116.

32. Eldridge, *Dying Adam* (2001). The full force of Eldridge's arguments have, as far as I can tell, not yet been given an adequate response by anyone who would still maintain a Christian provenance. His arguments also mean Anderson's recent hesitation about the Jewish origin of the *L.A.E.* (especially the Penitence Narrative) is really unwarranted (Anderson, "Adam and Eve," 21). Waddell's arguments for the pre-Christian dating of the Greek *L.A.E.* (*Messiah,* 186–99) also dovetail with those put forward by Eldridge.

33. Eldridge, *Dying Adam,* 250–56.

34. Levison, "Adam and Eve," 523.

35. For the Worship of Adam Story pre-Christian see now also J. Dochhorn, "Vit Ad 11–17." Rivka Nir, "Image of God," has recently argued that the Greek text is Christian in its treatment of the beast and Seth in Greek *L.A.E.* 10–12. Her discussion certainly shows how some aspects of the text could have been accommodated within a Christian world view. But the parallels she adduces also indicate that no Christian would create a story so patently devoid of explicit Christology and other key aspects of the gospel.

There are perhaps as many as four pre-Christian Jewish texts that know the story. Firstly, Philo is almost certainly a witness to it in his treatise *On the Creation of the World,* where he says that when man was created the other creatures were so amazed at the sight of him that they worshipped (*proskynein*) him as one by nature ruler and master (§83). This is a parallel to a reference to the Worship of Adam Story in the Armenian and Georgian versions of the *Life* where it is says the beasts (*not the angels*) worshipped Adam (Armenian and Georgian L.A.E. [44](16):2b—*Synopsis* §18). Secondly, a fragmentary Qumran text (4Q381 frag. 1, lines 10–11) refers to service and ministry to Adam. In the immediate context the angels and the creatures of heaven and earth ("all God's hosts") seem to be the only possible subject of the action.[36]

Michael Stone has argued that in *2 En.* 22 there is allusion to the story.[37] There Enoch has ascended to the highest heaven and is presented before the throne of God. The Lord God "sounds out" the angels in his throne room, commanding them to let Enoch join in and stand in front of his face forever (22:6). The angels then prostrate themselves and welcome Enoch. Stone suggests that the fact that God "sounds out" or "makes a trial" of the angels is an allusion to the motif of a refusal to worship the human being in L.A.E. 12–16. This is possible, though by no means certain. It would accord with other aspects of *2 Enoch.*[38] In *2 En.* 7 angels have already prostrated themselves to Enoch (v. 4) and pleaded his intercession on their behalf in a way that, in the Greco-Roman period, could be construed as a manifestation of their worship of him. Later on, after his exaltation to the highest heaven and his transformation to a heavenly or "divine" being, Enoch is certainly worshipped by his fellow human beings (57:2 and 64:3) (a feature of *2 Enoch* we shall consider in Part 5). And, crucially, Enoch is depicted in this apocalypse as one who recovers the identity that Adam lost when he sinned.[39] However, it is not clear that the angels actually prostrate themselves *to Enoch* in 22:7 and we do not know for certain when *2 Enoch* was written. It is much closer to the original Aramaic Enoch tradition (preserved in *1 Enoch*) than *3 Enoch,* and was probably composed sometime before 100 AD in a North African Jewish context. So again, *2 Enoch* is a possible, but by no means certain, witness to a pre-Christian version of the *L.A.E.* 12–16 story. On the

---

36. See Fletcher-Louis, *Glory of Adam*, 98–99, and for the text and comment, and for its official reconstruction, see *DJD* 11:92–94.

37. Stone, "Three Notes," 145–48.

38. The argument is taken up and developed by Orlov, *Dark Mirrors*, 91–104, with respect also to a possible witness to the Worship of Adam Story in *3 En.* (100–101).

39. On that recovery, see Fletcher-Louis, "2 Enoch".

other hand, we can be more confident that the author of Daniel did know the story (see below).

There are passages in the NT that may know the story. Chief among these is Heb 1:6, which says when God "brought the firstborn into the world, he said 'Let all the all the angels of God worship (*proskynēsatōsan*) him.'"[40] Given the ways in which Jesus undoes the disobedience of Adam in the Gospel temptation story, it is also possible that the reference to the angels serving him in Mark 1:13 and Matt 4:11 is an allusion to the story of the angelic worship of Adam that is meant to alert the reader to the fact that the angels already recognize his true identity as the one who inaugurates a new humanity, and in rendering him worshipful service they anticipate the future worship of him by his human followers.[41]

In addition to all these literary pointers to a pre-Christian provenance, the argument that follows will be that the Worship of Adam Story makes a vital contribution to an historically satisfying explanation of the origins and shape of "Christological monotheism." That will add further weight to an already cumulatively strong case that the story is pre-Christian.

I: A Jewish, Hebrew-Speaking Provenance?

There is a small detail of the Worship of Adam Story, and of the material that is related to it in other parts of the *L.A.E.* tradition, that points to a Semitic *Vorlage* behind all known witnesses.[42] In the Latin *L.A.E.* 14:1-2 (cf. Greek 10:3; 12:1-2; 33:5; 35:2) Adam is simply said to *be* God's image.[43] Steenberg and others have drawn attention to the way this sharpens up the relationship between God and Adam compared to the statement that God makes man *in* his image in Genesis 1. What has not been noticed is that this specification of Adam *as* God's image in all likelihood means *the story of the angelic worship of Adam was created out of a reading of the Hebrew*

---

40. For a reference to the *L.A.E.* story in Heb 1:6, see most recently Moffitt, *Epistle to the Hebrews*, 134-37 and cf. J. Dochhorn, "Vit Ad 11-17."

41. Compare Marcus, *Mark*, 168-71; Orlov, *Dark Mirrors*, 110-12. David Litwa has also suggested that "Ecce Adam" in *L.A.E.* 13:3 stands behind the "Ecce homo" of John 19:5 (in Litwa, "Behold Adam," 138-41).

42. The story of Adam's penitence in the river Jordan (Latin, Armenian, Georgian *L.A.E.* 8:1-3 and some mss of Gk. 29:11b-c—*Synopsis* §4) is also indebted to the Hebrew of Josh 3:16. See Anderson, "Penitence Narrative," 6 n. 9.

43. The view that Adam *is* the image is then reflected in the *Apoc. Sedr.* 13:3; *Gos. Bart.* 4:53-54; *Discourse of Abbaton* fol. 13a (Budge, *Coptic Martyrdoms*, 483) and *Encomium on Saint Michael* fols. 11b-12b (Budge, *Coptic Texts*, 903-4).

by a non-Christian Jewish author, not from the Greek version of Genesis by a Christian (or by a Greek-speaking Jew).

The Septuagint text of Gen 1:26–27 says that God made man *"according to (kat' eikona)* his image" (and "according to his likeness"). Why the Greek should want to remove any distinction between the Hebrew creation of humanity *in* God's image and *according to* God's likeness is not absolutely clear. The Greek seems to imply that God already had an image that functioned as a pattern or model *according to* which humanity at its creation was conformed (in shape, form, spiritual character, in essence, or in some other way).[44] The Greek of Gen 1:26–27 would then be similar in meaning to the Greek of Exod 25:40, where Moses is told to make the Tabernacle *"according to (kata)* the pattern *(typos)"* shown to him on the mountain. In other words, for the Tabernacle, there already existed in the heavenlies divinely ordained architectural drawings (a *pattern*) that Moses was to follow. In a similar way, the Septuagint of Gen 1:26 claims that God already had an image, *that in some way provided a model for the creation of humanity;* the earthly Adam is the *"Abbild"* or *"Ebenbild"* of the *"Urbild."*[45] Here the Greek is probably influenced by older texts that describe God's physical, anthropomorphic form (Gen 3:8; Ezek 1:26; Isa 6:1–2; Dan 7:9; *1 En.* 14:20–24). It is also possible that the Septuagint is consciously appealing to a Greek philosophical environment where, following Plato, humanity has an unchanging form, or idea, that is the model for individual human beings (see, e.g., *Parmenides* 130C).[46] In reliance on the LXX of Gen 1:26, Philo of Alexandria, who was so keen to accommodate the Bible to Greek philosophical categories, took humanity's creation *according to the image of God* to mean that there was an entity—the *Logos*—according to whose image humanity was created.[47] For others who read the Greek version of the Pentateuch with no particular interest in the Greek philosophical tradition, God simply created humanity *according to* his image (Sir 17:3), "making a copy from his own image" (*Sib. Or.* 1:23; cf. e.g., Wis. 2:23; Col 3:10; *T. Naph.* 2:5).

Some texts that evidently relied on the Hebrew of Genesis retained the statement that humanity was created *"in* God's image" (e.g., *Sib. Or.* 3:8; *Jub.* 6:8, the targums to Gen 1, and the second-century Greek translations of Aquila and Theodotian). But there are others besides the *L.A.E.* that know a translation, or *interpretation*, of the Hebrew according to which Adam

---

44. For this interpretation of LXX Gen 1:26 see Muraoka, *Lexicon,* 365.

45. For the distinction between the *Urbild* and *Abbild* in rabbinic Adam tradition see Jervell, *Imago,* 97–107; cf. Kim, *Origin,* 203–4.

46. So Rösel, *Übersetzung,* 49.

47. E.g., *Alleg. Interp.* 3:96, cf. *Heir* 231; *Spec. Laws* 1:81.

simply *was* God's image (1 Cor 11:7; the Latin text of *4 Ezra* 8:44; *2 En.* 30:10; *Sib. Or.* 8:403; Symmachus' Greek translation).[48] The key point here is that *this interpretation can only justifiably be made from the Hebrew*. In the Hebrew of Gen 1 the *beth* in ("*betsalmenu . . . betsalmo . . . betselem . . .*") can be treated either as a *beth essentiae* ("*as* our image . . . *as* his image . . . *as* the image") or as a *beth pretii* ("*in the place of, instead of our image . . .*" and, therefore, "*for* our image").[49]

Of course, theoretically, it is possible that the Worship of Adam Story was created by Christians who read Paul and followed the formulation in 1 Cor 11:7, where man "*is* the image and glory of God." However, there are several points that tell against that scenario. There is nothing else in the *L.A.E.* to suggest reliance on Paul's letters. That passage in 1 Cor 11:7 is hardly a prominent piece of Pauline theology and, in any case, Christian Greek literature from the subapostolic period shows a clear preference for the language of the Septuagint of Gen 1 (see e.g., *1 Clem* 33:4-5; *Barn.* 5:5; 6:12; *Ep. Apost.* 1:3). If the Pauline corpus is a reliable guide to early Christian faith, it is supremely Christ who *is* the image of God (2 Cor 4:4; Col 1:15; cf. Heb 1:3), Adam himself is the man of dust (1 Cor 15:49), whilst believers are remade "*according to* the image," that is Christ (Col 3:10; cf. Rom 8:29; 1 Cor 15:49). Nothing in the earliest Christian literature encourages us to believe that a Christian would have created the Worship of Adam Story and, as far as I am aware, no plausible *Christian* life setting has so far been proposed for it. And the fact that Adam *is* the image is consistent with other indications that the story was originally composed on the basis of the Hebrew of text of Genesis.

We shall see below that the identification of Adam *as God's image* is by no means an incidental detail of the Worship of Adam Story. Indeed, this is clear even at a cursory reading of the Greek and Latin versions of the *L.A.E.* Later on in the story of Adam's life, when Seth and Eve go in search of healing oil to help Adam, Seth is attacked by a wild animal (*Synopsis* §12). He is able to rebuke and overcome the beast because he *is* the image of God to whom the animal creature should submit. That story would not work quite so well if Seth were made *according to* God's image. The fact that

---

48. This strongly suggests then that *2 En.* 30:10 is one part of *2 Enoch* that reflects a Hebrew *Vorlage* to the Greek *Vorlage* of the Slavonic. Unlike the Latin, the Syriac at *4 Ezra* 8:44 seems to reflect a Septuagintal understanding of the Hebrew "made like your own image" (see Box, *Ezra-Apocalypse*, 187).

49. For the *beth essentiae* at Gen 1:26 see Clines, "Image of God," 76-80 and Joüon and Muraoka, *Grammar*, §133c. For the *beth pretii* here compare Ps 106:20 "they exchanged their glory *for the form (betabnit)* of an ox eating grass" and see Gruber, "God, Image of," 1760-61.

such an anthropology is based squarely on a reading *of the Hebrew* of Gen 1 means that both the Worship of Adam Story and the one about Seth's encounter with the beast were most likely composed in a pre-Christian, Hebrew-speaking, Jewish environment.

Theoretically, some Greek-speaking Christian author of the Worship of Adam Story could have relied on a different translation of the Hebrew of Gen 1:26 to the one extant in the LXX. But there is no evidence of Christians in the late Second Temple period using a Greek Pentateuch that had an "*as* our image" in Gen 1:26. Aquila and Theodosian (from the second century AD) both have "in our image (*en eikoni hēmōn*)." There is one Greek version of Gen 1:26—Symmachus—that does have God say that man is to be made "*as* our image (*hōs eikona hēmōn*)." But Symmachus is a Jew translating the Hebrew (possibly in Palestine) at the end of the second century AD.[50] If his translation of Gen 1:26 (which could be dependent on an older tradition) demonstrates anything, it is that Adam's identity *as* God's image was a Jewish, not a Christian understanding of the biblical text. If the story was created by a Christian—which we have seen seems unlikely—he must have been a Jewish, Hebrew-speaking Christian and in this case his story still testifies to an essentially Jewish perspective on Adam.

Notwithstanding the rather slim possibility of reliance on 1 Cor 11:7 (or a Christian reading of Genesis that stands behind 1 Cor 11) or some other explanation of the identification of Adam *as* the image of God, the overwhelming probability that the Adam story was composed by a reader of the Hebrew of Gen 1:26 is consistent with other reasons for thinking that the story was created by Jews, not by (Greek-speaking) Christians.

4: Is the Worship of Adam Story "Untypical" of Pre-Christian Judaism?

The second argument against the case (put forward by Steenburg) that the story prepared the way for the worship of Jesus is Bauckham's claim that the story is untypical for first-century Judaism. This is a somewhat surprising judgment after Bauckham's own admission that in the *Similitudes of Enoch* the Son of Man figure is worshipped because he participates in a key aspect of the divine identity. And it really is not a fair representation of what we know of Second Temple life and thought.

---

50. For the date and context of Symmachus see Salvesen, *Symmachus*, 283–97; Fernández Marcos, *Septuagint*, 122–26. For the different versions of Gen 1:26 see generally Salvesen, *Symmachus,* ad loc, and Wevers, *Genesis*, 15.

We have already noted some texts that exalt Adam to a position of glory and we have flagged up the possible Adamic identity of the Enochic Son of Man. In fact, the position given to Adam in the story is not without parallel in Jewish texts that are certainly pre-Christian and that point to a wider interest in Adam's sharing something of the divine identity, especially God's own (divine) glory. As Jarl Fossum pointed out, our story should be compared with texts that show that Jews meditated on the connection between the "*'adam*" of Gen 1 and the "likeness (*demut*) as an appearance of a man (*'adam*)" who is seated on God's throne in Ezek 1:26—over the heads of the living creatures (*hayyot*)—and who is also described as "the likeness of the glory of Yhwh (Ezek 1:28)."[51] The DSS text *Divre Hammerot*, or *Words of the Luminaries* (4QDibHam), fuses the language of the two texts with the statement in 4Q504 8 (recto) line 4 that "[Adam] you fashioned in the likeness (*demut*) of [your] glory (*ytsrth bdmwt kbwd*[*kh*])." The text is fragmentary and it is hard to judge what it exactly claims for Adam's identity. It is possible that it describe's "Adam's glory" as "an effulgence of God's own glory."[52] Alternatively, 4Q504 8 provides a witness to a Hebrew parallel to the Septuagint interpretation of Gen 1:26, where humanity is created "according to the likeness" of the divine form that preexisted humanity's creation. Either way, 4Q504 8 shows that Jews in the late Second Temple period were keenly focused on Adam's original and glorious identity in a way that is similarly reflected in the Worship of Adam Story. The text was likely composed in the first half of the second century BC, before the foundation of the Qumran community, and the fact that it is a piece of liturgy—a cycle of prayers for the different days of the week—brings the statement on Adam in fragment 8 into the context of worship and prayer. It is unfortunate that more of the text is not preserved, because it could shed valuable light on the way Adam figured in the Qumran community's cultic life. It is clear and worth noting, however, that the text connects Adam's original glorious identity to Israel, the true humanity, that is created "for the glory" (*lkbwdkh*) of God in another portion of the liturgy (4Q504 frags. 1–2, iii 4).[53]

---

51. Fossum, *Name of God*, 277–78.

52. Van Kooten, *Paul's Anthropology*, 18. Compare the discussion in Fletcher-Louis, *Glory of Adam*, 92–95.

53. See Fletcher-Louis, *All the Glory*, 94. F. Avemarie, "Image of God," 217–18, rather misses the point of my reading of 4Q504 1–2 col. iii, line 4. It is not that the Hebrew adjective *l* expresses identity ("You created Israel *as* your glory"). The *l* is final or purposive and, *in the literary context of* 4Q504, Israel serves God's divine glory by carrying it or participating in it, as did Adam (as in indeed Avemarie recognizes). The parallel that Avemarie cites in 1QM 13:9 ("Image of God," 218 n. 54) nicely illustrates my point: "you created us *for* y[ou] *as* an eternal nation," in other words: Israel's identity as an *eternal* nation carries or conveys something of God's own identity (as the truly

The Hebrew text of Ben Sira 49:16 says that "over all the living creatures is/was the beauty of Adam/a man." A reference to the first-formed Adam is expected at this point in the context of an account of the righteous heroes of old in Ben Sira 44:1—50:1. However, the reference to an "'*adam*" who is *over the living creatures* (*'al kol hay*) is highly suggestive of the "likeness of the appearance of *a man* (*'adam*) over (*'al*)" the living creatures (*hayyot*) in Ezek 1:26–28, a passage that Ben Sira has had in view a few verses earlier (49:8; cf. 50:7). So, Ben Sira seems to connect, or identify, in a more overt way than 4Q504, the Adam of Gen 1 and the "'*adam*" who is "the likeness of the glory of *Yhwh*" in Ezek 1:26.

Given that the "Chosen One," who is seated on the throne of glory in the *Similitudes of Enoch*, is called "the Son *of Man*," and that he is climactically identified with Enoch the *seventh* descendent from Adam (*1 En.* 71), we are also bound to wonder whether the way he manifests the divine identity owes something to the kind of Adam theology present in the Worship of Adam Story and these other pre-Christian Jewish texts. In the last chapter we noted the likelihood that the *Similitudes* identifies the Son of Man with the human-like figure on the throne in Ezek 1:26 (at *1 En.* 46:1). As Helge Kvanvig has recently pointed out, in some instances the Ethiopic expression (and its underlying Aramaic), that is usually translated "Son of Man," probably has in mind a connection to Adam: this is "the Son of Adam" (62:5; 69:29; 71:14) or "the offspring of the mother of the living (i.e., Eve)" (*1 En.* 62:7, 9, 14; 63:11; 69:26–27; 70:1; 71:17).[54] In this case, the Enochic Son of Man is a kind of "Second Adam"; an Adam who is also, mysteriously, a preexistent Adam seated on God's throne of glory.

There is no literary connection between the *L.A.E.* and the *Similitudes* (although the Armenian and Georgian versions have the intriguing comment that Adam is God's "chosen one"—21:2). But the Adamic contours to the Enochic Son of Man suggest that the worship of the Enochic figure may not be unconnected to wider traditions in which Adam was himself worshipped.

So connections to other Jewish texts suggest that the protological worship of Adam was not "untypical" of late Second Temple Judaism. And the connections between the Adam and Enochic Son of Man stories mean it is unwise to treat these as isolated *exceptions to the rule* that a "strict" Jewish monotheism excluded such worship. In what follows I will offer more textual evidence that first-century Jews certainly did not consider the Worship of Adam Story exceptional or theologically dubious. There are good grounds

---

eternal God).

54. Kvanvig, "Son of Man," 193–95.

for thinking it was well-known, regarded as theologically mainstream, and that it was created in an attempt to faithfully interpret the biblical text.[55]

5: Is Adam Actually "Worshipped" in this Story?

The third objection to the proposal that the Worship of Adam Story helps explain Christ devotion is Bauckham's claim that in fact the angels do not actually "worship" Adam. His reasoning at this point is twofold. First of all, he disputes the meaning of the word that English translators have usually rendered "worship." Behind the Latin *"adorare"* ("worship") we can be confident that the Greek version of the story had *proskynein* (the verb which in fact *is* used in some Greek manuscripts for the worship of Adam in Greek L.A.E. 16:2). Sometimes that Greek verb can describe a gesture in recognition of another's superiority *but not actual worship* (see, e.g., Matt 18:26). *Context determines its meaning.* Here the context means only that God wants the angels to express their obedience to Adam as their superior. And this brings us to Bauckham's second point. Whilst Adam is certainly superior to the angels, he is also inferior to God and, crucially, "Adam does not occupy the divine throne."[56] So what the angels do to Adam cannot be "worship."

As far as I know, Bauckham is the only commentator to doubt that worship is in view in this case and, for multiple reasons, I think he is wrong on this point. I will cover most of the reasons here and then return, towards the end of this chapter, to the issue once we have established the story's scriptural and theological context.

Before we engage his case, let us return to Steenburg's original argument—which Bauckham has not yet responded to in print—and clarify what it means to say that the text describes the "worship" of Adam by the angels. Steenburg, in his own way, justified the view that Adam is "worshipped" through a specific interpretation of the context of the angels' action. He argued that in the story *the reason for the angels' prostration is the fact that Adam is the visible or physical manifestation of God.*[57] In other words, the context of their action is the *presence of God in Adam* and so, on that basis, its meaning is "worship." (This, I should stress, is a worship of Adam that is not quite the same as the worship of Jesus Christ in earliest Christianity.

---

55. Cf. Jean-Pierre Pettorelli, "Adam and Eve, Life of," 305: there is "no compelling reason to deny the narrative a Jewish origin."

56. Bauckham, *God of Israel*, 204.

57. Steenburg, "Worship of Adam," 96–97. Chester, *Messiah*, 72–73, 113–15, also stresses the need to take seriously that part of Steenburg's argument.

Jesus' followers worshipped him as one *included* in the divine identity in a way that our text does not claim was the case with Adam.)

There are several details of the text that support this interpretation. Repeatedly the text focuses on Adam's identity *as God's image and likeness*. In two respects the tale gives greater specificity to the meaning of "image and likeness" than is apparent from a surface reading of Gen 1. First, there is an interpretative clarification of the meaning of Gen 1:26. Genesis 1:26 itself says Adam is made "*in (beth)* the image of God." The text at the Latin L.A.E. 14:1–2 and 15:2 interprets the biblical text to say that Adam simply *is* the image of God. This accentuates the focus on Adam as God's visible or physical form or manifestation. Secondly, 13:3 says what the biblical text itself does not say: that Adam's *countenance* is made in the image of God (Latin L.A.E. 13:3; cf. Georgian). This too accentuates the focus on Adam's role as God's visible and physical presence. The Greek version of the *Vita*, which probably originally contained the Worship of Adam Story, adds to this theme the notion that in Eden Adam and Eve were clothed with glory, even God's own divine glory (Gk. L.A.E. 20:2; 21:2, 6).

It is true that Adam is a distinct entity. But because the angels are commanded to respond to Adam *as the image and likeness of God,* the "worship" of Adam (if that is what it is) does not necessarily mean that God's singular, unique identity is now threatened by the worship *of another figure*.[58] Adam is presented "not as the ultimate object of veneration but rather as a representation or an icon of the deity *through whom* the angels are able to worship God."[59] The question, then, of Adam's *inferiority* to God does not enter the picture any more than it does in the case of a theology that gives to a sacramental signifier a genuinely divine real presence, or in the case of Jesus who is a clearly presented in the NT as both subordinate to God and also his "image." If we are to properly understand the story and its internal logic, it is simply a category mistake to quibble about Adam's inferiority to God or otherwise. To do so is like telling a Catholic that the eucharistic elements are not the body and blood of Jesus because they are actually baked flour and fermented grape juice, or to complain that the veneration of the eucharistic host entails the creation of additional divine entities that threaten the trinitarian economy. (For any number of reasons we may well judge that such practices misconstrue the nature of a genuine Christian worship, but *for those with a sacramental theology such problems simply do not arise*.) Adam is, to be sure, a creature and he himself worships God before the angels are told that they should now worship Adam (13:2). But the text's

---

58. As Hurtado implies it would do (*Lord Jesus Christ*, 39).
59. Orlov, *Dark Mirrors*, 105 (italics added); cf. Bunta, "Likeness of the Image," 72.

conceptual framework for "image and likeness" of God means worship of Adam himself is also appropriate, in the same way that, within a trinitarian theology, Christians can worship Jesus who himself worships the Father. Or, to put the matter another way, we should not be overly punctilious, from a particular Christian vantage point, about what "worship" can and cannot mean in a story that does not itself claim a Christian theological framework.

These observations also mean, by the way, that it is a mistake to rush to the conclusion that if Adam is worshipped here then this must be one of those texts that the rabbis had in their cross hairs when they inveighed against the "Two Powers in heaven" heresy.[60] This is unlikely because the story does not portray Adam as a *thoroughly separate*, individuated, divine being. He is not "a god" or "demigod." He exists solely at the service of God; *as God's image and likeness*. (Though in a later period the rabbis might well have been concerned that the story implied, or was taken by some to mean, the commendation of a worship of two divine beings.)

So, what we have here, as was the case with the *Similitudes*, is a text that challenges Bauckham's description of Jewish monotheism in a way that suggests that, however much it is based on an inductive study of the primary texts, it does not do justice to all the data and to the specific historical contexts of some of the primary texts. His construal of Jewish monotheism seems now to be circular.[61]

Bauckham says the strictly exclusive identity of the one God is defined by his authority over all things, a position that is often visually represented with God enthroned in the highest heaven.[62] In no text is it said of a messianic figure or "principal angel or exalted human in Second Temple Jewish texts... that he has authority over all things or over heaven and earth."[63] The Jewish messiah may be ascribed a position of universal rule, but according to Bauckham, that reign is limited to the earthly sphere (on the basis of Ps 2:8; Dan 7:14, and, for example, in *Sib. Or.* 5:416; *1 En.* 62:6). A position of universal *cosmic* authority is exclusive to God himself (and to Jesus Christ in the NT). So, the logic of Bauckham's argument is straightforward: Adam is *not* seated on God's throne and he is not said to have authority over "all things," so he is not included in the divine identity, so this is not really worship.

Bauckham has defined the divine identity (and therefore "worship") in a way that makes selective use of the primary texts. The existence of a

---

60. As I mistakenly concluded in my *Luke-Acts*, 142 (following Segal, *Two Powers*, 112–13).
61. As D. Litwa points out (*Being Transformed*, 278 n. 51).
62. See esp. Bauckham, *God of Israel*, 176 and 152–81 generally.
63. Ibid., 176.

text—such as the one presently under investigation—that, *on other grounds*, deems it appropriate that angels do genuinely "worship" the pre-fall Adam, forces us to question whether Bauckham's assessment of the data is sufficiently comprehensive and that it does justice to the theological sophistication of Jewish writers. Might it be that here we have Jewish evidence that an entity can be "worshipped" even if there is no interest in whether it does or does not possess a universal sovereignty? Might it be that, for some Jews, a figure could be "worshipped," not because he is "included" as a distinct entity within the divine identity, but because he is a unique, singular manifestation of the divine identity (visually and physically)?

If, as dispassionate historians, our assessment of these possibilities is to be guided by the biblical account of things, it is unfair to apply the sovereignty criteria to establish an entity's "divine identity" strictly and in all cases. God himself often appears without a throne in Scripture and in Jewish texts. Is he suddenly less divine for the lack of one? NT Christology expresses belief in the Lord Jesus Christ's inclusion in the divine identity in a variety of ways, with several key passages making no explicit mention of enthronement (1 Cor 8:6; Phil 2:6–11; Col 1:15–20; John 1:1–18). Are we now to say that Jesus is not actually worshipped in these texts? In fact, in quite a few passages Christ is praised precisely as the one who is the visible form or physical manifestation of God, as Steenburg and others have pointed out (Phil 2:6; Col 1:15; 2:9; 2 Cor 4:4; Heb 1:3), not as one who is enthroned with God.[64]

I am quite certain that the Worship of Adam Story, as it appears in the Primary Adam Books, is not primarily interested in Adam's authority. Crucially, *if the prostration simply acknowledges Adam's superiority to the angels then it is surprising that none of the versions of the story in the Primary Adam Books picks up the language of kingship and dominion that is clearly used for Adam in Gen 1* (language that does crop up frequently in postbiblical Adam traditions). There is no mention, that is, of God's command that Adam "have dominion" or that he "subdue" the earth (Gen 1:26, 28). It is true that some witnesses to the story outside the *L.A.E.* do include reference to Adam's rulership, and his superiority within creation is partly in view in those cases. But *the version in the Primary Adam Books shows that recognition of Adam's superiority and authority was not the primary focus of the angelic prostration for many of those who copied and retold the pseudepigraphical story.*

This is one of those texts that is easily misunderstood or ignored by the Reformed tradition, which emphasizes divine sovereignty as *the* key to a biblical understanding of divine identity. In keeping with another strand of

---

64. See also Chester, *Messiah*, 115.

biblical theology, the story is primarily interested in divine *presence*; before his fall Adam was created to bear divine presence *as God's physical and visual image*. As such, he is owed worship. I will return to say more about this shortly. But before I do so, it is worth making a few more observations that cast more doubt on Bauckham's own criteria for assessing such a case of a possible divine identity.

In the first place, Bauckham's claim that Adam does not have a position of cosmic authority *as one seated on God's throne* is obviously an argument from silence. The text does not say that Adam did not rightfully belong on God's throne before his fall. Secondly, the story itself probably does carry with it, at least implicitly, the notion that Adam has a cosmic authority.[65] *All the angels* are commanded to worship Adam. Given the way angels function in Second Temple literature, this gives Adam a position of cosmic rule. We should compare other texts where God (and Christ) are surrounded by all the angels of heaven and earth and submission to God's ultimate authority and worship of him are in view or assumed (e.g., Dan 7:9-10; Rev 5:11-14). It certainly cannot mean that Adam has only a rule on earth (mirroring God's rule in heaven). For Jews, a scene where *all the angels* worship must mean that all of heaven and earth does Adam obeisance. In their ability to worship, intercede, follow divine commands, and so forth, the angels serve as representatives of the totality of the cosmos (cf. Gk. *L.A.E.* 29:11c).

Thirdly, the Worship of Adam Story probably presumes a wider river of biblical interpretation in which Adam and Adamic figures are ascribed a position of universal, cosmic authority. Certainly, first-century messianism of the *royal*, Davidic variety does *not* usually entail the scope of universal sovereignty regularly given to Jesus Christ in NT texts.[66] However, in the case of Adam, *Ps 8 provides clear scriptural warrant for a true humanity that*

---

65. Cf. J. Dochhorn, "Vit Ad 11-17," 288-99, who sees the story as an example of a wider ancient Jewish interest in humanity's possession of a God-delegated cosmic authority.

66. Though Bauckham far too neatly draws a line between God's sovereignty (over all the cosmos) and the messiah's rule over just the earth. It *may* be true that in Ps 2:8 and Dan 7:14 the scope of dominion is limited to the earthly sphere (though this is by no means certain in the second text). However, the other texts Bauckham cites (in *God of Israel*, 176)—*Sib. Or.* 5:416 and *1 En.* 62:6—are hardly clear proof of his point. *Sib. Or.* 5:414-32 describes a "blessed man" who comes "from the plains of heaven" carrying in his hand a scepter given by God with dominion "over all" (*pantōn*). This preexistent messiah figure then exercises an authority on the earth that extends to the heavenly spheres; rebuilding the (Jerusalem) Temple with cosmic proportions so that the whole of creation praises the glory of God. Similarly, in *1 En.* 62:6, the Son of Man is not said to rule over "all the earth," but simply "over all," and there is much to suggest he has a sovereignty that extends beyond the earthly realm (as we noted in chapter 4). 4Q521 frag. 2 ii line 1 may also envisage all the heavens and the earth obeying a messiah.

has authority on the earth, in the heavens and over the seas (8:5-8 [Heb. vv. 6-9]); that is, over "all things" (*pantōn*) and all parts of the three-tiered biblical cosmos. Indeed, in 4Q381 frag. 1, which as we have seen perhaps includes a reference to the worship of Adam by the angels, the preceding passage quite likely bases a claim that Adam was to rule over all of heaven and earth on Ps 8.[67] Certainly, Ben Sira/Sirach 49:16 has in view humanity's sovereignty over the creatures of the earth, the seas, and the heavens that is described in Ps 8 when it says Adam was "over all the living (Heb.)"/"over every living creature in creation" (Gk.).[68] This is also an evocation of Ezekiel's "likeness as the appearance of an *'adam*" who is seated on God's throne over the four living creatures (Ezek 1:26).

Returning to the Worship of Adam Story, although it is true that Adam is not explicitly placed on God's throne, the angels' recognition of his superior position in the economy of creation most likely testifies to his divine identity in a way that is consistent with the presentation of Adamic or human figures in these other Jewish texts.[69] It may well presume the praise in Ps 8 where Adam and humanity are celebrated *precisely because they have authority over all parts of the cosmos*. There too, Adam is not explicitly enthroned, but royal language is used for the one to whom God delegates cosmic authority (see vv. 5-6 [Heb. 6-7]). In any case, whilst there is no enthronement of Adam in the L.A.E. version of the Worship of Adam Story, other witnesses to the tale do enthrone Adam, even next to God, and so we cannot exclude the possibility that that was a known part of the tradition—perhaps even with a debt to the enthroned Adam of Ezek 1:26—already in the first century.[70]

---

67. 4Q381 frag. 1 line 3 introduces a section devoted to God's creation of "heaven and earth" (lines 3-6). Line 7 then says "and by His Spirit (cf. Gen 1:2) he appointed them to rule (*lmshl*, cf. Ps 8:7) over *all* (*bkl*) these, on the ground and in the [. . .]" (the text is broken at this point). The fact that in lines 10-11 it is most likely "all his host and His angels" (cf. Gen 2:1) who serve Adam suggests that the heavenly sphere was included in the scope of Adam's rule in the preceding section. Furthermore, the rule (√*mshl*) of Adam is then echoed later on in the scroll's reference to Yhwh's ruling (*moshel*) over the raging of the sea (4Q381 frag. 15 line 4 quoting Ps 89:10) and to the nation of Israel that is called "to rule (*lmshl*) over all (*bkl*)" (4Q381 frags. 76 + 77, line 15).

68. For the reasons to see Ps 8 here see Fletcher-Louis, "Cosmology of P," 107.

69. Compare the comments of Chester, *Messiah*, 115.

70. See esp. the *Encomium on Saint Michael*, fol. 12a, where God also made everything subject to Adam (Budge, *Coptic Texts*, 903-4); *Discourse of Abbaton*, fol. 13a (Budge, *Coptic Martyrdoms*, 483), and compare *Gen. Rab.* 8:10 for Adam next to God in his chariot and the angels worshipping him. From another angle, in the *Apocalypse of Sedrach* the Worship of Adam Story has God say of Adam "I made him wise, the heir of heaven and earth and I subjected all things (*panta . . . hypetaxa*, cf. Ps 8:7 [LXX] *panta hypetaxas*) to him and every living creature fled from him and from his face" (6:2).

7. A JEWISH "DIVINE" ADAM

Whether or not the Worship of Adam Story really has any interest in Adam's cosmic authority, the angelic "worship" of Adam can be understood in terms of the specific details of the story—especially Adam's presentation as God's physical and visible image and likeness—and with reference to a wider set of texts that testify to a high view of humanity in its pre-fall, sinless state. On the other hand, nothing in the text demands that we have to follow Bauckham in concluding that the prostration is simply intended as an acknowledgement of Adam's superiority to the angels *but not his participation in, or expression of, the divine identity*. To be sure, Satan complains that what he is commanded to do is demeaning because Adam is inferior and subsequent to him. But his perspective on the prostration should hardly be assumed a complete or reliable guide to the author's (and God's) own understanding of the prostration.

In later rabbinic texts, the possibility of an angelic worship of Adam is firmly rejected. That rejection shows the rabbis knew something very much like the story in *L.A.E.* 12–16. In those rabbinic texts the angelic reaction to Adam is emphatically not commanded by God and it is simply deemed inappropriate altogether. So the rabbinic texts show that in the nonrabbinic (or older rabbinic) story the angels' behavior was definitely understood as "worship."[71]

I agree with Bauckham that ultimately what we have with the angels' action in this story "can be distinguished from properly divine worship" if, as confessionally committed Christians, we define "proper divine worship" by the grammar of worship prescribed by the NT.[72] Nevertheless, this story stubbornly resists the instincts of Christian scholars to define pre-Christian, Jewish worship through the lens of our own tradition. Or, to put the matter another way, here there is clear evidence that Jews at the turn of the eras could conceive of a created being possessing a distinctive kind of relationship to its Creator such that, *as the representative bearer of his presence*, that being deserved to receive the worshipful prostration that is rightfully God's own.

As such, the story offers a partial precedent for the worship of the man Jesus. Clearly, the story envisages a one-time event that was not repeated after Adam's fall. Nevertheless, there is every reason to believe that the earliest Jewish followers of Jesus could have interpreted worship of him through the conceptual and "historic" precedent provided by the angels' worship of Adam. If they believed Jesus was no mere creature like Adam they might have argued from the lesser to the greater that if Adam was worshipped,

---

71. See esp. *Pirqe R. El.* 11 and also *Gen. Rab.* 8:10; *Eccl. Rabb.* 6:9:1. On the rabbinic material, see esp. S. Bunta, "Likeness of the Image," 69–72.

72. The quoted words appear in Bauckham, *God of Israel*, 204.

how much more should Jesus (the preexistent one become human) be worshipped. And this brings us to the fourth objection to the Steenburg case.

6: The Story's Place in First-Century Jewish Practice and Belief

Hurtado understandably insists that if the Worship of Adam Story played a part in the origins of Christ devotion, then it needs to have had a genuine role in first-century Jewish cultic life. However, his own view that the story is simply a "literary scene set in the mythic past," and as such it in no way provides a precedent for Christ devotion, is overhasty.[73]

He claims that the story is simply an "etiological tale explaining the origin of Satan's evil disposition toward humanity."[74] It is true that this is one way the story is used in the Primary Adam Books, where the point is emphasized in the immediate literary frame given to the story (Latin *L.A.E.* 12:1—13:1; 15:3—17:1). But in the rest of the *Vita* it plays another role too. It contributes to an exploration of the nature of Adam's lost identity and his ultimate destiny. And, in any case, without that frame that explains the origins of Satan's hostility to humanity, the story itself is primarily concerned with Adam as God's visible and physical manifestation. In fact, some texts that include or know the story make no reference to it as an explanation of Satan's envy of humanity.[75] Even in the *Vita*, Satan's envy ends up later in the story bringing the focus back on to Adam's identity and destiny, with Adam promised that he will be exalted and given the throne that Satan now occupies (Latin *L.A.E.* 47:3; Gk. 39:1–3). *The story is about Adam, and who or what he is in relation to God and to the rest of creation*, especially its sentient, spiritual angelic realm. He and Eve used to live in paradise (see esp. Pericope §10). They used to eat the food of angels (Latin, Armenian, and Georgian *L.A.E.* 4:2). They were created with a name that reminds God of his majesty (Latin *L.A.E.* 27:1). And *as God's image* they rightfully have authority over all the beasts in creation (all versions—Pericope §12). And now they are

---

73. Hurtado, *Lord Jesus Christ*, 39. I do not understand what Hurtado means when he speaks of the story as an example of "imaginative scenes" that Jews "might pen for etiological or laudatory purposes" (ibid., 40).

74. Ibid., 40 n. 42.

75. See, for example, *Apoc. Sedr.* 5–7 and Philo *On Creation*, 83. If 4Q381 frag. 1 and Heb 1:6 refer to the story, they too seem uninterested in the "etiological" role Hurtado gives it. The rabbinic texts (*Gen. Rab.* 8:10; *Eccl. Rab.* 6:9:1; *Pirqe R. El.* 11) do not seem interested in the story's role as an etiology of Satan's envy either. It is generally reckoned that the reference to Isa 14:13–14 in Latin *L.A.E.* 15:3 has been added secondarily to the Latin text, since it is not present in the Georgian and Armenian versions.

tragically separated from these realities. But because they are God's specially chosen creature he will have mercy on them. In other words, the Primary Adam Books are preoccupied with the theme of the ideal and originally intended human identity, and its recovery. (A theme that has tended to be downplayed in the Western theology of recent centuries.)

Only secondarily is it a story that explains Satan's jealous opposition to humanity. Satan is jealous and rebels *because Adam has this extraordinary identity*. Furthermore, both the Worship of Adam Story and the material gathered with it in the Primary Adam Books illustrates the widespread Jewish interest in Adam's *identity*. That is an interest that arises, in part, from a desire to interpret Scripture, especially Gen 1–3, and, above all, to exegete Gen 1:26–28 (as we shall see in the next section). We can also assume that for its Jewish author(s) and original readers the question of Adam's *identity* is a question of human identity in general, but more specifically of Israel's own identity. In any case, here in this Jewish Adam material there is evidence that for Second Temple Jews the issue of Adam's original identity was every bit as important as the question of God's *identity*, that Bauckham has addressed.

Returning to Hurtado's demand that the text have some relation to pre-Christian worship practices, it is, of course, true that there is no Adam cult in the first-century Jewish world that could provide a neat and complete precedent for the Christ cult. The historical Adam belongs in the past and there was no sculptured image of him in Israel's Temple. However, there are strong *hints* that the prelapsarian Adam did play a role in Israel's liturgical life and that we should be open, therefore, to the possibility that in some way the angelic Worship of Adam Story was designed to anticipate the worship of a future new and true Adam (such as the one described in *1 En.* 37–71). In Part 5, I will lay out reasons to take those hints with the utmost seriousness. I lay them out here with a few basic observations and suggestions.

After his sin and departure from the garden, Adam has a place where he prays (Greek 5:3 [longer text]; Armenian and Georgian 30(5):3) or worships (Latin 30:3). And in the Latin there is a long passage that predicts the burning bush, the Tabernacle, and the Temple (25:1—29:10). It includes a statement that seems to be a prediction that God will raise up, from Adam's seed, a priesthood to minister in the true Temple.[76] According to the Georgian and Armenian version of the *L.A.E.*, after the initial act of angelic prostration at Adam's creation, there was a daily act of morning worship offered to God's image (44(16):2b).[77] How these passages functioned in a

---

76. This passage, which is focused on an imminent eschatological vindication of Torah and Temple piety strongly suggests that the Latin is a pre-AD 70 Jewish work.

77. The parallel reference to the worship of Adam in some, but not all, Greek texts at this point in the *L.A.E.* (Gk. 16:2) suggests that the Armenian and Georgian here bear

pre-Christian version of the story is not now clear, but they are suggestive of the possibility that the Worship of Adam Story was by no means a piece of detached imaginative speculation; that it had some concrete setting as narrative commentary on the theology of the Jewish Temple and its practices.

In 4Q381 frag. 1 the reference to service and ministry to Adam (line 11) follows a broken reference to monthly and daily festivals (line 8). The conceptually similar reflection on Adam's glorious identity in 4Q504 frag. 8 is part of a text that was used in a weekly cycle of prayers.[78] The cognate description of Adam exalted over all the creatures in Ben Sira 49:16 (that likely evokes Ezek 1:26) comes at the climax of a long hymn of praise (begun in 44:1) that reaches its crescendo with the hymn in 50:1–21 recounting the high priest's ministry in the Temple. This is a text to which we shall return. For now it is enough to note that in Ben Sira 49:16 the "*beauty* of Adam" is somehow transferred to the high priest Simon in 50:1 (who is the "*beauty* of his people"). This could mean that, in some sense, praise given to Simon is praise of him *as the true Adam*. There *is*, in other words, a kind of statue of Adam set up in memory of him in Israel's Temple: it is the high priest. We will return to this possibility in Part 5.

A praise of Adam, it should be remembered, is not without biblical basis. In Ps 8 humanity is praised as one whom God has crowned with glory and honor and under whose feet are the creatures of the earth, the heavens and the seas.[79] The LXX translation of the Hebrew superscription of Ps 8 gives it a liturgical setting. It is designated "for the winepresses" (v. 1; cf. LXX Pss 80:1; 83:1). Ben Sira/Sir 50:11–13, 15 reflects that setting when it echoes Ps 8 with a description of the priesthood ministering at the *altar* of burnt offerings (where the blood runs down to the ground like wine in a winepress) as if it is the true humanity ruling in all creation.[80] Again, this suggests that, as a hymn in praise of the high priest Simon, Ben Sira/Sir 50 also directs praise (albeit obliquely through Simon) to Adam. At any rate, here there is evidence that suggests the praise directed to "man . . . the son

---

witness to the normative, "original," Greek version of the story.

78. For comments on the liturgical setting of 4Q504 frag 8, and connections to wider liturgical traditions, see Fletcher-Louis, *All the Glory*, 92–95 (and the rest of that monograph).

79. In chapter 2 we noted how the numerical structure of Psalm 8 and the way the name of God (that has the values 17 and 26) is written into the Psalm. It is the sections of the Psalm that describe humanity that have seventeen words (vv. 3–4) and twenty-six words (vv. 5–8). This suggests the author sees humanity as a bearer, or visible image, of his name (*Yhwh*).

80. For Ben Sira 50 seeing the fulfillment of the vision for humanity in Ps 8 in the priestly ministry at the altar, see Fletcher-Louis, "Cosmology of P," 107.

of man" in Ps 8 cannot be treated merely as a piece of poetic literature: it is poetry that was echoed in Israel's Temple worship.

In his consideration of the Worship of Adam Story, Hurtado insists that for it to provide a "real precedent for the worship of Jesus" it needs to show that devout Jews "actually worshipped as a divine being [a] figure in addition to God" and that this worship functioned as something equivalent to the "full *pattern of* religious behavior practiced in early Christian groups, featuring Jesus, and made up of specific devotional actions" laid out in Hurtado's studies.[81] This is one example of the ways Hurtado makes unreasonable demands of historical data before it is given a fair hearing as possible precedent for Christ devotion—a problem that we identified back in chapter 4. If the Worship of Adam Story offers any explanatory precedent for the worship of Jesus all that needs to be shown is that *combined with other forces, factors, and events,* a belief that the prelapsarian Adam was worshipped by the angels can be seen to have given rise to the distinctive, and in many ways quite different, worship of Jesus Christ.

Also, Hurtado's insistence on genuine precedent being an actual Roman-period cult of a figure alongside Israel's God illustrates his inclination to emphasize practice at the expense of theology. But once we recognize that what a people believes—especially their hopes and expectations for the future—can prepare the way for new practices, it is better to allow the Worship of Adam Story to speak to the issue of the theological shape of Jewish monotheism: as such, it provides *conceptual* precedent for the worship of Jesus because it envisages a monotheism in which the worship of a human being *as God's image and likeness* is appropriate. This will be especially important for our quest for Christological origins if it is also the case that the worship of Jesus *as God's image* stands squarely at the front and center of "Christological monotheism."

Furthermore, there are reasons for thinking that the worship of Adam *at the beginning* was conceptually related for first-century Jews to the worship of a true human image of God in later history, especially at its eschatological consummation. We have already noted possible connections between the Worship of Adam Story and the worship of the Son of Man in the *Similitudes of Enoch*. They suggest that the former could be used to provide theological justification for the latter. Indeed, this possibility is consistent with the fact that, taken as a whole, the material in the *L.A.E.*, along with the other texts attesting a keen interest in Adam's original, sinless state in Second Temple Judaism, served as inspiration for the future destiny of the righteous. *The golden thread running through the various versions of the*

---

81. Hurtado, *Lord Jesus Christ*, 40.

L.A.E. is the claim that Adam and Eve have lost their original identity. They have lost the glory they possessed in Eden. They have lost the authority over a chaotic, rebellious creation, that they possessed as God's image (Pericope 12). They have lost freedom from sickness (see Pericopes 9–11). In that context, the Worship of Adam Story points to a future restoration of a right and proper, God-ordained worship of a true humanity (or of individual perfect human representative of the whole of humanity).

As N. T. Wright has perceptively observed, to speak of Adam is to speak of Israel and, in some cases, it is to speak of the nation's messiah. By the same token, for some Jews, a Jewish story that described a God-directed angelic worship of Adam could have nurtured the belief that in the eschatological future it would be right and proper to worship a second Adam (within the grammar of the right and proper worship of God). That possibility assumes a distinctively Jewish and biblical understanding of memory and of the past. The past is to be remembered not in the way that some of us in the last four hundred years have remembered Jesus' death in the celebration of the Lord's Supper—as a merely cognitive recognition of the past, once-and-for-all death of Jesus—but in order to nurture a (sacramental) connection between God's mighty acts of old and the present.[82] The Worship of Adam Story proclaims the creation of Adam as one such mighty act in the past and we should bear in mind the possibility that for Jews in antiquity it invited a particular kind of worship in the present or in the imminent eschatological future.

This way of understanding the story is confirmed by consideration of two other texts. We saw in the last chapter that in various ways Dan 7 suggests that the "one like a son of man" who appears with clouds in v. 13 is an Adamic figure (who reprises the Adamic Daniel himself of earlier chapters). As a figure of future hope, the "one like a son of man" cannot simply be Adam. But Dan 7:13–14 does serve as an example of the thesis that the messiah takes up the identity and calling of the original Adam. *And he will be worshipped* (especially in the Old Greek translation), just as Daniel himself received worship in Dan 2:46.

Similarly, in the *Animal Apocalypse* of 1 Enoch (1 En. 85–90) history looks forward to the climactic undoing of the effects of the fall and a return to the original purity and unity of creation that was briefly present with Adam. The closing scenes of the *Animal Apocalypse* have several parallels to Dan 7:9–14 and history's goal is reached with a new, Adamic humanity catalyzed by the birth of an individual white bull with huge horns (1 En.

---

82. For the problem of a Christian tradition that treats Gen 1 as a text that is simply "back there," obscuring its cultic and sacramental interpretative tradition, see the recent comments of S. L. Herring, *Divine Substitution*, 104–5.

90:37-38). The white bull reprises the identity of Adam in *1 En.* 85:3, 9-10 and "all the wild beasts and all the birds of heaven were afraid of it and made petition to it" (90:37). Their petition to the new Adam goes with the way all the nations of the earth (symbolized by animals and birds) "fall down and worship" the righteous (symbolized by sheep) "making petition to them and obeying them in everything" (90:30). The white bull does not have strongly royal characteristics, but he certainly has messianic characteristics and as such we should at least say he is an Adamic messiah.[83] For a text written in the Hellenistic era, the petition of the bull is most likely an expression of cultic devotion (given the way that petition of divine rulers was a component part of the Ruler Cult). The scene is overtly cultic with the previous section describing the creation of a new Temple (90:28-32),[84] and God himself is said to "rejoice over" the white bull and the rest of the newly transformed, restored humanity (*1 En.* 90:38, cf. Zeph 3:17).

Here too, then, in another part of the Enochic corpus there is suggestive evidence that a tradition in which Adam was worshipped has nurtured the belief that, at the climax of Israel's history, God would raise up another Adamic figure to lead his people. There is no way of telling whether the *Animal Apocalypse* knew the Worship of Adam Story as we now have it. *But it is unwise to treat the* Worship of Adam Story *as a textual pariah, marooned on its own isolated island of textual creativity. It may well have been more than welcome in communal gatherings of Jewish worshipers in the Second Temple period. It certainly has deep conceptual connections to other well-known Jewish texts.* Those connections will become clearer as our study proceeds, as will the likelihood that it had a quite specific cultic context.

7: A Scriptural, Theologically Coherent Explanation of the Story

If there is weighty evidence that the Worship of Adam Story is pre-Christian, known to various NT authors, and genuinely an account of angels *worshipping*, not just giving obeisance to, Adam, with conceptual connections to other texts that describe worship of a uniquely exalted human being, what

---

83. See the discussion of this passage in Nickelsburg, *1 Enoch 1,* 406-47; Olson, *New Reading,* 26-230, who emphatically rejects a royal interpretation. For an overhasty *royal* interpretation see, e.g., Horbury, *Jews and Christians,* 136. The image of a horned bull echoes language for Aaron in Ben Sira 45:7-8. For the connections to Dan 7 see K. Koch, *Vor der Wende,* 132, 249-50; Nickelsburg, *1 Enoch 1,* 405, 407.

84. Some have mistakenly viewed the vision of the new "house" in 90:28-36 as a vision of a new Jerusalem (e.g., Nickelsburg, *1 Enoch 1,* 404-5). The scene uses standard (post-)biblical language for the Temple.

then are we to make of its relationship to the theology of Israel's Scriptures? I have argued that Bauckham's analysis of the text does not do justice to the theological possibilities open to Jewish authors committed to a biblical monotheism. But how could the angelic worship of Adam possibly be compatible with a strictly biblical monotheism? There is no attempt in the story to deny that Adam is a creature, the last of God's works, nor that Jewish monotheism entails a firm boundary between the Creator (who is God) and the creature (who is not). In Gen 2–3, Adam and Eve are cast out of Eden because they eat of the forbidden tree in a bid for a divine identity like God's: how then could it possibly be right that God himself would have Adam treated by the angels as if he were indeed "divine"?

We shall return to all these important theological issues in Part 5. At this juncture, I bring discussion of this fascinating story to a close by sketching out an explanation of its conceptual heart that gives it a secure theological basis in Israel's Scriptures. This is an explanation that I first broached fifteen years ago and although my argument has not gone unnoticed, most have passed over it without comment or reasoned objection.[85] It is an explanation which means the story should be treated as a thoroughly mainstream, pre-Christian one in which Adam is most certainly "worshipped".[86]

In an important essay on the Worship of Adam Story, Corinne Patton observed two decades ago that the two words "image" and "likeness" used to describe Adam (in the Latin *imago* and *similitudo*) are words that are regularly used for the anthropomorphic or zoomorphic objects of non-Israelite cultic devotion. So,

> while these terms can mean things other than a central cult object, when this terminology is used of an object as the recipient of worship within sacred space, it is hard to see these terms as meaning anything other than that this object is the central cult object of a temple.[87]

---

85. Fletcher-Louis, "Worship of Divine Humanity." See, also, my *Glory of Adam*, 100–103. For acceptance of the conceptual thrust of my argument see van Kooten, "Transformation," 220; *Paul's Anthropology*, 27–32. Tilling acknowledges the argument, but seems unsure what to do with it (*Christology*, 202–6).

86. It far outweighs the possibility, adduced from parallels between parts of *L.A.E.* 12–16 and patristic exegesis of Ezek 28 (adduced by Anderson, "Ezekiel 28"), that the story is Christian. Anderson's observations on echoes of the expulsion of Satan from paradise in Ezek 28 in *L.A.E.* 12 and 16 are a little one-sided in suggesting the story is Christian. For example, there are indications that chs. 12 and 16 rely on the Hebrew of Ezek 28:14 (see Anderson, "Ezekiel 28," 146), and in any case those chapters are a frame around the actual account of the angels' worship—the core of the story for which Anderson offers no explanation from Christian parallels.

87. Patton, "Adam," 299.

The worship of Adam takes place in heaven and there are other indications within the *L.A.E.* that the place of Adam's worship is sacred space, with the angels behaving like priests.[88] While Patton could not confidently explain the overtly cultic nature of the angels' worship in relation to the biblical prohibition against idolatry, she suggested that the story best be understood as an ordination of God's own cult image (Adam). Her linguistic argument works equally well for the word *eikōn*, which will have stood behind the Latin *imago* in an earlier Greek version of the story (and indeed for a *tselem* if the story were originally composed in Hebrew or Aramaic), and *there are several reasons why this must be the conceptual heart of the story.*

In the first place, this reading immediately offers a theologically coherent, and biblically grounded, explanation of God's command to the angels. As we have seen, the Hebrew of Gen 1:26 can reasonably be taken to mean that Adam is created simply to *be* God's *tselem* and *demut*. Ever since the Hebrew was translated into other ancient languages, these words have been taken simply to mean humanity in some way possessed the (visual, ethical, moral, or spiritual) characteristics of God himself. But the Hebrew (and Aramaic) word *tselem* in the expression *tselem of a deity/God* normally means "divine cult statue" (of a deity/God).[89] In other words, Gen 1 itself says that at the climax of creation God created Adam to be his living cult statue or idol; not in the sense that he himself worshipped Adam, but *in the sense that the idol of a deity makes that deity manifest to the world.* The idol of the deities in the ancient world gave visible and physical form and presence to the god(dess) they represented. This is a reading of Gen 1:26 that has much to commend it and it is one that has been taken up by quite a few OT scholars in recent years.

One reason this reading of Gen 1 is likely to be faithful to the text's original intention is the fact that it provides the strongest possible theological justification for the biblical prohibition against idolatry. The worship of idols made by human hands is a foolish travesty, not just because it dishonors God the Creator, but also because it disregards and dishonors humanity whom God has already placed in the world to be his one and only image-idol. The Decalogue and other biblical texts outlawing idolatry, it should be noted, do not deny the possibility that God himself could place in the world a true image that would make him present within a particular space and time in ways analogous to non-Israelite beliefs about the role of an idol as the manifestation of a deity. Indeed, it now seems that in other parts of the

---

88. Ibid., 296–99.

89. See Num 33:52; 2 Kgs 11:18 = 2 Chr 23:17; Ezek 7:20; 16:17; 23:14; Amos 5:26; Dan 2:31, 32, 34.

Hebrew Bible, besides Gen 1, a polemic against idolatry is also grounded in the claim that only God's humanity can truly function as God's image.[90] What this all really means for OT theology and for the interpretation of Gen 1, which in so many ways is a trenchant polemic against polytheistic beliefs about the nature of the cosmos, need not detain us here. We shall return to make some further observations on this important new understanding of the theological anthropology at the heart of OT theology in Part 5.

For now it is enough to note that, whatever this understanding of *tselem*-as-idol meant exactly for the author of Gen 1, the language allowed later readers to conclude that Adam was indeed created to be God's image-idol. And if humanity is God's image-idol then it stands to reason that the kind of worship offered to the idols of false gods, as an expression of worship to the gods themselves, should in some way be offered to this image-idol as an expression of worship to the true God. There are no other humans to worship Adam so the angels or the beasts must have worshipped him. In the ancient world, this is what the idol of a deity is for: inter alia, it makes a god or goddess present so that through the cult statue the deity might receive the worship (s)he claims from human beings and from other entities within the cosmos.

There are a couple of details of the Worship of Adam Story that confirm the proposal that an image-idol-of-God anthropology always defined its conceptual heart. In the Greek version of the *L.A.E.* Adam is described as the "work of God's hands" in apposition to the statement that he is God's image (Gk. *L.A.E.* 33:5; cf. 37:2 and Georgian 45(33):5; Slavonic 40:1—41:6). A reference back to the Worship of Adam Story in an earlier version of the Greek that included that scene is quite likely because in many of the story's witnesses outside the *L.A.E.* it is said that Adam is the "work of God's hands."[91] To speak of Adam in this way in the context of a divine command that Adam be worshipped is fitting because many times the Scriptures say idols are "the work of *human* hands" (lit. ". . . of the hands of *'adam*").[92] As *the work of God's hands*, Adam then is the true image-idol.[93]

---

90. For this theology: in Ezekiel, see esp. Kutsko, *Between Heaven and Earth;* in prophetic call narratives see Glazov, *Opening of the Mouth,* and see Beale, *Biblical Theology,* 357–80 (esp. 378). See further now S. L. Herring, *Divine Substitution.*

91. See *Apoc. Sedr.* 5:2 ("the *creation* of your hands"); Coptic *Enthronement of Michael* (Anderson, "Exaltation of Adam," 85); Slavonic *3 Baruch* (Gaylord, "Satanael," 305); *Cave of Treasures* 2:10–14; Greek, *Didascalia,* 23 (Nau, "Didascalie," 240, 252); *Encominum on Saint Michael* fols. 11b–13a (Budge, *Coptic Texts,* 903–5); cf. *4 Ezra* 3:5 and *2 En.* 44:1.

92. Deut 4:28; 2 Kgs 19:18; Isa 37:19; Pss 115:4; 135:15; 2 Chr 32:19.

93. Israel is the work of God's hands in Isa 45:11; 60:21 and in *4 Ezra* 8:7. Implicitly, the psalmist is the work of God's hands in Ps 138:8, but the expression is never used of Adam in Israel's Scriptures.

Indeed, a more striking reference to the biblical rhetoric of idol manufacture may be intended in the version of the Worship of Adam Story in the Armenian *L.A.E.* At *L.A.E.* 14:1 the Armenian text has God say to the angels "Come, bow down to god whom I made." This is perhaps an allusion to the polemic against the foolish boast of the idol-manufacturer who "makes a god" in Isa 44:15 (cf. Isa 44:17; 46:6; Exod 32:1; Hos 8:6; Philo *Moses* 2:165; *Sib. Or.* 5:404).

I: The Worship of Adam Story and Daniel 2–7

There is further confirmation of this interpretation of the Worship of Adam Story when its plot line is compared with the account of an idol's dedication and worship in Dan 3. In that passage the Babylonian king Nebuchadnezzar makes an idol (described as a *tselem* eleven times in 3:1–18; Gk. *eikōn*) and has it set up on the plain of Dura. He summons satraps, prefects, governors, counselors, treasurers, justices, magistrates, and all the officials of the provinces of his empire to the "dedication ceremony" (Heb. *chanukkah*). A herald then proclaims to the assembled congregation of representatives from all strata of society (3:4–6):

> You are commanded, O peoples, nations, and languages, that when you hear the sound of the horn ... every kind of music, you are to fall down and worship (Ara. *tisgedun*, Gk. *proskynēsate*) the golden image that King Nebuchadnezzar has set up. And whoever does not fall down and worship shall immediately be cast into a burning fiery furnace.

The Jews Shadrach, Meshach, and Abednego refuse to worship and are dealt with as predicted. The exact nature of the idol (whether it is an image of the deified king himself or of a separate deity) is not clear, but scattered references to the rituals of cult statue dedication in antiquity suggest that this account follows a well-known script.

The Worship of Adam Story follows an almost identical script, only now some of the roles are reversed in the noncanonical tale because it claims that Adam is the *true* image-idol of God. Adam is the "image and likeness" made not by man, but by God himself. Where Nebuchadnezzar sends (presumably through messengers) to gather representatives from throughout his realm, God sends Michael to gather the angels who we may presume function, as they typically do in antique Jewish angelology, as representatives and guardians of different spheres of the cosmos, God's realm. Again, Michael plays the role of Nebuchadnezzar's herald commanding the assembled angelic company to worship the image. We assume that all but the Jewish heroes worship the statue in the Daniel story. In the Worship of Adam Story all the angels except Satan (and his minions) fulfill the divine command. The warning of fiery punishment in Dan 3 is parallel to the warning in the Latin *L.A.E.* 15:2 (and its parallels) that refusing God's commands will lead to divine anger and punishment (which Satan then experiences).

In all of this, no verbal allusion or citation of Dan 3 is necessary. The fact that the Dan 3 scene is stereotypical means Jewish readers of the Adam story would quickly understand the allusion to a scenario that for many of them was as immediate a challenge to their religious life and convictions as it was a life-threatening horror to Daniel and his friends. It may be that some biblically literate readers of the Worship of Adam Story would recall Dan 3 as they read.

But the lack of direct verbal reference to Daniel might in fact signal literary dependence in the other direction. Reading Dan 3:1–12—the idol dedication scene and Jewish refusal of worship—in its wider narrative context suggests in fact that the author of Daniel knows something very much like the Latin *L.A.E.* 12–16. Indeed, a careful examination of some intriguing parallels between the whole of Dan 1–7 and the component parts of the *L.A.E.* suggests the pseudepigraphical collection was either known to the author of Daniel or that they share a common formative life setting.

In the immediately preceding episode, at the end of chapter 2 (that we studied in the last chapter), Daniel himself accepts the worship of the king (and his exaltation of Daniel within the Babylonian political structure). We saw there that from the non-Jewish perspective—for readers in the new Hellenistic environment for which these chapters were written—Nebuchadnezzar gives to Daniel the honors befitting a divine benefactor. However, we were not able to supply a clear rationale for the acceptance of that behavior *from the Jewish perspective* of the text's author. We can now do so.

The biblically faithful author believes that *the pagan treatment of Daniel can be accepted because Nebuchadnezzar is not far from the truth:* as a leading member of God's people, Daniel is one who is truly human and who therefore acts as God's true image-idol. Like the prelapsarian Adam, he is possessed of the divine spirit (Dan 4:5–6, 15 [Eng. vv. 8–9, 18]; 5:11, 14; cf. Gen 2:7). So, even though the Babylonian king does not fully understand why his treatment of Daniel is appropriate, for Daniel (both for the author and for the actor in the drama) this is not idolatry because the king does to him what should be done to God's true living image-idol. In Dan 2:46, Nebuchadnezzar is to Daniel what the angels are to Adam in the Worship of Adam Story. Daniel is able to accommodate some of the conventions of the wider Hellenistic world in its cultic honoring of "divine" men because those conventions are legitimate insofar as the truly human being is created to be God's image-idol. This explanation of the otherwise puzzling scene at the end of Dan 2 has wider implications for the kind of material from which Horbury has argued for a Jewish openness to Greco-Roman cultic patterns. In *the specific (biblical) sense that some human beings (especially righteous Israelites) (partially) fulfill the Adamic role as God's living image-idol, for which Adam was created, we can say of some Jews that their monotheism had a strongly inclusivist logic.*[94] It sometimes meant that Jews were willing to acknowledge the partial truth of "pagan" patterns of worship. For one thing, it is better, after all, that a non-Jew sees and pays devotion to the presence of God in Israelites who function as God's living image-idols, than that they worship dead and dumb man-made idols. But, more than that, it really is appropriate to give praise and glory and honor to the righteous *because this is what human beings were always made for.*

There is a similar inclusivist logic to the Jewish understanding of the one God in the speech Luke ascribes to Paul in Athens in Acts 17. I will return to a fuller unpacking of Paul's argument there in Part 6. But even a casual reading of what Luke records Paul saying there shows his debt to the kind of theology that is present in Dan 2.[95] Paul acknowledges that the pagan Stoic poets had already perceived truths that prepared them for the gospel: human beings are created to participate in the divine life (v. 28) and so, because it is human beings that are created to make God present to the world, the making of man-made idols to represent the divine is foolish (v. 29). Unwittingly, it is the same truth of which the Greek poets *spoke*, out of which Nebuchadnezzar *acted*.[96]

There is much to be said for this reading of Dan 2. Throughout Dan 1–6 there is a critique of pagan idolatry and of the practices of mantic divination that went with it. As everyone in the ancient world knew, the Chaldean diviners relied on the use and manipulation of cultic images for the obtaining of divine "revelation." The mantic rituals of the Chaldeans were conducted before cult images of their gods, who were believed, through those rituals, to speak to the Chaldean priests. With Daniel there is no

---

94. In saying that, my point is really quite separate to the details of the argument between Horbury (see "Herodian Age") and Bauckham (*God of Israel*, 107–26) as to whether or not Jewish monotheism was "inclusivist" (so Horbury) or "exclusivist" (so Bauckham) in respect of the existence or nonexistence of other gods. I touch on that important debate in Excursus B at the end Part 3.

95. My reading of Acts 17 is largely anticipated now by J. Jipp, "Areopagus Speech."

96. Of course, there is then the intriguing and surely important contrast between Daniel's acceptance of divine honors (Dan 2:46) and the rejection of similar behavior by Peter (Acts 10:25–26), and Paul and Barnabas (Acts 14:8–18).

recourse to cultic images: Daniel himself functions as the divine image. Because he worships, obeys, and trusts the living God, and has his Spirit, the living God speaks through him.

Indeed, as with so much of the *L.A.E.*, the whole of Dan 1–7 is likely intended as a meditation on what it means that Israel is God's true *tselem*.[97] In the rest of Dan 3, Daniel's friends, Shadrach, Meschach, and Abednego, are inviolable against the destructive power of the superheated fiery furnace. Idols in the ancient world were made of inert materials. Fire could serve to make molten metal so that a cast idol came to life from the fire (Exod 32:24), but idols were supposed to resist the destructive force of the flames.[98] The wood used for idols was believed to be an "everlasting wood."[99] But Israel's prophets mock the idols that could be burned on a domestic fire (Isa 44:15–17) because only the living God speaks from the midst of the fire and is not consumed (Exod 3:2; Deut 4:12, 15, 33; 5:4, 24, 26; 9:10; 10:4). The idols of the nations can easily be purged from the land by fire (2 Kgs 23:4, 6, 15; Deut 7:5; 12:3). But God does have an entity that functions as his image-idol: the nation of Israel, as represented by Daniel and his friends, was "brought forth from the furnace of iron" (Deut 4:20; Jer 11:4; cf. Isa 43:2).

In Dan 6, Daniel is unharmed by the lions in a way that recalls the story in all versions of the *Life of Adam and Eve* where Seth exercises authority over a beast that tries to attack him. Seth is able to stop the mouth of the beast and banish it because he is the image God (Latin *L.A.E.* 37–39 = Greek *L.A.E.* 10–12—Synopsis §12). In Dan 6, in a similar way, an angel stops the mouths of the lions. A contrast between Daniel as God's true image and the false images of Israel's idolatrous neighbors is probably in view when the king seals the lion's den with his seal "that nothing might be changed concerning Daniel" (6:17). That seal would have carried an image of the king and/or his gods. Seals, like modern credit cards, were supposed to carry the authority of their owner. But as the story turns out, Darius' seal has no power when used against the image of the one God (that carries the authority and power of that true and living God).

That contrast can be seen again in Dan 4, where Nebuchadnezzar's fall recalls Adam and Eve's descent to the level of the animals who eat the plants of the field outside the garden (cf. Gen 3:18). That story also has a parallel in the Penitence Narrative that makes up the early chapters of the Latin,

---

97. For this reading of Daniel and a fuller argument to what follows, see Fletcher-Louis, "Religious Experience," 135–37.

98. This is a theme explored in particular in Pseudo-Philo's *Biblical Antiquities* (chs. 6, 26 and 38), on which see Fletcher-Louis, "Idols of the Gods".

99. See Dick, *Born in Heaven*, 22–23, on Isa 40:20, esp. 23 n. j.

Georgian, and Armenian versions of the *Life of Adam and Eve*. In those versions of *L.A.E.* chs. 2–6—*Synopsis* §2—there is an account of Adam and Eve's search for food outside of Eden that is based on Gen 3:18 where the curse means that Adam and Eve eat "the plants of the field." As Gary Anderson has shown, that story is a narrativization of an exegesis of Gen 1–3 that differentiates between the seed-bearing plants originally given to Adam by God in Gen 1:29 and the plants of the field given to Adam (and Eve) under the curse east of Eden.[100]

So, there are *three* passages in Dan 1–6 that correspond to three passages in the *L.A.E.* To these three there should be added a fourth; the likely connection between the Worship of Adam Story and Dan 7:13–14, which, as we have seen, picks up the worship of Daniel scene at the end of Dan 2. We have already noted the ways in which the Danielic "one like a son of man" fulfills God's original purpose for Adam at the climax of creation. We have also seen that there are good reasons for thinking that, especially in the Old Greek translation, but also in the Aramaic original, the man figure is worshipped by the nations. That worship, like the worship given to Daniel himself in Dan 2:46, is therefore equivalent to what the angels (and other creatures) do to Adam in the Worship of Adam Story.[101] It is just possible, also, that Dan 1–7 was composed for an audience that knew the Adam material that now appears in the *L.A.E.*[102] The connections between the two texts provide firm confirmation for the proposal that the theological heart of the Worship of Adam Story is biblical and that it belongs to the earliest stages of the interpretation of Gen 1:26–28. In turn, these connections also suggest that whoever or whatever the author of Daniel thought the "one like a son of man" character was, that the nations' worship of him would be in recognition of the fact that he functioned as God's image-idol. To this one

---

100. Anderson, "Penitence Narrative," 6–23. He notes the parallel to Dan 4 (p. 14). A direct linguistic link to Dan 4 may be present in the Armenian that says the first couple find only "food of beasts" in 4:2–3 and that Eve "eats grass" (18:1) (cf. Dan 4:15, 23, 25 [Eng.]). The Latin has a parallel to the "food of beasts" in 4:2, but not to the Danielic language in the Armenian at 4:3 and 18:1.

101. The "all glory" (*pasa doxa*) that serves or worships the "one like a son of man" in the OG of Dan 7:14 might specifically have in view the angelic realm (as a complement to the human realm signified in the "all the nations of the earth according to (their) kind" in the previous phrase).

102. This suggestion fits with the view of the editor of 4Q381 that that text originated in the Persian or early Hellenistic periods (Schuller, *Psalms*, 5–60). It also fits with evidence that traditions allegedly going back to Adam survived the flood and were well known in the Second Temple period (see Latin *L.A.E.* 50:1–2 and *Synopsis* §36 (= 51:1–9 in *OTP* vol. 2, 294); Josephus *Ant.* 1:69–71; *2 En.* 33:8–12; cf. *Jub.* 8:3).

it is fitting that God delegates authority over the bestial nations (Dan 7:3–8, 14; cf. *L.A.E. Synopsis* §12).[103]

Here then there is a wealth of evidence to suggest that the Worship of Adam Story was theologically unproblematic for biblically faithful Jews. Indeed, it expressed in a simple and dramatically memorable story a proclamation at the heart of Israel's Scriptures: the one true Creator God has no need of man-made images and that is partly because humanity itself was created to be his living cult statue. The Worship of Adam Story was composed to convey the conviction that, in the God-ordained order, the worship of God should, on occasion, be expressed through the worship given to his living image, just as pagan deities were worshipped through the worship of their idols. The story is so simple and yet theologically powerful that it could very well have circulated widely in Second Temple Jewish society. It would have served well as a pedagogical tool for the primary theological education of Jewish children (in homes, synagogues, or at the Temple) or of proselytes.

It may be that some Jews took theological exception to the story's implications. But we have no explicit evidence for a rejection of it until much later rabbinic texts have God step in to ensure that the angels do not mistakenly worship Adam as a figure separate to God. Perhaps already in the first century AD the forebears of the rabbis took exception to the story. We do not know. In Part 5 I will adduce reasons to suspect that the rabbinic opposition to the story reflects a loss of understanding of its original, Second Temple interpretative context.

But there is one thing of which we can now be certain. The language and imagery of the story must mean that what the angels do to Adam is "worship," not just obeisance. For the Greek text to use the verb *proskynein* and for the Latin to use the verb *adorare* to describe action towards Adam *as the "image" and "likeness" of God* must mean that worship is in view because this is divine cult statue language. Or, to put the matter negatively, if the original authors and tradents of this story had wanted their readers to see in the angels' behavior an act of submission, but not worship, they should have used verbs that could not possibly have been misunderstood ("obey" would have done the job). Every reader in antiquity knew that *proskynein/adorare* + "image" and "likeness" of a deity meant worship. If, as modern readers, we miss the cultic context of this language we fundamentally misunderstand the story and its meaning.

---

103. For a connection between the beasts (*thēria*) of Dan 7 and the beast (*thērion*) of Gk *L.A.E.* 10:3—12:3, see Nir, "Image of God," 329. These connections show that the theology of *Synopsis* §12 is biblical (contrast Magliano-Tromp, "Adamic Traditions," 301).

8: Conclusion

In conclusion then, there are important pre-Christian traditions surrounding the prelapsarian Adam and, a priori, there is every reason to believe that those traditions made a contribution to the formulation of earliest beliefs about Jesus. The most important of these is the Worship of Adam Story in the Primary Adam Books. There is very little reason to think that story is Christian and plenty of reason to place it squarely in a pre-Christian Jewish context. Indeed, some striking literary connections between the Primary Adam Books and the book of Daniel suggest it may even go back to the early Hellenistic period (if not to the Persian period). It remains to be seen, though, what role exactly the Worship of Adam Story could have had in the birth of "Christological monotheism" and Christ devotion. To a proper consideration of that question we will turn in the next chapter.

For now we may note, however, that this chapter adds weight to the argument we made in our third chapter (§3) that the expression Son of Man in the Gospels must have titular force. Given all this evidence for a keen Jewish interest in Adam and the recovery of his identity it cannot be that the Greek *ho huios tou anthrōpou* means not very much at all. On the contrary, because Jesus' use of that expression probably sounded (to Greek-speaking Jews) like a claim to be "the man," it would inevitably be heard as a claim to be some kind of true Adam. When Jesus stands before the Sanhedrin and answers Caiaphas' question, "Are you the Christ, the Son of the Blessed?" he says, in effect, "I am, and you will see *the Man*, seated at the right hand of Power, coming with the clouds of heaven" (Mark 14:62).

This chapter's investigation of Jewish Adam traditions also offers a potential answer to one of the questions that we left unanswered at the end of the chapters on Jewish expectations of a divine messiah and the pre-Christian accommodation of the patterns of Ruler Cult. There we concluded that the material collected by William Horbury and recent insights into the *Similitudes of Enoch* needed to be anchored in a well-defined social and theological context in Second Temple Judaism. In what way, if any, did traditions surrounding a divine messiah or ruler have a secure basis in Scripture? And can we be confident that the literary traditions that have come down to us (especially the strange material in *1 En.* 37–71) had a secure and prominent place in common or, even, in mainstream Second Temple Jewish life (in theology and in practice) such that they could have had any impact on early Christological origins?

In this chapter on Adam a partial answer to these questions has presented itself: some Jews believed, in faithfulness to their reading of Gen 1, that the true humanity should be worshipped the way the pagans would worship an image (*tselem*) of a deity. We have already found reason to believe that *theologically* a worship of Adam by the angels on this basis could be applied also to the worshipful treatment of other human beings (in the case of Nebuchadnezzar's "worship" of Daniel in Dan 2:46). And theologically the worship of a human being as God's "idol" might also help explain the "worship" offered to the "one like a son of man" in Dan 7:14. That would, obviously, then explain why it is that there are such clear and strong connections between the beginnings of Christ devotion and texts that say the first followers believed he was indeed Daniel's Son of Man figure (John 9:35-38; Acts 7:56; cf. Matt 28:16-20).

But more needs to be said about these possibilities. Is there any evidence that the theological framework that explains the Worship of Adam Story also explains the worship of the Son of Man figure in 1 *En.* 37-71? And does the true-humanity-as-God's-idol notion explain the peculiar ways the Enochic Son of Man manifests the divine identity? The portrayal of the Son of Man figure in the *Similtidues*—as a preexistent, premundane figure who plays the role of *Yhwh* in the eschatological scenario and who sits on God's own throne of glory—goes quite some way beyond both the plain sense of Dan 7:13 and what is said of Adam in the Worship of Adam Story. Should we conclude, then, that what we have in the *Similitudes* is really the product of an idiosyncratic imagination that has run away with the more modest ideas present in Daniel and in the Worship of Adam Story? What would a Saul the Pharisee or a Peter the fisherman have made of the Worship of Adam Story and of 1 *En.* 37-71? Given that there is now evidence that both these were mainstream pre-Christian Jewish texts, could they have prepared them to have viewed Jesus as a preexistent, incarnate, divine being who really belongs within—is *included* within—the singular unique divine identity?

To answer these questions properly we will come eventually, in later volumes, to the new paradigm. In the fourth section of this study (chapters 8-10) we will discover important, but frustratingly *equivocal*, evidence for the possibility that *both* the Worship of Adam Story *and* the material in the *Similitudes* contributed to the origins and shape of "Christological monotheism." I say "equivocal" evidence because in places there is reason to believe that the theological ideas, if not the actual texts examined in the last three chapters, stand behind NT texts. However, in our discussion in Part 4 we will also clarify the ways in which these Jewish texts *do not in themselves satisfactorily* explain either the origin or the shape of the distinctive "Christological monotheism" of the Gospels, Paul, and other NT texts.

EXCURSUS B

On the Absolute Distinction between Creator and Creation

BOTH THE JEWISH ADAM material and that strand of Jewish messianism that focuses on a *transcendent* and even a *"divine"* messiah presents a challenge to modern scholarship. Are such traditions compatible with a biblical presentation of the relationship between God and the world? Indeed, how are we even to speak of such texts? Until now, I have placed speech marks around the word "divine" in acknowledgement of the fact that such language for entities other than God himself is either inappropriate or that it begs questions about the nature of Jewish monotheism.

No two specialists in Christological origins agree on everything. There are so many issues that offer the possibility for distinctive viewpoints. But in the midst of all the noise coming from a multitude of voices arguing over a plethora of issues, there is one point for which it is possible to discern two distinct positions, or camps, ranged against each other. On the one side, there is a group of scholars who think that normative Jewish life—theology and practice—is committed to a clear and sharp distinction between God the Creator and his creation. On the other side, and in response to recent declarations on this point by the first group, there are others who reckon on a "fluid" or permeable boundary between the Creator and the creation, such that in some special cases there are figures who straddle the two categories.[104] The second group freely speaks of texts in which the messiah, or Moses, or some other figure is "divine." The first group avoids such language.

The questions posed by this disagreement now deserve a thorough investigation in their own right and in conversation across a range of relevant disciplines (Old Testament/Hebrew Bible studies, the study of Greco-Roman

---

104. Chester, in particular, likes to speak of such "fluidity" (*Messiah*, 51, 54, 58).

religion, and systematic and philosophical theology). I confine myself here to a brief overview of the state of debate. I will propose a third way between the two opposing positions currently taken by scholars and make some comments that I hope will situate my interpretation of the primary texts in relation to the quest for Christological origins.

As an excursus, this discussion is somewhat tangential to my train of thought and argument in the main chapters. The issue needs some comment because if I say nothing there is a danger some will misconstrue what I have already said and what I will go on to say. It may also be that a fixed position on the issue tackled here has meant, and will continue to mean, that some readers will struggle unnecessarily to grasp the meaning and implications of some of the primary texts.

This is not a *chapter* in its own right because I do not think that the earliest beliefs about Jesus are simply explained by the material in the last three chapters. Jesus was not simply slotted into preexisting Jewish categories. The material reviewed in the last three chapters is of inestimable historical importance. But none of it, either on its own or in some joined-up pattern, can explain the peculiar and unprecedented way in which Jesus was deemed to belong within the divine identity. Neither do I see any good grounds for thinking that a Christology in which Jesus was identified as a divine mediator on analogy to a "divine" Adam or a "divine" Son of Man served as one stage of an upward development towards a full blown "Christological monotheism." I will offer a paradigm in Parts 4 and 5 that incorporates the evidence of the last three chapters into a larger, comprehensive explanation of the origins and shape of "Christological monotheism." For now this excursus is an extended footnote on the theological issues raised by the material in Part 3.

1: An Absolute Qualitative Distinction between God and All Reality

To date, it is Richard Bauckham who has most eloquently argued that all Jewish talk of God drew "a firm line of clear distinction between the one God and all other reality" and that the Jewish world view was governed by an "absolute distinction between God and all other reality."[105] Bauckham

---

105. Bauckham, *God Crucified*, 16, 15 (= *God of Israel*, 13, 12): elsewhere a "qualitative difference" (*God Crucified*, 33; *God of Israel*, 24) and "an absolute difference in kind from all other reality" (*God of Israel*, 109, cf. 119). His language echoes K. Barth's recourse to S. Kierkegaard's "infinite qualitative distinction" between God and man (in, e.g., Barth, *Romans*, 10).

points to a wealth of evidence, from both Israel's Scriptures and from later Jewish texts, that shows that for Jews God is uniquely set apart from the rest of reality.[106] He has a unique *"identity,"* that is defined—on analogy with human identities—by his relationship to the rest of reality as Creator and Ruler of all (uncreated and subject to none). As one with a distinct identity, he has a name (*Yhwh*) and his identity is revealed through a special relationship with his people, Israel. In the Bible and in Second Temple Jewish theology, the one God is not conceived in terms of a collection of attributes or of his possessing a divine *nature*. The only exception to this rule is his *eternity*, which is one metaphysical attribute that often defines his identity in Jewish literature.[107]

In all this, *strict* Jewish monotheism is quite different from a Greco-Roman world view in which there was a sliding scale of degrees of divinity from the one high god, down through lower gods or demigods and daemons in the heavens, earth, and lower regions, alongside deified human beings; each possessing, in varying degrees, a divine status or nature recognized through the bestowal of cultic honors. That "gradient" view of divinity can be thought of as "inclusive": if Jewish monotheism were "inclusive" it would mean the one God worshipped by Israel belonged to—or stood at the head of—a class of divine beings. But Israel held to an "exclusive" monotheism in which the one God exists outside of any class of supernatural beings. For this exclusive monotheism "there is no class of beings to which God belongs and of which he can be the supreme instance."[108] In short, the normative Jewish view entailed a firm commitment to the strict monotheism of the biblical writers, especially of Second Isaiah and the Deuteronomist. In the literature of the late Second Temple period, biblical monotheism is reflected sometimes in new ways (in apocalyptic visions of God enthroned on high, for example), but it is everywhere assumed, nonetheless.

Because, Bauckham claims, Jews were so clear and unequivocal in their commitment to this understanding of the divine identity, as modern readers we should not be distracted by textual evidence that might give the impression that some Jews were content to "blur" the boundaries between God and the world. Bauckham insists, for example, that there really is not much interest in a class of divine mediators in Second Temple literature. In any case, what

---

106. This is the burden of the first chapter of Bauckham, *God Crucified* (1-22, = *God of Israel*, 1-17) and it is a theme taken up in several chapters of his longer book (*God of Israel*, 60-106, 107-26, 152-81).

107. Bauckham's comments on God's eternity in *God of Israel*, 234, seem to be a shift from his earlier denial that "eternity" is a case of God having a distinct "nature" (in *God Crucified*, 8 = *God of Israel*, 7).

108. Bauckham, *God of Israel*, 109.

evidence there is shows that Jews organized mediatorial figures according to two categories. On the one hand, there are expressions, *personifications*, of aspects of God's own character—such as Wisdom, Spirit, the Word—which belong firmly on the Creator side of the Creator-creation distinction. On the other hand, there are other beings—such as angels and exalted humans—who are *creatures* and who therefore cannot be said to be "divine."

This aspect of Bauckham's recent work on Christological origins is one way in which he now emphasizes Jewish commitment to theology over practice. He thinks, for example, that worship of God (practice) is simply done in recognition of who God is (belief).[109] Whilst Hurtado does not privilege theology over practice in the same way, a similar categorical distinction between God as Creator and sovereign also underlies his assessment of the Jewish material.[110] At any rate, quite a few recent contributors to the early Christology debate have explicitly endorsed Bauckham's view, sometimes with even stronger language to define the Creator-creature distinction.[111]

Bauckham's account of Jewish identity, including the novel proposal that we give up talk of divine nature and instead talk of divine *identity*, raises numerous questions (as does any new theory). There is much to be said for it, even whilst his method and philosophical assumptions (about divine *identity*, for example) invite critical scrutiny. His insistence on a clear and absolute distinction between the Creator and the rest of reality is the way Jewish (and biblical) monotheism has been traditionally understood by most, if not all, in the modern period. But in various ways the primary sources challenge Bauckham's interpretation of the distinction.

2: No Absolute Qualitative Distinction between the Creator and Creation?

Quite apart from the questions posed by Bauckham's divine identity theory, numerous specialists in the field (and certainly not a minority) have now

---

109. See esp. Bauckham, *God Crucified*, 13–16 (= *God of Israel*, 11–13), where he acknowledges (*God Crucified*, 14, n. 20 [= *God of Israel*, 11 n. 20]) a shift in his own position away from his earlier work where he gave worship greater significance.

110. This can be seen in the way, for example, that he handles the *Similitudes of Enoch*, in his categorical denial of any possibility of deification within Jewish monotheism (in Hurtado, *How on Earth?*, 46), and in his recent contribution to the debate over the difference between an "inclusive" versus an "exclusive" monotheism (Hurtado, "Ancient Jewish Monotheism").

111. E.g. Fee, *Pauline Christology*, 15; Tilling, *Christology*, 1–2; Gathercole, *Preexistent Son*, 55 and 74, 143–44, 148, 289; Wright, *Paul*, 652 and for an older representative of this view see, e.g., G. Theissen, *Theory*, 41.

EXCURSUS B: THE DISTINCTION BETWEEN THE CREATOR & CREATION

challenged the understanding of the relationship between God and the rest of reality in Second Temple Judaism that he and others adopt.[112] Also, other scholars exegete key Jewish texts in a way that implicitly rejects Bauckham's interpretation of the distinction between God and the rest of reality. In particular, there are quite a few types of (non-Christian) text that challenge Bauckham's view that there is no sense in which it is proper to talk of entities other than God himself as "divine." There are texts, in other words, which indicate that the distinction between the Creator and creation did not mean for Jews in antiquity that there was no sense in which God shared his identity or nature with others. Let us consider four types.

I: "Divine" Creatures as Creative Agents

Firstly, there are texts which belie Bauckham's insistence that for Jews Wisdom and the Logos can be neatly assigned to the divine side of a God-versus-rest-of-reality dividing line.[113] In Sirach 24 preexistent Wisdom plays the role of the Creator, but in Sir 24:8-9 Wisdom herself speaks of God as *"my Creator"* who "before the ages, in the beginning, . . . *created me*" (cf. Sir 1:4).[114] The ambiguity probably goes back to Prov 8, the great biblical Wisdom poem that is the inspiration for the poem in Sir 24. There Wisdom "is likely presented as both divine and a creature" and as a "created co-Creator."[115] In

---

112. For various forms of challenge see, e.g., Janowitz, *Magic*, 70-74; Horbury, "Early Christology," esp. 21, 31; *Jews and Christians*, 17, 19; "Monotheism," 31; Chester, *Messiah*, 20-27, 41; Klawans, *Purity*, 121-23; McGrath, *Only True God*, 12-15, 56; Dunn, *Worship*, 59-90, 141-44; Waddell, *Messiah*, 19-22; Litwa, *Being Transformed*, 86-116, 229-81; Peppard, *Son of God*, 11, 22-23, who discerns a Platonic conceptual framework at work for those who insist on a rigid distinction between Creator and creature. Both my *Luke-Acts* and *All the Glory of Adam* have sided with this second group of scholars in anticipation of my argument here.

113. Though Bauckham's categorization of Wisdom does suit Wis 7:25-26.

114. For Wisdom as Creator in Sir 24, see Sheppard, *Wisdom*, 25-26; Fletcher-Louis, "Cosmology of P," 80-94, and compare Wis 7:22; 8:5-6. This article of mine provides a more thoroughgoing case for Wisdom as (co-)Creator in Sir 24 than others have offered, but it builds on the often-noted connections between Wisdom and the Creator in the opening lines of the hymn (on which see also, for example, Chester, *Messiah*, 366-68).

115. Fretheim, *God and World*, 208 and 213, 215 respectively (see further 205-8, 211-18) and compare Collins and Collins, *King*, 178, on Wisdom as God's first creature in Prov 8:22-23. The meaning of the key parts of the Hebrew of Prov 8 is much debated, but certainly in the LXX Wisdom in Prov 8:22 is a created being. For Wisdom's role as premundane creative agent see the whole of Prov 8:22-30.

the case of the Logos we have, as James McGrath has stressed, a text in Philo where there is a clear straddling of the Creator-creature boundary.[116]

II: "Divine" Angels?

Secondly, there is language in Jewish texts for angels that suggests the older view that *Yhwh* as the highest god in a divine council, or pantheon, of lesser gods did not completely disappear in the Second Temple period. In the Dead Sea Scrolls in particular, angels appear frequently as *elim* ("gods").[117] More widely, the regular Hebrew word for God (*elohim*) can be treated as a plural in, for example, the interpretation that takes the statement that "Enoch walked with *elohim*" (Gen 5:22, 24) to mean that he walked or sojourned with the angels (in *1 En.* 1–36 [esp. 12:1-2], *2 En.* 1–38, 67; *Jub.* 4:21-23). This openness to the application of "god" language for angels in Hebrew texts finds a parallel in some Jewish Greek documents.[118] It is conceptually cognate to the remarkable description of the angel *Iaoel* in the (late-first-century) *Apocalypse of Abraham*, where even Hurtado recognizes it is appropriate to speak of a principal angel's "divinity" in virtue of its possession of the divine name.[119]

In all of this, it should be noted, that such texts describe beings who are clearly quite distinct from the gods worshipped by the nations (to whom some Scriptures deny any entitlement to "god" language[120]). So, for some

116. Philo *Heir* 206 (noted in McGrath, *Only True God*, 13). Philo uses similar language for the perfect man existing "on the boundary between the uncreated and the perishable nature" (*Dreams* 2:234, cf. 2:231 on the high priest on the Day of Atonement "belonging as to his mortal nature to creation, but as to his immortal nature to the uncreated God"). (See also Chester, *Messiah*, 49–51).

117. Esp. in the *War Scroll* (e.g., 1QM 1:10-11); the *Hodayot* (e.g., 1QH^a 15:31; cf. 4Q491c frag. 1, lines 5, 7, 11) and the *Songs of the Sabbath Sacrifice* (e.g., 4Q400 1 i 20).

118. In *Ezek. Trag.* 99 the angel at the burning bush is a "divine logos," an expression that appears also in *Let. Aris.* 99; Philo *Flight* 5; *Cherubim* 3; *Unchangeable* 182. Josephus writes for his non-Jewish readers of "a divine angel" (*theios angelos*) (e.g., *Ant.* 1:219, 332). In *Jos. Asen.* 17:9 some manuscripts have the archangel described as "a god," which is surely the *lectio difficilior* by comparison with those that have the angel simply represent "God" himself.

119. Hurtado, *How on Earth?*, 121. By contrast, Bauckham offers an idiosyncratic and, to my mind, implausible explanation of the name Iaoel in this text (*God of Israel*, 224-28) that fails to reckon adequately with the statement in 10:3, 8 that Iaoel has within himself the ineffable name of God (*Yhwh*) (cf. Exod 23:20-21). Neither does he comment on the fact that Iaoel is one of God's own names in the hymnic piece in 17:13. For a more plausible discussion see, e.g., McGrath, *Only True God*, 49; Chester, *Messiah*, 368-69.

120. E.g., Deut 32:17, 21. On those texts see Bauckham, *God of Israel*, 114.

Jewish writers, it was evidently right and proper that the *good* angels, who do God's bidding, be described with "god" language.[121] If we are to faithfully represent *the way the Jewish authors of these texts think* we have to say that they speak of angels as "(semi)divine" beings, even if we keep such language in scare quotes to flag up that a different understanding of divinity is present to the one we, as scholars steeped in (or committed to) Christian categories usually think it appropriate. As scholars with Christian convictions we may not like such language. We may complain that it lacks a systematic distinction between categories of identity. But we are not, I submit, permitted to insist that Jews in antiquity had to think about angels, God, and human beings the way most of us do today.

It is interesting and probably theologically significant that the NT nowhere reflects this wider openness to "god" language for angels. But if we are to be historiographically faithfully to the primary texts we should not assume that a NT understanding of angels represented the full spectrum of Jewish views. And when we consider the kind of material examined in chapters 4–6 we should be aware of this wider pool of texts that used "divine" language for beings other than God himself.

III: "Divine" Human Beings?

Thirdly, there are texts where many now reckon that certain righteous human beings are described in "divine" terms. Sometimes, this means the kind of "god" language that is used for angels is also used for the righteous. In other cases a richer visual and literary vocabulary, sometimes drawing on the language of the divine benefactor and ruler in the wider Greco-Roman environment, is used as Horbury has shown.[122] Some now freely talk of texts in which there is a "deification" or "apotheosis" of an exemplary human.[123]

---

121. With good reason, N. Mizrahi ("Seventh Song," 21) says the words *elim* and *elohim* for angels function as an emphatic expression of the view that "they are not simply part of the created world, but also partake, to some degree, in the divinity itself."

122. Horbury, *Jewish Messianism*. Notable examples of this phenomenon are *Artapanus* (9.27.6) on Moses and Dan 2:46 on Daniel.

123. See, e.g., Marcus, *Way of the Lord*, 82–83; *Mark*, 423, 1117, on Ezekiel the Tragedian; Horbury, "Ecclesiasticus," 278–83, for "apotheosis" in Ben Sira/Sirach and his criticism of Hurtado's lack of attention to evidence of deification in his "Review," 539; Chester, *Messiah*, 243; Dunn, *Worship*, 60, 84–89; M. Idel, *Ben*, 1, 6. The celebrated case of the misinterpretation of 4Q491c by its original editor M. Baillet (in *DJD* 7:26–30) serves as a cautionary tale to all who would deny that the dualistic assumptions of modern interpreters have sometimes prevented us recognizing highly exalted language for human beings (see Fletcher-Louis, "Deification," and J. J. Collins, "Apotheosis," and P. Alexander, *Mystical Texts*, 90, "possibly even apotheosis"). Van Kooten, *Paul's*

Prominent among those for whom Jewish authors were happy to use divine language is Moses, in large part, of course, because the Bible itself ascribes "god" language to him. God himself makes Moses "as God/a god to Pharaoh" in Exod 7:1 and Exod 34:29-30, where Moses descends from Sinai with a radiant face, can be taken to mean that he is transformed and given some kind of heavenly, glorious, or "divine" identity as a result of his time in God's presence.[124] But there are other cases where no obvious "divine" language is present in Scripture to provide warrant for what a postbiblical author has done to a figure or a community.[125]

To be sure, there are other texts that speak against the deification of a human being, but the existence of these cannot hastily be used to short-circuit discussion of the ones where deification is an appropriate label.[126] These are readily explained by a recognition that there are different kinds of "deification"; an acceptable form contrasted with others that offend a biblical theology. There are several reasons a deification might be judged illegitimate from a Jewish perspective.[127] Sometimes the texts speak against a

---

Anthropology, 18-19, 27, talks of "man's present divine glory" and a "type of divine anthropology" in Qumran literature. Hurtado rejects the possibility of a "deification" in Jewish texts in *How on Earth?*, 19, 46, without engagement with the data that speaks to the contrary.

124. For "god" and "divine" language used of Moses see: Exod 7:1 in 4Q374 frag. 2 col. ii (on which see Fletcher-Louis, "Deification," and *All the Glory*, 136-41; cf. 6-9); Philo *Moses* 1:155-58, *Sacrifices* 8-10, QE 2:29, 40; Josephus, *Ant.* 3:180 on Moses a "divine man" (*theios anēr*), cf. *Ant.* 2:232; *Ap.* 1:279; Tanhuma Buber *Beha'alotekha* 15 (26a-b). Bauckham offers an incomplete and one-sided discussion of the Philo texts (in his recent article "Moses"). See now, for a more balanced assessment of the ambiguities in Philo's treatment of Moses's real "deification," Litwa, *Being Transformed*, 106-9 and his "Deification of Moses." See further Artap. 9.27.6 and for Moses in a sense "divine" already in the biblical texts see the discussion in Herring, *Divine Substitution*, 150-64. For the connection between a divine Moses and the Israelite "divine" king see Wyatt, "Royal Religion," 72-73.

125. In the case, for example, of Joseph as "god, god, Mighty One of God" in *Jub.* 40:7 (cf. Pompeius Trogus 36.2.10), Isaiah as a "divine and wonderful man" in Josephus *Ant.* 10:35, Israel as a "divine and heavenly race" in *Sib. Or.* 5:249, the author and speaker of the Qumran hymn 4Q491c who boasts that he has a throne in the heavens and is "reckoned among the gods" (frag. 1 line 7) (discussed above, in chapters 5 and 6 and in Fletcher-Louis, *All the Glory*, 199-216; cf. 168-74, 187-89, 298-305, 326-38, 345-46, 350-55, 391-92) and the postresurrection deification in *Ps.-Phoc.* 103-4. I have argued that in 11Q13 (11QMelch) Melchizedek is a divine human (*All the Glory*, 216-21), though for others he is simply an angel. In any case, the words *elohim* and *el* are used of him in 11QMelch 2:10, 11.

126. What I say in this paragraph applies to texts that reject a pagan deification: e.g., *Let. Aris.* 136; Philo *Cherubim* 77; *Embassy* 111-12; *On Dreams* 2:129-33; *Decalogue* 61-69; Acts 12:20-23; Josephus *Ant.* 19:4.

127. For what follows see more briefly McGrath, *Only True God*, 50.

self-deification, where the glory goes only to the person, not to God. Where it is a pagan who is ascribed a divine identity there is the obvious problem for a Jew that such a person's character is quite at odds with the character of the one God. Israel is called to be holy just as God is holy and, in obedience to Torah, to reflect the character of the Creator. Pagans who would be divine live by a different ethic. So, unavoidably, their character cannot reflect or make present the character of the one true God. Furthermore, that ethical character difference inevitably means that if they were in fact "divine" they would pose a numerical and ontological threat to the supreme, unique identity of the one God.[128] Any human being who has no interest in bearing the character of the one true God (*Yhwh*) who would become "a god" is what the eternal gods of the pagan pantheon (Zeus, Apollo, Athena, Amun and the rest) are to the one God: a direct competitor.

By contrast, a human being whose core purpose (whose "why") and character (whose "how" and "what") is to bear the character of the one true God—to be his palpable image and likeness—and who, as such would be "divine," need be no threat to the unique identity of the one God. Indeed, such a human being might justly be deemed both a fitting subject, servant, and a representative of the one God who makes that God truly present in space and time. And so we may say he is "divine" *in this very specific sense.*

We should pay careful attention to what precisely Jews said in their passionate rejection of the "pagan" practice of deifying human beings. Their invective targets specific elements of that deification that have wider implications for the nature of religion and politics in an idolatrous and polytheistic environment. They criticize the personal, self-arrogating behavior of would-be "divine" rulers. And although they are willing to use "god" language for Moses, they did not make statues of Moses or treat him as an independent divine being. They do not offer him cultic veneration through songs and sacrifices. They do not, for example, celebrate his birthday (a normal aspect of the cult of the personality of the divine ruler in the Greco-Roman worlds—see e.g., 2 Macc 6:7). They emphasize that God chose Moses.

From my reading of the primary sources, I can see no reason to think that biblically faithful Jews could not believe that an individual human being has been deified *by God himself*—graciously, by the power of his presence, glory, divine spirit, or whatever—and that this deification is manifest in a *conformity to the character* of the one God *whom this individual now makes present* in a unique and particular way. This kind of deification would be entirely compatible with the Jewish critique of the idolatrous patterns

---

128. Compare the comments of McGrath in ibid., 19, 59–61.

of pagan deification: true deification is something God does (for his own glory), not something that the would-be deified do to themselves (for their own, independent, personal glorification and power).[129] Neither is it a deification that can be achieved by the individuals' devotees. So it is quite unlike the deification of the Roman emperor, who at his apotheosis (after death) and during his lifetime was deified by others (by the Senate's decree in the case of his apotheosis). It is the kind of deification that means that, on the one hand, no cultic veneration (through the songs, prayers, sacrifices, and a statue in a temple) is given to the individual (lest anyone think that he is a separate, independent divine being and he himself is the source of his own wisdom, virtue, and power), but, on the other hand, it is right and proper to use "divine" language for him.

Indeed, it might well be that in some of the texts "god" (or "God") and "divine" language for particular human beings simply reflects deeper theocentric commitments. Because the Jewish world view is so thoroughly *theocentric* it might be inevitable that sometimes there would be divine language for the righteous: *it is God*, not the individual (viewed as an *independent* created entity), whose presence, whose being, is manifest in and through a particular human being. In other words, because God is so jealous for his own self and glory, true human beings are taken up into and become an extension of his own being (not just his action).[130] Aspects of the individual human identity are (through ascesis or by whatever means) suppressed, occluded, or subordinated to God's own identity, not puffed up in self-exaltation. But in the process the individual human being becomes what can properly be called "divine"; even while they remain, paradoxically, a distinct, separate entity to God himself. To say that Moses, for example, is "divine" is a way of saying that his laws and his instructions for the building of the Tabernacle really are God's; they do not come from Moses himself. The legislator was so taken up into the divine purposes that it is God speaking and acting through him and so it is appropriate, in that sense, to say that he has "a higher than ordinary mortal nature" (as Josephus puts in it *Ant.* 3:320).

---

129. For this distinction between *self*-deification (with an allusion to Isa 14:13-14) and God's action of drawing a man to take hold of his own nature, see Philo *Alleg. Interp.* 1:38. In *Let. Aris.* 136, the Greco-Roman deification of benefactors is critiqued because inventors, in effect, steal the credit for their inventions that should go to the Creator himself (cf. Philo *Decalogue* 61). But a stolen glory does not exclude the possibility of possession of a divine glory graciously granted.

130. For this as a likely feature of some Qumran literature see Fletcher-Louis, *All the Glory*, 106-7.

In the Greco-Roman world, the words "god" and "divine" applied to a human being can have an "appallingly broad signification."[131] So, if Jewish authors are simply accommodating their views of the heroes of the faith to a non-Jewish audience we would be well-advised to be cautious about any straightforward adoption of their language in a quest to understand the shape of Jewish monotheism. For a non-Jew to hear it said that Moses was a "divine man" could mean no more than that he was a holy man. To say that the righteous become "gods" after the resurrection (as does *Ps. Phoc.* 103–4) could be no more than a way of saying that because they now have "eternal life" they are, in pagan terms, *immortals*. And if all the texts reviewed in the foregoing paragraphs reflected Jewish attempts to explain themselves to their Greco-Roman neighbors then they would in no way count as evidence against the construal of the relationship between God and the rest of reality put forward by Bauckham and others. The righteous become, in a sense, "immortal," but not *essentially* divine; not divine *in nature*.

However, there are too many texts—not least those written in Hebrew—where there is no reason to think the author is simply accommodating their language for the benefit of outsiders. And even in the case of Philo and Josephus, where a non-Jewish readership may be in view, there are good reasons to think that a "divine" Moses means far more than a "holy Moses."[132] It is hard to avoid the impression that sometimes Jews believed it was appropriate to use "god" language for the righteous in faithfulness both to the shape of biblical theological anthropology and the language of specific biblical passages.

IV: The Worship of "Divine" Agents?

The third category of text brings us nicely to the fourth, which is illustrated by the texts we have been concerned with in chapters 4 and 6: Adam in the Worship of Adam Story and the Son of Man-Messiah in the *Similitudes of Enoch*. In both texts, as we have seen, there is good reason to think that God is willing to share his identity or nature with another, even to the point that in *these* texts a worship of the *separate* figure (who is explicitly a *creature* in

---

131. Litwa, *Iesus Deus*, 22.

132. Consider, for example, the way that in Josephus *Ant.* 3:180 the claim that Moses is a "divine man" is predicated on his legislation for the Tabernacle as a little cosmos. Moses's "divinity" is a matter of his reflecting or actualizing the work of the Creator (cf. Philo *Moses* 1:158). In one passage, Philo's view that Moses was "divine" seems to be indebted to the kind of humanity-as-God's-image-idol notion that we have found the Worship of Adam Story (*Moses* 1:27).

the case of the Adam story) is appropriate. Our discussion of Dan 7:13–14 and Dan 2:46 in chapters 4 and 5 might also be included here.

My comments on the conceptual framework in which the "divine" human being texts most likely made sense also apply to these texts. Adam is not a second god. He is the image and likeness of the Creator himself. He does not try to make himself what he is. *He is simply created to manifest God's presence.* And so we may say he is "divine" and worthy of worship as such, in this very specific sense.

By the same token, the *Similitudes of Enoch* rejects an understanding of royal messianism that too easily accommodates the pagan patterns of the Ruler Cult. Instead, it puts forward a "divine" messiah whose identity is wholly given to the service of the one God.[133] The Son of Man-Messiah makes the one God present at the eschatological dénouement in a way that means he participates in and manifests the divine identity and action. Again, the Son of Man-Messiah does not exalt himself. Indeed, he stands over against the kings and the mighty who do exalt themselves (e.g., *1 En.* 46:7; 38:4; 62:1, 3). He is what he is from premundane preexistence and, like the Adam of Gen 1 and the Worship of Adam Story, from the ground of his being.

In both these cases there *is* a cultic veneration of the "divine" individual, but there is no sense of competition between that devotion and devotion to God. There is no worship of the creature *instead of the Creator.* In both cases there is a tight connection between God and the "second" figure that eliminates any sense of a multiplication of divine identities. And, of course, many of the normal trappings of cultic devotion to divine human beings in the Greco-Roman world are missing (cult statues, temples dedicated to the "god," and priests set apart for their service, for example).

In the light of all this material, the rigidly structured conceptual framework upon which Bauckham and others insist begins to crack under the weight of so many apparent exceptions to the putative rule that there is a clear, irrevocable, and *permanent* separation or distinction between Creator from the creature. Might there be another way of construing the relationship between God and the world that accommodates *all* the evidence? Might there be a conceptual model that explains *both* the evidence upon which Bauckham bases the claim that there is an absolute difference between God and the world, *and* the evidence that, on occasion, Jews could happily speak and act in ways that made it appropriate to use "god" and "divine" language for other entities, besides God himself?

---

133. For this explanation of the ontology of the Enochic Son of Man in terms of a particular political theology, see Fletcher-Louis, "*Similitudes*."

These are questions that deserve a much fuller consideration than is possible here.[134] There are some weaknesses in Bauckham's method and assumptions (which perhaps also reflect unwarranted assumptions of others on his side of the debate) that probably explain why some of the primary data does not fit his model. Some deeper probing of his proposals, I suggest, points in a new direction that will help prepare the ground for the new paradigm that I will outline in Parts 5 and 6.

V: Problems with Bauckham's Proposals

In the first place, Bauckham adopts a form of theological modeling that comes *from below*. Bauckham asks that we understand the Jewish (and biblical) God *on analogy to human notions of* identity. But what emerges is a decidedly modern notion of identity. In terms of the recent history of philosophy, God is a discrete, impermeable, Cartesian self. He is a billiard ball (albeit the supreme, master billiard ball), sending other billiard balls (humans, angels, and others) on their way. He has a hard exterior, that means he cannot share his life, nature, or identity with another entity: "Jewish monotheism could not accommodate . . . *divinity by delegation or participation.*"[135] Thinking about his description of God and the world on analogy to human organizational structures, his model is reminiscent of an older, and now much criticized, command-and-control approach to company decision-making. For such a highly autocratic model the workforce has little chance of a participation in the C-suite's powers: delegation does not come naturally.

It may well be that Bauckham's understanding of the self is true to the nature of the human self since that has a discrete, unshareable identity (though that is also debatable). But in any case, the issue is not what it means to have a human identity; what does it mean to speak of God and *his* identity? As it is, Bauckham's view of that question reflects a long philosophical tradition that tends to emphasize the biblical image of God as a sovereign and to interpret that sovereignty in terms of an absolute distinction of being that enables direct commands (a kind of command and control sovereignty).

But the primary sources, time and again (and we are going to see more of this in the rest of this study), point to another model. From Gen 1

---

134. McGrath's comments on a different kind of understanding of the boundary between God and the rest of reality partially anticipates some of what follows (see esp. *Only True God*, 56).

135. Bauckham, *Crucified God*, 27–28 (= *God of Israel*, 20) (italics added).

onwards there is a delegation of authority and power that frees creation itself to be creative and to contribute to the work of creation (though the active role of the land and the sea in the work of creation in Gen 1:11, 20, 24 is easily obscured by the English translations). And, as we have seen, the primary texts time and again take for granted the possibility, articulated in various ways—though hardly ever with any attempt at a technical philosophical precision—that God is willing and able to share himself and (something of) his identity with a few specifically chosen entities. What Philo says with regards to Moses' *standing* next to God (in Deut 5:31) applies equally to all the texts we have just considered: "God makes the worthy man sharer of his own nature, which is repose" (*Post.* 28).[136] In other words, when we work inductively from the primary sources we quickly have to conclude that the Jewish (and biblical) God does not have the kind of identity that can easily be accommodated to a Cartesian understanding of the self and that he has a strongly *inclusive* heart and mind. It has always been his intention to delegate and to share, even in some cases to delegate and share something of his nature or identity.

Perhaps because Bauckham works on analogy with human identities there is a second problem in the way he approaches the primary texts. He seems to be governed by a too-inflexible perception of what is possible with God. In one place he says,

> In the light of this understanding of divine uniqueness, we can now turn to the various intermediary figures who have seemed, to so many recent scholars, to blur the distinction between God and other heavenly beings. The key question to ask about such figures is: Is this figure included within the unique identity or not?[137]

But why should we approach the primary texts with just these two alternatives? Why must a figure be either "included" within the divine identity or not? Why this binary choice? As far as I can tell, Bauckham has never explained why, in a biblical or Jewish theology, God cannot "share his own nature" with another entity (to use Philo's language) in a way that means a second entity is, so to speak, "divine" but not *fully* included within the divine identity. Why cannot a particular entity "manifest" or "participate in" or "share" the divine identity without being fully "included" within it? Why would that necessarily entail a (pejorative) "blurring" of a distinction (any more than the inclusion of the Son and Spirit alongside the Father within a

---

136. On the theme of human "standing" firm as a reflection of God's own immutable "standing" see Fletcher-Louis, *Luke-Acts*, 174–75, and *All the Glory*, 146–48, for a parallel to Philo's exegesis of Deut 5:31 in the Dead Sea Scroll text 4Q377 frag. 1.

137. Bauckham, *God of Israel*, 158.

trinitarian divine identity means the lack of the kind of distinction between ordinary entities, including human selves, that we experience in our own contingent space and time reality)?

This second point leads to a third. Despite all the emphasis Bauckham places on God's sovereignty, there is the danger that Israel's God is not actually the supreme sovereign. There is the danger that in fact, on his construal of the evidence, Israel's God *is subordinate to categories or notions of identity to which his own identity must conform*.[138] This comes out in particular when he says (in words that others now quote as if it is a technical and authoritative statement) that Paul's Christ belongs "on the divine side of the line monotheism must draw between God and creation."[139] Why "must" monotheism draw that line? And why is "monotheism" doing the drawing, not God himself? Bauckham's language seems to say that actually the identity of the God revealed in Scripture is subordinate to another reality: that God is subordinate to an external necessity (the "must" of the quoted text) and agency (that "draws" a line between God and the rest of reality). In effect, his statement above gives the impression that a particular notion of what monotheism means (in terms of an absolute distinction between God and the rest of reality) has been deified.

One point of saying that God is the absolute sovereign (as indeed the biblical and Jewish texts say time and time again) is to say that he is free. And if he is free, he is free: to deify those whom he wills through a *transformation* of their nature and identity, and to *create* entities (Wisdom, Adam, a Son of Man-Messiah, or whatever) that in various ways share his identity (as Creator, ruler, judge) and who manifest his presence within the world.[140] He is not bound by some external notion or construct of his relationship to the world and its content.

The notion that God is unable to extend himself beyond himself in a way that implies divine change *is*, of course, found in the ancient world, even if it is not obviously present anywhere in Israel's Scriptures. That is to say, the Greek philosopher Plato rejected the popular Greek view that the

---

138. A similar point is made by the Jewish theologian Michael Wyschogrod in his important essay on the notion of incarnation ("Incarnation," 204), where he warns against the dangers of a Jewish a priori rejection of the Christian belief in the Incarnation (and see also Wyschogrod and Soulen, *Abraham's Promise*, 41–42, 214–16).

139. Bauckham, "Worship of Jesus," 335; cf. Tilling, "Misreading," 140, Bird, "Concluding Thoughts," 204.

140. Bauckham himself appeals to God's freedom to explain the *inclusion* of the human life of Jesus within the divine identity (*God Crucified*, 71–72 = *God of* Israel, 53). I suggest that, mutatis mutandis, that argument in respect of Jesus should be applied also to the pre-Christian Jewish and biblical view of other "divine mediators" who *participate in*, or *manifest*, or *share* the divine identity or nature.

gods could appear in multiple forms. Stories from Homer onwards, in the poets and in tragic theater of the gods taking human form are to be rejected as dangerous nonsense, not because God is a sovereign, but because deity must confirm to Plato's understanding of change. Working upwards by analogy to human experience, Plato argues that change implies a vulnerability and degradation of being that is entirely inappropriate for the deity.[141]

Fourthly, from another angle, and in anticipation of the proposals laid out in later chapters, it is also worth pondering a striking omission in Bauckham's account of the divine identity. Human identities are usually tied to a physical location; a house number and postal or zipcode. (Being "of no fixed abode" in Western societies raises the concern that an identity is unstable and dangerous.) Given the way that he approaches the divine identity on analogy to human identities, it is surprising that Bauckham's approach to the identity of Israel's God has nothing to say about his presence in the Tabernacle and his residence in the Temple in Jerusalem, places that function as his "house" and his "dwelling place (*mishkan*)."[142] In the same way that the God of the OT is constituted by a personal story in which he enters into a relationship with a people, so too the relationship with that people—indeed the relationship between this God, the rest of humanity, and of all creation—is constituted by his peculiar presence in a particular space and time. Because Bauckham attends so carefully to the primary texts, this omission is surprising.[143] But inasmuch as his understanding of Jewish theology seems in various ways to reflect a particular Christian theological tradition, it is not. As we have seen, he emphasizes God's sovereignty. The omission of any discussion of how God's *presence* on earth, in a temple, defines his identity means he also works with a particular kind of sovereignty; a detached one.

Israel's Scriptures, on the other hand, put forward a divine identity in which sovereignty is defined by a particular kind of presence. They claim the one God is King precisely in *this particular place* and *at particular salvation-historical times* (that are then celebrated in certain ongoing liturgical times). Place: he is present in his holy city, in his house (the Temple), where he is seated on his throne and his presence fills that building (e.g., 1 Kgs

---

141. See Plato *Rep.* 2:380d–381e.

142. Hurtado comes close to my point here in his rejection of an anachronistic disinterest in cult as definitive of religious identity (in "Ancient Jewish Monotheism," 391–92), but ultimately he shares Bauckham's understanding of exclusive monotheism that works with a particular understanding of divine sovereignty and the absolute difference between God and the rest of reality (see "Ancient Jewish Monotheism," esp. 398).

143. But by no means unusual. Several other recent contributions to the study of NT Christology also suffer for a lack of discussion of the Temple as a defining feature of pre-Christian Jewish monotheism (among them are Collins & Collins, *Son of God*, and Boyarin, *Jewish Gospels*).

8:1–13; Pss 46, 48, 76, cf. Exod 34:34–38; Lev 9, 16; 2 Macc 14:35; Josephus *Ant.* 3:202–3; *J.W.* 5:459).[144] Time: he is present in this place, and in the Tabernacle, *when* he comes to be with his chosen people, in intimate covenantal communion *from Sinai onwards*, and at the climax of their restoration (following his withdrawal from that intimate communion and their exile). Within the ongoing cycle of worship and festivals he is present, in peculiarly intense ways, at particular liturgical times (that celebrate his past actions and presence).

The way in which God takes up residence in the Temple, within creation, means that to speak of "a firm *line* of clear distinction" between God and the rest of reality is to miss the shape of the Bible's own way of thinking. To simplify matters grossly: the Temple consists of *concentric zones* of holiness and there is no one "line" dividing God, who resides in the holy of holies, from the world outside. Israel's high priest can enter fully into God's space (albeit once a year) and, conversely, God's presence—in the form of a cloud, for example (1 Kgs 8:10–11), or by virtue of his own garment (Isa 6:1) or his own palpable glory (e.g., Isa 6:3)—can fill the wider space outside the holy of holies. Language of a clear "dividing line" between God and the rest of creation sounds like the Western Christian vision of the Creator-creation relationship, wherein the notion that God is physically present in one particular building has disappeared. As it is, the role of Israel's Temple in her vision of the cosmos points to a more complex relationship between God's identity outside of space and time and his decision to enter within a particular space and time and to enter into an intimate communion with a particular people. The fact that the Temple speaks so loudly and clearly for the view that the one true Creator God can and does take up residence within a particular space and time suggests he was also more willing to take on concrete materiality than is sometimes assumed.

3: Towards a New Model of "Exclusive Inclusive Monotheism"

These comments on Bauckham's work lead me to propose some modifications to his model of the biblical and Jewish understanding of the divine identity. Rather than working our way from below, by way of analogy to human identities, I suggest we allow Israel's Scriptures (and late Second Temple Jewish texts) to speak from above in ways that inevitably challenge our own ordinary perceptions of identity. The first consequence of such an

---

144. And long before Sinai, in the age of the patriarchs, he is present in particular places and objects (see Sommer, *Bodies of God*, 38–57).

approach is a fresh perspective on what it means to say that God is radically and absolutely distinguished from the rest of reality.

Paradoxically, the absolute difference between God and the rest of reality serves, I suggest, as the philosophical warrant for the conviction that the difference, though absolute, can nevertheless somehow (and mysteriously) be transcended: *it is precisely because he is absolutely distinguished from, different in kind to, the rest of reality, and free from all external constraint, that God is able to enter into and take on the nature and identity of that reality, even on occasion, taking that reality up into his very own self.* His identity, as David Litwa has recently put it, is "shareable."[145]

Equally, he is perfectly free to enter into a particular space at particular times. Genesis 1 itself says that God enters into time. Each work of creation takes place over the course of a particular time (a day or part thereof). God *acts* in time. And on the seventh day it is not just divine *action* that takes place in time; God himself—in his identity—enters a particular time. God chooses, in his sovereign freedom, and in virtue of his acts on the previous days, to be at rest on the seventh day. Precisely because this is *not* acting in time, it is, paradoxically, a statement about what God *becomes; in time*. To be at rest is a statement about God's *being*. And insofar as this being takes place *on a particular day* it is a being that is becoming. In a similar way, I suggest, on the sixth day God enters a particular space—the human creature who is created to be his image and likeness. At least, that is the way some first-century Jews who read and cherished the Worship of Adam Story seem to have read the first chapter of their Bibles. In Part 4 I will outline the case for thinking that in reading Gen 1 that way those Jews were faithful, broadly speaking, to what Scripture intended.

Benjamin D. Sommer has recently argued that biblical texts often assume a notion of divine identity that prevailed in the ancient Near East according to which it is precisely the *"fluidity"* of divine being that makes the gods what they are.[146] Deities can be in more than one place at one time; they can inhabit a body (a cult object) and they can be in many bodies, in many sanctuaries, at any one time. Mutatis mutandis, Israel's god could be conceived as having a body—a notion that Sommer thinks is present in the image language in Gen 1:26–28.

Whilst Sommer sees a variety of stances towards this understanding of Israel's God within the biblical corpus, and there are questionable elements to the working out of the central thesis, his work nevertheless offers a conceptual model that would help explain the kind of textual evidence

---

145. Litwa, *Being Transformed*, 262, 267.
146. Sommer, *Bodies of God* (2009).

from the late Second Temple period that we have reviewed here. That is to say, traditions surrounding Wisdom, the Logos, "divine" angels, "divine" human beings, and uniquely designated entities that are deemed worthy of worship all attest to the view that God is both able and willing, *of his own free choice*, to share himself with, to extend himself into or through, created entities or to take up such entities into his own life; that they might be—by his grace, power, and presence—what he is in his own intrinsic and indefeasible nature.

Sommer's talk of divine "fluidity" is a little unhelpful and may not actually do justice to the way divine identities work in the biblical and wider ancient Near Eastern worlds. For one thing, the word suggests a divine entity has a fixed quantity. Fluids change shape and position, but not mass. But the way the deities of the ancient world interact with their "bodies" implies their "mass" (so to speak) is by no means fixed. The more idols a particular god has, the more bodies he has. Divine "being" is extendable, it can increase (and diminish—when cultic objects that a deity inhabits are destroyed or mutilated). As David Litwa points out in his discussion of material from the turn of the eras, the divine identity is not a zero-sum game.[147] To say that God shares his identity with Adam or the Son of Man-Messiah does not mean that he suffers a loss of being; on the contrary, it may be a way of saying that his identity is magnified and his glory extended.

It might be objected that the Bible itself rules out any possibility of God sharing his identity with others. After all, does not Isaiah loudly proclaim that God gives his glory to no other (Isa 42:8; 48:11)? But the same prophet a few verses later expressly says that he gives his glory to Israel, his chosen people (Isa 60:1-2). The "others" to whom the one God will not give his glory are other deities (cf. Exod 20:3; 34:14). In all probability Isaiah rejects the ancient Near Eastern notion that gods can share their identity with each other to form a kind of divine conglomerate where, for example, the god Ninurta has eyes that are the god Enlil and the goddess Ninlil, the god Anu and the goddess Antu are his lips, Ea and the goddess Daminka are his ears, and Adad the storm god is his head.[148] The God of Isaiah cannot be coopted to the purposes of the gods of other nations. But he is not against the sharing of himself with his own; with his people Israel. On the contrary, he looks to his "servant" and his people to carry his spirit and his glory as a light to the nations.

147. See Litwa, *Being Transformed*, 242, 270.
148. See further the Hymn to Ninurta in Foster, *Before the Muses*, 713–14, and the discussion in Livingstone, *Explanatory Works*, 101; Sommer, *Bodies of God*, 16–18.

Bauckham has presented a model of divine "identity" that he sets over against the usual view that we should talk of divine "nature" or being (ontology) and functions. He claims the historiographical high ground by arguing that "nature" language come from a later period that has lost sight of the way in which the biblical texts themselves operate. Nature language distorts the biblical world view through the introduction of a Greek philosophical concern for metaphysical attributes.[149] But if the Bible reveals a "shareable" divine identity then there are good reasons for thinking that actually "nature" language—which was already being used by pre-Christian Jews to describe God and his interaction with the world—makes a vital contribution to our understanding of biblical theology.

If we assume that the divine "identity" is defined by an understanding of human selves as nonshareable then we are bound to run aground when we encounter primary texts that work with a shareable divine identity. By contrast, in choosing to use the language of divine *nature* it may well be that the church fathers stood in continuity with a biblical and Jewish tradition that believed God chooses to share his identity, his life, and being with (some specifically chosen) entities, especially human ones. We should consider the possibility that the church fathers spoke of Christ's divine *nature*, not because they were selling out to Greek categories, but precisely because they believed deification reflected God's original intention for humanity from the beginning (before sin entered the story and created a need for salvation) and in so believing they stood in conceptual, theological continuity with the Old Testament itself.[150]

They certainly stood in continuity with the NT insofar as 2 Pet 1:4 speaks of believers becoming "partakers of the divine nature"; a statement that recent scholarship has shown is a positive affirmation of a distinctively Christian kind of present, this-life deification in many ways consistent with the shape of Pauline soteriology.[151]

The plausibility and precise shape of an alternative model to the one Bauckham espouses would require more extensive discussion, not least because it is likely that on the ground, at first-century street level, different Jewish groups took differing positions on the degree and ways in which the one God shared his identity with others. I introduce it here in part to prepare the way for the new paradigm to be outlined in later volumes which will

---

149. Bauckham, *God Crucified*, 8 (= *God* of Israel, 7).

150. Cf. Litwa, *Being Transformed*, 97: "if we see deification as the Jewish God's attempt to let his divine identity partially overlap with human beings, deification is in fact intrinsic to biblical thought."

151. See esp. Starr, *Sharers,* and "2 Peter 1:4." For deification in Pauline soteriology see esp. Gorman, *Inhabiting,* and Wright, *Paul,* 546, 781, 955, 1021–23, 1031.

contribute more color and detail to this initial sketch. But more importantly, I float these possibilities now to gain a hearing for an understanding of Jewish monotheism that is a third way between currently competing positions.

With Bauckham and others there is no gainsaying the unique *inclusion* of Jesus within the identity of the one God in NT texts. With Bauckham there can be no denying that late Second Temple Judaism is thoroughly committed both to Israel's Scriptures and the theological categories and patterns they articulate. Equally, with all those who are unconvinced by the argument for a neat and clear boundary between God and the rest of reality, we must give due recognition to the textual evidence that speaks for another model. A third way can also avoid capitulating to the Greco-Roman model of divine identity according to which there are degrees of divinity and a graduated hierarchy of divine beings each having in common certain divine attributes (power, eternity, and their own individual "brand value" as benefactors of note, for example), but quite separate, individuated identities. I see no evidence that, with a few possible exceptions at the fringes of Jewish society, Jews who took up Greco-Roman language and imagery for a "divine" human being thought they had departed from a biblically faithful theological framework. We have seen in the case of Nebuchadnezzar's worship of Daniel (Dan 2:46) a nice example of a text that is best explained as an expression of a fundamentally biblical theological anthropology through the language and behavior of the non-Jewish cult of the benefactor.

If we say that Jewish (and early Christian) monotheism was content to have God share his identity with others, that does not mean that we are signing up first-century Judaism to a Greco-Roman view of divinity in which the one God is merely "the highest member of a class of beings to which he belongs"[152] Any sharing or delegation of divine being and nature comes at the gracious *initiative* of this one God; it is not forced upon him by the already-determined rules of the divine hierarchy. As we have seen in chapter 5, there is good evidence that Jews (and the Bible itself in Dan 2) sometimes did use the language and imagery of the wider Greco-Roman world to express themselves. But I see no reason to assume that in using "divine" language for angels and human beings Jewish writers had departed from a "strict" biblical monotheism as some have claimed.[153]

---

152. As Bauckham charges those who have espoused what he calls an "inclusive monotheism" (*God of Israel*, 108).

153. E.g., A. Y. Collins, "Worship of Jesus," 236. Neither is there any reason (as Litwa thinks—*Being Transformed*, 258–61) to think that a monotheism in which the one God's identity is "shareable" cannot include belief in creation ex nihilo. For reasons beyond the scope of this study, I am persuaded that the traditional belief that God created the world out of nothing is securely grounded in the original author's intention

Perhaps the best evidence for this kind of third way in understanding how Jewish monotheism construes the relationship between God and the cosmos is the NT itself. The early Christian texts we have considered thus far are quite comfortable with the notion of a preexistent, even a premundane, divine being entering space and time as the individual man Jesus of Nazareth. And they let this be, we have argued, with a full identification of the preexistent divine Son with humanity. The ease with which the one who exists within the identity of the Creator God enters into creaturely existence comes, of course, to its most succinct expression in John's Gospel, where "the Word became flesh" (1:14). Similarly, in Phil 2:6–11, the way in which the one who is "in form of God" lives out an individual, personal, human life, even as one who suffers (through the shedding of blood) at the cross is a no less straightforward statement of incarnation. But for all the late-modern anxiety about the origins of such a notion (which has led the likes of James Dunn to conclude, against the natural reading of the texts, that the idea is not actually there), the texts themselves show no caution or anxiety that such a Christology is some kind of abrogation of the distinction between God and the rest of reality. Christological texts in the NT may, on occasion, reveal the battle wounds of controversy, but there is never any sign that an abrogation of an absolute theological distinction between God and the world was the cause of controversy.[154] Christological beliefs caused controversy because this Jesus died accursed on a cross, calling his worshippers to a radically different kind of community ethic to the one prevailing in the first-century Roman context—as the contexts of both Phil 2 and 1 Cor 8:6 show. Ultimately, those beliefs would cause a painful separation from the Jewish synagogue and Temple—as the contexts of Col 1:15–20 and Heb 1–2 both show (although portions of Acts, especially chapters 2–7 suggest the separation may not have been an automatic consequence of the beliefs). His divine life challenged that of the emperor. Jesus himself was accused of hubris in behaving like the emperor in *making himself* equal with God (John 5:18; 10:33; cf. 8:53). Some of his followers provoked a hostile reaction from

---

in Gen 1.

154. Bauckham says Hebrews makes statements about the Son's divinity and his partaking of human nature (in 2:11, 14) that "are straight contradictions" that can only be understood "by a notion of two natures at least embryonically related to that of later patristic Christology" (*God of Israel,* 249). Well, Hebrews may indeed exhibit continuity with later patristic Christology, but the text nowhere reveals that it is dealing with "straight contradictions" and so we are bound to wonder whether its author would have been puzzled by the premise of Bauckham's comment on the Son's divine and human "natures" (*sic!*). Hebrews' own reflections on Melchizedek in ch. 7 suggest he breathes a different philosophical air to one that would see any contradiction in an entity having both divine and human natures.

some Jews because of their stance on the Torah. But *there is no evidence that Christians were criticized, much less persecuted, because they now proclaimed and worshipped a messiah whose identity transgressed an uncrossable line that distinguished between God and the rest of reality.* (Controversy of that kind came at a later period when the church swam in thoroughly Hellenistic, not Jewish, waters.)

In chapters 3 and 4 we pointed to some weaknesses and flaws in Hurtado's work and we posed some questions to Bauckham's own model of Christological origins. A theme running through our critical observations was the sense that the *incarnational* shape of NT Christology is missed or downplayed by the emerging consensus. There are quite a few places where this is explicitly the case in Hurtado's model, and we have also flagged up the problem in Bauckham's work (especially in his treatment of the Gospel Son of Man sayings). Having now considered the philosophical issues at stake in the way the likes of Bauckham and Hurtado approach the relationship between Creator and creation we are bound to wonder whether their position on this important matter is related to their tendency to downplay the Incarnation. Might it be that the philosophical tail is wagging the dog of textual interpretation and historical modeling? Is it that surprising that the emerging consensus obscures the incarnational shape of the New Testament if, at the outset, it has decided that the relationship between God and the rest of reality must preclude God's delegation or sharing of his identity (with *the* Incarnation in Jesus simply a one-off special case)? Might it be a fundamental methodological mistake to start our analysis of ancient Jewish theology by considering God's "identity" on analogy to human identity? Might it be that, at the heart of the biblical "revelation" there is a full frontal challenge to human notions of identity?

In the third volume I will lay out a model of Christological origins that provides more evidence that Jews did *not* believe in the kind of sharp, immovable line between God and the rest of reality that Bauckham describes. In view of the evidence adduced by Bauckham, they *did* emphasize God's transcendence over the rest of reality, *but,* I will argue, they were equally committed to the good news that God's transcendence provided warrant for an immanence such that God would take *on* and take *up* materiality—even into his own life.

This does not mean that the earliest Christology—"Christological monotheism"—was simply slotted into a preexisting Jewish pattern or set of beliefs about a conglomerate of "divine mediators." As we have seen in the foregoing chapters, the way the NT *includes* Jesus within the divine identity has no precise parallel or precedent in Jewish traditions. Indeed, it is striking that nowhere in the NT—in its soteriology, not just it is Christology—is there the kind of divine mediator language that we find in the Jewish sources. Angels are angels; not "gods" or "divine angels." Believers are transformed and highly exalted; but only "partakers of the divine nature" (in 2 Pet 1:4), not "divine." Daniel 2 can happily have Daniel, the paragon of spirit-breathed wisdom, receive worship from his Babylonian overlords. But Peter the apostle resolutely rejects a similar worship from Cornelius the Roman centurion (Acts 10:25-26; cf. Acts 14:8-18). There is an intriguing contrast here between earliest Christianity and its Jewish environment. It is a contrast that should be allowed to stand and the temptation to collapse Jewish monotheism into the shape of a New Testament monotheism (minus Jesus) should be firmly resisted.

In this excursus I have merely addressed the need to reconsider the shape of Jewish monotheism in the light of some non-Christian primary texts and have proposed some new ways of thinking about biblical theology that could explain all the relevant data. In Parts 5 and 6 I will set out a paradigm that will further illustrate the ways in which what I have proposed here has explanatory power for biblical interpretation.

Bibliography

Adams, Edward. *The Stars Will Fall from Heaven: Cosmic Catastrophe in the New Testament and Its World.* Library of New Testament Studies 347. London: T & T Clark, 2007.

Aitken, James K. "The Semantics of 'Glory' in Ben Sira—Traces of a Development in Post-Biblical Hebrew." In *Sirach, Scrolls, and Sages: Proceedings of the Second International Symposium on the Hebrew of the Dead Sea Scrolls, Ben Sira, and the Mishnah, held at Leiden University, 15–17 December 1997,* edited by T. Muraoka and J. F. Elwolde, 1–24. STDJ 33. Leiden: Brill, 1999.

Alexander, Philip. *The Mystical Texts: Songs of the Sabbath Sacrifice and Related Manuscripts.* London: T & T Clark, 2006.

Anderson, Gary A., and Michael E. Stone, eds. *A Synopsis of the Books of Adam and Eve.* EJL 17. Atlanta: Scholars, 1999.

Anderson, Gary A. "Adam and Eve in the 'Life of Adam and Eve.'" In *Biblical Figures outside the Bible,* edited by Michael E. Stone and Theodore A. Bergren, 7–32. Harrisburg, PA: Trinity, 2002.

———. "The Exaltation of Adam and the Fall of Satan." In *Literature on Adam and Eve: Collected Essays,* edited by Gary A. Anderson, Michael E. Stone, and Johannes Tromp, 83–110. SVTP 15. Leiden: Brill, 2000.

———. "Ezekiel 28, The Fall of Satan, and the Adam Books." In *Literature on Adam and Eve: Collected Essays,* edited by Gary A. Anderson, Michael E. Stone, and Johannes Tromp, 133–47. SVTP 15. Leiden: Brill, 2000.

———. *The Genesis of Perfection: Adam and Eve in Jewish and Christian Imagination.* Louisville, KY: Westminster John Knox, 2001.

———. "The Penitence Narrative in the *Life of Adam and Eve.*" In *Literature on Adam and Eve: Collected Essays,* edited by Gary Anderson, Michael Stone, and Johannes Tromp, 1–42. Leiden: Brill, 2000.

Angel, Andrew R. *Chaos and the Son of Man: The Hebrew Chaoskampf Tradition in the Period 515 BCE to 200 CE.* London: T & T Clark, 2006.

Angel, Joseph. L. "The Liturgical-Eschatological Priest of the *Self-Glorification Hymn.*" *Revue de Qumran* 96 (2010) 585–605.

———. *Otherworldly and Eschatological Priesthood in the Dead Sea Scrolls.* STDJ 86. Leiden: Brill, 2010.

———. "The Traditional Roots of Priestly Messianism at Qumran." In *The Dead Sea Scrolls at 60: Scholarly Contributions of New York University Faculty and Alumni,* edited by Lawrence H. Schiffman and Shani Tzoref, 27–54. Leiden: Brill, 2010.

Allison, Dale C. *Constructing Jesus: Memory, Imagination, and History.* Grand Rapids: Baker Academic, 2010.

Ashton, John. *Understanding the Fourth Gospel.* Oxford: Oxford University Press, 1991.
Aune, David E. *Revelation.* 3 vols. WBC 52. Dallas: Word, 1997–99.
Avemarie, Friedrich. "Image of God and Image of Christ: Developments in Pauline and Ancient Jewish Anthropology." In *The Dead Sea Scrolls and Pauline Literature*, edited by Jean-Sébastien Rey, 209–36. Leiden: Brill, 2013.
Barclay, John M. G. *Jews in the Mediterranean Diaspora: From Alexander to Trajan (323 BCE–117 CE).* Edinburgh: T & T Clark, 1996.
Barker, Margaret. *The Great High Priest. The Temple Roots of Christian Liturgy.* London: T & T Clark, 2003.
———. "The High Priest and the Worship of Jesus." In *The Jewish Roots of Christological Monotheism. Papers from the St. Andrews Conference on the Historical Origins of the Worship of Jesus*, edited by Carey C. Newman, James R. Davila, and Gladys S. Lewis, 93–111. JSJSup 63. Leiden: Brill, 1999.
Barry, Kieren. *The Greek Qabalah: Alphabetic Mysticism and Numerology in the Ancient World.* York Beach, ME: Samuel Weiser, 1999.
Barth, Karl. *The Epistle to the Romans.* Oxford: Oxford University Press, 1933.
Bauckham, Richard, James R. Davila, and Alexander Panayotov. *Old Testament Pseudepigrapha: More Noncanonical Scriptures.* Grand Rapids: Eerdmans, 2013.
Bauckham, Richard. "Devotion to Jesus Christ in Earliest Christianity: An Appraisal and Discussion of the Work of Larry Hurtado." In *Mark, Manuscripts, and Monotheism: Essays in Honor of Larry W. Hurtado*, edited by Chris Keith and Dieter T. Roth, 176–200. London: Bloomsbury, 2014.
———. "The Divinity of Jesus Christ in the Epistle to the Hebrews." In *The Epistle to the Hebrews and Christian Theology*, edited by Richard Bauckham, Daniel Driver, and Trevor Hart, 15–36. Grand Rapids: Eerdmans, 2009.
———. "For Whom Were the Gospels Written?" In *The Gospels for All Christians: Rethinking the Gospel Audiences*, edited by Richard Bauckham, 9–48. Edinburgh: T & T Clark, 1998.
———. *God Crucified: Monotheism and Christology in the New Testament.* Carlisle, UK: Paternoster, 1998.
———. "Humans, Animals, and the Environment in Genesis 1–3." In *Genesis and Christian Theology*, edited by Nathan MacDonald, Mark W. Elliott, and Grant Macaskill, 175–89. Grand Rapids: Eerdmans, 2012.
———. *Jesus and the Eyewitnesses: The Gospels as Eyewitness Testimony.* Grand Rapids: Eerdmans, 2006.
———. *Jesus and the God of Israel: "God Crucified" and Other Studies on the New Testament's Christology of Divine Identity.* Milton Keynes, UK: Paternoster, 2008.
———. *The Jewish World around the New Testament: Collected Essays I.* WUNT 233. Tübingen: Mohr Siebeck, 2008.
———. *Jesus: A Very Short Introduction.* Oxford: Oxford University Press, 2011.
———. *Living with Other Creatures: Green Exegesis and Theology.* Waco, TX: Baylor University Press, 2011.
———. "Moses as 'God' in Philo of Alexandria: A Precedent for Christology?" In *The Spirit and Christ in the New Testament and Christian Theology: Essays in Honor of Max Turner*, edited by I. Howard Marshall, 246–65. Grand Rapids: Eerdmans, 2012.
———. "Review Article: Seeking the Identity of Jesus." *Journal for the Study of the New Testament* 32 (2010) 337–46.

———. "The Son of Man: 'A Man in My Position' or 'Someone'?" *Journal for the Study of the New Testament* 23 (1985) 23–33.

———. *The Testimony of the Beloved Disciple: Narrative, History, and Theology in the Gospel of John.* Grand Rapids: Baker Academic, 2007.

———. *The Theology of the Book of Revelation.* New Testament Theology. Cambridge: Cambridge University Press, 1993.

———. "The Worship of Jesus in Apocalyptic Christianity." *New Testament Studies* 27 (1983) 322–41.

———. "The Worship of Jesus in Philippians 2:9–11." In *Where Christology Began: Essays on Philippians 2,* edited by Ralph P. Martin and Brian J. Dodd, 128–39. Louisville, KY: Westminster John Knox, 1998.

Bauckham, Richard, ed. *The Gospels for All Christians: Rethinking the Gospel Audiences.* Grand Rapids: Eerdmans, 1998.

Beale, G. K. *A New Testament Biblical Theology: The Unfolding of the Old Testament in the New.* Grand Rapids: Baker Academic, 2011.

Beetham, Christopher A. *Echoes of Scripture in the Letter of Paul to the Colossians.* Leiden: Brill, 2008.

Bell, Richard H. "Sacrifice and Christology in Paul." *Journal of Theological Studies* 53 (2002) 1–27.

Bernett, Monika. *Der Kaiserkult in Judäa unter den Herodiern und Römern: Untersuchungen zur politischen und religiösen Geschichte Judäas von 30 v. bis 66 n. Chr.* Tübingen: Mohr Siebeck, 2007.

———. "Roman Imperial Cult in the Galilee." In *Religion, Ethnicity, and Identity in Ancient Galilee,* edited by Jürgen Zangenberg, Harold Attridge, and Dale Martin, 337–56. Tübingen: Mohr Siebeck, 2007.

Bird, Michael F. "Concluding Thoughts." In *How God Became Jesus,* edited by Michael F. Bird, Craig A. Evans, Simon Gathercole, Charles E. Hill, and Chris Tilling, 201–5. Grand Rapids: Zondervan, 2014.

Black, Matthew. *The Book of Enoch or 1 Enoch. A New English Edition.* SVTP 7. Leiden: Brill, 1985.

Blackburn, Barry. *Theios Aner and the Markan Miracle Traditions: A Critique of the Theios Aner Concept as an Interpretative Background of the Miracle Traditions Used by Mark.* WUNT 2.40. Tübingen: Mohr Siebeck, 1991.

Boccaccini, Gabriele. *Enoch and the Messiah Son of Man: Revisiting the Book of Parables.* Grand Rapids: Eerdmans, 2007.

———. "The Enoch Seminar at Camaldoli: Re-entering the Parables of Enoch in the Study of Second Temple Judaism and Christian Origins." In *Enoch and the Messiah Son of Man: Revisiting the Book of Parables,* edited by Gabriele Boccaccini, 3–16. Grand Rapids: Eerdmans, 2007.

———. "Jesus the Messiah: Man, Angel or God? The Jewish Roots of Early Christology." *Annali di Scienze Religiose* 4 (2012) 193–220.

Bond, Helen K. *Caiaphas: High Priest and Friend of Rome.* Louisville, KY: Westminster John Knox, 2004.

Bousset, Wilhelm. *Kyrios Christos. Geschichte des Christusglaubens von den Anfängen des Christentums bis Irenaeus.* FRLANT 4. Göttingen: Vandenhoeck & Ruprecht, 1913.

———. *Kyrios Christos: A History of the Belief in Christ from the Beginnings of Christianity to Irenaeus.* Nashville: Abingdon, 1970.

Box, G. H. *The Ezra-Apocalypse: Being Chapters 3–14 of the Book Commonly Known as 4 Ezra (or II Esdras)*. London: Pitman, 1912.
Boyarin, Daniel. "Beyond Judaisms: Metatron and the Divine Polymorphy of Ancient Judaism." *Journal for the Study of Judaism* 41 (2010) 323–65.
———. *Border Lines: The Partition of Judaeo-Christianity*. Philadelphia: University of Pennsylvania Press, 2004.
———. "Enoch, Ezra, and the Jewishness of 'High Christology.'" In *Fourth Ezra and Second Baruch: Reconstruction after the Fall*, edited by Matthias Henze and Gabriele Boccaccini, 337–62. Leiden: Brill, 2013.
———. *The Jewish Gospels: The Story of the Jewish Christ*. New York: New Press, 2012.
———. "Two Powers in Heaven; or, The Making of a Heresy." In *The Idea of Biblical Interpretation: Essays in Honor of James L. Kugel*, edited by Hindy Najman and Judith H. Newman, 331–70. Leiden: Brill, 2004.
Brown, Raymond E. *The Death of the Messiah: From Gethsemane to the Grave: A Commentary on the Passion Narratives in the Four Gospels*. 2 vols. The Anchor Bible Reference Library. New York: Doubleday, 1994.
Brown, William P. *The Seven Pillars of Creation: The Bible, Science, and the Ecology of Wonder*. New York: Oxford University Press, 2010.
Budge, E. A. Wallis. *Coptic Martyrdoms, etc., in the Dialect of Upper Egypt*. British Museum. London: Printed by order of the Trustees sold at the British museum [etc.], 1914.
———. *Miscellaneous Coptic Texts in the Dialect of Upper Egypt*. London: Printed by order of the Trustees of the British Museum, 1915.
Buitenwerf, Rieuwerd. *Book III of the Sibylline Oracles and Its Social Setting, with an Introduction, Translation, and Commentary*. SVTP 17. Leiden: Brill, 2003.
Bunta, Silviu. "The Likeness of the Image: Adamic Motifs and צלם Anthropology in Rabbinic Traditions about Jacob's Image Enthroned in Heaven." *Journal for the Study of Judaism* 37 (2006) 55–84.
Burney, C. F. "Christ as the ΑΡΧΗ of Creation." *Journal of Theological Studies* 27 (1925) 160–77.
Burridge, Richard A. "Gospel Genre, Christological Controversy and the Absence of Rabbinic Biography: Some Implications of the Biographical Hypothesis." In *Christology, Controversy and Community: New Testament Essays in Honour of David R. Catchpole*, edited by David G. Horrell and Christopher M. Tuckett, 137–56. Leiden: Brill, 2000.
Burkett, Delbert. *The Son of Man Debate: A History and Evaluation*. SNTSMS 107. Cambridge: Cambridge University Press, 1999.
Buth, Randall, and R. Steven Notley. *The Language Environment of First-Century Judaea*. Jewish and Christian Perspectives 26. Leiden: Brill, 2014.
Capes, David B. *Old Testament Yahweh Texts in Paul's Christology*. WUNT 2.47. Tübingen: Mohr, 1992.
Casey, P. M. "Monotheism, Worship and Christological Development in the Pauline Churches." In *The Jewish Roots of Christological Monotheism*, edited by Carey C. Newman, James R. Davila, and Gladys Lewis, 214–33. JSJSup 63. Leiden: Brill, 1999.
———. *Solution to the "Son of Man" Problem*. Library of New Testament Studies. London: T & T Clark, 2007.
———. *Son of Man: The Interpretation and Influence of Daniel 7*. London: SPCK, 1979.

Cassuto, Umberto. *A Commentary on the Book of Genesis*. 2 vols. Jerusalem: Magnes, 1961.

Charlesworth, James H. "Can We Discern the Composition Date of the Parables of Enoch?" In *Enoch and the Messiah Son of Man: Revisiting the Book of Parables*, edited by Gabriele Boccaccini, 450–68. Grand Rapids: Eerdmans, 2007.

———. "The Date and Provenance of the Parables of Enoch." In *Parables of Enoch: A Paradigm Shift*, edited by James H. Charlesworth and Darrel L. Bock, 37–57. London: Bloomsbury, 2013.

Chester, Andrew. "The Christ of Paul." In *Redemption and Resistance: The Messianic Hopes of Jews and Christians in Antiquity*, edited by Markus Bockmuehl and James Carlton Paget, 109–21. London: T & T Clark, 2007.

———. "High Christology—Whence, When and Why?" *Early Christianity* 2 (2011) 22–50.

———. "Jewish Messianic Expectations and Mediatorial Figures and Pauline Christology." In *Paulus und das antike Judentum*, edited by Martin Hengel and Ulrich Heckel, 17–89. WUNT 58. Tübingen: Mohr Siebeck, 1991.

———. *Messiah and Exaltation: Jewish Messianic and Visionary Traditions and New Testament Christology*. WUNT 207. Tübingen: Mohr Siebeck, 2007.

Clines, D. J. A. "The Image of God in Man." *Tyndale Bulletin* 19 (1968) 53–103.

Collins, Adela Yarbro, and John J. Collins. *King and Messiah as Son of God: Divine, Human, and Angelic Messianic Figures in Biblical and Related Literature*. Grand Rapids: Eerdmans, 2008.

Collins, John J., and Daniel C. Harlow. *The Eerdmans Dictionary of Early Judaism*. Grand Rapids: Eerdmans, 2010.

Collins, Adela Yarbro. "'How on Earth Did Jesus Become a God? A Reply." In *Israel's God and Rebecca's Children: Christology and Community in Early Judaism and Christianity. Essays in Honor of Larry W. Hurtado and Alan F. Segal*, edited by David B. Capes, April D. DeConick, Helen K. Bond, and Troy A. Miller, 55–66. Waco, TX: Baylor University Press, 2007.

———. "The Secret Son of Man in the Parables of Enoch and the Gospel of Mark: A Response to Leslie Walck." In *Enoch and the Messiah Son of Man: Revisiting the Book of Parables*, edited by Gabriele Boccaccini, 338–42. Grand Rapids: Eerdmans, 2007.

Collins, John J. *The Apocalyptic Vision of the Book of Daniel*. Missoula: Scholars, 1977.

———. *Daniel: A Commentary on the Book of Daniel*. Hermenia. Minneapolis: Fortress, 1993.

———. "Enoch and the Son of Man: A Response to Sabino Chialà and Helge Kvanvig." In *Enoch and the Messiah Son of Man: Revisiting the Book of Parables*, edited by Gabriele Boccaccini, 216–27. Grand Rapids: Eerdmans, 2007.

———. "King and Messiah as Son of God." In *Reconsidering the Concept of Revolutionary Monotheism*, edited by Beate Pongratz-Leisten, 291–315. Winona Lake, IN: Eisenbrauns, 2011.

———. "Messianism and Exegetical Tradition: The Evidence of the LXX Pentateuch." In *The Septuagint and Messianism*, edited by Michael A. Knibb, 129–50. BETL 195. Leuven: Leuven University Press, 2006.

———. *The Scepter and the Star: The Messiahs of the Dead Sea Scrolls and Other Ancient Literature*. New York: Doubleday, 1995.

———. "A Throne in the Heavens: Apotheosis in Pre-Christian Judaism." In *A Throne in the Heavens: Apotheosis in Pre-Christian Judaism*, edited by J. J. Collins and M. Fishbane, 43–58. Albany, NY: State University of New York Press, 1995.

Corley, Jeremy. "A Numerical Structure in Sirach 44:1—50:24." *Catholic Biblical Quarterly* 69 (2007) 43–63.

Cotter, Wendy. *Miracles in Greco-Roman Antiquity: A Sourcebook*. London: Routledge, 1999.

Cranfield, C. E. B. *A Critical and Exegetical Commentary on the Epistle to the Romans*. 2 vols. ICC. Edinburgh: T & T Clark, 1983.

———. "Some Reflections on the Subject of the Virgin Birth." *Scottish Journal of Theology* 41 (1988) 177–89.

Crisp, Oliver. *Divinity and Humanity: The Incarnation Reconsidered*. Current Issues in Theology. Cambridge: Cambridge University Press, 2007.

Crossley, James G. *Reading the New Testament: Contemporary Approaches*. Reading Religious Texts Series. London: Routledge, 2010.

Cullmann, Oscar. *The Christology of the New Testament*. London: SCM, 1963.

Culpepper, R. Alan. "Designs for the Church in the Imagery of John 21:1–14." In *Imagery in the Gospel of John: Terms, Forms, Themes, and Theology of Johannine Figurative Language*, edited by Jörg Frey, Jan van der Watt, and Ruben Zimmermann, 369–402. WUNT 200. Tübingen: Mohr Siebeck, 2006.

Danker Frederick, W. *Benefactor: Epigraphic Study of a Graeco-Roman and New Testament Semantic Field*. St. Louis, MO: Clayton, 1982.

Davies, W. D., and Dale C. Allison. *The Gospel According to Matthew*. 3 vols. ICC. Edinburgh: T & T Clark, 1991–97.

Davies, John A. *The Royal Priesthood: Literary and Intertextual Perspectives on an Image of Israel in Exodus 19.6*. JSOTSS 395. London: T & T Clark, 2004.

Davila, James R. *Hekhalot Literature in Translation: Major Texts of Merkavah Mysticism*. Supplements to the Journal of Jewish Thought and Philosophy 20. Leiden: Brill, 2013.

Deines, Roland. "Christology between Pre-existence, Incarnation and Messianic Self-Understanding." In *Earliest Christian History*, edited by Michael F. Bird and Jason Maston, 75–116. Tübingen: Mohr Siebeck, 2012.

Deissmann, Gustav Adolf. *Light from the Ancient East: The New Testament Illustrated by Recently Discovered Texts of the Graeco-Roman World*. London: Hodder & Stoughton, 1927.

Dick, Michael B., ed. *Born in Heaven, Made on Earth: The Making of the Cultic Image in the Ancient Near East*. Winona Lake, IN: Eisenbrauns, 1999.

Dittenberger, Wilhelm. *Orientis graeci inscriptiones selectae: supplementum sylloges inscriptionum graecarum*. 2 vols. Leipzig: Hirzel, 1903. (= *OGIS*)

Dochhorn, Jan. *Die Apokalypse des Mose: Text, Übersetzung, Kommentar*. TSAJ 106. Tübingen: Mohr Siebeck, 2005.

———. "Die Christologie in Hebr 1,1–2,9 und die Weltherrschaft Adams in Vit Ad 11–17." In *Biblical Figures in Deuterocanonical and Cognate Literature, Deuterocanonical and Cognate Literature Yearbook*, edited by H. Lichtenberger, F. V. Reiterer, and U. Mittmann-Richert, 281–302. Berlin: de Gruyter, 2008.

Drawnel, Henryk. *An Aramaic Wisdom Text from Qumran: A New Interpretation of the Levi Document*. JSJSupp 86. Leiden: Brill, 2004.

Dunn, James D. G. *Christology in the Making: A New Testament Inquiry into the Origins of the Doctrine of Incarnation.* London: SCM, 1980.

———. *Did the First Christians Worship Jesus? The New Testament Evidence.* London: SPCK, 2010.

———. "How Controversial Was Paul's Christology?" In *From Jesus to John: Essays on Jesus and New Testament Christology in Honour of Marinus de Jonge,* edited by M. C. de Boer, 148–67. JSNTSup 84. Sheffield, UK: JSOT, 1993.

———. *Jesus Remembered.* Christianity in the Making 1. Grand Rapids: Eerdmans, 2003.

———. *The Theology of Paul the Apostle.* Edinburgh: T & T Clark, 1998.

Ehrman, Bart D. *How Jesus Became God.* New York: HarperCollins, 2014.

Eldridge Michael, D. *Dying Adam with His Multiethnic Family: Understanding the Greek Life of Adam and Eve.* SVTP 16. Leiden: Brill, 2001.

Ellens, J. Harold. "The Dead Sea Scrolls and the Son of Man in Daniel, 1 Enoch, and the New Testament Gospels: An Assessment of 11QMelch (11Q13)." In *The Dead Sea Scrolls in Context: Integrating the Dead Sea Scrolls in the Study of Ancient Texts, Languages, and Cultures,* edited by Armin Lange, Emanuel Tov, and Matthias Weigold, 341–97. Leiden: Brill, 2011.

Elnes, E. E. "Creation and Tabernacle: The Priestly Writer's Environmentalism." *Horizons in Biblical Theology* 16 (1994) 144–55.

Eskola, Timo. *Messiah and the Throne: Jewish Merkabah Mysticism and Early Christian Exaltation Discourse.* WUNT 2.142. Tübingen: Mohr Siebeck, 2001.

Fee, Gordon D. *Pauline Christology: An Exegetical-Theological Study.* Peabody, MA: Hendrickson, 2007.

Fernández Marcos, Natalio. *The Septuagint in Context: Introduction to the Greek Version of the Bible.* Leiden: Brill, 2000.

Fine, Steven. *Art and Judaism in the Greco-Roman World: Toward a New Jewish Archaeology.* Cambridge: Cambridge University Press, 2005.

Finlan, Stephen, and Vladimir Kharlamov. *Theosis: Deification in Christian Theology.* Eugene, OR: Pickwick, 2006.

Fitzmyer, Joseph A. *Romans: A New Translation with Introduction and Commentary.* London: Chapman, 1993.

Fletcher-Louis, Crispin H. T. "2 Enoch and the New Perspective on Apocalyptic." In *New Perspectives on 2 Enoch: No Longer Slavonic Only,* edited by Andrei Orlov, Gabriele Boccaccini, and Jason Zurawski, 127–48. SJS 4. Leiden: Brill, 2012. (Also in Fletcher-Louis, *Collected Works, Volume 1*).

———. "4Q374: A Discourse on the Sinai Tradition: The Deification of Moses and Early Christology." *Dead Sea Discoveries* 3 (1996) 236–52.

———. *All the Glory of Adam: Liturgical Anthropology in the Dead Sea Scrolls.* STDJ 42. Leiden: Brill, 2002.

———. *Collected Works, Volume 1. The Image-Idol of God, the Priesthood, Apocalyptic and Jewish Mysticism,* forthcoming.

———. "God's Image, His Cosmic Temple and the High Priest: Towards an Historical and Theological Account of the Incarnation." In *Heaven on Earth: The Temple in Biblical Theology,* edited by T. Desmond Alexander and Simon Gathercole, 81–99. Carlisle, UK: Paternoster, 2004. (Also in Fletcher-Louis, *Collected Works, Volume 1*).

———. "The Gospel Thief Saying (Luke 12.39–40 and Matthew 24.43–44) Reconsidered." In *Understanding, Studying and Reading: New Testament Essays in Honour of John Ashton*, edited by Christopher Rowland and Crispin H. T. Fletcher-Louis, 48–68. JSNTSup 153. Sheffield, UK: Sheffield Academic Press, 1998.

———. "Humanity and the Idols of the Gods in Pseudo-Philo's *Biblical Antiquities*." In *Idolatry: False Worship in the Bible, Early Judaism, And Christianity*, edited by S. C. Barton, 58–72. Edinburgh: Continuum, 2007. (Also in Fletcher-Louis, *Collected Works, Volume 1*).

———. "Jewish Apocalyptic and Apocalypticism." In *Handbook for the Study of the Historical Jesus*, edited by Tom Holmén and Stanley E. Porter, 1569–607. Leiden: Brill, 2011. (Also in Fletcher-Louis, *Collected Works, Volume 1*).

———. "Jewish Mysticism and the New Testament." In *The New Testament and Rabbinic Literature*, edited by Reimund Bieringer, Florentino García Martínez, Didier Pollefeyt, and Peter J. Tomson, 429–70. JSJSup 136. Leiden: Brill, 2010. (Also in Fletcher-Louis, *Collected Works, Volume 1*).

———. *Luke-Acts: Angels, Christology and Soteriology*. WUNT 2.94. Tübingen: Mohr Siebeck, 1997.

———. "A New Explanation of Christological Origins: A Review of the Work of Larry W. Hurtado." *Tyndale Bulletin* 60 (2009) 161–205.

———. "Priests and Priesthood." In *Dictionary of Jesus and the Gospels*, edited by Joel B. Green, Jeannine K. Brown, and Nicholas Perrin, 696–705. Downers Grover, IL: IVP Academic, 2013.

———. "Religious Experience and the Apocalypses." In *Experientia Volume 1: Inquiry into Religious Experience in Early Judaism and Christianity*, edited by Frances Flannery, Colleen Shantz, and Rodney A. Werline, 125–44. Atlanta: Society of Biblical Literature, 2008. (Also in Fletcher-Louis, *Collected Works, Volume 1*).

———. "*The Similitudes of Enoch* (1 Enoch 37–71): The Son of Man, Apocalyptic Messianism & Political Theology." In *The Open Mind: Essays in Honour of Christopher Rowland*, edited by Jonathan Knight and Kevin Sullivan, 58–79. London: T & T Clark, 2014. (Also in Fletcher-Louis, *Collected Works, Volume 1*).

———. "The Temple Cosmology of P and Theological Anthropology in the Wisdom of Jesus ben Sira." In *Of Scribes and Sages: Early Jewish Interpretation and Transmission of Scripture*, edited by Craig A. Evans, 69–113. LSTS 50; SSEJC 9. Sheffield, UK: Sheffield Academic Press, 2004. (Also in Fletcher-Louis, *Collected Works, Volume 1*).

———. "The Worship of Divine Humanity and the Worship of Jesus." In *The Jewish Roots of Christological Monotheism: Papers from the St. Andrews Conference on the Historical Origins of the Worship of Jesus*, edited by Carey C. Newman, James R. Davila, and Gladys Lewis, 112–28. JSJSup 63. Leiden: Brill, 1999.

———. "The Worship of the Jewish High Priest by Alexander the Great." In *Early Christian and Jewish Monotheism*, edited by L. T. Stuckenbruck and W. Sproston North, 71–102. JSNTSup 63. Edinburgh: T & T Clark, 2004. (Also in Fletcher-Louis, *Collected Works, Volume 1*).

Fossum, Jarl E. *The Image of the Invisible God: Essays on the Influence of Jewish Mysticism on Early Christology*. NTOA 30. Göttingen: Vandenhoeck & Ruprecht, 1995.

———. *The Name of God and the Angel of the Lord: Samaritan and Jewish Concepts of Intermediation and the Origin of Gnosticism*. WUNT 36. Tübingen: Mohr Siebeck, 1985.

Foster, Benjamin R. *Before the Muses: An Anthology of Akkadian Literature*. 3rd ed. Bethesda, MD: CDL, 2005.
Fretheim, Terence E. *God and World in the Old Testament: A Relational Theology of Creation*. Nashville: Abingdon, 2005.
Frey, Jörg. "Eine neue religionsgeschichtliche Perspektive: Larry W. Hurtados *Lord Jesus Christ* und die Herausbildung der frühen Christologie." In *Reflections on the Early Christian History of Religion. Erwägungen zur frühchristlichen Religionsgeschichte*, edited by Cilliers Breytenbach and Jörg Frey, 117–69. AJEC 81. Leiden: Brill, 2013.
Gardner, Gregg. "Jewish Leadership and Hellenistic Civic Benefaction in the Second Century B.C.E." *Journal of Biblical Literature* 126 (2007) 332–37.
Garr, W. Randall. *In His Own Image and Likeness: Humanity, Divinity, and Monotheism*. CHANE 15. Leiden: Brill, 2003.
Gathercole, Simon J. "Paul's Christology." In *The Blackwell Companion to Paul*, edited by Stephen Westerholm, 172–87. Oxford: Wiley-Blackwell, 2011.
———. *The Preexistent Son: Recovering the Christologies of Matthew, Mark, and Luke*. Grand Rapids: Eerdmans, 2006.
Gaylord, Harry E. "How Satanael lost his '-el.'" *Journal of Jewish Studies* 33 (1982) 303–9.
Gieschen, Charles A. *Angelomorphic Christology: Antecedents and Early Evidence*. AGAJU 42. Leiden: Brill, 1998.
———. "The Name of the Son of Man in the Parables of Enoch." In *Enoch and the Messiah Son of Man: Revisiting the Book of Parables*, edited by Gabriele Boccaccini, 238–49. Grand Rapids: Eerdmans, 2007.
———. "The Descending Son of Man in the Gospel of John: A Polemic against Mystical Ascent to See God." In *The Open Mind: Essays in Honour of Christopher Rowland*, edited by Jonathan Knight and Kevin Sullivan, 105–29. London: Bloomsbury, 2014.
Glazov, Gregory Y. *The Bridling of the Tongue and the Opening of the Mouth in Biblical Prophecy*. JSOTSup 311. Sheffield, UK: Sheffield Academic Press, 2001.
Gooder, Paula. *Only the Third Heaven? 2 Corinthians 12:1–10 and Heavenly Ascent*. LNTS 313. London: T & T Clark, 2006.
Goodman, Martin. *The Ruling Class of Judaea: The Origins of the Jewish Revolt against Rome A.D. 66–70*. Cambridge: Cambridge University Press, 1987.
Gordley, Matthew E. *Teaching through Song in Antiquity: Didactic Hymnody among Greeks, Romans, Jews, and Christians*. WUNT 2.302. Tübingen: Mohr Siebeck, 2011.
———. "The Colossian Hymn in Context: An Exegesis in Light of Jewish and Greco-Roman Hymnic and Epistolary Conventions." WUNT 2.228. Tübingen: Mohr Siebeck, 2007.
Gorman, Michael J. *Cruciformity: Paul's Narrative Spirituality of the Cross*. Grand Rapids: Eerdmans, 2001.
———. *Inhabiting the Cruciform God: Kenosis, Justification, and Theosis in Paul's Narrative Soteriology*. Grand Rapids: Eerdmans, 2009.
Grabbe, Lester L. *An Introduction to First Century Judaism: Jewish Religion and History in the Second Temple Period*. Edinburgh: T & T Clark, 1996.
———. *Judaic Religion in the Second Temple Period: Belief and Practice from the Exile to Yavneh*. London: Routledge, 2000.
Greenfield, Jonas C., Michael E. Stone, and Esther Eshel. *The Aramaic Levi Document: Edition, Translation, Commentary*. SVTP 19. Leiden: Brill, 2004.

Gruber, Mayer. "God, Image of." In *The Encyclopaedia of Judaism*, edited by J. Neusner, 1757-62. Leiden: Brill, 2003.

Habermann, Jürgen. *Präexistenzsaussagen im Neuen Testament*. Frankfurt am Main: Lang, 1990.

Halbertal, Moshe, and Avishai Margalit. *Idolatry*. Cambridge: Harvard University Press, 1992.

Hannah, Darrell D. "The Elect Son of Man of the *Parables of Enoch*." In *Who is This Son of Man? The Latest Scholarship on a Puzzling Expression of the Historical Jesus*, edited by Larry W. Hurtado and Paul L. Owen, 130-58. London: T & T Clark, 2011.

———. *Michael and Christ: Michael Traditions and Angel Christology in Early Christianity*. WUNT 2.109. Tübingen: Mohr Siebeck, 1999.

———. "The Throne of His Glory: The Divine Throne and Heavenly Mediators in Revelation and the Similitudes of Enoch." *Zeitschrift für Neutestamentliche Wissenschaft* 94 (2003) 68-96.

Hayward, C. T. R. *The Jewish Temple: A Non-Biblical Sourcebook*. London: Routledge, 1996.

Hays, Richard B. *The Conversion of the Imagination: Paul as Interpreter of Israel's Scripture*. Grand Rapids: Eerdmans, 2005.

———. *The Moral Vision of the New Testament. A Contemporary Introduction to New Testament Ethics*. Edinburgh: T & T Clark, 1996.

———. *Reading Backwards: Figural Christology and the Fourfold Gospel Witness*. Waco, TX: Baylor University Press, 2014.

———. "The Story of God's Son: The Identity of Jesus in the Letters of Paul." In *Seeking the Identity of Jesus: A Pilgrimage*, edited by Beverly Roberts Gaventa and Richard B. Hays, 180-99. Grand Rapids: Eerdmans, 2008.

Heil, John P. *The Transfiguration of Jesus: Narrative Meaning and Function of Mark 9:2-8, Matt 17:1-8 and Luke 9:28-36*. Analecta Biblica. Rome: Biblical Institute Press, 2000.

Hengel, Martin. *Between Jesus and Paul*. London: SCM, 1983.

———. *Judaism and Hellenism: Studies in their Encounter in Palestine during the Early Hellenistic Period*. London: SCM, 1974.

———. *The Son of God: The Origin of Christology and the History of Jewish Hellenistic Religion*. Philadelphia: Fortress, 1976.

———. *Studien zur Christologie*. Kleine Schriften. 4. Tübingen: Mohr Siebeck, 2006.

———. *Studies in Early Christology*. Edinburgh: T & T Clark, 1995.

Henten, Jan Willem van. "The Honorary Decree for Simon the Maccabee (1 Macc 14:25-49) in Its Hellenistic Context." In *Hellenism in the Land of Israel*, edited by John J. Collins and G. E. Sterling, 116-45. South Bend, IN: University of Notre Dame, 2001.

———. "Royal Ideology: 1 and 2 Maccabees and Egypt." In *Jewish Perspectives on Hellenistic Rulers*, edited by Tessa Rajak, Sarah Pearce, James Aitken, and Jennifer Dines, 265-82. Berkeley: University of California Press, 2007.

Herring, Stephen L. *Divine Substitution: Humanity as the Manifestation of Deity in the Hebrew Bible and the Ancient Near East*. FRLANT 247. Göttingen: Vandenhoeck & Ruprecht, 2013.

Himmelfarb, Martha. *Between Temple and Torah: Essays on Priests, Scribes, and Visionaries in the Second Temple Period and Beyond*. TSAJ. 151. Tübingen: Mohr Siebeck, 2013.

———. "'He Was Renowned to the Ends of the Earth' (1 Macc 3:9): Judaism and Hellenism in 1 Maccabees." In *Between Temple and Torah. Essays on Priests, Scribes, and Visionaries in the Second Temple Period and Beyond*, 235-54. Leiden: Brill, 2013.

———. *A Kingdom of Priests: Ancestry and Merit in Ancient Judaism*. Philadelphia: University of Pennsylvania Press, 2006.

———. "The Wisdom of the Scribe, the Wisdom of the Priest, and the Wisdom of the King according to Ben Sira." In *For a Later Generation: The Transformation of Tradition in Israel, Early Judaism and Early Christianity*, edited by Randal A. Argall, Berverly A. Bow, and Rodney A. Werline, 89-99. Harrisburg, PA: Trinity, 2000.

Hofius, Otfried. "Das vierte Gottesknechtslied in den Briefen des Neuen Testamentes." *New Testament Studies* 39 (1993) 414-37.

Holladay, Carl R. *Theios Aner in Hellenistic Judaism: A Critique of the Use of This Category in New Testament Christology*. SBLDS 40. Missoula, MT: Scholars, 1977.

Horbury, William. "The Aaronic Priesthood in the Epistle of Hebrews." *Journal for the Study of the New Testament* 19 (1983) 43-71.

———. "Deity in Ecclesiasticus." In *The God of Israel*, edited by Robert P. Gordon, 267-292. University of Cambridge Oriental Publications 64. Cambridge: CUP, 2007.

———. "Jewish and Christian Monotheism in the Herodian Age." In *Early Jewish and Christian Monotheism*, edited by Loren T. Stuckenbruck and Wendy E. S. North, 15-44. London: T & T Clark, 2004.

———. "Jewish Messianism and Early Christology." In *Contours of Christology in the New Testament*, edited by Richard N. Longenecker, 3-24. Grand Rapids: Eerdmans, 2005.

———. *Jewish Messianism and the Cult of Christ*. London: SCM, 1998.

———. *Messianism among Jews and Christians: Twelve Biblical and Historical Studies*. London: T & T Clark, 2003.

———. Review of *Lord Jesus Christ: Devotion to Jesus in Earliest Christianity* by Larry W. Hurtado. *Journal of Theological Studies* 56 (2005) 531-39.

Horst, Pieter W. van der. "Greek in Jewish Palestine in Light of Jewish Epigraphy." In *Hellenism in the Land of Israel*, edited by John J. Collins and Gregory E. Sterling, 154-74. South Bend, IN: University of Notre Dame Press, 2001.

Hurtado, Larry W. "'Ancient Jewish Monotheism' in the Hellenistic and Roman Periods." *Journal of Ancient Judaism* 4 (2013) 379-400.

———. "The Binitarian Shape of Early Christian Worship." In *The Jewish Roots of Christological Monotheism: Papers from the St Andrews Conference on the Historical Origins of the Worship of Jesus*, edited by C. C. Newman, J. R. Davila, and G. S. Lewis, 187-213. JSJSup 63. Leiden: Brill, 1999.

———. *The Earliest Christian Artifacts: Manuscripts and Christian Origins*. Grand Rapids: Eerdmans, 2006.

———. "Fashions, Fallacies and Future Prospects in New Testament Studies." *Journal for the Study of the New Testament* 36 (2014) 299-324.

———. *God in New Testament Theology*. Library of Biblical Theology. Nashville, TN: Abingdon, 2010.

———. *How on Earth Did Jesus Become a God? Historical Questions about Earliest Devotion to Jesus.* Grand Rapids: Eerdmans, 2005.

———. *Lord Jesus Christ: Devotion to Jesus in Earliest Christianity.* Grand Rapids: Eerdmans, 2003.

———. *Mark.* NIBC 2. Peabody, MA: Hendrickson, 1995.

———. *One God, One Lord: Early Christian Devotion and Ancient Jewish Monotheism.* Philadelphia: Fortress, 1988.

———. "The Origins of Jesus-Devotion: A Response to Crispin Fletcher-Louis." *Tyndale Bulletin* 61 (2010) 1–20.

———. "Pre-70 C.E. Jewish Opposition to Christ-Devotion." *Journal of Theological Studies* 50 (1999) 35–58.

———. "Remembering and Revelation: The Historic and Glorified Jesus in the Gospel of John." In *Israel's God and Rebecca's Children: Christology and Continuity in Early Judaism and Christianity. Essays in Honor of Larry W. Hurtado and Alan F. Segal,* edited by David B. Capes, April D. DeConick, Helen K. Bond, and Troy A. Miller, 195–214. Waco, TX: Baylor University Press, 2007.

———. "Resurrection-Faith and the 'Historical' Jesus." *Journal for the Study of the Historical Jesus* 11 (2013) 35–52.

———. "Revelatory Religious Experience & Religious Innovation." *Expository Times* 125.10 (2014) 469–82.

———. "Son of God." In *Romans and the People of God,* edited by Sven K. Soderland and N. T. Wright, 217–33. Grand Rapids: Eerdmans, 1999.

Hurtado, Larry W., and Paul Owen, eds. "Summary and Concluding Observations." In *Who is This Son of Man? The Latest Scholarship on a Puzzling Expression of the Historical Jesus,* edited by Larry W. Hurtado and Paul Owen, 159–77. LNTS 390. London: T & T Clark, 2011.

———. *Who is This Son of Man? The Latest Scholarship on a Puzzling Expression of the Historical Jesus.* LNTS 390. London: T & T Clark, 2011.

Idel, Moshe. *Ben: Sonship and Jewish Mysticism.* Kogod Library of Judaic Studies 5. London: Continuum, 2007.

Janowitz, Naomi. *Magic in the Roman World: Pagans, Jews, and Christians.* London: Routledge, 2001.

Jeremias, Joachim. *Jerusalem in the Time of Jesus.* London: SCM, 1969.

Jervell, Jacob. *Imago Dei: Gen 1:26f. im Spätjudentum, in der Gnosis und in den paulinischen Briefen.* Göttingen: Vandenhoeck & Ruprecht, 1960.

Jipp, Joshua J. "Paul's Areopagus Speech of Acts 17:16–34 as Both Critique and Propaganda." *Journal of Biblical Literature* 131 (2012) 567–88.

Jonge, M. de. "The Christian Origin of the *Greek Life of Adam and Eve.*" In *Literature on Adam and Eve: Collected Essays,* edited by Gary A. Anderson and Michael E. Stone, 347–64. SVTP 15. Leiden: Brill, 2000.

Jonge, M. de, and J. Tromp. *The Life of Adam and Eve and Related Literature.* GAP. Sheffield, UK: Sheffield Academic Press, 1997.

Joüon, Paul, and T. Muraoka. *A Grammar of Biblical Hebrew.* Subsidia Biblica 27. Rome: Gregorian & Biblical, 2009.

Kim, Seyoon. *The Origin of Paul's Gospel.* WUNT 4. Tübingen: Mohr Siebeck, 1982.

Kister, Menahem. "Physical and Metaphysical Measurements Ordained by God in the Literature of the Second Temple Period." In *Reworking the Bible: Apocryphal and Related Texts at Qumran: Proceedings of a Joint Symposium by the Orion Center for the Study of the Dead Sea Scrolls and Associated Literature and the Advanced Studies Research Group on Qumran, 15–17 January, 2002*, edited by Esther G. Chazon, Devorah Dimant, and Ruth A. Clements, 153–76. Leiden: Brill, 2005.

Klauck, Hans-Josef. *The Religious Context of Early Christianity: A Guide to Graeco-Roman Religions.* Studies of the New Testament and Its World. Edinburgh: T & T Clark, 2000.

Klawans, Jonathan. *Purity, Sacrifice, and the Temple: Symbolism and Supersessionism in the Study of Ancient Judaism.* Oxford: Oxford University Press, 2006.

Knibb, Michael A. "The Septuagint and Messianism: Problems and Issues." In *The Septuagint and Messianism*, edited by Michael A. Knibb, 3–20. Leuven: Leuven University Press, 2006. Reprinted in *Essays on the Book of Enoch and Other Early Jewish Texts and Traditions*, 349–66. Leiden: Brill, 2009.

Knohl, Israel. "Sacred Architecture: The Numerical Dimensions of Biblical Poems." *Vetus Testamentum* 62 (2012) 189–97.

Koch, Klaus. "Questions Regarding the So-Called Son of Man in the Parables of Enoch: A Response to Sabino Chialà and Helge Kvanvig." In *Enoch and the Messiah Son of Man: Revisiting the Book of Parables*, edited by Gabriele Boccaccini, 228–37. Grand Rapids: Eerdmans, 2007.

———. *The Rediscovery of Apocalyptic.* London: SCM, 1972.

———. *Vor der Wende der Zeiten: Beiträge zur apokalyptischen Literatur.* Gesammelte Aufsätze 3. Neukirchen-Vluyn: Neukirchener, 1996.

Kooij, Arie van der. "The Greek Bible and Jewish Concepts of Royal Priesthood and Priestly Monarchy." In *Jewish Perspectives on Hellenistic Rulers*, edited by Tessa Rajak, S. J. Pearce, J. K. Aitken, and J. Dines, 255–64. Berkeley: University of California Press, 2007.

———. "A Kingdom of Priests: Comment on Exodus 19:6." In *The Interpretation of Exodus: Studies in Honour of Cornelis Houtman*, edited by Riemer Roukema, 171–79. Leuven: Peeters, 2006.

———. "LXX Exod 23 and the Figure of the High Priest." In *On Stone and Scroll: Essays in Honour of Graham Ivor Davies*, edited by James K. Aitken, Katharine J. Dell, and Brian A. Mastin, 537–49. Berlin: de Gruyter, 2012.

———. "Moses and the Septuagint of the Pentateuch." In *Moses in Biblical and Extra-Biblical Traditions*, edited by Axel Graupner, Michael Wolter, 89–98. Berlin: de Gruyter, 2007.

———. "The Old Greek of Isaiah 9:6–7 and the Concept of Leadership." In *Die Septuaginta—Text, Wirkung, Rezeption. 4. Internationale Fachtagun veranstaltet von Septuaginta Deutsch (LXX.D), Wuppertal 19.–22. Juli 2012*, edited by Wolfgang Kraus and Siegfried Kreuzer, 333–45. Tübingen: Mohr Siebeck, 2014.

Kooten, George H. van. *Paul's Anthropology in Context: the Image of God, Assimilation to God and Tripartite Man in Ancient Judaism, Ancient Philosophy and Early Christianity.* WUNT 232. Tübingen: Mohr Siebeck, 2008.

———. "Image, Form and Transformation. A Semantic Taxonomy of Paul's 'Morphic' Language." In *Jesus, Paul, and Early Christianity: Studies in Honour of Henk Jan de Jonge*, edited by Rieuwerd Buitenwerf, Harm W. Hollander, and Johannes Tromp, 213–42. Leiden: Brill, 2008.

Krentz, E. "The Honorary Decree for Simon the Maccabee." In *Hellenism in the Land of Israel*, edited by J. J. Collins and G. E. Sterling, 146–53. South Bend, IN: University of Notre Dame Press, 2001.

Kutsko, John. *Between Heaven and Earth: Divine Presence and Absence in Ezekiel.* Biblical and Judaic Studies UCSD 7. Winona Lake, IN: Eisenbrauns, 2000.

Kvanvig, Helge S. "The Son of Man and the Parables of Enoch." In *Enoch and the Messiah Son of Man: Revisiting the Parables of Enoch*, edited by Gabriele Boccaccini, 179-215. Grand Rapids: Eerdmans, 2007.

———. "Throne Visions and Monsters. The Encounter between Danielic and Enochic Traditions." *Zeitschrift für Alttestamentliche Wissenschaft* 117 (2005) 249-72.

Labuschagne, Casper J. *Numerical Secrets of the Bible: Rediscovering the Bible Codes.* North Richland Hills, TX: Bibal, 2000.

———. "Significant Compositional Techniques in the Psalms: Evidence for the Use of Numbers as an Organizing Principle." *Vetus Testamentum* 59 (2009) 583-605.

Leithart, Peter J. *1 & 2 Kings*. Brazos Theological Commentary on the Bible. Grand Rapids: Brazos, 2006.

Leivestad, Ragnar. "Der apokalyptische Menschensohn ein theologisches Phantom." *Annual of the Swedish Theological Institute* 6 (1968) 49-105.

———. "Exit the Apocalyptic Son of Man." *New Testament Studies* 18 (1971-72) 243-67.

Leonhard, Clemens. "'Herod's Days' and the Development of Jewish and Christian Festivals." In *Jewish Identity and Politics between the Maccabees and Bar Kokhba: Groups, Normativity, and Rituals*, edited by Benedikt Eckhardt, 189-208. Leiden: Brill, 2011.

Lenglet, A. "La structure litteraire de Daniel 2-7." *Bib* 53 (1972) 169-90.

Lenz, John R. "Deification of the Philosopher in Classical Greece." In *Partakers of the Divine Nature: The History and Development of the Deification in the Christian traditions*, edited by Michael J. Christensen and Jeffery A. Wittung, 47-67. Madison, NJ: Fairleigh Dickinson University Press, 2007.

Levenson, Jon D. *Creation and the Persistence of Evil: The Jewish Drama of Divine Omnipotence.* San Francisco: Harper & Row, 1988.

Levinson, Bernard M. "The Reconceptualization of Kingship in Deuteronomy and the Deuteronomistic History's Transformation of Torah." *Vetus Testamentum* 51 (2001) 511-34.

Levison, John R. "Adam and Eve in Romans 1:8-25 and the Greek *Life of Adam and Eve*." *New Testament Studies* 50 (2004) 519-34.

Lieberman, Stephen J. "A Mesopotamian Background for the So-Called Aggadic 'Measures' of Biblical Hermeneutics." *Hebrew Union College Annual* 58 (1987) 188-92.

Lincicum, David. "The Origin of 'Alpha and Omega' (Revelation 1.8; 21.6; 22.13): A Suggestion." *Journal of Greco-Roman Christianity and Judaism* 6 (2009) 128-33.

Lincoln, Andrew T. "The Letter to the Colossians." In *The New Interpreter's Bible: A Commentary in Twelve Volumes*, edited by Leander E. Keck, 531-85. Nashville: Abingdon, 2000.

Livingstone, Alasdair. *Mystical and Mythological Explanatory Works of Assyrian and Babylonian Scholars.* Winona Lake, IN: Eisenbrauns, 2007.

Litwa, M. David. "Behold Adam: A Reading of John 19:5." *Horizons in Biblical Theology* 32 (2010) 129-43.

———. "The Deification of Moses in Philo of Alexandria." *Studia Philonica Annual* 26 (2014) 1-27.

———. *Iesus Deus: the Early Christian Depiction of Jesus as a Mediterranean God.* Minneapolis: Fortress, 2014.
———. *We Are Being Transformed: Deification in Paul's Soteriology.* Berlin: de Gruyter, 2012.
Long, Charlotte R. *The Twelve Gods of Greece and Rome.* Leiden: Brill, 1987.
Van der Lugt, Pieter. *Cantos and Strophes in Biblical Hebrew Poetry.* 3 vols. Leiden: Brill, 2006–13.
Macaskill, Grant. "2 Enoch: Manuscripts, Recensions, and Original Language." In *New Perspectives on 2 Enoch: No Longer Slavonic Only*, edited by Andrei A. Orlov, Gabriele Boccaccini, and Jason Zurawski, 83–102. SJS 4. Leiden: Brill, 2012.
———. *Union with Christ in the New Testament.* Oxford: Oxford University Press, 2013.
Mack, B. L. *Wisdom and the Hebrew Epic: Ben Sira's Hymn in Praise of the Fathers.* Chicago: University of Chicago Press, 1985.
Magliano-Tromp, Johannes. "Adamic Traditions in 2 Enoch and in the Books of Adam and Eve." In *New Perspectives on 2 Enoch: No Longer Slavonic Only*, edited by Andrei A. Orlov, Gabriele Boccaccini, and Jason Zurawski, 283–304. SJS 3. Brill: Leiden, 2012.
Marcus, Joel. "Identity and Ambiguity in Markan Christology." In *Seeking the Identity of Jesus: A Pilgrimage*, edited by Beverly Roberts Gaventa and Richard B. Hays, 133–47. Grand Rapids: Eerdmans, 2008.
———. *Mark. A New Translation with Introduction and Commentary.* Vol. 1. AB. 27A. New York: Doubleday, 1999.
———. *Mark. A New Translation with Introduction and Commentary.* Vol. 2. AB. 27B. New Haven: Yale University Press, 2006.
———. *The Way of the Lord: Christological Exegesis of the Old Testament in the Gospel of Mark.* Louisville, KY: Westminster John Knox, 1992.
Martin, Ralph P. *A Hymn of Christ: Philippians 2:5–11 in Recent Interpretation & in the Setting of Early Christian Worship.* 3rd ed. Downers Grove, IL: IVP, 1997.
Mastin, B. A. "Daniel 2:46 and the Hellenistic World." *Zeitschrift für Altestamentliche Wissenschaft* 85 (1973) 80–93.
McDonough, Sean M. *Christ as Creator: Origins of a New Testament Doctrine.* Oxford: Oxford University Press, 2009.
McGrath, James F. "On Hearing (Rather than Reading) Intertextual Echoes: Christology and Monotheistic Scriptures in Oral Context." *Biblical Theology Bulletin* 43 (2013) 74–80.
———. *The Only True God: Early Christian Monotheism in Its Jewish Context.* Urbana, IL: University of Illinois Press, 2009.
Meadowcroft, T. M. *Aramaic Daniel and Greek Daniel: A Literary Comparison.* JSOTSup 198. Sheffield, UK: Sheffield Academic Press, 1995.
Menken, M. J. J. *Numerical Literary Techniques in John: The Fourth Evangelist's Use of Numbers of Words and Syllables.* NovTSup 55. Leiden: Brill, 1985.
Middleton, J. Richard. *The Liberating Image: The Imago Dei in Genesis 1.* Grand Rapids: Brazos, 2005.
Milik, Józef. *The Books of Enoch.* Oxford: OUP, 1976.
Millard, Alan. "Incense—the Ancient Room Freshener. The Exegesis of Daniel 2.46." In *On Stone and Scroll: Essays in Honour of Graham I. Davies*, edited by James K. Aitken, Katharine J. Dell, and Brian A. Mastin, 111–22. Berlin: de Gruyter, 2012.

Mizrahi, Noam. "The Cycle of Summons: A Hymn from the Seventh Song of the Sabbath Sacrifice (4Q403 1i 31–40)." *Dead Sea Discoveries* 21 (2014) 1–25.

Moffitt, David M. *Atonement and the Logic of Resurrection in the Epistle to the Hebrews*. NovTSup 141. Leiden: Brill, 2011.

Muraoka, T. *A Greek-English Lexicon of the Septuagint*. Louvain: Peeters, 2009.

Nau, F. "Une didascalie de Notre Seigneur Jésus-Christ." *Revue de l'Orient Chrétien* 12 (1907) 225–54.

Nickelsburg, George W. E., and James C. VanderKam. *1 Enoch 2: A Commentary on the Book of 1 Enoch Chapters 37–82*. Minneapolis: Fortress, 2012.

Nickelsburg, George W. E. *1 Enoch 1: A Commentary on the Book of 1 Enoch Chapters 1–36, 81–108*. Hermenia. Minneapolis: Fortress, 2001.

———. "Son of Man." In *Anchor Bible Dictionary*, edited by David Noel Freedman, 6:137–50. New Haven: Yale University Press, 1992.

———. "Son of Man." In *The Eerdmans Dictionary of Early Judaism*, edited by John C. Collins and Daniel C. Harlow, 1249–51. Grand Rapids: Eerdmans, 2010.

Nicholson, Ernest W. *Deuteronomy and the Judaean Diaspora*. Oxford: Oxford University Press, 2014.

Nir, Rivka. "The Struggle between the 'Image of God' and Satan in the *Greek Life of Adam and Eve*." *Scottish Journal of Theology* 61 (2008) 327–39.

North, J. Lionel. "Jesus and Worship, God and Sacrifice." In *Early Jewish and Christian Monotheism*, edited by Loren T. Stuckenbruck and Wendy E. S. North, 186–202. London: T & T Clark, 2004.

Novenson, Matthew V. *Christ among the Messiahs: Christ Language in Paul and Messiah Language in Ancient Judaism*. New York: Oxford University Press, 2012.

Oakes, Peter. "Re-mapping the Universe: Paul and the Emperor in 1 Thessalonians and Philippians." *Journal for the Study of the New Testament* 27 (2005) 301–22.

Olson, Daniel C., and Melkesedek Workeneh. *Enoch: a New Translation*. North Richland Hills, TX: BIBAL, 2004.

Olson, Daniel C. *A New Reading of the Animal Apocalypse of 1 Enoch: "All Nations Shall be Blessed."* Leiden: Brill, 2013.

Orlov, Andrei A. *Dark Mirrors: Azazel and Satanael in Early Jewish Demonology*. Albany, NY: State University of New York Press, 2011.

———. "Roles and Titles of the Seventh Antediluvian Hero." In *Enoch and the Messiah Son of Man: Revisiting the Book of Parables*, edited by Gabriele Boccaccini, 110–36. Grand Rapids: Eerdmans, 2007.

Osborne, Thomas P. "'Récitez entre vous des psaumes, des hymnes et des cantiques inspirés (Ep 5:19). Un état de la question sur l'étude des 'hymnes' de Nouveau Testament." In *Les Hymnes du Nouveau Testament et leurs Fonctions*, edited by Daniel Gerber and Pierre Keith, 57–80. Paris: Cerf, 2009.

Parsons, Mikeal C. "Exegesis 'By the Numbers': Numerology and the New Testament." *Perspectives in Religious Studies* 35 (2008) 25–43.

Patton, Corrine L. "Adam as the Image of God: An Exploration of the Fall of Satan in the *Life of Adam and Eve*." *Society of Biblical Literature Seminar Papers* (1994) 294–300.

Pettorelli, Jean-Pierre. "Adam and Eve, Life of." In *The Eerdmans dictionary of early Judaism*, edited by J. J. Collins and D. C. Harlow, 302–6. Grand Rapids: Eerdmans, 2010.

Pietersma, Albert, and Benjamin G. Wright. *A New English Translation of the Septuagint and the other Greek Translations Traditionally Included under That Title*. Oxford: Oxford University Press, 2007. (= *NETS*)

Piovanelli, Pierluigi. "'A Testimony for the Kings and the Mighty Who Possess the Earth': the Thirst for Justice and Peace in the Parables of Enoch." In *Enoch and the Messiah Son of Man: Revisiting the Book of Parables*, edited by Gabriele Boccaccini, 363-79. Grand Rapids: Eerdmans, 2007.

Peppard, Michael. *The Son of God in the Roman World: Divine Sonship in its Social and Political Context*. Oxford: Oxford University Press, 2012.

Pomykala, Kenneth. *The Davidic Dynasty Tradition in Early Judaism*. Atlanta: Scholars, 1995.

———. "Messianism." In *The Eerdmans Dictionary of Early Judaism*, edited by John J. Collins and Daniel C. Harlow, 938-42. Grand Rapids: Eerdmans, 2010.

Propp, William Henry. *Exodus 19-40: A New Translation with Introduction and Commentary*. AB 2A. New York: Doubleday, 2006.

Rand, Herbert. "Numerological Structure in Biblical Literature." *Jewish Bible Quarterly* 20 (1991) 50-56.

Regev, Eyal. *The Hasmoneans: Ideology, Archaeology, Identity*. Journal of Ancient Judaism Supplements 10. Göttingen: Vandenhoeck & Ruprecht, 2013.

Reumann, John Henry Paul. *Philippians: A New Translation with Introduction and Commentary*. AB 33B. New Haven, CT: Yale University Press, 2008.

Reynolds, Benjamin E. *The Apocalyptic Son of Man in the Gospel of John*. WUNT 2.249. Tübingen: Mohr Siebeck, 2008.

———. "The 'One Like a Son of Man' According to the Old Greek of Daniel 7, 13-14." *Biblica* 89 (2008) 70-80.

Rösel, Martin. *Übersetzung als Vollendung der Auslegung: Studien zur Genesis-Septuaginta*. BZAW 223. Berlin: de Gruyter, 1994.

Rooke, Deborah W. *Zadok's Heirs: The Role and Development of the High Priesthood in Ancient Israel*. Oxford: Clarendon, 2000.

Rowe, Christopher Kavin. *Early Narrative Christology: The Lord in the Gospel of Luke*. Grand Rapids: Baker, 2009.

———. "Romans 10:13: What is the Name of the Lord?" *Horizons in Biblical Theology* 22 (2000) 135-73.

Rowland, Christopher, and Christopher R. A. Morray-Jones. *The Mystery of God: Early Jewish Mysticism and the New Testament*. Leiden: Brill, 2009.

Rowland, Christopher C. "Apocalyptic, Mysticism and the New Testament." In *Geschichte - Tradition - Reflexion: Festschrift für Martin Hengel zum 70. Geburtstag*, edited by Peter Schäfer, Hubert Cancik, Hermann Lichtenberger, and Martin Hengel, 406-30. Tübingen: Mohr Siebeck, 1996.

———. "Apocalyptic Visions and the Exaltation of Christ in the Letter to the Colossians." *Journal for the Study of the New Testament* 19 (1983) 73-83.

———. *Christian Origins: An Account of the Setting and Character of the Most Important Messianic Sect of Judaism*. London: SPCK, 2002.

———. "A Man Clothed in Linen: Daniel 10.6ff. and Jewish Angelology." *Journal for the Study of the New Testament* 24 (1985) 99-110.

———. *The Open Heaven: A Study of Apocalyptic in Judaism and Early Christianity*. New York: Crossroad, 1982.

Salvesen, Alison. *Symmachus in the Pentateuch.* Journal of Semitic Studies Monograph 15. Manchester: Journal of Semitic Studies, 1991.

Safrai, Samuel. "Spoken and Literary Languages in the Time of Jesus." In *Jesus' Last Week: Jerusalem Studies in the Synoptic Gospels—Volume One*, edited by S. Notley, Marc Turnage, and Brian Becker, 225-44. Leiden: Brill, 2006.

Sanders, E. P. *Judaism: Practice and Belief 63 BCE-66 CE.* London: SCM, 1992.

Schäfer, Peter. *The Jewish Jesus: How Judaism and Christianity Shaped Each Other.* Princeton: Princeton University Press, 2012.

Schnelle, Udo. *Apostle Paul: His Life and Theology.* Grand Rapids: Baker Academic, 2005.

Schröter, Jens. "Trinitarian Belief, Binitarian Monotheism, and the One God: Reflections on the Origin of Christian Faith in Affiliation to Larry Hurtado's Christological Approach." In *Reflections on the Early Christian History of Religion. Erwägungen zur frühchristlichen Religionsgeschichte*, edited by Cilliers Breytenbach and Jörg Frey, 171-94. AJEC 81. Leiden: Brill, 2013.

Schuller, E. M. *Non-Canonical Psalms from Qumran: A Pseudepigrahic Collection.* HSS 28. Atlanta: Scholars, 1986.

Segal, Alan F. *Paul the Convert: The Apostolate and Apostasy of Saul the Pharisee.* New Haven: Yale University Press, 1990.

———. "The Risen Christ and the Angelic Mediator Figures in Light of Qumran." In *Jesus and the Dead Sea Scrolls*, edited by James H. Charlesworth, 302-28. New York: Doubleday, 1992.

———. *Two Powers in Heaven: Early Rabbinic Reports about Christianity and Gnosticism.* SJLA 25. Leiden: Brill, 1977.

Sheppard, G. T. *Wisdom as a Hermeneutical Construct: A Study in the Sapientializing of the Old Testament.* BZAW 151. Berlin: de Gruyter, 1980.

Smith, Morton. "Ascent to Heavens and Deification in 4QM^a." In *Archaeology and History in the Dead Sea Scrolls: The New York University Conference in Memory of Yigael Yadin*, edited by Lawrence H. Schiffman, 181-88. Sheffield: JSOT, 1990.

Sommer, Benjamin D. *The Bodies of God and the World of Ancient Israel.* Cambridge: Cambridge University Press, 2009.

Starr, James M. *Sharers in Divine Nature: 2 Peter 1:4 in Its Hellenistic Context.* Stockholm: Almqvist & Wiksell, 2000.

Steenburg, D. "The Worship of Adam and Christ as the Image of God." *Journal for the Study of the New Testament* 39 (1990) 95-109.

Sterling, Gregory E. "Judaism between Jerusalem and Alexandria." In *Hellenism in the Land of Israel*, edited by J. J. Collins and G. E. Sterling, 263-301. South Bend, IN: University of Notre Dame Press, 2001.

Stettler, Christian. *Der Kolosserhymnus: Untersuchungen zu Form, Traditionsgeschichtlichem Hintergrund und Aussage von Kol 1, 15-20.* Tübingen: Mohr Siebeck, 2000.

Stone, Michael E. "Enoch's Date in Limbo; or, Some Considerations on David Suter's Analysis of the Book of Parables." In *Enoch and the Messiah Son of Man: Revisiting the Book of Parables*, edited by Gabriele Boccaccini, 444-50. Grand Rapids: Eerdmans, 2007.

———. "The Fall of Satan and Adam's Penance: Three Notes on *The Books of Adam and Eve.*" *Journal of Theological Studies* 44 (1993) 143-56.

———. *A History of the Literature of Adam and Eve*. Early Judaism and its Literature 3. Atlanta: Scholars, 1992.

Stuckenbruck, Loren T. *Angel Veneration and Christology: A Study in Early Judaism and in the Christology of the Apocalypse of John*. WUNT 2.70. Tübingen: Mohr Siebeck, 1995.

———. "'Angels' and 'God': Exploring the Limits of Early Jewish Monotheism." In *Early Jewish and Christian Monotheism*, edited by Loren T. Stuckenbruck and Wendy North, 45–70. London: T & T Clark, 2004.

———. "'One Like a Son of Man as the Ancient of Days' in the Old Greek Recension of Daniel 7,13: Scribal Error or Theological Translation." *Zeitschrift für Neutestamentliche Wissenschaft* 86 (1995) 268–76.

Swartz, Michael D., and Joseph Yahalom. *Avodah: An Anthology of Ancient Poetry for Yom Kippur*. Penn State Library of Jewish Literature. University Park, PA: The Pennsylvania State University Press, 2005.

Theisohn, Johannes. *Der auserwählte Richter: Untersuchungen zum traditionsgeschichtlichem Ort der Menschensohngestalt der Bilderreden des Äthiopischen Henoch*. SUNT 12. Göttingen: Vandenhoeck und Ruprecht, 1975.

Theissen, Gerd. *A Theory of Primitive Christian Religion*. London: SCM, 2000.

Tilling, Chris. "Misreading Paul's Christology: Problems with Ehrman's Exegesis." In *How God Became Jesus*, edited by Michael F. Bird, Craig A. Evans, Simon Gathercole, Charles E. Hill, and Chris Tilling, 134–50. Grand Rapids: Zondervan, 2014.

———. *Paul's Divine Christology*. WUNT 323. Tübingen: Mohr Siebeck, 2012.

———. "Problems with Ehrman's Interpretative Categories." In *How God Became Jesus*, edited by Michael F. Bird, Craig A. Evans, Simon J. Gathercole, Charles E. Hill, and Chris Tilling, 117–33. Grand Rapids: Zondervan, 2014.

Toepel, Alexander. "Adamic Traditions in Early Christianity." In *New Perspectives on 2 Enoch: No Longer Slavonic Only*, edited by Andrei A. Orlov, Gabriele Boccaccini, and Jason M. Zurawski, 305–25. Leiden: Brill, 2012.

VanderKam, James C. *The Book of Jubilees: Text and Translation*. 2 vols. CSCO 510–11; Scriptores Aethiopici 87–88. Leuven: Peeters, 1989.

———. "Daniel 7 in the Similitudes of Enoch (*1 En*. 37–71)." In *Biblical Traditions in Transmission: Essays in Honour of Michael A. Knibb*, edited by Charlotte Hempel and Judith M. Lieu, 291–307. JSJSup 3. Leiden: Brill, 2006.

———. *From Joshua to Caiaphas: High Priests after the Exile*. Minneapolis: Fortress, 2004.

———. "Righteous One, Messiah, Chosen One, and Son of Man in 1 Enoch 37–71." In *The Messiah. Developments in Earliest Judaism and Christianity*, edited by James H. Charlesworth, 161–91. Minneapolis: Fortress, 1992.

Vollenweider, Samuel. "Christozentrisch oder theozentrisch? Christologie im Neuen Testament." In *Christologie*, edited by E. Gräb-Schmidt and R. Preul, 19–40. Leipzig, 2011.

———. *Horizonte neutestamentlicher Christologie: Studien zu Paulus und zur frühchristlichen Theologie*. WUNT 144. Tübingen: Mohr Siebeck, 2002.

———. "Hymnus, Enkomion oder Psalm? Schattengefechte in der neutestamentlichen Wissenschaft." *New Testament Studies* 56 (2010) 208–31.

———. "Die Metamorphose des Gottessohns: Zum epiphanialen Motivfeld in Phil 2, 6-8." In *Horizonte neutestamentlicher Christologie*, 285–306. WUNT 144. Tübingen: Mohr Siebeck, 2002.

———. "'Der Name, der über jedem anderen Namen ist' Jesus als Träger des Gottesnamens im Neuen Testament." In *Gott nennen. Gottes Namen und Gott als Name*, edited by Ingolf U. Dalferth and Philipp Stoellger, 173–86. Tübingen: Mohr Siebeck, 2008.

———. "Der 'Raub' der Gottgleichheit: Ein religionsgeschichtlicher Vorschlag zu Phil 2.6(-11)." *New Testament Studies* 45 (1999) 413–33.

Waaler, Erik. *The Shema and the First Commandment in First Corinthians: An Intertextual Approach to Paul's Re-reading of Deuteronomy*. WUNT 2.253. Tübingen: Mohr Siebeck, 2008.

Waddell, James Alan. *The Messiah: A Comparative Study of the Enochic Son of Man and the Pauline Kyrios*. London: T & T Clark, 2011.

Walck, Leslie W. "The Social Setting of the Parables of Enoch." In *A Teacher for All Generations. Essays in Honor of James C. VanderKam*, edited by Eric F. Mason, Kelley Coblentz Bautch, Angela Kim Harkins, and Daniel A Machiela, 669–86. Leiden: Brill, 2012.

———. "The Son of Man in the Parables and the Gospels." In *Enoch and the Messiah Son of Man: Revisiting the Book of Parables*, edited by Gabriele Boccaccini, 299–351. Grand Rapids: Eerdmans, 2007.

———. *The Son of Man in the Parables of Enoch and in Matthew*. London: T & T Clark, 2011.

Water, Rick van de. "Michael or Yhwh? Toward Identifying Melchizedek in 11Q13." *Journal for the Study of the Pseudepigrapha* 16 (2006) 75–86.

Watson, Francis. "The Triune Divine Identity: Reflections on Pauline God-Language, in Disagreement with J. D. G. Dunn." *Journal for the Study of the New Testament* 82 (2000) 99–124.

Watts, Rikki. "The New Exodus/New Creational Restoration of the Image of God." In *What Does It Mean to Be Saved?* edited by John Gordon Stackhouse, 15–41. Grand Rapids: Baker Academic, 2002.

Wevers, John William. *Notes on the Greek Text of Genesis*. SCS 35. Atlanta: Scholars, 1993.

Wright, N. T. *The Climax of the Covenant: Christ and the Law in Pauline Theology*. Edinburgh: T & T Clark, 1991.

———. *Jesus and the Victory of God*. London: SPCK, 1996.

———. "The Letter to the Romans." In *The New Interpreter's Bible, Volume Ten: The Acts of the Apostles, Introduction to Epistolary Literature, the Letter to the Romans, the First Letter to the Corinthians*, edited by L. E. Keck, 395–770. Nashville: Abingdon, 2002.

———. "Messiahship in Galatians." In *Pauline Perspectives. Essays on Paul, 1978-2013*, edited by N. T. Wright, 510–46. London: SPCK, 2013.

———. *The New Testament and the People of God*. Christian Origins and the Question of God 1. London: SPCK, 1992.

———. *Paul and the Faithfulness of God*. 2 vols. Christian origins and the question of God 4. London: SPCK, 2013.

———. *Paul: Fresh Perspectives*. London: SPCK, 2005.

———. *The Resurrection of the Son of God.* Christian origins and the question of God 3. London: SPCK, 2003.
Wyatt, Nicolas. "Royal Religion in Ancient Israel." In *Religious Diversity in Ancient Israel*, edited by Francesca Stavrakopoulou and John Barton, 61–81. London: T & T Clark, 2010.
Wyschogrod, Michael, and R. Kendall Soulen. *Abraham's Promise: Judaism and Jewish-Christian Relations.* London: SCM, 2006.
Wyschogrod, Michael. "A Jewish Perspective on Incarnation." *Modern Theology* 12 (1996) 195–209.
Zeller, D. "Die Menschwerdung des Sohnes Gottes im Neuen Testament und die antike Relgionsgeschichte." In *Menschwerdung Gottes—Vergöttlichung von Menschen*, 141–76. Göttingen: Vandenhoeck & Ruprecht, 1988.
———. "New Testament Christology in its Hellenistic Reception." *New Testament Studies* 47 (2001) 312–33.

Scripture and Ancient Document Index

Ancient Near Eastern Texts

Hymn to Ninurta   311n148

Old Testament/Hebrew Bible

Genesis

1–3	252, 277, 289	5:1–24	177, 235
1–2	62n1	5:22	298
1	52n50, 55, 145, 238, 242, 264, 267, 270, 280n82, 283–84, 291, 310	5:24	298
		12:1–3	237
		12:8	16
		14	195
1:1	52–53	14:14	46
1:2	242, 274n67	14:18–20	195, 235
1:11	145, 306	16:10	237
1:20–25	242	17:6	237
1:20	145, 306	19:24	22
1:24	145, 306	22:2	117
1:26–28	116, 236–37, 242, 277, 289, 310	22:12	117
		22:16	117
1:26–27	52, 164n9, 264	23:12	19
1:26	144, 242, 254–55, 264, 266, 270, 272, 283	26:4	237
		28:3	237
1:28	52, 145, 242, 272	31:13	23n49
1:29	289	33:3–7	19
2–3	282	34	225
2:1–3	145	35:11–12	237
2:7	235, 242, 254, 286	41:43	244
2:21–24	235	49:8–12	234
3:8	264	49:9	234
3:14–19	260	49:10	222, 223n41
3:18	288–89		
4:26	16		

Exodus

1:7	237n76
3:2	288
4:22	239
4:31	180
7:1	300
13:21	102n74
14:1	239
19:6	221n35
19:9	102n47
20:3	311
20:5	19
22:39	224
23	221n35
23:20–22	200
23:20–21	298n119
23:24	19
24:1	180
24:16	102n74
25:40	264
28–29	224, 229
28:2	232, 248
28:4	224
28:15	225
28:29–30	225
28:36	200
28:40	232, 248
28:41	221
29:6	224
32	165
32:1	285
32:24	288
32:27–29	225
33:3	135
33:5	135
34:5	102n74
34:8	180
34:9	135
34:14	19, 311
34:29–30	300
34:34–38	309
34:34	10n14
39:32	145
39:43	145
40:16–38	235
40:33	145

Leviticus

4:5	221
9	309
16	309
16:2	102n74, 235
16:12–13	235
19:19	232
26:1	19

Numbers

11:25	102n74
12:5	102n74
14:14	102n74
24:17	208, 229
25	225
27:21	225
33:52	283n80

Deuteronomy

1:33	102n74
4:12	288
4:15	288
4:20	288
4:28	284n92
4:33	288
5:4	288
5:9	19
5:21	306
5:24	288
5:26	288
6:4–9	53
6:4	10, 33, 37–38, 46, 54, 99, 139
7:5	288
9:6	135
9:10	288
9:13	135
10:4	288
12:3	288
13:1–5	19, 152
17:8–13	226, 229
17:8–9	225

17:14–20	221, 226, 229	3–4	236
20:2–4	225	3:13–14	231
21:5	225	3:16–28	226
22:11	231	3:9–28	225
32:9	195	8:1–13	308–9
32:17	298n120	8:1–22	234
32:21	10n14, 298n120	8:6–14	231
32:48	19	8:10–11	235, 309
33:7	226	9–12	228
33:8–11	227	10:9	225
		12:16	238n77

Joshua

3:16	263n42
18:1	237n76

2 Kings

1	118
10:16	136
11:8	283n80
11:12	224
19:18	284n92
23:4	288
23:6	288
23:15	288

Judges

3:9	94n61
3:15	94n61

1 Samuel

8–13	227–28
8:5	227
8:10–20	227
12:7–8	16

1 Chronicles

29:22	221
29:20	208
29:23	208
29:28	231

2 Samuel

1:10	224
1:19	232n62
7:14	11n15, 19
8:15	225
18:21	19
19:44	238n77
20:1	238n77
22:12	102n74

2 Chronicles

1:11–12	231
19:8–11	225
23:11	224
29:28–30	180
23:17	283n80
32:19	284n92
32:27	231

1 Kings

3–8	234

Nehemiah

9:27	94n61

Esther

3:1–6	19

Psalms

2	208, 214n23, 231
2:2	192n67
2:7	19
2:8	271, 273n66
3	42n30
3:7	182
4:1	18n38
6:1	18n38
7:7–8	195
8	44, 107, 112, 236–37, 252–53, 273–74, 278
8:1	278
8:2	44
8:3–4	278n79
8:4–8	237
8:4–5	44
8:4	107
8:5–8	236, 274, 278n79
8:5–7	237
8:5–6	274
8:5	253
8:6–9	44
8:6	140
8:7	274n67, 274n70
8:10	44
11	48n43
11:4	48
16	48n42
17:1	18n38
18	48n42
18:13–14	187
18:7–15	200
21:5	231
24:1	10n14
28:4	187n56
29	48n42
29:1	18n38
32:1–2	11n15
34:8	11n14
37	48n42
41:9	18n38
42:2	23
45	231, 234
45:2–3	231
45:6	56, 213, 208, 216
45:6–7	19
45:13	208
46	309
48	45, 309
48:3	45n36
48:12–13	45n36
53:1	18n38
54	48n42
58:6	182
60:1	18n38
62:12	187n56
63:1	23
67:2–3	48n42
67:7–8	48n42
68:2	182
68:16	51
72	231, 234
72:11	208
72:18–19	231
74:13–14	243
76	309
80	107
80:1	278
80:17	107
82:1	195
83:1	278
84:2	23
89	231
89:8–10	243
89:10	274
89:40	224
94	56n56
94:1–2	10n14
94:1	56n56
94:11	11n15
97:1	187
97:2	102n74
97:4–5	182, 187
97:9	187
97:12	187
102:25–27	11n14, 19
104:3	102n74, 198
104:32	182n40

106:20	265n49	11:2	191, 222
110	183n42, 195, 208, 233, 235–6	13:9–10	187
		14:4–20	212, 215
110:1	13, 56n56, 119, 138–41, 183, 190, 195, 225, 236	14:13–14	69, 254, 276n75, 302n129
		19:1	102n74, 198
110:2–3	234	22:23–24	231
110:2	139	24:12	187n56
110:3	208, 231	24:21–23	182
110:4	139, 225, 235	32:2	230n57
110:5–6	139	34:4	187
115:4	284n92	37:19	284n92
117:1	11n15	40:13	10n14, 11n15
132:18	224	40:20	288n99
135:15	284n92	42:8	248, 311
136	44	43:2	288
138:8	284n93	43:7	44
144:6	187	44:6	13
		44:9–22	164
		44:15–17	288
## Proverbs		44:15	285
		45:11	284n93
8	146, 297	45:14	179
8:22–31	52	45:18–19	11
8:22–30	145n36, 297n115	45:21–25	11
8:22–23	297n115	45:21–23	139
8:22	297n115	45:22–25	137
10:1—22:16	45	45:21	11
10:1	45	45:23	10n14, 22, 32, 71
25:2—29:27	45	45:24–25	11
25:1	45	46:6	285
25:2	231	48:11	248, 311
		48:12	13
		49:1	179
## Isaiah		49:7	179
		49:23	179
1:9	11n15	52:11	11n15
6	185n51	53:1	11n15
6:1–2	264	59:19	44
6:1	309	60:1–2	311
6:3	200, 231, 309	60:14	179
8:13	11n14	60:21	284n93
9:5	56, 208, 216	61:1	195
9:6–7	221	61:2	195
9:6	208	62:3	224
10:21	208	66:15–21	182n40
11:1–4	208	66:18	187n56

Jeremiah

4:13	102n74
9:23–24	10n14
10:3–15	164
10:5	161
10:8	161–2
11:4	288
22:3	225
23:5	225
32:18	208

Ezekiel

1	185
1:4	102n74, 200
1:13–14	200
1:24	200
1:26–28	184, 268
1:26	144, 185, 264, 267–68, 274, 278
1:28	184, 231, 267
7:20	283n80
16:17	283n80
21:26	224
23:14	283n80
28	282n86
28:12	224
28:12–16	236
28:14	282n86
34:11–12	103n75
34:16	103n75
34:22	103n75
44:7–9	135
44:24	225

Daniel

1–7	242, 286, 288–89
1–6	287, 289
1:3–4	242
1:3	241
1:4	240
1:8–20	242
1:17	241
1:20	241
2–7	243, 285–90
2	313, 316
2:20–23	240–41
2:31–32	283n80
2:34	283n80
2:46–48	242–43, 286–87, 289
2:46	169, 237–47, 280, 287, 289, 292, 299n122, 304, 313
2:47	240
2:48–49	240
2:48	241–42
3	285–86, 288
3:1–18	285
3:1–12	286
3:4–6	285
3:12	197
3:14	197
3:17–18	197
3:95	197
4	288–89
4:8–9	242, 286
4:15	289n100
4:23	289n100
4:25	289n100
4:18	242, 286
4:37	197
5:11	242, 286
5:14	242, 286
6	288
6:17	197, 288
6:21	197
6:27	197
7	107, 109–12, 119, 123–25, 127n112, 129n2, 174, 195–96, 202–4, 215, 234, 280
7:2	124, 242
7:3–8	234, 242–43, 290
7:9–14	103, 113–14, 177, 280, 195–96
7:9–11	14
7:9	101, 114, 124, 140, 196, 264
7:9–10	273
7:10	114

7:13	101–2, 106–7, 109–26, 140, 173, 175, 178, 186, 190, 195–99, 203–4, 233, 235–36, 292		Micah	
		1:3–4		182
		5:2		208
7:13–14	113–15, 118, 120, 122–23, 181, 186, 195–99, 234, 237–47, 280, 289, 304		Nahum	
		1:3		102n74
7:14	114–15, 118–20, 122, 181, 234, 242, 271, 273n66, 289n101, 290, 292		Habakkuk	
		2:19		162
7:17	234	3:6		182n40
7:18–27	242			
7:22	242		Zephaniah	
7:27	197, 242			
8–12	119	3:17		281
9:25–26	195			
			Zechariah	
	Hosea			
8:4	228	3–6		224
8:6	285	3:7		225
		6:11		224
	Joel	6:13		225, 231
		9:14		187
2:10	187	10:3		231
2:32	10	12:7		232n62
3 [LXX 4]:14–15	187	14:5		10n14, 186–87
	Amos		Malachi	
5:26	283n89	1:7		10n14
		1:12		10n14

Apocrypha

Tobit

Additions to Esther

12:15–22	19	13:12–14	19

Wisdom

2:18	239
2:23	264
5:5	239
7:22–26	146
7:22	145n36, 146, 297
8:5–6	145n36, 297
11:20	41, 55
14:17	164
14:21	162
14:23	161–62
14:28	161–62
15:4	162
18:24	224

Ben Sira/Sirach

1:4	297
17:3	264
24	145n36, 146, 297
24:8–9	297
35:24	187
36:1–2	222
44:1—50:1	268
44:1	278
44:16	228n55
45:7–8	232, 281n83
45:7	231, 232n63
45:12	224, 232n63
45:13	232
45:15	221
45:17	225
45:20	231–2
45:23	231
45:24–25	222, 228n55
47:11	228n55, 232n61
47:19–21	228n55
47:23–25	228n55
48:17–22	222
49:4–5	228n55
49:8	268
49:11–13	222, 278
49:14	228n55
49:16—50:1	228n55
49:16—50:13	236–37
49:16	252–53, 268, 274, 278
50:1–21	130n5, 278
50	26, 278
50:1	278
50:1–4	222
50:7	231–32, 268
50:11	231, 232nn62–63
50:13	231, 232nn62–63
50:15	278

Baruch

6:4–5	161
6:16	161
6:23	162
6:29	161
6:45	162
6:47	162
6:69	161

1 Maccabees

3	221
3:3–9	211, 218
3:3	217
4:30	218
8:14–15	239
14	221
14:4–15	211, 218
14:4–5	217, 232n62
14:9–10	217
14:10	231
14:21	217
14:25–49	211
14:29	217
14:35	217
14:39	217, 231
14:48	211
15:32	232n62
15:36	232n62

2 Maccabees

6:7	301
14:35	309
15:12–16	225

Pseudepigrapha

Apocalypse of Abraham

1–7	164
6:3	162
10:3	298n119
10:8	298n119
17:13	130n4, 298n119
23:5	252
31:1	173, 193

Apocalypse of Sedrach

5–7	276n75
5:1–2	260n28
5:2	284n91
6:2	274n70
13:3	263

Apocalypse of Zephaniah

6:14–15	19

Aramaic Levi Document (A.L.D.)

1 viii	222
14–15	225
67	222, 223n41
99	225

Artapanus

9.27.4	240n82
9.27.6	242n85, 299n121, 300n124

Ascension of Isaiah

10:14	138n23
11:32–33	138n23

2 Baruch

14:18	252
14:19	252
15:7	252
21:24	252
29:1—30:5	173, 193
39:7	173, 193
73:6	252

3 Baruch

4:16	252

1 Enoch

1–36	191, 223, 298
1:3–9	187
1:6	182
1:9	191
6–15	96
12:1–2	298
14	235
14:2	235
14:8—15:1	235
14:18–23	243
14:20	231
14:20–24	264
15:1	235n70
37–71	26, 33, 101, 109–10, 118, 143, 171–205, 209, 229, 246, 248, 271, 277, 279, 291–92
37:1	201
38:2	177
38:4–5	201
38:4	304
39:4–8	177
39:6	177, 200
39:8	52n50
39:12–14	185n51
40:5	177, 200
45:3	177, 179, 200

1 Enoch (continued)

46–70	112	61:5	182, 202
46–48	215, 235	61:8–9	184n47
46–47	174, 177	61:8	177, 179–80
46	184, 196	62–63	110
46:1–2	177	62:1	304
46:1	177, 184, 268	62:2–3	177, 192
46:3	177	62:3–5	110, 179
46:4–6	185	62:3	304
46:4–5	197	62:5	177, 179, 268
46:4	177, 182, 198	62:6	172, 177, 179–80, 184, 201, 271, 273
46:5	172, 177, 180	62:7	52n50, 112, 177, 268
46:7	180, 215, 304	62:9	172, 177, 179–80, 201, 268
48	143	62:14	268
48:1–7	185	62:15–16	250
48:2	177, 185	63:1	201
48:2–3	33n5, 177	63:11	268
48:3	52n50	63:12	201
48:4	182n38	65:3	183
48:5	172, 177, 179, 185, 214	67:12	201
48:6	33n5	69:11	250, 253
48:6–7	177	69:13–25	143, 185
48:6–4	177, 183	69:16–25	180
48:8	192, 201, 214	69:26	185
48:10	172, 177, 183, 191–92, 214	69:27	110
49:1–2	179	69:25–29	180
49:2	177	69:26–27	268
49:3–4	192	69:28	184n47
49:3	183	69:29	110, 179, 268
50:1	250	70:1	268
51:1	202	71	111, 177–78, 191, 250, 268
51:3	177, 179, 192	71:11–12	200–201
52:6	182, 187, 198, 200	71:13–17	177, 199
53:4	172, 177, 191	71:14	268
53:6	177	71:17	268
53:7	182, 187, 198, 200	85–90	280
55:3–4	182n39	85:3	281
55:4	110, 177, 179–80, 184n47	85:9–10	281
57:1	201	89:73–74	201
60:5	198	90:28–36	281n84
60:8	177	90:28–32	281
61:1	201	90:30	281
61:3	201	90:37–38	281
61:5	187	90:38	281
61:8–11	110	92:1	172
		93:9	201

2 Enoch

1–38	298
7:4	262
22	262
22:6	262
22:7	262
22:8–10	73, 199, 221
24:1	199, 225
30:8—33:2	253n10
30:10	265
30:11	252–3
30:13	252n7
33:8–12	252n6, 289n102
44:1	284n91
57	200
57:2	262
64	200
64:3	262
67	298

3 Enoch

1:3	224
2:3	224
4:8	200
6:3	200
9:1–5	200
10:1	200
10:2	200
12–13	185
12:1–4	200
12:3	224
13:1–2	200
14:5	200
15:1–2	200
16:1	200

Ezekiel the Tragedian

68–82	26n57, 235
99	298n118

4 Ezra

3:5	284n91
6:46	252
6:55	2522
7:28	132
8:1	252
8:7	284n93
8:44	252, 265
9:13	252
11:37	234
12:1	234
12:31–34	172
12:31–32	234
13	101, 109, 118, 172–73, 190, 193, 208, 229
13:2–13	200
13:3–4	182, 187, 198
13:25	172

Joseph and Aseneth

6:3	239
6:5	239
12:9	161
14:2	113
15:11–12	246n91
17:9	298n118
23:14–17	225
26:6	225
27:6	225

Jubilees

4:21–23	298
6:8	264
8:3	252n6, 289n102
30:8–21	225
31	232
31:11–20	227
31:15	225
36:7	143, 185n53
40:7	244, 246–47, 300n125

Life of Adam and Eve

Latin (and parallels to Latin)

1–22	260
2–6	289
4:2	276
4:2-3	289n100
4:3	289n100
8:1-3	252, 263n42
11:3	252
12-16	26, 254-92
12	282n86
12:1—13:1	276
13-14	26n57
13:2	270
13:3	263n41, 270
14:1-2	263, 270
15:2	270, 286
15:3—17:1	276
15:3	276n75
16	282n86
16:2	252
18:1	298
25:1—29:10	277
27:1	276
30:3	277
37-39	288
47:3	276
50:1-2	252n6, 289n102
51:1-9	289n289

Greek (*Apocalypse of Moses*)

5:3	277
10-12	261n35, 288
10:3—12:3	290n103
10:3	263
12:1-2	263
16:2	257, 260, 269, 277n77
20:1-2	252
20:2	270
21:2	252, 270
21:6	252, 270
29:11	263n42, 273
29:13-14	252
33:5	263, 284
35:2	263
37:2	284
39:1-3	276

Armenian, Georgian

14:1	285
21:2	268
30(5)3	277
[44](16):2b	262, 277
45(33):5	284

Slavonic

40:1—41:6	284

Letter of Aristeas

76	146n38
97-98	146n38
98	224, 232
136	300n126, 302n129

Prayer of Manasseh

3	143
	185n53

Pseudo-Philo *Liber Antiquitatum Biblicarum* (*L.A.B.*)

6	288
26	288
26:6-15	252
38	288
48:2	226n52
51:6-7	226n52
60:2	143, 185n53

Pseudo-Phocylides

103–4	300n125, 303

Psalms of Solomon

2:19	231n59
2:21	231n59
11:7	231n59
17–18	192, 220, 229, 234
17:23	208
17:27	239
17:31	231n59
17:36	94n61
17:46	208
18:18	208

Sibylline Oracles

1:23	264
1:24	252
3:8	264
3:286–94	234
3:286	193
3:702	239
5	144
5:249	300n125
5:404	185
5:414–33	173, 208, 234, 273n66, 193
5:416	271, 273n66
8:403	265

Testament of the Twelve Patriarchs

Testament of Dan

5:4	226n52

Testament of Gad

8:1	226n52

Testament of Joseph

19:11	226n52

Testament of Judah

21:1–5	226n52

Testament of Levi

2:3	223
3:4	231
4:5	223
5–6	225
5:1	113
8:2	224
8:9	224
8:10	225
8:17	225
18	223n42

Testament of Naphtali

2:3	41
2:5	264

Testament of Reuben

6:7–8	226n52
6:10–12	225

Testament of Simeon

71	226n42

Testament of Abraham

Recension A

11:4–12	252
16:8	146n38

SCRIPTURE AND ANCIENT DOCUMENT INDEX

Testament of Moses

10:2	224–25, 252

New Testament

Matthew

1:1	152, 171
1:1–17	42
1:17	171
2:2	20, 58
2:8	20, 58
2:11	20, 58
4:9–10	19
4:11	263
5:11	134
5:17	80
6:9–13	39
8:2	20
8:29	80
9:13	80
9:18	20
9:8	122
10:34	80
10:35	80
11:9	117
11:19	103, 146
11:25–27	80, 94
13:36–43	110, 114, 189
13:41	101
13:41–42	102, 114
14:5	117
14:33	20
15:2–6	136
15:25	20
16:27–28	110, 114, 187, 189
16:27	102, 114
16:28	101, 115
18:10	103
18:26	19, 269
19:28	101, 110, 114, 189
20:20	20
20:28	80
21:16	44
22:37	140n26
23:34	146
24:27	187
24:30–31	102, 110, 189
24:30	102, 189, 196n78
24:31	114
24:39	101, 115
25:31–46	102, 114, 189
25:31–32	187n56
25:31	101–2, 110, 114–15, 186
26:64	196n78
27:46	92
28:9	20, 58, 181
28:16–20	181, 292, 189
28:17	20, 58, 154, 181
28:18–20	204
28:18–19	181
28:18	181
28:19	15, 48

Mark

1:1	152
1:10	151
1:11	117
1:13	115, 263
1:14–15	122
1:15	116
1:16–20	122
1:24	80
1:35	92
1:44	122
2:1–10	120, 123
2:5	120
2:6	120–21
2:7	135
2:10	103, 114, 120–23, 125
2:17	80
2:28	103, 114, 123
3:13–19	122
3:22	121
4:1–32	116
4:10–12	123
4:21–23	123
5:6	20
6:4	117
6:15	117
6:46	92
7:3	136
7:5	136
7:8–13	136
7:10	122
7:1–13	121
8:27–38	121
8:29–30	77
8:29	104, 171
8:30	104
8:31—9:12	112
8:31–38	125
8:31	104
8:38	101–2, 104, 114, 186–87
8:38–91	187n56
9:2–9	103
9:9	104, 112
9:12	104, 112
9:30–32	125
10:30–34	125
10:45	80, 102, 115
12:18–27	154
12:35–37	77, 139
12:36	44, 101
12:37	140n26
13:13	134
13:24–25	187
13:24–27	187
13:26	101–2, 107, 113–14, 119–20, 186–87
13:26–27	101–2, 113–14
13:27	114
13:32	92
14:61–62	118
14:61	104, 171
14:62	101–2, 104–5, 107, 110–13, 119–20, 204, 291
15:19	20
15:34	87–88, 92
16:19	138n23

Luke

1–2	226n52
2:11	94
2:26	171
3:15	225n52
3:21	92
3:22	151
3:23—4:13	255
4:25–28	117
4:34	80
5:16	92
5:32	80
6:12	92
7:34	103, 112, 115
7:35	146
9:29	151
9:31	151
9:32	114, 151
9:51–56	118
9:58	112
10:18	152
10:21–24	80
10:21–22	80, 94, 152

Luke (continued)

11:2–4	92
11:20	116
11:29–30	117
11:49	146
12:8–9	102–3, 112, 115
12:10	103
12:39–40	104
12:49	80
12:51	80
13:4	40n23
13:11	40n23
13:16	40n23
13:26	119
13:31–35	80
17:20	116
17:22–30	187
17:24	102, 187
17:30	102
18:8	101–2, 115
19:10	80, 103, 115
20:43	140n26
21:27	113, 125
21:36	102
22:69	113, 125
24:19	117
24:34	18
24:47	16
24:50–53	20
24:52	58
24:36–43	151
24:53	20

John

1:1–18	17, 45, 72–73, 152, 272
1:1–3	86
1:1	56, 217
1:3–4	72
1:3	13n23, 22, 73
1:2–3	53
1:11–13	83
1:11–12	86
1:12–13	72–73
1:14–18	150
1:14	46, 94, 314
1:16	72
1:18	46, 56, 217
1:49	94
1:51	150
3:13	102–3, 150
3:16–17	83
3:17	94
5:17–23	77
5:18–23	135n16
5:18	314
5:19–23	136
5:22–23	156
5:23	82
5:27	102, 110, 114–15, 125, 181, 196n78
6	117
6:14	117
6:46	150
7:40	117
8:53	314
9:17	117
9:22	134n14, 135n16
9:35–38	81–82, 104–5, 125, 156, 181, 189, 292
9:38	20, 58
10:31–33	135n16
10:33	314
10:36	135n16
12:20	57
12:23	114
12:42	134n14, 135n16
12:45	150
13:31	114
14–16	149
14:9	150
14:13–14	156
14:26–27	149
17	46n39
17:1	94
17:11	94
17:21	94
19:5	263n41
19:7	135n16
20:24–29	154
20:28	56, 217
21:11	46

Acts of the Apostles

1:6	18
1:9–11	119
1:15–26	155
1:20	57n58
1:24	16
2–7	314
2:17–21	151
2:21	57n58
2:33–36	69n9
2:33–35	138n23
2:36	57n58
2:38	16–17
2:47	18, 57n58
3:20	57n58
3:22	57n58
4:2	134, 153
4:7	134
4:33	57n58
5:9	57n58
5:17	134
5:28	134
5:31	94n61, 138n23
5:40	134
6	25
6:11	134
6:14	134–35
7	113, 125, 149
7:41–43	135
7:48	135
7:51–52	135
7:54–60	28, 189
7:55–56	138n23, 149
7:56	113, 124–26, 181, 204, 292
7:59–60	16, 18, 149
8:16	17
8:27	57
9:14	16
9:21	16
10	154
10:19	148
10:25–26	246n91, 287n96, 316
10:34–43	153
10:39–41	155
10:43	16
10:44–48	154
10:46	18
10:48	17
11	154
11:12	148
12:1–4	134
12:20–23	300n126
13:2	16, 18, 57, 148
13:4	148
13:5–11	134
13:23	94n61
13:45	134
14:8–18	20, 287n96, 316
15	154
15:5	134
16:25	18
17	287
17:5	134
17:28	287
17:29	162, 287
18:13	134
18:24	50
20:25–26	20
21:28	134
22:3	136
22:16	16
22:21–22	134
23:6–10	134
23:9	137
24:6	134
24:15	134
24:21	134
25:19	134
26:6–26	134
25:26	94

Romans

1:1–4	94n59
1:3–4	67n4, 69n9
1:3	77, 94
1:7	14
1:8	92, 94
1:18–25	261
1:21–23	7, 162
1:31	10
2:6–7	251

Romans (continued)

2:6	187n56
3:1–8	133
3:21–26	59n65
3:25	59n65
3:30	7
4:7–8	11
5–7	84
5:1	35n15
5:11	35n15
5:12–21	255
6:4	17
7:25	92
8:2	84
8:3	59n66, 67n4, 84–85, 94, 255
8:3–4	83
8:4–10	84
8:4	84
8:6	84
8:7	36n17
8:10–11	84
8:11	14
8:14–16	83
8:14	85
8:17	94n59
8:18–32	85
8:29	85, 94
8:32–39	56n56
8:32–34	140n26, 253
8:34	56n56, 92, 138n23
9:5	36, 50, 55–56, 94n59, 216–17
9:27–29	11
9:28–29	11n14
10:2	136
10:9–13	10, 16, 48, 138
10:16	11
11:3	11
11:33–36a	39
11:34	11
11:36	12n19, 36n17, 38, 142
12:1	58
12:4–5	92
12:27	92
14:10	14
14:11	10n14
15:6	14, 91
15:7–12	94n59
15:11	11
15:30	35n15
16:20	16
16:27	92

1 Corinthians

1:2	10, 16
1:3	14
1:8	141
1:9	14
1:12	36, 50
1:13	16
1:15	16
1:24	146
2:16	10n14
3:4–6	36, 50
3:20	11
3:21	91
3:22	36, 50
4:6	50
6:11	17
7:11–12	35
7:32–34	23
7:35	23
8–11	34
8–10	36
8–9	34n13
8	9
8:3–6	9, 33
8:4–6	17, 58
8:4–5	34
8:4	7, 10, 33, 55
8:6	6, 10–14, 17, 22, 24, 31, 33–40, 44–46, 48–57, 77, 95, 99–100, 138–39, 141–42, 171, 204, 216, 272, 314
9:1	148
9:14	35
10:4	67n4
10:7	7
10:9	67n9
10:14–22	17

10:14	7	5:10	94n59
10:20	162	5:14–21	83
10:21–22	10n14	5:19	84
10:21	17	5:21	84, 255
10:26	10n14	6:17–18	11n15
11:3	91	6:18	11
11:7	265–66	8:9	67n4
11:20	17	10:17	10n14
11:23–25	35	11:31	91
12	151	12	150
12:2	7	12:1	151
12:3	16, 35, 134	12:1–4	28
12:4–6	19	12:4	15
14	151	12:8–9	16, 18
14:26	17, 148	12:8	16
15:1–7	35	12:9	151
15:5	50	13:14	16
15:22	255		
15:23–28	94n59, 104n78		
15:24–28	91	## Galatians	
15:25–27	140n26, 253		
15:25	138n23	1:3	14
15:27–28	13n23	1:8	151
15:27	44, 236	1:11–12	148
15:29	14	1:13–17	28
15:38	14	1:13–14	136
15:45	255	2:2	148
15:57	35n15	3:13	136
16:12	50	3:27	17
16:22–23	16, 52n50, 54, 73	4:4–7	83
16:22	24	4:4–6	84n36
		4:4	67n4, 94
		6:12	136
## 2 Corinthians		6:16–18	16
1:2–3	15		
1:3	91	## Ephesians	
1:20	92		
3:7—4:6	148	1:2–3	14
3:12—4:4	22	1:3	91
3:16	10n14	1:5	36n17
4:10–11	92	1:10	13n23
4:4	272	1:17	91
5	85	1:20–22	253
5:1	14	1:20	138n23, 140n26
5:8	23	1:22	13n23, 44, 236
5:10–11	14	2:6	251

Ephesians (continued)

3:16	94n59
4:6	7
4:15	36n17
5:14	17
5:18–20	17–18
5:19	18, 57
5:20	92
5:23	92
6:23–24	16
6:23	14

Philippians

1–3	34n13
1:20	23
1:23	23
2	35, 82, 104, 214–15
2:5–11	218
2:5	171
2:6	22, 32–33, 35, 98, 104, 217, 272
2:6–11	5n8, 12, 14,17, 24, 32, 38, 67, 69–72, 76, 80, 82–83, 94, 96–98, 169, 204, 207, 213, 215–16, 238, 255–56, 272, 314
2:6–8	46n39, 69, 72
2:6–7	72
2:7–8	72
2:9–11	11, 22, 46n39, 70, 72, 98, 137, 139, 141, 217
2:9–10	71
2:9	11n18, 71
2:10	20
2:10–11	10n14, 18, 32, 44, 70–71, 97, 213
2:11	16, 22, 33, 37n19, 70, 72, 77, 97, 171, 216
3:8–9	23
3:20–21	14, 70, 215
3:20	94n61
3:21	13n23, 22, 233
4:18	58
4:20–23	16

Colossians

1–3	34n13
1	35
1:3	91
1:6	52
1:9	52
1:10	52
1:13–15	22
1:13	171
1:15–20	12, 17, 33, 36n17, 39, 46n39, 51, 53–54, 72, 141, 218, 272, 314
1:15–17	12
1:15	35, 51–52, 171, 255, 272
1:16–18	72
1:16–17	13n23, 85–86, 95
1:16	22, 52
1:17	36n17, 52
1:18–20	86
1:18	52
1:19	22, 51, 150
1:20	13n23, 14, 36n17, 72, 95
1:24	92
1:28	52
2:3	52, 150
2:8—3:4	53
2:8	52, 136
2:9	272
2:18	150
2:23	52
3:1–3	251
3:1	138n23
3:10	52, 264
3:16–17	17–18
3:16	18, 52, 57
3:17	92
4:5	52

1 Thessalonians

1:9–10	7
1:10	104n78
2:19–20	104n78

3:11–13	16	1:3	13, 22, 86, 95, 138n23, 216, 233, 272
3:11	14		
3:13	10n14	1:4	13
4:6	10n14	1:5	94, 216
4:13–18	104n78	1:5–13	18, 39
5:1–11	104	1:6	20, 263
5:9–10	23	1:8	13, 56, 216–17
5:9	35n15	1:10–12	11n14, 13
5:19–22	151	1:12–13	59n65
5:23–28	16	1:13	13–14, 138n23
		2:5–18	86, 255
		2:5–9	14
## 2 Thessalonians		2:6–8	44, 236
		2:6–9	253
2:1–12	104n78	2:7	233
2:16–17	16	2:8	13n23
3:5	16	2:9	233
		2:11–13	91
		2:11	314n154
## 1 Timothy		2:14	314n154
		3:3	233
1:12	18	4:14–15	85
1:15	67n6	4:15	84
2:5	34n10	5:5	171
3:16	17, 67n6, 72	7	314n154
		7:14	171
		8:1	138n23
## 2 Timothy		9:11–14	59n65
		10:12–13	138n23
1:9–10	67n6	12:2	138n23
2:22	10, 16	13:21	18, 233
4:18	18		

Titus

James

2:13	56, 217	2:7	17

1 Peter

Hebrews

		1:1	56
1–2	67n6, 72, 85, 140n26, 314	1:3	91
		2:3	11n14
1:1	171	2:22	84–85, 255
1:2–3	13, 52, 146, 216	3:15	11n14
1:2	13n23, 22, 86, 94	3:22	138n23
1:3–4	13	4:11	18, 22

2 Peter

1:1	56, 217
1:4	312, 316
3:18	18

1 John

1:1	152
2:1	92
3:5	84, 255
4:1–6	152
4:9	83
5:20	56, 217

Jude

5–7	67n6
14–15	187n56, 190, 192
25	92

Revelation

1:5–6	18, 73
1:7–13	112
1:7	113
1:8	13
1:12–16	73
1:13–16	22, 114, 196, 204
1:13	113, 124
1:17	13
3:14	13
3:21	138n23, 140
4–5	13, 22, 28, 140
4:1	113
4:8–11	18
4:10	58
5	73
5:5	73
5:6	59n65
5:9–14	14, 18
5:9	73
5:11–14	273
5:12	59n65
5:12–13	233
5:14	20, 58
6:17	14, 23
7:9–17	18
7:14	59n65
7:15–17	13
9:20	20
11:15	14, 23
13:4	20
13:8	20
13:12	20
13:17–18	42
14:4	18, 21, 58
14:9	20
14:11	20
14:14–16	113, 196n78
16:2	20
19:10	20
21:6	13
22:1	23
22:3–4	13–14, 23, 48
22:3	13, 23
22:8–9	20
22:12	187n56
22:13	13
22:20	16

Dead Sea Scrolls

1QH[a]: *Hodayoth*

4:14–15	251
15:31	298n117
26:6–16	194

1QM: *War Scroll*

1:10–11	298n117
5:1	224n45
10:2–5	225
10:10–12	152

10:14	253n9
11	229, 234
11:6–7	224n45
12:8	231n59
13:9	267

1QpHab: *Habakkuk Pesher*

7:10—8:3	135
9:9–10	135
11:4–8	135

1QS: *Community Rule*

4–5	224
4:22–23	251
9:11	221

1QSb: *Blessings Scroll*

3:25	231
3:26–28	225
4–5	227
4:2–3	224
4:28	231–2, 251n3
5:18	231
5:20–29	231

4Q161: 4QIsaiah Pesher

8–10 iii 17–24	227

4Q171: 4QPsalms Pesher (4QpPsa)

3:1–2	251

4Q174: 4QFlorilegium

passim	220

4Q374

2 ii	300n124

4Q377

1	306n136

4Q381

passim	289n102
1	276n75
1 3–6	274n67
1 7	274n67
1 8	278
1 10–11	262, 274
1 11	278
15 4	274n67
76 + 77 15	274n67

4Q392

1 4–6	252

4Q400–407, 11Q17: *Songs of the Sabbath Sacrifice*

4Q400 1 i 20	298n117
4Q405 23 i 6	224
4Q405 23 ii	130n5
4Q405 23 ii 3	232, 251n3
4Q405 23 ii 8–9	232, 251n3

4Q408

3 + 3a line 5	232, 251n3

4Q417:4QInstruction

1 i 17	253

4Q418: 4QInstruction

81 2–5	237n74
81 5	251n3

Self-Glorification Hymn: 4Q491c, 4Q471b, 4Q427 7i, 1QHa XXVI)

4Q491c	175
4Q491c	
1 5–7	194
1 5–6	212, 225
1 5	298n117
1 7	298n117
1 11	298n117
4Q471b	212n15, 194
4Q471b 1–3, 5	195
4Q427 7	212n15, 194
4Q427 7 I + 9, 12	194n73
1QHa XXVI	212n15

4Q504: Words of the Luminaries

8	278

8 (recto) 4	267
1–2 iii 4	267

4Q521

2 ii 1	273n66

4Q541

frag. 9	224

11Q13: 11QMelch

passim	175
2:5	195
2:9–14	225
2:9	195
2:10–11	195, 300n125
2:18	195

11Q18: 11QNew Jerusalem

14 ii 2–5	224

11Q19: 11QTempleScroll (11QTS)

56:12–59:21	220, 224, 227

Josephus

Contra Apionem

1:59	227n54
1:279	300n124
2:187	225
2:193	34

Jewish Antiquities

1:69–71	252n6, 289n102
1:219	298n118
1:332	298n118
2:232	300n124
3:153–59	59n65
3:172	224
3:180	300n124, 303n132

SCRIPTURE AND ANCIENT DOCUMENT INDEX

3:187	224, 232n63	18:4	226n52
3:180–86	145	18:23	213
3:202–3	309	18:90–93	225
3:320	302	19:4	300n126
4:218	225	20:5–12	225
4:200–201	34	20:12	224
4:208	232	20:241	213, 225
10:35	300n125	20:244	225
10:211–12	241		
10:268	241		
11:326–38	130n5		*Jewish War*
12:258–61	211		
13:214	211	1:70	221, 225
13:282–83	225	2:57–59	229
13:284–87	225	5:218	142
13:301	221	5:235	224
15:404–18	225	5:459	309
17:273–84	229	6:284–300	152
18:1–10	229		

Philo

Abraham

119	146n38

Allegorical Interp.

1:38	302n129
3:96	265n47

Cherubim

3	298n118
77	300n126
127	142

Creation

78–79	252
83	262, 276n75
146	146n38

Decalogue

61–69	300n126
61	302n129

Dreams

1:227–29	23n49
2:129–33	300n126
2:231	298n116
2:234	298n116

Embassy

111–12	300n126
116–18	19
143–50	210

Flight

5	298n118
111	224
118	225

Heir

206	298n116
231	264n47

Migration

103	143, 185n53

Moses

1:27	303n132
1:155–58	300
1:158	242n85, 303n132
2:114	224
2:116	225
2:131	225
2:165	185

Planting

50	146n38

Posterity

28	306

Questions and Answers on Exodus

2:29	300
2:40	300

Sacrifices

8–10	300n124

Special Laws

1:81	264n47
4:123	146n38

Unchangeable

182	298n118

Rabbinic Writings

Mishnah

Aboth

3:23	42

Horayot

2:2	221
2:3	221
2:7	221
3:4	221

Kil'ayim

9:1	232

Other Rabbinic Literature

Genesis Rabbah

8:10	259n24, 274n70, 275n71, 276n75

Ecclesiastes Rabbah

6:9:1   259n24, 275n71, 276n75

Tanhuma Buber

Beha'alotekha 15 (26a-b)   300n124

Pirqe Rabbi Eliezer

11   259n24, 275n71, 276n75

Other Ancient Jewish Writings

Synagogue Service *Piyyutim*

Azkir gevurot elohah
161   224n48

Atah konanta 'olam be-rov ḥesed
101   224n48

Greco-Roman Writings

Aelian

Various Histories

5:12   212n17

Aristotle

Rhetoric

1410a   35n14

Hecataeus of Abdera

XL.3.5   225

Horace

Odes 3:3:9-12   212

Plato

Parmenides

130C   264

Republic

2:380d–381e   308n141
10:607a   218

Pliny the Younger

Epistles 10.96.7   15

Pompeius Trogus

36:2.10   300n125

Suetonius

Julius Caesar

88:1   212

Nero

39:2   51n46

Virgil

Eclogue 4   215n24
Aeneid 6:791–93   215n24

Ancient Inscriptions

OGIS

90A.3   217
90A.9   217
90A.37–38   217
90A.49   217
90A.51   217

New Testament Apocrypha

Apocalypse of Peter

6:1   138n23

Didascalia

23   284n91

Cave of Treasures

20:10–14   284n91

Gospel of Bartholomew

4:52–55   260n28
4:53–54   263n43

Early Christian Writings

1 Clement

36:5   138n23

Discourse of Abbaton

13a   263n43, 274n70

Athenagoras

Legatio

27:1   161

Encomium on Saint Michael

11b–13z   284n91
11b–12b   263n43
12a   274n70

Evagrius of Pontus,

De Oratione, Prologue   46n40

Gregory Nazianzen

Orations

40:11   259n23

Justin Martyr

Dialogue 56   22

Letter of Barnabas

9:7–8	40
9:8	46
12:10	138n23
16:5–6	191

Polycarp

Philippians

2:1   138n23

Printed in Great Britain
by Amazon